EPIC LIVES

One Hundred

Black Women

Who Made

a Difference

EPIC LIVES

One Hundred

Black Women

Who Made

a Difference

Jessie Carney Smith, Editor

**Foreword by
Stephanie Stokes Oliver**

DETROIT   WASHINGTON, D.C.   LONDON

Epic Lives:
One Hundred Black Women Who Made a Difference

Published by **Visible Ink Press**™
a division of Gale Research Inc.
835 Penobscot Building
Detroit, MI 48226-4094

Visible Ink Press™ is a trademark of Gale Research Inc.

Art Director: Cynthia Baldwin
Interior and Cover Design: Tracey Rowens

Cover photo of Bessie Coleman - lower right
    courtesy of Bettmann Archives/Newsphotos.
Cover photo of Angela Davis - top
    courtesy of Wide World Photos.
Cover photo of Ntozake Shange - left
    courtesy of Wide World Photos.
Poem "Still I Rise" by Maya Angelou
    copyright © 1978 Random House Inc.
    Reprinted by permission.

ISBN 0-8103-9426-X

CONTENTS

FOREWORD

How does a person become great? Can one aspire to greatness?

Or does it come naturally? How do you know when greatness has

occurred? Is it when you're given an Essence Award? Or when

you're asked to appear on "The Oprah Winfrey Show"? Or is it when

your biography appears in a reference book with ninety-nine other

*women who you **know** are great?*

Did anyone tell Harriet Tubman that she was great when she was being chased by yapping hounds and killer bounty hunters? Did anyone tell Fannie Lou Hamer that she was great when officers of the law beat her mercilessly in a Mississippi jail? Has anyone given Aretha Franklin her due respect yet?

For African-American women in particular, greatness has most often come through struggle. It has come from "making a way where there was no way." It has come in spite of the monumental odds of racism and oppression. It has come because of tenacity, perseverance, assertiveness, intelligence, giftedness, blessedness, "uppityness," and nerve.

It is important to document these lives. It is important to pass the stories down to our descendants. It is important that there are books like

You may write
* me down in history*
With your bitter,
* twisted lies,*
You may trod me
* in the very dirt*
But still, like dust,
* I'll rise....*

Out of the huts
* of history's shame*
I rise
Up from a past
* that's rooted in pain*
I rise
I'm a black ocean,
* leaping and wide,*
Welling and swelling
* I bear in the tide.*

Leaving behind nights
* of terror and fear*
I rise
Into a daybreak that's
* wondrously clear*
I rise
Bringing the gifts
* that my ancestors gave,*
I am the dream and
* the hope of the slave.*
I rise
I rise
I rise.

—Maya Angelou, "Still I Rise"

**Stephanie
Stokes Oliver,
editor of *Essence***

Epic Lives: One Hundred Black Women Who Made a Difference. This book can serve not only as a record of history, but as a volume of inspiration. The biographies give great detail into the lives of Americans who helped to shape our people and our country. We can read and be motivated. For each of us there may come a time when we will have to take a stand, a moment when we will have to make a hard decision that may change not only us, but also history.

For some women, such as Sojourner Truth, that moment comes with the courage to stand up and say things that need to be said. For others, like Rosa Parks, it comes with the wisdom to sit down and say nothing. Shirley Chisholm moved Congress to action; Bernice Reagon sang, "We shall not be moved."

Through the one hundred profiles in *Epic Lives*, editor Jessie Carney Smith celebrates the deeds of women in that unofficial sisterhood called Strong Black Women. The world acknowledges the sisterhood's reputation for strength in the face of adversity; and our own knowledge of this legacy—along with our continuing faith—gives us inner power. It's a heritage of survival and triumph that continues through generations; when a black woman is asked to name a strong woman, a woman she admires, she often responds, "my mother." The women in *Epic Lives* are representative of the thousands of African-American women who have come before, those who are with us now, and those who are yet to come. Strong black women just keep on coming.

Writer, poet, and professor Maya Angelou is one of those women. Her profile in this book places her autobiographical works, which include the ever-popular *I Know Why the Caged Bird Sings*, "firmly within the tradition of those of Frederick Douglass, Anne Moody, Richard Wright, and Malcolm X," and it notes that her books document the collective history of black American people in a way that takes the autobiographer "away from concentration on the individual 'I' and places her within the collective 'we.'"

Angelou's poetry gives us the same gift of "we." She understands that great and strong black women may not always be the ones for whom "gentlemen" rise, and that it is more important that we "rise" ourselves. In her poem "Still I Rise," excerpted here, she speaks for the women on these pages—and for all African-American women.

INTRODUCTION

"I was not born with a silver spoon in mouth; but instead with a

clothes basket almost upon my head," said Maggie Lena Walker, a   ***Tribute*** •

versatile woman whose achievements in the early part of this   ***to African-***

century as entrepreneur, feminist, civil rights advocate, newspaper   ***American***

founder, and lecturer brought her well-deserved respect, honor,   ***women***

and recognition.

Walker's wide range of interests and accomplishments reflect only some of the areas in which black American women have excelled. Whatever the circumstances of their lives, black American women share a rich and varied history that has been only partially told. *Epic Lives* tells their story by celebrating the lives of one hundred African-American women, both contemporary and historical, and both acclaimed and unsung. This book is a tribute to these women—as well as those not chronicled here— and to their accomplishments in the face of racial and gender discrimination and abuse.

The women celebrated in *Epic Lives* are not necessarily *the* one hundred most important African-American women—the number of influential black women is far too great to be narrowed so drastically. These women are, however, accomplished in their own right and representative of their sisters, mothers, and daughters, whose achievements may remain unknown but who have influenced the course of our shared history just the same.

Some of the individuals in *Epic Lives* stand alone in the magnitude of their accomplishments, such as abolitionist and preacher Sojourner Truth and Underground Railroad conductor Harriet Tubman. Others are pioneers who transcend boundaries both tangible and intangible, including turn-of-the-century aviator Bessie Coleman and present-day astronaut Mae C. Jemison. Cosmetics entrepreneur Naomi Sims and her foremothers, black beauty pioneers Madame C. J. Walker and Annie Turnbo Malone, have recognized and glorified the beauty of black women, while writers like Maya Angelou, Toni Morrison, and Alice Walker document and celebrate their lives.

Countless black women have influenced our country's musical heritage, from lyric soprano Leontyne Price and her idol, contralto Marian Anderson, to "The Divine" jazz voice Sarah Vaughan and "Queen of Soul" Aretha Franklin. Innovative dancer Katherine Dunham, Oscar-winning actress Whoopi Goldberg, and influential television host Oprah Winfrey are among the many who have contributed to the performing arts. Athletics, too, have seen the likes of tennis champion Althea Gibson and Olympic gold medalists Florence Griffith Joyner and Jackie Joyner-Kersee. Leading the professional realm are pediatrician Lucille C. Gunning, physicist Shirley Ann Jackson, and advertising executive Barbara Gardner Proctor.

Educators such as Mary McLeod Bethune, Johnnetta Betsch Cole, and Niara Sudarkasa, and humanitarians like Mother Clara Hale and Mother Charleszetta Waddles foster intellectual growth and racial pride among black youth. And to integrate and carry on the teachings of their fathers Malcolm X and Martin Luther King, Jr., Attallah Shabazz and Yolanda King work together to address young people and adults through their plays and lectures.

Reconstructing this country from its very foundations in constitutional law have been civil rights activists Rosa Parks and Coretta Scott King, Children's Defense Fund founder Marian Wright Edelman, Texas politician Barbara Jordan, Washington mayor Sharon Pratt Kelly, federal judge Constance Baker Motley, former NAACP and NOW attorney Althea T. L. Simmons, former Planned Parenthood president Faye Wattleton, and others equally important but too numerous to mention within the confines of this book.

Epic Lives celebrates the accomplishments of these and many other black women who have made a difference to us all. In commemorating the lives of these one hundred, *Epic Lives* pays tribute to the shared experiences of all African-American women. And in honoring their hard-earned triumphs, *Epic Lives* recognizes the vital influence of these women on our nation's history, on our future, and on our community as it exists today.

I am grateful to all those who contributed their time and expertise in writing the biographies in *Epic Lives*, from those who contributed a single essay to those who prepared multiple profiles.

It is impossible to thank individually all the libraries and repositories whose generous help made this work possible, but I cannot omit three: the Schomburg Center for Research in Black Culture, the Moorland-Spingarn Research Center of Howard University, and the Special Collections of Fisk University.

Standing alone in a special category is my Fisk faculty colleague Robert L. Johns, who edited each of the essays and shared the agony and ecstasy of producing this pioneer work. Additional proofreading aid was generously rendered by Laurie Collier, Anne Compliment, and Maureen Shepherd.

For exquisite design, thank you Tracey Rowens; for speedy and precise typesetting, thank you Casey Roberts; and for pulling the elements together, thank you Christa Brelin.

Expressions •

of gratitude

**Jessie Carney Smith,
editor of *Epic Lives***

PHOTO CREDITS

CONTRIBUTORS

A. B. Assensoh
Penelope L. Bullock
Floris Barnett Cash
Jean Elder Cazort
Arlene Clift-Pellow
Bettye Collier-Thomas
Grace E. Collins
Helen C. Cooks
Carolyn Cunningham
Nancy A. Davidson
Althea T. Davis
Alice A. Deck
Alan Duckworth
James Duckworth
Margaret Duckworth
Lois L. Dunn
Robert Dupuis
De Witt C. Dykes, Jr.
Maalik Edwards
Joan Curl Elliott
Sharynn Owens
  Etheridge
V. P. Franklin
Marie Garrett
Sandra E. Gibbs
Jenifer Lyn Grady
Jacquelyn Grant
Beverly Guy-Sheftall
Debra Newman Ham

James E. Haney
Violette J. Harris
Ruth Edmonds Hill
Carolyn R. Hodges
Mary R. Holley
Juanita R. Howard
Dona L. Irvin
Jacquelyn L. Jackson
Laura C. Jarmon
Margaret Jerrido
Robert L. Johns
Adrienne Lash Jones
Jo Ann Lahmon
Theresa A. Leininger
Thura R. Mack
Nellie Y. McKay
Genna Rae McNeil
Diana Marre
Dianne Marshall
Ronald E. Mickens
Rob Nagel
Dolores Nicholson
Stephanie Stokes Oliver
Lucius Outlaw
Margaret D. Pagan
Nell Irvin Painter
David H. K. Pellow
Margaret Perry
Marva Rudolph

Spencer G. Shaw
John C. Shields
Bonnie Shipp
Simmona E. Simmons
Oscar L. Sims
Robert E. Skinner
Elaine M. Smith
J. Clay Smith, Jr.
Jessie Carney Smith
Raymond R.
  Sommerville
Deborah Stewart
Lester Sullivan
Darius L. Thieme
Patricia Turner
Marsha C. Vick
Gloria Wade-Gayles
Virginia Wilson Wallace
Nagueyalti Warren
Carole McAlpine Watson
Monda Raquel Webb
Leslie Wilson
Emery Wimbish, Jr.
Phyllis Wood
Linda T. Wynn
Dhyana Ziegler

Heartfelt •

thanks to these

chroniclers

of history

EPIC LIVES

One Hundred

Black Women

Who Made

a Difference

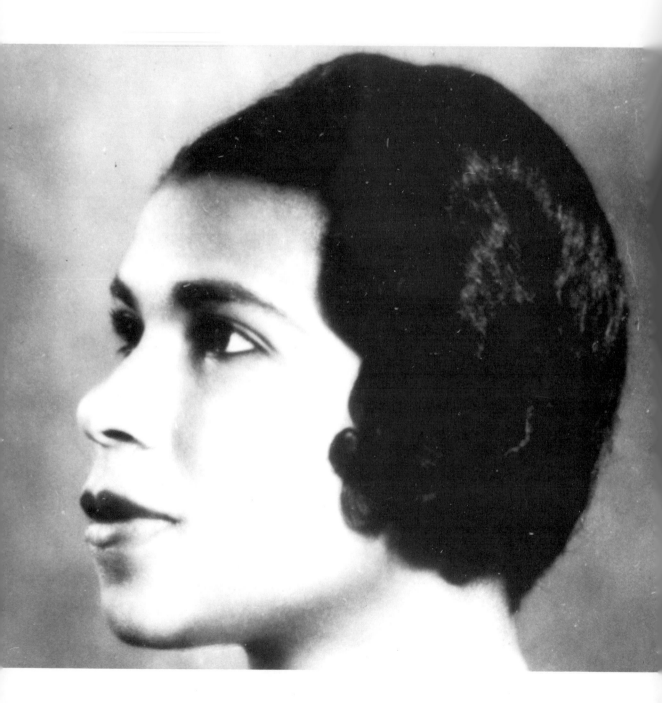

MARIAN ANDERSON

*M*arian Anderson rose from inauspicious beginnings to become

one of the twentieth century's most celebrated singers. In 1991 Ebony

magazine called Anderson "the standard bearer for grace and elegance

among Black singers, and many White singers as well." The contralto—

who first sang in her church choir—astonished audiences around the

world and in doing so became a symbol of the struggle to overcome

discrimination in the arts. Furthermore, she never compromised her

identity: she included beloved black spirituals among the traditional

pieces of her repertoire.

Anderson, the first of three daughters of John Berkeley Anderson and Anna D. Anderson, was born in Philadelphia, Pennsylvania, on February 27, circa 1900. (Anderson's birth year is most frequently reported as 1902, although some biographies show her birth year as

1908.) Anderson began singing at the Union Baptist Church, joining the senior choir by age thirteen, and she became known as the "baby contralto." Anderson further developed her voice during her high school years, when she took lessons from soprano Mary Saunders Patterson, joined the Philadelphia Choral Society, and embarked on a schedule of singing at nearby churches and schools that often meant missing classes. G. Grant Williams, editor of the *Philadelphia Tribune*, became her first manager. She continued voice study with Patterson while beginning to learn from Agnes Reifsnyder, a contralto, who helped develop Anderson's medium and low tones. Meanwhile, another well-respected instructor, Giuseppe Boghetti, also accepted her as a student. Boghetti remained her voice teacher for many years and continued as her musical advisor until his death.

Anderson graduated from South Philadelphia High School for Girls in 1921, and by 1924 she felt competent enough to make a New York concert debut. She sang to a very small audience at Town Hall in what she considered a major career fiasco. She sang lieder, and the critics' comments about her German so depressed her that she stopped studying music and put aside any hope for a musical career. Although this was not the first time her lack of extensive language study was mentioned, it was the most devastating. Anderson had studied French in high school, was tutored in French in Boghetti's studio, and was also coached in French songs by Leon Rothier in New York City. She learned Italian from Boghetti as well, and was urged by many to go to Europe to study and develop language proficiency.

Eventually Anderson returned to music, and by 1928 Anderson had saved enough money to go to England, intent on studying German lieder with Raimund von Zur Mühlen. She was also given the address of Roger Quilter, the English composer who had befriended Roland Hayes and other black musicians. She had only two lessons with the aged and ill von Zur Mühlen, but she did study with a student of his, Mark Raphael. She also sang for guests of Quilter and made her English debut at Wigmore Hall on September 16, 1930. A Rosenwald Fellowship allowed her to study in Berlin, where she lived with a German family in order to absorb and master the German language. She studied music for a short period with Sverre Joran and had more extensive coaching with Michael Raucheisen.

• **Berlin concert**

brings critical

acclaim

Anderson's concert in the Bach Saal in Berlin in October of 1930 brought her critical acclaim. She embarked on an extensive European career, making occasional returns to the United States, and she received a second Rosenwald grant in 1933. She credits Kosti Vehanen, her new accompanist, for her extended repertoire and her career advancement.

She sang more than 108 concerts in a twelve-month period in the Scandinavian countries, learning songs in Swedish, Norwegian, and Finnish. She visited the home of Sibelius and sang for him, and he dedicated his composition "Solitude" to her.

Anderson continued to study in Europe—French repertoire with Germaine de Castro and Mahler songs with Madame Charles Cahier (Sara Jane Layton-Walker), who had studied with Mahler. Her programs now showed works by the composers Handel, Scarlatti, Pergolesi, Strauss, Brahms, Schubert, Schuman, Dvorak, Rimsky-Korsakov, and Rachmaninoff. Audiences all over the world, including those in the Soviet Union, called for her to sing or repeat Schubert's "Ave Maria." Always a part of her concerts were spirituals. She usually sang those as arranged by her friend Harry Burleigh, but she also sang and recorded the spirituals of Lawrence Brown, Hall Johnson, Roland Hayes, R. Nathaniel Dett, and Florence Price.

At Salzburg in 1935, Arturo Toscanini made his often repeated remark regarding Anderson: "Arturo Toscanini told Mme Cahier, 'What I heard today one is privileged to hear only in a hundred years.' He did not say the voice he heard, but *what* he heard—not the voice alone but the whole art."

At a concert at the Salle Gaveau in Paris, the impresario Sol Hurok heard Anderson, introduced himself, and told her he wished to become her manager. On December 31, 1935, Anderson's career under Hurok Management began with a critically acclaimed concert at Town Hall in New York City, followed by a January 1936 concert at Carnegie Hall. Under Hurok, Anderson began a most intensive and extensive concert career. Vehanen retired as her accompanist in 1941; Franz Rupp became her accompanist from 1941 through her final farewell concert in 1965.

Events of February 1939 catapulted this serene and dedicated artist from the music review pages of newspapers to front-page stories. The refusal of the Daughters of the American Revolution to schedule Anderson in concert in their Constitution Hall captured the most headlines. Howard University, the original sponsor of the Anderson concert, was caught in the furor of the DAR refusal, the resignation of Eleanor Roosevelt from the DAR, and the subsequent Lincoln Memorial concert on April 9, 1939. This was a free concert given through the auspices of Harold Ickes, the Secretary of the Interior. The audience, estimated at seventy-five thousand, included congressmen, Supreme Court justices, and ordinary citizens.

In July 1939 Eleanor Roosevelt was selected to present the NAACP's Spingarn Medal to Anderson. Additional recognition came to Anderson

DAR actions •

stir controversy

when she received the ten-thousand-dollar Bok Award for the year 1940, presented in March of 1941. This award, created by Philadelphian Edward Bok in 1921, was designated for an individual making a contribution to Philadelphia and the surrounding community. Anderson used the funds to establish a scholarship award for young singers.

On July 24, 1943, at Bethel Methodist Church in Bethel, Connecticut, Anderson married Orpheus Hodge Fisher, a New York architect. Rumors of their impending marriage had surfaced over the years. "King," as she called him, was the boyfriend of her youth. She met him in Wilmington, Delaware, when they were both in high school; Anderson sang at a benefit concert and attended a reception at the Fisher home afterwards. The newlyweds purchased a farm in Danbury, Connecticut, and King designed and helped build their home. There Anderson had her music studio and engaged in her hobbies of photography, playing jazz piano, collecting jazz recordings, sewing, and upholstery.

Anderson's extraordinarily busy concert schedule continued in the 1940s with additional concerts for servicemen and for bond drives. One such concert was given at Constitution Hall in December 1942. She requested that on this occasion the audience not be separated in the usual racial seating; the DAR would not agree to this stipulation. In the end, Anderson chose to sing in the interest of the benefit for the Army Emergency Relief Fund.

Anderson

debuts at

Metropolitan

Opera

In September 1954 an extraordinary event occurred which, as with other events in Anderson's life, had implications in the broader musical world for other black singers. Langston Hughes wrote of this as "a precedent-shattering moment in American musical history." She was asked by Rudolph Bing, general manager of the Metropolitan Opera, to join the Metropolitan Opera in the role of Ulrica in Verdi's *Un Ballo in Maschera*. Anderson's 1955 debut at the Metropolitan Opera was of such significance in the history of American race relations that it was given a front-page story the next morning in the *New York Times* with a picture of Anderson and her mother taken after the performance. Critics have often written about Anderson's age and voice at this debut; few have commented on Bing's astute casting of her in the role of Ulrica, the sorceress/fortune-teller who need not have a youthful voice.

In her only operatic run, Anderson sang with the Metropolitan Opera for seven performances, including a performance in her home city at the Philadelphia Academy of Music. After *Un Ballo in Maschera* Anderson resumed touring, embarking in September of 1957 on a ten-week tour of south Asia and the Far East sponsored by the U.S. Department of State. This tour was filmed by the television crew of the CBS television program "See It Now" as the "Lady from Philadelphia."

Anderson's farewell tour began in 1964 at Constitution Hall in Washington, D.C., and ended with a concert at Carnegie Hall on Easter Sunday in 1965. After this extensive tour, in which she revisited cities of her many recitals over the years, Anderson generally lived in retirement on Marianna Farm in Danbury.

After her retirement Anderson sang in Paris at the Sainte Chappelle and on behalf of the First World Festival of Negro Arts, which was held at Dakar, Senegal, in 1966. She also appeared as narrator on several occasions with various orchestras in Aaron Copland's *Lincoln Portrait*. In 1977 a seventy-fifth birthday gala concert was sponsored by Young Artists Presents with performers including Clamma Dale, Mignon Dunn, Shirley Verrett, James Levine, and others. In 1982 an eightieth birthday concert in Anderson's honor was given at Carnegie Hall with Verrett and Grace Bumbry.

Anderson was also honored by the Danbury community and many others in a gala concert that served to establish a Marian Anderson Award, reestablishing the award she started in 1941 with the ten-thousand-dollar Bok Award. Musicians performing at this gala included Jessye Norman and Isaac Stern, with Julius Rudel conducting the Ives Symphony Orchestra.

Recordings by Anderson span four decades—from the acoustic recordings of the mid-1920s to the long-playing album of Brahms and Schubert lieder that was recorded at Webster Hall in New York City in 1966 and released by RCA in 1978. Several recent recordings are compact disk reissues of earlier works.

John B. Steane provides an overview that is valuable for mentions of Anderson's recordings of specific works:

> On records, where we can turn backwards and for-
> wards from one kind of song to another at will, the
> variety of her singing, and the conscious direction of
> the voice are still more impressive. One feature of the
> change is the appearance and disappearance of vibra-
> to. . . . Her performance of this on 78 is extremely fine:
> the breath-control is admirable, and the song makes
> great demands upon it. She grades and shades her tone
> with much skill, and captures too the kind of yearning
> happiness-in-melancholy which often proves elu-
> sive. . . . This, together with the range of the voice,
> makes us realise afresh what an operatic artist she
> might have been.

Anderson •

records for

four decades

In an article in *National Review*, Sweeley summed up Anderson's artistry and the symbolic place in America forced upon her:

> Marian Anderson has become an American symbol—so much so that one may forget how accomplished a singer she really was. The extraordinary range, power and richness of her voice were wedded to a remarkable musicality. The quick, bright vibrato in the middle range, the seemingly boundless top, and the wonderful depth of the lower notes were all combined into one marvelous vocal instrument.

**Profile by
Patricia Turner**

MAYA ANGELOU

A ny biography of Maya Angelou must necessarily rely on Angelou's

1928- •

own account of her colorful life. To date Angelou has written five

volumes of a serial autobiography: I Know Why the Caged Bird Sings,

writer, poet •

Gather Together in My Name, Singin' and Swingin' and Gettin' Merry

Like Christmas, The Heart of a Woman, *and* All God's Children Need

Traveling Shoes. *She has also written several volumes of poetry, and at*

various times in her life she's been a dancer, actress, scriptwriter,

director, producer, songwriter, and editor. She currently holds an

endowed chair as Reynolds Professor of American Studies at Wake

Forest University in Winston-Salem, North Carolina.

Maya Angelou was born Marguerite Johnson on April 4, 1928, in Saint Louis, Missouri. When she was three, she and her four-year-old

brother, Bailey, Jr., were sent on a train by their divorced parents, Bailey and Vivian (Baxter) Johnson, to live in Stamps, Arkansas, with their paternal grandmother. "Momma" Henderson, as they called her, supported her family on meager proceeds from her general store, and she taught Angelou "common sense, practicality and the ability to control one's own destiny that comes from constant hard work and courage." Although living during the depression years in the South was a struggle for blacks, Angelou found love and the sense of the black tradition there, primarily from her grandmother and the local church.

When Angelou was seven she spent eight months with her mother in Saint Louis. There Angelou's trust in the adult world crumbled: her mother's boyfriend, Mr. Freeman, raped her. After an initial close encounter with Freeman, she says that she thought "he held me so softly that I wished he wouldn't ever let me go. I felt at home. From the way he was holding me I knew he'd never let me go or let anything bad ever happen to me. This was probably my real father and we had found each other at last. But then he rolled leaving me in a wet place, and stood up."

On a subsequent encounter, when he did rape her, Angelou was confused and felt increasingly guilty, especially at Freeman's trial. When Freeman was kicked to death, Angelou, feeling responsible for his murder, entered a self-imposed world of silence that lasted five years. Annoyed by her daughter's stony silence, Vivian Baxter sent Angelou back to Stamps. However, just as an adult had forced Angelou to retreat into a world of silence, so an adult, Bertha Flowers, another role model, helped to draw Angelou out again. According to critic Dolly McPherson, "Mrs. Flowers throws Maya her 'first life line' by accepting her as an individual not in relation to another person." Angelou's grandmother remained equally supportive, but shortly after Angelou's graduation from eighth grade, at the top of her class, she and Bailey left the security of her home to live with their mother in San Francisco.

Rape prompts •

a vow of silence

Vivian Baxter, now a professional gambler, introduced Angelou to a world vastly different from Stamps. While attending George Washington High School and taking drama and dance lessons on scholarship at the California Labor School, Angelou met a variety of people at her mother's rooming house. From her mother, stepfather, and boarders, Angelou learned everything from etiquette to card-playing. A serious and permanent testing of her emerging adulthood was her unplanned pregnancy and motherhood at age sixteen. Angelou ends *Caged Bird* with the birth of her son, Guy, because "I wanted to end it on a happy note. It was the best thing that ever happened to me."

Motherhood as well as the growing need for independence from her own mother prompted Angelou to move from her mother's home.

Angelou first tried to get a job as a telephone operator, then tried to enlist in the WACS, and she finally accepted a position as a cook in a Creole restaurant even though she knew nothing about Creole cooking. A subsequent job as a nightclub waitress in San Diego inadvertently plunged Angelou briefly into the world of prostitution; for a short while, she "managed" two lesbian lovers. Angelou states:

> At eighteen I had managed in a few tense years to become a snob at all levels, racial, cultural and intellectual. I was a madam and thought myself morally superior to the whores. I was a waitress and believed myself cleverer than the customers I served. I was a lonely unmarried mother and held myself to be freer than the married women I met.

At age twenty-two Angelou married a white man, Tosh Angelos. The two-and-a-half-year marriage failed because of Angelou's insistent need for freedom from a constricting life, and Angelou began a career as a dancer in a bar. Soon performers from the well-known Purple Onion offered Angelou a job dancing at that establishment—a move that became a turning point in Angelou's halting career. It also modified her view of the white world: "There whites were treating me as an equal, as if I could do whatever they could do. They did not consider that race, height, gender or lack of education might have crippled me."

Angelou got more opportunities to develop as an entertainer, and in 1954-55 she toured Europe and Africa in *Porgy and Bess*. Around this time, Angelou adopted her present name, derived from her brother's nickname for her and a variation of her first husband's surname, Angelos. McPherson describes this time in Angelou's life as one of liberation, "the triumphal blooming of a talented, determined young Black woman into the adult self and into a fully liberated woman."

● **Angelou**

becomes social

activist

Returning to the United States after the tour, Angelou resumed her career as a nightclub performer. During this time, she also became a social activist and with comedian Godfrey Cambridge co-wrote a revue, "Cabaret for Freedom," a benefit for Martin Luther King's Southern Christian Leadership Conference. Recognizing her commitment to the civil rights cause, King asked her to serve as northern coordinator for the SCLC from 1960 to 1961.

By this time, according to Lynn Z. Bloom, "Angelou had made a commitment to become a writer." She was introduced to the Harlem Writer's Guild by social activist-author John Killens. Undoubtedly her close association with such noted authors as James Baldwin, Paule Marshall, and John Henrik Clarke inspired Angelou.

In late 1961, Angelou left the United States with her son and Vusumzi Make, a South African freedom fighter, who persuaded her to accompany him to Cairo, Egypt, saying that their union would be "the joining of Africa and Africa-America." Angelou never married Make, though they lived together for several years. Because of Make's poor financial management, Angelou did the unheard of—she sought employment as an editor of the *Arab Observer,* a move that infuriated Make. Their disagreement over her new independence as well as his adultery confirmed Angelou's decision to leave Make and move to Ghana. Although she had not planned to stay there long, her son Guy's automobile accident in Ghana changed her mind. In *All God's Children Need Traveling Shoes* Angelou connects Ghana with her past in Arkansas and California:

> Their skins were the colors of my childhood cravings:
> peanut butter, licorice, chocolate, caramel. There was
> the laughter of home, quick and without artifice. The
> erect and graceful walk of the women reminded me of
> my Arkansas Grandmother, Sunday-hatted, on her
> way to church. I listened to men talk, and whether or
> not I understood their meaning, there was a melody as
> familiar as sweet potato pie, reminding me of my Uncle
> Tommy Baxter in Santa Monica, California.

However, Angelou was never completely accepted by native Africans, who regarded her, despite her African heritage, as an outsider. While in Ghana, Angelou served as a feature editor of *The African Review* in Accra, wrote articles for the *Ghanian Times* and Accra's Ghanaian Broadcasting Corporation, and taught at the University of Ghana.

Since her return from Ghana, Angelou has demonstrated her versatile talent in several areas. In 1966 she had a part in Jean Anouilh's *Medea,* produced in Hollywood, and she wrote and acted in plays nationwide. She also was busy writing songs and a television series, and in 1972 Angelou became the first black woman to have a screenplay, *Georgia, Georgia,* produced. Five years later Angelou's performance in the television production of Alex Haley's *Roots* earned her an Emmy nomination, and in 1979 her first autobiography, *I Know Why the Caged Bird Sings,* was made into a television movie, for which Angelou wrote the script and music. In the national arena, the versatile Angelou was appointed by President Gerald Ford to the Bicentennial Commission and by President Jimmy Carter to the Commission of International Woman's Year. Her marriage in 1973 to Paul de Feu ended in 1981. Since 1981, Angelou has held the lifetime appointment position as Reynolds Professor of American Studies at Wake Forest University in Winston-

Salem, North Carolina. She is currently writing another volume of her autobiography, which she calls "a hard one to do, and it's coming very thin on the ground."

Angelou has also published several volumes of poetry about issues in the black experience and in society as a whole, including *Just Give Me a Cool Drink of Water 'fore I Diiie, And Still I Rise,* and *I Shall Not Be Moved.* Most critics agree that Angelou's outstanding works are *I Know Why the Caged Bird Sings* (nominated for the National Book Award in 1974) and *The Heart of a Woman.* Critics find that Angelou, in her autobiographies, "mixes fact with fantasy." However, in a 1989 interview, Angelou states that in telling her life, she tells the "truth" as distinguished from "facts": "There's a world of difference between truth and facts. Facts can obscure the truth. You can tell so many facts that you fill the stage but haven't got one iota of truth."

Most critics assess Angelou's autobiographies as a significant contribution to American literature of the self and to black American literature in particular. Placing the autobiographies firmly within the tradition of such black autobiographies as those of Frederick Douglass, Anne Moody, Richard Wright, and Malcolm X, critics appreciate Angelou's growing awareness of her external environment and of the self within that environment. Selwyn Cudjue, in particular, applauds Angelou's narration of the "collective experience," which takes the black autobiographer away from concentration on the individual "I" and places her within the collective "we." Eugenia Collier notes another achievement of Angelou's autobiographies:

> The pervasive theme, naturally developed in all the autobiographies, is the strength of the Black woman, her ability to prevail despite the awful hurting put upon her by the world, even by her own Black man, who often assuages his own hurt by further oppressing her. Yet there is no blatant preaching, no anti-male rhetoric.

Critics view Angelou's life as a journey to selfhood, the gradual appreciation of herself as a unique individual. In the same vein, Angelou's distinction between the "facts" and the "truth" of her life story emphasizes the special self-examination and insight into self that every black American woman needs to achieve in a male-dominated society. Angelou selects those events in her life that helped her to grow emotionally, psychologically, spiritually—the "stuff of life" that truly counts in building self-acceptance.

Profile by
Grace E. Collins

JOSEPHINE BAKER

*F*lamboyant and colorful on and off the stage, controversial, erratic, difficult, eccentric, and domineering, Josephine Baker was a singer, entertainer, dancer, French spy, and a woman who tried to create a utopian community in a world that doesn't allow such impracticalities. Baker was a consummate and working entertainer until the day of her death, a vigorous spokesperson for causes she believed in, and a brave woman who tried, but didn't always succeed, to make her dreams come true. An "icon of the Jazz Age," as biographer Phyllis Rose calls her, Baker was the first black woman to become an international star.

1906-1975 •

dancer, •

entertainer

Baker was born in Saint Louis, Missouri, on June 3, 1906. Her mother, who worked as a domestic, was Carrie McDonald, and she was not married to Baker's father, Eddie Carson, a local musician who played the drums. Abandoned by her real father and living with a

stepfather who was prone to violence and abuse, Baker developed a mistrust of men and a feeling that she must rely on herself. Her mother's temperament added little to the stability of the family, which lived in extreme poverty, moving often and struggling for survival. The law at that time permitted children of eight years old to be sent out to do domestic work, providing they were also sent to school, so Baker went to work at that age. She had the misfortune of encountering an abusive employer in her first job, which ended when the woman reached the final point in her continuing mistreatment of Baker by plunging the child's arm into a pot of boiling water. Her second employer treated her much better.

Before she was fourteen, Baker had run away from home, found a job supporting herself by waiting on tables, and married and left her first husband, Willie Wells. (She would marry several more times during her lifetime.) Her pregnancy by Wells ended either by early miscarriage or by abortion. Strongly attracted to show business, she then joined a street band that was eventually incorporated into the Dixie Fliers, a traveling show that featured Clara Smith. Baker worked as a dresser for Smith and developed her skills as a dancer. When the troupe reached Philadelphia, she met and married William Howard Baker in 1921, much to his family's dismay.

Baker was turned down for the original production of Sissle and Blake's *Shuffle Along* because she was not yet sixteen, the minimum age to work in New York theaters. However, she managed to get a job in the road company and eventually found a place in Sissle and Blake's new production, *Chocolate Dandies,* in 1924. When the show closed the next year, Baker found work at the Plantation Club. Caroline Dudley, a wealthy white Chicago woman with a passion for black shows, conceived the idea of taking authentic black performers to Paris. Dudley offered Baker a position, and after hesitating, she accepted. Originally, Baker was not the most important member of the troupe, but when she reached Paris the balance began to turn quickly. Paul Colin, who soon became her lover, selected Baker for the central figure of his poster for the *Revue Nègre* rather than the nominal star, Maude de Forest.

As rehearsals progressed, the producers became worried about the success of the show, and they persuaded Baker to dance nude. The *Revue Nègre* opened on October 2, 1925, at the Théâtre des Champs-Elysées. As Baker first appeared dancing the Charleston to "Yes, Sir, That's My Baby!" there were some hostile reactions from a small part of the audience scandalized by the "vulgarity" of the dancer, but Baker's nude dance with Joe Alex overwhelmed the spectators. Josephine Baker became the rage of Paris.

Baker embarked on a world tour in 1928. While traveling through Europe and South America, Baker also worked on her voice and her dancing, and by the time she returned to Paris in 1930, there was a genuine difference in her performances. The comic elements had disappeared; she struck many people as a much-changed performer, and not all people liked the change, seeing the toning down of her "vulgarity" as a loss of vigor.

Her performance for the revue *Paris Qui Remue* in 1930 represented a step upward in show business, since the Casino de Paris was considered to be a cut above the Folies Bergère. This advancement brought Baker into conflict with the aging but still-reigning queen of Paris music halls, Mistinguett; there was one public confrontation in which the two women spat at each other. The song that became Baker's theme, performed at every subsequent appearance, was written for this show—"J'ai Deux Amours," "I have two loves, my country and Paris." As publicity for the show, she led a baby leopard about Paris on a leash. The leopard's collar was a diamond choker that was later sold for twenty-two thousand dollars when Baker was desperate for money.

The time had come to try to return to the United States. After considerable hesitation, Baker accepted an offer to appear in the 1936 *Ziegfeld Follies.* She knew she was in her homeland when the Saint Moritz hotel in New York City gave her and her companion, Giuseppe Abatino, a suite but asked her to use the back entrance to avoid offending the sensibilities of visiting southerners. She returned to France later that year to appear in the Folies Bergère.

Baker now fell deeply in love with Jean Lion. The son of moderately prosperous Jewish parents, he had entered the stock exchange at the age of eighteen and found that he had a flair for making money. Blond, very handsome, and athletic, he was now a millionaire several times over. He taught Baker to fly and proposed one day while they were in the air. They were married in the spring of 1937, and after the shock of the wedding the family accepted her. This marriage brought Baker French citizenship. She became pregnant but had an early miscarriage, and the incompatibility of each partner's goals in the marriage soon became evident. They separated, but the divorce did not take place until 1942. Baker hoped for some time for a reconciliation, which never took place. Her grief over the breakdown of her marriage did not prevent Baker from taking new lovers, and it was while she was traveling with Claude Meunier, whose family fortune came from chocolate, that she saw and rented a château, Les Milandes.

Baker's opening in the Casino de Paris's revue *Paris-Londres* in September 1939 coincided with the onset of World War II. In the late spring of 1940 she was recruited as a spy by Jacques Abtey. Her potential lay in the fact that she was a persona grata at the Italian Embassy because of the favorable remarks she had made about Mussolini during her appearances in Italy in 1935. When the German invasion of France came, she and Abtey joined the flight from Paris. They went first to Les Milandes, and then they made their way to Lisbon. They returned to Marseille in late 1940 and set up operations there. Barred from performing in German-occupied France, Baker arranged a revival of *La Créole*. She cut short the run of the operetta to go to Casablanca in January 1940. As a performer she had freedom to travel from there to Portugal through Spain. During this period she continued to function as a spy; thus, she was a member of the French Resistance from the very beginning. Her conduct earned her the Medal of the Resistance with rosette at the end of the war, and later she was awarded the Legion of Honor.

In December 1941, Baker delivered a stillborn child in a Casablanca clinic; the father is unknown. There were complications, and to the doctor in charge an emergency hysterectomy seemed the only way to save her life. Until June 1942, Baker's life was in serious danger from the resulting complications; at one point United Press International carried the news that she had died. Even in the hospital, she continued to serve the Resistance, since visiting her offered a convenient pretext for Resistance workers to meet and exchange messages. When the American Army landed in Morocco on November 8, 1942, Baker had recovered. She spent the time after the landing entertaining the Allied troops in North Africa, striving in the face of the official segregation policy of the United States Army to see that black soldiers had a fair share in the seating.

Baker made a successful return trip to the United States in 1951. She attracted wide attention with her statements against segregation and her refusal to perform at segregated venues. Baker was the first African-American performer to appear before integrated audiences in a Miami Beach hotel and the first to house her entire troupe in a Las Vegas hotel; she canceled engagements in such places as Atlanta and Saint Louis when her conditions were not met. On May 29 Harlem turned out to honor her on Josephine Baker Day, and the NAACP honored her as the Most Outstanding Woman of the Year.

Baker continued working outside the United States and began to transform Les Milandes into a tourist center, the showpiece of the ideal community she wished to show the world. Between 1954 and 1965 she adopted twelve children of differing ethnic backgrounds and nationalities—ten boys and two girls, her Rainbow Tribe. After the success of the initial years, the efforts at Les Milandes began to unravel, due in large part to Baker's long absences performing and her management by caprice. Relations with the neighbors became very strained. By being unable to pay employees or by refusing to pay them, she made them feel entitled to steal what they could get their hands on. Lynn Haney states that between 1953 and 1963 Baker spent more than $1.5 million and was $400,000 in debt.

In August 1963 Baker returned to the United States to appear at the March on Washington. After a manager was found, she gave a benefit in New York on October 12 for the Student Nonviolent Coordinating Committee, the Congress of Racial Equality, and the NAACP. By this time it was not easy for her to find managers, since she had become notorious for refusing to pay them the money they had earned. Baker returned to Europe, where she had her first heart attack while performing in Denmark in 1964. Her financial affairs were becoming increasingly disordered, and she no longer automatically commanded the highest fees. Finally in the spring of 1969 Les Milandes was seized. Baker had to be carried out bodily. For seven hours she sat barefoot, cap on head, crying on the back-door steps until an ambulance removed her to a local clinic, where she was treated for exhaustion. The subsequent sale of the château and what remained of its furnishings brought in very little money.

Grace Kelly, now Princess Grace of Monaco, came to Baker's rescue by providing the down payment on a villa at Roquebrune, near the principality. The four bedrooms provided scant room for twelve children. Baker worked when she could; when she could not, she would from time to time wander the streets begging for her children. Without her fine clothes, makeup, and wig, she now appeared to be an old woman, but she retained the ability to appear glamorous and beautiful the moment she stepped onto the stage, a transformation that could surprise observers.

In the first part of 1973, Baker returned to the United States for a successful appearance at Carnegie Hall. Encouraged by her reception, she planned a seventeen-city tour beginning in the fall. In July while performing in Denmark, she had a second heart attack and a stroke that left her face partly paralyzed. In spite of her memory lapses, the United States tour went well until her Christmas season performances at the Palace flopped. In desperation she called in her nephew, Richard, from Saint Louis for support.

The Société des Bains de Mer, the company that runs the Monte Carlo casino, provided the last turn in Baker's career as a performer by sponsoring a show starring Baker and simply called *Joséphine* in August 1974. This revue was so successful that the company decided to take it to

Paris. No large theater would entertain the idea because of concerns about Baker's health. A small music hall was located and rehearsals begun. In rehearsal, Baker was still able to summon up immense energy and pay close attention to detail. She was to be on stage almost continuously, sing many songs, and dance the Charleston. *Joséphine* officially opened on April 8, 1975, after several trial runs. Performances sold out many days in advance. That evening a gala was held at the Hotel Bristol to celebrate Baker's fifty years as a performer in Paris. Two nights later she was the last to leave a party, where she had tried in vain to persuade someone to take her to see a young black man who was doing impressions of her in a nightclub.

The following afternoon she did not wake up from her regular nap; she had suffered a massive cerebral hemorrhage and was in a coma. She died early in the morning of April 14, 1975. Her televised state funeral the following day at the Madeleine church drew twenty thousand people, and she is the only American woman to receive an official twenty-one gun salute from the French government. A quiet, private funeral service attended by her children was held in Monaco, and Josephine Baker of Saint Louis finally found a resting place in the cemetery of Monaco. Current American interest in Baker is evident in the 1991 HBO Pictures production of *The Josephine Baker Story* and in the recent re-release of the movies *Zou-Zou* and *Princesse Tam-Tam*, which played to capacity crowds during a screening at Manhattan's Film Forum. The subtitled films are now available on videocassette as well.

**Profile by
Robert L. Johns**

MARGUERITE ROSS BARNETT

W hen Marguerite Ross Barnett was appointed president of the

University of Houston in 1990, she became the first black and the first

woman chief administrator of the flagship of the four-campus Houston

system. She had already made her mark at the University of Missouri-St.

Louis, where she was chancellor and tenured professor of political

science. This distinguished political scientist boosted the prestige of both

institutions with her scholarship, her leadership ability, and her fund-

raising efforts.

1942-1992 •

university •

president

Born May 22, 1942, in Charlottesville, Virginia, Barnett was the daughter of Dewey Ross and Mary (Douglass) Barnett. She attended Bennett High School in Buffalo, New York, and in 1964 graduated from Antioch College with a bachelor's degree in political science. She continued her studies at the University of Chicago, where in 1966 she received a master's and in 1972 earned a Ph.D. As a child, she had wanted to become a scientist, but a course on Indian politics changed her career plans. As a part of her doctoral studies, she conducted research in India for two years. This project resulted in a book on ethnic and cultural pluralism, *The Politics of Cultural Nationalism in South India,* for which the American Political Science Association awarded her its top book prize in 1981.

Barnett's career as teacher of political science began with her appointment as lecturer at the University of Chicago from September of 1969 to September of 1970. She then moved to Princeton University, where she was assistant professor of political science for six years, and (simultaneously) James Madison Bicentennial Preceptor for two years. She became professor of political science at Howard University in 1976. In 1980, while still at Howard, Barnett was co-director of the Ethnic Heritage Project, a study of an historic black community in Gum Springs, Virginia, funded by the United States Department of Education. She then moved to Columbia University, where she taught and directed the Institute for Urban and Minority Education. In 1983 she was appointed professor of political science and vice-chancellor for academic affairs at the City University of New York, a twenty-one college system that serves 180,000 students. She remained there until May of 1986, when she was named chancellor and professor of political science at the University of Missouri at St. Louis, a post she held for four years.

• University of Houston appoints its first woman president

Following her appointment to the presidency of the University of Houston in the spring of 1990, Barnett, the first black and the first woman to head that institution, continued to gain widespread press coverage. An article in the March 6, 1991, issue of the *Chronicle of Higher Education* kept her in the national spotlight as head of a university that she said was "literally on the cusp of greatness." Barnett was one of only three women to lead universities with more than thirty thousand students. She was also the only black heading a major research institution, though she believed this to be less significant to her than her agenda at the University of Houston and the role that she felt public urban universities ought to play in addressing a wide range of issues, from homelessness to space exploration. The role of modern urban research universities, she maintained, is to help society "solve its key conundrums . . . in the same way land-grant institutions helped solve the problems of the 19th century."

Barnett was described as "an animated woman" who outpaced even her most energetic colleagues, an effective school booster, and a woman with strong views as well as a willingness to hear the views of others before making a decision. Self-confident, though not conceited, Barnett was as comfortable in the corporate boardroom as she was in her staff meetings and was been praised equally by business people and academics.

During her career Barnett was involved with numerous community activities and served on a number of boards, including the Monsanto Company, the Educational Testing Services, the Student Loan Marketing Association (SALLIE MAE), the American Council on Education, and the Committee on Economic Development. Her cultural affiliations included memberships on the board of directors of the Houston Grand Opera and the board of advisors of the Houston Symphony. Her professional memberships centered on associations in political science and South Asian studies, and she was a member of the Overseas Development Council, the Council on Foreign Relations, and the Cleveland Council.

The author of fifty articles, Barnett was also writer or editor of five books. In addition to her award-winning volume on South India, she co-edited *Public Policy for the Black Community: Strategies and Perspectives; Readings on Equal Education; Comparing Race, Sex, and National Origin Desegregation: Public Attitudes of Desegregation;* and *Educational Policy in an Era of Conservative Reform.*

Barnett was the mother of one daughter, Amy Douglass Barnett, who was born on December 18, 1962. Barnett (who was previously married to Stephen A. Barnett) married Walter Eugene King on June 30, 1980; currently in real estate, he is a former member of Parliament in Bermuda and a former professional golfer.

In November of 1991, Barnett announced that testing and treatment for an unspecified neuro-endocrinological condition would require periodic absences from her duties at the University of Houston. She was on medical leave from the post when she died of a blood disorder involving hypoglycemia with metastatic cancer on February 26, 1992, at Maui Memorial Hospital in Wailuku, Hawaii.

**Profile by
Jessie Carney Smith**

DAISY BATES

*D*aisy Bates is one of the twentieth century's most important civil

1920- •

rights activists. A staunch advocate for integration, Bates played a vital

role in the integration of Central High School in Little Rock, Arkansas, in

journalist, civil •

1957. Daisy Lee Gatson Bates was born in 1920 in Huttig, a small town

rights activist

in the lumbering region of southeast Arkansas. She was raised by

adoptive parents, Orlee and Susie Smith, and she never knew her real

parents. In the autobiographical sections of her 1962 work The Long

Shadow of Little Rock, *Bates remarked that the circumstances of her*

biological mother's death and her father's subsequent flight were sur-

rounded by secrecy. When she was eight years old, some neighborhood

children taunted her for being "so uppity. If you knew what happened to your mother, you wouldn't act so stuck up." She inquired of a cousin what the children meant and was told that her mother was ravished and murdered, allegedly by three white men, and her body was found submerged in a local pond. Her father fled Huttig for fear of reprisals from whites should he attempt to prosecute the suspects.

The relationship with the Smiths was warm and close, and Bates was raised as a somewhat spoiled and willful only child. She was indulged by her loving mother and hardworking though extremely sensitive father. When she was fifteen years old and still in school, Bates met Lucius Christopher Bates, an insurance agent and close friend of her father. L. C. Bates had been born in Mississippi, attended the segregated county public schools, went on to Wilberforce College, the African Methodist Episopal church-supported school in Ohio, and majored in journalism.

In 1941, shortly after the death of Orlee Smith, L. C. and Daisy married and finally settled in Little Rock. L. C. soon convinced his wife to join him in a newspaper venture, and the couple used their savings to lease the *Arkansas State Press*. Initially, the paper was fairly successful, and within the first few months reached a circulation of ten thousand.

With the outbreak of World War II, nearby Camp Robinson was reopened at the request of local businessmen and politicians, and soon large numbers of black soldiers filled the streets of Little Rock on weekends. Incidents of police brutality involving blacks were regularly reported in the *State Press*, but on March 2, 1942, a particularly horrible incident occurred. According to eyewitness accounts, military police had taken Private Albert Glover into custody, and when Sargeant Thomas Foster inquired about the arrest, local policeman A. J. Hay intervened, struck Foster with his nightstick, threw him to the ground, and fired five shots into his prostrate form. Daisy was on the scene soon after and reported the details of the incident in the *State Press*. Subsequently, the black community filed protests with U.S. Army officials, but nothing was done to prosecute Hay, since this was the way the local police traditionally handled blacks. The newspaper coverage of the incident, however, enraged local white businessmen, who feared that the bad publicity could lead to the closing of Camp Robinson. Accordingly, they withdrew all their advertisements from the *State Press*, a potentially crippling blow to the fledgling newspaper. Instead of folding the paper, though, the Bateses tried "taking the paper to the people": they doubled their efforts, working twelve to sixteen hours a day, and gradually circulation began to increase. Within a year the newspaper reached twenty thousand readers.

The *State Press* gained the reputation of an independent voice of the people and worked for the improvement of social and economic circumstances for blacks throughout the state. In Little Rock, the paper continued to expose police brutality, and eventually changes were made. Black policemen were hired to patrol the black neighborhoods, and the state of race relations improved noticeably. As Daisy noted, by the end of the war, Little Rock had gained "a reputation as a liberal southern city.

When the U.S. Supreme Court declared segregation in public schools unconstitutional in May of 1954, Arkansas school officials felt obliged to respond publicly to the decision. Later in the month Little Rock school superintendent Virgil Blossom called several prominent blacks into his office to preview the school board's statement, which indicated the board intended to pursue this integration gradually. Daisy had been president of the state conference of NAACP branches since 1952; the expectation on the part of some NAACP officials in liberal Little Rock was that the city's public schools would be integrated by September 1954. The meeting with Blossom made it clear that any significant movement toward integration in local public schools would only come through activities launched by members of the black community.

The state and local NAACP decided to challenge the school board's policy of gradualism—a decision that placed Daisy and a group of children at the center of national and international attention for several months. To compile cases of denial of admission, Daisy and her "children," as they came to be known, would go to the white public school and attempt to enroll the black students. Their attempts and denials would be recorded in the *State Press* and other newspapers.

Bates involved •

in Little Rock

crisis

Meanwhile, white supremacists took every opportunity to denounce the growing possibility of race-mixing in the public schools. Outraged white citizens issued manifestos, resolutions, petitions, and legislative initiatives in vain attempts to slow or halt the coming integration of the Little Rock public schools. Battle lines were drawn in Hoxie, Arkansas, in the summer of 1955, when black parents demanded enrollment of their children in the white schools, and the Hoxie School Board, lacking sufficient funds to finance the dual system, was forced to integrate its public schools. White racists mobilized a broad-based opposition, but the Hoxie School Board, citing the Supreme Court decision, held its ground. In many ways the confrontations in Hoxie set the tenor and tone for white opposition to public school integration in Little Rock.

The "Blossom Plan" called for integration to start in the highest grades at Central High School, rather than at the elementary level where black students were more numerous, beginning in September 1957. In February 1956, NAACP attorneys Wiley Branton and U. Simpson Tate filed suit in federal court to gain the admittance of several of Daisy's children to white public schools at mid-semester. Federal Judge John Miller decided to go along with the Little Rock School Board's timetable for integration, but it confirmed the federal court's interest in overseeing the scheduled launch date of September 4, 1957.

During the 1956-57 school year, black students were polled and school officials estimated that "only about eighty out of several hundred eligible Negro children" applied for admission to Central High School. Seventeen were deemed eligible by school officials, and ultimately nine entered the pages of twentieth-century black history under the protective custody of the courageous and capable Daisy Bates: Carlotta Walls, Jefferson Thomas, Elizabeth Eckford, Thelma Mothershed, Melba Patillo, Ernest Green, Terrence Roberts, Gloria Ray, and Minnijean Brown.

- *Little Rock Nine*

begin

integration

efforts

Blossom insisted during a meeting with Daisy and the black students' parents that no parents or adults accompany the students to Central High School—a mandate that seemed more and more unreasonable as eyewitness reports described mobs of whites forming around the high school and in other areas of the city. Bates contacted the members of the Interracial Ministerial Alliance and ask that a group of ministers accompany the students to the school. They agreed to assemble at 8:30 a.m., so Bates called the parents of all the children except Elizabeth Eckford (who had no telephone) to inform them of the change in plans. The next morning Eckford went alone to Central High School and was taunted and berated, jeered at and accosted by hundreds of white students and citizens in front of cameras, reporters, and photographers from around the world. The photographs of Eckford's grace under pressure captured her agony and youthful determination, and she became a symbol of the oppression of black children in the United States. In the ensuing months and years there would be many other black teenagers and young adults who, when placed in similar circumstances, would demonstrate strength and commitment well beyond their years.

The attack on Eckford set off a round of mob violence in Little Rock that lasted for the next seventeen days. On September 22, 1957, following the issuance of a court injunction against the Arkansas National Guard's further interference with public school integration, Faubus went on television and asked that the black students make no attempt to enroll at Central High School. Chief of Police Marvin Potts was now in charge of the operation, and Daisy received his personal assurances that the police would protect the children. The next morning at 9:23 a.m., the children gathered at the Bates home and in two cars drove to a side entrance at Central High School while the white mob was attacking several black reporters. The nine students were quickly escorted into the building.

This touched off mob action in the downtown Central High School area and throughout Little Rock. Indiscriminate acts of violence were committed against northern reporters and photographers, television personnel, and any blacks the mob encountered. By two o'clock in the afternoon, Potts recognized that he could not guarantee the safety of the students inside the high school, and they were taken out secretly through a delivery entrance. Later that day, Potts declared that the city was experiencing a "reign of terror."

The students remained home the next day as crowds of whites surrounded the high school. Mayor Woodrow Wilson Mann and Potts requested help from the U.S. Department of Justice. Later that afternoon news filtered in that U.S. President Dwight D. Eisenhower had federalized all units of the Arkansas National Guard and ordered Secretary of Defense Charles Wilson to enforce the integration order issued by the U.S. District Court. Wilson ordered one thousand paratroopers from the 101st Airborne "Screaming Eagle" Division of the 327th Infantry Regiment to Little Rock. Later that evening Eisenhower went on national television and made it clear that the "disorderly mobs have deliberately prevented the carrying out of proper orders from the federal court . . . I have today issued an executive order directing the use of troops under federal authority to aid in the execution of federal law in Little Rock."

The paratroopers accompanied the black students to and from school the following day, and they remained at Central High School until September 30, when they were withdrawn to Camp Robinson, about twelve miles from Little Rock. The federalized Arkansas National Guard remained on patrol at the school as southern politicians made efforts to get Faubus to agree to protect the students in return for an end to federal occupation. Unfortunately, the governor had fallen under the spell of the state's staunch segregationists and would make no public concessions or guarantees of protection for the Little Rock Nine.

Meanwhile, Daisy's nine children were on their own inside Central High School, but they were not alone in their struggle for acceptance and equal treatment. Some of the students remembered that some white students made positive overtures, but diehard segregationists continually harassed them with name-calling, pushing, shoving, and overt threats of violence. Bates kept in close contact with them and their parents and always accompanied them to meetings with school officials when incidents occurred.

The crisis at Little Rock's Central High School in 1957 demonstrated to the nation and the entire world the strength and commitment of black youth to the attainment of full citizenship rights in the land of their birth. Little Rock was merely the first round of an extended struggle to desegregate the public elementary, secondary, and higher educational institutions throughout the United States. Black parents and children knew that their cause was just, and they were encouraged by the strength and persistence of Daisy Bates and the example set by her children.

Profile by
V. P. Franklin

MARY FRANCES BERRY

*M**ary Frances Berry is internationally recognized as a historian,***

educator, lawyer, public servant, and civil and human rights activist. A

member of the United States Commission on Civil Rights under both the

Carter and Reagan administrations and an expert on U.S. constitution-

al history, she has written such books as* Black Resistance/White Law *to

call attention to government-sanctioned racism in the United States.

1938- •

historian, •

lawyer,

government

official

The second of three children, Berry was born on February 17, 1938, to Frances Southall Berry (now Wiggins) and George Ford Berry in Nashville, Tennessee. Economic and personal hardships beset the family in Mary's earliest years; insurmountable difficulties compelled Frances Berry to place Mary and a brother in an orphanage for a time. While she was still a child, the ravages of poverty and the human capacity for cruelty, selfishness, and racial prejudice created for Mary Frances Berry a period in her life akin to a "horror story."

Neither poverty, hunger, nor inhumane treatment at the orphanage, however, prevented Berry from demonstrating at an early age exceptional determination, resilience, and intellectual ability. She obtained her first years of formal education in the segregated schools of Nashville and its environs. It was while Berry was in Pearl High School,

however, with "no idea of what [she] was going to do with [her] life," that a black teacher, Minerva Hawkins, saw in the teenager a "diamond in the rough" and changed Berry's life irrevocably. Berry recalls in *Ebony* that as a tenth-grade high school student she felt unchallenged:

> I would hang out of school, leave school early, leave for lunch. It wasn't that I couldn't do the work. I always finished ahead of the other students. I was just bored with school. When I got to Ms. Hawkins's class, she noticed that. She started giving me extra books and extra assignments. Then she would talk to me about it. She would even invite me over to her house after school. She then started talking to me about my life and got me interested in intellectual pursuits.

Upon graduation from high school (with honors), Berry sought and found work, and she began her college education at Hawkins's alma mater, Fisk University, and continued at Howard University. After graduating from Howard in 1961, she enrolled in its graduate school and then became a doctoral student at the University of Michigan, studying history. In addition to her Ph.D., Berry earned a J.D. in 1970.

Berry has enthusiastically and energetically developed a career in academe, which began with and continues to include teaching. One important objective has been to teach effectively whether in the classroom or another academic setting. Berry's teaching activities as a professor of U.S. history and legal history have included the incorporation of racially plural materials into traditional courses, the introduction of new courses, and instruction of young scholars pursuing graduate degrees in history. Berry's career as a scholar-educator has been marked by a series of noteworthy achievements beyond teaching. In 1972 she was named the first director of the Afro-American Studies Program at the University of Maryland and the interim chairperson of Maryland's Division of Behavioral and Social Sciences for the College Park campus. She was appointed provost for the same division in 1974, becoming the highest ranking black woman at College Park.

Berry takes •

the helm

in academe

In 1976 Berry accepted the invitation of the University of Colorado to become chancellor at that institution, thereby becoming the first black woman and one of only two women to join the ranks of presidents and chancellors of major research universities. (The only other woman at the time of Berry's appointment was Lorene Rogers, president of the University of Texas.) Unquestionably, the most prominent and significant academic administrative post in which Berry has served has been the chancellorship of this 21,000-student campus (then 3 percent black, 14 percent Hispanic), with a faculty of 2,300 members and an annual budget of $113.3 million. Her concerns and her goals during the chancellorship were best described by Berry on the occasion of the university's 163rd commencement: "My task . . . will be to foster and continue the effort to attain excellence in our academic programs, despite the increasing difficulty of explaining the value and power of knowledge and its creation, to . . . many constituencies." Berry has accepted two subsequent academic appointments. In 1980 she joined the faculty of her undergraduate alma mater, Howard University, as a professor of history and law and became a senior fellow at Howard's Institute for the Study of Educational Policy. After nearly a decade, Berry resigned from the faculty of Howard University to accept a professorship at the University of Pennsylvania, where she now serves as the Geraldine R. Segal Professor of Social Thought and Professor of History.

• *Race, gender,*

and law

explored in

publications

Berry has achieved particular distinction among scholars for her research, critical analyses, lucid writing style, coverage of timely issues from a historical perspective, and specific expertise in legal and African-American history. In addition to *Black Resistance/White Law*, which analyzes the practice of Constitutional racism, Berry has written five major books: *Military Necessity and Civil Rights Policy: Black Citizenship and the Constitution, 1861-1868; Stability, Security, and Continuity: Mr. Justice Burton and Decision-Making in the Supreme Court, 1945-1958; Long Memory: The Black Experience in America; Why ERA Failed;* and *The Politics of Motherhood.* John W. Blassingame, who co-wrote *Long Memory,* has perceptively argued that Berry's "works tend to close debate. Rarely does one put down a book she has written with the feeling that the subject should be explored again. Instead her books . . . [have become] standards in the field."

Beyond *Black Resistance/White Law,* two of Berry's works have made significant contributions to the field of black American history. In *Military Necessity and Civil Rights Policy,* Berry offers the thesis that blacks have gained the greatest benefits with respect to civil rights during times of national crises. Focusing on the Civil War period, she noted the federal government's concurrent need for black soldiers and the violation of their constitutional rights. In contrast to this monograph stands *Long Memory,* which interprets the black experience through 1980, offering "a wide historical sweep and masterful weaving of cultural, literary and social patterns," as *Library Journal* noted.

Why ERA Failed, a widely reviewed and successful book, has examined the legal process, gender, race, and cultural conflict as well as external and internal factors which affect social movements designed to amend the Constitution. Berry clearly and incisively identified the essential elements required to create the sense of need for alteration of the Constitution and, within a broad historical analysis, addressed specifically the problems of the movement to obtain an Equal Rights Amendment. As John Hope Franklin has commented, *Why ERA Failed* is "an excellent analysis of the historical as well as current forces that doomed this effort to extend equal rights to women by Constitutional amendment." Berry's next study, *The Politics of Motherhood,* presents a historical view of culture, gender, race, politics, and economics in an effort to facilitate understanding of the status of women as mothers, the policy and political questions germane to child care, and concepts of the good and just within society.

From 1977 to 1979, Berry was the first black woman to serve as chief educational officer of the United States. She is best known, however, in her public service as a commissioner of the United States Commission on Civil Rights. Berry's association with the commission preceded her appointment. In 1975 she had prepared for the commission an extensively researched and well-documented special study, *Constitutional Aspects of the Right to Limit Childbearing.* Subsequent to her service as assistant secretary for education, President Jimmy Carter appointed Berry to the United States Civil Rights Commission, which had been established in 1957 to function as an independent, bipartisan agency within the executive branch. Responsible for the investigation of discrimination, the commission had engaged in monitoring and fact-finding, but it had also been the recommending body for the Civil Rights Act of 1964 and Voting Rights Act of 1965.

However distinguished Berry's service as commissioner and vice-chairperson from 1980 to 1982, President Ronald Reagan sought to dismiss her before the 1984 election. This effort to remove Berry and two other appointees holding viewpoints opposed to Reagan's was characterized by Berry as the reduction of the commission from the "watchdog of civil rights" to "a lapdog for the administration," wrote the *Washington Post* in 1984. Berry's prestige and notoriety increased when she successfully challenged in federal court Reagan's attempt to remove her from the commission.

Berry •

challenges

Reagan

An outspoken critic of oppression, exploitation, and denials of human as well as civil rights, whether the victims be a race of people, a small nation, women, the poor, the marginalized or disabled, Berry has a record of and reputation for articulate, historically grounded advocacy of justice. At various periods the issues addressed by Berry have been the Vietnam War, women's rights, federal remedies for past institutionalized racism in the United States, black American civil rights and liberation, African liberation, or the specific recognition of black self-determination required by the principle of justice in South Africa.

Berry's leadership in the Free South Africa Movement—of which she is a founder—and her Thanksgiving 1984 arrest at the South African embassy while protesting apartheid and U.S. policy toward South Africa have catapulted Berry to greater national and international prominence. Viewed variously as either abrasive and radical or persuasive and factual, her responses to the government and the media on matters of justice for persons of African descent in the United States and for black Africans in South Africa gained her recognition throughout the United States. She is a spokesperson for justice, moving with ease from the terse, blunt statement to eloquent, research-rooted testimony. She consistently participates in protests, whether they be authorized public demonstrations or actions of civil disobedience. Her praxis has established Berry as one of the outstanding scholar-activists of the second half of the twentieth century. "When it comes to the cause of justice," she has explained, "I take no prisoners and I don't believe in compromising."

**Profile by
Genna Rae McNeil**

MARY McLEOD BETHUNE

A champion of humanitarian and democratic values throughout   **1875-1955** •

---

the United States for more than thirty years, Mary McLeod Bethune made

---

essential contributions to the development of black America. Through   ***government*** •

---

her prominent position in the administration of President Franklin D.   ***official,***

Roosevelt she assumed the role of race-leader-at-large, thus becoming   ***activist***

---

the most influential black woman in the annals of the country. Bethune

provided the leadership to raise black women from the social and

political invisibility they suffered to a sustained presence in national

affairs.

Born in 1875 in Sumter County near Mayesville, South Carolina, Mary McLeod Bethune was the fifteenth of seventeen children of Sam McLeod and Patsy (McIntosh) McLeod. Her father was of African and Indian descent, and her mother was African. Her parents and most of

her brothers and sisters were slaves emancipated through the Union victory in the Civil War. One major consequence of freedom for the McLeod family was the acquisition, in the early 1870s, of a farm of about thirty-five acres.

During the post-Reconstruction era in white-controlled Sumter County, the overwhelming black majority had little access to public schooling. Therefore, Bethune was fortunate to attend the rural Trinity Presbyterian Mission School four or five miles from her home when it opened in 1885. Three years later she attended Scotia Seminary (later Barber-Scotia College) in Concord, North Carolina. Bethune spent six years at this outreach of northern white Presbyterians. Beyond academics she was submerged in a regime emphasizing religious concerns, "culture and refinement," and "industrial education"—sewing, cooking, laundering, and cleaning.

Upon graduation, Bethune, who was preparing to be an African missionary, entered the Bible Institute for Home and Foreign Missions (later Moody Bible Institute), an interdenominational school in Chicago. Upon applying to the Presbyterian Mission Board for an assignment after a year's study, however, Bethune was greatly disappointed, learning that it did not place African Americans in such positions. Though time and again, life would jolt Bethune, she later certified that this blow was the greatest disappointment of her life.

Bethune's •

greatest

disappointment

Believing that foreign missions were closed to her, Bethune entered virtually the only field open to a black woman of her inclination and training—teaching black students. For the next five years she taught in Georgia and South Carolina, during which time she met Albertus Bethune, a tall and handsome man five years her senior. In May of 1898 the couple married, and they soon made Savannah their home. Here he found work as a porter, and their only child, Albert Bethune, was born. Though the couple remained together for at least eight years and were legally married until Albertus's death in 1918, theirs was not a happy union. Because marriage and family experiences were unsatisfying for her, Bethune ultimately failed to accord these institutions priority status in advancing black Americans.

Bethune saw education as the primary route to racial uplift, and this field consumed her youthful energies. In 1900 she established a Presbyterian parochial school in Palatka, Florida. Two years later, she opened an independent school that she maintained in conjunction with rendering volunteer social services and selling life insurance. After two more years she left the declining Palatka for greener pastures on the state's east coast.

In Daytona, Florida, on October 3, 1904, in a rented house sparsely furnished with dry-goods boxes for benches and other improvised essentials, Bethune founded the Daytona Educational and Industrial Institute, with her assets of "five little girls, a dollar and a half, and faith in God." In addition, she had her own five-year-old son and well-formed ideas of the school she wanted, a re-creation of "dear old Scotia." But she would modify the model by having her students work a large farm to put food on the institute's table and to provide cash income from the sale of produce. Bethune hoped in time to offer nurse training and advanced subjects and attain national respectability.

Fortunately, Bethune had chosen well the city in which to realize her ambition. Daytona's black leaders eagerly assisted her, particularly A. L. James, pastor of Mount Bethel Baptist Church, one of the two black houses of worship in this town of two thousand. In 1905, besides Bethune, he became the only other black member of the school's trustee board, which meant that the whites gave the institute critical assistance. Socially prominent white women frequently exerted hands-on influence in the school's regular activities and even more in special events. Beginning in 1905 the most energetic of them were organized into a Ladies' Advisory Board to the institute, consisting of both local residents and winter tourists. Though on occasion Bethune used her female supporters as a means of interesting their husbands in the Daytona Institute, her largest individual contributors were white males with whom she dealt directly, including James N. Gamble of Proctor and Gamble Manufacturing Company. By 1922, with black and white support, Bethune had developed a thriving institution that enrolled three hundred girls and had a dedicated faculty and staff of about twenty-five.

Beyond study, religion, and work, the girls at the Daytona Institute benefited from contact with an incomparable professional role model, Bethune. With her extremely dark skin, flat nose, and full lips, which clashed sharply with America's ideal of physical attractiveness and which both blacks and whites deemed liabilities to leadership in middle-class black America, Bethune transcended the restricted sphere that society usually assigned to one of her color and, for that matter, one of her gender. Her sense of an unfettered self was so great that she defied Jim Crow customs and ordinances, most notably in her insistence on desegregated seating at the Daytona Institute. And despite Ku Klux Klan threats, she and her entire faculty and staff voted in 1920 and afterwards. With a vision of better opportunities for blacks and black women in particular, Bethune extended her influence throughout black America.

In 1923 her school, then the Daytona Normal and Industrial Institute, merged with the coeducational Cookman Institute in Jacksonville, Florida. Though declining at the time, the latter claimed a distinguished fifty-one-year-old heritage and sponsorship of the Methodist Episcopal church. The church had arranged for the institutional marriage between Daytona and Cookman on the basis of developing the union, under Bethune's leadership, into a coeducational junior college. To reflect the collegiate direction, the institution officially changed its name to Bethune-Cookman College in 1929. By 1935, having weathered the worst of the Great Depression, the college's development won for Bethune the NAACP's coveted Spingarn Medal.

Bethune's relationship to her beloved school took a momentous turn in 1936 when she accepted a full-time government position in Washington, D.C. Consequently, the college suffered from her divided attention until 1942. At that time, after a life-threatening illness, Bethune resigned the presidency. Yet when a great measure of her political effectiveness in Washington ended, she worked her way back into the school's presidential office. In 1947, however, she seemed to have accepted the fact that the escalating rigors of the job required a younger person and consequently vacated the position. At this time Bethune basked in a phenomenal educational record. No other woman of her generation created an institution for disadvantaged youth and developed it into a senior college.

Establishing a school, the achievement for which traditionally Bethune has been best known, assumes greater significance when it is understood that it was the foundation of her exalted stature in the women's club movement. By hosting state and regional conclaves and channeling personnel and other resources into club work, Bethune progressively made her school a hub of clubwomen's activity. This occurred in tandem with her presidency of state, regional, and national federations, beginning with the Florida Association of Colored Women in June 1917. In keeping with self-help trends in other southern states, on September 10, 1920, Bethune led Florida's women in opening a home in Ocala for wayward and delinquent girls.

Like the best of patriotic leaders during World War I, Bethune directed her constituents into well-publicized war-support endeavors. Bethune's presidency of the Southeastern Association of Colored Women, which she established in 1920 and presided over for five years, encompassed especially a turning outward to the broader society. The striking development occurred in 1922 when the Southeastern's Interracial Committee became the black contingent of the Women's General Committee of the Atlanta-based Commission on Interracial Cooperation. In this way was formed the most representative female leadership corps in the South.

But from 1924 to 1928, in the presidency of the ten-thousand-member National Association of Colored Women, the premier black women's secular organization, Bethune found her greatest platform for leadership in the established voluntary organization. Bethune's stature within the NACW derived in part from her brilliant vision of an activist public affairs role for black women in both national and international arenas. Like some other association leaders, particularly Margaret Murray Washington, Bethune determined to reach out to "the scattered people of African descent." She declared to her members, "We must make this national body of colored women a significant link between the peoples of color throughout the world."

To achieve her primary goal—effective representation of black women in public affairs—Bethune sought to transform the amorphous NACW into a cohesive body with a common program in all constituent regional, state, city, and individual club entities. For her this necessitated, above all, a permanent, fixed, national headquarters employing an executive secretary. Bethune crossed the country raising money for the project. On July 31, 1928, in Washington, D.C., the association proudly dedicated its newly acquired headquarters. The NACW was the first all-black group geared to operate in the nation's capital as scores of other national organizations already did.

• *Bethune*

establishes

NCNW

Under the brutality of the Great Depression, Bethune's focus upon black women's energetic presence in national affairs and the mechanisms that she had vitalized to achieve this goal languished within the NACW. Increasingly reasserting its historic decentralized character, the organization retreated from her emphasis upon a cohesive body. Given these developments, coupled with Bethune's domineering personality and her belief in the necessity of linkages between the distaff leadership of black Americans and New Deal administrators, on December 5, 1935, in New York City, she established the National Council of Negro Women. Essentially Bethune transferred to the council the brilliant vision that she had once vested in the NACW. As council president for fourteen years, she poured into the new entity all of her fine-tuned organizational skills. By 1949, when Bethune left office, the NCNW included twenty-two national professional and occupational groups and sororities, with eighty-two metropolitan councils.

Bethune's NCNW success derived in part from her contacts and insider status in the Franklin Roosevelt administration. Her base was the National Youth Administration, an agency that race liberals in Washington shaped and administered. Established in 1935 to assist young people aged sixteen to twenty-four in the Great Depression, and continuing to exist during World War II primarily to provide youth with vocational training and placement in vital defense industries, the NYA served several million constituents for more than eight years.

Consequently, with administrative sanction, Bethune established herself as the director of the Division of Negro Affairs, an arrangement that the Civil Service Commission made official in January 1939. In this way she occupied a slot in government higher than that of any other black woman in the history of the country up to that time. Although it was only a low-echelon berth within the broad framework of the federal bureaucracy, it was one of twenty or so of the highest appointed positions held by women in the New Deal. Regardless of Bethune's place on an organizational chart, she consistently operated on a level requiring consummate political skill in navigating through disputes in which her white colleagues and her black constituents were at odds, and both expected her loyalty. She brought tremendously impressive assets to her job: a charismatic personality, an unexcelled platform style, keen insight into race relations, superb abilities to influence people, and a well-known reputation. Her accomplishments with the Civil Service Commission included the establishment of the Special Negro Fund and the advancement of qualified blacks in state and local organizations; by 1941 Bethune's diligent work had led to the employment of black assistants to state directors in twenty-seven states, including all of the South except Mississippi, as well as in New York City and the District of Columbia.

Aware of her impeccable race leadership credentials, the Roosevelt Administration drafted Bethune to help sell its policies to black America. In both depression and war she did so with gusto, and her efforts contributed to the improving stature of blacks at the national level in the Democratic party coalition. Holding Bethune in high esteem, President Roosevelt supported Bethune's NYA directorship, saw her when she deemed circumstances warranted it, on occasion called her in to visit, extended messages to black organizations when she requested them, and within very narrow limits beyond NYA business acquiesced to her requests as a race leader.

Bethune expands •

role in FDR

administration

Eleanor Roosevelt associated with Bethune in a much closer way both politically and personally. She gained from the black leader a sensitive understanding of the country's racial problems and expert counsel on them. In addition to bringing Bethune into government, Roosevelt championed all her priority causes—her college, the NCNW, the NYA, and civil rights in general. And unlike scores of white female appointees in government who excluded Bethune from their informal support network, the First Lady consistently accorded her every consideration.

Bethune's unrestricted access to the White House, her standing in black America, and the security of her NYA bailiwick augured well for her becoming race representative-at-large in the administration. In its broader context, such a position required an individual to keep track of proliferating federal programs, to devise strategies by which black Americans could best obtain a fair share from them, and to work towards implementing them. Though Bethune enjoyed no government authorization for at-large activity, she confidently took this responsibility upon herself.

Bethune understood that at-large effectiveness necessitated competent staff. For this reason, in 1936 she helped organize the Federal Council on Negro Affairs, popularly acclaimed as the Black Cabinet. This council was made possible through the New Deal's recruitment into government of more than one hundred black advisers. These professionals embodied the regeneration of a black American political presence which had been lacking in the nation's capital since the demise of Reconstruction. According to Bethune's plan, the cabinet did, in fact, effect a loose coordination of government programs for blacks. Leaders from the National Urban League, the NAACP, the black press, and other race institutions as individuals and groups often took part in it.

The Black Cabinet's most publicly acknowledged service was as facilitator to two precedent-setting national black conferences held in Washington at the Labor Department in 1937 and 1939. Bethune not only presided over the proceedings but also the process through which the findings of the conferences were disseminated throughout official Washington from the president on down.

The Black Cabinet's less publicized work also contributed an edge to Bethune's at-large status in government. Members of the black network notified Bethune on an ad hoc basis of any sticky situation that required action from higher-ups. Once alerted, Bethune usually contacted Eleanor Roosevelt, as she did in 1942 after influential whites had created a racial tinderbox in Detroit by attempting to transfer to whites a federally funded housing project built for blacks. Partly as a consequence of a meeting between Bethune and Roosevelt, word soon passed down to the appropriate parties that the Sojourner Truth Project would indeed house blacks. At regular cabinet meetings, Bethune's salient activity was often receiving information—frequently meticulous analyses and program proposals. Armed with them, she strode forth to interact authoritatively with white individuals and groups on particular aspects of black welfare.

Yet on occasion rejection stared her in the face. During the McCarthy hysteria, the Board of Education in Englewood, New Jersey, denied Bethune a school's platform because she had been labeled a Communist subversive. In response, Americans who knew the vision that had undergirded her life—a vision of a country eschewing segregation and discrimination so as to appreciate the value of individuals regardless of race, color, creed, or gender—rallied to her defense in a movement reversing the board's action. Honors and awards came to Bethune until her death from a heart attack on May 18, 1955. A memorial tribute to Mary McLeod Bethune stands in Lincoln Park on Capitol Hill in Washington, D.C. The bronze sculpture by Robert Berks was erected in 1974 and depicts Bethune leaning on a cane that President Roosevelt gave her, and handing her will to two children.

**Profile by
Elaine M. Smith**

GWENDOLYN BROOKS

With poetry that reflects changes in society and in her own life,

1917- •

Gwendolyn Elizabeth Brooks became the first African American to

receive a Pulitzer Prize. Her writing has been both celebrated and

poet •

criticized by audiences black and white, but her talent and skill with

language have made her voice impossible to ignore.

Brooks was born June 7, 1917, in Topeka, Kansas, the daughter (and second child) of David Anderson Brooks and Keziah Corinne (Wims) Brooks. She graduated from Wilson Junior College in 1936, and since then she has received more than fifty honorary doctorates. Brooks's autobiography, *Report from Part One,* gives a joyful accounting of the poet's youth, which helps to explain Brooks's attitudes about family, race, friendship, teaching, learning, and all that has gone into the making of an American poet of Brooks's talent and stature. According to Brooks's mother, young Gwendolyn started writing at age seven, and Brooks writes, "I have notebooks dating from the time I was 11, when I started to keep my poems in composition books. My mother decided that I was to be the female Paul Laurence Dunbar."

Brooks's high school years were punctuated with easily remembered highs and lows, some of which were recorded in her 1971 interview with Ida Lewis: "I'd gone to several high schools. . . . I'd spent one year at Hyde Park Branch, which I hated. It was my first experience with many whites around. I wasn't much injured, just left alone. I realized that they were a society apart, and they really made you feel it."

This was the social creature speaking; meanwhile, the poet was reading and learning about newer poets such as T. S. Eliot, Ezra Pound, e. e. cummings, William Carlos Williams, and Wallace Stevens. She received enthusiastic encouragement from Langston Hughes, who read her poems upon meeting her when she was sixteen. His enthusiasm served as inspiration to the young Brooks, and years later, she and her husband gave him a party in their two-room kitchenette.

The September following her high school graduation Brooks enrolled in the newly opened Woodrow Wilson Junior College, and two years after her college graduation she met her future husband, Henry Lowington Blakely II. Both were twenty-one: Blakely, one of two blacks who worked on the student newspaper, was told by more than one person that there was "a shy brown girl who attended Junior NAACP meetings and wrote poetry." When he went to a meeting where Brooks and her friend, Margaret Taylor (later Burroughs, of the DuSable Museum), were seated, Taylor called to Blakely: "Hey Boy . . . This girl wants to meet you." Brooks later told Blakely that on seeing him she confided to Margaret, "That's the man I'm going to marry." And marry they did, sharing the good and the bad for thirty years until they separated in 1969: "We understood that our separation was best for the involved. (That won't be enough for the reader but it is enough for me.)" In 1973 the Blakelys reunited, and they celebrated their golden anniversary on September 17, 1989.

The 1940s and 1950s proved to be a stimulating time for her writing. She received her first public award in 1943 from the Midwestern Writers' Conference, and two years later Harper & Brothers published a book of her poems, called *A Street in Bronzeville*. Reviewing this book, which launched her career, a *New Yorker* critic said of Brooks: "She writes with style, sincerity, and a minimum of sentimentality." And *Poetry* magazine noted: "She shows a capacity to marry the special quality of her racial experience with the best attainments of our contemporary poetry tradition." She also received friendly and encouraging letters from Claude McKay and Countee Cullen. Indeed, Brooks had arrived in the world of poetry.

In 1945 she was one of the ten women to receive the Mademoiselle Merit Award for Distinguished Achievement. This was, indeed, a heady time, for she went to New York where she met Richard Wright and Ralph Ellison, among others. She was a strong admirer of such contemporary poets as John Crowe Ransom, Wallace Stevens (who later asked, "Why did they let the *coon* in to Pulitzerland?"), James Joyce, T. S. Eliot, Langston Hughes, and Merrill Moore, as well as older writers within the accepted canon of universal expression, such as Anton Chekov and Emily Dickinson. The concerns in the poetry of her first book, to be sure, were of the black community, but the style of her writing was "white." Houston Baker remarks on this when he observes some of her writing possesses "the metaphysical complexities of Apollinaire, Eliot, and Pound."

Annie Allen appeared in 1949, a time when Brooks had been working hard on both poetry and prose. A proposed novel, *American Family Brown,* was rejected by her publisher in 1947, and thereafter she concentrated on the poetry that appeared in *Annie Allen,* including a long piece called "The Anniad." The promise of her book was fulfilled, although some critics took Brooks to task for the high tone of her language; her friend don l. lee (who later changed his name to Haki Madhubuti) even proclaimed the book to have been "unread by blacks."

The more serious criticisms of *Annie Allen,* however, did nothing to deter the awarders of the Pulitzer Prize in 1950. Brooks was the first African American to receive a Pulitzer Prize of any sort for this book of poetry.

Brooks receives •

Pulitzer for

poetry

1953's *Maud Martha* is an autobiographical novel and, in the author's belief, this form "is a better testament, a better thermometer, than memory can be." The novel remains a manipulation of Brooks's experiences and the people she had known or shared deep moments with, but not a record of absolutely true happenings. In a rereading of this book, scholar Mary Helen Washington suggests feminist values and techniques that were not acknowledged when the book was first published, saying: "Current feminist theories which insist that we have to learn how to read the coded messages in women's texts—the silences, the evasions, the repression of female creativity—have helped me to reread *Maud Martha.*"

Brooks's first of four books of children's poetry was published in 1956, and adult collections followed: *The Bean Eaters, Selected Poems,* and *Riot.* Ezekiel Mphahlele points out that "Brooks is essentially a dramatic poet, who is interested in setting and character and move-ment. . . . She is interested in bringing out in its subtlest nuances the color of life that conflict eventually creates." *The Bean Eaters* allowed Brooks the full range of her poetic involvement in the lives of blacks. She writes of the murder of Emmett Till, she cuts through the bravura of young black boys in "We Real Cool," she is biting and sardonic in "Lovers of the Poor," and she describes the visit of a black reporter to

Little Rock in 1957. *The Bean Eaters,* the last book before a spectacular and surprising new direction in her work, was seen by one critic as "Brooks's ascent to the foothills of her grand heroic style."

She had reached a high point in her writing career, but she was about to change her writing to follow more closely the moods of her own people.

• *Black Writers'*

Conference

influences

Brooks

In the Mecca seemed to burst upon the scene after a 1967 visit Brooks made to the Second Black Writers' Conference at Fisk University, which she described in 1971 as discovering "what has stimulated my life these past few years: young people, full of a new spirit. They seemed stronger and taller, really ready to take on the challenges. . . . I was still saying 'Negro,' for instance."

In the Mecca started out as a novel, and it had various revisions before appearing as it stands now: a book of poems that presents a microcosm of black life in an all-too-crowded urban setting. The title poem is long and poignant, detailing the search for Pepita, the young daughter of Mrs. Sallie Smith, who has just come home from working in some white person's fine house. The poems introduce the reader, bit by bit, to certain types of characters who inhabit the Mecca, that teeming crowded building that houses not only poverty and failed dreams, but violence. In search of Pepita, then, black life and thought are explored in vignettes of real-life situations during the mid-1960s.

Poems in the second section of the book are short and include the ones dedicated to Medgar Evers and Malcolm X. Brooks was moving more deeply and inextricably into her native black world. Before the late 1960s, she told Claudia Tate, "I wasn't writing consciously with the idea that blacks *must address* blacks, *must write* about blacks. . . . I'm trying [now] to create new forms, trying to do something that could be presented in a tavern atmosphere." *In the Mecca,* which received a National Book Award nomination, was Brooks's declaration of independence from integration, because by 1969 she had changed her relationships with Harper and was publishing exclusively with blacks. (Her last book published by Harper came out in 1971: *The World of Gwendolyn Brooks.*) As she told one interviewer: "I have no intention of ever giving my books to another white publisher."

Riot, Aloneness, Broadside Treasury, Jump Bad, Report from Part One, and *Beckonings* were published by Broadside, the Detroit-based press started by Dudley Randall, a black librarian and Detroit's poet laureate. *Blacks,* published in 1987 by the David Company (Brooks's own company), is an anthology of her published works through 1987.

The poetry of Brooks spans two distinct periods, pre-1967 and post-1967, or to quote Brooks: "The forties and fifties were years of high poet-incense; the language-flowers were thickly sweet. Those flowers whined and begged white folks to pick them, to find them lovable. Then—the sixties: independent fire!" Despite what seems a stated philosophical dichotomy in Brooks's work, her friend Lerone Bennett aptly points out: "She has always written about the sounds, sights and flavors of the Black community." And another close friend, Madhubuti, states: "Her greatest impact has been as key player in the literature of African-American people." What is important, then, is an understanding that Brooks's writings, whether poetry or prose, have been directly involved around the ethos of blacks.

Brooks is a generous poet who works with children and prisoners, and she uses her own money to sponsor a poetry contest. On June 11, 1989, she was feted at Navy Pier in Chicago by fifty poets reading to her in celebration of her seventieth birthday, and she was given a $48,000 lifetime achievement award that year from the National Endowment for the Arts. In 1990 she became the first scholar to hold the newly established Gwendolyn Brooks Distinguished Chair of Creative Writing at Chicago State University.

During April of 1989, Brooks participated in the celebration of National Library Week in her neighboring towns of Hammond and Gary, Indiana. She was scheduled to visit Gary after her session in Hammond, but she was nearly an hour late. The crowded room of children and others was warm, and the library board members, as well as the director, valiantly filled the time with information and shared concern about the importance of libraries and literature. Brooks finally arrived and came down a side aisle, smilingly, even though she had been kept overlong by her previous host (Brooks is a punctual person), and she said to her anxious audience: "Believe me, I'll stay as long as you want me. I'll sign each slip of paper, or book." And she did, with grace and charm and open good humor.

**Profile by
Margaret Perry**

MARGARET TAYLOR BURROUGHS

*M*argaret Taylor Burroughs's contributions to art, education, literature, and the preservation of black American history and heritage
seem almost limitless. She brought about a necessary focus on African-
American art, first through her own work, then through her founding
and directorship of the DuSable Museum of African-American History.
And through her teaching and lecturing, both in the United States and
abroad, she has helped promote human rights and expanded global
consciousness to an awareness of the beauty and permanence of black
art and culture.

1917- •

artist, •

writer,

museum

director

Burroughs was born to Octavia Pierre Taylor, a domestic, and
Alexander Taylor, a farmer, on November 1, 1917, in Saint Rose Parish,
Louisiana, a small town near New Orleans. Three years later, as part of
the great labor migration north, the family moved to Chicago. While

they did not gain the economic opportunities they sought, the Taylors did gain access to greater educational and cultural opportunities. In 1933, after graduating from high school, Burroughs began exhibiting her art work in local fairs. Two years later she participated in the production of Langston Hughes's *Don't You Want to Be Free?* by the Negro People's Theater. In 1937 she graduated with a primary teaching certificate from Chicago Normal College, then received a secondary art certificate in 1939. During that same year, at the age of twenty-two, Burroughs married artist Bernard Goss. She later gave birth to their daughter, Gayle Goss Toller.

During the following decade, Burroughs embarked on her lifelong career as an artist, educator, and community worker. In 1940 she became a charter member of the Chicago South Side Community Art Center, which provided a place for black Americans to take art classes and exhibit their work. Her own prints and watercolors were exhibited here. In the next few years, her work was displayed in cities across the nation, including exhibitions in Chicago, New York, and Atlanta. The latter exhibit proved to be most significant for Burroughs. It was one of a series of annual events initiated by Hale Woodruff in 1942 for the promotion of African-American art on a national level. It offered both young and older artists a chance to exhibit and to win awards, and it formed the basis of a permanent collection of African-American art at Atlanta University. Burroughs, who had won the third print award in the 1947 Annual, recalled what the occasion meant to her, as recorded by Winifred Stoelting:

> But for the Atlanta Show, I might not be here. I never would have seen the creative light of day. For most of us, the Atlanta Show provided the first memory, the first mention, and the first knowledge of the black arts presence. I saw in those catalogs the works of black artists like Jacob Lawrence, John Wilson, Elizabeth Catlett, Charles White, Aaron Douglas, William Artis, and many others. . . . To many of us coming up in the 40s . . . acceptance in the Atlanta Show helped to bring us Negro artists together from all over the country.

With a growing concern for the education of youth, Burroughs decided to increase her knowledge and skills toward that end. She returned to college, receiving a bachelor's degree in art education from the Art Institute of Chicago in 1946. That same year she began her first job as an art instructor at DuSable High School in Chicago, a position she held for the next twenty-two years. In 1947 she wrote and illustrated a children's book, *Jaspet, the Drummin' Boy*. The following year she received her master's degree in art education. On December 23, 1949, after having recently divorced Goss, Burroughs married Charles Gordon Burroughs, a poet and writer who had lived for seventeen years in Russia.

The 1950s brought international recognition to Burroughs's art. After being included in a group exhibition at the Market Place Gallery in New York in 1950, Burroughs had a one-woman show in Mexico City in 1952. On sabbatical leave from teaching, she and her husband lived in Mexico where she studied at the Esmerelda Art School and the Taller de Grafica (School of Graphic Arts). It was here that Burroughs, like her friend Elizabeth Catlett, studied the theory of art as a vehicle of social commentary. She was greatly influenced by the way the muralists Diego Rivera and José Clemente Orozco merged art with politics. Responding to the call for art for the masses, Burroughs developed her style of figurative imagery using the "democratic" media of linoleum cuts and woodblock prints. With this medium, multiple images can be made and sold inexpensively to working people. An example from this period is her *Moses,* a determined portrait of the abolitionist Harriet Tubman.

Thereafter Burroughs's work increasingly merited attention. She began to expand her repertoire of oils, acrylics, and prints to include sculpture and batik. Her art was exhibited in Mexico City again in 1955. That same year, Burroughs won a citation from the Commission for the Negro in Arts. Two years later her work was displayed at the Annual Lake Meadows Outdoor Arts and Crafts Fair, which she founded along with Bernard Goss, Marion Perkins, and others. In 1957 Burroughs received the First Annual Art Festival Citation from the Beaux Arts Guild of Tuskegee Institute (now University). Over the next few years, her prints were exhibited at numerous universities, often winning accolades and awards.

Maintaining her commitment to her role as an educator, Burroughs did postgraduate work during the summers of 1958-60 at Teachers College, Columbia University. She became increasingly disappointed with school texts, however, which ignored or trivialized the significant achievements of black people, and Burroughs was determined to enact concrete changes immediately. In 1959 she helped found the National Conference of Artists, remaining its chairperson until 1963. The NCA furnished a networking system to encourage black American artists throughout the United States. From 1960 until 1962 Burroughs was also the art director and assistant in research for the Negro History Hall of Fame, which was presented at the Chicago Coliseum by the *New Crusader* newspaper.

While the Negro History Hall of Fame gave much-needed recognition to blacks, Burroughs envisioned a permanent institution that would be "dedicated to preserving, interpreting and displaying our heritage." Thus, she and eleven others formed the National Negro Museum and Historical Foundation, which presented annual Negro history programs and exhibitions. In 1961 Margaret and Charles Burroughs opened the Ebony Museum of Negro History in their home in Chicago. Inspired by positive community response, Burroughs, as director, labored to raise funds for expansion of the museum's facilities and programs. The institution changed its name in 1968 to the DuSable Museum of African-American History. Jean Baptiste Pointe DuSable, a man of African descent, was recognized as one of the first settlers in northern Illinois in the 1700s. By acknowledging Chicago's founding father, the institution hoped for economic support from the city. The appellation achieved its goal: Chicago donated to the DuSable Museum an old administration building. Today, the museum encompasses more than 60,000 square feet of space, has a staff of twenty-one, and has a membership of over one thousand.

The DuSable's collection of art, papers, artifacts, and memorabilia includes more than ten thousand books related to black history and culture, as well as objects once owned by notable African-Americans. "We try to get personal items because they mean a lot more to children," Audrey Edwards quoted Burroughs. Highlights include the academic robe worn by W. E. B. DuBois when he received an honorary degree from the University of Ghana; Joe Louis's Golden Glove Championship gloves; and paintings, sculptures, and books from the collection of Langston Hughes.

Throughout her life, Burroughs remained an enthusiastic, tireless teacher. After her tenure at DuSable High School, she taught African and African-American art history at the School of the Art Institute of Chicago in 1986. Burroughs then accepted a position as professor of humanities at Kennedy-King City College, a position she held until 1979, when she officially retired from teaching. In 1972 Burroughs's lifelong commitment to art education was formally recognized: she received an honorary doctoral degree from Lewis University in Lockport, Illinois, the first of more than a dozen honorary doctorates she has received. In 1980 Burroughs was one of ten black artists honored by President Jimmy Carter at the White House.

Although Burroughs's art had first been seen in another country in 1952, it was not until 1965 that her work again gained similar attention, this time through one-woman shows in Poland and Russia. Her work was also included in the International Kook Art Exhibit in Leipzig,

Germany. The following year she returned to Russia leading a delegation of African-American artists. The country responded by displaying Burroughs's art at the House of Friendship in Moscow in 1967. Profoundly moved by her journeys, notes Jacqueline Fonvielle Bontemps, Burroughs declared, "I wish my art to speak not only for my people, but for all humanity. . . . My subject matter is social commentary and seeks to improve the condition of life for all people."

Joining with active nationalists and Pan-Africanists throughout the United States, Burroughs began to write poetry focusing on the legacies of Africans and African-Americans. Drawing on folk traditions and contemporary events, Burroughs writes in simple, direct language for a broad audience. Her themes concentrate on the historical and cultural accomplishments of black peoples, particularly African-American freedom fighters. "Brother Freedom" was her first significant published poem in this vein. It appeared in the 1967 anthology dedicated to Malcolm X, *For Malcolm; Poems on the Life and Death of Malcolm X.* The publication was significant for Burroughs: it placed her work on a par with that of forty-two other poets, including such distinguished writers as Amiri Baraka, Gwendolyn Brooks, Robert Hayden, and Margaret Walker. The following year Burroughs published her first volume of poetry, *What Shall I Tell My Children Who Are Black?*

Seeking a greater knowledge of black culture and inspired by her initial journeys abroad, Burroughs next secured a travel grant to West Africa from the American Forum for International Study in 1968. That summer in Ghana provided imagery for her second volume of poetry, *Africa, My Africa,* published in 1970. In eighteen poems, Burroughs explores the meaning of her personal background and African heritage in the larger context of the African-American experience as both a continuation of and division from Africa's history.

While Burroughs actively pursued writing in the 1960s and 1970s, she did not abandon the visual arts, continuing to produce material for exhibitions throughout the U.S. during the 1980s. She also continued her educational crusade, lecturing at schools, colleges, and universities. Ever devoted to safeguarding and enriching black culture, Burroughs's recent projects have included collecting African games and compiling a volume of poems in honor of Paul Robeson. Skilled in many fields in the humanities as well as in business and diplomatic relations, Burroughs is truly a renaissance woman.

Burroughs •

writes poetry

and short

stories

**Profile by
Theresa A.
Leininger**

MARY ELIZABETH CARNEGIE

Mary Elizabeth Lancaster Carnegie is a highly respected leader in

nursing of national and international prominence. Her career in

nursing spans more than five decades, during which time she has been

and continues to be a leader and an agent for change in the nursing

profession. Carnegie has an impressive career that encompasses bedside

nursing, nurse education, educational nursing administration, consulta-

tion, nursing research, editorial positions on various prestigious nurs-

ing journals, and numerous publications and professional presenta-

tions. Carnegie has championed the cause of equality for black women

in nursing and has written about the history of inequality black women

experienced.

1916- •

nursing •

administrator,

author

Carnegie was born April 19, 1916, in Baltimore, Maryland. She was the fourth child born to John Oliver Lancaster and Adeline Beatrice (Swann) Lancaster. She had two older sisters and a brother, and one younger brother. She grew up with her aunt and uncle, Rosa and Thomas Robison, in Washington, D.C., where she attended Dunbar High School, an all-black school. Carnegie graduated from high school at the age of sixteen and thereafter went to spend some time with family living in New York, where a relative who had attended Lincoln School for Nurses encouraged her to consider nursing as a career.

In 1934 Carnegie, too, began her nursing education at the privately-owned Lincoln School for Nurses. In 1936, during Carnegie's student years at Lincoln, she had the opportunity to hear Mabel Keaton Staupers, executive secretary of the National Association of Colored Graduate Nurses (NACGN), tell the story of the association and the struggle black nurses were having in obtaining recognition by all members of the nursing profession, in gaining admission to nursing schools, and in obtaining employment in hospitals and public health agencies throughout the country. From this encounter with Staupers, a feisty black nursing leader, Carnegie's interest in and concern for equal opportunities for black nurses was stimulated.

The Lincoln School for Nurses was one of the few schools in New York City that accepted black students, and Carnegie graduated from it in 1937. Since the economic depression was not over, the class of thirty graduates was, as described by Carnegie, faced with the problem of getting a job—a difficult prospect for anyone at that time. This undertaking was made more difficult because only four of the two hundred hospitals located in New York City employed black nurses. Carnegie and a few of her colleagues nonetheless found immediate employment as staff nurses at Lincoln Hospital, one of those four institutions. The monthly salary of $75 plus maintenance was considered a princely sum then.

As a graduate nurse, Carnegie was appointed to the Veterans Administration Hospital in Tuskegee, Alabama, one of the two federal hospitals in the United States that employed black nurses. (The other was Freedmen's Hospital in Washington, D.C., but assignment there depended upon the successful completion of one year's probation at the Veterans Administration Hospital in Tuskegee.)

With her goal of obtaining the best possible education, she attended West Virginia State College full-time in return for giving professional service in the school health program. This allowed her to graduate in 1942 with a bachelor of arts degree and an offer of a job as clinical instructor at the segregated Saint Philip Hospital School of Nursing, the black wing of the Medical College of Virginia.

At that time in the South, black nurses were addressed as Nurse and white nurses as "Miss," but Carnegie and her colleagues instructed their students to address each other as Miss and also to refrain from calling their black patients by their first names, even though the white nurses and doctors did.

Like many other black nurses during World War II, Carnegie wished to serve her country. However, in 1944 her application to the Navy Nurse Corps was rejected with the explanation that black nurses were not being assigned to the Navy. It was not until spring of 1945 that black nurses were accepted into the United States Navy, and in 1948 discrimination in the armed forces was eliminated by President Harry S. Truman.

During the 1940s and 1950s few black American nurses had bachelor's degrees and even fewer had master's degrees. Therefore, relatively few black nurses occupied leadership positions, and the administrators of many schools for black nursing students were white. Carnegie felt that these directors manifested little personal interest in the further development of their former black students, and the indifferent attitude she noted was reflected not only in the programs but in the community's reaction to the black nurse. Carnegie believed that if this invidious position was to be changed, it was necessary to develop college programs to train high-caliber educators and administrators capable of preparing quality black nursing professionals. The black unit of the National Council for War Service was able to encourage Hampton Institute (now University), a college for blacks, to establish in 1943 a collegiate nursing program. Carnegie was released from Saint Philip's through the efforts of the NACGN to serve as assistant director of this new program. Since some time passed before a white director was appointed, Carnegie sought assistance from consultants from the National Nursing Council for War Service and the United States Public Health Service. She initiated the groundwork to establish the school and admitted the first group of nursing students to the program. Carnegie is credited with initiating the nursing program at Hampton, which was the first baccalaureate program in the state of Virginia.

Black college •

educates

nurses

Before the end of that first year at Hampton, Carnegie was awarded a fellowship by the Rockefeller Foundation, and in 1944 she enrolled at the University of Toronto, Canada, as a student in nursing school administration. Uncertain about housing accommodations on campus, she contacted a former student, Bernice Carnegie, who arranged housing with her sister. While studying in Toronto, she met and married Bernice's brother, Eric Carnegie, in December of 1944.

On completion of this course, she accepted an offer to become dean of the nursing program at Florida Agricultural and Mechanical College in Tallahassee. This was considered a major challenge because the School of Nursing was one of two for blacks in the state and the only one administered by blacks. The challenge was accepted, and Carnegie set out to develop a high-quality nursing education program. Although the college was in Florida, students traveled one thousand miles to a hospital in Baltimore, Maryland, to obtain a one-year period of clinical experience in medical, surgical, pediatric, and obstetrical nursing because of Florida's segregation polices. This separation almost completely removed students from the supervision and control of the college.

One of the first tasks Carnegie undertook was to seek affiliation with hospitals closer to home; there, however, she met with racial discrimination. Although the nursing directors in the state accepted her request to visit, they discovered on her arrival that she was black, and everyone refused to shake the hand she extended in greeting. This ill-mannered rebuff confirmed Carnegie's concern that students should not be exposed unnecessarily to discriminatory practices, and therefore clinical facilities had to be found. Carnegie's continued faith in the human race, which at this point was badly shaken, was rewarded when the director of nurses at a large county hospital, Duval Medical Center in Jacksonville, Florida, agreed to the use of the hospital wards as a clinical facility for the black students. This agreement was later confirmed by the board of directors of the hospital, the college, and the Florida State Board of Nurse Examiners. However, this matter was not so easily settled, and the white nurses threatened to walk out if the black students were placed there. The walkout did not occur, a relief for the frightened students and others concerned.

Carnegie's involvement in and contributions to professional associations are significant. Although the American Nurses' Association (ANA) had never prohibited black nurses from membership, in Florida they could not belong because the Florida State Nurses Association (FSNA), which was the avenue for entry to the ANA, denied them full membership even though they had paid full dues. As the dean of the only collegiate school in the state whose immediate superior, President William H. Gray, was also black and supportive of her, Carnegie was able to champion the cause for black nurses. It was through her efforts that the president of the Florida State Association of Colored Graduate Nurses (FSACGN) was made a courtesy member by the board of directors of FSNA—although without voting privileges.

It was while serving as president of the FSACGN in 1948, and therefore as a courtesy member of the FSNA board of directors, that Carnegie was made a full member of the FSNA board. Later, through the fund-raising activities of the FSACGN and contributions from the FSNA, she was able to attend the fiftieth anniversary of the International Council of Nurses, which was held in Stockholm, Sweden, in 1949. Shortly after her return to Florida the decision was made to dissolve the FSACGN. In 1949 Carnegie sought and won election to the board of directors of the FSNA, becoming the first black nurse to hold this elected position in Florida. She was reelected in 1950 for a two-year term. Her election and reelection to the board of directors of the FSNA was an indication of the high regard in which she was held. The dissolution of the FSACGN meant that black nurses had to be accommodated at both district and state levels. Although this called for a major change in attitude by white nurses, integration of the FSNA was well on the way by 1952.

Even though the struggle for lowering the segregation barriers was taking place, Carnegie never lost sight of her goal of continuing her own education. She obtained a master of arts in administration in higher education from Syracuse University in 1952. On her return to Florida she was again instrumental in getting an extension program for black graduate nurses started at Florida Agricultural and Mechanical College, Jacksonville, and in Miami.

The year 1953 marked the beginning of a new role and career—nursing journalism. The American Journal of Nursing Company in New York, which publishes the *American Journal of Nursing* and other prestigious nursing journals and is owned by the American Nurses' Association, offered Carnegie a post as assistant editor of *Journal,* the official organ of the ANA. She remained in this position for three years before becoming associate editor and then senior editor of *Nursing Outlook.*

Career begins •

in nursing

journalism

In 1972 Carnegie earned a doctorate in public administration from New York University. Thereafter she became editor of the premier journal *Nursing Research*, continuing in that capacity until 1978, when she retired. She remains editor emeritus for *Nursing Research*, and her interest in research, particularly historical research, is well known.

Retirement has not diminished her interest in or commitment to the nursing profession. Carnegie has accepted numerous distinguished visiting professor appointments and occupied various endowed chairs at prestigious universities. During the 1989-1990 academic year she occupied the Loewenberg Chair of Excellence at Memphis State University, Memphis, Tennessee. Since the 1990-1991 academic year, Carnegie has served as distinguished visiting professor at Indiana University School of Nursing. While there, she continued work on the second edition of *The Path We Tread: Blacks in Nursing.*

Carnegie has had wide consultative experience, including the Allstate Foundation Project on Recruitment of Minorities in Nursing in 1973 and a long list of colleges and schools of nursing. Since 1943 she has lectured widely and participated in workshops and seminars. Many of her lectures are on the concerns of women in education, the state of nursing, women in the community, and women in the church. Her professional activities have taken her through the United States and to Ghana, Zimbabwe, Kenya, Europe, Asia, and North, Central, and South America. While occupying the Vera C. Bender Endowed Chair at Adelphi University, Garden City, New York, Carnegie wrote her autobiography in *Making Choices; Taking Chances: Nursing Leaders Tell Their Stories.*

Carnegie believes that nursing is leading the other professions in its commitment to equality for all its members. She is one of those remarkable women who have overcome tremendous obstacles through her courage, integrity, and intellectual ability. She has mentored many nurses, her career serves as a beacon, and she is an exceptional role model for black nurses and women.

**Profile by
Althea T. Davis**

ELIZABETH CATLETT

*C*elebrated internationally for her figurative sculpture and prints,

Elizabeth Catlett is one of the premier black American artists of the

twentieth century. Catlett is also known, however, as a cultural nation-

alist and civil rights activist. Her left-of-center political beliefs have led

her to become an expatriate, living in Mexico as a citizen of that country

since 1962.

1915- •

sculptor, •

painter,

printmaker

The grandchild of slaves, Elizabeth Catlett was born in Washington, D.C., on April 15, 1915, and grew up in a middle-class home built by her father's family. Catlett's father, a mathematics professor at Tuskegee Institute, died before she was born. She was encouraged by her mother and a high school teacher impressed with Catlett's skills in drawing and carving, and in 1933 she entered Howard University, the first black college to establish an art department. There she began to major in design under the tutelage of Lois Mailou Jones. She also studied printmaking with graphic artist James Lesene Wells and drawing with artist and art historian James A. Porter. Porter, as author of one of the first books on black American art, knew well the obstacles Catlett would face in her artistic career. He urged her to gain professional experience by working for the government-sponsored Works Progress Administra-

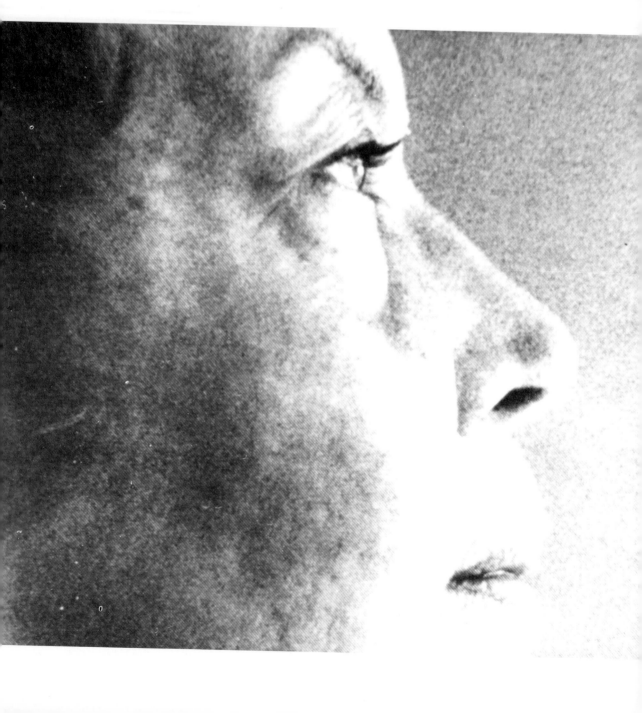

tion/Public Works of Art Project (called the Federal Art Project in 1934), where she worked in the mural division for two months. There she became aware of the Mexican muralists Diego Rivera and Miguel Covarrubias, whose political beliefs about the purpose of art would significantly influence her later work. Catlett's experience on the federal relief program profoundly affected both her art and her life. She declared her new major to be painting and gradually began her lifelong commitment to social change for the betterment of those less fortunate than herself.

When Catlett graduated cum laude with her B.S. in art in 1936, the United States was still recovering from the Great Depression. Few jobs in the arts were available, but she secured a position teaching high school in Durham, North Carolina, at fifty-nine dollars a month. Frustrated with a year of earning a wage less than that of white instructors, Catlett joined the North Carolina Teachers Association in an effort to equalize salaries for black faculty members. She was joined in this campaign by an NAACP attorney, Thurgood Marshall. Realizing the grim situation of the segregated South, Catlett returned to Washington, D.C., to earn money for graduate school.

At the University of Iowa in 1940, she was the first student ever to earn an M.F.A. in sculpture. After graduation Catlett taught at Prairie View College in Texas during the summer of 1940. That same year she won first prize in sculpture in the Golden Jubilee National Exposition in Chicago. She then worked as head of the art department at Dillard University in New Orleans for two years. There Catlett continued to campaign for higher wages for the faculty. Though not successful, she did win two other victories. Nude models were permitted in her life classes, and she persuaded a local museum to admit black students for the first time ever to see an exhibition of Picasso's works.

During the summer of 1941 Catlett took a ceramics class at the Art Institute of Chicago and while in Illinois met and married artist Charles White. In 1942 the couple moved to Hampton, Virginia, where Catlett taught at Hampton Institute and White executed a mural commission. The same year Catlett's work was exhibited at Atlanta University; she would be represented there again the next year and would win prizes later. The pair then moved to Harlem, New York.

Catlett supported herself in New York by teaching at a community institution for adult education, the George Washington Carver School. With her salary she continued her studies in several media, working privately with the French sculptor Ossip Zadkine in Greenwich Village and learning lithography at the Art Students League. She also continued to show her work around the country, at the Institute of Contemporary

Art in Boston in 1943; the Baltimore Museum of Art, the University of Chicago, the Renaissance Society, and the Newark Museum in New Jersey, all in 1944; and at the Albany Institute of History and Art in 1945.

• *Works honor*

black women

In recognition of Catlett's achievements, including winning second prize in sculpture at the Atlanta University Annual in 1946, the Julius Rosenwald Foundation awarded Catlett a fellowship to do a series of works honoring black women. At that time the Whites were having marital problems but accepted an invitation to work in Mexico City. At the Taller de Grafica Popular (TGP), they worked together with other artists on a volume of prints portraying life throughout the Mexican republic. The TGP was a graphic arts and mural workshop where artists collaboratively created art to aid socio-political change. It was founded in 1937 by Leopoldo Mendez, Luis Arenal, and Pabio Higgins. Catlett recalls to art historian Samella Lewis what the institution meant to her:

> The search for learning took me to Mexico, to the Taller de Grafica Popular, where we worked collectively, where we had strong artists and weak artists, and each one learned from the other. Everybody offered something—and when you saw the product, even if you were weak, you saw a collective product that you had helped form. It makes a difference in your desire to work and your understanding of what you're doing. At the same time we did individual work. I would say it was a great social experience, because I learned how you use your art for the service of people, struggling people, to whom only realism is meaningful.

It was at the TGP with the sponsorship of the Rosenwald grant that Catlett produced a significant portfolio of linocuts depicting black laborers, artists, and farmers. "The Negro Woman" earned Catlett her first solo show; the exhibition was held at the Barnett-Aden Gallery in Washington, D.C., 1947-48.

Although the sojourn in Mexico proved artistically beneficial for both Catlett and White, their relationship floundered and upon their return to New York City, they separated. Catlett then went back to work at the TGP and continued her studies with Francisco Zuniga. She also developed her wood carving at *la Esmerelda, La Escuela de Pintura y Escultura* in Mexico in 1948.

Among the members who joined the TGP in the 1940s was Francisco Mora, Catlett's second husband. Born in Uruapan, Michoacan, Mexico, in 1922 to an urban working-class family, Mora sympathized with the lower class, especially miners who were exposed to dangerous working conditions and poor wages. In oil painting, lithographs, and murals Mora depicted the life of the Mexican people and made a firm commitment to the practice of social art.

In 1947 when Catlett and Mora married, both of their countries were in political and social turmoil. In the United States leftist-oriented people in the arts continually battled the House of Representatives Un-American Activities Committee and Senator Joseph McCarthy. Despite the oppressive atmosphere during the following decade, the couple persevered in creating work with political content. Catlett won second prize again at the Atlanta University Annual in 1956 and received a diploma in printmaking from the First National Painting and Printmaking Exhibition in Mexico City in 1959. Mora executed three murals commissioned between 1950 and 1958: "Freedom of the Press" at the *El Sol de Toluca* newspaper office, "Folklore Map of Mexico" at the Hotel de Prado, and "Education for the People" at a primary school in Santa Maria Tarasquillo, Mexico.

Because their art and their association with the TGP were deemed radical, Catlett and Mora were suspected of being Communists. The charge became explicit in 1959. Accused of belonging to the Communist party, Catlett was arrested as an undesirable alien. Three years later she left the United States to become a Mexican citizen. Like Barbara Chase-Riboud, another black American sculptor who has made her permanent home abroad (in Paris, France), Catlett insists that her decision was not a condemnation of the United States, but instead a dedication to her adopted country where she could live as a responsible, active member of society. To Stephanie Stokes Oliver in *Essence,* she explained: "I changed my citizenship because I have been living in Mexico since 1946, and I'm a political person. . . . I couldn't do anything political in Mexico unless I was a citizen." Not pleased with her political statements, the United States government banned Catlett from traveling in the United States for nine years.

Nonetheless, Catlett thrived in her new environment. She had been hired in 1959 as the first woman professor of sculpture at the National School of Fine Arts in San Carlos, Mexico. Catlett served there as chair of the department and taught classes until her retirement in 1973, and she received numerous awards from the Latin American artistic community.

While Catlett is perhaps best known as a sculptor, she is also well recognized for her prints—a medium she appreciates because many originals can be made at relatively low cost and sold to people with low incomes. In 1969 she won the first purchase prize from the National Print Salon in Mexico. The following year she received a prize to study and travel in the German Democratic Republic and showed her work at the Intergrafic Exhibition in Berlin.

Inspired by her sojourn abroad, Catlett applied for and received a grant from the British Council to visit art schools in Britain in 1970. Her travels made her more firmly committed to what she termed the "worldwide drive for national liberation." While Catlett deeply appreciated the chance to see artistic developments in other countries, she emphatically stated in *Ebony* that art must address the needs of people around the world. "I don't think we can still keep going to Paris and Rome to see what the last word is in art and come back to our desperate nations and live in intellectual isolation from what's going on in our countries and ghettos."

• *Great black*

figures

portrayed

Joining many other black American artists in the 1960s and 1970s, Catlett sought to educate the public with her portrayals of great figures in black history. Her depictions ranged from abolitionists in the nineteenth century, such as Harriet Tubman, to contemporary heroes, as evidenced in *Homage to the Panthers* and *Malcolm Speaks for Us*. The latter work won a top purchase prize, was bought by the National Institute of Fine Arts, and now belongs to the Mexican government. Catlett explained the purpose of her portraiture in 1971 when she wrote in *American Women Artists,* "I have gradually reached the conclusion that art is important only to the extent that it aids in the liberation of our people. . . . I have now rejected 'International Art' except to use those if its techniques may help me make the message clearer to my folks."

Internationally recognized for her well-researched and sensitive renderings of black heroes, Catlett was commissioned to depict two historical black Americans in the land of her birth. In 1973 she produced a life-size bronze bust of Phillis Wheatley for Jackson State College in Mississippi. Two years later she created a ten-foot-tall bronze sculpture of Louis Armstrong for the City Park of New Orleans. The work was unveiled in the Bicentennial Celebration of 1976.

In addition to portrait studies, Catlett produced more abstract works with symbolic content and titles, such as *Black Flag* and *Magic Mask.* Works in this vein are powerful acknowledgements of a history of oppression, but also expressions of black pride. *Target Practice* is the head of a black man framed by a large rifle sight and mounted trophy-like on a wooden pedestal; *Black Unity* depicts two calmly dignified heads reminiscent of certain West African masks. Seen from the other side, however, the sculpture reveals a large clenched fist, a symbol of black power. Catlett affirms her heritage artistically in formal terms as well as in content. Rather than work in the Western medium of white marble, she seeks materials that reflect the beauty and diversity of skin tones among black peoples. She sculpts wood such as walnut, Spanish cedar, and mahogany, stones such as black marble and onyx, and she shapes terra-cotta and bronze.

By far Catlett's favorite theme is motherhood. Beginning with her master's thesis depiction of a mother and child, Catlett has spent years exploring the topic. She executed many pieces with the same title in terra-cotta and wood, as well as variations on the motif in lithography (such as *Black Maternity*) and marble (*Negro Mother and Child*). *Maternity* in black marble is a strong expression of that special bond. Catlett abstracts a woman's bust into a hollow shape reminiscent of West African heddle pulleys. Although the mother's uplifted head looks to the side, her arms cradle the fetus/child in a firm but open embrace. The small figure reaches towards life-sustaining breasts. Situated in this cavity, the baby is symbolically at once in the uterus, and always in the mother's heart. Catlett finds special pleasures in portraying motherhood for personal reasons. For ten years after her marriage to Mora and the birth of their three children, Catlett had no time to sculpt. Nonetheless, she believes that being a mother gave her work "immeasurably more depth." She maintained in *Ebony* that "raising children is the most creative thing I can think of." Other women concurred with Catlett's statement and held both her parental care and artistic creativity in high esteem. Women's groups on both coasts of the United States showed their appreciation of Catlett's work by giving her awards in the early 1980s. In 1981 she received an award from the Women's Caucus for Art at the national congress in San Francisco. And in 1985 she achieved a bronze sculpture award from the National Council of Negro Women in New York.

Catlett's art continued to merit attention from other groups as well. In 1976 Howard University commissioned her to create a twenty-four-foot-high bronze relief for the Chemical Engineering Building. The following year she was given an Alumni Award by that same institution, her alma mater. The next commission came from the Secretary of Education in Mexico City; in 1981 Catlett completed two life-size bronze sculptures, *Torres Bodet* and *Vasconcelos*.

Aptly called "La Maestra" by her students, Catlett continues to enrich our vision of the world with her art. Still residing in Mexico, she and her husband now devote their time to traveling and creating "art for liberation and for life." Catlett's credo, recorded by Lewis, is this:

> Art can't be the exclusive domain of the elect. It has to belong to everyone. Otherwise it will continue to divide the privileged from the underprivileged, Blacks from Chicanos, and both rural, ghetto, and middle-

class whites. Artists should work to the end that love, peace, justice, and equal opportunity prevail all over the world; to the end that all people take joy in full participation in the rich material, intellectual, and spiritual resources of this world's lands, peoples, and goods."

**Profile by
Theresa A. Leininger**

BARBARA CHASE-RIBOUD

*L*iving in Paris since 1961, Barbara Chase-Riboud has achieved

1939- •

international recognition for her remarkable contributions to the hu-

manities. She first distinguished herself in the art world with printmaking,

sculptor, •

and then became known for her distinctive abstract metal-and-fiber

writer,

sculptures, black-chalk drawings, and jewelry. Next, Chase-Riboud

poet

moved into the field of literature and won awards both for her fiction

and poetry; since 1974 she has published three novels, two volumes of

poetry, and several essays.

Chase-Riboud was born on June 26, 1939, in Philadelphia, Pennsylvania, to Vivian May (West) Chase, a histology technician, and Charles Edward Chase, a contractor; she was an only child. Her mother's ancestors were slaves who had escaped to Montreal, Canada, on the Underground Railroad. Chase-Riboud's talent in the arts was recognized at an early age; at five years of age she was taking dance lessons, at six there were piano lessons, and at seven art lessons. She began

working in sculpture and ceramics at Fletcher Art Memorial School in Philadelphia in 1946 and won her first prize at the age of eight. Chase-Riboud continued her studies at the Philadelphia Museum School of Art, from 1947 to 1954. By the time she was fifteen years old she won a *Seventeen* magazine award for one of her prints, which was purchased by the Museum of Modern Art from the exhibition organized by the ACA Gallery in New York.

The artist received a strong classical education, achieving her B.F.A. in 1957 from Tyler School at Temple University. The same year Chase-Riboud first exhibited her work at the Philadelphia Art Alliance and won its Purchase Prize. She also won first prize in the National College Board Art Contest from *Mademoiselle*. She then studied at the American Academy in Rome for a year under the sponsorship of a John Hay Whitney Foundation Fellowship. There she executed her first works in bronze and established her first contacts in Europe.

On Christmas 1957, Chase-Riboud's friends left her stranded on a dare in Egypt. Abandoned by them, she found herself rescued by the black American cultural attaché in Cairo. He befriended the artist and invited her to stay with his family. This three-month sojourn promoted a turning point in Chase-Riboud's traditionally academic art. She states in Eleanor Munro's *Originals:*

> I grew up that year. It was the first time I realized there was such a thing as non-European art. For someone exposed only to the Greco-Roman tradition, it was a revelation. I suddenly saw how insular the Western world was vis-a-vis the nonwhite, non-Christian world. The blast of Egyptian culture was irreversible. The sheer magnificence of it. The elegance and perfection, the timelessness, the depth. After that, Greek and Roman art looked like pastry to me. From an artistic point of view, that trip was historic for me. Though I didn't know it at the time, my own transformation was part of the historical transformation of the blacks that began in the 60s.

After her study abroad, Chase-Riboud continued her education at Yale University under the direction of Josef Albers and Paul Rudolph and received her M.F.A. in 1960. The same year she completed an architectural commission, a monumental fountain for the Wheaton Plaza, near Washington, D.C.

The first five years of the 1960s were a time of diminished artistic output for Chase-Riboud. After graduation from Yale, she went to

London, England, to marry her former professor. Disenchanted with the country, the climate, and the fiancé, she traveled to Paris for the weekend, then made the city her permanent home. At an exhibition of Yves Klein, she met the art director of the *New York Times,* who offered her the job of Paris art director. This ended when she married French photographer Marc Riboud on December 25, 1961, in Mexico. The next years were spent traveling with her husband on his assignments to Russia, India, Greece, and North Africa. Chase-Riboud was the first American woman to visit the People's Republic of China after the Revolution in 1949, including Inner Mongolia and Nepal. During these journeys, she became fascinated with Asian art and made mental notes for later work.

In the second half of the 1960s, Chase-Riboud resumed her artistic activity. Echoes of yin and yang symbolism appeared in the solo exhibition of her drawings and sculpture in Paris in November 1960; these works dealt with the union of opposites—male/female, negative/positive, black/white. Chase Riboud's sculpture quickly gained more notice and was exhibited in the New York Architectural League Show, 1965; the Festival of Negro Art in Dakar, 1966; L'Oeil Ecoute Festival of Avignon, 1969; and Americans of Paris, Air France, 1969. During this time Chase-Riboud also gave birth to two sons, David Charles and Alexei Karol.

- **African**

influence seen

in sculpture

Chase-Riboud's early sculptures are characterized by abstract organic shapes and poetic literary figurative compositions reminiscent of Germain Richier and Alberto Giacometti (for whom she wrote a poem after meeting him). She created compositions from two materials strongly contrasting in texture and finish—bronze and wool, steel and synthetics, or bronze and silk (see, for example, *Black Zanzibar Table* in *Forever Free,* and *She #1* in *Art: African American*). These sculptural compositions were constructed initially to hide the support system underneath the fibers. However, her expressive abstractions soon came to refer to certain West African dancing masks with their combination of diverse materials, such as wood, raffia, hemp, leather, feathers, and metal. Journeys to Africa, beginning with participation in the Pan-African festival in Algeria in 1966, strongly affected Chase-Riboud's artistic development, notes Marilyn Richardson. "I found myself there," Chase-Riboud says of the Pan-African festival in Nigeria of 1969, "with all the freedom fighters and liberation groups—the Algerians, the South Africans, the Black Panthers from America. A kind of historical current brought all of these people together in a context that was not only political but artistic."

Chase-Riboud began to employ bricolage as well as ancient lost-wax casting techniques and African symbols in her work. The combination of these formal concerns with modern materials and contemporary events was developed in her *Malcolm X* series of 1969-1970 and expanded exhibition at the Massachusetts Institute of Technology, "Four Monuments to Malcolm X" in 1970. Rather than make political art, Chase-Riboud pays tribute to the struggle of the 1960s with elegiac elegance. Françoise Nora quotes her in *Art News:* "Sculpture should be beautiful, each element has an aesthetic as well as a symbolic and spiritual function. My idea is to reinterpret the aesthetic function in contemporary terms, using modern materials." Her sculptures are powerful studies in contrasts—unyielding metals supported by braided, knotted, and wrapped fibers that interchange functions. The soft wool and silk become hard and the rigid bronze and steel seem to dissolve into softness.

Chase-Riboud was influenced by Albers's color studies at Yale as well as Minimalist approaches prompted by the New York School, such as the work of Eva Hesse, Robert Graves, and Robert Morris (the artist was also friends with Ken Nordland). However, she developed a unique style in the 1960s and 1970s that she described as "maximal." Her insistence on beauty and finish alienated her from contemporary trends in American art. Still, Chase-Riboud's revolt against styles such as Pop (and its concern with white mass culture) freed her to explore other possibilities in sculpture. She found her art more analogous to the density and complexity in avant-garde music of the 1960s. John and Alice Coltrane, Steve Reich, Terry Riley, and John Cage, like Chase-Riboud, incorporated African and Asian elements in their work, paying careful attention to texture and evocative qualities. Chase-Riboud found that such art approached the power of classical West African sculpture.

Chase-Riboud's art continued to win her recognition through the 1970s, with a National Endowment for the Humanities fellowship in 1973 and solo and group shows both nationwide and worldwide. At the invitation of the United States Department of State in 1975, she gave poetry readings and slide lectures of her art in Senegal, Mali, Ghana, the Ivory Coast, Tunisia, and Sierra Leone. For her many contributions to the arts, including her first novel, *Sally Hemings,* Chase-Riboud was awarded an honorary doctorate of arts and humanities from Temple University in 1981. After her divorce from Riboud that same year, on July 4, she married Sergio G. Tosi, an Italian art dealer and publisher.

In recent years Chase-Riboud's creative output has centered more on writing than the visual arts. Her first book of poems, *From Memphis to Peking,* published in 1974, was inspired both by her visits to Egypt and to the People's Republic of China. With the unifying theme of physical and spiritual journeys, it focuses on the writer's family origins and the quest for mystical knowledge.

Chase-Riboud produced her first novel, *Sally Hemings*, in 1979. Well researched and written, it concerns the alleged slave mistress of President Thomas Jefferson. The author was captivated by the mystery surrounding the Jefferson-Hemings relationship upon reading Fawn Brodie's biography of Jefferson. She tried to convince numerous friends to write the novel, then finally did it herself at the suggestion of Toni Morrison, her poetry editor at Random House. *Sally Hemings* won Chase-Riboud the Janet Heidinger Kafka Prize as best novel written by an American woman and was subsequently translated into French, German, Italian, Spanish, Swedish, Danish, Finnish, and Slavonic. Chase-Riboud was also honored with a gold medal by one of the Italian academies in 1979.

Her second book of poems, *Love Perfecting,* appeared in 1980. Although the volume received less notice than *From Memphis to Peking,* Chase-Riboud continued to write poetry for herself. According to Richardson, she says the genre "is very close to a discipline both familiar and dear to me: drawing. Both are dangerous searches for perfection . . . drawing prepared me for the demands of poetry." Chase-Riboud's perseverance paid off. In 1988 she won the Carl Sandburg Poetry Prize as the best poet for her book, *Portrait of a Nude Woman as Cleopatra, a Meloloque.* The writer won more acclaim, however, for her novels and sculpture, than for her poetry and drawings.

Chase-Riboud continued her exploration of slavery in her second novel, *Valide,* which was promptly translated into all the major European languages. The piece focuses on a Martiniquian slave who became the most powerful woman in the Ottoman Empire during the late eighteenth and early nineteenth centuries. The protagonist, as mother of the sultan, directs his harem. Issues that predominate in this novel and Chase-Riboud's other writings include constructions of power involving race and gender, liberty, history, and myth-making. In 1980, a year after the publication of *Valide,* Chase-Riboud carried on those themes with her third novel, *Echo of Lions.* This work is based on the true story of an extraordinary West African called Cinque who led a successful rebellion on board the Spanish slave ship *Amistad* in the early nineteenth century. After killing the captain and his crew, these men attempted to sail back to Sierra Leone but landed on the East Coast of the United States and subsequently endured four years of trials before being declared free. Coming full circle, Chase-Riboud wrote about a fight for liberty that occurred in the town where she received her graduate education, New

Haven, Connecticut. For this book she was cited by the Connecticut State Legislature and the governor for excellence and achievement in literature in 1989. Additionally, both *Echo of Lions* and *Sally Hemings* have been optioned by movie companies.

Chase-Riboud has authored several other novels that are pending publication and she continues to write and produce visual art. Chase-Riboud and her husband now divide their time between Paris and Rome. In the latter city, her studio in the Palazzo Ricci was reputedly also used by the sixteenth-century goldsmith Benvenuto Cellini. The artist does not believe in expatriatism, however, and does not see herself as one who lives in another country because she does not love her own. Instead, she declares in *Essence* of the City of Lights:

> Paradise it is not, but a view from another country is a precious gift, and I have always taken advantage of it. I detest criticism of America from Parisians, yet I accept my own critical view of the United States from this side of the ocean.

Chase-Riboud continues to contribute to the rich legacy of African-American culture in Paris, in the tradition of such artists as painter Henry O. Tanner, sculptors Augusta Savage and Nancy Elizabeth Prophet, and writers such as Countee Cullen, Langston Hughes, Richard Wright, and James Baldwin. She explains, "for me, the mystique, the verve, the sense of liberation persist here."

**Profile by
Theresa A. Leininger**

SHIRLEY CHISHOLM

*S*hirley Chisholm was, in her own words, "the first American citizen

1924- •

to be elected to Congress in spite of the double drawbacks of being female

and having skin darkened by melanin." Elected to the House of

politician, •

Representatives in 1968, she was the first black woman to be elected to

author

the United States Congress, and in 1972 she became the first woman or

black to seek a major party nomination for President. She describes her

precedent-setting life in her autobiographies, Unbought and Unbossed

and The Good Fight.

Shirley Anita St. Hill Chisholm was born in Brooklyn on November 20, 1924, to Charles and Ruby St. Hill. At the age of three, she and her two younger sisters, Muriel and Odessa, were sent to Barbados to live with their grandmother, Emily Seale, to allow the St. Hills to save some money. Chisholm's Aunt Myrtle and Uncle Lincoln helped the grandmother care for the three girls, and the children stayed in Barbados seven years. It was here that Shirley Chisholm received the foundation for her further learning. "Years later I would know what an important gift my parents had given me by seeing to it that I had my early education in the strict, traditional, British-style schools of Barbados. If I speak and write easily now, that early education is the main reason."

Eventually the three sisters returned to Brooklyn, where the depression had kept the St. Hills from realizing their financial goals. In 1934, after seven years, Ruby St. Hill had gone to Barbados to retrieve her children. Back in Brooklyn, they were introduced to their new baby sister, Selma. After years of living in warm and beautiful Barbados, the transition to New York—and an apartment with only cold water and heated by a coal stove—was difficult.

The return was made easier by caring and stimulating parents. Charles, the father, was an impressive man who, despite having finished only the equivalent of the fifth grade, read voraciously. He read several newspapers a day in addition to anything else he could get his hands on; in later years, Chisholm recalled that "if he saw a man passing out handbills, he would cross the street to get one and read it." During these early years, his daughter grew to idolize him, and his effect upon her was lifelong. Her mother also had a profound impact upon her life; she worked to make her daughters renaissance women: "We were to become young ladies—poised, modest, accomplished, educated, and graceful, prepared to take our places in the world." Although living in the depression, her parents sought to provide the best they could for their daughters.

Chisholm's initial experience in New York schools was very different from the positive situation in Barbados. A sixth grader in Barbados, Chisholm was placed in grade Three-B with children two years her junior due to a deficiency in her knowledge of American history and geography. However, she eventually was provided with a tutor and in a year and a half, she caught up to her peers. During her high school years, her mother kept a tight rein on her, forcing her to develop good study habits. This allowed her to graduate with a grade point average that draw several scholarship offers, including ones from Vassar and Oberlin. However, finances forced her to enroll in Brooklyn College.

Brooklyn College was a period of immense growth for Chisholm. She chose to become a teacher, believing there was no other career option for a young black woman. She majored in psychology and minored in Spanish. During her sophomore year, she joined the Harriet Tubman Society, where, she says, "I first heard people other than my father talk about white oppression, black racial consciousness, and black pride."

As her college career progressed, her immense abilities became evident. Chisholm later recalled, "More and more people, white and black, began to tell me things like, 'Shirley, you have potential. You should do something with your life'." Her belief that she needed to do something important strengthened her resolve to become a teacher. She believed she could better society by helping children, and she also had a growing desire to help alter the treatment of her race. It was during this period that the seed for a political career was first planted, by a blind, white political science professor, Louis Warsoff. One of Chisholm's favorite teachers, he suggested she go into politics. At the time, however, this seemed impossible for her, and she responded, "You forget two things. I'm black—and I'm a woman." But the seed, not yet ready to sprout, was planted.

Upon receiving her diploma, Chisholm began looking for a job. Despite her graduation cum laude, the search was difficult. Small and young-looking, she did not look old enough to be a teacher and was repeatedly told so. Ella Hodges of the Mount Calvary Child Care Center in Harlem hired her on probation, and she stayed there seven years. During this time, she also enrolled in Columbia University night school to seek her master's degree in early childhood education. At Columbia she met a graduate student who had recently migrated from Jamaica, Conrad Chisholm. During their early conversations, he attempted to convince her there was more to life than work—such as spending time with him. Easy-going Conrad was a perfect match for the outgoing, ambitious, driven Shirley. The year after they met, they were married, and theirs was a strong and happy union.

Chisholm's became active in politics in 1960, when she helped form the Unity Democratic Club. Its plan was to defeat the Seventeenth Assembly District political machine and take over the district. While pushing for reform, the Unity Democratic Club teamed with the Nostrand Democratic Club to push for the election of two committee members. Despite good showings, both men were defeated. With long-range planning, the groups were more successful in 1962. Both their candidates were elected, and control of the Seventeenth Assembly District fell to them. This victory would be particularly important when in 1964 their candidate was appointed to the bench. A new candidate for assemblyman had to be chosen, so Chisholm immediately began campaigning for herself. The campaign was difficult; she recalls that "it was a long, hard summer and fall. I won by a satisfying margin, in a three-way contest, with 18,151 votes to 1,893 votes for the Republican, Charles Lewis, and 913 votes for the Liberal, Simon Golar." As a result of her victory, Chisholm spent the next four years in the New York State Assembly. Her baptism in public life began.

Chisholm began her service in the New York State Assembly with flair, quickly establishing her own independence from the state party structure. At the beginning of her first term, there was a highly contested race for party leader between Anthony Travia, the former minority leader, and Stanley Steingut. Bucking expectation, Chisholm sided with Travia, one of only two Brooklyn assemblypersons to do so. She also was an active legislator, and two of her bills are particularly noteworthy. The first created a SEEK program, which made it possible for disadvantaged young people to go to college. Her other bill created unemployment insurance for domestic and personal employees. During her tenure, she won acclaim as one of the most militant and effective black members of the Assembly. With this experience behind her, she was ready to move on to the next challenge.

The Congressional campaign was made possible by the correction of an old evil. When the Supreme Court ordered redistricting because of previous gerrymandering, a primarily black Twelfth District of New York was created. Chisholm was the choice of a citizens' committee because of her independent and indomitable spirit. She entered into a primary race with William Thompson, the party machine candidate, and Dolly Robinson. Facing odds like these, she seemed to need a miracle. She launched a campaign effort, and this rigorous schedule paid high dividends. She won by about one thousand votes following a small voter turnout. The Republican candidate was James Farmer, the former national chairman of CORE, the Congress of Racial Equality. His campaign was well-staffed and financed.

About the time his nomination was announced, Chisholm became seriously ill and was diagnosed as having a massive tumor. It was benign, but surgery was still necessary; this took place in late July. After a short convalescence, Chisholm began campaigning again. Many women's organizations offered assistance, particularly after Farmer began to turn the campaign into a gender issue. Despite Farmer's money and his attempt to use her gender against her, Chisholm was too powerful. In the November election, Chisholm beat him decisively. Washington was the next stop for Congresswoman Chisholm.

Chisholm quickly demonstrated that the rebelliousness she displayed in the New York State Assembly was still prevalent. "Her House tenure started in controversy in 1969," explains Alan Ehrenhalt in *Politics in America,* "when House leaders put her on the Agricultural Committee, believing they were doing her a favor because of the committee's jurisdiction over food stamps." She demanded to be taken off this committee, feeling that it was not where she could best serve her constituency. Surprisingly, she was successful in her attempt and was switched to the Veterans' Affairs Committee. She stayed on this committee for only two years, switching in 1971 to the Education and Labor Committee, which is where she wished to be. Here is an example of Chisholm learning to work within the system, for the appointment may have been part of a deal. "She was widely believed to have won that assignment by supporting Hale Boggs of Louisiana in his successful campaign for majority leader against the more liberal Morris K. Udall of Arizona," noted Ehrenhalt. On that committee she campaigned for the poor, working for minimum wage increases and federal subsidies for day care centers, a bill that President Ford vetoed. Even before this, Congresswoman Chisholm had decided it was necessary to change the power structure from the top. Thus, she campaigned for the United States Presidency in 1972.

She was the first black and the first woman to seek a major party nomination for President. She began the race as she had all her previous political ventures—as a poorly funded and hard-working underdog. This time, however, her work ethic and drive were not enough to succeed. She attempted to put together a coalition of blacks, feminists, and other minority groups, but this effort failed. She failed even to win the support of the Congressional Black Caucus, creating a rift between her and them. By the time the convention rolled around, a loss was already assured. Chisholm went to the 1972 convention with 24 delegates. In the end she got 151 votes, released to her by Hubert H. Humphrey and other candidates who had given up on the "stop George McGovern" campaign. Her campaign cannot be deemed a true failure because of the ground-breaking nature of the endeavor. "In terms of black politics, I think an effect of my campaign has been to increase the independence and self-reliance of many local elected black officials and black political activists from the domination of the political 'superstars'." Never shy to suggest her own importance or the importance of her actions, Chisholm spoke on the further impact of her campaign:

Chisholm seeks •

presidential

nomination

> The United States was said not to be ready to elect a Catholic to the Presidency when Al Smith ran in the 1920's. But Smith's nomination may have helped pave the way for the successful campaign John F. Kennedy waged in 1960. Who can tell? What I hope most is that now there will be others who will feel themselves as capable of running for high political office as any wealthy, good-looking white male.

Chisholm remained in Congress and in 1977 moved to the powerful House Rules Committee. She also was elected secretary of the Democratic Caucus, a largely honorific post. In 1980 she went against tradition when she and two Democrats joined the committee's Republican members to force a floor vote on a bill calling for twice-yearly cost-of-living raises for federal retirees. She voted this way despite intense lobbying from Speaker Thomas "Tip" O'Neal. A more important disappointment to her party is her failure to support strict environmental laws that she feels would cost people jobs. However, as the years have passed, she has gradually become a more loyal party member. In her first two years in Congress, she only supported the party on 97 of 127 bills. In 1979 and 1980, she voted the party way on 154 of 163 bills.

The years passed and Chisholm gained more power in Congress. Her increasing length of tenure moved her up in the seniority system. Also, her position in the House of Representatives was safe. Even during the late seventies, when the conservatives were beginning to win elections, her power base in the Twelfth District remained secure. Her personal life was not as uniformly successful: she and Conrad Chisholm divorced in February, 1977. She did not remain single long, remarrying later that same year. This time she wed Arthur Hardwick, Jr., a black businessman she had met ten years earlier when both of them were in the New York State Assembly. In 1979 he was almost killed in a car accident. During his convalescence, she was regularly called away to perform her Congressional duties, and these demands began to weigh heavily upon her. "Her husband's accident and the new conservative climate in Washington prompted Shirley to think about her own goals," wrote biographer Catherine Scheader. On February 10, 1982, Chisholm announced her retirement.

She remained active on the lecture circuit and also was named the Purington Professor at Mount Holyoke College, where she taught classes in political science and women's studies. In 1985 she was visiting scholar at Spelman College. In 1986 Arthur Hardwick died of cancer, and following the 1987 spring semester, she retired from teaching.

She didn't abandon politics, though. When Jesse Jackson started his campaign for the presidency in 1984, Chisholm began working for him. With more time available, her support increased for his 1988 campaign. In the eyes of many, his campaigns were a direct result of her earlier attempt. Jackson's New Jersey chairman, Newark Mayor Sharpe James, credits Shirley with Jesse's successes. "If there had been no Shirley Chisholm," Scheader quoted him, "there would have been no 'Run, Jesse, run' in 1984 and no 'Win, Jesse, win' in 1988." Working for the Jackson campaign was not the extent of her political activities.

Following several disappointments at the 1984 Democratic Convention, Chisholm was determined to continue the struggle. She gathered nine black women together. This led to a major four-day convention of five hundred black women who created a new organization, the National Political Congress of Black Women (NPCBW), with Chisholm as its first leader. The group grew fast, with 8,500 members in thirty-six states by 1988. By this point, it was beginning to wield some real political power. According to Scheader, "The group sent a delegation of 100 women to the 1988 Democratic National Convention to present demands for promoting civil rights and social programs." Chisholm has remained a potent force in politics.

Chisholm has been active in the League of Women Voters, the Brooklyn Branch of the NAACP, the National Board of Americans for Democratic Action, and Delta Sigma Theta Sorority. She has been on the advisory council of the National Organization of Women and an honorary committee member of the United Negro College Fund. Among her many achievements, her most lasting may be her books. The first, *Unbought and Unbossed,* details her early life and her rise, culminating in her election to the House of Representatives. The second book, *The Good Fight,* details her unsuccessful run for the 1972 Democratic party nomination. Both works express her confidence in her ability and her beliefs and hopes for the future of blacks and women.

Chisholm has been a maverick her entire life, refusing the role society created for her. By rebelling, she has achieved many great things. She has been elected to offices and honored with awards and degrees. But, as biographer Catherine Scheader recorded, these achievements are not what she considers important:

> I do not want to be remembered as the first black woman to be elected to the United States Congress, even though I am. I do not want to be remembered as the first woman who happened to be black to make a serious bid for the presidency. I'd like to be known as a catalyst for change, a woman who had the determination and a woman who had the perseverance to fight on behalf of the female population and the black population, because I'm a product of both, being black and a woman.

**Profile by
Alan Duckworth**

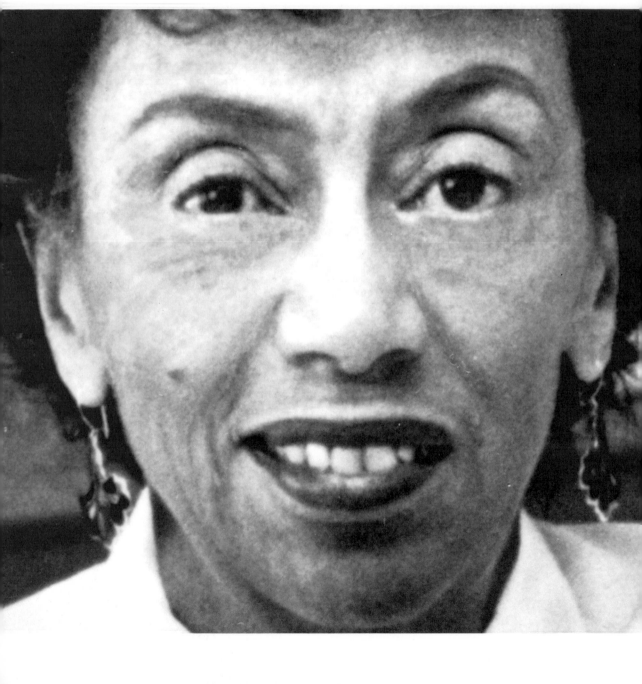

JEWEL PLUMMER COBB

ewel Plummer Cobb, president emeritus of California State University at Fullerton, successfully negotiated the world of the research laboratory before turning her energies to teaching and university administration. She has been an advocate of increasing minorities' and women's entry into scientific fields, and her own research efforts focused on cancer cell biology. In addition to holding a university presidency, she has served as dean of Douglass College and Connecticut College and held several teaching posts, among them positions at the University of Illinois College of Medicine, Sarah Lawrence College, and Connecticut College.

1924-

biologist, university president

Cobb was born in Chicago, the only child in an upper-middle-class home which emphasized the concerns and accomplishments of black people nationwide. Her father, Frank V. Plummer, was born in Washington, D.C., and graduated from Cornell University, where he was one of the founders of Alpha Phi Alpha Fraternity. After he completed medical training at Rush Medical School in Chicago in 1923, he began practicing in that city, serving the great wave of newly arrived black migrants from the South. He set up an office at Fifty-ninth and State streets, a streetcar transfer point for commuting stockyard workers. This made it convenient for them to use the transfer time allowance to visit the doctor without paying an additional transportation fare and without a special trip into town.

Cobb's mother, Carriebel (Cole) Plummer, moved with her family as a child of three from Augusta, Georgia, to Washington, D.C. She studied interpretive dance, which had been made famous by Isadora Duncan, at Sargeants, a physical education college affiliated with Harvard University. After she and her husband settled in Chicago she worked as a teacher of dance in the public schools and in Works Projects Administration projects. She later enrolled in the Central YMCA College (which became Roosevelt University) and received a bachelor's degree the same year her daughter graduated from Talladega College.

Despite the upper-middle-class status Cobb enjoyed, she remains aware of the limitations placed on black people in the United States. From her earliest memory she heard discussions of racial matters—the hopes and frustrations of her family and their associates. She became familiar with the aspirations, successes, and talents of black people. Her mother was a friend of historian Carter G. Woodson and writer/librarian Arna Bontemps, and her uncle, Bob Cole, was a musician and well-known producer of musicals in New York. Allison Davis, the black anthropologist, lived in their apartment building in Chicago, as did Alpha White, the director of the YWCA. Other important black American artists and professional people lived in the vicinity. Cobb never lost sight of the fact that she was a black person living in a white-dominated society. Through the years the Plummer family changed their place of residence more than once, always to a better location, and always after the white population had fled, thereby making a choice part of the city available to minorities for the first time.

In spite of the covert racial segregation that was apparent in her schools, Cobb felt that her pre-college education was good and that it was sufficient preparation for the demanding studies that lay before her. All through public school she was a member of the honor society. There was no question about her continuing on to college; the only decision to be made was which college. Based on her excitement and exhilaration when she first looked into the lens of a microscope, she chose a career as a biologist in her sophomore year of high school.

After high school Cobb decided to attend the University of Michigan because many of her friends were going there, and she was attracted to the glamour of the Michigan football team led by Tom Harmon. At that time, in 1941, the dormitories were segregated, and all black students, undergraduate as well as graduate, were required to live in one house. At the end of her third semester at Michigan, with the encouragement of Hilda Davis, dean of women, Cobb transferred to Talladega College, Talladega, Alabama. Talladega did not accept transfer credits, but students were allowed to take examinations for completion of a course whenever they felt prepared to satisfy course requirements. Cobb entered an accelerated program in which she took summer classes, had private sessions, and took examinations. She graduated three-and-a-half years later, in 1944, with a major in biology. Because of the wartime call for college-age men into the armed forces, only four men were among the thirty-two graduates.

Having been awarded the baccalaureate degree, Cobb accepted the advice of a Talladega professor and enrolled in New York University. Before she left Talladega she had applied unsuccessfully to New York University for a teaching fellowship there. However, when she appeared at the institution, armed with her excellent credentials and poise, she was offered a fellowship that she held for the next five years. From 1944 to 1950 she continued as graduate student and teaching fellow, working toward the master's degree, which she completed in 1947, and the doctorate, completed in 1950, both in cell physiology. With the Ph.D. in physiology from New York University, Cobb was ready to begin her career in science, education, and administration.

Rather than pursuing a medical career, Cobb elected to work in biology because of her preference for the theoretical research approach to biology as opposed to the pathological approach. She considers herself primarily a cell rather than a molecular biologist. While the major concerns of the molecular biologist are atoms and molecules, the cell biologist observes the action and interaction of living cells that are the components of life.

Cobb is most interested in tissue culture of cell biology; cells are grown outside of their native habitats—in test tubes or flasks—and studied under the microscope. Cobb's research experience has been in cancer cell biology, with human tumors and cancer chemotherapeutic agents. Her studies concentrated on human and other mammalian melanomas, and the effects of cancer chemotherapeutic agents and hormones on human and mouse melanomas in tissue cultures. The

From cell •

biologist to

college

president

93 •

research project she is most proud of involved growing human tumors in culture at the Cancer Research Foundation. With Dorothy Walker Jones (then Cobbs's research assistant, and now a professor of biology in the graduate school at Howard University) Cobb studied the effects of newly discovered cancer chemotherapy drugs on human cancer cells. The results of this work are still valued in medical research. In addition, Cobb has conducted pioneering laboratory work in the study of drugs used with cancer treatment.

Within cell biology, Cobb's concentration is pigment cell research, specifically, research on melanin, a brown or black pigment that colors skin. She was interested in melanin's ability to shield human skin from ultraviolet rays and the possibility that it evolved in Africa. All of Cobb's investigative work after the doctorate had some involvement with melanin, mostly with melanoma, a usually malignant skin tumor. Cobb held a post-doctoral fellowship at the National Cancer Institute from 1950 to 1952, and an instructorship in the anatomy department of the University of Illinois College of Medicine from 1952 to 1954. During her appointment as professor of biology at Sarah Lawrence College from 1960 to 1969 and as dean and professor of zoology at Connecticut College from 1969 to 1976, Cobb's research included work on mouse melanoma.

Because of Cobb's love of things scientific, she continued her research for many years after entering college administration. She found teaching satisfying but preferred the laboratory. Cobb would spend the early morning hours in the laboratory; from there she would turn to her administrative tasks, and then devote the remaining hours of the workday to the classroom. At Douglass College, where she assumed the deanship in 1976, a post she held until 1981, administrative demands forced her to give up her investigative work, but as professor of biological sciences at Douglass she taught tissue culture for three of the five years of her tenure there.

In 1981 Cobb accepted the presidency of the University of California, Fullerton. Of all her professional appointments, this was the most rewarding to Cobb. There she established the first privately funded gerontology center in Orange County, lobbied the state legislature for the construction of a new engineering and computer science building and a new science building, installed the first president's opportunity program for students from ethnic groups that are not fully represented on campus, and made the change from a strictly commuter campus to one with an apartment complex for student residences.

While Cobb has done no research since 1976, she reads current research literature regularly and is committed to the advancement of the study of the sciences by groups underrepresented in those fields: women and minorities. She has analyzed the "reasons behind the fact that women, who constitute 52 percent of the population, make up only 20 percent of the scientists but less than one percent of the engineers." In her article "Filters for Women in Science," published in the *Annals of the New York Academy of Sciences* in 1979, Cobb likened the situation of women to a filter, a familiar tool in the research laboratory, through which a filtrate passes according to the filter's pore size. She spoke of women as the filtrate that must pass through filters that have smaller pores than those for men.

Cobb also called for a meaningful change in the ingrained assumptions about the role of women in society and their ability to complete a successful course of study in the sciences. She listed a number of remedies—her own and those of others—starting with support for girls in elementary through high school to broaden their interest and guide them into the sciences. Among the steps that can be taken is providing positive information about the study of science. For women who are already in college, Cobb endorses informal discussions between established women scientists and women undergraduates and graduates. Other suggestions include special funding for the needs of women in graduate study, such as assistance for young mothers who want to teach part-time.

Cobb is saddened by the knowledge that in one recent year, in all of the universities in the United States, only four doctorates in mathematics were awarded to African Americans. She is very proud, however, of the privately funded pre-medical and pre-dental programs for minority students that she founded at Connecticut College. They served approximately forty students, with about 90 percent being accepted into medical or dental schools. While the president of the college dropped the programs after Cobb left Connecticut, the model has been duplicated at more than twenty colleges across the country.

Jewel Plummer Cobb was married in 1954 to Roy Raul Cobb of New York and divorced in 1967. They had one son, Roy Jonathan Cobb, born in 1957. By the time her son was fourteen, Cobb had given him her father's stethoscope and the collapsible field microscope he had used as a medic in World War I. The young man kept the microscope in his room, using it to examine such things as grass and dirt, and using the stethoscope to listen to the heartbeats of living things. On Saturday mornings he would go to his mother's laboratory at Sarah Lawrence College. From Phillips Exeter prep school Roy went to Wesleyan College, graduated with a major in biology, and then went to Cornell Medical School for the M.D.

Profile by
Dona L. Irvin

There is a strong history of medical and scientific study in Cobb's family, beginning with her paternal grandfather, Robert Francis Plummer, who graduated from Howard University in 1898 as a pharmacist, followed by her father, the medical doctor. Cobb represents the third generation, and Roy the fourth; he is a New Jersey radiologist who specializes in magnetic resonance images.

JOHNNETTA BETSCH COLE

*J*ohnnetta Betsch Cole, educator, anthropologist, and the first black

1936- •

woman president of Spelman College, is known as a magnetic and

affirmative force in the lives of her students. In the community of higher

college •

education administrators, Cole is considered an effective advocate for

president,

the liberal arts curriculum who is knowledgeable about keeping it

anthropologist

rigorous and relevant to a changing world. In the words of interviewer

Paula Giddings, Cole "has a sensibility born of an affectionate middle-

class family, a supportive Black community and the unforgotten pain of

the segregated South of the 1940s."

Cole was born October 19, 1936, in Jacksonville, Florida. Her maternal great-grandfather, Abraham Lincoln Lewis, cofounded the Afro-American Life Insurance Company of Jacksonville in 1901. Her father, John Betsch, Sr., worked with Atlanta Life Insurance Company

but later joined his wife's family business, Afro-American Life. Mary Frances (Lewis) Betsch, Johnnetta Betsch's mother, an educator and graduate of Wilberforce, taught English and was registrar at Edward Waters College before joining the family insurance business after her husband's death.

Cole spent her formative years in Jacksonville and entered Fisk University in the summer of 1952 at age fifteen under the school's early admissions program. She went to Fisk because of strong encouragement from her parents and high grades on the entrance examinations. After only one year there, however, she joined her older sister at Oberlin College. During her first year there, 1953, she took an anthropology class on racial and cultural minorities, which inspired her to major in sociology and pursue a career in anthropology. Class discussions of the retention of African culture in the New World had a profound impact on Cole's intellectual development and subsequent academic interests.

Her interest in anthropology was sparked in part because it was new and unfamiliar. "I became an anthropologist in a sense because then I was *exposed* to a possibility, because there was an option out there that I had never dreamed of," she told Giddings. Later when she went home and informed her grandfather that she wanted to be an anthropologist—a most unusual aspiration for an African-American woman during the 1950s—he was startled and looked at her and exclaimed, "What's THAT?" He was really saying, "Why that?" because he had every expectation that she would join the family insurance business. Cole stood her ground because she really wanted to become an anthropologist who "studies people and understands us and goes away and lives with these people—and in my case it would be to go to Africa, and understand Africa. And then to finally understand what happened to us here."

After graduation from Oberlin in 1957, Cole went to Northwestern University to pursue a master's degree in anthropology, which she earned in 1959. She continued her graduate study as a doctoral student there and also met Robert Cole, a fellow graduate student and the white son of a dairy farmer from Iowa. They married in 1960 and when he came to Jacksonville to meet Cole's parents, threats from the white community indicated that the family's insurance company would be bombed and the family would suffer. The first two years of Johnnetta's marriage to Robert, an economist, were spent in Liberia, West Africa, where they worked together on research for their respective dissertations. He conducted economic surveys, and she engaged in fieldwork in the Liberian villages and towns. In 1962 their first son, David, was born in Monrovia. The couple returned to the United States in 1962, and

Robert took a teaching job at Washington State University. Johnnetta Cole worked part-time, had a second son, Aaron, in 1966, and completed her dissertation on "Traditional and Wage Earning Labor in Liberia." In 1965 she was named Outstanding Faculty Member of the year at Washington State.

She was awarded a Ph.D. in anthropology in 1967 from Northwestern University, where she studied under noted anthropologists Melville J. Herskovits and Paul J. Bohannan. Later she joined the faculty at Washington State, where she was assistant professor of anthropology and director of black studies, a program she helped create. She stayed at Washington State until 1970, when she was offered a tenured faculty position at the University of Massachusetts, Amherst, where she was also invited to play a critical role in the ongoing development of their Afro-American Studies program. Robert Cole taught economics at Amherst College and the University of Massachusetts; a third son, Che, was born in 1970. In 1982, after twenty-two years of marriage, Robert and Johnnetta Cole divorced.

For thirteen years, Cole remained at the University of Massachusetts, Amherst, where she was assistant professor of Afro-American Studies, later full professor of both Afro-American Studies and anthropology, and then provost of undergraduate education (1981-1983). When the full history of the development of black studies in the American academy is written, Cole's important role in its evolution will surely be mentioned. Her association with *Black Scholar* during this period is an important manifestation of her interest in the development of the new discipline of black studies.

After a distinguished career at the University of Massachusetts, Cole was named 1983 Russell Sage Visiting Professor of Anthropology at Hunter College of the City University of New York. From 1983 to 1987 she was a full professor in the anthropology department and from 1984 to 1987 she was director of the Latin American and Caribbean studies program. In 1986 she was appointed to the graduate faculty of the City University of New York. Previously, she held two visiting posts—one at Williams College as Luce Visiting Professor, and another as visiting professor of women's studies at Oberlin College.

While at Hunter College, Cole's landmark book, *All American Women,* was published, breaking new ground in women's studies because of its sensitivity to the intersections of race, ethnicity, class, and gender. Cole started thinking seriously about gender on her first visit to Cuba with a delegation of African Americans. Widely published during her outstanding academic career, her scholarship focuses on cultural anthropology, Afro-American studies, and women's studies. Her fieldwork includes studies of a South Side Chicago black church, labor in Liberia, racial and gender inequality in Cuba, Caribbean women, female-headed households, the ways women age, and Cape Verdean culture in the United States. A rich source of biographical information on Cole can be found in *Composing a Life,* written by her friend and colleague, Mary Catherine Bateson, the anthropologist and daughter of Margaret Mead. Bateson and Cole were faculty colleagues at the University of Massachusetts at Amherst. The text is an analysis of Bateson's own life and those of four friends, all of whom faced "discontinuities and divided energies, yet each has been rich in professional achievement and in personal relationships—in love and work." The portrait that emerges is the result of Bateson's ten-day stay at Reynolds Cottage, the president's residence, shortly after Cole was named president of Spelman College in 1987.

On April 5, 1987, Cole was named the first black woman president of Spelman College, the oldest institution of higher learning for black women in the United States. Shortly thereafter, she gained the affectionate title "Sister President," a label that appeared in *Ms.* magazine's interview of October, 1987. She came to the presidency at midpoint in a career that spanned significant scholarship and distinguished administration. William Strickland, director of the W. E. B. Du Bois Collection and assistant professor of political science at the University of Massachusetts, Amherst, where Cole had spent thirteen years, asserted that she would bring a new style of leadership. "Her gift is her vision, which is non-narrow, nonchauvinistic, and internationally humane." She represents much more hope than is common in most leaders. The students at Spelman describe her as "approachable, accessible, visible, and a real sister who cares about us," writes Audrey Edwards in *Working Woman.*

When Cole assumed the leadership of Spelman College, she expressed her hope that scholars, teachers, artists, policy analysts, and community leaders would turn to Spelman for comprehensive information on the rich and diverse history, struggles, conditions, and accomplishments of black women. In fact, she intends to help Spelman become a renowned center for scholarship by and about black women and also the premier institution for educating and nurturing black women leaders from around the world.

In December 1988, Cole married a childhood friend, Arthur Robinson, Jr., in Reynolds Cottage. A public health administrator, Robinson brought to their new family two sons, Arthur J. III and Michael. Cole is now the mother of five sons and the surrogate mother of seventeen hundred Spelman daughters.

Spelman names •

first black

woman

president

**Profile by
Beverly Guy-Sheftall**

BESSIE COLEMAN

1893-1926 •

Overcoming a number of obstacles, Bessie Coleman became the first

black woman to earn her pilot's license and soon was known across the

United States for her flying talent. Not only did she excel as a perform-

aviator •

ance flier, but she was also dedicated to assisting other young black

Americans who wanted to work in the field of aviation. Her hard work

and determination was and continues to be an inspiration for black

aviators—men and women alike.

Coleman was born in Atlanta, Texas, on January 26, 1893. Her family moved to Waxahachie, near Dallas, while she was still a toddler. When she was seven years old her father, who was three-fourths Indian, moved back to Indian territory, leaving her mother to rear four daughters and a son. Susan Coleman supported her family by picking cotton and taking in laundry, and the children helped her in her work. She could not read or write at that time, but she encouraged her children to learn as much as they could.

When Coleman finished high school she wanted to go to college, so her mother let her keep the money she earned from washing and ironing for her college expenses. Coleman enrolled in Langston Industrial College (now Langston University) in Oklahoma. Her money lasted for only one semester, when she had to drop out of school. She then moved to Chicago, where she took a course in manicuring and started working at the White Sox Barber Shop on Thirty-fifth Street near State Street. Later Coleman managed a chili restaurant on Thirty-fifth Street.

Always an avid reader, Coleman kept abreast of current events and developments. She became interested in the fledgling field of aviation. Always ambitious for new challenges, she decided to pursue a career in aviation and set three goals for herself.

Coleman's first goal was to learn to fly and earn a pilot's license. She became discouraged, though, when all of her applications for admission to aviation schools were rejected. But she was encouraged by Robert S. Abbott, founder and editor of the *Chicago Defender* newspaper, who became her staunch supporter and promoter. At his suggestion, she learned French and went abroad to study aviation. Coleman took flying lessons from French and German aviators. She studied under the chief pilot for Anthony Fokker's aircraft corporation and learned to fly the German Fokker airplane.

When Coleman returned to the United States in 1921, she had earned her pilot's license. After another trip to Europe, she returned in 1922 with her international pilot's license. She was the first black woman to earn pilot's licenses, only ten years after the first American woman had earned a license and less than twenty years after Orville and Wilbur Wright had made the first successful flight in 1903.

- *Barnstorming*

proves

successful

Coleman's second goal was to become a recognized stunt and exhibition flier. Barnstorming was, in fact, the main area of aviation open to women in the United States. She achieved success in this field almost immediately. During the Labor Day weekend of 1922 Coleman made her first appearance in the United States in an air show. This event, which took place at Curtiss Field near New York City, was sponsored by Abbott and the *Chicago Defender*. Six weeks later she repeated her performance in Chicago at the Checkerboard Airdrome (now Midway Airport), again under the sponsorship of Abbott. Her manager was David L. Behncke, founder and president of the International Airline Pilots Association.

The two air shows were attended by thousands of spectators, who marveled at the daring stunts performed by this petite and attractive young lady. Coleman soon came to be known as "Brave Bessie." She participated in air shows in many cities throughout the United States, including her hometown of Waxahachie, Texas. While in California, she did some aerial advertising for the Firestone Rubber Company. She also gave lectures on the opportunities in aviation at schools and churches wherever she went.

Coleman did not live long enough to achieve her third goal, which was to establish an aviation school where young black Americans could learn to fly and prepare for careers in aviation. The main sources of funds for this endeavor were her barnstorming and lecturing activities. Early in 1926 she wrote to her sister Elois that she was on the threshold of opening this school. But she was not to realize these plans. Coleman met an untimely death on April 30, 1926, at the age of thirty-three.

Coleman was in Jacksonville, Florida, at the invitation of the local Negro Welfare League to perform in an air show for the Memorial Day celebration. On the evening of April 30, she and her mechanic were making a practice run, with her mechanic piloting the plane. During one of the maneuvers the controls of the plane jammed. Coleman was catapulted out of the plane and fell to her death. One of the last friends she had seen in Jacksonville was her friend Abbott, the Chicago newspaper publisher. She had chanced to meet him in a restaurant, and they had a happy reunion the day before her death. After services in Jacksonville, Coleman's body was flown to Chicago. Last rites were held at the Pilgrim Baptist Church at 33rd Street and Indiana Avenue, with the burial at the Lincoln Cemetery in southwest Chicago.

Coleman dies in •

aviation

accident

Although Coleman did not achieve all of her goals, her pioneering accomplishments were an inspiration to other black men and women who became active in aviation. Within a few years after her death, black fliers were perpetuating her memory through the Bessie Coleman Aero Clubs and the *Bessie Coleman Aero News,* a monthly periodical first issued by these clubs in May of 1930, with William J. Powell as the editor. Powell was also the author of a 1934 book about black Americans in aviation, *Black Wings,* which had as its frontispiece a photograph of Coleman in her flying uniform. Powell dedicated this book to "the memory of Bessie Coleman . . . who although possessed of all the feminine charms that man admires in the opposite sex, also displayed courage equal to that of the most daring men."

Black men and women aviators also remembered Coleman every Memorial Day by flying in formation over Lincoln Cemetery and dropping flowers on her grave. In 1975 the Bessie Coleman Aviators organization was formed in the Chicago area by young black American women who were actively interested in aviation and aerospace.

The first monument recognizing black Americans' achievement in aviation from 1917 to 1990 was unveiled in 1990 at Lambert-Saint Louis

International Airport. The 51-foot-long mural was done by Spencer Taylor and titled "Black Americans in Flight." It features 75 men and women pioneers in aviation, including Coleman and Mae Jemison, the first black woman astronaut.

Profile by
Penelope L. Bullock

CARDISS COLLINS

W hen Cardiss Collins was elected to the United States Congress in

1973 as a representative of Illinois's Seventh District, she was the first

black congresswoman from her state and the fourth black woman ever

to serve in Congress. Two years later, she became the first woman to serve

as leader of the Congressional Black Caucus. Throughout her career,

Collins has been noted for her close bonds with her constituency, her

unifying effect within governmental groups, and above all, for her

steady advocacy of minorities, the poor, women, and the elderly.

1931- •

politician •

Cardiss Hortense Robertson Collins was born in Saint Louis, Missouri, on September 24, 1931, the only child of Finley Robertson, a laborer, and Rosia Mae (Cardiss) Robertson, a nurse. She spent part of her childhood in Saint Louis but moved to Detroit, Michigan, when she was ten years old. After graduating from high school, Collins moved to Chicago where she lived with her grandmother. There she worked odd jobs until she became a secretary with the Illinois Department of

Revenue. Enrolling in evening accounting classes at Northwestern University, she eventually became an accountant and then an auditor with the department, where she worked for twenty-two years.

In 1958 Cardiss married George Washington Collins, a politician. While retaining her own career and raising their son, Kevin, she helped organize her husband's campaigns for Democratic committee member and then alderman in Chicago. Enjoying the involvement, Cardiss Collins also undertook the task of representing the Democratic party as committee member in Chicago's Twenty-fourth Ward.

With his wife's support and assistance, Collins went on to become the representative for Illinois's Sixth, and then Seventh, Districts in the United States Congress. He was known for helping people and keeping in close contact with his constituents. But on December 8, 1972, while flying into Chicago, George Collins's plane crashed. The congressman, then forty-seven, was killed.

Amidst her grief and the many adjustments to be made following her husband's death, Collins had a major decision to make. Chicago's Mayor Richard Daley offered to back her if she would seek to fill the remainder of her husband's term. She later recalled, according to reporter Jacqueline Trescott, "I never gave politics a thought for myself. When people started proposing my candidacy right after the crash, I was in too much of a daze to think seriously about running." Although she liked the thought of carrying out the work that her husband had begun and was committed to the Democratic party, she was concerned about her son Kevin's welfare. But when Kevin expressed his encouragement and her mother agreed to stay with Kevin in Chicago, Collins proceeded with the unexpected challenge.

Collins won the congressional race with a large majority of the votes, and she went to work immediately. While organizing her office she began work on a bill to combat credit discrimination against women. Despite the victory and the challenge before her, the first days were filled with grief over the loss of her husband and separation from her son. She later admitted to Trescott that if she had to make the decision again, she would not choose the same path: "I was lonely and alone. My son was alone. I regret that lost time."

Congressional •

seat easily won

Adjusting to life in Congress was no small challenge in itself. Helping her husband in his career had given her some exposure to the system, but she still had much to learn: "I guess I must have been a member of Congress all of 24 hours when I realized that, as the wife of a politician, I had just been a political spectator—not really playing the game. The difference started rolling in, like a sledgehammer, believe me," she told Audrey Edwards. Congressional procedures were a mystery to her. "I had to learn just the elementary things of how to get attention from the chair so I could get up on the floor to talk. . . . I had to learn what was meant by an 'open rule' and a 'closed rule.' Ultimately I'd find myself whispering to the congressmen next to me, 'Now what do you do if you want to do so-and-so?'" In 1979 she reflected, "In the last six years my biggest roadblock has been shyness. I was basically an introvert, but once people learned I had something to say, I gained confidence."

• *Collins heads*

Congressional

Black Caucus

Just two years after her election to Congress, Collins became the first woman and the first black in two important positions: first as Democratic whip-at-large, and later chairwoman of the House Government Operations Subcommittee on Manpower and Housing. One of her biggest challenges was overcome when her colleagues in the Congressional Black Caucus unanimously elected her to be the first woman ever to lead that group.

As caucus leader, Collins had specific goals. She thought that the caucus should be "Black people-oriented" and that it should be unified in its efforts. In guiding the group, she carefully avoided singling out her own voice. Rep. Parren J. Mitchell, her immediate predecessor, was quoted by Alex Poinsett in 1979: "One of the things that I admire most about her as chairperson is that she is completely democratic. . . . Very often chairpersons tend to become kind of autocratic. She almost bends over backwards not to do that. That doesn't mean she can't be tough when she wants to be, but it's a fair hearing always, even though she may have a very firm position on something."

Although Collins's approach as leader was democratic, her voice was strong and clear in her efforts to mobilize the caucus. She aggressively attacked President Jimmy Carter's proposal for budget cuts in social welfare programs, threatening the withdrawal of black support. "In no previous election season has so formidable a Black leader issued such an ultimatum," reported *Jet* magazine. Under her vigilant leadership, the caucus, among other important accomplishments, caused the defeat of an anti-busing amendment to the Constitution.

Collins has consistently represented the concerns of African Americans and other minorities. She strongly criticized the Reagan Administration for its civil rights policies. She refused to look aside when the United States Justice Department, the Federal Trade Commission, and the National Endowment for the Humanities failed to submit required goals and timetables for hiring women and members of minority groups. Nor has she allowed discriminatory hiring practices among private agencies, such as airlines and the broadcasting industry, to be overlooked. Along

with sponsoring legislation to help small and minority-owned businesses, Collins works to meet the needs of the poor (through welfare reform
and day care services, for example) and the elderly (through laws
protecting older Americans against violent crimes and for better Medi-
care coverage).

Collins believes, according to Barbara Reynolds, that "any woman
can overcome obstacles if she possesses a healthy dose of faith in her
own abilities." Edwards agrees, noting that in overcoming the shyness
and uncertainty of those first days in Congress, Collins "seems to have
learned her lessons well and moves with the easy assurance of one who
has found the cloak of office a comfortable fit."

**Profile by
Marie Garrett**

JANET COLLINS

*R*ecognized at an early age as a gifted artist, Janet Faye Collins went

on to become one of the most versatile and highly acclaimed dancers of

her time. She is equally acclaimed for her impressive talent in choreog-

raphy and dance instruction. Born on March 2, 1917, in New Orleans,

Louisiana, Collins was one of six siblings (five girls and one boy) in a

large family of modest means. Like her hard-working father and

mother, a tailor and seamstress who managed to provide each of their

children a college education, Collins combined supreme talent with

utmost effort in building a career that transcended racial boundaries.

1917- •

dancer, •

choreographer

When Collins was four years old, her family settled in Los Angeles, California, where she spent her formative years attending school and training in both classical ballet and modern dance. She began toe-dancing at the age of ten at a Catholic community center near her home. With amusement she describes this early start in dancing as a matter of "butterflies, bees, and flowers," according to Morris Gilbert: "Little tots bobbing around to the thump of an exaggerated piano beat." Serious ballet studies began when she was twelve. Her mother sewed costumes for dance pupils preparing for dance recitals so Collins could acquire training in ballet technique under the guidance of famed instructors Louise Beverly and Charlotte Tamon. This was but the beginning of study under a succession of illustrious teachers who trained her in ballet, modern dance, and choreography. Other notables who followed Beverly and Tamon included ballet dancers Carmelita Maracchi, Maria Slavenska, Adolf Bolm, Madam Toscanini, and Dorothy Lyndall; modern dancer Lester Horton; Angel Casino, a dancer of Spanish forms; and choreographers Doris Humphrey and Hanya Holm.

- *Youngster*

debuts in

Vaudeville

Making her professional debut in vaudeville shows while she was still in junior high school, Collins gradually achieved recognition and opportunities for work. After high school, she completed her formal education at the Los Angeles City College and Arts Center School, while continuing her dance training under established professionals. Her career as a concert and theatrical dancer gained momentum in 1940, when she worked as a principal dancer for Los Angeles Musical Productions. Her appearances included *Run Little Chillun* and *Mikado in Swing.* In 1941, while touring the West Coast for a production of *Cabin in the Sky,* Collins auditioned for and was immediately hired as a principal dancer for the then three-year-old, world-famous black dance troupe formed and directed by Katherine Dunham. Collins remained with the group for two years, after which she left with another of Dunham's premier dancers, Talley Beatty, to form a dance duo. The duo performed for one year in California before separating to follow individual pursuits.

While Collins was gaining experience as a theatrical and concert dancer, she continued to become ever more versatile by expanding her repertoire. In 1945 she won a Julius Rosenwald Fellowship, which allowed her time to develop her own dance compositions. For one of her several projects she conducted research on Hebraic dances, in which she received the assistance of Ernest Bloch, eminent Swiss-born composer of Hebrew music. Spirituals constituted another area of her studies, which she later rendered, along with her marvelous Biblical portrayals, into many inspired interpretations, such as *Three Psalms of David.* In 1946 Collins had a role in a film produced by Jack Cole, *The Thrill of Brazil,* but national recognition was to come later when she migrated from California to New York.

The break that propelled Collins to the zenith of her career came in 1947, when she had her first solo recital at Las Palmas Theater in Los Angeles. As a result of her performance, she received a scholarship to study composition under Doris Humphrey in New York, where she made her debut, in 1949, in a performance at the Young Men's and Young Women's Hebrew Association (92nd Street "Y"). On the basis of two solos during that performance, she was propelled to stardom, with reviewers touting her as "the most highly acclaimed gifted newcomer in many a season" and "the most exciting dancer in a long time."

Collins was subsequently sought out increasingly for lead roles in theatrical productions and solo concert performances. She performed in a concert for the Young Men's Hebrew Association and was selected as the principal dancer in the 1950 Cole Porter musical *Out of This World.* That performance earned her the prestigious Donaldson Award for the best dancer of the theater season, an award she was able to place alongside her Dance Magazine Award and the Mademoiselle Magazine Award for the 1950 "Woman of the Year." She also received scholarships for ballet (to work under Madam Toscanini, daughter of the famed Italian conductor Arturo Toscanini) and one for modern dance (to work under Hanya Holm, who choreographed her role in *Out of This World*). Collins's vastly growing repertoire was further spread through television, where she appeared regularly on variety shows such as "The Admiral Broadway Review,"), "This Is Show Business," and the "Paul Draper" and "Jack Haley" shows.

By the early 1950s, when she was at the height of her career, Collins "broke down more barriers than any dancer of her color," proclaimed *Ebony.* She had indeed done so in 1951, when she was hired as the first black prima ballerina of the Metropolitan Opera, a position that she retained for three years. In 1954, while reminiscing on her early days as a ballet dancer, Collins remembered her dejection when the director of the Ballet Russe of Monte Carlo, on tour in Los Angeles, declined to hire her despite an impressive audition because "they couldn't take me along for specialty roles. It would have been too expensive. And for the *corps de ballet* he said he'd have to paint me white," she told Norma Stahl. Briefly disappointed, but undaunted and more determined, she returned to practicing and performing. Years later, when Zachary Zolov, choreographer for the Metropolitan Opera, approached Rudolph Bing, the Metropolitan's general manager, with the proposal to hire her for lead dancer in *Aida,* skill was their single consideration and she was immediately hired. Her fame rapidly spread as audiences marveled at her technique. Again and again, audiences and reviewers alike cheered and rhapsodized about her outstanding performances. She is particular-

Collins is first

black prima

ballerina

ly noted for her memorable appearances in *Aida, Carmen, La Gioconda,* and *Sampson and Delilah.*

Concurrent with her position with the Metropolitan Opera, Collins performed between 1952 and 1955 under Columbia Artists Management in a number of solo concert dance tours in the United States and Canada. She then abandoned stage and concert tours and rejected offers to tour Europe in order to devote herself full time to teaching and developing plans for her own dance troupe. Always the perfectionist, Collins was very demanding of the students with whom she worked, expecting no less of them than she would of herself. She insisted that they study human anatomy, that they undergo rigorous physical conditioning, and that they devote the utmost concentration to every movement. The benefit of her expertise has been enjoyed by students at a number of schools where she taught, including the Modern Dance School of American Ballet, Saint Joseph School for the Deaf, Marymount Manhattan College, Manhattanville College of Sacred Heart, and Mother Butler Memorial High School.

Collins's abilities as a dancer and teacher were further augmented by her considerable talent as a costume designer and choreographer. From her work with Doris Humphrey and Hanya Holm she developed her own style and choreographed operas and several concert works, including *Blackamoor, Eine Kleine Nachtmusik, Spirituals, Three Psalms of David, The Satin Slipper, Genesis, Fire Weaver,* and *Sunday and Sister Jones.*

Characterizations of Collins's dance technique are filled with superlatives that emphasize her seldom-matched "incredible artistry and breathtaking movements," as described in *Ebony.* At once cool and exotic, a study in perfectly controlled power and tension, she exudes a harmony of spirit by achieving a perfect marriage of art and science, of precise technique and creativity in dance. Questioned by Morris about her formula for keeping separate the presumably conflicting techniques of ballet and modern dance, Collins denied there was such a conflict and insisted instead that knowledge of both were essential:

> To extend the range of the body . . . the illusion you communicate while dancing depends on what you feel about your dance. For instance, I love Mozart. For that I need elevation and lightness, which I've learned from ballet. I love spirituals, too, and for that there is modern dance and a feeling of the earth.

Collins's ability to spellbind her audiences and to convey the emotional content of her works so powerfully as to move people to tears—as with her performance of the spiritual "Nobody Knows the Trouble I've Seen"—has not only been recognized with many awards, but lauded in verse. Nerissa Milton, in a tribute to her in *The Negro History Bulletin,* reflects in verse on Collins's ability to use her art form to support truth. In a poem called "To a Dancer," Milton declares that upon seeing the magic, overwhelming beauty expressed in Collins's dance: "Then even those who doubt / Would see a symphony, enriched by / Truth." The verse proposes that Collins's artistry inspires not only pride in race but draws universal appeal that, by its magnificence, must force one to abandon bigotry and hatred.

Profile by
Carolyn R. Hodges

MARVA COLLINS

*M*arva Collins, the founder of Chicago's Westside Preparatory

1936- •

School, is renowned as an innovator in education. Using instruction

methods based upon her own philosophy as to how children should be

school founder •

taught rather than the dictates of the American public school system, her

maverick style has yielded remarkable results in teaching disadvan-

taged children that were formerly labeled uneducable by other schools.

Nonetheless, despite her success in bringing her students' test scores up

while national averages continued to drop, Collins has drawn fire from

those who resent her defying the status quo. Because of the attention she

receives from the media, some have labeled her an opportunist who

considers herself better than her peers. She has even been criticized by the black community, which has on occasion accused her of catering to a white-dominated media. Yet Collins's record as an educator has vindicated her approach to education, and her school continues to grow through the enrollment of students whose parents are eager to see their children gain an advantage over those who attend ordinary public schools.

Born on August 31, 1936, Collins was raised by parents who were financially well off and highly supportive of their daughter. She lived in Monroeville, Alabama, until she and her mother moved to Atmore, a nearby town, after her parents divorced. Although Brian Lanker quotes her as saying "I don't want to be wealthy. I don't need that kind of power," Collins's autobiography is a paean to her family's status in the community due to the accumulated wealth of her grandfathers and father, Henry Knight, Jr. Her father's business acumen earned him the respect of white businessmen and the envy of other blacks. It was largely because of her father, who had managed to become enormously successful despite a fourth-grade education, that Collins came to respect and have faith in such qualities as self-pride, nonconformity, strong values, uncompromising beliefs, and strength.

In high school Collins began to show traits of a feisty, strong-willed spirit by refusing to take a home economics course required of all female students. Believing that black girls taking home economics bore out white people's expectations that they could only be domestics or homemakers, she stood firm in her resolve. In 1953 Collins graduated as the only female from Escambia County Training School who did not take the required course. As the first person in her family to go to college, Collins chose Clark College in Atlanta, Georgia, even though she had no notion about her future. She graduated with a bachelor's degree in secretarial science, since that seemed a sensible choice.

Finding no suitable secretarial position open to blacks, Collins turned to the one profession she never planned to enter: teaching. At Monroe County Training School, she taught four business courses and got her basic teacher-training from her principal, who stressed knowing one's students and their capabilities. After a two-year teaching stint, Collins went to Chicago for a visit and decided to remain there.

Finding a position as a medical secretary, she soon married a draftsman, Clarence Collins, with whom she would have three children: Eric, Patrick, and Cynthia. She eventually realized that she missed teaching and applied for a position in the Chicago public school system. Due to a teacher shortage, Collins was immediately hired despite not having taken any education methodology courses. As a full-time substitute teacher, she was assigned to Calhoun South Elementary

School to teach second grade. Here, without any prior teaching experience at that level, Collins began to come into her own as an innovative, creative teacher who planned and taught according to learner needs rather than slavishly adhering to a preplanned curriculum guide. And here was where she began to run afoul of the "system," one she believed insensitive to black children, particularly those of low socioeconomic background in inferior schools. Collins became known as a maverick and a troublemaker and soon became the target of emotional abuse from other teachers. Collins stayed at Calhoun for only a year. By that time she and her husband were beginning a family and adjusting to life in an interracial neighborhood, Garfield Park.

After the birth of her first child, Collins returned to teaching with an assignment to Delano Elementary School. In *Marva Collins' Way*, Collins describes her initial satisfaction with a school headed by a strong principal. To her, he was an excellent role model who espoused knowledge and understanding of classical literature and poetry as well as the need to always continue learning. But when a new principal came to the school the working environment began to change for the worse. A by-the-book administrator, the principal demanded standardized testing and the exclusive utilization of the "look-say" method of teaching reading. Under this leadership, teachers became apathetic and disrespectful to children; internecine bickering and professional jealousy also became the norm. This last factor proved the most damaging to Collins because it resulted in slanderous and vicious attacks on her character. One such written assault read: "You think you're so great. We think you're nothing [signed] a colleague." Collegial envy and little or no support from a weak principal led to dizzy spells, insomnia, self-pity, doubt, and even guilt.

In 1975 Collins left the Chicago public school system and opened her own school, the Daniel Hale Williams Westside Preparatory School, in the basement of Daniel Hale Williams University, a Chicago community college. She and some neighbors received advice from the Alternative Schools Network, which also paid Collins's salary as director and curriculum developer. The college provided free space and equipment. Collins made appeals to private donators for books and supplies, no matter the condition, age, or appearance. She even foraged in the Delano School garbage dump. Ironically, some of the books she found were from the Open Court Reading Series she had long favored for its phonics approach to reading. Beginning with only four children, including her own daughter, Collins was teaching nearly twenty children four months later. Although small in number, they were too many for such cramped quarters. Because of this space problem, Collins moved her school to the top floor of her home, which her husband renovated for

Collins founds •

school for

alternative

learning

the purpose in 1976. That fall, Collins began teaching a class of eighteen students.

It was Collins's teaching method that first began to win her support from parents. First and foremost, Collins instills confidence, pride, and self-esteem in children who had never had or who had lost these vital self-determinants of character. Some had been systematically ignored, some mislabeled as "slow" and "retarded," and some were verbally and emotionally abused. Collins constantly assures them that she loves them and demands that they live up to and fulfill her high expectations of them. She does this via the hands-on approach. Known as a teacher who never sits down, Collins walks the aisles, hugs, cajoles, and keeps up a running commentary of maxims designed to encourage and uplift the spirits of children broken and defeated by the very institutions meant to do just the opposite. Furthermore, she espouses the basics of learning and demands that learners meet her high expectations. Using herself as a model, Collins teaches self-respect, self-reliance, and moral character, in addition to the three R's, especially reading.

Two years after Collins relocated her school, the media discovered her. The *Chicago Sun-Times* featured a story based on her claims that the Westside Preparatory students' standardized test scores in reading and language skills had jumped from below to as much as four years above grade level. Subsequently, *Time, Good Housekeeping, People, Newsweek, Black Enterprise, Ebony,* and a variety of educational journals ran feature stories on the "miracle teacher." The clincher, though, was a 1981 Hallmark Hall of Fame CBS television special entitled "The Marva Collins Story," starring Cicely Tyson and Morgan Freeman. The one hundred thousand dollars Collins received for this movie, in addition to a fifty-thousand-dollar grant from W. Clement Stone, helped her to move the school again, this time to two office buildings on the edge of Garfield Park. Television coverage from a 1979 "60 Minutes" story with Morley Safer helped, too. Soon, Collins had two hundred students and a staff of five teachers.

With all the new-found prestige, the miracle teacher became a candidate for jobs with high visibility. After the airing of the 1979 "60 Minutes" show, Collins was offered positions as Secretary of Education in the Ronald Reagan administration, Chicago School Board member, and Los Angeles County School System superintendent. She declined all nominations to remain with her children. By 1982, instead of continuing to bask in her new-found glory, Collins discovered that the wounds from old jealousies were still festering, that her detractors had not forgotten the one who, in their eyes, was still acting like "some kind of god." *Substance* magazine, a publication for substitute teachers, published the findings of George Schmidt, a teacher recently released from his position. He claimed that Collins had received $69,000 in CETA funds from 1975 to 1979 through the Alternative Schools Network, the same organization that had guided her efforts in opening the first school. This was newsworthy because Collins had long insisted that she would never resort to accepting federal monies that would allow the government to mandate rules and regulations for her to follow.

As if this were not enough, an apparently disgruntled former Westside Preparatory teacher accused Collins of inflating standardized test scores, an accusation harder to prove since private schools were not required to give those tests or report scores. Collins was also accused of plagiarism and pressuring parents who were delinquent with tuition payments. She appeared on the "Donahue Show" twice to answer these charges. A prevailing perception by some Chicago teachers and local media persons was that they had been deceived by a larger-than-life persona who, after all the hoopla had died down, was a human being with the same human frailties as everybody else. But her defenders were still behind Collins one hundred percent. For example, in support of her claims about Westside Preparatory student test results, the admissions director of a noted Chicago private school verified those claims for forty-five students he tested over a four-year period, all Westside students.

Today, Collins envisions extending Westside Preparatory to meet her students' educational and personal needs. Not only a high school, but a day-care center and an adult-education facility for the Garfield Park citizens are in the plans for an educational complex. She also now owns a school in Cincinnati, Ohio, and has bought a school building in the Park Forest area of Chicago with money donated by rock star Prince. In an article in *Essence* magazine Collins stated that there was no need to leave Chicago's West Side: "For what? Now all the cab drivers know me . . . [and] they are honking and blowing even when I don't need them. Leave the West Side—why? Something good is happening here." Since she fervently believes that there is good wherever one chooses to find it, Collins will succeed on her terms, in her own way—Marva Collins's way.

**Profile by
Dolores Nicholson**

ANNIE J. COOPER

*T*hroughout a lifetime that spanned slavery, the Civil War, Recon- **c. 1858-1964** •

struction, segregation, two world wars, a great depression, and an era of

civil rights struggle, Annie J. Cooper expressed strong concerns for racial **Pan-African** •

justice and equality for women. On her century-long quest to under- **scholar,**

stand and thereby improve human social interaction, Cooper traveled **feminist**

extensively throughout the world and, at the age of sixty-six, was among

the first African-American women to earn a doctorate. Through her

teaching and writing, Cooper communicated a global, historical, and

highly modern view of racism and sexism in Western civilization.

Anna "Annie" Julia Haywood Cooper was born on August 10, 1858 or 1859, in Raleigh, North Carolina, the daughter of Hannah Stanley (Haywood), a slave, and probably George Washington Haywood, the owner. A precocious child, Cooper went to Saint Augustine's Normal

School and Collegiate Institute. There she soon distinguished herself and became a tutor and then a teacher. In 1877 she married George A. C. Cooper, a fellow teacher from Nassau who had entered Saint Augustine's in 1873 to study theology. He died in 1879, just three months after his ordination, and Annie Cooper never remarried.

In 1881 Cooper entered Oberlin College, one of the few institutions accepting blacks and women at the time. After earning her bachelor's degree in 1884 and her master's degree in mathematics in 1887, she accepted a position in Washington, D.C., at the Preparatory High School for Colored Youth, which in 1891 became the M Street High School. Most of her career as an educator would be at this distinguished institution.

During the 1890s, while racist terrorism escalated, Cooper and other black intellectuals mobilized to arouse public action. Although teaching full time, Cooper found time for other commitments. She attended numerous conferences, presenting papers to diverse organizations. Early in the decade she went to Toronto on a summer exchange program for teachers, and in 1896 she visited Nassau. Cooper traveled to London in July of 1900 to attend the first Pan-African Conference, where she spoke about racism in America. Her London stay was followed by a tour of Europe.

Cooper was principal of the M Street School from 1902 until 1906. When she disputed the board of education's design to dilute the curriculum of "colored" schools, she was dismissed from her position. She served as chair of languages at Lincoln University in Jefferson City, Missouri, from 1906 to 1910, then returned to the M Street School as a teacher of Latin. Later, she became president of Frelinghuysen University, a unique institution that only briefly became a university before socio-economic conditions and accrediting requirements combined to close it.

During her stint as principal of M Street School, Cooper had impressed a visiting French educator, who served as an important contact when she decided to pursue the doctorate in France. By studying summers at the Guilde Internationale in Paris and then at Columbia University, Cooper was able to finish her course requirements for a Ph.D. She successfully defended her dissertation at the Sorbonne on March 23, 1925, and at age sixty-six she was the fourth known African-American woman to earn a doctorate. Remarkably, she managed to find time for research and study despite working full time, raising two foster children while in her forties, and adopting her half brother's five orphaned grandchildren in her late fifties.

Cooper died in her 105th year, on February 27, 1964. She was interred in the Hargett Street Cemetery in Raleigh next to her husband, whom she had outlived by eighty-five years.

Cooper's earliest writings, collected in *A Voice from the South* in 1892, mark her as a dedicated feminist and an advocate for African Americans. Her concern for women's rights grew out of her own experiences, when as a student she was not encouraged in her schoolwork. In fact, her announced intention of going to college "was received with . . . incredulity and dismay." Of the colleges that would admit women in those days, only a handful had ever graduated any African-American women. In *A Voice from the South,* Cooper challenged the then-prevalent argument that education ruined a woman's chances to marry, arguing that all of humanity would benefit from the education of women:

> The cause of freedom is not the cause of a race or a sect, a party or a class—it is the cause of human kind, the very birthright of humanity. . . . Woman's strongest vindication for speaking [is] that *the world needs to hear her voice.* It would be subversive of every human interest that the cry of one-half of the human family be stifled.

L'Attitude de la France à l'égard de l'esclavage pendant la Révolution, Cooper's doctoral thesis and best known work, studies the social and racial complexities of the Americas in a global and historical framework. Nominally a study of French racial attitudes, the dissertation is equally a study of the successful struggle of slaves in Saint Domingue to throw off an oppressive system and to create a new order. And although this work centers on Haiti and France, Cooper shows that it is not limited geographically or historically. Events that took place in antebellum North Carolina, in pre-1843 Bahamas, and in revolutionary Saint Domingue/Haiti were all chapters in the same book of history.

Cooper's *L'Attitude* is one among many studies of the establishment of a black state by slaves who revolted in Saint Domingue. Yet Cooper's work possesses the unique characteristic of its point of view. As the work of an African-American scholar who was born a slave, the dissertation has insight and sensitivity that elude most histories. Cooper's position is that of direct identification with the oppressed, whom she sees as victims of Western civilizations—civilizations she often describes as "barbarian." One of her most memorable references is this quote, describing white invaders in the new world:

A dedicated •

feminist and

black advocate

Huge white bodies, cool-blooded, with fierce blue eyes, reddish flaxen hair; ravenous stomachs, filled with meat and cheese, heated by strong drinks. Brutal drunken pirates and robbers, they dashed to sea in their two-sailed barks, landed anywhere, killed everything; and, having sacrificed in honor of their gods the tithe of all their prisoners, leaving behind the red light of burning, went farther on to begin again.

Cooper believed that social equality is inherent to human nature, but that Western civilization, by stressing force, has destroyed the natural balance of things. "Progress in the democratic sense is an inborn human endowment—a shadow mark of the Creator's image, or if you will an urge-cell of the universal and unmistakable hallmark traceable to the Father of all," she wrote in *The Third Step*. She concluded that equality should not be the equilibrium of force, conceded only when one cannot crush or exploit the other, but the equilibrium that comes when "the big fellow with all the power and all the controls" respects others as being as good as he is.

Civilizing the powerful seems to have been one of Cooper's primary motivations. "Let the Ruler bear in mind that the Right to Rule entails the duty and the inescapable responsibility to Rule Right," she invokes in *The Third Step*. "Let him recognize the differences among men ... not as obstacles to fulfillment of destiny ... [but as] the providential contribution to that heterogeneity which offers the final test of our civilization, harmony in variety." Cooper suggests that the task of rebalancing the power will likely fall on those who are not abusing power: the cultivated. "If the cultivated black man cannot endure the white man's barbarity," Cooper observed in *A Voice*, "the cure, it would seem to me, would be to cultivate the white man."

Cooper's intellectual evolution mirrored her social development. From the confined environment of a small, newly emancipated rural community, she grew to become a highly educated and knowledgeable scholar and teacher. From a young woman concerned with sexism and racism, she expanded her horizons to international proportions. Cooper's lifetime pursuit of knowledge and understanding had a humanistic basis. As an educator, she wanted to pave the way for a better, more rational, more "cultivated" world. As she researches, learns, and teaches, she once told a reporter: "I am soundly convinced that every scrap of information I may gain in the way of broadening horizons and deepening human understanding and sympathies, means true culture, and will redound to the educational values of my work in the school room."

**Profile by
David W. H. Pellow**

ELIZABETH "LIBBA" COTTEN

lthough Elizabeth Cotten did not make her professional debut as a

folk singer until she was sixty-seven years old, the self-taught musician

had a great influence on many folk artists. The composer of such classics

as "Freight Train" and "Washington Blues," whose unique style of

guitar playing was imitated by many, worked many years as a domestic

servant before being discovered by Pete Seeger and hailed as an

important artist of the folk revival.

1892-1987 •

folk •

musician

Cotten, frequently called Libba, was born in January 1892 in Chapel Hill, Orange County, North Carolina. She was the youngest of five children of George Nevills and Louisa (Price) Nevills. Her father, a dynamite setter in an iron mine, who made liquor to supplement the family income, was the son of a slave. Her mother was a midwife, the daughter of a farmer landholder from Siler City, North Carolina. Louisa Nevills was ten years old when the slaves were freed, and her family reacted to the Emancipation Proclamation with concern for protecting their horses from the Union Army.

Cotten was raised in Chapel Hill in the North Carolina Piedmont, an area that Bruce Bastin describes as having a strong blues and pre-blues tradition. He noted in *Red River Blues* that her "repertoire reflects the pre-blues dance pieces and tunes that were common in her girlhood." Willie Trice, one of Bastin's informants, explained that the blues and rags played in the Orange County area at the time, when performed by banjo players, were called reels rather than blues. The music from her youth informed Cotten's later style.

Cotten's was a musical family. She sang at home with her mother, and her uncles played fiddle and banjo. Although she would have preferred to learn to play the organ and piano, the first instrument she learned to play was the banjo, because her brother owned one, wrote Wilma Grand Chalmers in *$2 at the Door*. She recalled learning to play it when he was at work:

> Times when my brother'd go to work, I'd grab his banjo and turn the pegs and try to play it. Always ended up breakin' the strings. After dinner that night he'd roll a cigarette and go to get his banjo. I'd head for the bedroom and hide under the bed. There'd be a silence, then I'd hear him say, very quietly to himself, "She done it again." But he never would get after me to my face.

Cotten quit school when she was eleven years old to earn money to buy a guitar. When she had saved enough money, storing up seventy-five cents to a dollar a month, she bought a demonstrator Sears and Roebuck Stella for $3.75.

What distinguished Cotten's guitar-style was her manner of playing left-handed on a guitar strung for right-handers. Her upside-down style of playing the banjo and guitar is said to bring "the rhythmic effect and emphasis inherent in the thumb to the middle and upper strings, while sustaining the traditional alternating bass with the fingers." Cotten explained how she acquired this style:

"Cotten picking" •

guitar style

developed

> I had learned a banjo upside down and I couldn't change [the strings] because it belonged to my brother. Then when I bought the guitar, so much was said like, "You better change the strings, you can't play it left-handed," that they was changed as much as two or three times. And I could not play it. I couldn't play it, I couldn't tune it, I couldn't do anything with it. So I just sat down and took all the strings off, then I put 'em back on the old way and I stopped askin'. I started

playing, learning different little tunes on it. I'd get one little string and then add another little string to it and get a little sound, then start playing.

"I banged that guitar all day and I banged it all night so nobody could sleep." Cotten recalled to Chalmers. "Nobody helped me. I give myself credit for everything I learned." What she developed from her self-instruction was, according to Kristin Baggelaar and Donald Milton, "two-finger and 'banjo' stylings for which her name is most famous. In addition to this 'Cotten style' of guitar picking, she plays a broken rhythm style, using three or four fingers and chording up the neck."

Cotten's early musical career was by no means professional. Although she composed the classic "Freight Train" when she was only eleven and had a great future in music before her, two factors stifled her musical development. One was her marriage to Frank Cotten, and the other was the religious community. After their first date, they eloped and subsequently lived in her mother's home until they could afford to rent a house. Married at fifteen and a mother at sixteen—to a daughter, Lillie—Cotten could no longer devote herself to music. Cotten's musical development yielded to her religious experiences.

For the next fifty years, until she began to perform professionally in 1959, Cotten lived in various places and held several jobs. She moved with her husband and daughter between New York and Chapel Hill until her husband, a chauffeur, opened his own business in New York. Cotten worked as a domestic servant. In about 1947 the Cottens divorced, and she moved to Washington, D.C., where her daughter was living. There, Cotten worked during the holiday season at Lansburgh's Department Store, on the fifth floor where dolls were sold.

In Lansburgh's, Cotten found a young girl who had wandered away from her mother. The girl's mother, Ruth Crawford Seeger, was a composer and music teacher and wife of the ethnomusicologist Charles Seeger. Serendipitously, Ruth Seeger proposed that if Cotten chose to stop working at the store, she could come work for the Seeger's in Chevy Chase, Maryland. Cotten accepted her offer. At the Seeger home, Ruth Seeger was compiling a folksong collection for children, and her own children were learning music. Mike Seeger recalls that Cotten would use the young Peggy's guitar and practice in the kitchen, which she was doing when they first heard her play. Thus, Ruth Seeger "collected a few songs from Libba" for her compilation.

Cotten made her professional debut with Mike Seeger at a concert at Pennsylvania's Swarthmore College in 1959. She was sixty-seven years old. From that time to her death, Cotten was a professional folk artist and a part of a steadily increasing movement toward folk music appreciation. Bob Groom notes that by 1964, Cotten had appeared at the Newport Folk Festival with such notables as John Hurt, Skip James, John Estes, Muddy Waters, and Otis Spann. She appeared there again in 1968. From 1968 to 1971 and again in 1975, she performed at the American Folklife Festival in Washington, D.C. In 1968, according to Pete Seeger, "Libba Cotten, seventy-two years old and black, got a standing ovation from 3,000 white students at Duke University in March." In 1969, she performed at the Smokey Mountain Folk Festival in Gatlinburg, Tennessee, and at Washington Square Church in New York City.

In November 1978, Cotten performed at the first Washington Blues Festival, a benefit for black blues musicians held at Howard University, where she was listed among such blues luminaries as Furry Lewis, John Estes, and Hammie Nixon. Also during the 1970s Cotten performed at Canada's Mariposa Folk Festival, the Philadelphia Folk Festival, McCabe's in Santa Monica, California, Washington's Kennedy Center, and at the Folklife Festival on the Eno River in Durham, North Carolina. In 1978, she played New York City's Carnegie Hall.

During the 1980s Cotten continued to perform steadily, and at age ninety toured Europe and America with Taj Mahal. Later she toured on her own, traveling roughly four months of the year.

Besides her performances at coffee houses, folk festivals, universities, and concert halls, Cotten developed a full recording career. She cut her first solo album, *Negro Folk Songs and Tunes*, in 1957, for Folkways. She also recorded on Folkways *Elizabeth Cotten, Volume II: Shake Sugaree*, 1967, *Elizabeth Cotten, Volume III: When I'm Gone*, 1975, and *Elizabeth Cotten Live!*, 1983. She also appeared in Pete Seeger's videotape "Rainbow Quest" as well as in the Grass Roots Series videotape "Old Time Music," 1974, and on PBS-TV's "Me and Stella," 1977.

Cotten's accomplishments have not been ignored. On July 29, 1972, she received the Burl Ives Award from the National Folk Festival Association to commemorate her "unique contribution to folk music." In 1984, she received a National Heritage Fellowship from the National Endowment for the Arts. More recently, she received a Grammy.

Cotten's most famous song, "Freight Train," has an interesting history. Composed by Cotten at the age of eleven, it has, according to Pete Seeger, "gone around the world." The song, often attributed to other performers, was first recorded by Peter, Paul, and Mary in the early 1960s. Peggy Seeger also performed the song, and according to Groom, the version The Vipers and the Chas. McDermitt Skiffle Group performed as "Freight Train Blues" they received through Peggy Seeger.

Court action was required in order for Cotten to secure the copyright for the song, and it was not until 1957 that she was granted the rights.

Besides the influential "Freight Train," Cotten is also well known for her instrumental "Washington Blues," transcribed and commented on by Janet Smith. Smith contends that "Washington Blues" is a ragtime piece that rivals "Freight Train" for its exemplification of the range of Cotten's playing style. Observing that Cotten "literally invents all of her hand-positioning techniques," Smith suggests that the skill revealed in "Washington Blues" goes "far beyond the ever-familiar 'Freight Train'." "Washington Blues" was one of the early compositions of Cotten's professional career and was performed on various occasions in and around Washington, D.C., in the 1960s.

Chalmers notes that audience participation was an important part of Cotten's performance: "Libba, after a few verses, demands of the audience 'Now you-all sing'." Chalmers adds, "the soul of her music is inseparable from the audience, for whom it is recreated in each time and space." She attempted to respond to her audiences' expectations of her and included facts about her own life. Indeed, her album *Elizabeth Cotten Live!* illustrates this stylistic point: each side contains a personal story relating to Cotten's experiences. Side A contains "Banjo Story" and side B contains "Guitar Story" and "Elizabeth Story." The album ends with "'Til We Meet Again," described as "a traditional hymn which Elizabeth always includes as an expression of her deep religious faith and her love for her audience." Appropriately, it is a traditional benedictory hymn of some black church services. Cotten's music reflects a deep spiritual interest while sustaining her reputation as a blues artist. When she entered the world of professional song, she was "convinced that the Lord loved folk music." It seems to be such love that provided for Cotten the joy of performing. Cotten died on June 29, 1987, at age ninety-five.

**Profile by
Laura C. Jarmon**

ELLEN CRAFT

Ellen Craft and her husband, William, are most famous for their

remarkable escape from slavery, fleeing north to Philadelphia and

Boston and even to England to avoid being returned to their former

owners. They eventually returned home to Georgia, where they opened a

school for black children.

c. 1826-c. 1897 •

escaped slave, •

school

founder

Ellen Craft was born about 1826 in Clinton, Georgia, the daughter of a slave named Maria. Her father was Major James Smith, the mother's owner. When she was eleven, Craft was removed from the household and taken to Macon, Georgia, having been made a wedding gift for a Smith daughter. In Macon, she met her future husband, William Craft, also a slave.

Ellen and William Craft recount their flight in *Running a Thousand Miles for Freedom,* published in 1860. In a daring journey, Ellen posed as a young male slave owner and William as "his" slave. The determination to flee came from Ellen. She was particularly adamant about not wanting to bear children into slavery. William noted that being separated from her own mother at an early age had strengthened Ellen's resolve: "She had seen so many other children separated from their parents in this cruel manner, that the mere thought of her ever becoming the mother of a child, to linger out a miserable existence under the

wretched system of American slavery, appeared to fill her very soul with horror."

In December 1948 they plotted their escape. The plan was as follows: Given the great distance they would have to cover, they could not hope to make a successful journey on foot. Since Ellen looked white, however, they might be able to travel by train and other public transportation with William posing as Ellen's slave. She needed to play the role of a male because a white woman would not be traveling alone with a male slave. Suspicion would be aroused in that Ellen would be beardless and effeminate. She would also be expected to sign in at hotels, something she could not do since she could not write. Her disguise was that of a sickly young man whose face was almost completely covered in a poultice of handkerchiefs and whose writing arm was in a cast. She also wore eyeglasses with green shades. With her hair cut short, and wearing men's clothing, she became "a most respectable looking gentleman."

Traveling primarily by train but with steamer and ferry connections, they went through Georgia, South Carolina, North Carolina, and Virginia. Baltimore, Maryland, was their last stop in slave territory. They reached Philadelphia on Christmas Day in 1848. From plan to completion, the trip took eight days.

Despite understandable fears, Ellen carried out her part with fortitude and quick thinking, not faltering when faced with the challenges of maintaining her disguise. For example, when she boarded the train in Georgia, she was "terror stricken" to see sitting beside her an old white man who knew her well and had in fact dined at Ellen's owners' home the previous day. Rather than have him recognize her or her voice, she gazed out the window, pretending to be deaf. Forced to say something when the old man talked louder and louder, she answered in a single word, lessening the chances of her voice being recognized.

In Baltimore, threatened with detainment for being without documentation of William's ownership, Ellen questioned the official "with more firmness than could be expected." Once they reached the safety of Philadelphia, William remembered Ellen's weeping "like a child"; he also remembered that she "had from the commencement of the journey borne up in a manner that much surprised us both."

In Philadelphia, the Crafts were befriended by Quakers and free blacks. At first, Ellen Craft was distrustful of all whites. She did not believe that the Barkley Ivens family, white Quakers, could mean them any good. But the Ivens's generosity and gentle ways won her over during the three weeks she and William spent with them recuperating from the strain of the journey. While regaining their strength, the Crafts received tutoring in reading and writing. William noted they learned the alphabet "by stratagem" while enslaved. In their time at the Ivens's home, they began to learn to read and they learned to write their names.

The Crafts then moved on to Boston. They were assisted by abolitionists, including William Lloyd Garrison, Theodore Parker, and William Welles Brown. Brown arranged appearances for them, "sometimes charging an admission fee, an almost unprecedented practice in abolitionist circles," according to Benjamin Quarles. Continuing to develop her skills as a seamstress, Ellen Craft studied with an upholsterer. (She had already made good use of her ability to sew by making the trousers she wore in the escape from Georgia.)

- *Fugitives flee*

to England

The Crafts remained in Boston two years. They became the center of highly publicized events once again in 1850, when they fled to England because of attempts to return them to slavery by means of the Fugitive Slave Law. Their former owners sent two slavecatchers with warrants for their arrest, but abolitionists in the Vigilance Committee of Boston helped to shelter the Crafts and get them out of the city.

Once again, Ellen Craft showed firm resolve even as she recognized the depth of the danger. William Still records the observations of Mrs. George Hilliard, who informed Craft of the new threat: "My manner, which I suppose to be indifferent and calm, *betrayed* me, and she threw herself into my arms, sobbing and weeping. She, however, recovered her composure as soon as we reached the street, and was *very firm* ever after."

Before fleeing Boston, the Crafts were married for a second time. Theodore Parker performed this ceremony on November 7, 1850. Because the ports in the Boston area were being watched, the couple went by land to Portland, Maine, and then on to Nova Scotia before they were able to book passage on a steamer from Halifax to Liverpool.

In England by December 1850, the Crafts continued to evoke interest. An interviewer for *Chambers' Edinburgh Journal* retold the story of their escape. Although the Crafts were clearly "on really free soil" for the first time, as the interviewer stated, attitudes toward skin color showed consistency with American views. The interviewer described Ellen Craft as "a gentle, refined-looking young creature of twenty-four years, as fair as most of her British sisters, and in mental qualifications their equal too." William, on the other hand, was described as "very dark, *but* of a reflective, intelligent countenance, and of manly and dignified deportment" (emphasis added).

For six months after their arrival in England, the Crafts and William Welles Brown (who had gone to England in 1849) gave immediacy to the antislavery cause in travels within England as well as in Scotland. When they attended the Crystal Palace Exhibit in London with Brown several times during the summer of 1851, the ex-slaves were something of an exhibit themselves. White abolitionists made a point of promenading with them "in order that the world might form its opinion of the alleged mental inferiority of the African race, and their fitness or unfitness for freedom."

In the fall of 1851, the Crafts continued their education at the Ockham School near Ripley, Surrey—a trade school for rural youth founded by Lady Noel Byron. The Crafts were able to teach others manual skills as they themselves improved their literacy.

In October of 1852, Ellen Craft gave birth to Charles Estlin Phillips. The Crafts had four other children, all born in England: Brougham, William, Ellen, and Alfred. True to her resolve, Ellen Craft bore no children into slavery. And if there were any question about her continued determination to be free, she spoke clearly in a letter published shortly after Charles's birth. In response to rumors that she was homesick for family still enslaved and would like to return to that life, Ellen Craft wrote that she would "much rather starve in England, a free woman, than be a slave for the best man that ever breathed upon the American continent."

Running a Thousand Miles for Freedom was published in London, where the Crafts made their home beginning about 1852. William Craft remained a primary spokesman and the more public figure of the two. During the American Civil War, he was active in working against support for the Confederacy, and between 1862 and 1867 he made two trips to Dahomey. Ellen participated in the British and Foreign Freed-men's Aid Society. In November 1865, the Lushingtons, English abolitionists who had helped the Crafts attend the Ockham School, brought Ellen Craft's mother to London.

In 1868 the Crafts returned with two of their children to the United States. After working for a while in Boston, they returned to Georgia, where they purchased land in Bryan County, near Savannah. They opened an industrial school for colored youth. Ellen Craft "forbade whippings in her school," according to Dorothy Sterling, and insisted that "when the parents wanted to whip their children, they should take them into the grave yard, and when they got there to kneel down and pray."

In the 1890s Ellen Craft made her home with her daughter, who had married William Demos Crum, a physician and later United States minister to Liberia. Ellen Craft died about 1897 and, at her own request, she was buried under a favorite tree on her Georgia plantation. William Craft died in Charleston in 1900.

The Crafts' achievements as a couple stand out against the backdrop of more typical examples of the fragmented families in slavery. At the same time, Ellen Craft stands out on her own as a talented, determined, intelligent, resourceful woman.

**Profile by
Arlene Clift-Pellow**

ANGELA DAVIS

A sensitive child of the 1950s who became a militant revolutionary   **1944-** •

in the 1960s, Angela Davis fights for women's and civil rights and

against poverty and racism with a passion that inspires millions. Davis   **social** •

was born on January 26, 1944, in Birmingham, Alabama, the oldest of   **activist,**

four children. Her father, B. Frank, was an automobile mechanic who   **educator**

owned a gas station. He had been a teacher, but gave up the profession

because of the meager salary. Davis's mother, Sallye E., was also a

teacher and taught Angela to read, write, and calculate before she

began the first grade.

In class-conscious Birmingham, Davis experienced the disadvantages and advantages of a segregated school system. She faced old, dilapidated school buildings that lacked facilities and outdated textbooks discarded by white schools. However, blacks could run the schools the way they wanted (except when the superintendent for "colored"

schools visited). Davis and her classmates learned about black history—about the lives of Frederick Douglass, Sojourner Truth, Harriet Tubman, Denmark Vesey, and Nat Turner—and learned "traditional" Negro material, such as James Weldon Johnson's "Lift Ev'ry Voice and Sing" (often referred to as the Negro National Anthem). These cultural activities instilled in her a sense of pride. Nevertheless, Davis eventually realized that segregated schools provided few opportunities for the total development and growth of black children.

Davis's mother was politically involved and influenced her daughter considerably. In college Sallye Davis protested against the imprisonment of the Scottsboro boys and participated in the activities of the NAACP, even though the organization was outlawed in Birmingham in the mid-fifties. Davis learned from her mother's activism that she could protest against the system and count on her mother's moral support. Her grandmother, who constantly talked of slavery so that her grandchildren "would not forget about it," also influenced Davis. In the mid-fifties Davis and her mother took part in civil rights demonstrations in Birmingham, and in high school she assisted in the organization of interracial study groups that the police disbanded.

Political •

activism

begins early

During her childhood, Davis spent several summers with her mother, who at that time was studying for a master's at New York University. At the age of fifteen, when she was in her junior year at Parker High School in Birmingham, Davis received a scholarship from the American Friends Service Committee and moved to New York to enter the more academically stimulating Elizabeth Irwin High School, a progressive private school in Greenwich Village. Many teachers at this school had been blacklisted by the public schools because of their political ideology. Her parents had made arrangements for Davis to live in Brooklyn with the family of William Howard Melish, an active Episcopalian minister and winner of the 1956 Stockholm Peace Prize. While in New York, Davis was introduced to socialist ideology and consequently joined Advance, a Marxist-Leninist group.

In 1961 she entered Brandeis University in Waltham, Massachusetts, and developed into an excellent student. She majored in French and spent her junior year at the Sorbonne in Paris. It was here, in conversations with students from Algeria, that Davis became aware of revolutions against French colonialism and struggles for first-class citizenship among oppressed people. Her sensitivity to oppression was further ignited in September, 1963, when four girls Davis knew were killed during the bombing of a church in Birmingham. Davis's philosophy of life also altered considerably as she began to study under the philosopher Herbert Marcuse at Brandeis in 1964. He felt that it was the duty of the individual to resist and rebel against the system—an idea that influenced Davis profoundly.

A magna cum laude graduate of Brandeis with Phi Beta Kappa membership, from 1965 to 1967 Davis studied with the faculty of philosophy at the Johann Wolfgang von Goethe University in Frankfurt, West Germany, and with Oskar Negt and Theodore Adorno. In addition to philosophy, Davis mastered French and German.

• *Davis's radical*

activism ignites

Davis then enrolled at the University of California at San Diego, where Marcuse was teaching after his retirement from Brandeis. She obtained her master's degree in philosophy in 1969, and by the end of the following year she had completed all requirements for her doctorate except for her dissertation. There she began her active involvement with the civil rights movement, assisting in the development of the Black Students Council, developing a program for an experimental college for minorities, and supporting the San Diego Black Conference, an organization dominated by Ron Kerenga's rebellious group "Us."

In 1967 she attended a workshop in Los Angeles sponsored by the Student Nonviolent Coordinating Committee, which altered her life radically. There she met Franklin and Kendra Alexander. Alexander was involved with the SNCC, the Black Panthers, and the Communist party, while his sister, Charlene, was the leader of the Che-Lumumba Club, an all-black community cell in Los Angeles.

In 1968 Davis moved to Los Angeles and grew close to the Alexanders, who influenced her considerably. She became deeply involved with radical protests and rallies, although she eventually grew disillusioned with the SNCC and especially Stokely Carmichael, "Us," and the Black Panthers. Davis complained about the male chauvinism in these groups: women did all the work when a protest was organized, only to have the men complain that the women were taking over. After reflecting about the groups who were in tune with her political and social philosophy— her sensitivity for oppressed and repressed people and her distaste for racism and discrimination—she decided to join the Communist party in June, 1968.

In the spring of 1969, Davis joined the faculty of the department of philosophy at the University of California at Los Angeles and developed four courses in philosophy, politics, and literature. In spite of the popularity of her courses, Davis ran into conflict because of her membership in the Communist party. On July 1, 1969, an ex-FBI informer revealed in a letter published in the UCLA *Daily Bruin* that a communist was on the faculty. Eight days later a Los Angeles *Examiner* reporter identified Davis as the person. In spite of the recommendations of the department of philosophy and the chancellor of the university, the board of regents—under pressure from the governor of California, Ronald Reagan—fired her. Eventually the courts reinstated her since the dismissal violated her constitutional rights.

Although the administration of UCLA continued to monitor and evaluate Davis's courses, students found the instruction excellent and unbiased. The board of regents was determined to terminate her contract, however. At the end of the academic year of 1969-70, the board denied her a new contract because she lacked a doctorate and because of her allegedly inflammatory rhetoric in the community.

Davis outraged the UCLA Board of Regents with her speeches made in the defense of the "Soledad Brothers." George Jackson and W. L. Nolen were two inmates at Soledad Prison in California who organized a Marxist-Fanonist revolutionary cell. In January of 1970 Nolen and two other prisoners got into a fistfight and were killed by shots from the guard tower. When a white guard was found murdered, Jackson and two other prisoners were indicted.

The Soledad •

Prison Incident

Davis reacted emotionally to the event and threw herself energetically into the cause, organizing, picketing, and making speeches to raise defense funds. Without ever having seen Jackson, she fell in love with him—through a secret correspondence. He was killed by the guards during an alleged escape attempt, although charges had been dropped against him.

By now Davis symbolized the radical outlaw. Then she was indicted because she owned several guns that were used in a murder. Davis had bought the guns because of threats on her life, but, on August 7, 1970, Jonathan Jackson, George's brother, took the guns to the Marion County Courthouse in San Rafad, where prisoner James McClain was on trial for stabbing an inmate at San Quentin. Jackson pulled out the guns, took hostages, and made a run for a van in the parking lot. Before the van could pull away, Jackson, a judge, and two prisoners were killed. Since the guns found in the van were registered in Davis's name, a federal warrant was issued for her arrest. Rather than accept the warrant, Davis went into hiding. On August 18, 1970, the FBI placed her on the ten-most-wanted fugitive list, charged by the State of California with kidnapping, conspiracy, and murder. The FBI's hunt for Davis became high drama across the world. After a two-month search, the FBI found her in a motel in New York. Extradited to California, she remained in jail without bail until the movement for her release boomed into a worldwide protest. Rallies took place everywhere from Los Angeles to Paris to

Sri Lanka. The slogan "Free Angela" appeared on billboards, in newspapers, and on posters worldwide. Protests took place outside her jail cell. On February 23, 1972, a judge released Davis on $102,000 bail.

At the trial, Davis' lawyer argued that since Davis was not at the scene of the murder, there was insufficient evidence to prove she was part of the murder plans. After thirteen hours of deliberation, the jury of eleven whites and one Mexican American acquitted her on all counts. After the acquittal she held a mass benefit in New York to defray her legal expenses. The National Alliance Against Racist and Political Repression grew out of the "Free Angela" movement. She has spoken on behalf of the organization and has led demonstrations on various issues since 1972.

Because of her militant activities, the California state Board of Regents and Governor Reagan voted in 1972 that Davis would never teach at a state-supported university. The American Association of University Professors censured UCLA at the time for lack of due process in its failure to renew Davis's contract. Although the university's department of philosophy requested her services, the board refused. For a year, beginning in 1975, Davis was a lecturer in black studies at Claremont College in Claremont, California; in 1976 she lectured in philosophy and political science at Stanford University; from 1983 to 1985 she lectured in ethnic studies at California College of the Arts and Crafts in Oakland; and in 1984 she lectured in history of consciousness at the University of California at Santa Cruz. From 1978 to the present, she has been a lecturer in women's and ethnic studies at San Francisco State University, and in the humanities at San Francisco Art Institute.

Davis received several honorary degrees in 1972, and in 1979 she was awarded the Lenin Peace Prize. She has been a professor of philosophy at Moscow University and of political science at Havana University. In 1980 and again in 1984, the Communist Party, U.S.A., nominated her as its vice-presidential candidate. From 1985 Davis has been a member of the executive board of the National Political Caucus of Black Women. She has served on the board of directors for the National Black Women's Health Project since 1986.

Davis has written numerous essays and books on political and judicial reform, the rights of women, sexism, violence against women, and the rights of prisoners and mental health patients. She has also written *Ma Rainey, Bessie Smith and Billie Holiday: Black Women's Music and the Shaping of Social Consciousness*. A documentary on Davis, "Portrait of a Revolutionary," has been produced by one of her students at UCLA. Because she is constantly in demand as a speaker and she publishes extensively in journals and books, she has never finished her dissertation on eighteenth-century German philosopher Immanuel Kent. She remains in the doctoral program in the department of philosophy of Berlin's Humboldt University.

**Profile by
Joan Curl Elliott**

JULIETTE DERRICOTTE

*D*ean of women at Fisk University and a member of the general

1897-1931 •

committee of the World Student Christian Federation, Juliette Aline

Derricotte was born on April 1, 1897, in Athens, Georgia, the fifth of

college dean, •

nine children of Isaac and Laura (Hardwick) Derricotte. Her father was

organization

a cobbler and her mother a seamstress, and they managed to provide a

official

home that was warm, affectionate, and secure. The lively and sensitive

Derricotte, growing up in Athens, soon became aware of the racial

mores of a small southern town in the early 1900s, learning, for

example, that her family would always be the last to be waited on in a

store. Her desire to attend the Lucy Cobb Institute, located in a section of

Athens with spacious homes and tree-lined streets, was dashed when her mother finally had to tell her that it would be impossible because of her color. The recognition of that limitation was traumatic for Derricotte but critical in forging her determination to do whatever she could to fight discrimination.

After completing the public schools of Atlanta, Derricotte hoped against all odds that she would be able to go to college. A recruiter was able to convince her parents to send her to Talladega College. They could just manage the fifteen dollars a month for tuition and room and board, and that fall Derricotte made the long, rumbling train ride across the red hills of Georgia and Alabama to the town of Talladega. It was love at first sight when she saw the campus, with its large trees and graceful buildings, but she was shocked almost to the point of returning home when she discovered that all of the professors were white.

At Talladega Derricotte was a popular student and her warm personality made her many friends. One of her professors, recognizing her potential, suggested that she try for a public-speaking prize that included tuition. "Of course, I can't do it," she almost managed to convince herself. But with some coaching, she won the contest and self-confidence as well. Derricotte became the most important young woman on campus, always in charge of something. She joined the intercollegiate debating team, made speeches, became president of the YWCA, and helped to plan student activities. When disputes arose between students and faculty, as they often did, Derricotte would be the spokesperson for whichever side she felt to be correct, yet she maintained the goodwill of both. It was during her years at Talladega that she came to the realization that one should work for something bigger than oneself.

After graduation from Talladega in 1918, Derricotte went to New York to enroll in a summer course at the National YWCA Training School and in the fall was made a secretary of the National Student Council of the YWCA. In this position she visited colleges, planned conferences, and worked with student groups, bringing ideas and building leadership. She is credited with pioneering the methods of work and organizational structure that made the council an interracial fellowship. Through the warmth and forcefulness of her personality, she succeeded in making people understand each other in the most practical manner. She remained in this post for eleven years.

Derricotte had become a member of the general committee of the World Student Christian Federation and in 1924 was sent to England— one of two black delegates—to represent American college students. Four years later she was sent to Mysore, India. In these international settings, among representatives from around the world, Derricotte was always a curiosity and the center of attention, which gave way to respect. In India she learned first-hand from her fellow delegates of the worldwide extent of repression and discrimination in all forms. She learned from a young Indian woman who had been told upon entering church that all the whites must be seated before she could be seated; from a young Korean tentmate who kept her awake until early morning telling her that to know the meaning of prejudice, segregation, and discrimination, she would have to be a Korean under Japanese government. She remained in India for seven weeks, living in YWCAs, student hostels, mission schools, the furnished camp of a maharajah, a deserted military camp with five hundred students from India, Burma, and Ceylon, and in Indian homes. She gained valuable insights, as she wrote in *Crisis,* for she came to realize that the general committee, with its ninety or so delegates from around the world, was prophetic in the sense that:

> This is what can happen to all the world. With all the differences and difficulties, with all the entanglements of international attitudes and policies, with all the bitterness and prejudice and hatred that are true between any two or more of these countries, you are here friends working, thinking, playing, living together in the finest sort of fellowship, fulfilling the dream of the World's Student Christian Federation "That All May Be One."

Derricotte proceeded to China and Japan for meetings with students there, and returned home to share her experiences with American students. Summing it all up, she wrote in *Crisis:*

> Of course it was most interesting, but how can I say that I am no longer free; that the wealth as well as the poverty of India haunts me; I ache with actual physical pain when I remember the struggles of all India today: religious, caste, economic, social, political; how can I tell of the control which oil and rubber and jute have in the relations of East and West, or explain how back of oil and rubber and jute are the more fundamental and eternal puzzles of economics, race, and religion? My head whirls but every now and again I remember "that there is so much more to know than I am accustomed to knowing and so much more love than I am accustomed to loving."

In 1927 she received a master's degree in religious education from Columbia University, and from 1929 to 1931 she was the only woman trustee of Talladega College. Feeling a special call to participate in black education in the South, Derricotte resigned from the YWCA in 1929 and went to Fisk University as its dean of women. She entered a campus toiling with the problems of change and in revolt against long-outdated rules, particularly for young women. She eventually gained the confidence of the female students and gradually began to introduce the idea of freedom of action and responsibility for oneself. The students were beginning to feel comfortable. In November of 1931, almost fully recovered from illness that had troubled her all summer, Derricotte decided to go to Athens to visit her mother. Making the trip with her were three Fisk students from Georgia. One of them, a young man, was to do the driving. They stopped for lunch with friends in Chattanooga and headed south towards Atlanta with Derricotte driving. About a mile outside Dalton, Georgia, their car collided with that of a white couple. The details of the accident have never been known. Derricotte and a student were seriously injured. They were given emergency treatment in the offices of several white doctors in Dalton, and two students were released. As the local tax-supported hospital did not admit blacks, Derricotte and the seriously injured student were then removed to the home of a black woman who had beds available for the care of black patients. The student died during the night, and Derricotte was driven by ambulance to Chattanooga's Walden Hospital, where she died the next day, November 7, 1931.

Perhaps Derricotte is best remembered today for her death and the national outrage it caused. There was a series of investigations; the NAACP became involved; the Commission of Interracial Co-operation of Atlanta made an investigation at the request of Fisk University and other organizations. Memorial services were held all over the country, and her friend, noted theologian Howard Thurman, delivered the eulogy at the service held in her hometown, reading her haunting words from the Mysore Conference.

Profile by
Jean Elder Cazort

KATHERINE DUNHAM

T aking a bow to a standing ovation for her leadership of Treemon-

isha, performed at Southern Illinois University's Carbondale campus in

1972, Katherine Dunham had again lived up to her title as the "Grand

Dame of American Dance." And Dunham is still taking bows. She has

traveled the world as the guest of kings and rulers, performing not only

her brilliant dances but also teaching through them the universal truths

that intermingle and bind together the many cultures of the world.

1909- •

dancer, •

anthropologist

Her path has carried her far from Glen Ellyn, Illinois, where she was born on June 22, 1909, to Albert Dunham and Fanny June (Taylor) Dunham. Through her ancestral heritage of African, Madagascan, Canadian-French, and American Indian, she was a "small League of Nations—largely black," Terry Harnan observed.

Dunham opened her first dance school with the help of friends and her Russian dance teacher, Madame Ludmila Speranzeva, during the Great Depression. For the first time, she began to work seriously on choreography. In 1931 Dunham's dancers put on "Negro Rhapsody" as

the first act at the Chicago Beaux Arts Ball and received hearty applause from the audience. However, the good friends who had helped finance the studio were soon out of money, and it was closed. Feeling lonely and perhaps bereft, Dunham married Jordis McCoo, a fellow dancer. In a very short time she realized that she really was unready to forget her dreams and settle down. Fortunately, the marriage demanded very little since she went to school in the daytime and her husband worked nights at the post office. After school she and her friend Ruth Attaway, a drama teacher, looked for an inexpensive place to rent for a studio. They found an old stable with large, open spaces for their classes. It became a gathering place for such personages as Charles Sebree, Charles White, Langston Hughes, Sterling North, Arna Bontemps, Horace Mann, and others. All went well until winter came, lacking fuel to heat the stable properly, they were forced to close.

Dunham's next school, the Negro Dance Group, was a good stepping-stone, mainly because Madame Speranzeva allowed Dunham the use of her studio for pupils, and she coached Dunham privately in ballet and mime. Through Speranzeva, Dunham was introduced to the Isadora Duncan Dance Company and Fokine. She met Argentina, the famous Spanish dancer, and her partner Escudero. Though the school appeared to flourish, the parents of her black students wanted their daughters to study ballet for the sake of social graces and were concerned that the name of the school meant that they would be taught African dances. Though Dunham knew that the basic steps of the popular lindy hop, cakewalk, and black bottom had their origins in African tribal dances, she was also aware that she was unable to explain this easily to these parents. This whole dilemma worked out for her benefit, however, for through a presentation of Robert Redfield, a professor in ethnology, Dunham decided to study anthropology. Through this door perhaps she could teach blacks not to be satisfied only with imitating others but rather to develop their own natural talents through hard work and technical training.

In 1933 Dunham was chosen to hire and train 150 young blacks to present a program for the 1934 Chicago Century of Progress Exposition. From this honor came an invitation to a Julius Rosenwald Foundation reception. At this reception, she met Eric Fromm, a prominent psychiatrist, and the two became lifelong friends. After later seeing a performance by Dunham's dance group, Mrs. Alfred Rosenwald Stern invited her to appear before the foundation's board of judges to present her views on black dance. If they approved, she would receive a scholarship that would enable her to further her studies. On the appointed day, Dunham met the board. After the necessary preliminaries, the chairman asked: "Now, Miss Dunham, just what sort of dance study would you like this committee to finance for you?" Dunham asked if she might demonstrate some of the dance forms, since they were difficult to verbally describe, and the committee assented. Dunham started unsnapping hidden hooks on her primly tailored suit, and momentarily stood before them in dancing tights. She began to dance. When she had finished, she explained both the need and the cultural significance of studying the dances of Africa and the West Indies in their native environments. On February 15, 1935, Dunham received her Rosenwald Foundation travel grant. As part of her grant, she was to study for approximately three months with Melville Herskovits, head of Northwestern University's African studies, before beginning her travels. This time was invaluable to her, according to Harnan, and Dunham later called Herskovits "a fantastic guide for getting to the bottom of things, the heart of the matter." At twenty-five years of age she began a career that would take her many times to Europe, Mexico, South America, Africa, Australia, and Japan. This first journey was to take her to Jamaica, Martinique, Trinidad, and Haiti.

Upon returning home, Dunham appeared again before the Julius Rosenwald Foundation and spent a memorable evening reporting with music, dancing, pictures, and speech the many experiences of her trip. A short time after this, the Rockefeller Foundation granted her a fellowship for further studies toward her master's degree under the direction of Herskovits. In August of 1936, Dunham graduated from the University of Chicago with a bachelor's degree in anthropology. She later earned a master's degree from the University of Chicago and a Ph.D. from Northwestern University.

One evening in 1938, Dunham, as dance director of the Federal Theatre Project in Chicago, opened a program with *Ballet Fedre*. The next morning's newspapers praised all of the program, according to Harnan, but were wild about the "firey folk ballet with choreography by Katherine Dunham," saying that *L'Ag'Ya* was "danced with enough abandon to make some of the preceding events seem pallid by comparison." Dunham's artistry was beginning to be seen and appreciated. The teachings of Madame Speranzeva with their emphasis on acting and story line as well as the dancing skill, and the work that Dunham had done in Martinique where she had first seen *L'Ag'Ya*, the fighting dance, were very important background influences.

On this same evening came honors for the man who designed the sets and costumes, John Pratt. This 1938 presentation was the first time Pratt and Dunham had worked together as a team, but they later became known throughout the world. Born in Canada, John Pratt was a very tall, handsome white man who was then twenty-four years old. He had designed sets and costumes while studying at the University of Chicago, as well as having his art work exhibited at a Chicago gallery and university shows. Working together for many months strengthened the ties between Dunham and Pratt. After Dunham received her divorce, she and John Pratt were married in a private ceremony July 10, 1939, in Tecade, Mexico. Happily, in the world of artists in which they moved, color, creed, and nationality mattered little.

In February 1940 the Katherine Dunham Dance Company opened at the Windsor Theatre, West 48th Street, with Dunham's own *Tropics and Le Jazz Hot*. The show was a phenomenal success. Harnan recalled one critic's words: "Katherine Dunham flared into unsuspecting New York last night like a comet. Unknown before her debut, she is today one of the most talked-about dancers." From this night her name and her dances took her behind the footlights of the world's greatest stages. Her unique technique and stylistic perfection were the forces that propelled her toward that magic moment where the dancer, the dance, and the cultural story become one.

Soon after this success, an offer came for the Dunham Dance Company to take part in an all-Negro musical entitled *Cabin in the Sky*. The salary was three thousand dollars a week, more than any of them had ever dreamed of earning as dancers. Dunham's role was Georgia Brown, and for the first time she had the opportunity not only to dance, but to sing and act as well. The drama had a long and successful run.

Near the end of a most rewarding and successful tour of Mexico and Europe, 1947-1949, Dunham, Pratt, and the members of the troupe welcomed an opportunity to return to Haiti through an invitation from her old friend, Dumarsais Estimé, now president of the island. The warmth and blue water offered a much-needed rest. Before Dunham's first trip to the islands in 1935, she had received the sad news that her brother, Albert, had apparently suffered a mental breakdown. He was under the care of the best doctors available, and it was believed that given time, rest, and treatment, he would recover completely. In May, 1949, however, she received the news in Europe that her beloved brother had died. As the year 1949, filled with both joy and sorrow, closed, Dunham received the sad news of her father's death, and also learned that her friend, President Estimé, had been forced to resign and was now exiled from Haiti. Katherine Dunham and John Pratt returned to the United States, and in 1950 she was dancing again to Broadway fans.

In December of 1952 Pratt and Dunham adopted Marie Christine Columbier, a five-year-old French Martinique girl of mixed heritage. For a while she accompanied her new parents on their travels but was

"Le Jazz Hot" •

deemed a

phenomenal

success

eventually sent to school in Switzerland. In the succeeding years, Dunham choreographed several movies and the opera *Aida;* performed all over the United States; toured Europe, Australia, South America, and the Orient; and opened a medical clinic in Haiti. In 1959 *A Touch of Innocence,* the story of the first eighteen years of her life, was published.

Dunham, at the request of President Leopold Sedar Senghor, went to Africa to help train the Senegalese National Ballet and serve as technical cultural advisor to him in preparation for the First World Festival of Negro Arts at Dakar, Senegal, in 1965 and 1966. Here in Africa, the mother country of all of the dance studies Dunham had made, she felt quite at home. It was in Dakar, in a house that she and Pratt rented, that she finished her frank, captivating, personal narrative *Island Possessed,* about Haiti and its people. In 1969 she and Pratt gave up their house in Dakar to return to the United States. The political unrest was one factor in this decision, but a proposal, the East Saint Louis project, which Dunham had presented to Sargent Shriver in March 1965, was the main impetus of their return.

With this project, Dunham faced one of the biggest challenges of her life. Funding came from several philanthropic organizations who were willing to support the work of Southern Illinois University, but getting to those students she wanted to help was still an unsolved problem in her mind. Through her daughter, Marie Christine, now nineteen years old, and Jeanelle Stovall, a vacationing United Nations interpreter, Dunham's door to the students was opened. By December, 1967, Dunham had become cultural affairs consultant to the Edwardsville campus of Southern Illinois University. She was also named director of the Performing Arts Training Center and the Dynamic Museum. Her home was located in the East Saint Louis ghetto among the people with whom she expected to work.

The Dynamic Museum was a wonderful teaching aid, for here the objects that the Dunham Dance Company had collected all over the world were displayed, touched, and used. John Pratt was the curator of the museum and his own artistic costumes were on display, along with books, foreign theater posters, programs, records, and films of the dancers at the zenith of their fame. Having started schools of dance, theater, and cultural arts in Chicago, New York, Saint Louis, Haiti, Stockholm, Paris, and Italy, Dunham knew both the rewards and the difficulties that a school can bring; this one offered specific knowledge to students that could not be found elsewhere.

After Dunham retired, she opened the Katherine Dunham Center in East Saint Louis. Here she has her school and museum. The two main features that she directs each year are the Children's Workshop and the

Dunham Technique Seminar and Institute for Interculture Communication. Her husband, John Pratt, died March 3, 1986. Their daughter, Marie Christine, lives in Rome, Italy. Dunham, now eighty years old, divides her time between East Saint Louis and Haiti, avoiding the cold winter months that increase the pain of her arthritic condition.

Early in her career Dunham said: "I would feel I'd failed miserably if I were doing dance confined to race, color or creed. I don't think that would be art, which has to do with universal truths." Her life is a testimonial to those universal truths and she surely has not failed. She has not only distinguished her own race, but has also enriched every other race through the deeply moving, exquisite message of her dance.

**Profile by
Phyllis Wood**

RAMONA HOAGE EDELIN

*R*amona Hoage Edelin's devotion to education can be traced to the

work of her parents and her mother in particular, and to her upbringing

in the academic community. As an educator as well as an advocate for

quality education, Edelin has produced positive results through her

work with the National Urban Coalition and development of its "Say YES

to a Youngster's Future" program.

1945- •

organization •

executive

The only child of George Hoage and Annette (Lewis) Hoage (later Annette Lewis Phinazee), Edelin was born on September 4, 1945, in Los Angeles, California, and grew up in the academic settings of South Carolina State College, Atlanta University, and Southern Illinois University. Always a strong student, Edelin blazed her way through Fisk University, starting with her reception of the Sarah McKim Maloney Award in 1964, and continuing through her graduation in 1967 with a bachelor's degree magna cum laude in philosophy, with departmental honors; Edelin was also elected to Phi Beta Kappa and the Gold Key Honor Society, and received general university honors. On the dean's list for outstanding academic achievement virtually every semester, Edelin was also a regular participant in the university's honors program. In addition, she also conceived and helped implement a voluntary honor code that allowed those students who signed a pledge to be bound by their honor while taking unproctored examinations, an option available at few other institutions of higher education in the country at the time. Without question, Edelin was among the most stellar minds and talents that passed through Fisk University during the mid-1960s, astounding both her peers and faculty by her brilliance.

• *Edelin*

continues to

excel

Fisk University, however, was neither sufficient nor intended to contain her prodigious capabilities. Between her junior and senior years she was one of a small number of persons from around the country selected for intensive studies at Harvard University. Married to Kenneth Edelin, a medical doctor, after her graduation from Fisk University, she went on to earn a master's degree in philosophy from the University of East Anglia in Norwich, England, in 1969 while the family (a son, Kenneth, Jr., had been born) was stationed there as Kenneth Edelin, Sr., completed a tour of military service. After the family returned to the United States, Edelin entered the doctoral program in philosophy at Boston University, receiving her Ph.D. in 1981 after completing her studies with a dissertation on W. E. B. Du Bois.

A daughter, Kimberley, was born during these years. This enlargement of her family, to which she continues to be deeply dedicated, brought additional joys and responsibilities but did not prevent Edelin from building a noteworthy career in education as a teacher and administrator. She taught in the European division of the University of Maryland while in England and at Emerson College, Brandeis University, and Northeastern University during her years in Boston. While at Northeastern she was founder and chair of the Department of African American Studies.

Several themes are evident in Edelin's life. First, education—serious, demanding education—has been a consistent, nurturing, and central factor in her life, as both student and teacher. Second, Edelin's own educational experiences, and those she has provided for others, have been guided by an unwavering commitment to excellence. Third, from her undergraduate years, through her doctoral dissertation, and continuing today, Edelin has been devoted to achieving the most insightful and impassioned understanding possible of the histories and lives of African people, which she uses to help realize their potential for, in her words, "mastery" and "greatness." These elements of her life, long in the making, come together to form the woman who is now devoted to shaping and institutionalizing agendas to secure the lives and well-being of black Americans into the next century:

> A certain quickening of the will is moving through the
> African-American group as the dawn of the new

millennium approaches. This quickening heralds a process of cultural renewal, development, and the rebirth of mastery, greatness, and perfect equality for a people whose humanity itself has, by grace, survived what might have been utter devastation. The job of the 1990s is to leave four hundred-plus years of bare survival behind so that a new African being—in the United States and throughout the world—will cross the threshold into the year 2000.

Edelin is perhaps best known as president and chief executive officer of the National Urban Coalition, an action and advocacy organization founded in 1967 and based in Silver Spring, Maryland. Since joining the coalition in 1977 as executive assistant to the president, she has held the positions of director of operations, vice president of operations, senior vice president of program and policy (when she directed programs in housing and economic development, health and urban education, and advocacy), and chief executive officer. She became respected for her insight into a broad range of urban issues and has been especially identified for her contributions to the development and implementation of the coalition's "Say YES to a Youngster's Future" program, an early intervention, family-learning program aimed at exposing black American, Latino, native American, and female children, ages four to nineteen, to mathematics, science, and computer technology to help prepare them for the high technology jobs of the next century. Under Edelin's guidance as president and chief executive officer, the National Urban Coalition has instituted a Leadership Strategy Series, named in honor of the late M. Carl Holman, past president of the coalition, which assembles leaders from national organizations, business, labor, Capitol Hill, foundations, educational institutions, and community-based and youth groups for strategic sessions on pertinent issues of public policy and organizational development. It is from this important organizational position, drawing on her wealth of experience and considerable intellectual capabilities, that Edelin has sounded the call-to-arms for, and taken a front-line position in, what she has termed the "cultural offensive": a national effort to bring about cultural renewal as a crucial endeavor devoted to community and economic development and political empowerment for black Americans.

Edelin heads •

National Urban

Coalition

Why a "cultural" offensive? It is necessary, according to Edelin, because black Americans, at present, are on the whole without cultural integrity or a harmonious group identity that insures wholeness and self-sufficiency. Drawing insights from her chief intellectual mentor, W. E. B. Du Bois, Edelin is convinced that black Americans still must resolve

Du Bois's dilemma of "twoness," which he describes in *The Souls of Black Folk:*

> an American, a Negro; two souls, two thoughts, two unreconciled strivings; two warring ideals in one dark body, whose dogged strength alone keeps it from being torn asunder. . . . This waste of double aims, this seeking to satisfy two unreconciled ideals, has wrought sad havoc with the courage and faith and deeds of ten thousand people, has sent them often wooing false gods and invoking false means of salvation, and at times has even seemed about to make them ashamed of themselves.

Cultural integrity will, Edelin argues, provide the foundation for the formation of a "profound new identity" that will incorporate, among other things, a recovery of African legacies crucial to black's understanding of themselves. Only on this foundation will black Americans be able to move from bare survival to the rebirth and development that will bring mastery and greatness. And only in the context of an appropriate culture—"the vehicle that moves . . . human groups forward," as Edelin says—will this be possible. Without it, she argues, "we will never sit at the table of cultures as equals with the rest of the world's people."

• Cultural

offensive

sweeps the

nation

Edelin has assumed a leading role in assembling key persons from around the nation to carry out the cultural offensive. The coalition's "Say YES to a Youngster's Future" family development program, through its educational agenda, is devoted to arresting the decimation of young people by helping to create an environment where children can form wholesome self-perceptions. The program implements new programs to replace those that are inadequate for either group advancement or participation in the economic mainstream. One of Edelin's major concerns analyzing successful approaches to education—identified, tested, and certified by successful educators of black American youth—and assessing them for their value in facilitating the shift from survival to the appropriation of a new identity, cultural integrity, mastery, greatness, and equality. Through the Coalition's Leadership Strategy Series, Edelin is committed to countering the lack of unity in leadership and in resource accumulation by promoting leadership styles strong enough to achieve unity and consensus on an agenda for the cultural offensive that will emphasize such an educational program.

These concerns were prominent during Edelin's participation in the 1989 African American Summit, where she served as program chairperson. The focus of the summit was the development of a unified agenda for political and economic development. She has other concerns pertinent to the national black American community as well, among them the condition of family life, health and health care, economic development, politics, criminal justice, foreign policy, housing and urban policy, entertainment and information media, and the continuing struggle for maintaining and acquiring civil rights.

Edelin has been and continues to be actively involved in numerous agencies and organizations, including the District of Columbia Humanities Council, the Board of Elders of the African Heritage Institute, Delta Sigma Theta, Women in Politics, and many others. She is the author of a number of publications, and she contributes weekly to the commentary page of the *Afro-American* newspaper chain through her column "On the Cultural Offensive." Through these efforts and her leadership of the National Urban Coalition, this nation—and black Americans in particular—are beneficiaries of one of the country's most capable, devoted, and notable black Americans.

**Profile by
Lucius Outlaw**

165 •

MARIAN WRIGHT EDELMAN

*T*he children—*my own and other people's—became the passion of*

my personal and professional life. For it is they who are God's presence,

promise, and hope for humankind," Marian Wright Edelman, attorney

and founding president of the Children's Defense Fund, wrote of her

vocation in her 1992 book The Measure of Our Success: A Letter to My

Children and Yours. *Edelman has been an advocate for disadvantaged*

Americans for her entire professional career and is known primarily as

a crusader for children's rights.

1939- •

children's rights •

crusader

Edelman was born the youngest of five children on June 6, 1939, the daughter of Arthur Jerome Wright and Maggie Leola (Bowen) Wright in Bennettsville, South Carolina. Her father was the minister of Shiloh Baptist Church and had been influenced by Booker T. Washington's self-help philosophy. He expected his children to get an education and to serve their community. "The only bad thing about that is that none of us learned how to relax," Edelman recalled in an interview for a lengthy profile that appeared in a 1989 issue of the *New Yorker.* "Working for the community was as much a part of our existence as eating and sleeping and church." Arthur Wright established the Wright Home for the Aged in the segregated town of Bennettsville, and Maggie Wright ran it. Edelman recalls that her father probably never made more than two hundred dollars a month, "but none of us ever felt poor, and compared to the people around us, we weren't." Her father also believed in black role models, and whenever prominent blacks came to town, the Wright children were taken to hear them. Marian was named for Marian Anderson, whom she heard sing as a child. Her father, who had a profound impact on her development and her priorities, died when Edelman was only fourteen.

After graduating from Marlboro Training High School, Edelman was persuaded by her mother and brother, Harry, to attend Spelman College in Atlanta, Georgia, though her first choice was Fisk University in Nashville, Tennessee. "I hated the idea of going to a staid women's college," she observed, "but it turned out to be the right place for me after all." She entered Spelman in 1956. Because of her outstanding scholarship, she won a Charles Merrill grant for study abroad during her junior year. She spent the first summer at the Sorbonne University studying French civilization but decided to spend the remainder of the academic year at the University of Geneva in Switzerland.

During the second semester, Edelman studied for two months in the Soviet Union under a Lisle Fellowship; because of her interest in Tolstoy, she had always wanted to go to Russia. After her travels in Europe over the course of a year and two summers, she returned to Spelman a different person: "It was a great liberating experience. After a year's freedom as a person, I wasn't prepared to go back to a segregated existence," she recalled. In 1959, the year of sit-ins and the first student protests in the South, she returned to Atlanta for her senior year and became active in the embryonic civil rights movement that was to alter profoundly United States race relations in the South. During her senior year in 1960, she participated in one of the largest sit-ins in Atlanta at City Hall. Fourteen students were arrested, including Edelman. It was during this time that she decided to go to law school instead of pursuing graduate work in Russian studies at Georgetown University, which would have prepared her for a career in foreign service. During this time she also became aware that civil rights lawyers were scarce and sorely needed.

After graduating as valedictorian of her Spelman class in 1960, she applied to Yale University Law School and entered as a John Hay Whitney Fellow. In 1963, during spring break of her last year in law school, she went to Mississippi and got involved in the voter registration drive, which her friend, Robert Moses, led as a field secretary for the Student Nonviolent Coordinating Committee. She returned to New Haven, graduated from Yale in 1963, and after a year's training in New York went to Jackson, Mississippi, as one of the first two NAACP Legal Defense and Educational Fund interns. In the spring of 1964 she opened a law office and continued civil rights work, which consisted largely of getting students out of jail. During this time she was threatened by dogs, thrown into jail, and, before taking the Mississippi bar, refused entry into a state courthouse.

Asked if at that time she despaired about the law as a viable instrument of social change, she replied, "Sure, like every morning. But one keeps plugging, trying to make our institutional processes work." At age twenty-six, she became the first black woman to pass the bar in Mississippi. Her civil rights crusading continued when she headed the NAACP Legal Defense and Education Fund in Mississippi from 1964 to 1968. Edelman wrote about her intense commitment to liberation and struggle after her return from a year abroad in an article that appeared in the Spelman *Messenger:*

> I realize that I am not fighting just for myself and my people in the South, when I fight for freedom and equality. I realize now that I fight for the moral and political health of America as a whole and for her position in the world at large. . . . as I push the cause for freedom a step further, by gaining my own. . . . I know that I, in my individual struggle for improvement, help the world. I am no longer an isolated being—I belong. Europe helped me to see this.

Edelman fights •

for freedom

and equality

While in Mississippi, she met Peter Edelman, a Harvard law school graduate and one of Robert Kennedy's legislative assistants, who was working in 1967 on the Senate's Subcommittee on Employment, Manpower, and Poverty. She was going through a transition realizing that in order to change things in Mississippi, she had to affect federal policy. After receiving a Field Foundation grant to study how to make laws work for the poor, she moved to Washington, D.C., in March 1968 and started the Washington Research Project. This was a difficult time for the nation and the movement. Martin Luther King, Jr., had been assassinated in April, and Robert Kennedy was shot two months later. In July Marian Wright married Peter Edelman, one of the Kennedy aides who, after Kennedy's death, received Ford Foundation grants to help in the transition to other careers.

In 1971 the Edelmans left Washington and moved to Boston, where Peter became vice-president of the University of Massachusetts and Marian became director of the Harvard University Center for Law and Education. She flew to Washington weekly to oversee the activities of the Washington Research Project. By this time their interracial marriage had produced two sons—Joshua and Jonah. Ezra was born in 1974.

- **Edelman founds**

- *child advocacy*

- *group*

In 1973 Edelman founded the Children's Defense Fund, a nonprofit child advocacy organization based in Washington, D.C. Its mission was to provide systematic and long-range assistance to children and to make their needs an important matter of public policy. Her work with the CDF and her passionate devotion to the rights of children have brought her national recognition as "the children's crusader." The Edelmans returned to Washington in 1979, where Peter Edelman obtained a teaching post at the Georgetown University Law Center.

Teen pregnancy, especially in the black community, became a major issue in 1983. "I saw from our own statistics that fifty-five and a half percent of all black babies were born out of wedlock, a great many of them to teen-age girls. It just hit me over the head—that situation insured black child poverty for the next generation." In 1983 CDF launched a major long-term national campaign to prevent teenage pregnancy and provide positive life options for youth. It included a multimedia campaign that consisted of transit advertisements, poster, television, and radio public service announcements, a national prenatal care campaign, and local volunteer Child Watch coalitions in more than seventy local communities in thirty states around the country. CDF was also largely responsible for the Act for Better Child Care, which Senator Alan Cranston, a liberal Democrat from California, introduced in November 1987.

Under Edelman's leadership, CDF has become one of the nation's most active and effective organizations concerned with a wide range of children's and family issues, particularly those that most affect America's poorest children. CDF's mission is to teach the nation about the needs of children and encourage preventive investments in them before they get sick, drop out of school, suffer too-early pregnancy or family breakdown, or get into trouble. CDF has become an effective voice nationwide in the areas of adolescent pregnancy prevention, child health, education, child care, youth employment, child welfare and mental health, and family support systems.

In 1971 *Time* magazine named Edelman one of America's two hundred young leaders. That year, she became the first black woman elected to the Yale University Corporation, and for the next five years she was on the board of the Carnegie Council on Children. In 1980

Edelman became the first black and second woman to chair the Board of Trustees of Spelman College, her alma mater. Currently she serves on the boards of the NAACP Legal Defense and Education Fund, Citizens for Constitutional Concerns, Joint Center for Political Studies, United States Committee for UNICEF, Center for Budget and Policy Priorities, Spelman College, and others. She is also a member of the Council of Foreign Relations, and in 1985 she received the prestigious MacArthur Foundation Prize Fellowship.

A 1987 *Time* magazine article called Edelman "one of Washington's most unusual lobbyists" whose "effectiveness depends as much on her adroit use of statistics as on moral persuasion." In the same year Harvard University Press published *Families in Peril: An Agenda for Social Change,* based on Edelman's William E. B. Du Bois lectures delivered at Harvard in 1986. In this pioneering book Edelman states that "the tide of misery that poverty breeds and that Blacks have borne disproportionately throughout history has now spread to a critical mass of white American families and children."

An extensive writer, Edelman is also author of *Children Out of School in America; School Suspensions: Are They Helping Children?; Portrait of Inequality: Black and White Children in America;* and *The Measure of Our Success: A Letter to My Children and Yours.*

Profile by Beverly Guy-Sheftall

EFFIE O'NEAL ELLIS

A woman who has worn many hats in the medical field, some of

them firsts for a black woman, Effie O'Neal Ellis has become a major

national influence in the area of maternal and child care. Having

served in important positions in medical organizations on the state and

federal level, she has been particularly interested in the care of children

who come from lower-class families.

1913- •

physician, •

health

administrator

Ellis was born in Hawkinsville, Georgia, on June 15, 1913, to Joshua P. O'Neal, a builder, and Althea (Hamilton) O'Neal. Her primary education was obtained in Atlanta, Georgia. A conscientious and brilliant student, Ellis went through her undergraduate and graduate programs in a quiet but spectacular manner. She received a bachelor's degree with honors from Spelman College in 1933, then went on to Atlanta University and graduated with a master's degree in biology in 1935, the same year she married Arthur W. Ellis.

Because of her outstanding research work at Atlanta University, Ellis was awarded a study grant to go to Puerto Rico, where she studied diseases and parasites. Pleased with her efforts, she seriously considered specializing in parasitological research. Her work, however, gave her an opportunity to observe the health care that was available for the poor. As a result, she changed her career plans and decided she could be of greater service by working in the medical field.

Ellis was admitted to the University of Illinois College of Medicine, where she demonstrated remarkable abilities during her medical school years. She graduated from the University of Illinois College of Medicine in June of 1950. Out of the 160 medical graduates, Ellis was among 23 to graduate with honors, and she ranked fifth in her class.

During the 1950 to 1951 academic year Ellis served her internship at the University of Illinois Hospital, and she did a residency in pediatrics at Massachusetts General Hospital the following year. In keeping with her exceptional achievements, Ellis was awarded a postdoctoral fellowship to study heart trouble in children at the Johns Hopkins University School of Medicine from 1952 through 1953. While at Johns Hopkins, Ellis was also hospital staff physician. During the midst of her fellowship program, on March 23, 1953, Ellis married her second husband, physician James D. Solomon, who later became director of the laboratory at Saint Elizabeth Hospital in Washington, D.C. The Solomons have one daughter.

Ellis is first

black woman

administrator

in the AMA

Juggling marriage, motherhood, and a demanding career, Ellis was director of medical education and house pediatrician at Provident Hospital in Baltimore, Maryland, from 1953 to 1961. She then became director of maternal and child health for the Ohio State Department of Health in Columbus, Ohio, a post she held for four year. Always concerned about the welfare of children, Ellis felt she could have a positive impact on policy making and decisions regarding the poor by serving in a number of capacities for the federal government. She was chairperson for a panel group at the 1969 White House Conference on Food and Nutrition; she served in the Department of Health, Education, and Welfare as its first regional commissioner for social and rehabilitation service; and she was also regional medical director of the HEW Children's Bureau. The highlight of her career, however, was being selected to serve in the newly created post of special assistant for health services to the American Medical Association. In this capacity, Ellis became the first black woman to hold an administrative or executive office within the AMA. As the special assistant for health services, she became a special advisor on child and maternal health matters and health care of the poor. She served in this position from 1970 to 1975.

The tasks Ellis has performed have been well within her expertise. As an influential figure in medical policy she has stressed comprehensive services for maternal and child health. In addition, she believes in family planning as the greatest preventive tool in obtaining better maternal and child health care. She has emphasized that family planning should involve more than contraceptive measures, and she has traveled around the country speaking to community groups, medical organizations, health associations, and other educational audiences on the subject of prenatal care for mothers and health care for the poor. When it comes to prenatal care, Ellis believes every mother should be taught family planning, prenatal and postnatal care, nutrition, sanitation, and acute and preventive health care.

Ellis, who currently lives in Chicago, Illinois, is a member of numerous organizations, including the National Medical Association, American Public Welfare Association, American Association on Mental Deficiency, American Association for Maternal and Child Health, and the Alpha Omega Alpha and Delta Sigma Theta sororities. Among her awards and honors, Ellis is an honorary fellow of the School Health Association. She received the prestigious Trailblazer Award from the National Medical Association in 1970.

**Profile by
Margaret Jerrido**

ELLA FITZGERALD

Ella Fitzgerald's voice has been described as sounding more like an

instrument than any other voice in this century. Her voice is appreciated

internationally and her work continues to impress and please her

audience. In more technical terms, she has an impeccable and sophisti-

cated rhythmic sense, flawless intonation, and an extraordinary har-

monic sensibility. Henry Pleasants in his book The Great American

Popular Singers *describes Fitzgerald as "endlessly inventive," saying*

that "new melodic deviations and embellishments are as varied as they

are invariably appropriate." These facts, coupled with her classic sim-

plicity and genuine humility, make Fitzgerald a one-of-a-kind

entertainer, a true legend in her own time.

1918-

"First Lady

of Song"

Fitzgerald was born April 25, 1918, in Newport News, Virginia. Both of her parents were interested in music. Her father, who died shortly after she was born, filled their house with his guitar playing and singing, and her mother had a beautiful soprano voice. When Fitzgerald's father died shortly after World War I, the rest of the family moved to Yonkers, New York. Mrs. Fitzgerald had a sister there and hoped to find a better life in the North, close to relatives.

Fitzgerald grew up just across the Hudson River from the Bronx and in the shadow of a Harlem that was then in vogue. Yonkers was a mixed neighborhood, and Fitzgerald had a variety of friends. She studied music in school, sang in the junior high school glee club, and took piano lessons. But the five dollars a month for lessons soon became too much for her mother to afford. Forced to quit, Fitzgerald soon forgot how to read music, a loss she recalls with regret.

In her early teens, Fitzgerald discovered Harlem and its night magic firsthand. She and her girlfriends went there on weekends to hear celebrities sing and to beg for autographs. On one such occasion, she found herself at the Harlem Opera House on Amateur Night. It was 1934; Fitzgerald was sixteen, tall, and awkward. Her friends dared her to enter the talent contest. She accepted the challenge. In her hand-me-down dress and ill-fitting shoes, she entered the spotlight. The audience laughed. She had intended to dance, but her knees were knocking together so rapidly that she chose not to move from the spot where she stood, rooted in fear. She decided to sing instead. The audience ceased laughing as Fitzgerald sang "The Object of My Affection." She had learned the song from a Connie Boswell record, but the voice that emerged was a genuine talent of her own. She won first prize and received three encores.

This was the first of many talent contests she was to win. Fitzgerald went on to appear at the Lafayette Theater on Seventh Avenue and 132nd Street. Her repertoire consisted of only three songs: "Believe It, Beloved," "The Object of My Affection," and "July." She sang these songs in every talent contest she entered in Harlem.

In 1935 Fitzgerald entered another competition at the Harlem Opera House. Winning first prize, she landed a week's work singing with Tiny Bradshaw and his band. This engagement landed her an audition at the CBS Radio Network, and they offered her a guest appearance on the Arthur Tracy radio show. Her mother gave permission, as Fitzgerald was still underage, but before anything could come of it, Fitzgerald's mother died. Because she was now an orphan, the contract with CBS was no longer valid. Despite the fact that Fitzgerald went to live with her aunt, the authorities were dissatisfied, and she was forced into the Riverdale orphanage in Yonkers.

Institutional life bored Fitzgerald, and she often escaped to Harlem to enter amateur contests. Finally she made her way into the Apollo Theater. Nervous as usual, Fitzgerald walked on stage, sang her three songs, and won first prize. Her reward was fifty dollars. Appearing at the Apollo opened another door for her. The night of the amateur contest, Bardu Ali, who directed Chick Webb's band, had been in the audience. Hearing Fitzgerald sing, he is reported to have said, "This chick sings just like a horn." A few days later, Fitzgerald sang for Webb, unaccompanied: she had perfect pitch. Webb was amazed by her talent and ignored her old clothes and dull appearance. Even though "swing was really a man's thing" and he already had a singer, Webb hired her, and she began her rise to stardom.

In the male-dominated world of jazz and swing, Fitzgerald was a rare asset, one that many men could not seem to evaluate in other than physical terms. Donald Bogle writes in his book *Black Sugar: Eighty Years of America's Black Female Superstars* that if Fitzgerald had been "sexier" she might have developed into a "legendary public heroine." He seems unaware that she did. Sid Colin seems impelled to continually comment on Fitzgerald's physical appearance in his book *Ella: The Life and Times of Ella Fitzgerald*. Of a later British performance he writes: "Ever since her film appearance in *Ride 'em Cowboy*, she had been putting on weight in quite an alarming fashion. Now, at the age of thirty, she must have appeared almost matronly. To the British, who were wont to think of American entertainers as resembling the frenetic Betty Hutton, it must have come as a profound shock." But from the start, Chick Webb, Fitzgerald's guardian and mentor, saw a jewel.

At age seventeen Fitzgerald turned professional, singing with Webb's band at the famed Savoy Ballroom. It was not long, however, before her legal status became a problem. To solve this problem, Webb and his wife decided to adopt her, thus becoming her legal guardians. Webb groomed Fitzgerald for success slowly and carefully, telling her to relax, not to rush, and "go with the beat, always go with the beat," according to Colin. Under his tutelage Fitzgerald blossomed and her confidence grew, but she never ever quite mastered her nervousness before a performance. Proud of his protégée, Webb demanded that band members and other jazz musicians treat Fitzgerald with respect. She responded by always behaving like a lady.

Fitzgerald's first record was *Love and Kisses*, recorded with Chick Webb on June 12, 1935. It has since disappeared without a trace. Possessing a remarkable ear for music and the ability to imitate almost

Fitzgerald •

turns

professional at

seventeen

179 •

any musical instrument, Fitzgerald began "scat" singing. In October 1936 she recorded "If You Can't Sing It, You'll Have to Swing It" or "Paganini," using this unique style of singing.

Although still a teenager, Fitzgerald's confidence had increased to the point where she began writing songs. On February 18, 1937, Billie Holiday recorded a song composed by Webb with lyrics by Fitzgerald. Titled "You Showed Me the Way," the song stands among Holiday's classic recordings of this period. The lyric is often described as "Tin Pan Alley love song conventions," but reveals Fitzgerald's genuine simplicity.

Continuing to write songs, in the 1940s Fitzgerald wrote the lyrics to Duke Ellington's "In a Mellotone" and to Nat King Cole's "Oh, But I Do." She gained membership in the American Society of Composers, Authors, and Publishers in 1943, becoming the youngest person ever admitted to membership in this organization.

• *First bit*

record

is released

While in Boston during the spring of 1938, Fitzgerald was tinkling around on the piano singing the words to a nursery rhyme from her childhood days: "A-Tisket-A-Tasket, a brown and yellow basket." Al Feldman, a pianist and arranger for Webb, helped her, and together they came up with the song—a smash hit that by September of that year sold a million records. Excited by her sudden success, Fitzgerald momentarily lost her head. She married someone whose name she later had trouble recalling. Webb insisted that she have the marriage annulled, and she complied without argument.

Webb's death of spinal tuberculosis in 1939 was a great loss to the jazz world and to Fitzgerald. Webb had been a good guardian and confidant, and Fitzgerald credits him for the positive influence he had on her musical technique. At age twenty-one, Fitzgerald found herself the leader of Chick Webb's band. She kept the band going for three years. During this period, according to one source, she was married to Bernie Kornegay.

In 1942 the Chick Webb Band dissolved. Fitzgerald continued on her own, singing at various night spots. In 1944, Fitzgerald and the Ink Spots had a million-selling hit with "Into Each Life Some Rain Must Fall," and by 1945 they enjoyed another million seller, Duke Ellington's "I'm Beginning to See the Light."

In 1947 Fitzgerald married Ray Brown, a bass player from Pittsburgh. The pair adopted an infant and named him Raymond Brown, Jr. When their marriage ended in 1953, Ray Brown, Jr., continued to reside with Fitzgerald. In 1967 they moved to California, and Fitzgerald purchased a home in Beverly Hills. Ray Brown remarried, and today Ray Brown, Jr., is also married and lives in Seattle, where he sings, plays guitar and drums, and leads a band. Fitzgerald never remarried. She lives with her two dogs, and Doreen, her housekeeper, and works forty weeks of every year.

Fitzgerald's numerous honors and awards bear witness to her amazing talent. She is the recipient of twelve Grammy awards; the Pied Piper Award presented by ASCAP; the George & Ira Gershwin Award for Outstanding Achievement; the American Music Award (1978); the National Medal of the Arts 1987 (presented at the White House); and innumerable popularity awards from *Downbeat Magazine, Metronome Magazine,* and *Jazz Award Poll.* She was named number one female singer in the sixteenth International Jazz Critics Poll in 1968 and Best Female Jazz vocalist years later, in 1981. More recently Fitzgerald was honored on February 14, 1990, at a benefit concert at New York's Avery Fisher Hall for the American Heart Association.

Among Fitzgerald's greatest recordings are the famous *Gershwin Songbook,* a five-record set released in 1958, and the album *The Best Is Yet to Come,* for which she won her twelfth Grammy Award. Renowned jazz impresario Norman Granz has been Fitzgerald's close friend and personal manager since 1954. Buying out her long-term contract from Decca Records, Granz began to record her on Verve Records, his label, in the late 1950s. Since 1972 she has recorded exclusively for Pablo, Granz's classic jazz label. To date she has twenty-five albums to her credit on this label.

Fitzgerald •

winner of

twelve

Grammys

**Profile by
Nagueyalti Warren**

ARETHA FRANKLIN

*A*retha Franklin was crowned the Queen of Soul in 1967, the year

1942- •

that saw her five singles for Atlantic Records sell over a million copies

each. Among the songs to catapult Franklin to fame were "I Never Loved

"Queen of Soul" •

a Man," "Baby, I Love You," and her signature work, "Respect." Her first

album for Atlantic, I Never Loved a Man, *also topped the million mark in*

sales, and she was proclaimed the year's top female vocalist by Billboard,

Cashbox, *and* Record World *magazines. The accolades continued into*

1968, when the city of Detroit—her hometown—named February 16 of

that year Aretha Franklin Day. The Southern Christian Leadership

Conference responded to her rendition of Otis Redding's "Respect" with

a special citation, and Time *magazine honored Franklin with a cover* on June 21. Since this explosion into superstardom her career has had its peaks and valleys, but Franklin has maintained her position as one of the world's greatest musical treasures.

The influence of gospel is unmistakable in Franklin's music. Born the fourth of five children to noted evangelist preacher and singer Clarence La Vaughn Franklin, and Barbara (Siggers) Franklin, also an accomplished vocalist, she began life in Memphis, Tennessee, on March 25, 1942. Two years later the family moved to Detroit, where Aretha has lived most of her life. She grew up in a substantial and comfortable residence but felt acutely the absence of her mother, who left when Aretha was six and died four years later. Family friend Mahalia Jackson's observation is recorded in Mark Bego's biography of Franklin: "After her mama died, the whole family wanted for love."

Jackson, Clara Ward, and Dinah Washington formed close relationships with Franklin; as famous singers and houseguests of her father's, each exerted a powerful influence on her. The Reverend Franklin also welcomed a number of other musicians into his home, including James Cleveland, Arthur Prysock, B. B. King, Dorothy Donegan, Lou Rawls, and Sam Cooke. Cleveland had a particular influence on the family, tutoring young Aretha on the piano and encouraging the girls in their formation of a gospel group that appeared in local churches for a span of eight months. With the influence of so many talented friends, as well as that of her father, Franklin thrived musically. "I had a piano right off the back porch, and sometimes I'd sing all day, every day, with my sisters and my friends," she recalled. She began playing the piano at age eight or nine but rebelled at formal lessons. A moment of realization came at her aunt's funeral when Franklin heard Clara Ward's emotional singing: "Clara knocked me out!" she said. "From then on I knew what I wanted to do was sing."

Two years later Franklin began traveling with her father's revival, an experience that exposed her to drinking, carousing, all-night partying, and the prejudice of Southern whites. At age fourteen, and at that time strictly a gospel singer, she made her first solo recording for Chess Records. A startling set of hymns recorded at her father's church, the record was reissued by Sugar Hill in 1984 with the title *Aretha Gospel*.

Also during this time also she joined a gospel quartet directed by Reverend James Cleveland, one of her first mentors; he taught her how to reach notes unknown to her and to imbue her singing with expression. Her range reached five octaves, providing an incredible forty notes at her command. Traveling on gospel caravans from age thirteen to sixteen and singing with the true giants of gospel gave Franklin with invaluable experience for later concert tours of her own.

At the age of fifteen Franklin was a talented pianist and a gospel-singing sensation, and was just beginning to get over her childhood disappointments and the loss of her mother when she became pregnant. She named her son Clarence Franklin, after her father. Bego comments, "What happened to Aretha as a teenager set a pattern of victimization by the men in her life. At the age of fifteen, Aretha Franklin had already earned her right to sing the blues."

Having dropped out of high school to have her baby in 1958, Franklin spent a lot of time at home listening to music and playing the piano. She was fascinated by the blues, especially by the singing of Dinah Washington. Far from an idle time for her, it was at this point that Franklin began planning to leave her family to strike out on her own. With her father supporting her decision, Franklin moved to New York City at age eighteen, hoping to sing secular music and become a successful blues singer like Washington.

Franklin's talent was immediately recognized by John Hammond of Columbia Records, who exclaimed, "This is the best voice I've heard in twenty years!" He signed her to a five-year contract and became her manager. She was also recognized by the media early on, and in July 1962 she was among the headlining acts at the Newport Jazz Festival. Already, she was being compared with Ray Charles and Dinah Washington.

Despite her popularity among jazz critics, Columbia kept Franklin on a nightclub repertoire of pop songs with heavy orchestration, an arrangement that did not suit her and led to artistic and personal frustration. The dreary rounds of engagements in second-rate clubs worsened the situation; Franklin and her husband, Ted White, who had replaced Hammond as her manager, waited out the expiration of her contract while her records maintained modest sales.

After fulfilling her contractual obligation to Columbia, Franklin switched to Atlantic Records, a move well-timed for her popularity and earning power. She was already popular with black consumers, and white consumers were ready for her, having been exposed somewhat to black music through white performers like Elvis Presley. The crossover market made Motown Records and its stars giants in the business, and prompted Atlantic to follow the same path. As a result, Franklin was given the freedom to choose her own material and pursue her own style, allowing her to reach a wide audience without abandoning the qualities that made up her unique appeal to the black consumer. Thus a constantly widening circle of listeners was exposed to her vocal capabilities, characterized by Jim Miller: "[Franklin's] voice, a robust yet crystalline alto, is remarkable for its reliable intonation, expressive vibrato, and great range of pitch dynamics, and expression. She is able to execute changes of register, volume, and timbre with dexterity and fluency, often altering the entire color of her voice in successive verses of a song as the text demands."

A marked discrepancy exists between Franklin's shyness as a person and directness and inhibition as a singer, a quality that a *Time* cover story, among others, emphasized:

> She does not seem to be performing so much as bearing witness to a reality so simple and compelling that she could not possibly fake it. In her selection of songs, whether written by others or by herself, she unfailingly opts for those that frame her own view of life. "If a song's about something I've experienced or that could have happened to me, it's good," she says. "But if it's alien to me, I couldn't lend anything to it. Because that's what soul is about—just living and having to get along."

• *First Grammys*

won early in

career

Between 1967 and 1969, Franklin won four Grammy awards: best R&B recording and best female R&B performance, both in 1967, for "Respect"; best female R&B performance in 1968 for "Chain of Fools"; and best female R&B performance in 1969 for "Share Your Love with Me." She produced at least one million-selling song each year from 1967 to 1973.

The 1970s brought six Grammys for Franklin, for "Don't Play That Song for Me," "Bridge Over Troubled Water," "Young, Gifted and Black," "Amazing Grace," "Master of Eyes," and "Ain't Nothing Like the Real Thing."

Throughout her career Franklin has found herself challenged with personal problems. Her marriage to White ended in 1969, a situation she found difficult to handle. Her next relationship, with Ken Cunningham, lasted six years and produced many positive changes for her. With Cunningham's encouragement, Franklin was able to lose weight, cut back on alcohol, and focus more closely on her work. He also provided photography for her albums. She ended the relationship in 1977.

Franklin was again married in 1978, to actor Glynn Turman; the marriage ended in 1982, with little explanation. At the time Franklin moved back to Detroit to care for her father, who had been shot by a burglar in 1979. The tragedy deeply affected Franklin, who spent $1500 a week for nursing care and a total of over $500,000 on his medical support. She gave two benefit performances, in 1979 and 1981, to raise funds for his hospitalization. Her father remained in a coma until his death on July 24, 1984.

Franklin traditionally contributes large sums to charity through benefit concerts. Causes worthwhile to her have included the Relief Center at her father's church, Mother Waddles's Perpetual Mission, the United Negro College Fund, and the NAACP. She also used her voice to raise funds for the Joffrey Ballet in a 1982 performance at Carnegie Hall. The Joffrey in turn honored her with a ballet choreographed to her music. In 1988 she recorded a public-service announcement against driving under the influence of drugs and liquor. Her hit record, "Think," was used in the spot, entitled "Think . . . Don't Drive with Drugs or Drink!"

In 1986 Michigan legislators proclaimed Franklin's voice one of the state's natural resources. In August of 1989, Senator Carl Levin of Michigan presented Franklin with a plaque and a Senate resolution honoring her achievements and her contributions to the fight against drunk driving. Levin said, "For this dedication to her craft, and her community, she earned what all of us covet—"R-E-S-P-E-C-T." In 1991 Franklin's home state again honored her, this time with an honorary Doctorate of Humane Letters degree from Detroit's Wayne State University.

In her more than thirty years in the record business, Aretha Franklin has had a career that other female vocalists can only dream of matching. She is to contemporary pop and soul music what Ella Fitzgerald is to jazz singing. Her vast wealth of creative achievements is staggering; her fans await what the future holds.

Profile by Virginia Wilson Wallace

MARY HATWOOD FUTRELL

*A*s Mary Hatwood Futrell finished her sixth year as president of the

National Education Association, she made a number of observations.

"We know that our responsibility is not just to the children of America,

but to the children of the world. We know now that the destiny of the

American family is intertwined with the destiny of the human family.

And we know we can observe that misery or help halt that misery. Let us

not be observers." She challenged NEA members to bring about "a

massive reduction of worldwide illiteracy by the year 2000." Futrell is a

woman of her convictions—not just a talker, but a woman of action

who was brought up to achieve.

1940- •

educator, •

organization

leader

On August 31, 1989, Futrell stepped down from an unprecedented third term, or six years, as president of the NEA, the national organization that she has served in various capacities over the past twenty years, including three as its secretary-treasurer.

Born May 24, 1940, in Alta Vista, Virginia, Mary Hatwood Futrell is the second daughter of Josephine Hatwood (Austin). She lost her father, John Ed Calloway, at age four. Josephine Austin had left school to work after sixth grade, because her parents died, and she was determined her children would not have the same problem. When her husband died, she was determined that they would succeed through her love, attention, and discipline. Josephine Hatwood had wanted to be a nurse, but was forced to abandon this idea to support her children. She did domestic work for three families and cleaned churches to feed and clothe her children.

Discipline and perfection were demanded of Mary Futrell by her tenth grade teacher at Dunbar Public High School in Lynchburg, Virginia. As a punishment for too much talking, she had to write a thousand-word essay on education and its impact on the economy. She was forced to rewrite it with each paragraph beginning with a topic sentence. The second time she had to rewrite it to correct the grammar. The third time, the spelling. The fourth time, it was punctuation. The fifth time, it wasn't neat enough. The sixth time, it was accepted. Her teacher entered the final paper in an essay contest where the student won third prize. Futrell explained, "Except for mama, she was the person I most wanted to please in this world."

Futrell's education continued at Virginia State University, where she received a B.A. in business education. To begin college, she received a scholarship of fifteen hundred dollars. "My tenth grade teacher, Miss Jordan, nodded her head as if to say, 'See now, what you can do with discipline?'" She earned her M.A. at George Washington University, did additional graduate work at the University of Maryland, the University of Virginia, and Virginia Polytechnic Institute and State University, and has received a number of honorary doctorates. She is married to Donald Futrell.

Mary Futrell is a twenty-year veteran classroom teacher of business education in the Alexandria, Virginia, schools. She moved through the ranks in the NEA to become president of the 1.9 million-member organization and was twice reelected, serving an unprecedented third term. She is regarded as a tireless educator who has spent almost all her adult professional life providing and attempting to assure quality education for the youngsters in the nation's schools.

In August 1989, Futrell became a senior fellow and doctoral student at George Washington University, where she is pursuing educational policy studies. She also assumed the post of Associate Director of the Center for the Study of Education and National Development, an organization she describes to Bender as "a budding educational think tank, research center, and clearinghouse."

Her monthly essays in *NEA Today* reveal seven categories of concerns on which Futrell focused during her six years as president of the organization: reduction of the dropout rate, improvement and expansion of the Head Start program, child care programs for young families, effective programs to deal with drugs in schools, adequacy of resources, expanded use of computers in teaching, and funds for college loans. She was concerned as well about NEA membership. The many issues raised by the report, *A Nation at Risk,* which highlighted the inadequacy of American education, had a major impact upon her thinking.

Dropouts are a pressing issue in Futrell's mind. In March 1988, she addressed the topic of "National Dishonesty" regarding pushouts, a part of the dropout problem. She said, "The thousands of students pushed out of school by in-school discrimination demand and must have relief." The Robert F. Kennedy Memorial and the Southern Regional Council issued a call to action in 1973. She stated, "Their report, 'The Student Pushout: Victim of Continued Resistance to Desegregation,' charged that school districts had created a new category of classroom exile." She believed that pushouts include linguistic minority students, many of whom are learning English for the first time in high school. She elaborated on this issue in *NEA Today:*

> When these students can no longer endure messages that erode their self-esteem and demean their native heritage, they seek escape. We add these students to the dropout statistics. They don't belong there. They're pushouts. Only when we're honest enough to call them pushouts will we begin to solve their problem, which is our problem.

Amid all the headlines about drug abuse, there is one piece of good news. The number of students using drugs, according to a new national survey, is dropping, because, as experts say, drug abuse education efforts are beginning to pay off. There is only so much one can do for young people already hooked on drugs, because adequate treatment programs simply do not exist. The nation can try to convince young people to try to kick their addiction, but there often is no place to send them for help. Futrell observed in 1989, "Nationally, there are now more than six million Americans dependent on drugs, and only 250,000 slots in treatment programs." Twenty-four times as many slots are needed.

Problems exposed by Futrell show that political leaders say they're for a national campaign against drug abuse, but they're just not willing to fully fund it. In February of 1989, $441 million was proposed in spending for new education programs. Overall federal aid to education was not raised, even to keep up with inflation. Therefore, existing federal education efforts received almost half a billion dollars less than they need to operate at current levels.

Futrell continued, "The budget proposed for 1990 included what budget officials call a freeze on military spending, but it actually went up four percent, and the military budget lost no buying power." The education budget was increased with money for some new programs. Yet, Futrell observed, "In real dollar terms, education ends up with less federal support. . . . The only true national security is a well-educated American people." Less federal support will not solve the drug problem. With the reestablishment of the National Federation for the Improvement of Education as a major foundation, the primary issue is on dropout and literacy problems.

IBM is providing every school in the NEA's Mastery in Learning Project with a personal computer, a modem, a printer, and an experimental software package called People Sharing Information Network. All twenty-six Mastery in Learning schools nationwide will be electronically linked. "Our challenge now," Futrell wrote in *NEA Today*, "is to nurture and expand the relationship we've begun. Our challenge is to merge the traditional 3 R's with a new technological three R's. For whether as Resource tools, Research vehicles, or—most importantly—Restructuring mechanisms, computers offer our schools the promise of profound change." Because of President Bush's election, Futrell felt she could count on his educational promise and was proud that the NEA cooperated with IBM to take the first steps toward the expanded use of computers in education.

George Bush and Michael Dukakis differed in their views on education. Although Futrell had preferred Dukakis for president, she worked well with Bush's support. Futrell was enthusiastic about the program of the Democratic candidates in the 1988 presidential election for the continuation and expansion of college loans. Thus, she expressed disappointment later that college loans were so drastically cut. She said in early November, 1988, before the election, "Senator Lloyd Bentsen, way back in 1971, proposed a program, called COSTEP that brought businesses and banks together to provide college loans to needy students. To date, the COSTEP program has granted more than $100 million dollars in college loans to students in need. The cost to taxpayers: not one cent." She felt that the surest path to national security is support for programs that offer opportunity to youth. Futrell liked Bentsen's maxim: "If you think education is expensive, try ignorance."

Another issue on which Futrell experienced success was the phenomenal increase in NEA membership under her direction. In November 1989, the NEA announced its 1.98 millionth member. She built the NEA into the largest union in America. From September 1983 until September 1988, the NEA added two hundred fifty thousand members under her leadership. She succeeded in moving the staff from a position of traditionalism and from a go-slow attitude on reform to a position of leadership in that effort. Her successes have astounded even her most severe critics.

Futrell believes, "Each time NEA adds a new member, a new advocate is added for America's children, a new voice to speak on behalf of those who cannot vote, a new ally in our struggle for professional dignity and professional compensation." Her ambitious all-embracing goal was to open the NEA's ranks to all who contribute to the life of the schools and the welfare of students. She wished to include teacher assistants, nurses, counselors, librarians, bus drivers, cafeteria workers, clerical staff, maintenance workers, custodians, and higher education faculty. This idea, she believes, gives dignity and pride to all who are cogs in the wheel.

In 1983 the landmark report *A Nation at Risk* called for a new commitment to education. The report spoke to all Americans and challenged the federal government. It bluntly urged the federal government to help make sure all schools had the resources they needed. Although that has not happened, attention has been focused on education. The share of the federal budget devoted to education has actually decreased to below two percent. Therefore, education reform is dying, Futrell said in May of 1988. In July of the same year, she asked seven thousand NEA delegates to approve a bold initiative for education reform. She asked all NEA state affiliates to meet with their governors, state school officials, and state legislators and, with them, to designate at least one entire school district in every state as a living laboratory for restructuring America's schools. Working with school boards, parents, and civic leaders to develop programs to improve education, the NEA could have more clout for reform.

In a 1989 interview with Michael E. Howard, Futrell reviewed her accomplishments:

> During the last six years one of my goals reached has been to help the NEA assume a more forceful and more positive position on teachers' union rights. Secondly,

we increased union membership from 1.6 million to just under 2 million. Another has been our efforts to bring a higher visibility of teachers into the current talk about changing the curricula of today's schools. In addition, Operation Rescue, our dropout prevention and intervention program, implemented projects in 26 schools in 10 states engaging 15,000 students in enrichment and mastery projects.

Futrell has obtained a great deal of influence in the national educational arena, and she has had both the energy and the bravery to tackle any task. "When you live in poverty," she told Blount, "you learn how to deal with an adversarial situation and survive . . . and prove them wrong."

Profile by Virginia Wilson Wallace

ZELMA WATSON GEORGE

Z elma Watson George has combined careers in many diverse fields **1903-** •

with outstanding success. She is an opera singer who has studied black

music from a sociological standpoint, and she is a speaker and educator **sociologist,** •

who has advocated the interests of women and blacks as a public **musicologist**

servant. George views each of these activities not as separate careers, but

as different aspects of a single purpose: promoting communication

between those of different races, cultures, and nations.

George was born December 8, 1903, in Hearne, Texas. George's parents were both trained musicians, and she developed an interest in opera singing at an early age. George's father was the principal of a boarding school, and George was taught by her mother. Later her father became a Baptist minister, and George moved with her family to his various pastorates. In Topeka, Kansas, George attended an integrated high school where a white guidance counselor attempted to dissuade her from applying to the University of Chicago, leaving her all the more determined to attain this goal.

George was accepted at the University of Chicago, although she was refused dormitory housing because of her race. She auditioned for the university choir but was told her singing voice was too good for their standards. When George appealed this decision, the chaplain confirmed that she had been rejected because she was black, stating that "to put [her] in the choir would be like putting a lame person in it. The people who came to worship would be distracted by [her] physical presence." This was only one of many such barriers George encountered as a student.

Yet in spite of these negative experiences, George still regards the time she spent at the University of Chicago as some of the best years of her life. An enthusiastic student, she flourished in the academic setting, honing and broadening her research skills. George also widened her circle of friends to include men and women from every part of the country and from many foreign nations. It was here that she first came to know the "fellowship of the world," preparing her for her life's work in communication.

George revels •

in fellowship

of the world

After graduation, George worked as a social case worker and later served as a probation officer for a juvenile court. She also pursued her interest in music, studying organ at Northwestern University and voice at the American Conservatory of Music. In the early 1930s, George became the dean of women and director of personnel administration at Tennessee Agricultural and Industrial State College.

After spending five years in Nashville, Tennessee, George married Baxter Duke, a young minister whom she had known when both were teenagers in Topeka. The wedding took place in her father's former church in Chicago, and the couple moved to Los Angeles, where Duke had accepted a position as a minister at Avalon Christian Church. In addition to becoming a minister's wife, George accepted the role of developing the Avalon Community Center. As the executive director, she came into contact with a staff of two hundred blacks, Asians, Hispanics, and whites, ranging in age from teenagers to older adults. George had received her master's degree in personnel administration from New York University, and now she began working toward her Ph.D. in education at the University of Southern California. Her first year, described in Rowena Woodham Jelliffe's book *Here's Zelma,* "confirmed her desire to make a comprehensive study of Negro music and to explore its sociological impact." She acquired a two-year Rockefeller Foundation grant to research the songs of black America and to "discover the purposes to which they had been put." George received her Ph.D. in sociology and intercultural relations from New York University in 1954. Her dissertation, "A Guide to Negro Music: An Annotated Bibliography of Negro

Folk Music and Art Music by Negro Composers or Based on Negro Thematic Material," was a seminal work in that it catalogs twelve thousand titles written or inspired by black Americans.

George's marriage to Duke had failed after five years, and in 1944, she married Clayborne George, a well-known and respected lawyer who chaired the Civil Service Commission. George moved with him to Cleveland, Ohio, where she combined several careers while donating her time and skills to volunteer groups, including the Young Women's Christian Association, Council of Church Women, Girl Scouts of America, Conference of Christians and Jews, Council on Human Relations, League of Women Voters, American Society for African Culture, National Association for the Advancement of Colored People, and the National Council of Negro Women.

George fulfilled her life-long dream in 1949 when she received rave reviews in the title role of Gian-Carlo Menotti's opera *The Medium* at the Karamu Theatre in Cleveland, a performance she later repeated on Broadway. George went on to star in other operas, such as Menotti's *The Consul* at the Cleveland Playhouse in 1951, and Kurt Weill's *Threepenny Opera* at the Karamu.

While she pursued her singing and attended to her active social and community life, George was also gaining national and international recognition in the public service arena. In 1956, she was named to the Defense Advisory Committee on Women in the Armed Services, a post that involved extensive touring of nationwide military installations. George also participated in conferences, including the Minority Youth Training Incentives Conference, sponsored by the President's Committee on Government Contracts and the American Personnel and Guidance Association, and the Washington Conference on the Community's Responsibility for the Development of Minority Potential. In 1958, President Dwight D. Eisenhower appointed George to the President's Committee to plan the 1960 White House Conference on Children and Youth. The following year, she received a United States State Department grant for a six-month lecture tour of thirteen countries in the Far East, Southeast Asia, Europe, and Africa. The tour received press coverage praising George's ability to connect with her audiences in personal ways.

In 1960 George was approved by the United States Senate as an alternate to the United States Delegation to the Fifteenth General Assembly of the United Nations, where she represented the U.S. on the Economics and Finance Committee. During her term, a resolution was proposed by the African and Asian delegations, recommending a "speedy and unconditional end of colonialism." When this resolution was

• George

becomes

delegate to the

United Nations

passed—despite an abstention vote by the United States—George burst into spontaneous applause. Reflecting on this action—which drew the attention of the press—George points out that it was not planned in advance. "Your personal integrity is all you've got. . . . It was just something that, to be honest, I had to do."

Following her United Nations appointment, George became an even more highly sought speaker and lecturer. Eventually, she became a full-time lecturer under the auspices of the Danforth Foundation and the W. Colston Leigh Bureau. Between 1964 and 1967, she visited fifty-nine colleges as a Danforth visiting lecturer. In 1966 George was named executive director of the new Cleveland Jobs Corps Center for Women, a residential vocational training program for young women from low income backgrounds who have dropped out of school. George retired from this position in 1974 but has continued to speak and lecture, and she also taught at Cuyahoga Community College for a number of years in the 1980s.

George's success in promoting communication through forums as diverse as the lecture hall, the United Nations, and the Broadway stage is reflected in the multitude of awards and honors which she has received. These include the Dag Hammarskjold Award for Distinguished Service to the Cause of World Peace through World Law; the Dahlberg Peace Award from the American Baptist Church; the Mary Bethune Gold Medallion from Bethune-Cookman College; United States Department of Labor Distinguished Citizen Award; James Dodman Nobel Award in Human Relations; Lifetime Achievement Award by the Black Professional Association of Cleveland; and selection as one of a group of seventy-five contemporary black American women seventy years of age or older whose memoirs and biographies are included in the Black Women Oral History Project at Schlesinger Library, Radcliffe College. Most recently, a shelter for homeless women and children was named in George's honor.

**Profile by
Sandra E. Gibbs**

ALTHEA GIBSON

*G*rowing up on the streets of Harlem in the late 1930s and early   **1927-** •

1940s was not easy for Althea Gibson, an incorrigible child who was

constantly in trouble with her father and her teachers. Yet a talent for the   **world** •

game of tennis and a desire to be "somebody" spurred Gibson to   **tennis**

complete her education and fight for the life she wanted. She became the   **champion**

first black international tennis player in the world, winning at Wimbledon

and Forest Hills. After a successful tennis career, she played professional

golf and became the only black member of the Ladies Professional Golf

Association.

As a girl growing up in a congested Harlem tenement, Gibson developed a preference for movies over studies; truancy permeated her teenage years. Gibson graduated from junior high school in 1941, a surprise to her because of her low attendance, but was disappointed when her request to transfer to a downtown high school to be with her friends was denied. Embittered and lonely, Gibson's truancy resurfaced, but this time she found solace and comfort at the Society for the Prevention of Cruelty to Children, a place for troubled and homeless children. The social workers were kind to Gibson, but they had a serious message for her: if her aberrant behavior continued, a girls' correctional facility would be her next home.

Gibson heeded this warning, but instead of returning to school full time, she requested and received working papers on the condition that she attend night school for a designated number of hours per week. Gibson admits that she kept the school portion of her promise for only two weeks. She worked, feeling for the first time a sense of importance, at several jobs ranging from counter girl at a restaurant chain to mail clerk at the New York School of Social Work. She liked the latter position best, but it lasted only six weeks. Instead of going to work as expected, Gibson went to the Paramount Theatre to see artists such as Sarah Vaughan. Eventually she was fired.

While employed at the school, Gibson met boxer Sugar Ray Robinson and his wife, Edna, and sought their council on many occasions. They encouraged her to complete her high school education to secure better employment and later provided guidance in her tennis career. Despite the Robinsons' advice, Gibson remained restless and unhappy, and lost numerous jobs in quick succession. Meanwhile, she loitered on the streets and came to the attention of the Welfare Department. Staff personnel made arrangements for Gibson to live in a less crowded home and look for a job. She recalls, "It was while I was living in a never-never land through the courtesy of the City of New York that I was introduced to tennis."

Gibson exhibited a talent for tennis in all of the games sponsored by the Police Athletic League on 143rd Street in her neighborhood. Although she faced uncertainty about the future, it is evident that she had a flair for spirited competition. She played fast and pressing basketball on the neighborhood court; she hustled at stickball and excelled at paddleball, a form of conventional tennis played with a wooden paddle.

Buddy Walker, a musician who worked for the city recreation department in the summer, noticed Gibson's skill and bought her a second-hand racket. After Gibson practiced batting balls at the handball court in Morris Park, Walker judged her skills sufficient to play a few sets at the New York Cosmopolitan Club with professional Fred Johnson. Gibson's performance was above average; club members, impressed with her natural ability at tennis, provided a junior membership and financed her lessons.

The game of tennis changed Gibson's life dramatically, and within a year, after lessons with Johnson, she won her first tournament, the girls' singles in the New York State Open Championship in 1942. Still interested in Gibson's welfare and success, the Cosmopolitan Club members pooled their financial resources and sent Gibson to the American Tennis Association's national girls' championship, a predominantly black competition at Lincoln University in Pennsylvania. Gibson went to the finals but lost to Nina Davis. In later years, Davis recalled this 1942 match with humor: "Althea was a very crude creature. She had the idea she was better than anybody. I can remember her saying, 'Who's this Nina Davis? Let me at her.' And after I beat her, she headed straight for the grandstand without bothering to shake hands. Some kid had been laughing at her, and she was going to throw him out." After this loss, Gibson practiced more fiercely on the Cosmopolitan courts; however, World War II forced the cancellation of the American Tennis Association national tournament due to travel restrictions. The tournament resumed in 1944 and Gibson won the girls' singles in 1944 and 1945.

In 1946, at the age of eighteen, Gibson became eligible for the women's singles and played at Wilberforce College in Ohio. She lost to Roumania Peters, a teacher at Tuskegee Institute. Despite the loss, Gibson attracted the attention of two black surgeons who were leaders in the American Tennis Association, Hubert Eaton of Wilmington, North Carolina, and Robert W. Johnson of Lynchburg, Virginia. Eaton and Johnson recognized her potential and offered this proposal: they would feed, clothe, and educate her at their own expense. During the school year, Gibson lived with Eaton's family in Wilmington, attended high school, and practiced with him on his private court, the only one for blacks in the city. In the summer, Gibson received similar, though more intensive, instruction from Johnson and traveled with him to tournaments.

Before Gibson finished high school, Florida Agricultural and Mechanical College at Tallahassee offered her a tennis scholarship and encouraged her to spend the summer playing tennis on the campus. At twenty-two, Gibson entered college eager and mindful of what her mentors, Eaton and Johnson, had done: "Nobody could have been more grateful than I was to both doctors for everything . . . but it was good to feel a little bit independent again."

At Florida A&M, Gibson continued to hone her tennis skills, and she accepted invitations to play in Eastern and national indoor championships. She was not the first to break the color barrier in these matches; a black preceded her two years earlier—Reginald Weir. In both of Gibson's tournaments, Nancy Chaffee emerged the clear victor.

Gibson waited—in vain—for an invitation from the United States Lawn Tennis Association to play in the prestigious summer grass court tournament at Forest Hills, Long Island. Alice Marble, a white tennis player, also waited for Gibson's invitation. When none came, Marble wrote an editorial condemning "the injustices perpetrated by our policy-makers" in the July 1950 issue of *American Lawn Tennis* magazine that, as biographer Sylvia Dannett put it, "kicked up a storm from one end of the tennis world to another."

Marble succeeded; doors began to open for Gibson. Her application to enter the New Jersey State Championship at the Maplewood Country Club was rejected; however, the Orange Lawn Tennis Club in South Orange, New Jersey, one of the outstanding clubs on the Eastern circuit, accepted Gibson's application to play in the Eastern Grass Court Championship, a tournament ranked second to the nationals in the tennis circles of the Atlantic seaboard. Gibson defeated one player but was eliminated by Helen Pastall in the second round. She reached the quarterfinals in the National Clay Courts Championships at Chicago, where Doris Hart beat her 6-2, 6-3. It was after this match that Harold Blair of the United States Lawn Tennis Association "passed the word to Mr. Baker (President of the USLTA) that if I applied for entrance into the Nationals, I would be accepted. I filled out the entry blank as fast as I could get hold of one."

- *Gibson plays*

in Nationals

Gibson remembers vividly the moment when Lawrence Baker announced that "I was one of the fifty-two women whose entries had been accepted for the national championship tournament. . . . He added meaningfully, 'Miss Gibson has been accepted on her ability.' That was all I had ever asked." Although Gibson won the first-round match easily against Great Britain's Barbara Knapp in straight sets (6-2 and 6-2) in August 1950, she lost to Louise Brough, Wimbledon champion and former United States champion. Gibson became the first black to play major lawn tennis, but it took seven years for her to win the nation's tennis championship at Forest Hills.

Gibson graduated from Florida A&M with a degree in physical education, and pushed tennis aside temporarily to join the physical education department faculty of Lincoln University in Jefferson City, Missouri, where she taught for two years. When she returned to the game, the fact that she had played at Forest Hills was still of some significance, and it continued to present opportunities for her, such as tours in Mexico and Southeast Asia. Winning tournament after tournament in quick succession, Gibson played in Sweden, Germany, France, England, Italy, and Egypt. She won sixteen out of eighteen tournaments.

In 1957 Gibson became the first black woman to compete and to win at Wimbledon and Forest Hills. Facing Darlene Hard at Wimbledon, Gibson won the singles match 6-3, 6-2 and teamed with Hard to win the doubles championship. At Forest Hills, Gibson emerged victorious over Louise Brough, 6-3, 6-2. The following year, Gibson returned to Wimbledon and defeated Britain's Angela Mortimer 8-6, 6-2 in singles. Paired with Maria Bueno of Brazil in doubles, Gibson beat Margaret Gaborn du Pont and Margaret Varner 6-3, 7-5. In the decade after second victories at both Wimbledon and Forest Hills, Gibson admits having "so many prospects on the horizon that the future had no anxiety for me at all."

Gibson retired and dabbled in several activities before settling on golf as her next profession, playing in several tournaments from 1963 to 1967. For Gibson, golf offered the best chance to secure a good living. Unlike today's top tennis players, Gibson had not retired a rich woman. She commented, "I was born too soon," referring to the fact that now it is possible for women to earn a living at either tennis or golf.

No black woman on the tennis circuit has achieved what Gibson did more than thirty years ago. As the first black to capture titles in tennis and one of the greatest athletes of her time, she gathered and retained world dominance in a sport that few blacks deemed a viable option for themselves. Althea Gibson wanted to be "somebody," and she succeeded.

**Profile by
Sharynn Owens
Etheridge**

NIKKI GIOVANNI

Groundbreaking, prolific, and sometimes controversial poet Nikki

Giovanni maintains two guiding forces in her poetry and in her life: a

willingness to change and grow, and an emphasis on pride in her black

heritage, which she shares with young people and adults alike. Yolande

Cornelia "Nikki" Giovanni, Jr., was born in Knoxville, Tennessee, on

June 7, 1943, the daughter of Jones "Gus" Giovanni and Yolande

(Watson) Giovanni. At age seventeen she entered Fisk University, where

she majored in history. After a break in her studies, she received her

bachelor of arts degree with honors in 1967. She then did graduate work

at the University of Pennsylvania School of Social Work and undertook

additional study at the Columbia University School of Fine Arts.

1943- •

poet, writer, •

activist,

educator

It is customary to discuss Giovanni's development in terms of decades. In the sixties, militancy characterizes her writing; in the seventies, greater introspection and attention to personal relationships; in the eighties and nineties, a more global outlook with a greater concern for humanity in general. However, the various themes reflect changes in emphasis rather than wholesale abandonment of one concern for another. Giovanni's overall approach—seeking and telling the truth and growing in the process—is grounded in her family heritage. Her strong grandmother, Luvenia Terrell Watson, was "terribly intolerant when it came to white people." As a result of her outspokenness, Luvenia Watson was smuggled out of Albany, Georgia, under the cover of darkness by her husband, John "Book" Watson, and other family members, who had good reason to believe her life was in danger. Luvenia and John Watson had hoped to reach the North, but settled in Knoxville, Tennessee, "the first reasonable-sized town" on their way. A teacher, John Watson returned to Albany to finish the school term— "Grandfather was like that." He then joined his wife in Knoxville, where they made their home.

Giovanni's mother, Yolande Watson, was the oldest of three daughters. Yolande met Jones "Gus" Giovanni at Knoxville College. From their subsequent marriage, two daughters were born. Jones Giovanni's roots were in Cincinnati, where Nikki Giovanni spent some of her formative years. Of the family surname, she has observed, "It just means that *our* slave masters were Italian instead of English or French." Along with her grandparents, Giovanni's parents and her older sister, Gary, have been strong, positive influences on her development, even though Giovanni does not depict them (or herself) idealistically.

Giovanni has warned against reading her work—poetry or prose— as strictly autobiographical. Even so, because she assesses life from a personal perspective, her own experiences are essential starting points and often remain central themes for her writing. She states that *Gemini* merely "comes close" to being autobiography—truth being larger than merely what we remember. Nevertheless, Giovanni's summary of the importance of her heritage in *Gemini* is illustrated in her work as a whole:

> Life/personality must be taken as a total entity. All of
> your life is all of your life, and no one incident stands
> alone. . . . My family on my grandmother's side are
> fighters. My family on my father's side are survivors.
> I'm a revolutionist. It's only logical.

It was as a revolutionary poet in the 1960s that Giovanni first came to national attention. During this period she became known as the

"Princess of Black Poetry." The poetry in *Black Feeling, Black Talk* and in *Black Judgement* capture the spirit of the times. Other poets who became prominent during that period included Don L. Lee (later Haki Madhubuti) and Sonia Sanchez. Like her contemporaries, Giovanni found traditional poetic themes and techniques inadequate for the times.

Giovanni's activism revealed itself not only on paper. As a student at Fisk University in the mid-sixties, she had been a founding member of the university's Student Nonviolent Coordinating Committee chapter. Establishing the chapter was not an easy task, and her commitment is an example of her acting on principles rather than out of conformity.

Giovanni began her college studies at Fisk University in 1960, but she was "released" because she went home for Thanksgiving without asking permission of the dean of women. This incident is an example of her making decisions based on her values, in this case the primacy of family. Giovanni wanted to be with her grandparents, the Watsons, knowing that her grandfather was ill and that her grandmother needed her support. Looking back on the experience, Giovanni points out that she knew what the outcome would be, but if she had not gone to Knoxville, "the only change would have been that Fisk considered me an ideal student, which means little on a life scale." When she returned to college, it was because she felt ready. Grandmother Watson said she would live to see Nikki finish college, and she died about one month after Giovanni graduated.

The significance of family and family-oriented themes deepened for Giovanni with the birth of her son, Thomas Watson, in August 1969. "Don't Have a Baby till You Read This" recounts the experience. Giovanni has noted: "I had a baby at 25 because I *wanted* to have a baby and I could *afford* to have a baby. I did not get married because I didn't *want* to get married and I could *afford* not to get married."

As a mother, Giovanni had even more impetus to provide positive images for black children. Her response included establishing her own publishing company, Niktom, in 1970. At least in part, this endeavor can be read as an extension of the work she began in the sixties—to create literature that speaks directly to black people and that celebrates positive features of black life. In short, the concerns of the revolutionary were rechanneled rather than abandoned.

The titles of many of Giovanni's books of poetry published in the 1970s—*Re-Creation, My House, The Women and the Men, Cotton Candy on a Rainy Day*—have an introspective, thoughtful focus. Paula Giddings finds *The Women and the Men* a "coming of age. For the first

Revolutionary •

poet attracts

national

attention

209 •

time, the woman-child is virtually absent," replaced by an adult. Themes of relationships, of womanhood, and of motherhood are stressed. Again, Giovanni's themes are not easily summarized. The more personal themes are relevant to the wider world in that they suggest the values that should apply in making the world a better place. And Giovanni includes themes other than the personal. In *The Women and the Men,* the final section, "And Some Places," reflects her travel to Africa, which she visited with her friend Ida Lewis in 1971.

Giovanni's interest in exploring others' ideas is illustrated in the books that transcribe her conversations with James Baldwin and Margaret Walker. Both these dialogues demonstrate mutual respect even in the presence of clear generational differences. Topics are wide-ranging; both volumes include attention to black writing and to relationships between black men and women.

Record albums have served as another effective medium of expression for Giovanni. *Truth Is on Its Way* (1972) helped launch Giovanni's lasting popularity as a speaker and reader of her own poetry. The album consists of Giovanni's reading her poems to background gospel accompaniment.

The conversations and the albums underscore the importance of the spoken word for Giovanni. In a postscript to her conversations with Walker, Giovanni sums up the importance of such an exchange: "I rather like the immediacy of talking . . . the mistakes . . . the insights . . . the risks inherent in hot conversation. Life is all about that balance between risk and inertia . . . that poetic equation."

The very title *Sacred Cows and Other Edibles,* Giovanni's 1988 collection of short prose pieces, captures the author's continued readiness to take on and devour society's myths, or to "go naked and see what happens." *Sacred Cows* gives attention to sports, supplying special help to women in negotiating the terrain: "If they are in their underwear—it's Basketball; if they have on their pajamas—it's Baseball; if they wear helmets—it's Football." Lighthearted without being trivial, insightful without being ponderous, Giovanni considers the implications of sports as an expression of culture. *Sacred Cows* covers a range of other topics, including selections on writing and on her relationship with her mother. Much of the book is centered on her time as a resident of Cincinnati, where she lived with her parents in 1978 after her father became ill.

Once she has written something, Giovanni moves on. She has acknowledged that she lacks discipline. On that point, William J. Harris observes in *Black Women Writers:* "She has the talent to create good, perhaps important, poetry, if only she has the will to discipline her

- *Giovanni*

honors the

spoken word

craft." Finally, however, there can be no disagreement that Giovanni is a productive, talented writer. Her wit and candor as she stays "on the case," whatever the fundamental issues of the times may be, help explain why she remains consistently stimulating and significant.

Giovanni has clearly earned a prominent place in American life and letters. Since she first rose to national attention in the sixties, she has been consistently outspoken and charismatic. Characteristically expressing her ideas with charm and good humor, she allows for opposite points of view as well: "I don't think everyone has to write the way I write nor think the way I think," she was quoted in *Black Women Writers*. "There are plenty of ideas to go around."

**Profile by
Arlene Clift-Pellow**

211 •

WHOOPI GOLDBERG

*F*rom her childhood home in a housing project in New York City,

Whoopi Goldberg has emerged as one of America's best-loved comedi-

ennes and actresses. She has exhibited her wide-ranging talents in

films, television shows, theatrical performances, and recordings, and in

the process has won a host of major awards—an Oscar, a Grammy, a

Golden Globe award, and the NAACP Image award. Combining her

burgeoning career with a deeply felt social conscience, Goldberg has

used her vast popularity to combat a number of social ills. Her Comic

Relief benefits with Robin Williams and Billy Crystal, for instance, have

become annual events that have raised millions of dollars for the

homeless. Despite her many career triumphs, though, Goldberg's path to

c. 1950- •

actress, •

comedienne

success has not been without obstacles, from poverty and dyslexia to racism and sexism. Much of her work, especially her comedy routines, reflects those struggles. "I told my mother I don't want to be black no more. You have to have blond hair to be on *Love Boat*," says one of Goldberg's most poignant and powerful comedic characters, described by Mary Unterbrink as "a 9-year-old street urchin who covers her tight braids with a white skirt that she pretends is long blond hair."

Goldberg was born Caryn Johnson in about 1950 (some sources say 1949) in New York City, where she and a younger brother, Clyde, lived with their mother, Emma Johnson, in a housing project in the Chelsea section of Manhattan. Goldberg notes that her father abandoned them early on and that her mother had to work a variety of jobs, including as a Head Start teacher and nurse, to take care of them. Goldberg claims that she is "half Jewish and half Catholic," according to Unterbrink, and that one day she received her name by divine revelation: "One day I saw this burning bush and it said, 'Your name is boring, but have I got a name for you!'" Of her invented name, Goldberg says:

> It was a joke. First it was Whoopi Cushion. Then it was French, like Whoopi Cushon. My mother said, "No-body's gonna respect you with a name like that." So I put Goldberg on it. Goldberg's a part of my family somewhere and that's all I can say about it.

Goldberg attended the parish school of Saint Columbian Church on West Twenty-fifth Street, under the Congregation of Notre Dame. She demonstrated a propensity for performing at age eight, when she started acting at the Helena Rubenstein Children's Theatre at the Hudson Guild, having been influenced early by watching Gracie Allen, Carole Lombard, Claudette Colbert, and other established actresses in old movies on television. By age seventeen she had dropped out of high school, convinced that she was unable to grasp subject matter but unaware that she had dyslexia, which interfered with her performance. In the 1960s she hung out with hippies, but later she asked herself if she was going to keep on doing drugs and kill herself or figure out what to do with her life. She decided on the latter: "I didn't stop altogether at once. It took many, many tries. . . . You fall a lot because it's hard," she told Laura B. Randolph.

Goldberg became involved in "hippie politics" and was active in civil rights marches and student protests at Columbia University. She also worked as a counselor at a summer camp on Ethical Culture held in Peekskill, New York. But she soon found her true calling. She had been born a mimic "with a natural, flawless eye and ear for details of character," and her career was set to blossom when she found work on

Broadway in the choruses of *Hair, Jesus Christ Superstar,* and *Pippin.* From a brief marriage to her drug counselor during her drug rehabilitation period in the 1970s, she had one daughter, Alexandrea Martin.

Goldberg moved to the West Coast in 1974 to start over with her daughter and her childhood ambition to act—something she felt confident she could do. Before becoming a star, she held a series of jobs that were somewhat less glamorous than acting, such as styling hair at a mortuary and laying bricks. She was also a licensed beautician and a bank teller. She spent some time on relief—an experience she found disconcerting. "The welfare workers used to make these surprise visits because you weren't allowed to have friends," particularly if you gave them food, she recalled to Randolph. If the welfare worker saw "a friend in the house with a plate of food in front of them, it would be deducted from your money the next month. . . . Getting off welfare, like getting off drugs, was a sweet triumph."

Frustrated by the dearth of work for black character actors in the straight theater, Goldberg began to create her own varied repertoire and collection of offbeat social types whom she presented as believable individuals. "Although her antic monologues contain elements of improvisational standup comedy," relates *Current Biography,* "the pseudonymous Miss Goldberg is essentially a character actress [or actor, as she sometimes insists] whose original routines are really seriocomic plays, written in her head." She also performed in more conventional theatrical pieces, such as her 1986 role in the one-woman show *Moms,* in which she played the late comedienne Moms Mabley. Goldberg wrote the play with Ellen Sebastian and won a Bay Area Theatre Award for her performance.

Goldberg's popularity grew as she moved from the theater to film, making her debut as Celie, a victim of spouse abuse in *The Color Purple.* Steven Spielberg's choice to cast Goldberg in a lead role made her an unforgettable face and an instant movie star. For her performance in the film she won a Golden Globe Award, the NAACP Image Award, and an Academy Award nomination.

Goldberg moves •

from theater to

film and

television

Following *The Color Purple,* Goldberg continued her work as a comedienne, and in 1985 she won a Grammy Award for best comedy album. She wasn't quite as successful with her film career at the time, appearing in a number of movies that were not big hits, including *Jumpin' Jack Flash, Burglar, Fatal Beauty, The Telephone, Homer and Eddie, Clara's Heart,* and *Beverly Hills Brats.* Then, in 1990, with her acting career in a lull, Goldberg appeared in the hugely successful film *Ghost.* That film catapulted her career to a new level and earned Goldberg her first Academy Award (as best supporting actress). In

October of 1990, Goldberg was named winner of the Excellence Award of the sixth annual Women in Film Festival. And when the NAACP held its twenty-third annual Image Awards program in December 1990, she was named Black Entertainer of the Year.

Following *Ghost,* Goldberg solidified her prominence as an actress with roles in several well-received films, including *The Long Walk Home, Soap Dish, The Player,* and *Sister Act,* a surprise hit in the summer of 1992.

Not limited to the theater and film, Goldberg has also worked on television. She joined Jean Stapleton in 1990 on the short-lived situation comedy, "Bagdad Cafe," in which she played the hot-headed, softhearted cafe owner. She has also appeared on an irregular basis as a member of the crew of the starship *Enterprise* in "Star Trek: The Next Generation," and she was nominated for an Emmy for a guest appearance on *Moonlighting.* Goldberg, who sounds off on sex, drugs, race, and various other topics, has become one of the most sought-after black actresses. Basking in stardom and notoriety, Goldberg does not want to follow a traditional path for her career or to be labeled a black actress. As she said in *Newsweek,* "People have small minds. . . . I think of myself as an actor. I've said before, I can play a man—or a dog or a chair."

Life in the limelight has not always been kind to Goldberg. Despite her acclaimed performance in *The Color Purple,* for instance, some in the black community criticized her language and appearance in the role of Celie. In addition, she has been criticized for her romances with whites, such as her marriage to the Dutch cameraman David Claessen, whom she married in 1986 but divorced less than two years later.

Known for her "do-do braids," as she calls the locks of hair that she wears, Goldberg, whose main purpose for entertaining is to make people laugh, is a highly gifted performer who clearly achieves her purpose on stage. Short in stature and mild-mannered in appearance, she has been described as having "the face and personality of a wise child—with ingenuous eyes and a puckish smile." She admits, however, that she is temperamental—"cranky as I wanna be," as she said herself. A grandmother by the age of thirty-five, Goldberg is glad that her unmarried teenaged daughter made her own decision to have a baby. "This baby was a choice and not a forced issue," she explained in *Ebony.* Goldberg's triumph over dyslexia, drugs, welfare, and divorce is an example of the strength of her own determination and her will to succeed and excel—the mark of a survivor.

Profile by Simmona E. Simmons

ANGELINA WELD GRIMKÉ

*A*ngelina Weld Grimké has received little more than a passing

1880-1958 •

glance from literary scholars. Like most black female writers of the early

twentieth century, she and her works have had very little visibility

poet •

compared with her more highly acclaimed male contemporaries. None-

theless, Grimké is a notable writer whose works include two dramas,

several short stories, a few articles, and a great number of poems. Of

these, her poems represent her best creative energies, even though they

were primarily written as outlets for the pathos of her own being rather

than for publication.

Being born into the distinguished biracial Grimké family gave Angelina Grimké a place of prominence in Bostonian society. The daughter of Archibald Grimké and Sarah (Stanley) Grimké, she had both abolitionists and slaveowners in her father's immediate family.

Born February 27, 1880, Angelina was named after a beloved aunt, a white Quaker who openly acknowledged Archibald (who was biracial) as her nephew.

It is known that Sarah's family (they were white) opposed her biracial marriage, and it is generally believed that their influence caused her to leave Archibald in 1883 and return to their home. She kept Angelina until 1887, at which time she returned her seven-year-old daughter to her father. Though they corresponded often, Sarah Grimké never saw Angelina again.

Despite the fact that her mother had abandoned her, as a child Grimké was surrounded by love and comfort. She loved her father intensely and sought always to please him. Being light-skinned and living in a congenial environment, she was sheltered from the poor living conditions and racial prejudice that most blacks experienced in the years following Reconstruction. However, by the time she wrote the drama *Rachel,* produced in 1916, and a short story, "The Closing Door," published in 1919, she had become acutely aware of the racial problems, and her anger and sense of helplessness are evident in the dialogue of her characters.

Grimké attended several upper-class schools, liberal both educationally and politically, including Carlton Academy in Northfield, Minnesota, and Cushing Academy in Ashburnham, Massachusetts. Many times Grimké was the only black student in her classes. In 1902, she graduated from the Boston Normal School of Gymnastics and began teaching English in Washington, D.C., first at Armstrong Manual Training School and then at Dunbar High School. Her summers from 1906 to 1910 were spent as a student at Harvard. During the years in Washington, she produced most of her better-known writings. She retired from teaching June 30, 1926, because of ill health stemming from a back injury sustained in a railway accident in July, 1911.

In the face of all the seeming advantages of Grimké's life, the sad tone of her work suggests that deep unhappiness and frustration were always present within her. In many poems and in her diaries, she expresses the inner turmoil that her lesbianism created. Unfulfilled desire and thwarted longings are themes in much of her work. A note written to Mamie Burrill in 1896 seems to bear out the fact that she did have an adolescent relationship with her, for in it Grimké says: "Oh Mamie if you only knew how my heart beats when I think of you and yearns and pants to gaze, if only for one second upon your lovely face." In this same letter she asks Mamie to be her "wife" and ends it with: "Now may the Almighty Father bless thee little one and keep thee safe from all harm, Your passionate lover." After this relationship ended, it is

Sadness

pervades

emotional life

219 •

not known if Grimké had others. It appears, rather, that as she matured she suppressed these desires and alluded to them only in her poetry.

Grimké was small, weighing only ninety-two pounds in 1899 and one hundred pounds in 1912, after she was a mature woman. Her demeanor was solemn and demure, with a wistful sadness that was characteristic of her both as a child and as an adult. She had many acquaintances, but her father was seemingly the one person she considered to be her true friend. The following diary excerpt, written in 1912, emphasizes this:

> My father . . . is so much a part of me he is so all and all
> so absolutely necessary that I am taking him I find as a
> matter of course. This is wrong. I wonder, though,
> whether when some people are as one there may not
> be some little excuse. This I know now and I have
> always known it and felt. I have no desire absolutely
> for life without him.

Her father's final illness from 1928 until his death in 1930 was a decisive turning point in her life, during which she grew increasingly irritable and isolated. After her father died, Grimké moved to New York, supposedly for her writing, but she produced nothing. She spent the last years of her life almost a recluse in her New York City apartment. Her obituary in the *New York Times* on June 11, 1958, begins: "Miss Angelina Weld Grimké, poet and retired school teacher, died yesterday at her home, 208 West 151st Street, after a long illness. She was 78 years old."

Though Grimké had been writing since her childhood, only a few of her works were published during her lifetime, a few short stories, her play *Rachel,* some nonfiction efforts, and a few of her poems and lyrics that appeared in newspapers, journals, and anthologies.

In Grimké's works the external forms are focused and orderly, while the internal meanings present themselves to the reader as distorted reflections evoking questions whose answers lead directly back to both her sad personal life and to the following explanation of her own creative process:

> I think most [poems] that I do are the reflections of
> moods. These appear to me in clearly defined forms
> and colors—remembered from what I have seen, felt.
> The mood is the spiritual atmosphere. Symbolic also. I
> love colors and contrasts. Suggestion. Whatever I have
> done it seems to me is a reflection of some mood which
> gives the spiritual atmosphere and significance. The

• Grimké

publishes

poetry, stories,

and plays

mood has a physical counterpart in Nature in colors concrete imagery brought out by contrasts. Often to me the whole thing is not only a mood but symbolic as well. The more vivid the picture the more vivid the vibrations in the mind of the reader or listener. Each work has its different wavelength, vibration. Colors, trees flowers skies meadows. The more concrete, definite vivid the picture the more vivid the vibration of word in the reader or listener. And what is word? May it not be a sort of singing in the harp strings of the mind? Then on the principle of sympathetic vibration is there not in nature a harp singing also to be found.

Her definition of poetry is comparable to those of Coleridge and Wordsworth. Most of Grimké's poems bear greater similarities to those of the romantic and Victorian poets than to those of her contemporaries, insofar as her themes are more personal and traditional.

Much of Grimké's poetry portrays unconsummated, unrequited love. It is filled with isolation, hopeless longing, and rejection. Its tone is hushed and quiet with a subtle touch of delicate, mysterious fog covering the intensity of her double-edged images. Her greatest poetic tool is the juxtaposition of opposite images with such textual tension that they become parts of each other. The tensile strength thus created produces a force greater than either can ever have separately. In many of her poems the beauty of nature, both in its dying and rebirth, becomes an integral matrix into which her subjects are placed or from which they are drawn. Death is often depicted as the only means of satisfaction and completion to Grimké's lesbian desires. In "A Mona Lisa" the speaker would like "to creep / Through the long brown grasses / That are your lashes . . . [and] poise / On the very brink / Of the leaf-brown pools / That are your shadowed eyes . . . [and] cleave / Without sound, / Their glimmering waters . . . [and] sink down / And down . . . / And deeply drown."

Her most radical work, in terms of her deep belief that black women should not bring children into this tormenting world, is "The Closing Door." In this short story a pregnant black woman hears of her brother's lynching, and the fear that her baby will be a male bears constantly on her mind. After her baby son is born, she goes totally insane and kills the child, thus saving him from the possible fate of all black men—and anticipating a prominent theme of Toni Morrison.

Radical work •

anticipates

Toni Morrison

Grimké's best-known work is *Rachel*, a three-act drama that was staged in 1916 and 1917 and published in 1920. This work shows how prejudice in America demeans and almost destroys a very respectable black family. The play program for the Washington, D.C., premier performance advertised: "This is the first attempt to use the stage for race propaganda in order to enlighten the American people relative to the lamentable condition of ten million of colored citizens in this free Republic."

As a drama, *Rachel* presents the social problem of racism and shows the emotional effects of the problem but offers no satisfactory solutions. The setting for all three acts is a tenement apartment in a "northern city" between the years 1900 and 1910, and the focus is on Mrs. Loving, a widowed seamstress, and her children, all of whom are well educated but cannot find promising employment. In the course of the play the children learn how their father had died years before—he was killed by a lynch mob of so-called Christians—and Mrs. Loving's daughter Rachel vows never to bring children into such a terrible world.

Today's theater audience might find the painful futility and sentimentality of the play tedious. One son, Tom, becomes angry over the situation but his anger serves no purpose. Another, John, tries to look at the circumstances with some objectivity, but in truth he cannot envision anything better for himself than his life as a headwaiter. Rachel, who is unable and unwilling to confront life and the prejudices it holds, withdraws into isolation. It was a generation later that leaders came forward to confront these issues and seek solutions to them.

Grimké's second and last drama, *Mara*, has four acts, and its theme is also racial prejudice. A much-beloved only child, Mara, the daughter of retired black physician Dr. Marston is raped by a white man. Insanity, murder, and lynching are the sad results in this drama. As an epigraph, Grimké uses the Biblical text from Ruth 1: 20, "Call me Mara for the Almighty hath dealt bitterly with me." Grimké has definitely matured as a writer in this drama. Her characters have more variety in their personalities, and the conversations between them are more engaging than those in *Rachel*. The plot, while having the same theme, does not contain superficial sentimentality, and the scenes fall into a more natural, rhythmic pattern without long lapses. Though *Mara* is definitely better than *Rachel*, there exists no record that Grimké ever attempted to have it published.

Though she lived during a time when black writers were beginning to claim attention in the literary world, black female writers were not published often, nor were they usually given the attention that their male counterparts received. The main criticism of most of her works is that almost all of them contain the same sad themes of unfulfilled longings and deep inner frustration. However, this must be considered through the pathos of her life and social circumstances. Her family's prominent social position did not allow her the freedom to act on many of her deepest feelings, particularly to live openly as a lesbian. This unfulfilled desire drained her emotional well of creativity, and finally dried it up completely. What Grimké's success might have been had she lived later than June 10, 1958, can only be speculation. In her own life she rarely felt the rhythmic enchanting vibrations or heard the mystic sympathetic tones of nature's aeolian harp. Yet through her beautiful, imagistic works she allows readers to become active participants in its ethereal performance.

**Profile by
Phyllis Wood**

LUCILLE C. GUNNING

A specialist in treating chronic illnesses in children—particularly

1922- •

mental retardation and other handicapping conditions—Lucille C.

Gunning has aspired to establish in the Harlem community a pediatric

pediatrician •

hospital with a rehabilitation service. She contends that disabled child-

ren should be with other children and not with disabled adults, as their

emotional and psychological needs are different from those of adults.

Commenting on her achievements and goals, Gunning believes she

benefitted from the time when "teachers took you by the hand and

molded you into the kind of doctor they wanted you to be" and feels that

although she has grown in the profession, she never lost the lessons

taught by her role model teachers.

225 •

Gunning was born in New York City on February 21, 1922, the oldest of two children born to Roland and Susan Gunning. Her parents met in Jamaica, West Indies, where her father was a practicing pharmacist and her mother was a teacher. Seeking better opportunities, they came to New York City in the early 1920s. Unable to secure a position as a druggist, her father worked as a druggist's assistant. He supplemented his income by becoming the superintendent of the building where they were living in Harlem, while her mother taught school.

When Gunning was about thirteen months old, because of her poor health, she was taken to live with her paternal grandmother in Jamaica. When she was approximately five years old, her paternal aunt, a midwife of considerable repute in their community, took Gunning with her on a late-night delivery. Gunning waited as her aunt ministered to the patient, and heard considerable commotion and activity. She learned later that the baby died. What registered with her then was that, as the crying and screaming proceeded, a doctor with a black bag arrived, driving his horse-drawn carriage. Gunning sensed that in everyone's mind was a given: had the doctor arrived earlier, the baby would not have died. The scene remains vivid in her memory. She realized later that sometimes there is nothing anyone can do, but she did not know that at the time. Gunning didn't discuss the incident, but her determination to become a doctor was firmly established in her mind.

Her parents worked tenaciously so her father could realize his dream of becoming a doctor. Although older than most applicants, he gained admission to medical school in Edinburgh, Scotland. Upon completing his studies he returned to New York with the intention of taking the family to Jamaica. He did begin his practice in New York City, but he didn't return to Jamaica, remaining instead in New York until his death.

Gunning completed high school in Jamaica and would have gone to college in England, but because of the war she came to live with her parents in New York City. She told her family she wanted to study medicine, but her father and grandmother felt she should pursue nursing or teaching. Her mother was very supportive of her choice, though, and when her father realized that Gunning was determined, he too gave her his complete support.

Gunning wanted to study premedicine at Barnard College in New York City and to attend Columbia University College of Physicians and Surgeons. But in her interview she was told that she could study nursing or teaching but not premedicine, so she studied at New York University, graduated with a bachelor's degree in 1945, and went on to Woman's Medical College of Pennsylvania, graduating with a master's degree in

1949. She served as chief resident in the department of pediatrics at Harlem Hospital from 1951 to 1952. The following year she was pediatric chief resident at Woman's Medical College of Philadelphia Hospital, and from 1953 to 1954 she was a fellow in pediatric cardiology at Yale's Grace New Haven Hospital.

In 1954 Gunning opened her private practice in pediatrics from offices in the Bronx and in New Rochelle, New York. During these years she also served as a child health physician for the Department of Health in New York City in the divisions of infant and preschool and child guidance. She was visiting attending physician in the pediatric departments of various hospitals, then in 1964 obtained a fellowship in medicine at the Albert Einstein College of Medicine at Montefiore Hospital and Medical Center in the Bronx. There, she established and directed the pediatric rehabilitation division from 1966 to 1971 and also assumed the job of chief of pediatric rehabilitation at the Harlem Hospital Center in New York Center in 1971.

While at Harlem Hospital, Gunning was an assistant professor in clinical rehabilitative medicine at Columbia University. This position gave her the opportunity to teach and discuss issues in pediatric rehabilitation. She was aware that this area of practice was not in the curriculum or a part of the rotating internship even of a pediatric residency. Despite hardships, frustrations, and resistance at all levels, within this traditionally acute-care hospital that was committed to acute-care delivery Gunning found many children with handicapping conditions. These children were the nucleus for the pediatric rehabilitation service. Getting her program started "was like breaking the ice, I was constantly on the defensive because this was a new field, it was not popular and had no prestige. Today it is an ever-expanding field."

At Harlem Hospital, Gunning gained experience working with Downs Syndrome children. She established a developmental center which gave parents a place to play with their children while the parents and Gunning observed the children's development. Gunning found that parents practiced the training techniques that they saw in an attempt to make their children as self-sufficient as possible. This reinforced her belief that the parents had to be significantly involved in the treatment of the child and needed support in their efforts. Gunning feels that throughout her professional career parents and their children have been her most valuable mentors, teaching her even more than her many studies.

Gunning served as field-work supervisor for the Sophie Davis School of Biomedical Education of the City College, City University of New York, from 1976 to 1979. This program provides for minority

Gunning

establishes

developmental

center

students' admission into any New York State medical school upon successful completion of the premedical college courses. Gunning is also one of the founders of the Susan Smith McKinney-Steward Medical Society of New York City, an organization of black American women physicians who, in addition to other activities, provide counseling and mentoring to minority female students who have chosen medicine as a career. Her association with the Sophie Davis program and the Susan Smith medical society enabled Gunning to be of great value to aspiring medical students involved in both programs.

Gunning has published numerous articles on the subjects of childhood disabilities, pediatric rehabilitation, physical medicine and rehabilitation, child abuse, growth and development of the child with sickle-cell anemia, and mental retardation. In her work with disabled children, she has suggested that the person who cares for the chronically ill child should work with the psychologist or psychiatrist and take a much more active role in the habilitation of the child. "If the child is retarded we should review the whole issue of 'retardation' as well as the issue of retardation of the black child; rather than dealing with the intellectual impairment, deal with their asset profile and see what they are good at." While they may not be good in reading, writing, and mathematics initially, she has found the children to be extremely good at body mechanics, the arts, and music. However, she found it very difficult to secure funds to develop programs that could enhance these children's chances. In spite of these difficulties, through her developmental center Gunning was able to establish the first mothers' support group. Such groups have continued to function in the pediatrics department.

• Chronically ill

children need

their families

While she was at Harlem Hospital, Gunning also envisioned establishing an extended-care facility for children with chronic illnesses in the Harlem community, similar to Blythedale in Westchester. She believes that when chronically ill children are sent away from the community and the family is unable to visit the child, they become alienated from each other and from the community. As a result any gains from being at the facility (she does not want to call it a hospital) tend to be lost when the child goes home. This extended-care facility in the Harlem community would be the children's equivalent of a nursing home.

In 1981, Gunning resigned from Harlem Hospital to become the director of physical medicine and rehabilitation in the Children's Medical Center in Dayton, Ohio, where she developed a program which incorporated her ideas of children with disabilities being with other children in the hospital, and being cared for in a collaborative effort by members of the various disciplines. Within her two-year contract Gunning developed a multidimensional pediatric rehabilitation service that was active, completely comprehensive, and professionally and personally validating and rewarding.

Although her stay in Dayton was for only two years, she had realized her dream and was able to demonstrate that with the money and, above all, the commitment on the part of the hospital, her ideas could work.

At present, Gunning is the deputy director of medical services for the New York State Office of Mental Retardation and Developmental Disabilities in Tarrytown, New York. Her responsibility is to insure the best care of developmentally disabled persons in various residences in which the state has placed them—in communal homes rather than in institutions. Her commitment is "to the art of medicine; you must go that extra step to provide quality care for the patient."

Gunning married in 1953 on completion of her pediatric residency. Her husband, Carlton E. Blackwood, also a native Jamaican, attended New York University where he received a Ph.D. in chemistry. He was a biochemical researcher at Columbia University, then a staff member in the department of chemistry at New York's Iona College. He died in 1974. He and Gunning had four children: Elaine Blackwood, J.D., M.B.A.; Alexander Blackwood, M.D. and Ph.D., pediatrician; Lydia Blackwood, Ph.D., clinical pediatric psychologist; and Ann Blackwood, M.D., in residency at Montefiore Hospital and Medical Center and research at Columbia Medical College of Physicians and Surgeons in New York City.

**Profile by
Juanita R. Howard**

CLARA HALE

*F*or fifty years Clara McBride Hale, known as "Mother Hale," has

been the guardian of young children abandoned or born to addicted

mothers since 1932, when her husband died and she began to care for

other people's children to earn extra money. Since then Hale House,

located on 122nd Street in Harlem, has welcomed more than eight

hundred babies.

1905- •

humanitarian, •

institution

founder

Hale, the youngest of four children, was born on April 1, 1905, in Philadelphia, Pennsylvania. Her father died when she was an infant, so her mother assumed the economic responsibility of rearing four children by providing board and meals to lodgers. After Clara completed high school she married Thomas Halem, and they moved to New York City where he opened a floor-waxing business. Since the income from the business was insufficient to cover all the expenses, Hale obtained employment as a domestic worker—cleaning theaters. Her husband died of cancer when Hale was twenty-seven, and she was left alone to rear three small children: Lorraine, Nathan, and Kenneth. She doubled her domestic duties and cleaned homes during the day and theaters at night, but she was not satisfied with this arrangement, for it meant leaving her children without adult supervision. Subsequently, she began to care for other people's children during the day. Of her child-care role, Hale told Tom Seligson:

> The parents paid me. I didn't make a whole lot, but I wasn't starving. And the kids must've liked it because once they got there, they didn't want to go home. So what started as day care ended up being fulltime. The parents would see the children on weekends.

Hale reared forty foster children until she retired in 1968. Initially, she began to care for children who were wards of the city, receiving two dollars a week per child. All of her foster children, black and white, pursued a college education.

In 1969, after Hale retired from foster care, Hale's daughter, Lorraine, encountered a young woman who was a heroin addict nodding off in a Harlem park. A two-month-old baby girl was falling from her arms. Lorraine gave the young woman her mother's address as a place to go for help.

• Home for

drug-addicted

babies opened

The young woman took her child to Hale, and thereafter news spread that Hale's home was open to addicted babies. For a year and a half, Hale's three children provided the initial financial support for the addicted babies. In 1970 Percy Sutton, president of the Borough of New York City, began funding the project. Hale House assumed its present location at 154 West 122nd Street in 1975. The vacant five-story brownstone was rebuilt and has a floor for play and preschool activities, a nursery for detoxified babies, and a third floor where Hale keeps new arrivals during the withdrawal period.

The main objective of Hale House is to take drug-dependent children at birth, rear them until their mothers complete a drug treatment program, and reunite the mother and child when treatment ends. Hale observes that during withdrawal the children suffer from stiff legs and backs, diarrhea, and vomiting. They also scratch themselves and cry constantly. Hale's cure is based on the healing power of love and positive reinforcement. Each day by 6 a.m. Mother Hale is up and giving bottles to several drug-addicted infants. She cleans and feeds the babies, and when they cry from the pains of withdrawal, she walks the floor with them and talks to them, but she gives them no medicine, not even aspirin. Hale told Herschel Johnson:

> The children here know that someone loves them and they're happy. I make sure that they're always clean and well fed and comfortable. I tell them how pretty they are and what they can accomplish if they get an

education. And I tell them to be proud of their Blackness, to be proud of one another, and to pull together.

Her philosophy has a major positive effect: Hale House has been home
to eight hundred unwanted babies since 1969. The house receives
referrals from the police, clergy, hospitals, and social workers. Children
are admitted, regardless of ethnicity, religion, or gender, ranging in age
from ten days to four years.

Hale believes that color is not a factor in achieving one's goal. Brian
Lanker records her contention that:

> Being black does not stop you. You can sit out in the
> world and say, "Well, white people kept me back, and I
> can't do this." Not so. You can have anything you want
> if you make up your mind and you want it. You don't
> have to crack nobody across the head, don't have to
> steal or anything.

Hale's appearance is undoubtedly reassuring to her "children."
She is short and slight and looks younger than her years. She has thin
white hair, few facial wrinkles, and bright eyes, and her voice is warm
and confident.

For Hale's unselfish commitment to babies who are born addicts,
former President Ronald Reagan identified her as a "true American
hero" during his State of the Union Address before Congress on February
6, 1985. Hale was awarded an honorary Doctorate of Humane Letters
degree by John Jay College of Criminal Justice in June 1985. She received
the Salvation Army's highest award, the Booth Community Service
Award, on December 5, 1990. Hale's response to this public adulation
was that she does not feel like a hero; rather, she is involved in her life's
work and likes it. She contends that everyone has a role to assume in the
world, and hers has been to love and care for children.

Hale House •

helps 800

babies

**Profile by
Mary R. Holley**

FANNIE LOU HAMER

*T*he spirited civil rights activist Fannie Lou Townsend Hamer was

born on October 6, 1917, in Montgomery County, Mississippi, the

twentieth child born to sharecropper parents. Hamer was deprived of

many of the conveniences and benefits common to twentieth-century

America, and when her father was finally able to work the family out of

abject poverty, an envious white neighbor poisoned the Townsend mules

and cows, destroying the family's prospects.

1917-1977 •

civil rights •

activist

For black sharecroppers, education was secondary to the needs of the plantation. Because of this, Hamer had only six years of school, for at that time the school period extended from December to March, the four months corresponding to the time black labor was not needed in the fields. Still, because of the lack of adequate clothing during the cold months, only about one month of schooling was possible.

In 1942 she married Perry "Pap" Hamer, a tractor driver from another plantation. Because they were unable to have children, they adopted two girls, one of whom died in 1967. Inheriting the impoverished tradition of her sharecropper family, she and her husband continued in the cycle of poverty. But Hamer was a hard worker, and eventually she was promoted from strenuous cotton-picking to the less strenuous but still low-paying job of timekeeper on the plantation.

• *Civil rights*

activities

attract Hamer

Because black life was considered cheap, blacks suffered many abuses. Hamer's life was a reflection of that continued abuse, pain, and suffering. L. C. Dorsey in the *Jackson Advocate* describes other dimensions of her suffering: "Mrs. Hamer knew about another kind of pain; the pain [of] watching your offspring die from poverty, related illnesses, and of suffering because of a handicap that had she not been poor, could have been corrected." Her life took a turn in 1962 when she met workers of the Southern Christian Leadership Conference and the Student Nonviolent Coordinating Committee, who began mobilizing people to fight for freedom in Mississippi. As a result of this empowering encounter, Hamer became active in politics in Mississippi, especially in Ruleville. It all began at a rally led by the Reverend James Bevel of the SCLC and James Forman of SNCC held in August 1962. Forman spoke specifically about voter registration, challenging the people to action to effect change in their political leadership as a route to positive changes in their living conditions.

When the call came for volunteers to challenge the unjust voting laws, Hamer was among the recruits; she failed her first two attempts to register but passed her third. She subsequently taught other blacks how to register and pass the literacy test.

Life as a registered voter was not easy, for it became difficult for the Hamer family to get and maintain employment. Hamer then became a field worker in the civil rights movement. Following a civil rights workshop in Charleston, South Carolina, on their return trip to Ruleville on a Trailways bus, Hamer and a group of nineteen stopped at a bus terminal in Winona, Mississippi, to get something to eat. Challenging the "white only" practice, they were attacked by state troopers, arrested, and charged with disorderly conduct. In that Winona jail, Hamer suffered one of the worst beatings of her life. She was taken to a cell with two black male prisoners who were given a black leather clutch loaded with metal and ordered to beat her or suffer severe consequences for refusing to follow the demands of the white prison guards. Hamer was later returned to her jail cell, where she and the other civil rights workers were released following the intervention of James Bevel and Andrew Young. The incident left Hamer permanently injured.

Hamer came out of this experience more determined to change the unjust, oppressive, and racist system in Mississippi. In the spring of 1964 the Mississippi Freedom Democratic Party was established after unsuccessful attempts to gain participation in the Mississippi Democratic party. Hamer's work catapulted her to the position of vice-chairperson of the Mississippi Freedom Democratic Party, under which she campaigned for Congress from the Second Congressional District of Mississippi. Even more importantly, it was as a leader of the MFDP that she gained national attention when the group challenged the white Mississippi delegation to the 1964 National Democratic Convention in Atlantic City. The challenge resulted in the nation hearing her story as she testified before the credentials committee. Her story included atrocities such as her loss of employment because of her attempts to register to vote; the beatings such as the Winona, Mississippi, incident; her arrest with a busload of citizens trying to register; and the many other brutalities perpetrated against blacks by whites.

Hamer gains •

national

attention

The MFDP delegation did not obtain what it wanted; instead, a so-called compromise was made. The compromise in effect gave two seats to the sixty-eight-member delegation. Some saw this as a moral victory. Hamer, along with other MFDP delegates, took exception to this interpretation of the compromise and reportedly said, "We didn't come all this way for no two seats when all of us is tired."

As Hamer's horizons broadened and her involvement deepened, she became global in her interests and was able to see the injustices of the Vietnam War, becoming one of its early critics. Of that war she said, "We are sick and tired of our people having to go to Vietnam and other places to fight for something we don't have here." Consequently, she was able to draw a critical connection between war, racism, and poverty: "We want . . . to end the wrongs such as fighting a war in Vietnam and pouring billions over there, while people in Sunflower County, Mississippi and Harlem and Detroit are starving to death."

Hamer's life was not just about destroying racist and oppressive structures; she also was involved in much community building. She helped to bring to Ruleville the Head Start Program, the most successful of the War on Poverty efforts. In actuality, because she felt that the War on Poverty programs were actually war on the poor—keeping them dependent—she concentrated on building alternative structures that would promote self-reliance. For workers displaced by mechanization, she organized the Freedom Farm Cooperative; two-hundred units of low-income housing were built in Ruleville because of Hamer's fundraising ability. She helped in starting a low-income day care center, and she was involved in bringing to Ruleville a garment factory that provided jobs.

Hamer's motivation was her deep-seated religious conviction. She spoke often of her Christian faith, which undergirded her commitment to the struggle for human dignity for black people. She constantly challenged those who professed to be Christian in their actions, saying: "We serve God by serving our fellow [human beings]; kids are suffering from malnutrition. People are going to the fields hungry. If you are a Christian, we are tired of being mistreated."

Hamer's views on a variety of social issues are detailed in her speeches and interviews. She had a special interest in feeding, clothing, and housing the poor. In 1969 she founded Freedom Farm in Sunflower County, Mississippi, and fed fifteen hundred people with the food that was grown. She became involved with the Young World Developers, an organization that built homes for the poor, including impoverished whites. She had an interest in education, and when Shaw University asked her to teach a course in black contemporary history, she agreed. When her class met, "sometimes parents would be there. Sometimes teachers would be there. It was a great experience for me," she said.

Hamer addressed the role and responsibility of black women: "To support whatever is right, and to bring in justice where we've had so much injustice." The special plight and role of the black woman had existed for 350 years, she noted, and she had seen it in her grandmother, a former slave who was 136 years old when she died in 1960. In reference to middle-class black women who a few years earlier had failed to respect the work that she did, Hamer made a statement that was to become widely known and used frequently in other lectures:

> Whether you have a Ph.D., or no D, we're in this bag together. And whether you're from Morehouse or Nohouse, we're still in this bag together. Not to fight to try to liberate ourselves from the men—this is another trick to get us fighting among ourselves—but to work together with the black man, then we will have a better chance to just act as human beings, and to be treated as human beings in our sick society.

For her devotion to the full cause of the civil rights movement and the uplift of black people, many colleges and universities awarded Hamer honorary doctoral degrees. These include Shaw University, Tougaloo College, Columbia College in Chicago, Howard University, and Morehouse College. Though her life had been endangered and threatened many times over, her death actually came on March 15, 1977, from diabetes, heart trouble, and breast cancer.

Hamer was not just a woman of words but a woman of deeds. In fact, it was her struggle against poverty that was the real war on poverty. She dedicated her life not only to challenging unjust political, social, and economic structures but to creating conditions that facilitated the development of self-reliance and self-determination among blacks and other poor people of the world. L. C. Dorsey's "Action Memorial" to Hamer not only makes this clear, but makes equally clear the challenge that Hamer left to us:

> A proper memorial would be one in which all of us
> who loved her would dedicate and rededicate our lives
> to serving others and helping all of us achieve a greater
> measure of freedom, justice and love.

In Hamer's memory, Dorsey's plan called for the organization of registration drives, voter education programs, and campaigns against hunger, executions, police brutality, ignorance, poverty, and oppression. Addressing these issues will keep Fannie Lou Hamer's life and contributions to humanity at the forefront.

**Profile by
Jacquelyn Grant**

VIRGINIA HAMILTON

*T*hose who write for young people are often relegated to a type of

literary ghetto, because writing for children has been marginalized.

Often, the writers are perceived as vague, sexless persons who exist in

life's shadow, rarely participating with any zest. Virginia Esther Hamil-

ton defies these characterizations. She is not a marginalized author

lurking in a literary inner-city. Critics have had to place Hamilton

within the mainstream of literature because her inventive use of lan-

guage, her complex weaving of theme, character, and form, and her use

of various mythologies have raised children's literature to new heights of

excellence.

1936- •

writer •

At her best, Hamilton is a *griot*, a word sorcerer whose power is
evident in her written texts and her oral presentations. Her storytelling

voice, undoubtedly, was acquired within the loving confines of her childhood home in Yellow Springs, Ohio, an area rich in mystery and history because of its role in the Underground Railroad. Here, Hamilton acquired a sense of "the known, the remembered, and the imagined," words she uses as the title of a 1987 article in *Children's Literature in Education*.

Hamilton was born March 12, 1936, the fifth and youngest child of Kenneth James Hamilton, a college graduate and musician, and Etta Belle (Perry) Hamilton, a homemaker. Living up to family expectations, Hamilton performed well in the small country school she attended although she lamented its limited curriculum. After graduating from high school, Hamilton received a five-year scholarship to attend college. She enrolled in Antioch College, a school noted for its academic and liberal reputation, and later attended Ohio State University and the New School for Social Research.

Hamilton lived in New York for fifteen years. While there, she worked in a number of occupations ranging from bookkeeper to singer. Her plan was "to find a cheap apartment, a part-time job, write, and have a good time. And it all came together," she wrote in *Something about the Author*. She lived in a community in the East Village among musicians, writers, and artists, a sort of modern-day Bohemia. During this period Hamilton met a kindred spirit, Arnold Adoff, a Jewish teacher, poet, graduate student, and manager of jazz musicians. They married on March 16, 1960. Adoff, too, has received critical praise for his poetry and a National Council of Teachers of English poetry award. In addition to his literary work, he serves as Hamilton's manager. Virginia and Arnold Adoff are the parents of a daughter, Leigh Adoff, and a son, Jamie Adoff. Hamilton currently resides in Ohio.

As many women writers are required to do, Hamilton combined familial and career responsibilities. While living in New York, she wrote constantly, sending manuscripts to magazines such as the *New Yorker*, and in 1967 her first book, *Zeely*, was published. *Zeely* is the story of a sensitive, intelligent, and inquisitive girl named Elizabeth (who renames herself Geeder) who, along with her brother, goes to visit an uncle who lives on a farm. While rummaging in her uncle's attic, Elizabeth discovers some old magazines, one of which contains pictures of African people that enthrall her. Later, Elizabeth spies a gorgeous six-foot-tall African-American woman, Zeely, who bears an eerie resemblance to one of the women pictured in the magazine. Elizabeth is immediately attracted to Zeely and plots different ways of meeting her.

Zeely is important because of its literary quality and its depiction of a "normal" black American family whose members were not beaten down by poverty and hopelessness and because of its authentic cultural images. *Zeely* garnered the Nancy Block Memorial Award from the Downtown (New York) Community School Awards Committee (1967), which was the beginning of a continuous stream of awards.

Hamilton has written twenty-six books, including two biographies, six collections of folktales, and numerous works of fiction ranging from science fiction/fantasy to historical fiction. Most of these have won multiple awards ranging from the Coretta Scott King Award for *Sweet Whispers, Brother Rush*, to the Edgar Allan Poe Award for *The House of Dies Drear*, to the Newbery Medal for *M. C. Higgins, the Great*. Few authors have won as many awards for literary excellence as has Hamilton; no author has won the Newbery Medal, the Boston-Globe Hornbook Award, the Lewis Carrol Shelf Award, the National Book Award, and the International Board on Books for Young People Award for a single book. Hamilton achieved this distinction with the publication of *M. C. Higgins, the Great*.

That novel chronicles the quests of Mayo Cornelius Higgins as he attempts to forge his identity as a young man, share a friendship with an outcast neighbor, experience a bittersweet first love, and save his family from a possible disaster. The story, set in the mountains of Ohio, symbolizes a host of realities: love, freedom, community, heritage, and danger. Hamilton's portrayal of M. C.'s family—his mother, Banina, his father, Jones, his sister, and brothers, is arguably the best and most complex portrayal of a black American family in children's literature.

Hamilton does not sidestep controversial topics in her books. Two of her recent books, *A Little Love* and *White Romance,* broach subjects such as teenage sex, heavy metal music, drugs, and psychically disturbed youngsters. However, Hamilton cannot be classified as a writer of "problem" novels. The problems in her novels are a part of a multi-textured narrative. Similarly, Hamilton occasionally defies conventions in content in her novels such as *Sweet Whispers, Brother Rush, The Planet of Junior Brown,* and *Anthony Burns.* For children's books, these novels contain complex stylistic features, such as stream-of-consciousness ruminations, multiple settings, and shifting time periods; combinations of differing genres; and major characters in psychic and emotional distress. These books have challenged critics, who sometimes state that Hamilton is writing for adults or is too sophisticated for even the most advanced child reader. Hamilton responds to those criticisms thus:

> These adults would keep the young at a safe and quasi-literate level, where their responses to life and the world remain predictable and manageable. The way I counteract such backwardness is by keeping fresh my

Hamilton •

writes in

many genres

awareness of young people's keen imaginations and by responding to their needs, fears, loves and hunger in as many new ways as possible.

Hamilton shares her knowledge with teachers, students, and writers as she makes presentations at conferences sponsored by the National Council of Teachers of English, the International Reading Association, and the Ohio State University Children's Literature Conference. In addition, she teaches occasionally at colleges and universities, most recently Queens College and Ohio State University.

Essentially, Hamilton has accomplished what she dreamed about as a child. She is a unique writer who has a valuable and valued gift that she shares in unexpected, delightful, and intellectually challenging ways. She remains the storyteller and has become the knowledge-giver:

> Through character, time, and place, I've attempted to portray the essence of a race, its essential community, culture, history and traditions, which I know well, and its relation to the larger American society. I endeavor to demonstrate the nexus the black group has with all other groups, nationalities and races, the connection the American black child has with all children and to present the best of my heritage.

**Profile by
Violet J. Harris**

She does so in a triumphant manner that ultimately leaves the reader not with a happily-ever-after ending, but rather with a hopeful ending.

LORRAINE HANSBERRY

*L*orraine Vivian Hansberry knew about making painful choices. She

lived a life of commitment, conviction, and conflict and deserves to be

recognized as a revolutionary, as a political activist, and as an intellec-

tual of uncompromising integrity. During her brief lifetime, she wrote

insightful dramas about the most controversial issues of her day, one of

them certain to be remembered and revived as a classic. She also left

numerous essays on such challenging topics as racism, homophobia,

black art and history, the Cuban missile crisis, and world peace. She was

one of the sharpest observers and most brilliant intellects, as well as one

of the most talented theater artists, of her time.

1930-1965 •

playwright, •

activist

Hansberry was born on Chicago's South Side, May 19, 1930, to Carl
A. and Nanny Perry Hansberry. The Hansberrys were a very prominent

family, not only in the black community of Chicago, but also in national black cultural and political circles. Hansberry was introduced to some of the most important black political and cultural figures of her time when she was still a little girl. She knew Paul Robeson, Duke Ellington, Walter White, Joe E. Louis, and Jesse Owens, who were visitors of her parents.

In 1948 Hansberry decided to attend the University of Wisconsin instead of Howard University, where her parents wanted her to go. But she grew increasingly dissatisfied with the curriculum at Wisconsin, feeling that most of her classes were irrelevant to her interests as a black intellectual, so she left in 1950 to pursue another kind of education in New York. She went to work as a reporter for Paul Robeson's radical black newspaper, *Freedom,* writing politically astute articles as well as book and drama reviews. She became an associate editor of the newspaper in 1952. That year she went to the International Peace Congress in Uruguay as Paul Robeson's representative because the State Department had denied him a passport.

Sometime during the 1950s Hansberry acknowledged her lesbianism, although this fact was never made public. Her awareness of feminist issues was ahead of her time, as well as her realization that homophobia, sexism, and racism were linked. She grasped the connections between the struggle for gay rights, rights for people of color, and rights for women long before such terms as *homophobia* and *feminism* had come into the vernacular.

Racism, sexism, •

homophobia

linked

Her marriage in 1953 to Robert Nemiroff, a white Jewish intellectual and member of the Communist Party, caused friction between her and the black nationalists whose cause she supported all her life. But the black nationalists and the Communist Party, with which Hansberry also sympathized (though she never became a party member), both have strong lines against homosexuality. Partly because of these attitudes, and partly because her family would not have been supportive of Hansberry's sexual preference, she chose to keep her separation from Nemiroff in 1957 a secret. She and her former husband maintained the closest possible professional and personal relationship until her death, and Nemiroff still maintains control over her papers, as well as holding the rights to her published works. In a personal interview conducted with Nemiroff in San Francisco in 1986, he indicated that the reason for their separation had to do with Hansberry's sexuality, but it was clear that their commitment to each other never diminished in any other way. The fact that Hansberry trusted him with revisions of *Les Blancs* (her last play, left unfinished at the time of her death), and named him as her literary executor would seem to support this interpretation of their separation.

• *A Raisin*

in the Sun

In 1957 Hansberry completed a play whose title she had taken from Langston Hughes's poem "Harlem." The poet warns that a "dream deferred" will "dry up / like a raisin in the sun," or it will explode. The title points out the hopeless social conditions that force the black family in her play to defer their dreams until their own strength and pride help them struggle toward opportunity. One of Nemiroff's associates in the music business, Philip Rose, was so impressed by the play that he wanted to produce it on Broadway, but he could not persuade any of the well-known producers in New York to take a chance on it; they thought nobody would come to see a serious play about a black family. Instead, Rose raised enough money to give the play trial runs in New Haven and Philadelphia. Sidney Poitier lent notoriety to the cast, but the rest of the outstanding performers, including Claudia McNeil, Ruby Dee, Diana Sands, Louis Gossett, Ivan Dixon, Glynn Thurman, Douglas Turner Ward, Lonnie Elder III, and director Lloyd Richards, were all virtually unknown to mainstream audiences. After a brief but successful run in Chicago, the play finally opened at New York's Ethel Barrymore Theatre on March 11, 1959.

Nobody, not even the play's staunchest supporters nor the author herself, could have predicted the impact *A Raisin in the Sun* was to make on the American public. Twenty-five years later, the play was revived across the country and given important productions at the Kennedy Center and on PBS, with Esther Rolle and Danny Glover in the leading roles. Its status as a classic is now assured. In May of 1959, Lorraine Hansberry became the first black playwright and one of the few women to win the coveted New York Drama Critics Circle award for Best Play of the Year. The screenplay that followed, which Hansberry also wrote, received a Screenwriters Guild nomination for Best Screenplay of the Year, and the film won a special award at the 1961 Cannes Festival.

• *Hansberry's life*

and work

misinterpreted

Hansberry was a frequently misinterpreted artist, partially because of a quote attributed to her by Nan Robertson in a *New York Times* interview about her Broadway hit: "I told them this wasn't a 'negro play.' It was a play about honest-to-God, believable, many-sided people who happened to be Negroes." This statement, which distorted her real views, was twisted even further by Harold Cruse in his widely read book *The Crisis of the Negro Intellectual:* "I'm not a Negro writer—but a writer who happens to be a Negro." Hansberry's real position on this question was articulated to interviewer Eleanor Fisher in an attempt to silence these infuriating misrepresentations. She said that "it is impossible to divorce the racial fact from any American Negro." Concerning the family in *A Raisin in the Sun,* she explained to the *New York Times:*

> From the moment the first curtain goes up until they make their decision at the end, the fact of racial oppression, unspoken and unalluded to, other than the fact of how they live, is through the play. It's inescapable. The reason these people are in the ghetto in America is because they are Negroes.

There is no doubt that Hansberry's choice of themes for the play make it a drama about the black struggle for liberation. But the play also contains universal themes, among them marital and generational conflict, women's rights, idealism versus cynicism, the American Dream, the dangers of materialism, and Christianity versus atheistic humanism. The play is also very well-constructed, clear and direct, and full of wonderful roles for actors. All these things, including Hansberry's wit, flair for dialogue and stage business, and solid dramaturgy, help locate *A Raisin in the Sun* among the best plays of this century. It opened the door for black Americans in theater and paved the way for the black theater movement of the 1960s and beyond. When pressed in a personal interview, Ed Bullins admitted that "Lorraine made a lot of things possible."

Ironically, the white press criticized the play for being a formula money-maker and tried to attribute its success to white liberal guilt over "the Negro question." Representatives from white culture felt free to attack Hansberry for everything and anything related to the issue of racism. In an interview, Mike Wallace grilled her about "Negro anti-Semitism" and tried to blame blacks for the violence in Kenya. Keeping her composure, she replied that it was a mistake to "equalize the oppressed with the oppressor."

Alarmed at the vogue these ideas enjoyed among the intellectuals of her age, Hansberry created her second drama, *The Sign in Sidney Brustein's Window,* produced in 1964. It was not nearly the commercial success that her first play had been, for a number of reasons. The intellectual content of the piece was over the heads of most of her audience, and the critics lost patience with it. Even more significantly, critics were frustrated because they could not "type" this playwright. Here was a black woman writing a play about a white male Jewish intellectual. Hansberry disappointed those who expected a sequel to *A Raisin in the Sun* and defied all attempts at classification, not limiting herself to one issue, one form of expression, or one style of writing.

Hansberry signified several dangerous things to the dominant culture, particularly after her fame gave her national exposure. She was a lesbian (although never publicly), she was a Pan-Africanist (although not a separatist), and in 1961 she donated money for the station wagon used by James Chaney, Andrew Goodman, and Michael Schwerner, who were Freedom Riders in Mississippi at the time of their murder. In 1962 she gathered support for the Student Nonviolent Coordinating Committee and was a vocal critic of the House Un-American Activities Committee and the Cuban missile crisis. She stood up to Otto Preminger in her criticism of *Porgy and Bess* as a racist play in a highly publicized interview, and on May 24, 1953, she and several prominent blacks met with Attorney General Robert Kennedy.

The meeting did not go well. Kennedy seemed to expect these successful black artists and intellectuals to endorse America as a land of freedom and opportunity, while the participants had no such intention. Everything in America was not "all right," and Hansberry led the walk-out with the statement that she was not worried about the state of oppressed black people "who have done splendidly . . . all things considered," but about "the state of the civilization which produced that photograph of the white cop standing on that Negro woman's neck in Birmingham," reported James Baldwin in *Freedomways*.

It is not clear exactly when the FBI opened its file on Hansberry, but she was classified as a member of "black nationalist-hate groups." The dominant culture began to put pressure on her, which made it increasingly important that she maintain alliance with supportive groups such as SNCC, the black nationalists, and the Communist Party. She was forced to prioritize her issues so that the issue of gay liberation took a back seat to black liberation and world peace. She also had her life cruelly curtailed by cancer at the age of thirty-four. Given her prolific output in such a short lifetime, we can only speculate what contributions she would have made to her many fields of interest had she lived.

Hansberry was a fighter. She suffered a paralyzing stroke six months before her death and lost her speech and eyesight. But she fought back and regained both, leaving her sickbed to raise money for SNCC, to meet with Robert Kennedy, and to deliver a speech on what it meant "To be young, gifted and black" to winners of a United Negro College Fund writing contest. She went through two unsuccessful operations and had heavy treatments of radiation and chemotherapy, yet she continued to work for the causes that concerned her throughout 1964.

During that year she published a radical volume called *The Movement: Documentary of a Struggle for Equality*, with powerful photographs of racist brutality including lynchings and an equally potent text. She continued work on two plays, *Les Blancs* and *The Sign in Sidney Brustein's Window*, and a play about the eighteenth-century feminist, Mary Wollstonecraft. On June 15 she left the hospital to participate in the famous Town Hall debate between black militant artists and white liberal intellectuals on "The Black Revolution and the White Backlash."

When it became clear that she would never be able to finish *Les Blancs*, she had many long conversations with her former husband so that he could finish it after her death. Though their divorce had become final on March 10, 1964, they continued to see each other daily until the end. Robert Nemiroff and influential friends of his and Hansberry's kept *The Sign in Sidney Brustein's Window* running for 101 performances, a remarkable achievement given its mixed reviews. It closed with the author's death on January 12, 1965.

**Profile by
Diana Marre**

BARBARA HARRIS

*O**n Saturday, September 24, 1988, the Reverend Barbara Clementine***

1930- •

Harris was elected suffragan bishop of the 110,000-member diocese of

Massachusetts. She became the Right Reverend Barbara Clementine   **Anglican bishop** •

Harris on February 12, 1989, the 834th and first female bishop, thus

breaking more than four hundred years of tradition in the Anglican

Communion with her elevation to the episcopate, a two-thousand-year

apostolic succession. This black American woman made history and

was transformed into a symbol for the 2.5-million-member Protestant

Episcopal church and for Anglicans the world over.

Philadelphia, Pennsylvania, the birthplace of this "Church of Presidents," is also the birthplace of the Right Reverend Harris. She, her older sister, Josephine, and younger brother, Thomas, were born to Walter Harris and Beatrice (Price) Harris. Lifelong Philadelphians, the

Harris family has lived in the same Germantown home for more than seventy years. Harris, born on June 12, 1930, graduated from Philadelphia High School for Girls in 1948 and attended Villanova University from 1977 to 1979 and Hobart and William Smith College in 1981. At the latter two institutions, she completed college courses and special training designed for mid-career clergy recruits.

As a "cradle Episcopalian," Harris gave early notice of her intention to make the church the instrument of Jesus's dictate to "love the Lord your God with all your heart, with all your soul, and with all your strength" and to "love your neighbor as yourself." Baptized and confirmed at St. Barnabas Church in Germantown, as a teenager she played the piano for church school and started the Young Adults Group. At the time, it had between fifty and seventy members and was the largest such youth group in the city. It still exists, with some of the original members, as the Adult Fellowship. As an adult, Harris was an active volunteer with the St. Dismas Society and succeeded her rector, the Reverend Canon Charles L. L. Poindexter, as board member of the Pennsylvania Prison Society, the oldest such group in the nation. Poindexter's involvement stemmed from his concern over an embarrassing lack of black clergy in prison ministry. He recruited Harris, who carried on this volunteer ministry for some fifteen years, longer than anyone else. The racially mixed St. Dismas Society visited prisons on Sunday evenings and weekdays to hold services, provide counseling, and be special friends to the prisoners.

In 1968, St. Barnabas merged with St. Luke's, a predominantly white parish; it is now St. Luke's Church, the largest parish in Philadelphia and still the home church of Harris's family. According to Poindexter, Harris, feeling that St. Luke's was too staid, transferred her membership to the North Philadelphia Church of the Advocate with the blessings of her rector. Once the way was open for women's ordination, Harris began to fulfill a lifetime dream by studying for the ministry. She was ordained to the diaconate in 1979, served as deacon-in-training at the Church of the Advocate in 1979-1980, and was ordained to the priesthood in 1980. Harris's parish-based ministries were as priest-in-charge at St. Augustine-of-Hippo in Norristown from 1980 to 1984 and as interim rector at the Church of the Advocate, where she was serving when elected as suffragan bishop of the diocese of Massachusetts.

The controversy over Harris's election revolves around several basic issues. First, she is a divorced female, and it is ironic that a male competitor and her predecessor as suffragan are divorced males over whose marital status no such ruckus was raised. Secondly, traditionalists believe that because the apostles were men, the position of bishop must be reserved for men. Others criticized her educational background and experience. Harris's educational, theological, and ministerial qualifications differ from the more traditional and formal university and seminary-based training and parish-based ministry heretofore considered as prerequisites to the episcopate. Harris's tenure as executive director of the Episcopal Church Publishing Company and as frequent contributor to its liberal and highly controversial publication *The Witness* cause detractors to view her as a dangerous activist.

The issue of gender has no validity in light of the 1976 General Convention action opening all orders (deacon, priest, and bishop) to women. The issue of her educational qualifications and experience is likewise invalid, as Harris attended college and completed seminary requirements through an approved alternate route quite to the satisfaction of the diocese of Pennsylvania, by whose canons she was deemed fit for ordination. The new bishop also spent over ten years as senior staff consultant and as a chief public relations executive at Sun Oil Company. In addition, Harris had eight years of parish experience; as suffragan bishop—an assisting bishop—Harris's main responsibilities focus on pastoral care for a specific geographical area of the Massachusetts diocese. She will help people in local parishes deal with typical parish issues such as calling rectors and parish growth and development.

In combining her spiritual quest for social justice and the editorial skills she honed as a public relations executive, Harris has long utilized not only the pulpit but also the media to prophesy against social ills demanding attention and rectification by the church. As ECPC executive director, Harris regularly authored the controversial column *"A Luta Continua:* The Struggle Continues," which became the barometer for the rise and fall of subscription renewals and cancellations. Readers have never been lukewarm about Harris's views; they were and remain either wholeheartedly supportive or rabidly indignant over her commentaries. In "A Double Standard," for example, Harris wrote about the bombing of public facilities, especially those serving women seeking family planning and/or abortion counseling and services. She chided the federal government for labeling bombings by freedom fighters as acts of terrorism and conspiracies while dismissing bombings of the above facilities as "the work of 'fanatics' spurred on by . . . religious zeal," according to *Witness.* Since her elevation to the episcopate, Harris has continued to speak out on issues the church cannot ignore. A recent *Witness* article, "The Politics of AIDS," was excerpted from a keynote speech to the National Episcopal AIDS Coalition and focused on three paramount concerns: the politics of AIDS affecting medical breakthroughs, the legal and civil rights of AIDS sufferers and others for whom testing is required, and the rise of the AIDS epidemic among teenagers.

Although the new bishop has always been known as a staunch advocate for women's rights, not all women were ready for her election as bishop; there still exist many women who fervently believe in the male-only succession in the apostolic line. Nonetheless, many distaff Episcopalians long resented their status, or lack of it, especially since their financial support of the church added millions to the its coffers. Foremost among their grievances was the long struggle to be approved as deputies to the General Convention. Although a woman was provisionally seated in 1946, the approval for a constitutional change to allow women deputies was not forthcoming until 1967. Constitutional changes to approve women's ordination to the diaconate and priesthood were not effected until 1970 and 1976, respectively.

• The

"Philadelphia

11" force action

The year 1974 proved to be one of crisis for the Episcopal Church: That was the year of the"Philadelphia 11," the group of eleven female deacons who sought ordination to the priesthood in spite of the church's stalling on the issue. Harris was there as a participant in the ordination service held at the now historic site of the Church of the Advocate, and the host rector was the Episcopal priest who would preach her consecration sermon fifteen years later.

Three retired bishops ordained the "Philadelphia 11," but the House of Bishops declared the ordinations invalid some two weeks later at an emergency meeting. In 1975, four additional female deacons were ordained to the priesthood at the Church of St. Stephen and the Incarnation in Washington, D.C. Both irregular ordinations were the focal point at the 1976 Minneapolis General Convention, and the following year both Houses endorsed the ordination of women to the priesthood. In 1977 the fifteen "irregulars" were regularized.

Another strategy to urge the church to be more responsible to its diverse membership was the convening of the "Consultation" by the then-Reverend Harris. This early 1980s group was comprised of nine Episcopal groups that formed a coalition to "raise concerns [to] shape the identity and mission of the Church at General Convention and beyond." Its Vision Statement focused on the need to address the four systemic ills of racism, sexism, class discrimination, and imperialism by challenging the church to recognize, define, and act on the inherent evil in systems allowing the continuation of deprivation and injustice.

Bishop Harris has also been a long-time supporter and member of the Union of Black Episcopalians, a group formed to promote the participation of blacks throughout the church and to eradicate racism in the church and society. The UBE was founded in 1968 by seventeen black clergy at St. Phillip's parish in Harlem as the Union of Black Clergy. There being no female clergy at the time did not deter the wishes of women to become members, and a few black women asserted themselves, among them Harris and Mattie Hopkins of Chicago, and joined the "brothers." As more black women sought membership, the group became the Union of Black Clergy and Laity and, finally, the UBE.

Harris has been described in terms of her effectiveness as a catalyst for social justice in the church and as a larger-than-life symbol for people who have long been marginal and impotent members of societal institutions, including the church, but she is also witty, lively, and very human. The 1948 Philadelphia High School for Girls yearbook described Harris as "slim, spirited, happy-go-lucky Bobby." The Reverend Florence Li Tim-Oi, first ordained female Anglican priest, met Harris at the 1988 Lambeth Conference and described her as being neat and well-groomed, sharp-featured with bright eyes and a radiant smile, but a *U.S. News & World Report* writer described Harris as friends know her. Mentioned were the bishop's three-inch-heel patent-leather pumps, her spiky mauve fingernails, a magnificent gold and diamond ring, and the signet ring of the episcopate. To those wanting to kiss the ring, the bishop replied, "Forget the ring, sweetie, kiss the bishop!"

In reply to the very real concern of the Church of England's ongoing refusal to recognize the status of female priests and bishops, Harris answered with a rejoinder displaying rapier-sharp wit rather than anger: "I could be a combination of the Virgin Mary, Lena Horne and Madame Curie and I would still get clobbered by some." Further described as "someone you'd like to invite down to the corner bar to dish the dirt over a beer," Harris is also the person who, during the summer of 1964, registered black voters in Mississippi in lieu of her summer vacation; in addition, she was a participant in the Selma, Alabama, march with Martin Luther King, Jr.

Myrtle Gordon of Atlanta, Georgia, national church consultant on aging and UBE consultant on clergy wives, characterized Bishop Harris as "a strong black woman, small in stature, fiercely strong in her beliefs, loyalties, and concern for people's welfare in relation to the witness of the church; a dynamo in her strong convictions; one motivated and propelled to rectify situations caused by the church's failure to perceive and attend to people's needs."

Bishop shows •

her human side

**Profile by
Aleathia Dolores
Nicholson**

MARCELITE J. HARRIS

1943- •

Marcelite Jordan Harris, a brigadier general, is vice-commander of

the Oklahoma City Air Logistics Center at Tinker Air Force Base,

Oklahoma. She was the U.S. Air Force's first woman aircraft mainte- **military officer** •

nance officer and one of the first two women to be "air officers

commanding" at the Air Force Academy in Colorado. Not only was she

the first woman appointed maintenance squadron commander in

Strategic Air Command, she also became Air Training Command's first

woman wing commander. After setting other records as a woman

"first," she reached the rank of brigadier general in 1990, thereby

becoming the first black woman general in the Air Force.

Born January 16, 1943, in Houston, Texas, Harris is the daughter of Cecil O'Neal Jordan, Sr., a postal supervisor, and Marcelite (Terrell)

Jordan, a high school librarian. She has one sister, Elizabeth, and one brother, Cecil O'Neal, Jr. Her maternal great-great-grandfather, Pierre Landry, was the son of a slave woman and her master born on the Provost plantation in Ascension Parish, Louisiana. Pierre Landry lived the first thirteen years of his life virtually free, and after being sold he opened a plantation store to sell approved items to other slaves and became head carpenter for the plantation. After the Civil War and freedom came, he moved to Donaldsonville, the parish seat, where he was elected mayor in 1868. Between 1870 and 1884 he served in the state house of representatives and in the state senate, and then left politics to practice law. Harris's maternal great-grandfather, I. M. Terrell, was an educator who founded the first school for blacks in Fort Worth, Texas.

Harris graduated in 1960 from Kashmere Gardens Junior-Senior High School and in 1964 from Spelman College in Atlanta, Georgia, with a bachelor of arts degree in speech and drama. Later she earned a bachelor of arts degree in business management at the University of Maryland, Asian Division. She completed the Air Force's Squadron Officer School by correspondence and Air War College by seminar. She also completed Harvard University's Senior Officers National Security in residence as well as the Defense Department's CAPSTONE course for general officers.

In September 1965 Harris entered the U.S. Air Force through the Officer Training School at Lackland Air Force Base, Texas, and graduated in December of that year. She was then assigned to the position of assistant director for administration at the 60th Military Airlift Wing at Travis Air Force Base, California.

First female

aircraft

maintenance

officer

Harris became administrative officer for the 388th Tactical Missile Squadron in January 1967, based at Bitburg Air Base, West Germany. In May 1969 she was reassigned as the maintenance analysis officer with the 36th Tactical Fighter Wing at the same air base. After completing her German tour, Harris became the first woman in the Air Force to become aircraft maintenance officer upon graduating from the Aircraft Maintenance Officer Course at Chanute Air Force Base, Illinois, in May 1971. Three months later she became the maintenance supervisor for the 469th Tactical Fighter Squadron located at Korat Air Base, Thailand.

After returning to the United States, Harris was assigned as the job control officer for the 916th Air Refueling Squadron located at Travis Air Force Base, California. She became the squadron's field maintenance supervisor in September 1973. Two years later she was assigned as a personnel staff officer at the Air Force Headquarters in Washington,

D.C., where, among other assignments, she served as White House social aide to President Jimmy Carter. In May 1978 she became commander of Cadet Squadron Thirty-nine at the United States Air Force Academy, Colorado, and thus was selected as one of the first two women to be "air officer commanding."

Returning to the maintenance career field, in July 1980 Harris became maintenance control officer for the 384th Air Refueling Wing at McConnell Air Force Base, Kansas. A year later she became the first woman maintenance squadron commander in Strategic Air Command, assuming command of the 384th Avionics Maintenance Squadron, McConnell Air Force Base. Eight months later Harris assumed command of McConnell's 384th Field Maintenance Squadron.

In November 1982, Harris was assigned to the Pacific Air Forces Logistic Support Center, Kadena Air Base, Japan. She became the Air Force's first woman deputy commander for maintenance when she assumed the position at Keesler Air Force Base, Mississippi, in March 1966. She served as commander of the 3300th Technical Training Wing, Keesler Technical Training Center, Keesler Air Force Base, Mississippi, assuming the position on December 3, 1988. At that time she became the first woman wing commander in Air Training Command. On September 8, 1990, Harris attained the rank of brigadier general, and she is currently vice-commander of the Oklahoma City Air Logistics Center at Tinker Air Force Base, where she helps oversee 26,000 workers who maintain all types of military aircraft and missiles.

Brigadier •

General

oversees

26,000 workers

Among the numerous military honors Harris has received are the Bronze Star, Meritorious Service Medal with three oak leaf clusters, Air Force Commendation Medal with one oak leaf cluster, Presidential Unit Citation, Air Force Outstanding Unit Award with eight oak leaf clusters (one with valor), Air Force Organizational Excellence Award with one oak leaf cluster, National Defense Service Medal, Vietnam Service Medal, Air Force Overseas Ribbon—Short Tour, Air Force Overseas Ribbon—Long Tour with one oak leaf cluster, Air Force Longevity Service Award Ribbon with four oak leaf clusters, Republic of Vietnam Gallantry Cross with Palm, and the Republic of Vietnam Campaign Medal.

She married Maurice Anthony Harris, a native of Portsmouth, Virginia, and now a retired lieutenant colonel from the Air Force. They are the parents of a son, Steven, and a daughter, Tenecia.

**Profile by
Jessie Carney Smith**

PATRICIA HARRIS

P atricia Roberts Harris made history during her lifetime and achieved

many firsts. American history will remember her as the first black

woman to serve in a United States president's cabinet, both as secretary

of Housing and Urban Development and as secretary of Health, Educa-

tion and Welfare; she was also the first black woman to serve her nation

as ambassador and to lead an American law school.

1924-1985 •

lawyer, •

government

official

Harris was born on May 31, 1924, in Mattoon, Illinois, to Bert and Chiquita Roberts. Early in her life, Patricia's father, a dining car waiter for the Illinois Central Railroad, abandoned the family, leaving her and her brother, Malcolm, to be raised by their mother. In her formative years, Harris became aware of the importance of an education, saying, "We didn't have a lot of money [but] we believed in education and . . . in reading." Since hers was one of the few black families in Mattoon, Illinois, she also came to know about racism when one of her grade school classmates called her a nigger.

After receiving her secondary education in Chicago, Illinois, Harris entered the School of Liberal Arts at Howard University in 1941, from which she graduated summa cum laude in 1945 with a bachelor's degree. Later she was elected into Phi Beta Kappa. It was during her college days at Howard that Pat Harris gained a social consciousness about the ramifications of segregation in the American society. In 1943 she joined other Howard students in one of the first student sit-ins at the Little Palace Cafeteria, which refused to serve blacks in the midst of the black community.

Harris entered graduate school and worked several years at the Chicago YWCA before becoming executive director of Delta Sigma Theta in 1953. She subsequently married William Beasley Harris, a lawyer who encouraged her to attend law school. In 1957 she enrolled in the George Washington University School of Law, where she excelled. She was a member of the law review and was elected to the Order of the Coif, a national legal honor society, and graduated first in her class of ninety-four students in 1960. After graduation, Harris joined the appeals and research staff of the criminal division of the United States Department of Justice, where she remained until she joined the Howard University Law School faculty on a part-time basis as a lecturer in law in 1961. The rest of her time was spent as associate dean of students at Howard University. The appointment of Harris to the law school faculty made her the fifth woman to teach at Howard's law school.

Around 1963 Harris was appointed to Howard's law faculty on a full-time basis, one of two women on the law faculty. In June of 1965 Harris, a Democrat, took leave from her teaching responsibilities to accept an appointment by President Lyndon B. Johnson as ambassador to Luxembourg. She held the position until 1967, and that year she received the Order of Oaken Crown for her distinguished service in Luxembourg.

After retiring as ambassador, Harris returned to Howard's law school as a professor on a full-time basis, serving simultaneously as United States alternate delegate to the Twenty-first and Twenty-second General Assembly of the United Nations and as United States alternate to the Twentieth Plenary Meeting of the Economic Community of Europe.

• *Harris receives*

federal

appointments

In 1969 Harris, then a professor of law, was appointed dean of the Howard University School of Law, a position from which she resigned within thirty days after being appointed. Although her deanship was short because of a host of issues, ranging from a student uprising and faculty disagreements to a disagreement with the president of Howard University, she was the first black woman to head a law school. She later joined the Washington, D.C., law firm of Fried, Frank, Harris, Shriver, and Kampelman, where she practiced corporate law until President Jimmy Carter appointed her as secretary of Housing and Urban Development in 1977. She served in this position for three years. In 1980,

Carter appointed Harris as secretary of the Department of Health, Education and Welfare, a position in which she served until Carter was defeated in the presidential election of 1980.

In 1982 Harris ran for, but lost, a bid to become the mayor of the District of Columbia. The campaign was tough and bitter. She lost the Democratic primary to Marion S. Barry, Jr., receiving 36 percent of the vote. In 1983, twenty-three years after receiving her law degree from George Washington University, she was appointed as a full professor of law in its law school. She held this position until she died of cancer on March 23, 1985, shortly after the death of her husband.

From a very early age Harris never allowed her aspirations or personhood to be controlled by racism or sexism. Rather, her philosophy, one that carried her to extraordinary heights, was to do "what I think I ought to be able to do." That blacks faced barriers of discrimination in America troubled Harris because segregation "limited . . . the experiences that they were permitted to have." Although a lawyer, Harris was "suspicious of those who believe that the protector of minorities is in the courts" and that it took "a combination of action—the enactment of legislation and the courts—to protect the rights of minorities" in America. She believed that social change could be influenced through corporate responsibility, a belief that she practiced as a member of the board of directors of several major corporations, including Chase Manhattan Bank, Scott Paper Company, and IBM, and as a trustee of the Twentieth Century Fund.

Harris is perhaps best known for her response to Senator William Proxmire, who, during her Senate confirmation hearing in 1977 for secretary of Housing and Urban Development, questioned whether Harris was "sympathetic to the problems of the poor." Harris's response made every major newspaper in the country:

> You do not understand who I am. . . . I am a black woman, the daughter of a Pullman car waiter. I am a black woman who even eight years ago could not buy a house in parts of the District of Columbia. I didn't start out as a member of a prestigious law firm, but as a woman who needed a scholarship to go to school. If you think that I have forgotten that, you are wrong.

As a public official, Harris clearly demonstrated a concern for good government, racial harmony, and the elimination of racial and sex discrimination. As secretary of Housing and Urban Development, Harris's words speak for themselves. Speaking on the subject of jobs for minorities and minority youth, Harris stated:

It should not be new to you that the minority unemployment rate is consistently higher than the unemployment rate for whites, and it generally approaches a factor of two to one. For minority youths, conditions are even worse with unemployment in some areas reaching as high as 30% to 40%. . . . I am concerned that an entire generation may grow up without the opportunity to hold a decent job. We cannot allow that to happen.

In a speech addressing racial discrimination in housing, Harris noted:

If a Black person looking through newspaper advertisements for an apartment to rent or a house to purchase, were to select four apartments or brokers to visit, the probability of encountering discrimination would be 75 percent in the rental market and 62 percent in the sales market. There is clear probability that discrimination is even more prevalent, especially in view of the fact that the forms it takes have become more extensive and more sophisticated in recent years.

In a speech touching on her visions and the uniqueness of the American people as relates to the world, Harris stated:

We are a unique nation and a unique people. We are more tied to all the nations and peoples of the world than any other nation in this world. That is why we are more concerned with what happens around the world than any other nation. . . . Because of this, Americans are concerned that the violence, the terrorism, the wars, the threats of war, the poverty, the ignorance, the disease—that all of these things could in time spill over to our own cities and neighborhoods, and threaten our way of life.

Finally, in a speech on the role of women in the future, Harris stated:

I want to hear the Speaker of the House addressed as Madam Speaker and I want to listen as she introduces Madam President to the Congress assembled for the State of the Union. I want Madam President to look down from the podium at the women of the Supreme Court who will be indicative of the significant number of women judges throughout the Federal and State judicial systems.

Profile by
J. Clay Smith, Jr.

DOROTHY HEIGHT

*D*orothy Irene Height, president of the National Council of Negro

Women since 1957, has helped the council grow significantly and

expand its focus to include global issues that affect women. She was also

national president of Delta Sigma Theta sorority for nine years, has

served on numerous United States committees concerned with women's

issues, won countless service awards, and has traveled extensively for

the cause of women's issues worldwide. She spent the majority of her

professional life as a staff member of the Young Women's Christian

Association's National Board. Through her professional and voluntary

responsibilities, Height has fought to improve the status of women and to

empower women to speak in their own behalf.

1912- •

organization •

leader,

social servant

Height was born on March 24, 1912, to James Edward Height and Fannie (Borroughs) Height. The family moved from Richmond, Virginia, to Rankin, Pennsylvania, a small mining town, in 1916. Height attended Rankin High School, and upon graduation she applied to Barnard College in New York City. She was informed by the school, however, that they already had two black students and therefore she would have to wait a term or more. She chose instead to attend New York University, using a one-thousand-dollar scholarship she had won from an Elks Fraternal Society's national oratorical contest. While attending New York University, she lived with her sister and worked at odd jobs to support herself. Height finished her undergraduate course work in three years and in her fourth year worked to receive her master's degree in educational psychology. She completed this course work in 1933.

After completing her formal education, Height took a practice teaching position at Brownsville Community Center in Brooklyn. Also, following the founding of the United Christian Youth Movement in 1935, she became an active member and quickly became one of its leaders. This position enabled her to travel widely throughout the United States and to Europe. In 1937 she represented the organization at the International Church Youth Conference in Oxford, England, as well as serving as a youth delegate at the World Conference of Christian Youth in Amsterdam, Holland. In 1938 Height, acting as a representative of the Harlem Youth Council, became one of ten American youths to help Eleanor Roosevelt plan the 1938 World Youth Congress that met at Vassar College in Poughkeepsie, New York.

In 1938 Height accepted a position with the YWCA after her return from Europe to the United States. By this time she had decided she could use her skills more productively in an organization that was inclusive of the races and international in character. This new job took her from Brooklyn to Harlem, where she became assistant director of the Emma Ransom House, a place of lodging for black women.

In her new capacity, Height was immediately confronted with the plight of large numbers of black American women in domestic service jobs working under deplorable conditions. She became their advocate, speaking up, for example, in 1938 when she testified before the New York City Council about the despicable practice occurring in Brooklyn and the Bronx daily. Here on the streets, in what she called a "slave market," young black girls would bargain with passing motorists for a day's housework at substandard wages. The battle for fair wages for domestic workers is one that she maintains to this day, urging them to organize and form unions.

Plight of •

domestic

workers

addressed

This period of her life set the course for much of her future work. In 1937 Height not only began working with the YWCA but she also met Mary McLeod Bethune, president and founder of the National Council of Negro Women. This meeting was life-transforming, as she joined the organization that she was to lead for more than thirty years.

In 1939, Height relocated to Washington, D.C., to take a new position as executive secretary of the YWCA Phillis Wheatley Home. At this time she also became a member of Delta Sigma Theta sorority. She immediately made her presence and ideas known. At an executive committee meeting in June 1940, Height proposed that the Delta Sigma Theta Sorority adopt as a national project a job analysis program that would analyze the reasons black women were excluded from so many of the jobs open to other women, increase the number of positions for black women on jobs already accessible to other women, and improve conditions under which many unskilled workers were forced to work.

During 1944 Height was elected vice-president of Delta Sigma Theta, and three years later she became national president. During the nine years she held the position, according to Paula Giddings's history of the organization, "neither the direction nor the substance of the initiatives changed under [her] leadership, but the breadth and interest in them did." She expanded the sorority into one more focused on the relationship between black women in America and in Third World countries. When she was invited by the World YWCA to teach for four months at the Delhi School of Social Work in India in 1952, for example, she relayed the similar conditions of women in India and convinced her sorority members to establish a scholarship for two Hindu women.

The creation of international Delta chapters can be directly attributed to Height. Following her participation in the bicentennial celebration of Haiti in Port-au-Prince in 1950, she organized the sorority's first international chapter. Further, the organization established a Haitian relief fund, which after only four years proved invaluable when the island was hit by the destructive Hurricane Hazel. Height also increased the board's international and political consciousness by taking them to meet members of the United Nations' Department of Information and the Political and Economic Committee on the Rights of Women.

After her term as sorority head ended, Height could not long remain outside of club politics. In 1957 she became president of the National Council of Negro Women. The council, created by Bethune, is an umbrella group for local and national women's organizations. Through the organization, Height became an integral part of the leadership of the civil rights movement in the United States and abroad. Beginning in 1948, when Governor Nelson Rockefeller of New York appointed her to

• *Height leads*

NCNW

the state Social Welfare Board, she has held a variety of official and unofficial positions, representing black American women's issues.

In 1960, in the wake of major changes in the African political scene, the Committee on Correspondence sent Height to study women's organizations in five African countries. As a result of that travel she acted as a consultant to the secretary of state. She also sought both American funding for the African nations and the promotion of a sense of unity between blacks in this country and in African ones.

During the early years of the civil rights movement, Height was known to take a rather moderate stance on matters of integration and civil rights. She did not support the call for black power as a means to attain the rights promised to all citizens of the United States. By 1972, however, she altered her position, stating that:

> White power in the system in which we live is a reality. . . . We have to see that we have been treating the symptoms instead of causes. I think this does call for the more direct approach to the societal conditions.

This change in attitude was evident in her activities in the council and the YWCA. The council was finally coming closer to "bringing all the fingers together in a mighty fist," which was the vision of Bethune at its inception. According to author Jeanne Noble, Height was able to build financial and administrative capabilities that positioned the NCNW to become eligible for large foundation grants, a first in the history of black women's organizations.

The Ford Foundation granted the council three hundred thousand dollars to begin Operation Woman Power, a project to help women open their own businesses and to provide funds for vocational training. During the same period, the United States Department of Health, Education, and Welfare supplied the means for a job training program for teenagers. The council spent time in areas where community needs were not being met, calling them to the attention of those in power. It went to rural areas and bought seed and feed for poor farmers and communities and started food cooperatives.

During the past three decades the council has remained diligent in its role as a catalyst for effecting change in the position of black women. Currently, their focus has been on the revival of black family life, with annual celebrations that they call Black Family Reunions. These events are intended to encourage and renew the concept and admiration of the extended black family. This once-powerful barrier against racism and its attendant ills, such as juvenile delinquency, drug use, and unwanted teen pregnancy, is seen by Height and the NCNW to be the key to restoring the community.

Under Height's leadership the council publishes *Black Woman's Voice* and runs a Women's Center for Education and Career Advancement for minority women in nontraditional careers, an Information Center for and about black women, and the Bethune Museum and Archives for black women's history. It has offices in West and South Africa, working to improve the conditions of women in Third World countries. Height has spoken extensively on the responsibilities of the United States, United Nations, and local organizations in pursuit of these improvements.

Height has been central in the success of three influential women's organizations. As president and executive board member of Delta Sigma Theta, Height left the sorority more efficient and globally focused, with a centralized headquarters. Height's work with the Young Women's Christian Association led to integration and sincere and productive participation in the civil rights movement. The National Council of Negro Women is now a competent umbrella for 240 local groups and thirty-one national organizations. In different ways each organization has been striving toward the unified goal of equal rights for black women all over the world. Through diligence, excellent managerial skills, good use of contacts, and use of authority, she has left an undeniable mark in each endeavor she has undertaken.

**Profile by
J. L. Grady,
M. Edwards, and
A. L. Jones**

AILEEN HERNANDEZ

A ileen Clark Hernandez is one of the most influential women of her   **1926-** •

time, especially in the areas of labor relations, women's rights, and

equal-opportunity employment. Her numerous achievements include   **feminist,** •

serving as the only woman on the Equal Employment Opportunity   **labor relations**

Commission, founding her own public relations and management firm,   **specialist**

and becoming president of the National Organization of Women.

Hernandez was born in Brooklyn, New York, on May 23, 1926. She was the middle of three children and only daughter of Charles and Ethel Clark, both of Jamaican descent. The Clarks did not treat their children differently because of gender: all three learned to cook, sew, and care for their personal belongings. These early seeds eventually blossomed into a philosophy that has guided Hernandez's personal and professional life—the belief that people should be treated equally in the world of employment regardless of their race or gender.

Hernandez attended Bay Ridge Public School 176 in Brooklyn, graduating as class valedictorian, and Bay Ridge High School, graduating as class salutatorian in 1943. With a scholarship in hand, Hernandez pursued a college degree at Howard University in Washington, D.C.,

majoring in political science and sociology. She also participated in various extracurricular activities that reflected her personal interests and commitment to solving racial problems. As a member of the campus branch of the National Association for the Advancement of Colored People, for example, Hernandez picketed the National Theater, the Lesner Auditorium, and the Thompson restaurant chain. She wrote a column for the *Washington Tribune* that dealt with university activities, and during her junior and senior years she served as editor of *The Hilltop,* the university paper.

After graduating from Howard University, Hernandez worked briefly as a research assistant in the political science department there. Over the next twelve years, from 1947 to 1959, she continued her education at various schools, including the University of Oslo, where she participated in the International Student Exchange Program and studied comparative government; New York University, where she took classes in public administration; the University of California at Los Angeles, where she studied adult and nursery education; and the University of Southern California. In 1959 she obtained a master's degree in government from Los Angeles State College, and she also married an African-American garment cutter from Los Angeles, though she was divorced by 1961.

One of the many areas of interest Hernandez pursued was labor relations. Her interest in this field originated in the early 1950s, when she became an intern with the International Ladies Garment Workers Union. At that time, the ILGWU was trying to expand educational programs for its membership by providing qualified staff to conduct classes in such diverse areas as languages, the fine arts, and government. After completing her internship, Hernandez was assigned to work the West Coast office in Los Angeles. From 1951 to 1961, according to biographer Walter Christmas, she performed various duties that put her in direct contact with people:

Work in labor •

relations begins

> Her activities ranged from planning picnics and dances to organizing legislative mobilizations, political rallies, strikes, and picket lines. She also taught principles of unionism and pre-naturalization classes in English and citizenship to foreign-born union members at the University of California's adult education extension at Los Angeles.

During 1960, Hernandez represented the State Department as a specialist in labor education. In this position she toured South American countries—including Venezuela, Columbia, Chile, Peru, Argentina, and Uruguay—discussing American trade unions, the position of minority groups in the United States, the status of women, and the American political system. As a result of her work with ILGWU, Hernandez was named "Woman of the Year" by the Community Relations Conference of Southern California.

In 1961 Hernandez left ILGWU to serve as campaign coordinator for Democrat Alan Cranston in his bid for state comptroller. After Cranston was elected, he appointed Hernandez assistant chief of the California Fair Employment Practice Commission. Serving ably in this capacity, Hernandez supervised a staff of fifty, covering activities in the San Francisco, Los Angeles, Fresno, and San Diego field offices. One of her main contributions was the development of a technical advisory committee to study the effects of industrial testing in hiring minority group members.

Because of Hernandez's educational background and breadth of experience in both labor relations and fair-employment legislation and guidelines, President Lyndon B. Johnson appointed her to the Equal Employment Opportunity Commission. The commission was charged under the 1964 Civil Rights Act with enforcing federal laws that prohibit employment discrimination because of race, color, religion, national origin, and sex. Hernandez's appointment was both logical and note-worthy, for she became the only woman on this five-member commission. Hernandez's reaction to her appointment is recorded in *Essence:*

> I think when people in politics make appointments to commissions they are always trying to balance out various parts of the community. So they sort of hit the jackpot when they get someone who's black, who is a woman, who has a Mexican-American last name, who comes from California, and who's been in the labor movement.

Though she believed in its purpose, Hernandez resigned her position with EEOC within eighteen months of her appointment. She felt the commission lacked true enforcement powers and therefore could not effectively implement its policies. One noteworthy change that did occur during Hernandez's tenure, however, was that commercial airlines reversed their standard policy of terminating women flight attendants whenever they married.

In 1966 Hernandez started her own public relations and management firm, Hernandez and Associates. Through this vehicle, Hernandez pooled her knowledge, resources, and interests to advise private business, government, labor, and other organizations on programs to employ minority groups and women.

Perhaps Hernandez is most noted for being the first black woman appointed to a position with the National Organization of Women. Initially appointed in 1967 as NOW's western vice-president, in 1971 she succeeded Betty Friedan, NOW's founder and first president. The appointment came at a time when many black women regarded NOW and the women's liberation movement as an unwelcome element of competition. Some typical comments regarding the movement as it related to blacks were recorded in *Ebony:*

Succeeds •

Friedan as

NOW president

> We should stand behind our men, not against them. . . .

> This movement won't be any different from the Woman Suffrage theory: White women won the right to vote way back then but black people, including black women, didn't win this right until more than 100 years later. . . .

> Just a bunch of bored white women with nothing to do—they're just trying to attract attention away from the black liberation movement.

To Hernandez, NOW and its activities represented a natural evolution of the civil rights movement. She spurned the idea, according to *Essence,* that NOW was just for elitist white women who had nothing to do:

> In our Statement of Purpose, though, NOW is much broader. We say very clearly that we consider the women's movement as an extension of the civil rights movement, that is, a movement for all people. It's not in contradiction to the black movement or to any other effort that's trying for the inclusion of people in society. We see it as a natural outgrowth of the black movement. As a black woman, I particularly think that it is important to be involved in women's liberation, largely because black women are desperately needed in the total civil rights movement. Until women, black as well as others, gain a sense of their own identity and feel they have a real choice in the society, nothing is going to happen in civil rights. It's not going to happen for blacks; it's not going to happen for Mexican-Americans; it's not going to happen for women.

Hernandez's involvement in community and national affairs is encompassing and represents a compendium of organizations. She is or has been a member of: the Board of Directors of the National Committee Against Discrimination in Housing; the Steering Committee of the National Urban Coalition; Task Force on Employment of Women of the Twentieth Century Fund; American Civil Liberties Union; NAACP; Board of Trustees for Working Assets Money Fund; Board of Overseers for Civil Justice, Rand Corporation; Black Women Organized for Action; the National Hook-up of Black Women; and many more associations. She has also received numerous awards for her service, including a doctorate from Southern Vermont College, the Equal Rights Advocate Award, and the San Francisco League of Women Voters Award.

Hernandez continues to lecture on civil rights, equal-employment opportunity, trade unionism, and issues related to these themes. She also continues to wield influence through her public relations agency, Hernandez and Associates, located in San Francisco. Her clients have included United Airlines, Standard Oil, United Parcel Service, National Alliance of Businessmen, University of California, and the California cities of Richmond, Berkeley, and Los Angeles.

**Profile by
Marva Rudolph**

CLEMENTINE HUNTER

Like Grandma Moses, to whom she was often compared, Clementine

(1886-1988) •

Hunter began painting late in life, though she was a practicing folk

artist long before that. The prolific Hunter, who became known as one of

folk •

the century's leading "primitive" artists, stopped painting only one

artist

month before her death. The quality and importance of her work is still

being studied and discovered by new generations of artists and art

historians.

Clementine (pronounced "Clementeen") Reuben Hunter was born in late December, 1886, at Hidden Hill, a cotton plantation near Cloutierville, Louisiana. Her mother, Antoinette Adams, was of Virginia slave ancestry. Her father, Janvier (John) Reuben was a Louisiana Creole of native American, African, French, and Irish descent. She was originally given a French name, "Clemence," which appears in United States census records. But her Roman Catholic baptismal record gives the Latin "Clementiam."

In Cloutierville, Hunter experienced her only taste of formal education at a small Catholic elementary school. She attended school only

briefly, remaining illiterate all her life. After a few years, the family moved near Natchitoches, the oldest town in the state, to Melrose Plantation on the Cane River. Melrose, formerly called Yucca Plantation, had been owned by the Metoyers, the wealthiest free black family in the United States before the Civil War. By Hunter's day, however, Melrose was owned by a white family. The dynamic mistress of the plantation since 1898 was Carmelite "Cammie" Garrett Henry, who sought to restore the antebellum structures, revive local arts and crafts, and develop a library of Louisiana history.

Hunter had two children with Charlie Dupree, an eccentric Creole with a mechanical aptitude approaching genius. He died about 1914. She had five more children with Emanuel Hunter, a hardworking Christian whom she married in 1924. After first working in the fields, Clementine Hunter moved to full-time domestic duties in the main house sometime in the late 1920s. She developed a creative flair for cooking, decor, basketmaking, sewing, and quiltmaking.

At the same time, Hunter doubtless experienced the influence of the many prominent visitors to Melrose, including Lyle Saxon, Roark Bradford, and Richard Avedon. When François Mignon, the single most influential person in her artistic life, became a resident of Melrose in 1939, Hunter was ready for what would follow. A Frenchman whose career in foreign trade through New York City was disrupted by the outbreak of World War II, Mignon became curator of Cammie Henry's collections and a friend to Hunter. Sometime around 1940, one evening about seven o'clock, Hunter, then already in her late fifties, showed up at Mignon's door with some nearly empty tubes of paint discarded by an artist visiting Melrose. Hunter told him that she figured that she could "mark" a picture of her own if she set her mind to it. He cast about and came up with an old window shade, and the next morning at five o'clock she presented him with a completed picture. Although this was not the first picture that she had produced, it was the first that she had ever shown to another person. Indeed, one of her earliest recognized works is a quilt from 1938 depicting black life on the plantation. Field hands and boatmen surround a central panel in which the main house is depicted. The solid red, blue, and golden yellow pieces of fabric employed in this quilt strongly resemble the broad, flat areas of similar color that were soon to appear in her painting.

With Mignon's encouragement, Hunter began to paint untiringly on anything that she or he could scrounge—cardboard boxes, paper bags, scraps of wood, and eventually canvas. Mignon had little money himself, but somehow he managed to come up with enough for an occasional Sears and Roebuck mail order. Additionally, Hunter used bottles, an old chest, gourds, and even old iron pots—anything that could hold paint. She also continued to make a number of outstanding quilts. By the time of her death, her paintings numbered in the several thousands.

Over the years Hunter's technique changed little, and many regard her earliest works as her best. They are uncluttered and generally better composed. Later works by comparison sometimes appear crowded, repetitive, or clumsy. She appears always to have used oils. Claims that she tried watercolor in some of her early pictures can be attributed to oil paint that was thinned in order to stretch scarce supplies. In time the subjects of her painting widened, but they rarely strayed from her own memories. She said that she always preferred to paint from memory or from dreams rather than from life.

• **Painter's works**

form three

categories

Hunter's topics may be grouped into three categories. First and foremost, there are the memory pictures. They show people gathering and cooking food, washing, tending children, attending school, playing games, dancing and honky-tonking, and attending revival meetings, weddings, baptisms, funerals, and the like. In addition, there are scenes of birds, ducks, chickens, and cats and still lifes of flowers, most of these also apparently from memory. The second category, comprising what are perhaps her most poignant pictures, consists of the religious scenes of the Nativity, the Flight to Egypt, angels flying, and the Crucifixion. In these the figures are almost always depicted as black. The so-called *Cotton Crucifixion* remains probably the most provocative painting in this category. (Hunter did not name most of her works, so owners have assigned names that may or may not reflect the artist's original intentions.) In *Cotton Crucifixion*, Jesus is black, but the thieves are white, and at the foot of the cross black field hands drag full sacks through rows of cotton. The third category is difficult to define because it incorporates such dissimilar and atypical works. These pieces, including abstract paintings, all were presumably prompted by some sort of outside influence.

Hunter's reputation began to develop in the late 1940s and 1950s. In 1955, the Delgado Museum (now the New Orleans Museum of Art), gave her a solo exhibition, the first it offered to a black artist. At the same time, Northwestern State College in Natchitoches held its first all-Hunter show. However, she was not allowed to view her work with the white patrons and had to be slipped in by the back door when the gallery was closed.

In 1956 Hunter created one of her most important works, the African House Murals at Melrose. Mignon had the idea for her to paint nine large plywood panels, each four-by-eight feet, and several small connecting ones, to be installed in the circa 1800 African House, so-called because of its similarity to traditional buildings of central Africa, with a steep roof and a wide overhang unsupported by posts. Hunter's realization of Mignon's idea is an all-inclusive, knowing, and witty view of plantation life along the Cane River, a remarkable achievement for a self-taught sixty-eight-year-old. She also painted murals for Ghana House and Yucca House, two other buildings at Melrose.

Throughout the 1950s Hunter's subjects and their treatment developed very little. The exceptions are the few collage-like pieces that reflect continued influence from her quiltmaking. A good example is her 1958 *Going to Church,* which has multi-colored borders that look like applique on a quilt. Collage did not entirely enter into her work, however, until the 1960s, when James Register moved to Natchitoches. Second only to Mignon as an early supporter of Hunter, Register was a writer, sometime artist, and teacher at the University of Oklahoma. After visiting Melrose in the early 1940s, he began sending Hunter small cash payments and art supplies. In 1944 he secured for her a Julius Rosenwald Foundation grant. When Emanuel Hunter died in August of that year, Register helped to pay the funeral costs. Register and Mignon both acted as agents for the sale of Hunter's work.

By the time that Register settled permanently in Natchitoches in 1962, he had decided to try an experiment to test the talent and broaden the scope of the elderly artist whom he regarded as "almost a genius." During a period of two years, he cut up color advertisements from old magazines and pasted them to cardboard to form collages. He would take the pasteups to Hunter, one at a time, along with art supplies, to see what sort of work they would inspire, according to biographer James L. Wilson. "Sometimes the montage would be so difficult, being only a series of color patterns," said Register, "the outlines would have to be traced on the board for her." On its face alone, the whole project constituted an interference with Hunter's own vision. Certainly, the names of these 1962-1963 paintings probably have more to do with Register than Hunter. The pictures eventually came to number about one hundred, including titles such as *Chanticleer and the Moon Bird, Alice in Wonderland, Uncle Tom,* and *Porte Bouquet.* The Register experiment prompted new work, however, with new, splashier color and patterns that eventually influenced her other painting, especially her flower pictures. Although she readily admitted that she did not like painting Register's "abstract" commissions and happily quit after the two years, the influence of renewed color if not also the collage technique continued to spill over into her later work. This may be seen in the last decade of the artist's life in her *Chicken Hauling Flowers,* which she painted in 1980 at the age of ninety-four. All in all, the abstract period is the briefest and least-known of her career but one of the most influential.

It also raises the issue of profit in Hunter's art. In the late 1960s Mignon reported that Hunter still routinely sold pictures for as little as six dollars each. Early patrons do not appear to have made much on her work. After Register died in 1970, his collection of 110 paintings were valued altogether at only ten thousand dollars. By the mid-1970s Hunter's paintings were becoming so valuable that more than one artist was forging them. Yet, as late as 1975, *Reader's Digest* reported that Hunter received only a fraction of the two hundred to eight hundred dollars that her more sought-after pieces brought in big-city galleries. "Like many other folk artists, she has done most of her work for the people in her own area—and at prices they can afford. They love her for it," wrote Allen Rankin.

How much the charm of Hunter's story contributed to her popularity among collectors may never be known. For white patrons, at least, she filled a niche in the art market, as the black Grandma Moses, according to Verdis Dowdy. Very few of Hunter's patrons were black. Some black community leaders in Natchitoches suspected white patrons of finding virtue in her art because of her illiteracy. Her unwillingness to leave the neighborhood of her youth, coupled with her illiteracy, probably precluded her having direct relations with major galleries and direct participation in the larger profits for her art since the mid-1970s. By her late eighties, however, she was able at least to save enough to get a house trailer to replace her old cabin and buy space in a mausoleum with a fine coffin. In December 1987 she stopped painting and took to her bed. On January 1, 1988, at the age of 101, she died.

During her lifetime, Hunter had some two dozen solo exhibitions at galleries of such institutions as Fisk University, Dillard University, and the University of Texas at Arlington, and numerous major group shows. Hunter's work is part of more than a score of permanent collections, including those of the Amistad Research at Tulane University, the Birmingham Museum of Art, the Dallas Museum of Fine Art, the High Museum in Atlanta, Illinois State University, the Louisiana State Museum, the New York Historical Association, Radcliffe College, and Vassar College.

**Profile by
Lester Sullivan**

ZORA NEALE HURSTON

*T*he list of words accurately describing the thirty-year career of Zora

1891-1960 •

Neale Hurston includes anthropologist, dramatist, essayist, folklorist,

novelist, short story writer, and autobiographer. She is noted as the first

folklorist •

black American to collect and publish African-American and African-

Caribbean folklore. Her study of black folklore throughout the African

diaspora shaped her entire career as an essayist and creative writer in

that she wrote numerous articles on various aspects of black culture—its

dialect, religious rituals, and folk tales—and three of her four published

novels deal with the common black folk of her native southern Florida.

Hurston was born on January 7, 1891, in Eatonville, Florida, to Reverend John Hurston and Lucy Ann (Potts) Hurston. In her autobiography, *Dust Tracks on a Road,* Hurston credits the adult "lying sessions" (daily exchanges of folk tales) on Joe Clark's store porch in Eatonville for

giving her important insights into the nature of human behavior. While many of the adults engaged in exchanging tales, singing songs, and "lying" were unemployed at various times during Hurston's childhood, when Hurston described these sessions in various of her writings she studiously avoided protesting economic discrimination against blacks in America. She chose to demonstrate that black life in America was much more creative and vibrant than the surface poverty and one-dimensional acts of social protest. The poet and critic Arna Bontemps, one of Hurston's contemporaries during the Harlem Renaissance, stated in his review of her autobiography that Hurston "deals very simply with the more serious aspects of Negro life in America—she ignores them."

One of Hurston's earliest published essays, "How It Feels to Be Colored Me," states in no uncertain terms her refusal to spend her life lamenting the social plight of the black American:

> I do not belong to the sobbing school of Negrohood who hold that nature somehow has given them a lowdown dirty deal and whose feelings are all hurt about it. Even in the helter-skelter skirmish that is my life, I have seen that the world is to the strong regardless of a little pigmentation more or less. I do not weep at the world—I am too busy sharpening my oyster knife.

We can attribute this defiant confidence in her capabilities and in America's positive responses to her talents to her early life in Eatonville and her mother's encouragement to "jump at the sun" even if she could not land there. Furthermore, her statement reflects her unwavering belief in the fundamental equality between the races: there were good and bad, strong and weak individuals among both races, and no one group was perfect.

At age thirty in 1925, after studying for a time at Howard University, Hurston migrated to New York City and immediately became involved with the Harlem Renaissance, the black literary and cultural movement of the 1920s. During that time Harlem was the mecca for creative blacks from all over the United States and the Caribbean. Writers such as Claude McKay arrived from Jamaica, Eric Walrond from Barbados, Wallace Thurman from Salt Lake City, Jean Toomer and Sterling Brown from Washington, D.C., Rudolph Fisher from Rhode Island, and Langston Hughes from Kansas. Hurston, who befriended and worked along with all of these writers, was the only one to arrive in New York from the rural southeast—the cradle of black folk life that the renaissance celebrated. The sociologist Charles S. Johnson, who in 1925 founded *Opportunity: A*

Journal of Negro Life, and Alain Locke, who edited the anthology *The New Negro,* each admired and published Hurston's stories. She collaborated with Langston Hughes and a few other poets to publish *Fire!,* a one-issue literary magazine of black culture. Primarily because of the attention her stories attracted, Hurston received a scholarship in 1925 to attend Barnard College.

• *Folklore study*

is unique

Awarded a bachelor of arts from Barnard in 1928, Hurston continued her graduate studies at Columbia University under the direction of anthropologist Franz Boas. It was Boas who encouraged Hurston to return to Eatonville to collect black folklore, which she did with the assistance of a private grant from a New York socialite, Mrs. Osgood Mason. *Mules and Men* is a collection of the folklore Hurston gathered in Florida and Alabama between 1929 and 1931 and includes a revision of an essay on hoodoo (or voodoo) she had written in 1931 for the *Journal of American Folklore. Mules and Men* is unique in that it is the first such collection of folklore published by a black American woman, and it is by a woman indigenous to the culture from which the stories arise.

The traditional practice among academicians in anthropology is to study cultures that are unfamiliar to the researcher to insure a scientific objectivity. Boas assumed that Hurston's familiarity with her native village, Eatonville, and the rural South in general would prove advantageous to collecting African-American lore. The manuscript Hurston produced after her trips proved Boas correct. In his introduction to *Mules and Men,* Boas praised her work as invaluable because it "throws into relief the peculiar amalgamation of African and European tradition which is so important for understanding historically the character of American Negro life." Yet several black reviewers did not share Boas's enthusiasm for the affirmative, sometimes happy, side of black rural life represented in *Mules and Men.* Complaints about the absence of bitterness over racism and economic exploitation in Hurston's works recurred throughout her career.

• *Their Eyes*

Were Watching

God

Hurston published what critics agree is her best novel in 1937. Written in seven straight weeks in the Caribbean after a love affair ended, *Their Eyes Were Watching God* takes as its theme a black woman's search for an identity beyond that which prevailed in her small rural town. The main character, Janie (Crawford) Killicks Starks Woods, is a coffee-and-cream-colored quadroon. Raised by her maternal grandmother, a former slave, Janie rejects the community's expectations that she aspire to be the dutiful wife of a prosperous black farmer. From the onset of puberty, when Janie awakens under a blossoming pear tree, she yearns for an emotionally fulfilling union with another. This pear tree and Janie's expressed yearning to search beyond the horizon of her hometown symbolize her quest for a natural and unconstrained existence.

The novel insists on Janie's complete freedom to such an extent that she lives a feminist fantasy of expressing her sexual passion without facing its natural consequences of conception. This is a radical idea for the 1930s: that a beautiful black woman like Janie, left a widow living happily alone in her house at the end of the novel, can and should realize her fullest potential sexually and intellectually by and for herself.

Notwithstanding Hurston's suppression of the biological truisms of human sexuality in *Their Eyes Were Watching God*, the novel is a brilliant study of black folk and their language, their stories, and their mannerisms. All of this works symbolically as a measure of the characters' integrity and freedom, which in turn demonstrates a contrast to the image of the carefree "happy darky" that prevailed in the fiction of many American novelists.

Despite her literary descriptions of fulfilling relationships, Hurston's own all-consuming passion was collecting and studying African-American and African-Caribbean folklore. She pursued this with such intensity that she had difficulties maintaining long-term relationships with men. She was married twice, once in 1927 to Herbert Sheen, a musician, and again in 1939 to Albert Price III, with whom she had worked in connection with the Works Project Administration. These marriages each ended in divorce, primarily because Hurston refused to give up her career as a folklorist to remain at home. According to Hurston's biographers, she was at first passionately in love with both of her husbands, but that love was not enough to replace her passion for studying the folkways of blacks and her desire to succeed as a creative writer. She used any money awarded to her (two Guggenheim Fellowships, 1936 and 1938, granted by Mrs. Osgood Mason, a wealthy white socialite) or earned through the sale of her novels to travel throughout the southern United States and the Caribbean.

Hurston's •

passion

remains

folklore

Hurston's second collection of folklore, *Tell My Horse,* was published in 1938 following two trips to the Caribbean, and her third novel, *Moses, Man of the Mountain,* came out in 1939. *Moses* is a retelling of the biblical legend from the African-American point of view, with the Israelites cast as dialect-speaking southern blacks and Moses as a black voodoo doctor. The story blends fiction, folklore, religion, and comedy, and most critics assess it as a minor classic in African-American literature.

At her publisher's request, Hurston wrote an autobiography, *Dust Tracks on a Road,* which was published in 1942. Notwithstanding the inaccuracies that her biographers cite, Hurston does offer a straight linear narration of her life, from her birth and nurtured early childhood among the black folk in Eatonville through her turbulent adolescence and her life as a vagabond after her mother's death and her father's remarriage. She outlines her pursuit of an education at Howard University and Barnard College and summarizes her ethnographic research and the writing of her novels. Hence Hurston does attempt to adhere to the conventional innocence-to-experience plot of autobiography, even though she demonstrates an aversion to specific dates and rigorously avoids mentioning many intimate details of her life, such as her two failed marriages.

The 1950s marked the beginning of the end of Hurston's career; her income from her novels and folklore dropped significantly, forcing her to take on a series of menial jobs in various small towns in southern Florida. Moreover, Hurston published only a few articles and reviews during this time. None of her book-length manuscripts made its way into print. On October 29, 1959, after suffering a stroke, Hurston was forced to enter the Saint Lucie County Welfare Home in Fort Pierce, Florida. Her fiercely independent nature kept her from asking friends and family for shelter. She died in poverty at Saint Lucie on January 28, 1960, and was buried in an unmarked grave in a segregated cemetery. The novelist and poet Alice Walker, who identifies Hurston as her own literary foremother, traveled to the Fort Pierce, Florida, grave site in August 1973 and placed a stone marker on the approximate spot of Hurston's grave.

**Profile by
Alice A. Deck**

SHIRLEY ANN JACKSON

S hirley Ann Jackson is one of today's most distinguished young black

1946- •

American scientists. She has made important contributions to several

areas of theoretical physics; these include the three-body scattering

physicist •

problem, charge density waves in layered compounds, polaronic aspects

of electrons in the surface of liquid helium films, and the optical and

electronic properties of semiconductor strained layer superlattices.

Born in Washington, D.C., on August 5, 1946, Shirley Ann Jackson was the second daughter of Beatrice and George Jackson. She credits her continuing interest in science to the help provided by her father in the construction of science projects and the strong belief in education held by both parents. In addition, excellent mathematics teachers and an accelerated program in mathematics and science at Roosevelt High School provided a strong background that prepared her for the rigors of college. Of even more importance were the healthy environments of the home and secondary schools; they provided the necessary basis for the intellectual sharpness and psychological toughness needed to pursue a career in scientific research.

Graduating from Roosevelt High School in 1964 as valedictorian, she entered the Massachusetts Institute of Technology, from which she

received a bachelor's degree in physics in 1968. In 1973 she became the first black woman to earn a Ph.D. from the Massachusetts Institute of Technology; her research was in theoretical elementary particle physics and was directed by James Young, the first full-time tenured black professor in the physics department.

After earning her doctorate, Jackson was a research associate at the Fermi National Accelerator Laboratory in Batavia, Illinois, and a visiting scientist at the European Center for Nuclear Research in Geneva, Switzerland. At both institutions she worked on theories of strongly interacting elementary particles. Since 1976, Jackson has been at AT&T Bell Laboratories in Murray Hill, New Jersey, where she has done research on various topics relating to theoretical material sciences.

Jackson has received more than ten scholarships, fellowships, and grants, including the Martin Marietta Aircraft Company Scholarship and Fellowship; a Prince Hall Masons Scholarship; a National Science Foundation Traineeship; and Ford Foundation Advanced Study Fellowship and Individual Grant. She has studied at the International School of Subnuclear Physics in Erice, Sicily, and the Ecole d'été de Physique Theorique in Les Houches, France.

Shirley Jackson has received numerous honors, including election as a fellow of the American Physical Society, the CIBA-GEIGY "Exceptional Black Scientists" Poster Series, and the Karl Taylor Compton Award of MIT. Her professional society memberships include the American Physical Society, the American Association for the Advancement of Science, Sigma Xi, and the National Society of Black Physicists, of which she is a past president.

In 1985, New Jersey Governor Thomas Kean appointed Jackson to the New Jersey Commission on Science and Technology, and she was reappointed for a five-year term in 1989. She has also served on committees of the National Academy of Sciences, American Association for the Advancement of Science, and the National Science Foundation, promoting science and research and women's roles in these fields. Jackson is a trustee of MIT, Rutgers University, Lincoln University, and the Barnes Foundation.

Jackson has published more than one hundred scientific articles and abstracts. Her papers have appeared in *Annuals of Physics, Nuovo Cimento, Physical Review, Solid State Communications, Applied Physics Letters*, and *Journal of Applied Physics*.

First black •

female to earn

Ph.D. at MIT

**Profile by
Ronald E. Mickens**

MAE C. JEMISON

M ae C. Jemison, thus far this country's single black woman astro-

1956- •

naut and scheduled for a shuttle flight in August 1992, is a versatile

scholar whose primary interests are science and exploration of the

astronaut, •

universe. She has blended her skills in chemical engineering, medicine,

physician

and health care to become involved in one of the nation's leading

experimental projects, survived the rigorous training programs neces-

sary for space research, and emerged as a science mission specialist,

which allows her to experiment with metals and new compounds and to

study the effects of gravity on the human body.

One of three children, Jemison was born on October 17, 1956, in Decatur, Alabama, to Charlie Jemison, a maintenance supervisor, and Dorothy Jemison, a schoolteacher. The family moved to Chicago when she was three to take advantage of educational opportunities. The

Jemisons had a profound influence on their children's development and encouraged their talents and abilities. In addition, when she was four, Jemison's uncle, a social worker, helped stimulate her interest in science. She became especially interested in anthropology and archaeology. In school Jemison spent considerable time in the library reading and learning all she could about extinct animals, theories of evolution, science fiction, and particularly astronomy. Her family and friends constantly fostered her interest in these areas, and as result "I ended up being constantly aware of the world around me because of my own interest," she told Maria C. Johnson.

While she was in Morgan Park High School, one of Jemison's classes visited a local university, creating in her a curiosity about the biomedical engineering profession. She reasoned that such a position would require her to study biology, physics, and chemistry. Consistently on the honor roll, she graduated from high school in 1973 and entered Stanford University on a National Achievement Scholarship, later earning a degree in chemical engineering. Her versatility extended to nonscientific activities, including participation in dance and theater productions and representing Stanford in Carifesta '76 in Jamaica; she also enrolled in courses in African-American studies and earned a second bachelor's degree in that field. Jemison's views on becoming a well-rounded person were firm then, as Johnson reported:

> Science is very important to me, but I also like to stress that you have to be well-rounded. One's love for science doesn't get rid of all the other areas. I truly feel someone interested in science is interested in understanding what's going on in the world. That means you have to find out about social science, art, and politics.

After graduating from Stanford, Jemison entered Cornell University's medical school in the fall of 1977. Her interest in exploring the world and helping people led her to volunteer during medical school for a summer experience in a Thai refugee camp. She saw people who were malnourished, ill with tuberculosis, and asthmatic, and who suffered from dysentery and other maladies. On a grant from the International Travelers Institute, she was engaged in health studies in Kenya in 1979. In that same year she organized the New York City-wide health and law fair for the National Student Medical Association.

After graduating from medical school in 1981, Jemison completed her internship at Los Angeles County/University of Southern California Medical Center in July 1982, and worked as general practitioner with INA/Ross Loos Medical Group in Los Angeles until December of that year. From January 1983 through July 1985 she was the area Peace Corps medical officer for Sierra Leone and Liberia in West Africa. There she was manager of health care for Peace Corps volunteers and United States Embassy personnel as well. In addition to handling medical administrative issues by supervising medical personnel and laboratories, she developed curricula and taught volunteer personnel, wrote manuals for self-care, and developed and implemented guidelines on public health and safety issues for volunteers. In conjunction with the National Institutes of Health and the Center for Disease Control, Jemison developed and participated in research projects on hepatitis B vaccine, schistosomiasis, and rabies. In 1985 she returned to the United States and joined CIGNA Health Plans, a health maintenance organization in Los Angeles.

Jemison reached a decision early on that she wanted to be an astronaut. Here again she could "blend skills" and at the same time continue to develop her talents and abilities. The idea of space travel fascinated Jemison, who was already adventuresome, inquisitive, and eager to learn. While working as a general practitioner in Los Angeles, she applied to the National Aeronautics and Space Administration (NASA) and enrolled in night courses in engineering at the University of California at Los Angeles. During this period an unfortunate turn of events occurred: Spaceship Challenger failed on January 28, 1986, and NASA temporarily suspended its astronaut selection process. Saddened but not deterred, Jemison told *Ebony:* "I thought about it . . . because of the astronauts who were lost, but not in any way keeping me from being interested in it or changing my views." Later, Jemison reapplied, and NASA invited her to join the program. She was one of fifteen candidates chosen from a field of approximately two thousand qualified applicants.

Jemison joins •

space program

Jemison joined NASA's space program in 1987, completing a one-year training and evaluation program in August, 1988, which qualified her as a mission specialist. Her technical assignments included astronaut office representative to the Kennedy Space Center at Cape Canaveral, Florida, which involved processing space shuttles for launching by checking payloads and the thermal protection system (tiles), launch countdown, and work in the Shuttle Avionics Integration Laboratory (SAIL) to verify shuttle computer software.

The United States and Japan have developed a joint mission to conduct experiments in life sciences and materials processing called Spacelab J, scheduled for launching in August of 1992, and Jemison has been selected as a mission specialist on the space team. As science mission specialist, she will experiment with new compounds and metals and at the same time study the effect of gravity on the human body.

Currently, there are 104 astronauts, of whom eighteen are women and five are black. She is the only black woman. Looked upon as a role model, Jemison says that "if I'm a role model, what I'd like to be is someone who says, 'No, don't try to . . . be like me or live your life or grow up to be an astronaut or a physician unless that's what you want to do'." She admits that she never had a role model, and she is concerned about blacks and the NASA program. She readily acknowledges that blacks and other Americans have benefited from the space program, advances in communications, medicine, and the environment. "Some might say that the environment is not a Black issue, but I worked in Los Angeles and I saw more Black and Hispanic children with uncontrolled asthma as a result of pollution. Just as many of us get sick from those types of things," she told Marilyn Marshall, "and, in fact, we have more problems with them because many of us don't have the availability of health care."

Jemison's distinguished career has brought recognition from many groups. In addition to her busy speaking engagements, particularly in colleges and schools, she was honored by *Essence* magazine in 1988 when she received the Essence Science and Technology Award. In 1989 she became Gamma Sigma's Gamma Woman of the Year. The mural *Black Americans in Flight* by Spencer Taylor, unveiled in the Lambert-Saint Louis International Airport, honors Jemison as the first black woman astronaut. She is a member of the American Medical Association, the American Chemical Society, and an honorary member of the Alpha Kappa Alpha Sorority. Jemison is now based at the Lyndon B. Johnson Space Center in Houston, Texas. For her concern with social needs of the community as well as with the space program, Jemison has been called a national asset.

**Profile by
Jessie Carney Smith**

BARBARA JORDAN

What makes Barbara so special? It's that along with all her superior

1936- ●

intelligence and legislative skill she also has a certain moral authority

and a . . . presence, and it all comes together in a way that sort of grabs

politician, ●

you, maybe you're kind of intimidated by it, and you have to listen when

lawyer,

she speaks and you feel you must try and do what she wants. What

educator

Barbara has is not something you learn and develop, it's something that

God gave her and it's something you can't really describe."

So said Congressman Charles Wilson in 1975 about Barbara Charline Jordan, whom he called "the most influential member of Congress." Jordan gained national recognition as a politician first in the Texas State Senate and then in the United States House of Representatives, where she had a nationwide television audience as the House Judiciary committee considered articles of impeachment against President Richard M. Nixon.

Jordan was born February 21, 1936, in the segregated city of Houston, Texas. After graduating from Phillis Wheatley High School in

1952 she attended Texas Southern University, where she earned a degree in government before enrolling in Boston University's Law School. Once in Boston, Jordan competed with white students in a nonsegregated setting for the first time, and the adjustment was not easy. She felt that she "learned at twenty-one that you just couldn't say a thing is so because it might not be so, and somebody brighter, smarter, and more thoughtful would come out and tell you it wasn't so. . . . I was doing sixteen years of remedial work in thinking." She worked hard to overcome her perceived deficiencies. Her religious life began to change also from a focus on God's prohibitions to one on God's love under the influence of Howard Thurman's sermons. She was one of just two black women in the graduating class of 128. Shortly after graduation in 1959, she passed both the Massachusetts and Texas bar exams.

Although Jordan was offered a job in Massachusetts, she opted to open a private practice in Texas. She was soon involved in the 1960 presidential campaign, working for the Kennedy-Johnson ticket. Her first political success came when she developed a highly organized black-worker program for the forty predominantly black precincts of Harris County and managed to get an eighty percent voter turnout, the most successful get-out-the-vote campaign in Harris County that anyone could recall.

Jordan became increasingly involved in Texas politics in the early 1960s: she was speaker for the Harris County Democratic Party and ran unsuccessfully for the Texas House of Representatives in 1962 and 1964. Jordan's family pressured her to marry, but she made a decision to commit her life to politics. "I couldn't have it both ways," she said. "I reasoned that this political thing was so total in terms of focus that, if I formed an attachment [like marriage], this total commitment would become less than total."

In 1965 Harris County was reapportioned and Jordan found herself in a newly created Eleventh State Senatorial District. In the new district, she won against a popular liberal by a two-to-one margin. Harris County elected two blacks that year—Jordan to the senate and Curtis Graves to the house. When she went to Austin, the state capital, Jordan worked hard to fit in, because she was the first black elected to the Texas State Senate since 1883 as well as the first woman ever elected. She took this opportunity to hone her political skills. One aspect of this was to know how things worked; she later said: "If you're going to play the game properly, you'd better know every rule." This meant knowing the unwritten rules as well. In an *Ebony* article, Charles Sanders describes her skills in the game:

301 •

She not only dazzled [members of the Texas delegation] with her intellectual brilliance but also with her knowledge of their kind of rough-and-tumble politics. . . . She never permitted the men of the "club" to feel uncomfortable around her. She could smoke and drink Scotch—just like them. She could tone down her Boston University kind of speech and talk Texas lingo—just like them. She knew as much as they did, or more, about such things as oil depletion allowances and cotton prices and the Dallas money market, but she never, says one member of the "club," made men "feel like we had a smart-aleck, know-it-all women on our hands." He explains: "Now Barbara doesn't try to play possum on you; she doesn't mind letting you know that she's got a very, very high I.Q. But she doesn't embarrass you by making you feel that you're nowhere close to being as smart as she is. It's an amazing thing how she can be standing there schooling you about something and still make you feel that you knew all that right along."

In her six years in the Texas Senate, she "sponsored most of the state's environmental legislation, authored the first Texas minimum wage law, forced the state to place antidiscrimination clauses in all of its business contracts, and pushed the first package of urban legislation through a rural-minded state government dominated by white males," *Ebony* noted. She served in the Texas Senate until 1972, when she chose to run for the U.S. House of Representatives and won, taking office in January of 1973.

• *Defense of the*

Constitution

brings national

acclaim

When Jordan was elected to Congress, she asked Lyndon Johnson's advice on what committee assignments to request. Johnson advised her to request the Judiciary Committee and made arrangements to assure her assignment. In retrospect, that assignment turned into a major task; the Watergate Scandal put pressure on Congress, prompting the Judiciary Committee to initiate impeachment proceedings against President Richard Nixon. Although she originally argued against public speeches on the subject, she got no support for that position and her fifteen-minute, nationally televised speech on the duty of elected officials to defend the Constitution catapulted her into the public eye as nothing she had ever done before. Jordan disliked the idea of impeachment but felt that the evidence demanded that an indictment of Nixon be presented to the Senate. In her July 25, 1974, speech in favor of impeachment she used all her skills as a lawyer and as an orator to defend the constitutional issues that she felt were pertinent to her decision, and to persuade others of the rectitude of her position. *Newsweek* called her speech "the most memorable indictment of Richard Nixon to emerge from the House impeachment." She began by saying:

> "We the people"—it is a very eloquent beginning. But when the Constitution of the United States was completed on the seventeenth of September in 1787, I was not included in that "We the People." I felt for many years that somehow George Washington and Alexander Hamilton just left me out by mistake. But through the process of amendment, interpretation, and court decision, I have finally been included in "We the people."

> Today I am an inquisitor. I believe hyperbole would not be fictional and would not overstate the solemnness that I feel right now. My faith in the Constitution is whole. It is complete. It is total. I am not going to sit here and be an idle spectator in the diminution, the subversion, the destruction of the Constitution.

She then moved through the case against Nixon, concluding:

> Has the President committed offenses and planned and directed and acquiesced in a course of conduct which the Constitution will not tolerate? That is the question. We know that. We should now forthwith proceed to answer the question. It is reason and not passion which must guide our decision.

In the first session of her first term the Omnibus Crime Control and Safe Streets Act came up for renewal. Jordan proposed a civil rights amendment to mandate the use of federal funds in a nondiscriminatory fashion. She also introduced a bill proposing the repeal of the Fair Trade Laws, which allowed manufacturers to establish retail prices and to enforce them, a price-fixing mechanism that interfered with free competition.

Her reputation as one of the great orators of the twentieth century was sustained by her keynote address to the 1976 Democratic National Convention. She said that "we cannot improve on the system of government handed down to us by the founders of the Republic, but we can find new ways to implement that system and realize our destiny." She went on to quote Abraham Lincoln, evoking his idea of "a national community in which every last one of us participates; 'As I would not be a *slave,* so I would not be a *master.*' This expresses my idea of democracy. Whatever differs from this, to the extent of the difference, is no democracy."

In 1978 she decided against running for Congress again and, in effect, retired into a teaching position at the Lyndon B. Johnson School of Public Affairs, University of Texas at Austin. In 1982 she was appointed to the Lyndon B. Johnson Centennial Chair in National Policy. She serves as a faculty advisor, as a minority recruiter, and as teacher at the University of Texas at Austin.

Jordan said that she left Congress because she "felt more of a responsibility to the country as a whole, as contrasted with the duty of representing the half-million people in the Eighteenth Congressional District. I felt some necessity to address national issues. I thought that my role now was to be one of the voices in the country defining where we were, where we were going, what the policies were that were being pursued, and where the holes in those policies were. I felt I was more in an instructive role than a legislative role."

An academic invitation was the catalyst that led her to the decision to leave political office. She received a letter from Harvard University saying they had voted to give her an honorary doctorate at the next commencement. A month later another letter came from Harvard inviting her to speak at that commencement. Thinking about the speech at Harvard led her to the conclusion that she had to "leave elected politics . . . to free my time in such a way that it could be structured by the country's needs as I perceived them."

**Profile by
James Duckworth**

The JOYNERS

Olympic •

O n the surface, they couldn't be more different: one is warm and

outgoing, sometimes ebullient; the other is quiet, self-contained. One is

gold

conservative in style; the other is flashy to the point of garishness. But

medalists

sisters-in-law Jackie Joyner-Kersee and Florence Griffith Joyner,

considered the world's greatest female athlete and the world's fastest

female sprinter, respectively, share a common beginning—both were

born into poverty—and a firm, moral upbringing, which imprinted

upon them both the desire and the necessary dedication to excel. They

have fulfilled their life goals of becoming not only the best in their field,

but perhaps the greatest the world has ever seen.

Joyner-Kersee, the daughter of Alfred, a construction worker, and
Mary, a nurse's assistant, was born Jacqueline Joyner on March 3, 1962,

in East St. Louis, Illinois, an industrial city along the banks of the Mississippi River. In an environment filled with desperation and destruction, alcohol and drugs numbed the residents to the bleak conditions of living and dying. Before she was twelve years old, Joyner-Kersee witnessed the murder of a man on the street. A few years later, her drunken grandfather shot her grandmother to death. Her childhood was darkened further by the severity of her family's poverty. In the winter, she and her three siblings slept by the kitchen stove to keep warm. Water pipes froze. Sometimes there was no food or very little; mayonnaise sandwiches were a complete meal. She often wore the same dress to school three or four days in a row. But Joyner-Kersee never fell prey to the consuming despair of the streets around her, inheriting from her mother instead "a kind of old-fashioned decency that encompassed a host of values—modesty, faith, perseverance—that seems almost anachronistic today, especially in the bitter, cynical ghetto where she was raised," Pat Jordan pointed out.

Personal achievement became Joyner-Kersee's goal. When she was nine years old she entered a track event at a community center across the street from her home. She finished last. But she practiced, persevered, and, with her talent slowly emerging, began winning events. By the time she was twelve years old, she had long-jumped an incredible seventeen feet. Throughout high school, she continued her athletic ascent: she won four consecutive National Junior Pentathlon championships, led her basketball and volleyball teams to titles, set a state of Illinois high jump record in her junior year, and was viewed as the finest athlete in the state. Mindful of her mother's teachings, Joyner-Kersee combined these athletic achievements with scholastic ones as well. She graduated in the top 10 percent of her class in 1980 and won a basketball scholarship to the University of California at Los Angeles.

Griffith Joyner also grew up poor. The daughter of Robert, an electronics technician, and Florence, a seamstress, Florence Delorez Griffith was born on December 21, 1959, the seventh of eleven children. She and her siblings were raised in a housing project in the Watts section of Los Angeles by their mother after their parents divorced. Oatmeal three times a day was a standard fare. But the family was nourished by a loving, creative, and moral atmosphere. Every Wednesday evening Mary would gather her children for a family powwow, using the Bible as a touchstone to discuss the family's behavior of the last week. In addition, being a single parent, she stressed independence and individuality. "My mother had no choice but to be independent," Griffith Joyner was quoted as saying in *Contemporary Heroes and Heroines,* "and I think I got that from her—being able to stand on my own two feet.

She taught us all that nothing is going to be handed to you—you have to make things happen."

Being independent also meant standing apart from others. Griffith Joyner related to Stephanie Mansfield how her mother always told her, "It's easy to look alike; but when you look different, that's special." From a young age, Griffith Joyner found pleasure and escape in cosmetics and fashion design, creating unique styles for both her dolls and herself. At the age of seven, she began running track, first as a way to do something her other siblings didn't, then, when she began winning, for fun and a sense of individual achievement. Her father lived in the Mohave Desert, and she improved her speed by chasing jack rabbits when she visited him. By the time she graduated from high school in 1978, Griffith Joyner had set school records in sprints and in the long jump. She subsequently enrolled at California State University at Northridge.

• **Bob Kersee**

inspires both

runners

One man proved fateful in recognizing and nurturing the athletic abilities of both Griffith Joyner and Joyner-Kersee. When Griffith Joyner attended college, she majored in business, but a lack of money forced her to drop out after only one year and work as a bank teller. Bob Kersee, an assistant track coach with California State University whose "genius [was] recognizing raw talent and channeling it in its natural direction," Jordan emphasized, convinced her to return to the university, secured financial aid for her, and worked with her on the 200-meter dash. In 1980 Kersee accepted an assistant coaching position at UCLA. At his urging, she reluctantly followed him (UCLA didn't carry her major), aware that her track career was just beginning.

The summer before she began college, Joyner-Kersee earned a spot on the U.S. Olympic team in the long jump, but the subsequent U.S. boycott of the 1980 games in Moscow cut her dream short. In her freshman year her world was further shattered by her mother's death from meningitis. She found solace and direction in Bob Kersee. He sought her out for two reasons: to console her (he had lost his mother when he was also young) and, astonished by her overall athletic ability, to convince her to focus on her abilities on the heptathlon, a two-day track event consisting of a 200-meter dash, a 100-meter hurdles race, an 800-meter run, and the high jump, shot put, long jump, and javelin throw competitions.

Under Kersee's direction, both athletes flourished. In 1982, Griffith Joyner won the NCAA championship in the 200-meter dash with a time of 22.39 seconds, and became known as one of the country's most promising amateur athletes. In 1983 Joyner-Kersee qualified to compete in the world track and field championships in Finland, but had to withdraw after a hamstring injury. The following year, both Griffith

Joyner and Joyner-Kersee qualified for the Summer Olympics held in Los Angeles. Portending future achievements, both athletes earned silver medals in their respective events. Even with a second place finish (hampered by another hamstring injury), Joyner-Kersee set a U.S. heptathlon record of 6520 points. She had lost the gold in the final event, the 800-meter run, by .06 seconds.

But the two athletes' reactions to their 1984 Olympic accomplishments vastly differed. Joyner-Kersee was determined to improve her score and continued to train diligently, competing at various track meets around the world. But Griffith Joyner, upset by her loss, secured a full-time position as a secretary in a bank, worked at night as a hair stylist, and began writing children's books. Her training schedule was cut severely; she gained weight. Pete Axthelm quoted Griffith Joyner's physical therapist Robert Forster on her sudden change in direction: "Florence is not a typical athlete. The rest of them sit around and watch soap operas. Florence wants to stretch for something more." Finally, in 1986, upon the urging of Bob Kersee and her boyfriend Al Joyner, a 1984 Olympic triple-jump gold medalist and Joyner-Kersee's brother, Griffith Joyner resumed her training in preparation for the 1988 Olympic games in Seoul, South Korea.

Within two years, both athletes' personal and athletic lives underwent an exponential jump. Joyner-Kersee married Bob Kersee on January 11, 1986. That same year, at the Goodwill Games in Moscow, she shocked the world by becoming the first heptathlete to break the 7,000 point mark, only to then break that mark a month later at a meet in Houston, Texas, with a final point total of 7,161. She was hailed as the world's greatest female athlete, champion of an event that is "the equivalent of learning seven different languages, and Joyner-Kersee speaks all of them fluently, a few brilliantly," Alice Gabriel ventured. These winning performances earned her the 1986 Sullivan Award (given to the nation's best amateur athlete), the 1986 Jesse Owens Award, and the *Track and Field News* "Athlete of the Year" award. The following year, Joyner-Kersee won two gold medals at the world track and field championships (a prelude to an upcoming Olympics), and was subsequently named Female Athlete of the Year for 1987 by the Associated Press.

Meanwhile, Griffith Joyner was marking her own achievements. She married Al Joyner on October 10, 1987. And, as she told Craig A. Masback, "When you've been second-best for so long, you can either accept it, or try to become the best. I made the decision to try and be the best in 1988." In July of that year, at the Olympic Trials, she eclipsed the world record in the 100-meter race by running a 10.49 second pace, .27

Athletes' lives •

leap forward

seconds better than the previous record. In addition, Griffith Joyner grabbed newspaper headlines and magazine covers for her unorthodox and sexy racing outfits: florescent colored bodysuits with one leg sheared off covered by fetching bikini bottoms. With her long hair flowing like a lion's mane and her three-inch highly manicured fingernails painted an assortment of bright colors, Griffith Joyner brought "unprecedented glamour to a taxing and sweaty sport," Axthelm believed.

At the 1988 Summer Olympics, Joyner-Kersee and Griffith Joyner provided the world with their greatest performances. Joyner-Kersee won two gold medals: in the long jump, she soared 24 feet, 3.5 inches, the second best of her career; in the heptathlon, she broke her own world record point total again. Griffith Joyner won three gold medals (for the 100-meter and 200-meter dashes and the 400-meter relay) and one silver (for the 1600-meter relay), the most medals an American female track athlete has won. But it was her performances in the 200-meter races that were truly astounding: in the first heat she broke the Olympic record; in the semi-final the next day, she broke the world record; in the final, less than two hours later, she set a new world record of 21.34. In a four-day span at the Olympics, she had broken four records. "Blessed with speed and style and defiant sexuality," Mansfield noted, "Florence Griffith Joyner has broken down the barrier between vanity and athletic prowess and is living proof that one needn't cancel out the other." For her achievement, she was named Female Athlete of the Year for 1988 by the Associated Press and also received the 1988 Sullivan Award.

Griffith Joyner subsequently became the most widely recognized American athlete. Phil Hersh pointed out how the public "saw in Griffith Joyner the embodiment of a new ideal in American women. She was beautiful, physically fit, daring enough to race in a costume that looked like a negligee and talented at more than running." It was exactly these extra talents and her desire to pursue them, however, that forced Griffith Joyner to announce her retirement from track and field on February 25, 1989, at the peak of her career. She listed acting, designing, modeling, and writing as areas of interests that left little time for her to train. But her feats were tarnished later in the year when American runner Darrell Robinson and others accused her of using anabolic steroids, drugs that enhance athletic prowess. The charges, however, were never verified, and Griffith Joyner has vehemently denied them, citing determination and hard work for her achievements.

Joyner-Kersee also had to defend her reputation against drug charges, continually proving them false with numerous urine tests and a standard of living that she holds up to others as a litmus test. Despite the debilitating effect of asthma—and the fact that she cannot take the best medication available to control the condition—Joyner-Kersee has continued to maintain her world-class standing, both as a sense of personal accomplishment and as a motivation to others. Between training and track meets, she finds time to tour the country, lecturing youth and civic groups and lending inspiration and insight. She has also extended her philanthropic work to her hometown, establishing a community foundation that raises funds to maintain recreation centers for disadvantaged youth.

**Profile by
Rob Nagel**

ELIZABETH KECKLEY

*B*orn into slavery, Elizabeth Hobbs Keckley bought her freedom, established a sewing business, and eventually became seamstress and friend to first lady Mary Todd Lincoln. One biographer, John E. Washington, said that "Madam Keckley was the most celebrated colored person ever connected with the White House."

c. 1824-1907 •

White House •

modiste

Keckley was born in Dinwiddie, Virginia. The exact date of her birth is unknown. Many sources give the year 1818; others list 1820, 1824, 1825, and even 1840. In a document dated April 18, 1863, signed by Keckley, she stated that she was thirty-nine years old—which would suggest 1824 or 1825 may be accurate.

As with many slave families, Keckley's home was divided. Keckley and her mother, Agnes, belonged to the Burwell family. Her father, George Pleasant, belonged to "a man named Hobbs," according to biographer John E. Washington, and was allowed to visit his family only at Christmas and Easter. Just when Colonel Burwell was making plans for the family to be together, her father's master moved west. "The announcement fell like a thunder-bolt" on a family that had already endured painful separation. For some time Keckley's parents corresponded with each other, but they never were reunited. The letters from her father became special keepsakes for Elizabeth Keckley.

Early in life the young slave girl began to strive for specific goals and encountered the painful realization that the path would not be an easy one. An especially painful memory was associated with her teenage years, which she recalled in her memoir *Behind the Scenes: Thirty Years a Slave and Four Years in the White House:*

> I was regarded as fair-looking for one of my race, and for four years a white man—I spare the world his name—had base designs upon me. I do not care to dwell upon this subject, for it is one that is fraught with pain. Suffice it to say, that he persecuted me for four years, and I—I —became a mother.

The man was Alexander Kirkland. The son, named George, was Keckley's only child. Later, as a young man, he became a Union soldier during the Civil War and was killed in battle.

Keckley said of her early life, "Notwithstanding all the wrongs that slavery heaped upon me, I can bless it for one thing—youth's important lesson of self-reliance." Throughout her life, Keckley not only relied upon her own resources but also served as a source of strength for others. She began her venture in the sewing business to prevent her master from hiring out her mother. Although her own health suffered, she "kept bread in the mouths of seventeen persons for two years and five months."

While serving her master's family, the Garlands, in St. Louis, Elizabeth Hobbs became reacquainted with James Keckley, who had moved from Virginia. He proposed marriage, but she declined his first offer because she was reluctant to bring children into slavery. Eventually, however, she accepted his proposal and married him in a brief ceremony in the Garlands' home. Later she wrote:

> The day was a happy one, but it faded all too soon. Mr. Keckley—let me speak kindly of his faults—proved dissipated, and a burden instead of a helpmate. More than all, I learned that he was a slave instead of a free man, as he represented himself to be. With the simple explanation that I lived with him eight years, let charity draw around him the mantle of silence.

• *Keckley buys*

freedom

Longing to be free, Elizabeth Keckley spoke often to Mr. Garland about purchasing freedom for herself and her son George. Her master, tired of hearing her request, forbade her to ask again, but Keckley could not refrain from renewing her campaign. Garland eventually set the price of freedom for Keckley and George at twelve hundred dollars.

When Garland died and his estate was being settled, the need for Keckley to raise the money became immediate. Keckley decided to go to New York and appeal to the benevolence of the people. But Mrs. Le Bourgois, one of her patrons, told her, "It would be a shame to allow you to go North to *beg* for what we should *give you*." Le Bourgois raised the funds by petitioning other patrons, Keckley accepted the money as a loan, and on August 13, 1855, she and George became free citizens. Entitled now to the money that she earned, she soon repaid the loan that had enabled her to reach the goal of freedom.

In 1860 Keckley attempted to earn a living by teaching young ladies to sew, first in Baltimore, then in Washington, D.C. In Washington, she quickly developed a clientele that included many of the most prominent ladies of the city, such as Mrs. Jefferson Davis, Mrs. Stephen A. Douglas, and Mrs. E. M. Stanton. "Ever since arriving in Washington I had a great desire to work for the ladies of the White House, and to accomplish this end I was ready to make almost any sacrifice consistent with propriety," Keckley stated. The primary sacrifice was hard work. She patiently built the sewing business, which she operated from rooms she rented. Eventually, she employed as many as twenty young ladies, teaching them not only dressmaking but also charm and elegance.

Keckley's business success came not only from her sewing and teaching skills, but also from her bearing and personality. These personal qualities, combined with Keckley's talent with a needle and thread, helped her to become "one of the most sought-after seamstresses in all of the capital," according to an *Ebony* feature.

Keckley's opportunities to fulfill her goal of sewing for the ladies of the White House came less than a year after she started her business. The Lincolns moved to the capital, and "within two weeks after President Lincoln arrived in Washington in late February 1861, Mrs. Keckley had moved into the family orbit," wrote Benjamin Quarles. The haste was occasioned by Mary Todd Lincoln's having spilled coffee on her dress for the inaugural reception. Mrs. McClean, a friend of Mrs. Lincoln's, had assured Keckley that she could provide an opportunity for Keckley to work in the White House, and this was an appropriate opportunity. Of the four seamstresses Mary Lincoln interviewed, she chose Keckley—with the provision that her services were not too expensive. Keckley completed her first project in time for the reception, and eventually she served not only as a dressmaker but also as a fashion designer, personal maid, and traveling companion to Mary Lincoln.

It was probably shared grief that drew them together initially. Early in their acquaintance, Keckley suffered the loss of her only son. Reserved and independent, Keckley bore her grief quietly but admitted, "It

Keckley's •

White House

years begin

was a sad blow to me, and the kind womanly letter that Mrs. Lincoln wrote to me when she heard of my bereavement was full of golden words of comfort." Just months later, Willie Lincoln, his mother's favorite son, caught a cold that developed into a fever. Keckley helped attend him during his illness and washed and dressed him when he died. Her own pain still fresh, she helped Mary Lincoln through the sorrow that threatened to overwhelm her. The experience of encountering grief together during those early days of their association strengthened their friendship.

The depth of the friendship between Keckley and Mary Lincoln was especially apparent on April 14, 1865, and in the days that followed. Hearing that Abraham Lincoln had been shot while attending a production at Ford's Theatre, Keckley unsuccessfully attempted to enter the heavily guarded White House to comfort Mary Lincoln. The next day she learned that Mary Lincoln had sent for her; however, three different messengers had failed to locate her.

In her grief, the president's widow refused contact with the world. She was unable to attend the funeral, and confined herself to her room for five weeks while she began to pack her belongings. Aside from the company of her own sons, the only person whose presence Mary Lincoln desired during those trying days was Keckley. Keckley helped Mary Lincoln with the packing, accompanied her to Chicago, helped her get settled there, and then returned to Washington to resume her business. With a reputed debt of seventy thousand dollars to be met, Mary Lincoln could not afford to retain Keckley.

The two ladies corresponded with each other, however, and when Mary Lincoln decided to secretly sell some of her clothes, she once again requested Keckley's assistance. In 1867 they met in New York, posing as Mrs. Clarke and a friend, and conducted an unsuccessful attempt to raise the needed money without attracting attention. Their identities were quickly discovered and highly publicized, and both women much criticized.

Behind the Scenes

Keckley continued her sewing business for a while in New York and then back in Washington. But she also entered into a new venture, hoping to solve the financial problems that she and Mary Lincoln faced. In 1868 G. W. Carlton and Company issued Keckley's book *Behind the Scenes,* in which she attempted to defend both Mary Lincoln and herself from the harsh criticism that was being heaped upon them.

Exposed along with Mary Lincoln's qualities and faults were private matters of the Lincoln family life, a detailed account of the "old-clothes scandal," personal letters written by Mary Lincoln, and many of her private opinions about important people. Biographer Ruth Randall commented:

> There is no reason to doubt that Mrs. Keckley told the story with the idea of helping Mrs. Lincoln, and told it with what appears to be, with the testing of modern research, a high degree of accuracy. But the publication of the book, which stepped on a lot of prominent toes which were very much alive, resulted in another furor. A viciously clever parody called *Behind the Seams* by "Betsey Kickley," who was represented as a Negro woman who could sign her name only by making an X for her mark, was rushed into the print the same year.

Robert Lincoln, humiliated by and enraged at the publication of his mother's private letters, refused to hear any explanations or apologies. According to some accounts, he persuaded the publisher to suppress the book. Although Keckley believed that Mary Lincoln bore her no grudge, she only heard from her "in a roundabout way" for the remainder of her life. Two attempts to help Mary Lincoln financially had failed, and now no avenue existed for the giving or receiving of emotional support.

No records indicate that the authorship of Keckley's book was seriously questioned during her lifetime. More recently, however, researchers have questioned the authenticity of the work. For example, in 1953's *Mary Lincoln, Biography of Marriage,* Ruth Randall says that "the Keckley book has the unsatisfactory status of a ghostwritten product; it has inaccuracies as all recollections have; it should be checked wherever possible; but when critically used it has considerable value for the careful scholar."

As recently as 1982, Benjamin Quarles stated that the book was ghostwritten by James Redpath or Hamilton Busbey. However, even if Keckley had help, or if the book was actually written by someone else, enough evidence exists to substantiate the information as memories of Keckley. Recognizing the value of those memories, Arno Press reprinted her book in 1968. In the beginning pages of the work, Keckley remarked, "I had been raised in a hardy school—had been taught to rely upon myself, and to prepare myself to render assistance to others." The information contained in her autobiography will continue to serve research needs of Lincoln scholars for many generations.

Keckley's last years were spent in the Home for Destitute Women and Children in Washington, an institution that she had helped create.

**Profile by
Marie Garrett**

Except for a weekly ride, Keckley spent most of the time in her room, where a picture of Mary Lincoln hung on the wall above the dresser. Keckley died of a paralytic stroke at the home on May 26, 1907, and was buried in Harmony Cemetery. An excerpt from Psalm 127 was engraved on her tombstone: "For So He Giveth His Beloved Sleep." A portrait of Keckley remained in the home for some time.

LEONTINE KELLY

Leontine Turpeau Current Kelly is a minister, church official, and the first black American woman elected bishop of a major religious denomination. She was strongly influenced by her parents, who were both active in the Methodist church, and encouraged by her husband, whose ministry she carried on after his death.

1920- •

religious leader •

Kelly was born March 5, 1920, in the parsonage of Mount Zion Methodist Episcopal Church in Washington, D.C. She was the seventh of eight children born to the Reverend David De Witt Turpeau, Sr., and Ila (Marshall) Turpeau. The Turpeaus had settled in Cincinnati by the late 1920s, and Kelly received her basic education in the public schools there. Her principal at the Harriet Beecher Stowe School, Jennie D. Porter, inspired Kelly to believe that sex or race should not be barriers to achievement. Porter was a pioneer: Cincinnati's first black principal and the first black person to earn a doctorate at the University of Cincinnati. Kelly later graduated from Woodward High School. Growing up in a parsonage, she learned how Methodist churches functioned and imbibed values from her parents about religion, race, gender, society, and the individual that would influence her life and later career.

During Kelly's youth and young adulthood, the Methodist church, like most Christian churches, maintained racial segregation in local churches and in its administrative structure. David Turpeau explained to his children that it was the duty of black Americans to be racial missionaries to the larger white church and change the attitudes of white Christians about racial issues and race relations as one step toward improving American society as a whole, racially and spiritually.

After graduating from high school, Kelly attended West Virginia State College (later West Virginia State University) between 1938 and 1941. She married Gloster Bryant Current, a fellow student at West Virginia who graduated in 1941, after completing her junior year, but by the mid-1950s Leontine and Gloster Current were divorced, leaving Leontine devastated. She sensed a need for personal renewal, believing the faith system she developed while growing up was insufficient. So she disciplined herself "through prayer, meditation and Bible study," according to biographer Barbara Reynolds, resulting in a deeper, more mature faith rooted in the spirituality of her ancestors.

In 1956 she married James David Kelly, a Methodist minister who was then pastoring East Vine Avenue Methodist Church in Knoxville, Tennessee. In June 1958 the Kelly family moved when James was transferred to Leigh Street Church in Richmond, Virginia.

In this new location, Leontine Kelly took the steps that eventually led her to high achievement within the ordained ministry. Her husband encouraged her to complete her college degree and to develop her credentials within the Methodist church. She enrolled in Virginia Union University in Richmond, receiving a B.A. in 1960. Concurrently, she became a certified lay speaker in the Methodist church. She then worked as a social studies teacher from 1960 to 1966. Being a teacher fulfilled some of the social goals of her father's religious philosophy of personal involvement in enhancing the lives of others and improving society.

By the 1960s, Kelly had been active in church affairs and became a popular speaker whose style was described as "preaching" rather than speaking. Yet, up to 1969, she had no plans to become an ordained minister in spite of her closeness to several ministers: her father, her brother, her first husband, who became a minister in the 1950s, and her second husband.

The death of James Kelly in 1969 led the congregation of Galilee Church in Edwardsville, Virginia, to ask Leontine Kelly to succeed her husband. She accepted, serving as a layperson in charge of the church. Less than a year after her husband's death, Kelly felt herself called by God to become an ordained minister. She began theological studies, first through the Conference Course of Study, then through summer school at Wesley Theological Seminary, Washington, D.C., in 1970 and 1971, and finally through enrolling in Union Theological Seminary in Richmond, receiving the master of divinity degree in 1976.

Kelly's status within the Methodist church began to advance as she received her first ordination as a minister, becoming a deacon in 1972. She filled positions of increasing responsibility and respect throughout the 1970s and 1980s, eventually becoming a member of the national staff of the United Methodist church, and filling the position of evangelism executive on the Board of Discipleship. By 1984, she had attained the prominence necessary to be considered a candidate for bishop.

The Methodist church was a leader in appointing women to positions of responsibility in the church, approving the full acceptance of women as ministers in 1956 and becoming the first major religious denomination to elect women to their top ministerial office—bishop. In 1980 Marjorie Swank Matthews was elected bishop at the age of sixty-four, becoming one of the forty-six bishops of the church. Because church policy requires bishops who reach age sixty-six to retire at the end of their four-year term, Bishop Matthews retired in 1984 at the age of sixty-eight.

• *Methodists elect*

first black

woman bishop

Faced with the retirement of the only woman bishop in the church, Methodist clergywomen were seeking candidates to put forward for the position. Though few women satisfied the traditional conditions for promotion to bishop, Methodist clergywomen sought competent female candidates who not only had experience as pastors and administrators but also had achieved enough prominence to gain broad-based support among male and female clergy and laypersons.

Kelly's personal maturity, her long-term involvement in the clergywomen's movement, and her administrative experience as a staff member in the Virginia Conference and on the National Board of Discipleship made her a viable candidate for bishop. As early as 1982, the national caucus of clergywomen had identified Kelly as the primary candidate to replace Bishop Matthews. In 1984 the clergywomen asked if they could place her name in nomination and Kelly consented. However, because the Southeast Jurisdiction race was deemed too difficult, Kelly was nominated in the Western Jurisdiction. By the thirteenth ballot, Kelly was clearly one of the frontrunners, and she was elected on the seventeenth ballot. She and the other new bishops were consecrated on Friday, July 20, 1984.

Kelly became the second woman to be chosen bishop in the United Methodist church and the first black woman bishop in any major United

States denomination. She remained the only one until the Episcopal church elected Barbara C. Harris a suffragan bishop in 1989. Black men had been elected as bishops in the Methodist church since the first two were chosen in 1920, the number increasing to seven by the mid-1970s. In 1984 Kelly and four black men were elected, bringing the total number of black bishops to eleven.

In September, 1984, at the age of sixty-four, Kelly assumed her duties as bishop of the San Francisco area. She supervised the California and Nevada conferences of the United Methodist church, which included one hundred thousand members in 386 churches in Northern California and Nevada. It was Kelly's responsibility, with the advice of her cabinet, to make appointments of four hundred ministers and numerous other positions, to preside over conferences and meetings, to ordain ministers as deacons and elders, and subsequently to supervise their status.

As bishop, Kelly developed her own distinctive style of leadership based on her personal interpretation of the Bible. "As a black person, what I look for in the Bible is a sense of my own freedom and acceptance by God and the sense of liberation," she told Brian Lanker. The Bible also gave her "the strength and . . . patience to wait for freedom" while actively seeking it, and the insight to share power in such a way as to encourage others to develop their full potential while she retained her ultimate responsibility for decisions and consequences.

Kelly is considered a dynamic preacher whose intellectually cogent messages are powerfully delivered. Her "soul-stirring sermons" surprise those who expect a small, grandmotherly Methodist to be less than forceful, observed Marilyn Marshall in *Ebony*. Her leadership prompted fellow bishop Melvin G. Talbert to say that she "has proven herself a very competent leader at various levels of the church." Through her career, Kelly has striven for high quality in all her activities, knowing that others would see her as a role model and as an example. The strong sense of self-confidence, nurtured in her childhood and sustained throughout her continually deepening religious faith, is balanced by a sense of humor about life in general and humility about her personal achievements.

On August 31, 1988, at the age of sixty-eight, Kelly relinquished her position in charge of the San Francisco area and retired as bishop. She became a part-time teacher, serving as visiting professor of Evangelism and Witness at the Pacific School of Religion in Berkeley, California. In addition, she became president of the newly organized AIDS National Interfaith Network, which had plans to coordinate activities designed to minister to victims of AIDS, including training pastors and caretakers of

AIDS sufferers. Kelly also has worked with "Choose Peace," an organization headed by Bishop C. Dale White. She continues to speak out, this time on how politics and the church can come together to bring about effective change, saying:

> How can you transform system and political structures if you stand outside? We shouldn't be afraid to be political, in our church or in our world. Nothing is more political than Moses being sent to tell Pharaoh to let the Hebrew people go!

**Profile by
De Witt C. Dykes, Jr.**

SHARON PRATT KELLY

Sharon Pratt Kelly lives by a motto that is illustrative of her genuine character: "In order to be a good leader, one must have skillfully mastered the art of compassion." At five feet two inches, Kelly, Democratic mayor of Washington, D.C., may be short in height, but she is a giant in personality and charisma. She is warm, dedicated, committed to service, and possesses an infinite strength and iron will.

1944- •

Mayor of •

Washington,

D.C.

Kelly was born January 30, 1944, in Washington, D.C., to Carlisle and Mildred "Peggy" Pratt. Peggy Pratt died of breast cancer when Sharon was four. Her grandmother, Hazel Pratt, and aunt, Aimee Elizabeth Pratt, served as mother figures to Kelly and her sister, Benaree. Their father, a former Washington, D.C., superior court judge, held high expectations for his daughters. "He is the person who shaped my philosophies of life," Kelly recalls. "My father stressed developing the mind, hard work, and a commitment to public service." And her life is exemplified by the early lessons imparted by him.

Kelly attended Washington, D.C., public schools and enjoyed team sports—especially baseball. An all-boys baseball club even asked her to join, but she declined. "I was at that adolescent stage when you worry

about looking good," she jokes, "so I turned them down." An average student at first, Kelly began to work feverishly on her studies after enrolling at Roosevelt High School. She disciplined herself and studied five hours every night, graduating in 1961 with honors.

Kelly loved the silver screen and the seemingly glamorous life of its actors and actresses. But upon enrolling at Howard University in Washington, D.C., political science outweighed an acting career. "I always wanted to be an actress," she says wistfully. "But my commitment to public service steered me in a direction in which I could initiate change."

While an undergraduate, Kelly became the first woman to run for student council president and was honored as a member of Pi Sigma Alpha national political science honor society and named a Falk Fellow in political science. In 1965 she graduated with a B.A. in political science and then continued her studies at Howard University's School of Law, earning her law degree in 1968. In 1966, while in law school, Kelly married Arrington Dixon, who later became Washington, D.C., council chairman. The year she graduated, 1968, daughter Aimee Arrington Dixon was born, and in 1970 the Dixons were blessed with another baby girl, Drew Arrington Dixon. The Dixons were divorced in 1982, and in 1991 Sharon Pratt Dixon married banker-turned-businessman James Kelly III.

From 1970 to 1971 Kelly was house counsel for the Joint Center for Political Studies in Washington, D.C., and from 1971 to 1976 she was an associate with the law firm Pratt and Queen. While in private practice, she fought for the rights of children involved in custody battles, provided juveniles with strong and competent legal representation, and protected the rights of families.

In 1972 Kelly joined the faculty at the Antioch School of Law, a position she held for four years. During this time, former Speaker of the House Thomas "Tip" O'Neill appointed her to the District of Columbia Law Revision Commission, "which transferred the city's criminal code from Congress to the District," according to the *Washington Times.*

In 1976 Kelly accepted a position in the general counsel's office at Potomac Electric Power Company (PEPCO). Eventually she was appointed vice-president for public policy, the first black American and first woman vice-president of consumer affairs. During Kelly's term, many new programs were initiated and implemented for the improvement of low-income Washington, D.C., residents as well as for senior citizens. Dixon also created jobs with new satellite branches of PEPCO. "I wanted PEPCO to adopt new policies and a general approach of how to deal with changing methods," she explains. "Ideas, concepts and policies drive me!"

Kelly's interest in politics stems from her early childhood. "I've always been fascinated by people who shape public policy, such as Franklin Delano Roosevelt and Martin Luther King. Mr. King had excellent communication skills. He took complex issues and made them simple for everyone else." She also admires Malcolm X for his boldness, search for truth, and his willingness to share his knowledge with others. Mentors Patricia Roberts Harris, who served in the Carter Administration, and astute businesswoman Flaxie Pinkard were her female role models. Kelly also served as campaign manager for Harris in her bid for the mayoral seat in Washington, D.C., in 1982.

Kelly has been actively involved in Democratic politics for more than twenty years. She was elected to four terms as the Democratic National Committeewoman from the District of Columbia, 1977-1980. From 1980 to 1984 she served as the Democratic National Committee Eastern Regional Chairwoman. Already accustomed to breaking gender barriers, Kelly was the first woman to serve as the Democratic National Committee Treasurer from 1985 to 1989. She has also been a member of the American Bar Association, Unified Bar of the District of Columbia, and the District of Columbia Women's Bar Association. Organizations that recognized Dixon for her work include the Washington, D.C. chapter of the NAACP, the United Negro College Fund, and the Association of Black Women Attorneys.

• Nation's capital

elects its first

woman mayor

On November 6, 1990, Kelly became the first woman to win the mayoral race in the District of Columbia. Perturbed by the city's looming fiscal problems, its soaring crime statistics, record homicide rate, and drug addiction, Kelly entered the race committed to helping rectify these problems. "I set the goal to win the nomination, then I set the goal to serve. The key is to put yourself in a position to effect the changes you want to take place."

As mayor, Kelly wants to set new standards for public service, responsibility, and leadership. Her main goal is to facilitate black and Hispanic ownership of business and community properties. She plans to create solid programs that will assist both the city's seniors and its youth. Appalled by the drug problem and other crimes in the city, she proposes to "implement a Fresh Start drug treatment program to be administered by local church and community groups; target seized drug capital for drug fighting units and treatment programs and establish a Neighborhood Oriented Policing program where churches, community groups, businesses and the police work together," reports the *Georgetowner.*

Concerned that women have been expected to derive influence from their proximity to men with power rather than be influential as power figures themselves, Kelly notes: "We need a political genesis, a renaissance in which masculine politics and the 'dog eat dog' mentality that earmarked it, is replaced by a feminine kind of politics in which you do what is right, not what is expedient," the *Washington Post* quoted her. Of the mayor's position, she says: "The office is a means to an end, not the end."

**Profile by
Monda Raquel Webb**

FLO KENNEDY

*H*er name is Florynce Rae Kennedy—Flo to friend and enemy

1916- •

alike—and she is the biggest, loudest and, indisputably, the rudest

mouth on the battleground where feminist-activists and radical politics

lawyer, •

join in mostly common cause." So wrote Patricia Burstein in 1974.

feminist,

Nearly twenty years later, Flo Kennedy is still a very distinctive part of

civil rights

today's society, wearing the many hats of lawyer, activist, feminist,

activist

humanist, and spokesperson for civil rights issues.

Kennedy has been described as intelligent, outrageous, outspoken, energetic, aggressive, dynamic, profane, prophetic, and/or shocking, but she simply says of herself:

> I'm just a loud-mouthed middle-aged colored lady with a fused spine and three feet of intestines missing and a lot of people think I'm crazy. Maybe you do too, but I never stop to wonder why I'm not like other people. The mystery to me is why more people aren't like me.

In her autobiography, *Color Me Flo: My Hard Life and Good Times,* Kennedy describes her family as part of the "pooristocrats" of the black community. Kennedy, born February 11, 1916, in Kansas City, Missouri, was the second of five daughters. She spent her formative years primarily in Missouri and California, lived in New York City from 1942 to 1972, then moved to San Francisco, California, where she still resides. Her father, Wiley Kennedy, at various worked as a Pullman porter, waiter, and the owner of a own taxi business. Her mother, Zella, was "awfully smart" and was educated in the normal schools at a time when very few black people went to school. For the most part, Zella stayed at home and raised the children, but she went to work as a domestic during the Great Depression.

"Our parents had us so convinced we were precious that by the time I found out I was nothing, it was already too late—I knew I was something," Kennedy wrote. Neither parent used excessive discipline, says Kennedy; "both parents taught each of us never to take any s— from anyone." She recognizes this style of discipline as the major factor for her outspoken, aggressive nature:

> The whole concept of authority is what I think Women's Lib and Black liberation is about. The reason I have a pathological attitude toward authority, is because my parents did not establish their own authority, and did not require us to see the government, our teachers, or any of these people as unquestionable authority.

Kennedy was educated in the public schools of Missouri and California. "I must have been almost ready for high school when I decided to become a lawyer. My theory has always been that whatever the people who have all the money don't want you to do, that's what you ought to do," she declared. After excelling in high school, Kennedy moved to New York City in 1942 to live with her sister Grayce. In 1944, at the age of 28, she entered Columbia University and four years later graduated with a bachelor's degree in pre-law. She then applied to Columbia Law School but was denied admission. When Kennedy alleged that she was rejected because of her race and threatened to bring action against Columbia, the university admitted her. She obtained her law degree in 1951, passed the New York Bar in 1952, and by 1954 had established her own private practice.

Though not a staunch supporter of the institution of marriage, Kennedy married Charles Dudley Dye in 1957 when she was 31 and he 41. She describes Dye as a "Welsh science-fiction writer and a drunk."

The marriage dissolved after a short period of time and Dye eventually died an alcoholic. Kennedy never remarried.

While partners with lawyer Don Wilkes, Kennedy handled the estate of entertainer Eleanora McKay (Billie Holiday). Holiday's agent, Associate Booking Corporation, neglected to advise the singer of a federal statute that required persons convicted on charges of narcotics, such as Holiday, to register each time they left the country. Holiday had failed to do so and as a result, the United States attorney threatened to indict her when she returned from a European tour. A long, grueling legal battle ensued between the United States government and Holiday. Wilkes was able to persuade the United States attorney not to indict Holiday, but she died just a few days after winning this major victory.

Racism in •

justice system

is contested

Kennedy continued to represent the Holiday estate and later took on the estate of Charlie Parker. According to Kennedy, both persons were fighting to recoup monies in royalties and sales denied them by their record companies and agents because they were black.

At this time Kennedy also served as lawyer to the activist H. Rap Brown, who in Kennedy's estimation was not dealt with fairly by the courts. In an interview with *Reconstruction* magazine, Kennedy spoke about Brown's struggle with the legal system, stating, "The courts are so racist and so bigoted. As a lawyer, you're looking for justice for people, but if you know there's no justice, what are you going to go looking there for? There's absolutely no justice for anybody I'd want to defend."

These kinds of battles forced Kennedy to reevaluate her profession and led to an eventual change in careers—a change that has spanned almost three decades. According to Kennedy:

> Handling the Holiday and Parker estates taught me more than I was really ready for about government and business delinquency and the hostility and helplessness of the courts in rectifying the imbalance between the talented performers and the millionaire parasites who suck their blood. These experiences . . . marked the beginning of a serious disenchantment, if indeed I ever was enchanted with the practice of law. By this time I had learned a good deal about the justice system, and had begun to doubt my ability to work within it to accomplish social changes.

Kennedy believes that all types of oppression are related, and that they are expressed in four forms: personal, private, public, and political. Kennedy asserts that racism is the most blatant type of oppression in the country, that it pervades all the forms of expression, and that is something that everyone must combat on all fronts at all times. To do her part, she participated in several black power conferences held in the late 1960s and early 1970s. In addition to speaking out against racism, she stood on the forefront of a myriad of civil liberty causes and served as spokesperson for diverse groups—including homosexuals, prostitutes, minorities, women, and the poor—at a time long before it was in vogue to do so. Kennedy, a mover and shaker by anyone's definition, put before the public eye relevant and oftentimes unspoken issues that affected the lives of many.

In 1966 Kennedy founded the Media Workshop to confront racism in media and advertising. She was an original member of the National Organization for Women but broke away when, as she put it, "NOW got to be so boring and scared." Early on she spoke out on black women joining the women's liberation movement:

> It is obvious that black women are not prepared to work with white in liberation because of the divide and conquer techniques always employed by an exploitative society. However, in many towns there are movements where black and white women are working one to one [in the movement]. It's the same wherever you are. Whether you're fighting for women's lib or just black lib, you're fighting the same enemies.

• Steinem calls

Kennedy a

political

touchstone

To support Shirley Chisholm as a presidential candidate in 1972, Kennedy formed the Feminist Party. Regarding Kennedy's important role in such budding political movements, journalist Gloria Steinem says:

> For those who had been in the black movement when it was still known as the civil rights movement or in the consumers movement that predated Ralph Nader, or in the women's movement when it was still supposed to be a few malcontents in sneakers, or in the peace movement when there was more worry about nuclear fallout than about Vietnam, Flo was a political touchstone—a catalyst.

Infuriated when a group at a 1967 antiwar conference tried to suppress the comments of one of her colleagues, Kennedy went on a tirade that resulted in an invitation to address a crowd in Washington. In her autobiography Kennedy regards the event as the start of her speaking career. By the mid-seventies, Kennedy had lectured at more than two hundred colleges and universities and at rallies dealing with numerous issues.

Kennedy moved her residence from New York to California in 1972. During that same year, she filed a complaint against the Catholic Church (Archdiocese of New York, Terence Cardinal Cooke, Birthright, and Knights of Columbus) with the Internal Revenue Service. She alleged that the Catholic Church violated the tax-exempt requirements by spending money to influence political decisions, particularly those that dealt with the abortion issue.

The class action suit she filed to test New York's abortion laws is described in *Abortion Rap,* a book that Kennedy cowrote. As a part of the legal team that challenged the constitutionality of the New York law, she collaborated on briefs and cross-examined witnesses in pre-trial hearings.

In 1985, on her seventieth birthday, Flo Kennedy was roasted by her friends. At the celebration she was regarded as a civil rights activist, attorney, writer, television producer, and national director of activist groups. A fitting tribute to Kennedy—a woman of many words and deeds—is the poem "She Is Everywhere," written by Leonard Cohen, civil court judge, and published in *Color Me Flo*. Kennedy is still on the speaking circuit and can be found wherever there is a cause she believes needs to be championed and brought before the public consciousness.

**Profile by
Marva Rudolph**

CORETTA SCOTT KING

*A*lthough she first achieved prominence as the wife of Dr. Martin

1927- •

Luther King, Jr., a famous and charismatic leader, Coretta Scott King

"has made the transition from the supportive spouse to establishing

civil rights •

herself as a leader in her own right," observed biographer Lynn Norment.

activist

Coretta Scott was born in Marion, Alabama, on April 27, 1927, one of

three children of Obadiah and Bernice McMurry Scott. Upon her

graduation from the Marion Lincoln High School, King traveled to

Yellow Springs, Ohio, to attend Antioch College, where in 1951 she

earned a bachelor's degree in music and elementary education. Further

study at the New England Conservatory of Music brought a music degree

in 1954—and marriage to Martin Luther.

After they met through a mutual friend, Coretta Scott's and King's relationship blossomed. On June 18, 1953, they were married in the garden of Scott's Alabama home in Marion. The Reverend Martin Luther King, Sr. (affectionately known as Daddy King) officiated at the wedding and the Reverend A. D. King, his younger son, was the best man.

Coretta King wrote about the early years of her marriage in her memoirs, *My Life with Martin Luther King, Jr.:*

> In September, 1953, after our marriage, Martin and I went back to Boston, he to finish the residence requirements and write the thesis for his doctorate and I to finish my musical education at the conservatory. We rented an apartment in a very old house right around the corner from the one Martin had when we were courting. It had four rooms—kitchen, bedroom, den and living room. Martin worked on his research in the den and I studied in the bedroom, though in order not to bother Martin or the neighbors, I never practiced my singing at home but used the practice rooms at the conservatory.

In June of 1954 Coretta King earned a Mus.B. degree in voice from the New England Conservatory of Music. By that time, her husband had completed his residency requirements at Boston University and was free to accept a job outside Boston while writing his dissertation. He completed his doctoral comprehensive examinations in August.

King had decided to return to the South to work at a church, and he had been interviewed for the position of the pastor of Dexter Avenue Baptist Church in Montgomery, Alabama. Among those who received him warmly during his first visit to Montgomery was the Reverend Ralph David Abernathy, who was at the time the pastor of First Baptist Church in the city and had met him before in Atlanta. King was impressed with the officials of the Montgomery church, so he and Coretta moved to Montgomery, and he started his pastoral work there in September of 1954.

• Civil rights

protests begin

When Coretta King and her husband arrived in Montgomery, the officials of Dexter Avenue Baptist Church were still working feverishly to refurbish its parsonage at 309 South Jackson Street, so the couple had to stay with a church member. Their first child, Yolanda Denise King, born on November 17, 1955, was barely three weeks old when the Reverend King was chosen to lead the historic Montgomery bus boycott. The Kings were actively involved in the incident in sympathy with Rosa Parks, the originator of the event. From that time on, Coretta Scott King stood beside her husband in every civil rights protest meeting and demonstration from Montgomery to Memphis. Eventually, three other children were born to them: Martin III, Dexter, and Bernice.

Coretta King accompanied her husband on his travels throughout the United States and abroad. In March, 1957, the couple made their maiden overseas journey, a trip to Ghana to attend the country's independence celebrations, at which the British handed over the colony to the indigenous government headed by the late President Kwame Nkrumah. In 1960, the Kings would visit Nigeria, another British colony that achieved its independence. Accompanied by Professor Lawrence D. Reddick, an eminent black historian, the Kings visited India in 1959. And in December, 1964, Coretta King, other family members, and friends traveled with Martin Luther King, Jr., to Oslo, Norway, where he accepted the Nobel Peace Prize. At age thirty-nine, he was the youngest recipient of the prize.

Before going to Norway, King and his entourage of forty Americans visited London, where he fulfilled several speaking engagements, including the preaching of a sermon at the famous St. Paul's Cathedral. In her memoirs, King captured the essence of the Nobel ceremony:

> We had quite a time getting him ready. He had to wear formal dress, striped trousers and a gray tailcoat. While several of us were working on the ascot, Martin kept fussing and making funny comments about having to wear such a ridiculous thing. Finally he said, "I vow never to wear one of these things again."

Dr. and Mrs. King were received by King Olav of Norway on December 9, 1964. The next day they shared one of the high points of the American civil rights movement. Of the gathering afterwards, Coretta King wrote in 1969:

> We were all very emotional, and each of us felt we must say something, and in a very real sense this tribute from his friends meant as much to Martin as the formal [Nobel] ceremony which had preceded it. When my turn came, I talked about what my role had been— simply giving support to Martin over the years. I explained what a great privilege it had been, what a blessing, to live at the side of a man whose life would have so profound an impact on the world. It was the most important thing I could have done, and I had wanted to do it. I said, "This great experience has given

me renewed faith. I will continue to give what support I can to my husband, and to the struggle."

• *Coretta King*

pursues civil

rights interests

In the quest for civil rights for all minorities in America, Coretta King's support of her husband was unlimited. Through their indefatigable efforts, President Lyndon B. Johnson signed the Voting Rights Bill on August 6, 1965. In Coretta King's assessment, this bill and the 1964 Civil Rights Act comprised a major step in the legal protection of the rights of black Americans. On several occasions, she traveled to civil rights events on her own. In 1967 she visited Chicago several times to participate in the Reverend Jesse Jackson's "Operation Breadbasket" program.

> I attended one of Rev. Jesse Jackson's meetings in Chicago in October, 1967, and I heard him give his regular message. It was terribly meaningful to me. I came home and said to Martin, "I think that Jesse Jackson and Operation Breadbasket have something that is needed in every community across the nation."

On April 4, 1968, Martin Luther King, Jr., was shot to death by an assassin at the Lorraine Motel in Memphis, Tennessee. King had gone to the city to take part in a demonstration to support striking garbage workers. After King's death, Coretta King did not retire from the civil rights movement. Instead, on Monday, April 8, 1969—barely four days after her husband's assassination—she and her children, accompanied by civil rights leaders, led a mammoth demonstration in Memphis, where she called for a "peaceful society." In June of the same year, Coretta King and several civil rights leaders went to Washington, D.C., to take part in the so-called "Poor-Man's March." She was the keynote speaker at the Lincoln Memorial program of more than 50,000 people.

To protect and expand the legacy of her late husband, Coretta King founded the Martin Luther King, Jr., Center for Nonviolent Social Change in Atlanta, Georgia. As founding president and chief executive officer of the center, she states that its purpose is to serve as a living memorial to King, to preserve his legacy, and carry forward his unfinished work. Through the planning and lobbying efforts of Coretta King, the twenty-three-acre neighborhood surrounding King's birthplace in Atlanta was, in 1980, declared a National Historic Site by the National Park Service. The King center is situated in the area on historic Auburn Avenue.

Coretta King led the twentieth-anniversary March on Washington in 1983, bringing together more than five hundred thousand people and eight hundred human rights organizations to form a "New Coalition of Conscience." In 1984, Coretta King was elected the chairperson of the Martin Luther King Holiday Commission, which was established by an

Act of Congress to formalize plans for the first official celebration of the holiday honoring Dr. King (1986). Since then, she has coordinated the public observance of her late husband's holiday at home and abroad.

Coretta King has received numerous local and international honors. She was the first woman to deliver the Class Day address at Harvard University and the first woman to preach at a regular service at St. Paul's Cathedral in London, England, in 1969. For her indefatigable efforts, Coretta King has been the recipient of several prestigious honors, including more than one hundred honorary doctoral degrees. President Jimmy Carter appointed her the alternate delegate of the United States delegation to the United Nations. And in July 1977, Coretta King, accompanied by Daddy King and other family members, traveled to Washington, D.C., to receive the Presidential Medal of Freedom, awarded posthumously to her husband.

Coretta King has shown staunch support for the anti-apartheid movement. In addition to making public statements and writing a syndicated weekly newspaper column advocating social, economic, and political causes, she travels extensively. In April, 1990, for example, she paid a visit to the so-called frontline nations of southern Africa, where she met with leaders of Namibia, Zimbabwe, Zambia, and the recently released African National Congress leader, Nelson Mandela. In Zimbabwe, she participated in the observance of the country's ten years of independence. Her presence amply confirmed her abhorrence of colonialism and all forms of domination.

Today, Coretta King serves in various capacities. In addition to functioning actively as chief executive officer of the King Center, she is also co-chairperson of the Full Employment Action Council and an active member of both the Black Leadership Forum and the Black Leadership Roundtable, speaking in support of human rights campaigns and social justice.

**Profile by
A. B. Assensoh**

KING and SHABAZZ

Yolanda •

M ajor civil rights leaders Martin Luther King, Jr. and Malcolm X

King

seemed, on the surface, to espouse antithetical approaches for the

African-American community in its quest for recognition and dignity:

Attallah

one advocated passive resistance, the other fiery anger; one wanted

Shabazz

integration, the other separatism. But before their tragic assassinations,

both at the age of thirty-nine, their once-divergent views were begin-

ning to coalesce. The force behind this possible convergence did not

dissipate with their deaths, but has been carried on through their eldest

daughters. For Yolanda King and Attallah Shabazz, it has been a

natural progression. "For me it's like the shape of the letter Y," Shabazz

told Ellen Hopkins. "Two supposedly opposing paths meet and become one. When our fathers died, they were approaching that fork. Yolanda and I closed the gap and became the stem." King and Shabazz are not, however, simply messengers. Distilled through them and infused with their own spirit, their fathers' beliefs have become their message, one message of hope and faith based on who and what they are, offered not as political discourse but as artistic vision.

As the daughters of historical leaders, both King and Shabazz were raised in surprisingly normal households; for the most part, their fathers were simply their fathers. Yolanda King, the eldest of four children born to King, a minister, and Coretta Scott King, was born on November 17, 1955, in Montgomery, Alabama. While growing up, she had no insight as to who her father was or what he was doing. "Till I was about eight or nine, I had no awareness he was anybody special," she recounted to Hopkins. "Since all our friends were in the movement, I thought what Daddy did was natural. Everybody went to jail, right?" Only after her father took her on a Get Out the Vote! campaign when she was nine did King begin to realize his importance by the reception people gave him. But this dawning of recognition didn't change her relationship with her father. Four years after her father's assassination, King explained to Robert E. Johnson that, though conscious of the demonstrations and the jail terms, she best remembered her father for something different:

> I knew my father as the man who came home and kissed us, sat down at the table with us, joked with us, and took us places now and then and taught us so much about life and people and living in particular—the things that he felt were necessary in leading a good life and a life that would contribute to society.

Born on November 16, 1958, in New York City, Attallah (Arabic for "gift of God") Shabazz was raised in a similar atmosphere. The eldest of three daughters born to Malcolm X, a one-time leader of the Nation of Islam, and Betty Shabazz, her childhood was unencumbered by any political divisiveness that surrounded her father's activities. It was, instead, a life filled by a father with playfulness, understanding, direction, and tolerance. Shabazz grew up cross-cultural, made fully aware of her African, Arabic, Caribbean, and Native American racial heritage. She was also raised Muslim, but was sent to a Roman Catholic school in order to learn to empathize with other religious beliefs. Contrary to popular perception, she admits repeatedly that she never heard her father vilify white people. Her diverse, complex upbringing was a direct result of the diverse, complex individual her father was. She explained to Lawrence Christon how people only have a two-dimensional, exploited picture of her father:

People only see pieces, the fiery speaker, the street
hustler of Boston and New York. But it seems that every
five years of his life he went through a radical change.
In the end, he was so much more than anyone knew. I
can tell you, no picture on a T-shirt captures him.

The assassinations of both fathers—Malcolm X on February 21,
1965; Martin Luther King Jr. on April 4, 1968—had an incalculable
effect on both daughters. Shabazz, who was only six years old at the
time, witnessed her father's murder at the Audubon Ballroom in
Harlem. King was 12 years old when she learned about her father's
shooting from a news bulletin on television. Both daughters turned
inward emotionally and it took many years for them to fully compre-
hend the loss. "As you grow older, you realize how young thirty-nine is,"
Shabazz related to Hopkins. "I don't remember if it was his birthday or
his memorial day, but a day came when I realized he's *dead*. I never
knew till then how much the void . . . nauseated me."

Emotional release for King and Shabazz in their childhoods came
through the arts, specifically acting. King, who penned her first play at
the age of seven, began acting in plays in grade school. At the age of 15
she caused a stir in her hometown by portraying a prostitute in *The Owl
and the Pussycat*. King then realized the serious implications such a
career choice would have. "As an artist and a Black woman coming out
of a background that emphasizes service, there are certain responsibilities I must assume," she told a reporter for *Ebony* a few years later. "I see
these responsibilities not as a burden, but as an extension of what I am."
Shabazz was also drawn to the arts early, sculpting, writing, and acting
since she was in grade school. By the time she had finished high school,
she too decided to pursue an acting career.

In what some may call historical fortuity and others simply predesti-
nation, both budding actresses were studying their craft in New York in
1979 (King was working toward a MFA degree from New York University) when a mutual friend introduced them to each other. The initial
atmosphere at the meeting was curious but cautious. "Both of them felt
that sense of awe one has when meeting another who is connected to
legend and pain and greatness," A. Peter Bailey noted. The preliminary
hesitation soon gave way to an easy, warm feeling when both found
they shared not only the common traits of friends—age, career goals,
outlook in life—but the previously untapped tragic emotions about
their respective fathers' deaths. Shabazz detailed this feeling to Hopkins:

Fate •

unites

daughters

So in meeting Yolanda, she wasn't so much a stranger,
because we have each other's history. We both know
what it is to catch your breath when a bulletin inter-

rupts on TV. We know what it is to sit through tributes.
For Yolanda and I, April 4, 1968, is February 21, 1965.
As we are different, we are the same.

Recognizing their mutual regard and histories, and feeling the pull of shared destiny, Shabazz and King decided to collaborate on a play that would meld both their artistic and social concerns. "Through the arts you can impact upon people's attitudes, values, and understandings," King explained to Lynn Norment. "Perhaps in that way it is more effective than the podium and the traditional means of education." The result was *Stepping into Tomorrow,* a 75-minute blending of comedy, drama, and music that uses the ten-year reunion of six high school friends as a vehicle to motivate youth to overcome the dangers faced when growing up. "All of the things that we fall prey to—peer pressure, drugs, gang violence—the reason is because of low self-esteem, not liking yourself, and having a small will or none at all," Shabazz explained to Bob Pool. "We show characters who have gone through that in their lives," King elaborated to Dawn Clayton. "We show the triumph and completeness they are beginning to find—with the hope that these kids will also find some hope."

Shabazz and King also collaborated on *Of One Mind,* a play hypothesizing on the possible shared dreams and goals of their fathers had both men been given the chance to live. Shabazz pointed out to Christon that before the assassinations, both men were coming toward singular principles: "They were moving closer in their analysis of the problem. They were beginning to see racism, sexism, and ethnic division as symptoms of a deeper conflict, the haves versus the have-nots."

But it has been *Stepping into Tomorrow,* realized through their performing arts troupe Nucleus, Inc., which they founded in 1980, that has carried their unified and unifying message farther and longer. Touring the country, Nucleus renders the play in about 50 cities a year—in schools, churches, community centers, local theaters. In 1988 the Los Angeles County Board of Supervisors honored King and Shabazz for their motivational play, which the Board deemed "entertaining and enlightening."

Both King and Shabazz continue to perform their play and co-direct Nucleus. They have also branched out in the acting community, taking on credits as producers of theatrical and other productions. In the early 1990s, Shabazz was an associate producer of gospel music's Stellar Awards and the National Association for the Advancement of Colored People Image Awards. King, as director of cultural affairs, plans and produces artistic events for the Martin Luther King, Jr. Center for

Nonviolent Social Change in Atlanta. Both also tour the country, separately and together, lecturing on civil rights, the arts, and their respective fathers' dreams and visions. It is impossible, as King explained to Norment, to be who they are and to let those dreams fade:

> When you grow up in an environment where that kind of commitment and dedication is not just talked about but lived so fully, so honestly, there is no way that it does not take root in your being. They say that the best lessons, the best sermons, are the ones that are lived. There is no way I could be true to what is so much a part of me if I did not feel a responsibility to carry on and do what I can to further the unfinished work.

**Profile by
Rob Nagel**

JEWEL STRADFORD LAFONTANT

Ambassador Jewel Stradford Lafontant, a former Chicago attorney, **1928-** •

is an ambassador-at-large and United States coordinator for refugee

affairs. Lafontant, who reports directly to President Bush, was appointed **lawyer,** •

to this position in August 1989. Lafontant was born in Chicago on April **ambassador**

22, 1928, the younger child of Francis Stradford and Aida Arbella

(Carter) Stradford. Her mother, an artist, was born in Camden, South

Carolina, on November 14, 1895, and died April 29, 1972. Francis

Stradford, a lawyer, was born in Lawrenceburg, Kentucky, on Septem-

ber 3, 1892, and died April 29, 1963. Jewel Stradford was married to

Ernest Lafontant, an attorney who was born on March 1, 1924, and

died in October of 1976. She has one son, John W. Rogers, Jr., from this marriage. Nurtured by an environment of excellence and achievement, Lafontant's son, a Princeton graduate in economics, is president and chief executive of Ariel Capital Management. Jewel Stradford Lafontant is now married to Naguib S. Mankarious, an international business consultant.

Lafontant, who received a bachelor of arts degree from Oberlin College and a doctor of laws degree from the University of Chicago, was a trial attorney with the Legal Aid Bureau from 1947 to 1954. From 1955 to 1958 she was an assistant United States District Attorney in Chicago. An article in the Washington *Star News* notes that "Lafontant is very conscientious in following her father's footsteps to the Supreme Court." The article further notes that it was because of her father that she attended Oberlin. As a young practicing attorney, Lafontant worked with her father. Francis Stradford's credits include the Hansberry case he won before the Supreme Court in the mid-1940s, which allowed blacks to live in previously segregated sections of Chicago. The case was that of Carl and Nannie Hansberry, the couple who moved their family to an all-white neighborhood on Chicago's South Side. The Hansberry family and the Stradfords were very close. Jewel Lafontant recalled sitting in the Hansberry's living room as bricks came through their windows. Lafontant believes that social changes can and should be made through the law.

• *Legal history*

embraces

Lafontant

Lafontant's distinguished career as an attorney includes a senior partnership in the firm of Vedder, Price, Kaufman and Kammholz and executive vice president and director of the Ariel Capital Management Company. These connections were suspended when she became the first female deputy solicitor general of the United States during the Nixon administration. In this capacity, she argued cases before the United States Supreme Court and also served as United States representative to the United Nations. Lafontant's achievements and accomplishments have been numerous, including directorship of Equitable Life, Revlon, Mobil Oil, Midway Airlines, the Hanes Corporation, Trans World Airlines, Pantry Pride, and TBG Broadcasting.

Lafontant, who was a fellow of the International Academy of Trial Lawyers and the American Bar Association, has served on numerous boards and civic interest groups as chairperson of the Illinois Advisory Committee to the United States Civil Rights Commission, commissioner of the Blue Ribbon Commission on the Administration of Justice in Cook County, commissioner of the Martin Luther King, Jr., Federal Holiday Commission, and commissioner of the Chicago Tourism Council. She has been a member of the Labor Relations Committee of the United States Chamber of Commerce, the President's Commission on Executive Exchange, the visiting committee of the University of Chicago Law

School, the board of overseers for the Hoover Institution, director of the Capital Development Board of the State of Illinois, director of Project HOPE, director of the Council on Foreign Relations, director of the Illinois Humane Society—Serving Vulnerable Children, a trustee of Howard University, a member of the Chicago Committee, the Citizen's Committee on the Juvenile Court and the national advisory board of the Salvation Army, and an honorary member of Rotary International.

A guiding force in the recruitment of black entrepreneurs, Lafontant encourages blacks to build skills and pursue independence. In an interview in *Dollars and Sense*, Lafontant articulated her position that black entrepreneurs should encourage blacks to be producers as well as consumers. Because of her prowess, acumen, and experience, Lafontant is respected by the corporate world as well as by members of the black community for her candor and influence. In the *Dollars and Sense* interview, she stated:

> They say that blacks don't measure up. Then you ask them where are they recruiting and they begin reciting all the black schools. I don't want to be treading on anyone's toes but I am partial to Oberlin College because I finished Oberlin and my father and his father, since it was the first college to admit blacks. . . . Some of the companies exclude schools like Oberlin and recruit from the all-black colleges in the deep South, where they have both good and bad schools. You also have some very poor ones that are barely accredited. So if you recruit at those you might have a legitimate reason for not hiring. . . . I asked them not to exclude black colleges, but include schools such as Oberlin. I hate those self-fulfilling prophecies, those "I gave you a chance and you couldn't make [it]" kind of generalizations. So I see recruitment efforts as part of my role and I am not doing nearly enough.

Addressing the difficulty of overcoming certain misconceptions and biases blacks encounter in the corporate world and a racist attitude that is pervasive at the middle-management level, Lafontant believes that individuals must be educated so that they do not place people in stereotypical roles, recognizing that even though people may look different, they can achieve as well as other groups. As she said in *Dollars and Sense*, "Incompetence is not distinguishable by color."

**Profile by
Simmona E.
Simmons**

ELMA LEWIS

*E*lma Lewis worked as a dancer, actress, dance teacher, director, choreographer, and speech therapist, put herself through college and graduate school, and then found her true niche when she opened the Elma Lewis School of Fine Arts in Roxbury, Massachusetts. Her determined fund-raising and belief in the importance of her work led to the founding of the National Center of Afro-American Artists. According to one admirer, Lewis "has almost single-handedly forged what is probably the nearest thing there is to a national center for Black culture and art in the United States today."

1921-

arts

administrator,

educator

Elma Ina Lewis was born in Boston, the only child of Edwardine (Jordan) Corbin Lewis and Clairmont Richard McDonald Lewis, both of whom had emigrated from Barbados. She had two older brothers born of her mother's first marriage; their father had died when the boys were still infants. One of her brothers helped Lewis learn to read by the age of three. At that same age, at a meeting of Marcus Garvey's Universal Negro Improvement Association, she recited a poem about the beauty of black women taught to her by her father. Her parents were ardent followers of Garvey and regular attendees at the Sunday meetings in Boston. Her mother was a Black Cross nurse, and her father was a member of the African Legion. Lewis herself belonged to the Girl Guides, and her brothers were newsboys for the Garvey newspaper. The *Washington Post* quoted her as saying, "I really believe that being in the Garvey Movement gave me a sense of self."

Lewis attended Boston public schools, graduating from high school in 1939. As a child she studied dance, voice, and piano and also received elocution lessons for one dollar a week. By the age of eleven she was earning as much as fifty dollars a week and could support herself through dancing and dramatic performances. She also taught dance from 1935 to 1941 at the Doris W. Jones School of Dance in Boston and was a speech therapist at Roxbury Memorial High School for Girls in Boston from 1942 to 1943. In addition, she worked as a student speech therapist for the Massachusetts Mental Health Habit Clinic in Boston. With income from performances and other jobs Lewis was able to pay her own way through Emerson College, from which she graduated with a bachelor's degree in literature interpretation in 1943. She played the role of Julie in Ferenc Molnar's *Liliom* in 1945 at the Copley Theatre in Boston. She wanted to become an actress but realized there were very few opportunities for blacks at the time and that such roles that were available were likely to be as menials. Being practical, she attended the Boston University School of Education, specializing in the education of exceptional children and receiving a master's degree in 1944.

In 1945 Lewis taught in the Boston public schools. Then she became a speech therapist again at the Massachusetts Mental Health Habit Clinic and from 1945 to 1949 was a fine-arts worker at the Harriet Tubman House, a social-work agency in Boston's South End. From 1946 to 1968 she worked with the Robert Gould Shaw House, also a social service agency, as director and choreographer for twenty-one operas and operettas presented by the Robert Gould Shaw House Chorus.

In 1950 Lewis founded the Elma Lewis School of Fine Arts in a six-room apartment in a racially mixed area in Roxbury, according to Susan Quinn in *Ms.*, to "offer quality education in the arts to children in the neighborhood." With three hundred dollars from her father, some folding chairs and tables, and a rented second-hand piano, she began her school with four teachers and twenty-five students, teaching them dance and drama. The school moved several times until 1968, when she purchased for a token one dollar a former Hebrew synagogue and school valued at more than one million dollars, with the intention of using these facilities for her increasing activities. The population in the area had undergone a change with the influx of the black middle-class into a primarily Jewish community. Previously, the school had survived with the support of the black community through tuition, bake sales, and some gifts. Now having obtained property, Lewis began fund-raising in earnest for rehabilitating the buildings and for an endowment. After renovations, the doors of the Elma Lewis School of Fine Arts opened in January, 1969, with 250 students.

Lewis stayed in Roxbury, her own community, working with friends and neighbors. Usually operating with very little money in hand, the staff often went unpaid for long periods of time. Although there was a constant need for monetary and other contributions, Lewis developed an institution that the larger community began to notice and to consider worthy of support. The *Boston Globe,* Eastern Gas and Fuel, New England Telephone, the Permanent Charities of Boston, and other local agencies have given financial support over the years. The Rockefeller Foundation gave a grant in 1969 "to foster young talent in theatre and dance," reported the *New York Times,* and in 1973 gave a $350,000 grant to the dance company. The Kresge Foundation and the National Endowment for the Arts have also been supporters. In 1969 the Ford Foundation gave a four-year grant of $400,000 that "had to be matched dollar to dollar the last three years (a feat accomplished within the first year)," the *Boston Globe* noted. The Ford Foundation in 1974 offered a $650,000 challenge grant toward endowment if Lewis could raise $1.3 million by August 1977.

On the occasion of the twenty-fifth anniversary of the school in 1975, Lewis sent out a call for more than six thousand alumni to come and celebrate. In introducing her at the anniversary dinner, Judge Harry Elam, quoted in the *Boston Globe,* called her "an indomitable spirit who told her students over and over when something went wrong, that all they had to do was to pick themselves up, brush themselves off, and start all over again." In addition to their studies, students at the school participate in many social events that would ordinarily be unavailable to them. They have been junior hostesses for an opening party of Ossie Davis's *Purlie Victorious,* they have heard presidential candidate Shirley Chisholm, they have met many international visitors, and designed a gown for singer Odetta. The school has done very little advertising; word-of-mouth has been the main vehicle of promotion. The tuition is minimal and flexible. Most of the students come after school to take classes, but there are also evening programs for adults. Lewis has said, "I believe in Black artists rather than Black art." The Parent's Organization has been a strong support for the school, especially helping those young people who go to New York to further their development.

In 1968 Lewis became founder/director of the National Center of Afro-American Artists, of which the Elma Lewis School is now a subsidiary. She hopes that the center will evolve into a national repository for the study and dissemination of black culture. The center at various times has included an experimental theater, both jazz and classical orchestras, and "Playhouse in the Park," a summer theater in Franklin Park. From 1969 to 1980 Lewis was producer, and at times choreographer, for many of the programs and events offered.

An article in the *New York Times* stated that Lewis "could be Black America's version of Sol Hurok, Tyrone Guthrie and P. T. Barnum—all fused into one generous package." In 1975 artist John Wilson, quoted in the *Boston Globe,* said of the Elma Lewis School:

> It's a landmark. In terms of developing tangible Black art, exposing a community to the arts, and stimulating involvement, I can't think of any other institution like this. The school has grown from nothing. I have seen it happen as [Lewis] has been instrumental in getting it off the ground.

Lewis has been consultant to the Office of Program Development for the Boston public schools, to the National Educational Association, and to the National Endowment for the Arts. She has been involved in numerous civic organizations, boards, councils, and commissions, and has received more than one hundred citations and awards for her accomplishments in history, art, and public service. In 1981 she was among the first to receive a MacArthur Foundation Fellowship, a five-year grant of $280,000 that enabled her to have necessary surgery on her eyes, to travel, and to develop a curriculum on black culture. When interviewed at the end of the five-year grant period, she said that she wanted the National Center of Afro-American Artists to become "worthy to be called a world institute."

Lewis has received more than twenty-five honorary degrees, including degrees from Bates College, Brown University, Colby College, Emerson College, Harvard University, New England Conservatory of Music, Northeastern University, and the University of Massachusetts.

Although it was not Lewis's intention to train professional artists, many of her students have become professionals in the fields of dance, drama, and singing. "Our goal is to develop good human beings, human beings who can hold their heads up high and be proud of being black; if in the process we develop good artists, that's all right too," she told *Black Enterprise* writer Zarine Merchant. In a story in *Essence,* Lewis said, "It is not in the realm of *luxury* but of *necessity* that the creative energies of the nation's Black population will be nurtured and preserved for prosperity."

The mission of the National Center of Afro-American Artists can best be described in Lewis's own words, cited in the *Boston Globe:* "We expose the students to all of the art disciplines, and if they want to specialize they can do this and become professionals. But I like to think that the Center, most importantly, is a process during which the child, that most marvelous of human beings, not only learns cultural pride, but learns too, how to deal with the world."

**Profile by
Ruth Edmonds Hill**

AUDRE LORDE

It is impossible to categorize the poet Audre Lorde, for the layers of

complexity in her works and Lorde's courage in touching the center of

her personal pain transcend labels. She writes as an African American,

as a woman, as a mother, and as a lesbian, saying, "I cannot be

categorized." Critics "have always wanted to cast me in a particular

light," she explains, to narrow her so that she can fulfill their

expectations.

1934- •

poet, •

essayist,

librarian

If we cannot categorize Lorde, then, we can name her as she names herself. She is, in the world of art, the black unicorn she describes in one of her most popular poems—a rare individual. Like the unicorn, she is "greedy" and "impatient." She was "mistaken / for a shadow / or symbol. . . . / It is not on her lap where the horn rests / but deep in her moonpit / growing." She is "restless" and "unrelenting" and, like the black unicorn, "not / free."

Lorde's avenue toward freedom is her writing. She began writing as a young woman, she says, because "there was no one saying what I wanted and needed to hear" and as a means to work through the very personal pain that continues to inform her poetry. She is the woman outsider, as Joan Martin records in *Black Women Writers:* "Child-woman seeking still a mother's love. Black mother agonizing the fated issue of her womb. Black lesbian feminist poet." Her themes are often—though not exclusively—of love, frequently lesbian love. But, in Martin's words, "one doesn't have to profess heterosexuality, homosexuality, or asexuality to react to her poems. . . . Anyone who has ever been in love can respond to the straightforward passion and pain, sometimes one and the same, in Lorde's poems."

Lorde's personal, private pain is a transforming experience for her readers. It transcends her childhood in Brooklyn and her reality as a lesbian, and it invokes the spirit of ancestral women. In her poetry Lorde travels to Africa, where there are women whose faces are her own. She celebrates the courage of defiant women, like Harriet and Assata, who give testimony to the strength of black women as survivors in such poems as the powerful "A Litany of Survivors."

Lorde is not a message-poet, but "the question of social protest and art is inseparable" for her. "Art for art's sake doesn't exist for me," she says in *Black Women Writers.* When she airs her pain, which is not hers alone, she declares, "that's the beginning of social protest." As a black woman she protests racial oppression and sexual oppression. As a socialist she protests class oppression. As a lesbian she protests them all, bringing into focus the sharp edges of homophobia. More powerfully than any other writer, living or dead, Lorde broke the silence on lesbian love. In her autobiography *Zami: A New Spelling of My Name* she writes vividly of her love-making with several women, most especially Afrekete, "whose print remains" upon Lorde's life "with the resonance and power of an emotional taboo."

> Afrekete Afrekete ride me to the crossroads where we shall sleep, coated in the woman's power. The sound of our bodies meeting is the prayer of all strangers and sisters, that the discarded evils, abandoned at all crossroads, will not follow us upon our journeys.

It is not only the passion and joy of her personal relationships Lorde celebrates in her writings; it is also "the erotic urge, the place that is uniquely female." She writes: "Within a woman's capacity for feeling, our ability to love, to touch the erotic, lies so much of our power, our ability to posit, to vision."

For a woman who feels "a duty to speak the truth as I see it and to share not just my triumphs, not just the things that felt good, but the pain, the intense, often unmitigating pain," sharing her battle with cancer is another example of her courage and her commitment to truth. *The Cancer Journals* is, therefore, another gift from Lorde to those who would understand that only by walking through pain can we name ourselves, claim ourselves, and make a difference in the world. The *Journals* consist of poetic prose entries: "I want to write of the pain I am feeling right now, of the lukewarm tears that will not stop coming into my eyes."

Lorde was born in New York City on February 18, 1934, the daughter of Frederic Byron Lorde and Linda Belmar Lorde. She is the former wife of Edward A. Rollins, whom she married in 1962, and has two children, Elizabeth and Jonathan. Lorde studied for a year, 1954, at the National University of Mexico, received a B.A. from Hunter College in 1959, and an M.L.S. from Columbia University in 1961. By training a librarian, Lorde worked at Mount Vernon Public Library, 1960-62; Saint Clare's School of Nursing, 1965-66; the Towne School, 1966-68; City College of the City University of New York, 1968-69; Lehman College, 1969-70; John Jay College of Criminal Justice, 1970-80; and, since, 1980, at Hunter College.

Lorde's honors and awards include a National Endowment for the Arts grant, 1968; Creative Artists Public Service Award, 1972, 1976; Honorary Commission from the governor of Louisiana, 1973; Woman of the Year Award from Staten Island Community College, 1975; Broadside Press Poet's Award, 1975; and Creative Artists Public Service Book Award for Poetry, 1974, for *From a Land Where Other People Live.*

Poetry reflects •

triumphs and

pain

**Profile by
Gloria Wade-Gayles**

ANNIE TURNBO MALONE

*A*nnie Minerva Turnbo Pope Malone, a pioneer in black beauty

culture, was acclaimed as the nation's first black millionairess. In the

1920s at the peak of her career, she was said to be worth fourteen million

dollars; at her death her wealth had dwindled to a mere one hundred

thousand dollars. The significance of Malone as an entrepreneur,

philanthropist, and founder of the first center for the study and teaching

of beauty culture specifically related to African Americans is virtually

unknown to this generation of Americans and rarely mentioned in

general black American histories.

1869-1957 •

beauty culture •

specialist

Malone was born on a farm in Metropolis, Illinois, on August 9, 1869, the tenth of eleven children of Robert Turnbo and Isabella (Cook) Turnbo. Orphaned at a very young age, she was reared primarily by an older sister in Peoria, Illinois.

Concerned about the styling of her coarse hair, she rejected the hair-straightening techniques of Peoria women who, like many late-nineteenth-century black women, used soap, goose fat, and other heavy oils on their hair. In the late 1890s she began to experiment with chemicals to develop a product that would straighten kinky hair without damaging the hair follicles or burning the scalp like so many hair-straightening products at the turn of the century. By 1900 Malone had developed successful straighteners, hair growers, tetter reliefs, and special hair oils.

Acknowledged by some sources as the first to develop and patent the pressing iron and comb in 1900, Annie Malone manufactured and sold Wonderful Hair Grower while residing in Lovejoy, Illinois. In 1902 she moved her business to Saint Louis, Missouri, where she and three trained assistants sold her products door-to-door, providing free hair and scalp treatments to attract clients. In that same year, during the World's Fair, Malone opened her first business location. Within a year her products were being widely distributed to black women throughout the Midwest. During this period Malone developed marketing strategies aimed at the national black consumer. Advertisements were placed in key black newspapers, press conferences were held, and women were recruited as agents to sell her products. Malone toured the South in an effort to expand her business to the nation's primarily black market. Also at this time, in 1903, she married a Mr. Pope; they soon divorced after he attempted to interfere with her business activities.

Coinciding with Annie Malone's expansion effort was the rise of Madame C. J. Walker. A former washerwoman and one of Malone's first students, Walker was employed as an agent for Poro products (Malone's business) by 1905. Not content to sell Poro products and to work for Annie Malone, Madame Walker began to perfect a hair formula similar to that of Malone's, to develop a complexion cream, and to market the hot iron as the primary straightener of black hair. In 1906 Walker moved to Denver, Colorado, where she organized her first office. In 1908 she organized a second office in Pittsburgh, Pennsylvania, and in 1910 she consolidated the two in Indianapolis, Indiana, where she built a plant to manufacture her products. At her death in 1919, Walker was an acknowledged millionaire.

Walker is cited in numerous historical sources as the first successful major manufacturer of black beauty products. However, many sources indicate that Malone's business predated the Walker Company. In 1906 Malone copyrighted the trade name "Poro" in order to safeguard her products and merchandising systems from imitators. (Poro is a West African word for an organization dedicated to disciplining and enhancing the body physically and spiritually.) In the early 1900s Poro products did well against those of many competitors, due in part to Malone's system of exclusive franchised agent-operators, a system also utilized by Madame Walker.

In 1902 the Poro business was located in Saint Louis at 2223 Market Street. In 1910 it was moved to larger quarters at 3100 Pine Street. Although Annie Malone was an entrepreneur, her special focus was the development of Poro College. In 1917 she built the Poro College complex in Saint Louis, which served as a center for education and employment and became the social hub of the city's black community. It was used by diverse local and national organizations for special functions and as office space. In 1927 during the Saint Louis tornado disaster, Poro College served as one of the principal facilities of the Red Cross where storm victims were sheltered, clothed, and fed. The main building and its annex contained classrooms, barbershops, laboratories, an auditorium, a dining room, a cafeteria, an ice cream parlor, a bakery, a theater, and a roof garden. The equipment and furnishings of the Poro plant, which included the Poro College Building, were valued at over a million dollars.

In the early twentieth century, black leaders stressed the need for race improvement and the presentation of a positive self-image. Malone, imbued with the values of the black middle class, felt that one's deportment was just as important as education. Poro students were taught how to walk, talk, and eat properly. The college trained women as agents for the Poro System and provided jobs for workers and high school students. By 1926 Poro claimed to have 75,000 agents located throughout the United States, the Caribbean, and other parts of the world. The Poro College employed 175 people. In 1930 the business and college were moved to Chicago. Located at 44th Street on South Parkway, the area was called the Poro Block.

Following a period of major growth in the 1920s, Poro became a vast hair care empire. Shortly after the boom, however, Malone's enterprise suffered from poor decisions made by incompetent and dishonest managers. While Poro was showing its first signs of decline, Malone was also engaged in a power struggle with her husband, Aaron Malone, who was the chief manager and president of Poro until 1927. For almost six years prior to their much-publicized divorce in 1927, they maintained a facade of happiness. Their troubled relationship adversely affected the operation of the business.

Prior to suing Annie Malone for divorce, Aaron Malone actively courted Poro supporters, national black leaders, and key community sources for personal support that would be an effective weapon in wresting control of Poro from his wife. In the divorce suit, Aaron Malone asserted that Poro enterprises had succeeded because of his business acumen and ability to market the company through an extensive network of contacts developed prior to their marriage. He demanded one-half of the business assets. The black leadership was divided in their support for Annie and Aaron Malone. However, Annie Malone had the backing of powerful black clubwomen like Mary McLeod Bethune, who in 1927 was the national president of the National Association of Colored Women. Since Poro products were marketed primarily to women and Annie Malone's philanthropic efforts affected many of these elements, she gained the edge. Annie Malone kept the business from going into receivership, negotiated a settlement of two hundred thousand dollars with Aaron Malone, and got a divorce. On the surface, she appeared victorious; however, Malone's self-image and the business had suffered.

Following the divorce, Malone's reputation was marred; and her resources were further depleted by other legal battles, one of which forced the sale of her St. Louis property. Between 1943 and 1951 Malone was also involved in lawsuits filed against her to claim thousands of dollars in excise taxes, which the Federal government required for all luxuries and cosmetics. By 1951 the government had taken control of Poro. Malone's failure to pay real estate taxes led to the sale of most of the Poro property.

* *Nation's first*

major black

philanthropist

Annie Malone was the nation's first major black philanthropist. Because of her extensive philanthropy, she became known as a "freak giver." At one time she reportedly was supporting two full-time students in every black land-grant college in the United States. Numerous black orphanages received five thousand dollars or more annually. She purchased homes for her brothers and sisters and educated many of her nephews and nieces. Howard University's Medical School Endowment, the St. Louis Colored YWCA, and Tuskegee Institute benefited greatly from Malone's generosity, receiving well over sixty thousand dollars during the 1920s. When Poro College opened in 1918, it was said that the Malones had contributed more to charity and Christian associations than any hundred black Americans in the United States.

Malone's philanthropy extended to employees. Her concern for their welfare was demonstrated in lavish gifts. At annual Poro Christmas banquets she gave diamond rings to five-year employees, gold awards to real estate investors, and prizes for punctuality and attendance. As noteworthy as Malone's philanthropy was, it too created a financial problems that plagued her from beginning to end.

Throughout her life Malone was intensely concerned about the material and cultural uplift of her race. She held memberships and served offices in a number of organizations, including the National Negro Business League and the Commission on Interracial Cooperation. She served as chairman of the board of directors of the Saint Louis Colored Orphans Home, an institution later named after her, and president of the Colored Women's Federated Clubs in Saint Louis.

Annie Turnbo Malone died of a stroke on May 10, 1957, in Chicago's Provident Hospital. She had no children.

**Profile by
Bettye
Collier-Thomas**

BIDDY MASON

Biddy Mason, who lived during an era when African Americans

had few legal rights and even fewer opportunities, fought for her

freedom from slavery and then prospered as a nurse, midwife, landown-

er, and entrepreneur. Mason's transformation from slave to successful

businesswoman created a secure future for her family and provided

inspiration for those who came into contact with her. A profoundly

religious woman, Mason also housed the needy, visited local jails, and

co-founded the Los Angeles chapter of the First African Methodist

Episcopal church. She is recognized today as a trailblazer who allowed

neither her gender nor her race to hamper her many endeavors, and one

who generously contributed to the good of her community.

1818-1891 •

entrepreneur, •

nurse,

humanitarian

369 •

Born August 15, 1818, and named Bridget, this former slave quickly came to be known as Biddy. The exact place of her birth, thought to be in Georgia or Logtown, Mississippi, is not known for certain. Biddy Mason was the slave of Robert Marion Smith and Rebecca (Crosby) Smith, who owed a plantation in Mississippi. She eventually had three children, Ellen, Ann, and Harriet, who were possibly fathered by Smith.

Smith became a Mormon convert in 1847 and decided to migrate to the Utah Territory to make his contribution to building the Kingdom of the Saints in Salt Lake City. On March 10, 1848, Mason began her strenuous cross-country journey with the Smith family and others, including another slave of Smith's named Hannah, who had several daughters. Mason exhibited great endurance and an impressive variety of skills as organizer of a camp of fifty-six whites and thirty-four slaves. She herded the two yoke of oxen, seven milk cows, and eight mules that belonged to the party. She also prepared the meals, cared for her own children, and acted as midwife for several births during the arduous two-thousand-mile trek.

The Smith clan and their slaves, including Mason, remained in the Mormon environs for only a few years, from 1848 to 1851. During this brief period, however, Mason witnessed and was subjected to the indignities of the Mormons' firm and often outspoken belief in the inferiority of blacks. Robert Smith learned of a newly established Mormon community in San Bernardino, California, and decided to leave the Salt Lake Valley and move to this new community in September 1851, taking his slaves with him.

Smith obviously did not know of the legislation that had passed in California. The California state constitution, as drafted in 1849, forbade slavery. The debates between the pro- and antislavery forces continued until September 1850, when California was admitted to the Union as a free state. Despite being a free state, the status of people of color who entered the state as slaves both before and after the admission of California was ambiguous. Mason's owner became alarmed over the confused status of slaves and began making preparations to move his family and slaves to Texas, a slave state.

Mason told two free black men of Los Angeles her fear of being forced to leave California and remaining hopelessly entrapped as a slave. The two men, Charles Owens and Manuel Pepper, were determined to keep Smith from separating them from Biddy's and Hannah's young daughters, with whom they had romantic relationships. Owens's father, Bob Owens, was an influential and well-known businessman in Los Angeles. These gentlemen decided that Smith's plot to keep his slaves in bondage, particularly Mason, Hannah, and their daughters, had to be thwarted. They, along with sheriffs and others, disrupted Smith's plan by invading his hideout in the Santa Monica Mountains of Los Angeles. There, Smith was served with an order to appear in court by Mason and her family.

Mason was compelled to remain silent during the court proceedings to rule on her petition for freedom because of an 1850 California law that did not allow the testimony of blacks, mulattos, or Native Americans against white people in either criminal or civil cases of law. When Smith failed to appear in court on January 21, 1856, Mason's petition for manumission was approved. Not only did Mason gain her own freedom, but Judge Benjamin Hayes, who presided over the two-day hearing, also freed all members of her family when he rendered the final decision against Smith.

Upon her entry into the life of a free person of color, Mason was invited by Robert Owens to remain in Los Angeles. Mason accepted his invitation for her and her daughters to live with him, his wife, Winnie, and their children—Charles, Sarah Jane, and Martha. The strong bond between these two families culminated in the marriage of Charles Owens and Ellen Mason. They had two sons, Robert Curry Owens and Henry L. Owens.

Mason's reputation as an adept nurse and midwife was quickly established and respected among newly arrived Anglo immigrants, Native Americans, and the wealthy. Mason's finely honed midwifery and nursing skills were probably learned on the Southern plantations from older slaves and knowledgeable practitioners of successful treatments through the use of herbs, roots, exercise, and diet. Her consistently high standards in the practice of midwifery among all social classes allowed her to gain economic independence.

Nurse/midwife •

becomes

entrepreneur

Through her work and her thrift, Mason achieved her dream of owning a home for her family only ten years after gaining her freedom. She bought a site on Spring Street, now a bustling commercial center in the heart of downtown Los Angeles. The purchase price was $250 and she was one of the first black women to own land in Los Angeles. From the time of purchase, she referred to the lot as "the Homestead" and sternly instructed her children that it was never to be abandoned. Mason actually rented a small dwelling for eighteen years after the purchase of her land. Although she was not a speculator, she was saving money to build a revenue-producing structure on part of her property.

By 1884, at the age of sixty-six, Mason moved onto her own land. She also sold a parcel for $1,500 and built a commercial building with rental spaces in this rapidly developing urban center of Los Angeles.

Mason had made wise decisions regarding her business and real estate transactions, establishing a secure and financially independent future for herself and her family. Through her insightful observations of the struggles of ethnically diverse groups of Americans, it became clear to her that those who were beginning to prosper in nineteenth-century Los Angeles possessed skills that enabled them to acquire land and to educate their children. These observations of success among newcomers to Los Angeles helped to inspire Mason's goal of possessing a homestead in perpetuity for her family. Mason's acquisitions of land provided her heirs with wealth and status in the Los Angeles community. Her grandson, Robert, a real estate developer and politician, was described at the turn of the century as the richest black man in Los Angeles.

Mason's homestead was more than a secure place for her family. She used it as a base for her generous charitable work with the poor, often providing a refuge for needy people of all races. Mason was well known for her frequent visits to the jails, and those who were incarcerated often found that they were neither abandoned nor forgotten. People seeking her assistance often formed lines at 331 South Spring Street.

In addition to being a philanthropist, Mason was a deeply religious woman. She, along with her son-in-law Charles Owens, invited a group of people to her home to found in 1872 the Los Angeles branch of the First African Methodist Episcopal church. Mason's legacy of legal precedents, social philanthropy, civic participation, familial nurturing, and the spiritual enrichment of the Los Angeles community has been appropriately acknowledged in a recent series of community celebrations of her life.

Although many mourned Mason's passing when she died on January 15, 1891, she was interned in an unmarked grave at Evergreen cemetery in the Boyle Heights area of Los Angeles. The grave remained unmarked for nearly one hundred years. On Palm Sunday, March 27, 1988, Mayor Tom Bradley and about three thousand members of the First African Methodist Episcopal church paid homage to her by unveiling an impressive tombstone to mark her grave.

Thursday, November 16, 1989, was declared Biddy Mason Day, and a ceremony at a new multipurpose building called the Broadway Spring Center unveiled a memorial depicting the highlights of her lifetime achievements in nineteenth-century Los Angeles.

**Profile by
Oscar L. Sims**

Queen Mother AUDLEY MOORE

A tireless crusader for civil rights, women's rights, and Pan African

nationalism for nearly eighty years, Audley Moore has been involved in

almost every important political group, organization, and movement

that worked toward these aims, as well as acted as the driving force

behind a great many economic and political efforts for the improvement

of the lives of African Americans.

1898- •

Pan-Africanist, •

feminist

Audley Moore was born in New Iberia, Louisiana. She was the oldest of three daughters born to Henry and St. Cyr Moore. Her father, a onetime sheriff's deputy in Iberia Parish, had married three times and fathered eight children. Her mother, the granddaughter of an African woman raped by her white owner, died when Audley Moore was only five, leaving Moore and her sisters, Eloise and Lorita, to live with their maternal grandmother in New Iberia while their father moved to New Orleans. Moore recalls that her mother's father had been lynched, and she witnessed the lynching of her grandmother's husband. A few years later the sisters were reunited with their father in New Orleans; he died when Moore was in the fourth grade. She then dropped out of school to take care of her sisters, selling some of her father's mules to rent a house and lying about her age in order to become a hairdresser to support the family.

Moving to New Orleans around the turn of the century proved to be a bittersweet experience for Moore and her sisters. It was here that they would experience the brunt of racial violence and segregation but also the awakening of racial pride. In a *Black Scholar* interview, Moore vividly recalls the violence and segregation of their early years in Louisiana:

> I remember when I was a kid in Louisiana, the Catholic convents took black girls but no black boys for the priesthood. . . . Then I remember police rounding up our men just because they were standing on the corner . . . talking to one another, hauling them in for vagrancy . . . rounding them up at fish fries. They would take all the men and put them in a van, then go back and rape the women.

It was the repressive climate of racial violence and segregation that led many outraged blacks in New Orleans to flock to a local meeting hall in 1919 to hear a little-known Jamaican, Marcus Garvey, call for the establishment of an independent black nation. Garvey's appearance in New Orleans provoked a local disturbance. At first the police prohibited Garvey from speaking to the incensed crowd. The following night, the crowd came back again to hear him—most armed with guns. According to her comments published in *I Dream a World: Portraits of Black Women Who Changed America*, Moore carried two—"one in my bosom and one in my pocketbook." This time when the police attempted to silence Garvey, they met armed resistance. The crowd stood on benches, waved their guns, and exhorted Garvey to speak. Moore recalls the police "turned red as crawfish and filed out like wounded puppy dogs." Garvey's impact on Moore was immediate and lasting; it set her on a lifelong quest for black consciousness and nationhood. She became a life member of Garvey's United Negro Improvement Association (UNIA), buying stock in the ill-fated Black Star Shipping Line. In an interview for *Black Women Oral History*, she says Garvey "raised in me a certain knowledge of the history of the wealth of Africa."

Moore, her husband, and her sisters joined thousands of other blacks fleeing the South in search of freedom and employment in the West and the North. After traveling to California and Chicago, they eventually settled in Harlem in 1922, only to discover the same appalling conditions they were trying to escape in the South. From 1900 to 1930, the black population of New York City grew dramatically by 250 percent, from 91,709 in 1910 to 327,706 in 1930. Although most of these migrants came from the South, a large influx also came from the West Indies, creating a dynamic fusion of Afro-American cultures. As the geographic and cultural boundaries of Harlem took shape, "Black Manhattan" emerged as the mecca of black life. But beneath the glamour and appeal of Harlem lay a gloomy underside consisting of congested housing conditions, widespread unemployment and job discrimination, and poor health conditions.

Moore was particularly disturbed by the exploitation of black working women in Harlem, most of whom were domestic workers in white homes. She compares labor conditions in Harlem to slavery in the South. White women would meet African-American women on the street corners in the Bronx, examine their knees for crust (a sign of a hard worker), and hire them for as little as fifteen cents a day. She set out to organize these women by founding the Harriet Tubman Association, one of the many organizations she would found and head in her lifetime.

● *Organizes*

community

uplift activities

By 1930 Moore's organizing efforts in Harlem led to a twenty-year affiliation with the Communist party, which recruited strongly in the African-American community in the 1920s and 1930s. Moore initially joined the International Labor Defense, thinking it was the Communist party because of its large number of Communist members. She officially joined the party in 1933, encouraged by its involvement with the Scottsboro Case (1931-1933) and its advocacy of voters' rights and civil rights. The party helped her to hone her organizational skills among working-class people and gave her an in-depth understanding of capitalism. While active in the party, she fought racial segregation on a number of fronts, helping to integrate major league baseball and the Coast Guard, fighting evictions, and organizing early rent strikes in Harlem.

She also served as the campaign manager to Benjamin E. Davis, Jr., an African-American Communist leader in New York, who served two successive terms on the New York City Council in the 1940s. In 1950 she resigned from the party, denouncing it as "racist to the core," and became an advocate of poor people in the South, returning to her home state of Louisiana to lead a successful campaign to restore 23,000 black and white families to the welfare rolls after they were cut off by state authorities. Through her organization, the University Association of Ethiopian Women, she also sought to overturn the death sentences of African-American prisoners.

Moore's affiliations with the Garvey movement, the Communist party, and other grassroots organizations did not prevent her from associating with or joining more mainline groups such as Mary McLeod Bethune's National Council of Negro Women, organized in 1935 in Washington, D.C., as an umbrella organization for black women's organizations. Personally acquainted with the renowned educator and reformer, Moore was present at the organizational meeting of the NCNW. She credits both Bethune and historian Lawrence Reddick with helping her to develop confidence in public speaking by providing speaking opportunities for her in Washington; both were impressed with Moore's persuasive oratory and clear analysis.

Moore's associations with prominent black male leaders from 1930 to 1950 were less than favorable because she objected to their sexism and class consciousness. She claims that African-American women were wrongly excluded from the first two Pan-African Congresses (1919 and 1921), organized principally by W. E. B. Du Bois. It was not until the founding of the Organization of African Unity that Moore says she got an opportunity to participate in the Pan-African Movement and to travel to Africa. She claims that Elijah Muhammad, the head of the Nation of Islam, was unreceptive to developing any cultural or political ties with Africa. In fact, she notes it was she and her sister Eloise who introduced Malcolm X to African history and Pan-Africanism.

Beginning in the 1950s, Moore's Pan-African nationalism broadened to include such issues as economic reparations, cultural identity, and education. Although she was hardly the first African American to issue a call for reparations, she was instrumental in making it a central issue prior to the inauguration of the civil rights and the black power movements. She launched her campaign for reparations in 1955 while in New Orleans, after reading in "an old Methodist encyclopedia" that "a captive people have one hundred years to state their judicial claims against their captors or international law will consider you satisfied with your condition." With the one-hundredth anniversary of the Emancipation Proclamation just five years away, Moore launched a national crusade to rally support for reparations, even going to the White House in 1962 to meet with President John F. Kennedy. She organized and directed the Reparations Committee of the Descendants of United States Slaves, which filed a claim in California in late 1962. Though the Civil Rights Act of 1964 and the Civil Rights Bill of 1965 fell far short of her demands for five-hundred million dollars, she had persisted in her efforts. As she declares in *I Dream a World:*

Moore calls for •

reparations

> They owe us more than they could ever pay. They stole
> our language, they stole our culture. They stole our
> mothers and fathers and took our names away from us
> . . . It's past due. The United State will never be able to
> pay us all they owe us.

For Moore reparations were also a constructive step in the rebuilding of African-American cultural identity—the first step in black nationalist ideology. She founded and headed a number of organizations to achieve her goal of teaching racial pride and cultural identity in African Americans. With Harlem as her base, she organized the African-American Cultural Foundation, which led the fight against the names "Negro" and "black." She contends that both terms are pejorative labels used by white oppressors to brainwash African Americans; she advocates the use of "African" as a more appropriate term.

Moore also founded the World Federation of African People and was a founding member of the Ethiopian Orthodox Church of North and South America, the Congress of African Peoples, and the Republic of New Africa, which were in part inspired by her trips to Africa, the West Indies, and Europe. On her first trip to Africa in 1966, she attended the funeral of Kwame Nkrumah. The trip was a memorable experience for Moore, as she notes in her *Black Scholar* interview:

> When the plane landed such a thrill came over me, I became hysterical. For some reason, I couldn't keep it in any longer. All the years, all I had suffered, all of the separation, all of the whips on our back, all the rapes . . . came before me. I cried and cried.

Moore would return to Africa many times, visiting the heads of states of Uganda, Nigeria, Guinea, Tanzania, and Zimbabwe, and participating in such conferences as the All-African Women's Conference in 1972 and the Sixth Pan-African Conference in 1974—both in Tanzania. While in Ghana, she was initiated as "Queen Mother" of the Ashanti people in recognition of her lifetime service to the African people.

One of Moore's most tangible contributions to people of African descent has been the Eloise Moore College of African Studies, founded on a two-hundred-acre plot of land in Mount Addis Ababa, New York. Named in honor of her sister, the fledgling school is designed to "embrace the cultural, education, and industrial needs" of African Americans, as Moore describes in *Black Scholar:*

> We wanted to buy a school to teach our children, who are being severed from public schools—so called drop-outs. . . . We wanted to give our children skills that automation could not eradicate like soil conservation, skills like pruning trees, like landscaping, like poultry rearing. . . . Africa needs those skills. So if we could teach our children to be teachers—to go to Africa to teach the young ones their skills, we could have a flow of interests and collective work reaching across the seas.

Although the school burned down in 1961, Moore's vision of a school promoting African identity and vocational training has not diminished.

More recently Moore has been campaigning to establish a national monument in memory of the millions of Africans who died during the trans-Atlantic slave period. She has also been active in the Ethiopian Orthodox church of North and South America, which she cofounded with her sister Lorita. Although raised as Catholics, the two sisters became disenchanted with the Roman Catholic church in 1935 when the Pope blessed Italy's ammunition used to invade Ethiopia. The Moore sisters joined with a number of other African-American groups in organizing for Ethiopia's defense. In 1969 Moore was baptized by Abuna Tehopholis, head of the Ethiopian Orthodox Church, and became an abbess and later an archabbess.

Profile by Raymond R. Sommerville

TONI MORRISON

*T*oni Morrison is considered by many critics to be one of the most

1931- •

significant novelists of the twentieth century. Often compared to literary

giants such as William Faulkner and James Joyce, she is noted for her

writer, editor, •

mastery of language—especially her achievements in voice and narra-

educator

tive style and her control of verbal nuance, metaphor, and image. But in

spite of formal literary training, Morrison perceives her creativity as

emanating from central forces in black American culture and not from

the Eurocentric traditions of most authors to whom she is likened. She

explains that writing novels gives her a sense of encompassing that

ineffable "something" in black culture that, so far, has been best

expressed by black musicians. Morrison herself insists on the highest standard—the "irrevocably beautiful"—in her own craft and believes that the best art is political. One function of her novels, she points out, is to tell the stories of black people—stories articulated and memorized long before they appeared in print. In telling these stories, Morrison makes a conscious effort to transpose the orality of black language into the written text. In finely crafted "meandering" dialogue, her fiction articulates a full spectrum of complex meanings and emotions.

The second of the four children of George and Ramah Wofford, Morrison was born in Lorraine, Ohio, shortly after the onset of the Great Depression. Morrison's father was from Georgia, where racial violence made such an indelible impact on him that throughout his entire life he found it impossible to trust or believe in the humanity of white people. However, her mother disagreed and approached each new encounter with whites with patience and reason. Although she grew up in an integrated community in which everyone was poor and blacks were not social outcasts, Morrison learned a great deal about racial history from her family. Morrison's most vivid memories of childhood include learning about black folklore, music, myths, and the cultural rituals of her family and community. Her mother sang in the church choir; her grandfather, an artist, once supported his family by means of his violin performances; her grandmother decoded dreams from a book of symbols and played the numbers based on her translations; and there were signs, visitations, and ways of knowing well beyond traditional wisdom. Storytelling was a major form of family entertainment during her young life.

Not surprisingly, Morrison learned to read at an early age and was the only child in her first-grade class to enter with reading skills. As a teenager, she read widely, from Jane Austen to the great French and Russian novelists to literature of the supernatural. Morrison graduated from high school with honors and went on to study literature and the classics at Howard University. She also joined the Howard University Players and traveled with the student repertory troupe in the summers, performing in plays across the South. These trips, her first contacts with that region, brought her face to face with the kinds of experiences she had heard about in childhood.

Following her graduation from Howard in 1953, Morrison entered Cornell University, where in 1955 she earned a master's degree in English. For the next two years she taught at Texas Southern University and in 1957 she accepted an appointment at Howard and married a Jamaican architect named Harold Morrison. Among her most well-known students at Howard were the acclaimed author Claude Brown, and Stokley Carmichael, the famous civil rights activist of the 1960s.

Morrison's marriage lasted only a few years; by 1964 she was a divorced mother of two young sons.

In 1965, Morrison began an eighteen-year career in publishing with Random House. After moving to New York City in 1968 as senior editor in the trade department, she used her influence to bring the works of several young black writers to publication. Even with the demands of editorship, novel-writing, and single parenthood, Morrison still found time to teach Afro-American literature and creative writing at such schools as the State University of New York at Purchase, Yale University, and Bard College. In 1984 Morrison left publishing to accept a chair in humanities at the State University of New York at Albany, a position she held until 1989, when she accepted a chair at Princeton University.

Morrison first began writing in the late 1950s when she joined a group of ten black writers in Washington, D.C., who met monthly to read each other's works. Once she brought a hurriedly written story about a young black girl who wanted blue eyes. The idea originated from a conversation she had as a child with another black girl who rejected the existence of God after she had prayed unsuccessfully for two years for blue eyes. At the time, Morrison did not think seriously of becoming a writer. Later, living alone with her sons in Syracuse, she turned to writing as a means of coping with loneliness. She developed more fully her idea of the pain of yearning for a dominant, but unrealizable standard of physical beauty, and published *The Bluest Eye* in 1970.

Morrison •

begins writing

Set in the Midwest, *The Bluest Eye* is the story of nine-year-old Claudia McTeer, her ten-year-old sister, Frieda, and their friend, Pecola Breedlove. Feeling unloved by her family and the black community, Pecola surmises she is flawed by the ugliness of her blackness. Thus convinced, she transforms her need for love into an obsession for a symbol of beauty: blue eyes. She yearns to be like Shirley Temple, whom everyone adores. Conversely, Claudia and Frieda, living with their parents in a poor but emotionally secure home, learn to love themselves without a sense of inherent unworthiness. In telling the story of Pecola Breedlove, Claudia comes to better understand herself, the community, and why she and Frieda survived while Pecola did not.

Morrison's next novel, *Sula,* focuses on the relationship between two black girls in the 1920s and 1930s, Nel Wright and Sula Peace. In their extraordinary friendship, Sula is a social rebel and town scandal who lives "an experimental life"; Nel is a conformist who uncritically accepts the stereotypical woman's role as her life. In the juxtaposition of Nel and Sula, Morrison explodes old ideas of good and evil by showing them to be intricate parts of each other.

Although reviewed in many well-known magazines and newspapers, neither *The Bluest Eye* nor *Sula* was an instant success. In fact, the earlier book was out of print by 1974, when *Sula* appeared. While the handful of predominantly white critics who reviewed *The Bluest Eye* were unanimous in praise of Morrison's vision of black life and the power of her poetic prose, their reactions to the plot were guarded, ambivalent, and sometimes negative. Only two black women, writing for *Black World* and *Freedomways,* openly admired *The Bluest Eye. Sula,* with more notice from black reviewers, fared better than its predecessor. Most reviewers called the second novel "thought-provoking" and a bold attempt to address the black female situation within the black community.

The emergence of her first two novels, however, gained Morrison national recognition as a critic and scholar of literature and African-American culture. Between 1971 and 1972 she wrote twenty-eight book reviews and an essay on the women's movement for the *New York Times*, and since then has become a prominent voice in academia and the media. In addition to her fiction, Morrison's publications include a textbook, as well as many essays and articles on American literature, black American writing, and black women. In 1992 Morrison published *Playing in the Dark,* a critical investigation of the way that race has shaped the white "classics" of American literature. She also edited a book of essays on the controversial confirmation hearings of Supreme Court Justice Clarence Thomas.

Wide-spread recognition as a fiction writer came with Morrison's third novel, *Song of Solomon*. With the guidance of his magically insightful aunt, Pilate, "Milkman" Dead moves from a restless alienation in a Northern community to some sense ancestral grounding in the American South. *Song of Solomon* includes themes of flight, family, and male violence, and embodies black culture's social codes, superstitions, fables, myths, and songs. Featured on the front page of the *New York Times Book Review, Song of Solomon* received considerably more notice than Morrison's first two novels combined.

Morrison's next work, *Tar Baby,* is a fusion of fantasy and realism which has roots in the black American folktale of the white farmer who uses a tar baby to trap a troublesome rabbit and is himself outwitted by the clever animal. Most of the novel occurs on the exotic Isle des Chevaliers, an Edenic Caribbean locale invaded by wealthy white Americans. The landscape of *Tar Baby* encompasses the sophistication of Paris, the excitement of New York City, and the certainty of Philadelphia, presenting an overview of the black experience in confrontation with white America. A month after its publication, *Tar Baby* was on the

New York Times best-seller list and remained there for nearly four months.

The idea for Morrison's fifth novel, the Pulitzer Prize-winning *Beloved,* grew from a newspaper clipping about a slave woman, Margaret Garner, who in 1851 escaped from Kentucky to Ohio with her four children. Facing capture and a return to slavery, Garner killed one of her children and unsuccessfully attempted to kill two others. Morrison was struck by the reports of a calm, quiet, and self-possessed Garner while she was in prison. She expressed no remorse for her actions, explaining only that she did not want her children to live in slavery.

In *Beloved,* Sethe, a mother recently escaped from slavery, kills her older daughter to save her from trackers and a return to slavery. Beloved, the daughter, reappears as a ghost and forces her mother to remember the past. In Sethe's search for love and healing, Morrison indicates that her pain is not hers alone to bear: only when Sethe's ties with the community are reestablished does she heal. *Beloved* is about a community confronting its collective past of slavery, suffering, endurance, and strength. A meditation on the legacy of slavery, Morrison describes the book as an effort to rescue the "sixty million and more" to whom she dedicates it from the oblivion to which they had been consigned by history. From Morrison's point of view, no suitable memorial previously existed to remind Americans of those who endured the terrible experience of slavery.

Jazz, Morrison's sixth novel, is set in Harlem in the 1920s, where the rhythm and yearnings of a community in the process of creating itself embody the ineffable power of improvisational jazz. Before the novel opens, Joe Trace, a fifty-year-old cosmetics salesman, shoots and kills his eighteen-year-old lover, Dorcas, in a fit of jealousy. At the funeral home, Joe's wife, Violet, tries to mutilate Dorcas's face with a knife. *Jazz* explores the pasts of these three people, revealing the complexities and suffering of their lives prior to the incident. As the narrative moves back in time to the South of Joe and Violet's childhoods, an anonymous narrator ponders community life in the city and the country, and the nature of family love, romantic love, and desire. Morrison has received widespread praise for the beauty of her articulation of this novel's profound insight into human emotions and history.

Although critics have praised Morrison's storytelling—with its illuminating metaphors, graceful syntax, and haunting images—the author says that she writes mainly for her own satisfaction. Writing affords her an opportunity to find coherence in the world, and the discipline it requires helps her to sort out the past—her own as well as the collective past of black people in America. One of her great desires is

**Profile by
Nellie Y. McKay**

that her writing continues to develop an element she admires in black music, especially in jazz—the absence of a final chord that keeps listeners on the edge, always wanting something more.

CONSTANCE BAKER MOTLEY

Constance Baker Motley served as an associate counsel for the

NAACP Legal Defense Fund for twenty years, becoming part of a civil

rights movement that achieved spectacular legal victories against segre-

gation. She later became a senior district judge for the Southern District

of New York, which covers Manhattan, the Bronx, and six counties

north of New York City.

1921- •

lawyer, •

politician,

judge

Motley was born on September 14, 1921, in New Haven, Connecticut. Her parents, Willoughby Alva and Rachel (Huggins) Baker, immigrated to the United States from the Caribbean island of Nevis. Although blacks composed only about two percent of the total population of New Haven at the time, Motley was exposed to black history and culture through her religious affiliation. She attended Sunday school at an Episcopal church where the minister offered lectures on black history. The minister and his wife, who was from the South, served as mentors to her.

When Motley entered New Haven High School at the age of fifteen, she was well-prepared for the rigors of academic life, but she encountered her first instances of racial discrimination. The first incident

occurred when she and a group of friends went to Bridgeport, Connecticut, for a picnic and were refused admission to the roller-skating rink. On another occasion, Motley and several friends were prohibited from swimming at a local beach in Milford, Connecticut, because their group was interracial. These experiences raised her consciousness on racial discrimination and helped influence her decision to join the civil rights movement. When she was fifteen Motley began participating in local community affairs, becoming president of the New Haven Youth Council and secretary of the New Haven Adult Community Council. Both organizations were established to promote civil rights.

Motley graduated from high school with honors in 1939. As one of nine children in her family during the depression era, however, college seemed a remote possibility. A year and a half later, a businessman who contributed to many black causes, Clarence Blakeslee, offered to pay Motley's college expenses after hearing her speak at a New Haven community center he had built. This generosity enabled Motley to attend Fisk University in Nashville, Tennessee, from February, 1941, to June, 1942. She transferred during World War II to New York University, graduating from its Washington Square College in October, 1943, with a major in economics. Motley began her studies at Columbia Law School the following year. There were very few women there, but they persevered. As Motley recalled, "When I graduated in 1946, you would not have been able to find a single person willing to bet twenty-five cents that I would be successful in the legal profession."

Motley, like her sisters from the nineteenth century—Mary Church Terrell, Mary Ann Shadd Cary, Charlotte Ray, Harriet Tubman, and Sojourner Truth—dreamed of helping black people. The dream became reality in Motley's last year of law school when she was selected as a law clerk for Thurgood Marshall, the chief counsel of the NAACP Legal Defense and Education Fund, future Solicitor General of the United States and Supreme Court Justice. Motley observed gender and racial prejudice as she worked in this capacity:

> During the course of my work with the NAACP Legal Defense and Educational Fund, I traveled around the country trying school and other kinds of desegregation cases. One of the early cases in which I appeared as a trial lawyer was a case in Mississippi . . . involving the equalization of black teachers' salaries in 1949.

The local newspapers ran a big story on the day the trial began because there were two black lawyers from New York who were going to try the case, and one was a woman. The courthouse was packed; not only because this was the first case in this century in which blacks in

Mississippi sought to attack the establishment and try to end segregation, but because, as the paper stated, it featured "a black woman lawyer from New York."

Motley noted a distinct connection between the black struggle for equality and justice and the increasing momentum for civil rights following World War II. She claimed that World War II "created a type of psychological stress whereby segregation in the armed forces became a national embarrassment." The returning servicemen brought a new sense of pride in their American citizenship and this gave them the strength to unite in the struggle against discrimination and oppression. According to Motley, people joined the NAACP in unprecedented numbers.

• *School*

segregation

laws attacked

in court

In 1954, Motley helped write the briefs filed in the United States Supreme Court in the school desegregation case *Brown* v. *Board of Education*. After this historic case, the Supreme Court declared segregation unconstitutional in a series of cases in other areas where restrictive state statutes and polices were based exclusively on race. "The Brown decision was the catalyst which changed our society from a closed society to an open society and created the momentum for other minority groups to establish public interest law firms to secure their rights," Motley recalls. In addition, she notes that it provided the impetus for the women's rights movement, the poor people's movement, and other public interest concerns, including prisoners' rights, consumer rights, and environmental law.

Setting a record of personal achievement unequaled by most lawyers, Motley argued ten civil rights cases in the Supreme Court and won nine. Among others, Motley represented James Meredith in his long fight to enter the University of Mississippi (*Meredith v. Fair*), Charlayne Hunter and Hamilton Holmes in their fight to enter the University of Georgia (*Holmes v. Danner*), and similar college and professional school-level cases.

In court, Motley was a keen and perceptive lawyer, always firm and forceful in her legal presentations. During her years as associate counsel of the NAACP Legal Defense Fund, she appeared before state and federal courts in eleven southern states and the District of Columbia in numerous cases involving public school desegregation, public and publicly aided housing, transportation, recreation, and public accommodations (the sit-in cases). Jack Greenberg, who succeeded Thurgood Marshall in 1962 as NAACP Legal Defense Fund director-counsel, regarded Motley as "anchor woman of his team," as he is quoted in *Crisis*. She and other attorneys of the NAACP Legal Defense Fund represented Martin Luther King, Ralph Abernathy, Fred Shuttlesworth, and other demonstrators in the civil rights protest movement of the 1960s, and succeeded in having various injunctions against them lifted.

As a result of Motley's work in civil rights during the 1950s and early 1960s, her legal career broadened and future appointments opened to her. In February 1964 she was elected to the New York State Senate, setting a precedent as the first black woman to hold the office. During her first seven weeks in the state legislature, she began a campaign for the extension of civil rights legislation in employment, education, and housing. However, Motley's tenure in Albany was brief. In a special election in February 1965, called by the New York City Council, she was elected to fill a one-year vacancy as president of the Borough of Manhattan. Motley was reelected in the city-wide elections of November 1965 to a full four-year term. As the first woman and the third black to hold the office of borough president, Motley made tremendous accomplishments. For example, in this office she drew up a plan to revitalize Harlem and other underprivileged areas of the city.

In 1966, Motley received national recognition for her achievements in civil rights when President Lyndon B. Johnson appointed her to the United States District Court for the Southern District of New York. There was tremendous opposition to her appointment, not only from southern senators but from other federal judges as well, but as Motley later noted, she "finally made it through the Senate" and was confirmed in August 1966. She became the chief judge of her court on June 1, 1982, and served as such until October 1, 1986, when she took senior status.

Motley's appointment to the federal judiciary marked the climax of a distinguished career in politics and civic affairs. Throughout the years she exerted honest, determined, and frank leadership in the legal field.

Motley receives support and encouragement from her husband, Joel Motley, and from their son, Joel Motley, Jr., a graduate of Harvard, a lawyer, and an investment banker. In *Ebony,* Joel Motley claims that he maintains his own identity by "being considerate and understanding of his wife's career."

Motley is optimistic about the future of the legal profession, especially the increasing demand for black lawyers. "Most of the problems blacks now face require political solutions. The most pressing need among blacks is the need for greater political power," she concludes. "Lawyers are natural leaders and activists in the black community. More and more blacks will become involved in policy making agencies, in government, in politics, in business and diplomacy—in areas where blacks have not been before and where decisions and changes are going to be made."

Motley •

appointed

federal judge

**Profile by
Floris Barnett Cash**

PAULI MURRAY

*P**auli Murray's career and interests transcended categories. In the*

1910-1985 •

course of achieving noteworthy stature in the fields of literature, law,

and religion, she became a distinguished educator and an ardent

lawyer, •

leader in the civil rights and women's movements. In her writings, legal

scholar,

arguments, lectures, sermons, and personal activities she demonstrated

religious leader

that knowledge must be committed to the search for freedom and justice

if it is to contribute fully to society.

Born in Baltimore, Maryland, on November 20, 1910, Murray was the fourth of six children. Her father, William Henry Murray, was a graduate of Howard University and a teacher and principal in the Baltimore public schools. Her mother, Agnes (Fitzgerald) Murray, was a graduate of the Hampton Training School for Nurses. Christened Anna Pauline Murray, she was the namesake of her paternal grandmother, Annie Price Murray, and her maternal aunt, Pauline Fitzgerald Dame. When her mother died of a cerebral hemorrhage in 1914, Murray went to live with her Aunt Pauline and her maternal grandparents, Robert George Fitzgerald and Cornelia (Smith) Fitzgerald, in Durham, North

Carolina. Her father, who suffered from long-term effects of typhoid fever, was too ill to care for his six children and was committed to Crownsville State Hospital.

Determined to attend college, Murray studied in a New York high school to gain the credentials to qualify for admission to Hunter College. She graduated with honors but returned to Durham and worked for a year before entering the freshman class at Hunter College in the fall of 1928. Though she had to leave school temporarily in her sophomore year after the stock market crash, she graduated from Hunter College in January, 1933, with a major in English and a minor in history. She was one of only four black students in her class of 247 women.

Always ahead of her time, Murray was an innovator in the movements toward racial and sexual equality in the United States. Beginning in the late 1930s, her activism in the civil rights movement was so influential that it could be considered a career in itself, but for her it was a logical involvement that grew out of her everyday struggle to overcome social injustice. Her first protest against the Jim Crow practices in the South occurred when as a young girl she would walk miles in Durham rather than ride the segregated city buses. Her first overt stand against racial segregation came when she refused to consider attending a segregated college after she graduated from high school.

Innovation in

civil rights

movement

begins

In the fall of 1938, Murray took an even more unorthodox step in attacking racial discrimination in regard to her own education, a step unthinkable for a black person to take at the time: she applied for admission to the graduate school at the University of North Carolina. She was rejected on the grounds that "members of your race are not admitted to the University," as she recalls in *Song in a Weary Throat: An American Pilgrimage.* Her personal quest for admission to the university suddenly became public news because the Supreme Court ruled in the *Gaines v. Canada* case that it was the duty of a state to furnish graduate and professional training to all the residents of the state based on an equality of right. Only the second black person ever to apply to the university, Murray received wide publicity, which resulted in black students' filing applications almost immediately at other southern universities. With the admission of several black students to the University of North Carolina law school in 1951, Murray began to see the importance of her role as a pioneer in this struggle for equality of opportunity in higher education.

As Murray recounts in her autobiography, the irony in her battle for admission to the university began forty years later, in 1978, when the university decided to award her an honorary degree. Although she initially accepted the honor, Murray later declined because of the university system's refusal to implement a more adequate desegregation plan for its sixteen campuses, which it had been directed to do by the United States Department of Health, Education, and Welfare. In 1990, the University of North Carolina established the Pauli Murray Scholarship to be awarded annually to an undergraduate student with documented financial need who has made significant contributions to the improvement of race relations.

Murray's serious interest in a career in law was sparked in March of 1940 when she was arrested on a Greyhound bus in Petersburg, Virginia, and charged with disorderly conduct and creating a public disturbance. Although she and a friend, Adelene McBean, had observed the Jim Crow laws on the bus, they had refused to move further back to a broken seat where the driver had directed them. They were jailed for three days, and despite efforts of the NAACP attorneys, they were found guilty and had to pay a fine.

Rights violation •

spurs interest

in law

While in jail, Murray and her friend drafted a "Statement of Facts" about the case, which their attorneys praised for its form and accuracy. Murray found herself able to follow and anticipate the legal arguments that the attorneys made, and to envision her case as part of a larger effort to overthrow all segregation laws. Vindication came in 1946 when the United States Supreme Court held the Virginia Jim Crow statute invalid in the *Morgan v. Virginia* case.

In the fall of 1941, Murray enrolled at the Howard University law school with the intent of becoming a civil rights lawyer. She worked for the defense of Odell Waller, a black Virginia sharecropper who had been sentenced to death for killing a white landowner, Oscar Davis. With Murray Kempton, she published "All for Mr. Davis: The Story of Sharecropper Odell Waller" to acquaint the nation with the facts of the case, but all appeals failed and Waller was executed in 1942.

Murray's interest in fighting racial discrimination remained steady as she worked with the NAACP and joined the Congress of Racial Equality (CORE), a pacifist organization experimenting with Gandhian techniques, led by Bayard Rustin and James Farmer. Murray also developed a close friendship with Eleanor Roosevelt that lasted for more than twenty years.

During her senior year of law school Murray was elected president of her class and chief justice of the Court of Peers at Howard University. Her senior law thesis was significant because of her argument that the "separate but equal" doctrine did violence to the personality of the minority individual. The lawyers for Oliver Brown, et al. used her argument successfully ten years later to help win the *Brown v. Board of Education of Topeka* case before the United States Supreme Court. In May 1944 Murray graduated cum laude from the Howard University law school and won a Rosenwald Fellowship for graduate study in law at Harvard University. After the public announcement, however, she was rejected by Harvard law school on the basis of gender.

That fall Murray entered the Boalt Hall of Law at the University of California, Berkeley. In 1945, she received an LLM degree in law and passed the California bar examination. In January 1946 she became the first black deputy attorney general of California, but she had to leave the job shortly thereafter because of a personal illness and the illness of her Aunt Pauline.

In 1951 Murray published her first book, *States' Laws on Race and Color*. Thurgood Marshall affirmed the importance of this book, calling it the Bible for the civil rights lawyers who were fighting segregation laws. In the early 1950s, Murray and James Baldwin were the first black writers admitted to the famous McDowell Colony for artists in Peterborough, New Hampshire. In 1956 Murray published *Proud Shoes: The Story of an American Family*, her biography of her grandparents. *Proud Shoes* established a new genre in American literature—the Afro-American family history—preceding by twenty years Alex Haley's *Roots*.

In 1956 Murray was hired as an associate attorney in the nationally prestigious law firm of Paul, Weiss, Rifkind, Wharton and Garrison in New York City, where she worked until 1960. In February 1960, Murray left New York for an eighteen-month sojourn in Ghana to teach at the Ghana School of Law and to explore her African cultural roots. In 1961 she and Leslie Rubin published an original textbook, *The Constitution and Government of Ghana*. Murray returned to the United States and began graduate study at Yale law school in the fall of 1961.

In 1962 Murray, whose stature as a legal scholar and educator and as an activist in a number of civil rights groups had become well-known, was selected as a member of the Committee on Civil and Political Rights, one of seven study committees set up by the President's Commission on the Status of Women.

- *Murray helps*

found NOW

In 1965, Murray received the degree of Doctor of Juridical Science from Yale law school, the first black person awarded this degree. She met Betty Friedan that fall and mentioned an idea for an independent national civil rights organization, like the NAACP, for women. In October of 1966, Murray was one of the thirty-two women who met in Washington and founded the National Organization for Women.

In 1972 Murray was named Louis Stulberg Professor of Law and Politics at Brandeis University, where she served a five-year tenure as professor of American Studies. The following year, her friend Renee Barlow died in New York. With no priest available, Murray ministered to Barlow when she died, as she had with her aunt Pauline in 1955. After this experience, Murray felt the call of service in the church. She applied for admission to holy orders and entered the General Theological Seminary in September, 1973, the only black woman and the oldest student enrolled.

The last decade of her life, a time usually reserved for retirement, saw the full flowering of Murray's talents and gifts—ongoing study, the writing of her autobiography, ordination in the ministry of the Episcopal church, and speaking engagements across the country. In 1976 she received the Master of Divinity degree, cum laude, from the General Theological Seminary and was ordained to the Holy Order of the Deacons of the Episcopal Church, USA. On January 8, 1977, Murray was ordained an Episcopal priest at the National Cathedral in Washington, D.C. She was the first black woman ordained a priest in the two-hundred-year history of the Protestant Episcopal Church. On July 1, 1985, Murray died of cancer at her home in Pittsburgh. Funeral rites were held in Washington, D.C., at the National Cathedral, where she had been ordained.

Murray's last literary contribution was her autobiography, *Song in a Weary Throat: An American Pilgrimage,* which was published posthumously in 1987 and which documents her career and her search for personal identity. In 1988 this work received both the Robert F. Kennedy Book Award and the Christopher Award. In 1989 it was reprinted as *Pauli Murray: The Autobiography of a Black Activist, Feminist, Lawyer, Priest, and Poet.*

Murray's entire life was one of broadening interests, multiplying talents, and response to new challenges. In an age of the deliberate oppression of America's black citizens, she contributed to the reordering of the national agenda, insisted on rational discourse, and fostered conciliation among all people. Her observation in a 1976 interview with Genna Rae McNeil that she had "lived to see [her] lost causes found" stands as a convincing testament to her contributions to the betterment of American society.

Episcopal •

Church ordains

first black

woman

**Profile by
Marsha C. Vick**

ELEANOR HOLMES NORTON

E leanor Holmes Norton has always been a forerunner in politics,

1938- •

law, and human rights. The championship of equality and advocacy for

the rights of poor and working people have guided her career as a

lawyer, •

constitutional, civil rights, and labor lawyer; as Human Rights commis-

government

sioner of New York City; as chair of the Equal Employment Opportunity

official

Commission during the Carter administration; and in every other phase

of her career.

Norton, the oldest of three girls, was born April 8, 1938, in Washington, D.C. Her father, Coleman Holmes, was a civil servant in the housing department of the District of Columbia; her mother, Vela Holmes, was a schoolteacher. Both parents were college graduates and instilled in their children the importance of hard work and a good education.

In 1955, after graduating from high school, Norton enrolled in Antioch College in Yellow Springs, Ohio. She went on to Yale University, where she earned both a master's degree in American studies in 1963 and a doctor of jurisprudence degree in 1964. When she completed her education Norton moved to Philadelphia, where she worked for a year as a clerk for a federal judge. There she met Edward Norton, whom she married on October 9, 1965. "He liked the fact that I was a highly educated woman," she told Greta Walker in an interview for *Women Today.* "Nobody would have married me who didn't want a woman with a career. By the time my husband met me, a career was totally built into my being. I would never have attracted a man who wanted a wife to stay home." Later that year the Nortons moved to New York City, where she took a job as the assistant legal director of the American Civil Liberties Union.

During her career with the ACLU, Norton represented alleged criminals, Vietnam War protesters, civil rights activists, Ku Klux Klansmen, politicians, and feminists. In one case she won promotions for sixty women employees who accused *Newsweek* magazine of job discrimination based on sex. Norton specialized in cases involving freedom of speech. She was a member of the team of lawyers that drew up a brief in defense of Julian Bond when the Georgia House of Representatives voted to deny the young black legislator his seat for his outspoken opposition to the Vietnam War. When Governor George C. Wallace, the American Independent party's candidate for the presidency, was denied a permit to hold a rally at Shea Stadium during the 1968 election campaign, Norton asked to represent the governor in his lawsuit against the city. "If people like George Wallace are denied free expression, then the same thing can happen to black people," she explained in *Current Biography.* "Black people understand this. No black person ever said to me, 'Sister, how come you're representing George Wallace?' They knew how come." Wallace's ACLU lawyers won their case, but when New York City appealed the decision, Wallace moved the rally to Madison Square Garden to save the time and expense of litigation.

In October 1968 Norton argued and won her first case before the Supreme Court as the legal representative of the National States Rights Party, a white supremist group that had been denied permission to rally in Maryland two years earlier because local authorities thought that the group's vocal denunciation of Jews, blacks, and others might provoke angry responses from nonparty members. During these years, in addition to practicing law, Norton taught courses in black history at the Pratt Institute in Brooklyn, New York.

In April 1970 Mayor John V. Lindsay appointed Norton chairman of the New York City Commission on Human Rights. Norton accepted the position mainly because the Human Rights Commission, by law, acts as the representative of and advocate for the complainants. Shortly after the appointment, she stated her goals at a press conference:

> As commissioner, I will attempt to see that no man is judged by the irrational criteria of race, religion, or national origin. And I assure you that I use the word "man" in the generic sense, for I mean to see that the principle of nondiscrimination becomes a reality for women as well.

Because many working women do not see themselves as objects of discrimination, Norton observed, women are more exploited by business than any other group. "Most people think civil rights today is about 'whether or not I'm turning down somebody at the door because he is black or female,'" Norton explained. "It doesn't happen that way anymore. It is more subtle. It happens when women are asked at a job interview, 'Do you intend to get pregnant within the next two years?' And it happens to women much more than it happens to blacks, because blacks have spent more than 300 years trying to educate the country about how perverse it all is."

As the first woman to head New York City's most powerful anti-discrimination agency, Norton became known for her ability to obtain federal grants to assist in her efforts to end all forms of discrimination. In support of working women's individual complaints, she obtained liberal maternity benefits, including maternity leave for single women, from an airline company, a major bank, and a blue-collar employer; convinced another company to allow a pregnant secretary to remain on the job past her seventh month of pregnancy; won for a woman sports reporter the right to sit in the press box at hockey games; forced the chic Twenty-one Club to serve women on an equal basis with men; and ordered the Biltmore Hotel to change the name of its Men's Bar and open it up to women. Working closely with national and local women's groups, Norton promoted the revision of outdated federal and state laws regulating workmen's compensation and minimum wages, the liberalization of abortion laws, and the establishment of adequate day care centers.

To address the particular problems of black women who have had to contend with both racial and sexual discrimination, Norton helped found the National Black Feminist Organization in August 1973. In an effort to combat job discrimination against blacks, Hispanics, Vietnam veterans, ex-offenders, and older employees, Norton urged businessmen to give these people access to "higher-level, skilled, and better-paid jobs in every industry," according to *Current Biography*. Norton noted that while most companies had made an effort to recruit minority group members for entry-level positions, few offered these employees any real chance for advancement.

Norton helped get the nation's strictest law prohibiting discriminatory real estate practices through the New York State legislature. She also convened public hearings on the New York City Schools Board of Education's employment practices in January 1971. Citing a 1959 Board of Education survey that showed that minority groups comprised fifty-five percent of the students, nine percent of the teachers, and four percent of the principals, she ordered Human Rights Commission investigators to look into recruitment, appointment, and promotion procedures and to outline constructive proposals for improvement.

In 1988 Norton was designated by the Reverend Jesse Jackson to handle platform discussions during his presidential campaign. Her appointment was greeted with some relief by Democratic party leaders; according to the *New York Times*, her appointment seemed to be symbolic of Jackson's desire to make peace with the party and help it win the election.

• *Civil rights*

record leads

to federal

appointment

Norton was among the members of a distinguished panel appointed by President Gerald Ford to investigate the American welfare state. Among the ideas endorsed by this panel was a "limit on the length of time that those who can work are entitled to welfare benefits." Welfare mothers who bumped up against the time limit would be offered a public-sector job and told by the government to choose "between the job we offer and making it on your own." Norton and other prominent black figures endorsed kicking mothers off welfare if they would not work.

Norton was also among the one hundred scholars and experts who produced the study "A Common Destiny: Blacks and American Society," released by the National Research Council in 1989. "Americans face an unfinished agenda," states the report, regarded as the most substantial study of black life in America since World War II. "Many black Americans remain separated from the mainstream of national life under conditions of great inequality."

In an *Essence* article, Norton contends that affirmative action has been effective in the advancement of blacks:

> Affirmative action is the most important modern anti-discrimination technique ever instituted in the United States. It is the one tool that has had a demonstrable effect on discrimination. No one who knows anything about the subject would say it hasn't worked. It has

certainly done something, or else it wouldn't have provoked so much opposition. In just one decade—the 1970s—the number of sales, technical and professional jobs Blacks hold increased by 50 percent. Affirmative action, by all statistical measures, has been the central ingredient to the creation of the Black middle class.

In 1990 Norton was elected to replace Walter Fauntroy as Congressional delegate representing the District of Columbia, despite a controversy that arose during her campaign and cost her some votes. Norton and her husband, a lawyer who once headed the city's Board of Elections and Ethics, had failed to file local income tax returns for eight years. Norton boldly confronted the crisis at a tearful press conference, claiming that she did not know that her husband never mailed the 1982 through 1989 tax returns she signed. Her husband explained that he was personally responsible for the oversight. As she ran for public office, Norton gave up her tenured position as professor in the Georgetown University Law Center and her seat on several corporate and philanthropic boards. She became one of three black women in the United States Congress.

Since taking office, Norton has achieved a political turnaround. She has been hailed as a successful delegate who has helped the District of Columbia get $300 million in federal aid. In October 1991 Norton was one of seven Congresswomen who stormed the Senate floor in support of Anita Hill. Early in 1992, Norton announced plans to seek reelection.

Among her many other accomplishments, Norton has been awarded nearly fifty honorary degrees, including honorary doctorates from Howard University, Gallaudet College, the University of the District of Columbia, and Georgetown University.

**Profile by
Jo Ann Lahmon**

ROSA PARKS

*R*osa Louise McCauley Parks, a long-time advocate of civil rights, is best known for her December 1, 1955, refusal to surrender her seat to a white passenger in a crowded Montgomery, Alabama, bus. Parks's landmark act is described as having "breathed life" into the civil rights movement. Recently, three thousand black leaders, government dignitaries, entertainers, and social leaders honored Parks with a seventy-seventh birthday celebration in Washington, D.C.

1913- •

civil rights •

activist

Parks was born February 4, 1913, in Tuskegee, Alabama, one of two children of Leona (Edwards) and James McCauley. Her father was a carpenter and her mother taught in rural schools. Her parents separated in 1915, soon after Parks's brother, Sylvester James, was born. After her father went north to live, she had very little contact with him. Her mother returned with her children to Pine Level, Alabama, to live with her parents.

Parks helped with the household chores, not only because her mother was teaching much of the time, but also because her mother and both grandparents were not in good health. In fact, Parks often had to take care of everyone. She especially liked making quilts and cooking. Her mother taught in rural one-room schools and other buildings where classes could be held, and for about three years was Parks's teacher. When Parks was eleven years old, she went to a private school, the Montgomery Industrial School for Girls, and lived with her aunt, Fanny Williamson.

The teachers at the Montgomery Industrial School for Girls were liberal women from the North. In exchange for tuition, Parks cleaned two classrooms. With her duties at school and at home, there was little time for Parks to enjoy childhood. She entered Booker T. Washington High School but dropped out when her mother became seriously ill. Parks learned about the hardships of slavery and about emancipation from stories told by her maternal grandparents. From her family's teaching, her own observations as a child, and from her experiences at school, Parks realized that segregation and discrimination were wrong.

Although Parks's mother hoped she would become a teacher and offered financial support so she could attend Alabama State Teachers College, Parks thought more about nursing as a possible career. In December 1932 she married Raymond Parks, a barber from Montgomery, Alabama. He had very little formal education, as there was no nearby school for blacks in his youth, but he attended Tuskegee Institute when he was about twenty-one years old. He often talked about the poverty and cruelty of his childhood. After their marriage, Rosa Parks held a variety of jobs to supplement her husband's income. She sewed at home, worked as a domestic, as an insurance salesperson, and as an office clerk.

Raymond and Rosa Parks shared a common interest in the problems of inequality and segregation in the South. As a member of the National Committee to Save the Scottsboro Boys, who were charged with raping two white girls, Raymond often brought food to the young men while they were in jail awaiting trial.

In 1943 Parks became a member of the Montgomery Chapter of the NAACP, one of the first women to do so, and she joined the Montgomery Voters League and encouraged blacks to register to vote. In the summer of 1955 Parks attended workshops at the integrated Highlander Folk School in Monteagle, Tennessee, which had been engaged in the civil rights struggle since the 1930s. Whenever she could, Parks avoided the segregated drinking fountains, the "Colored Only" elevators, and other reminders of the low status imposed on blacks in the South. She often walked home from work.

The incident that changed Parks' life occurred on Thursday, December 1, 1955, as she was riding home on the Cleveland Avenue bus from her job at Montgomery Fair, a downtown department store where she worked as an assistant tailor. The first ten seats on the city buses, which were always reserved for whites, soon filled up. She sat down next to a man in the front of the section designated for blacks, when a white male got on and looked for a seat. In such situations, the black section was made smaller. The driver, who was white, requested that the four blacks move. The others complied, but Parks refused to surrender her seat, so the driver called the police. Parks had been evicted from a bus twelve years earlier by the same driver, but this time it was different. In a *Black Women Oral History Project* interview, she said, "I didn't consider myself breaking any segregation laws . . . because he was extending what we considered our section of the bus." And in *Black Women* she explained, "I felt just resigned to give what I could to protest against the way I was being treated."

At this time there had already been fruitless meetings with the bus company about the rudeness of the drivers and other issues—including trying to get the bus line extended farther into the black community, since three-quarters of the bus riders were from there. In the previous year three black women, two of them teenagers, had been arrested for defying the seating laws on the Montgomery buses. The community had talked many times about a citywide demonstration, such as boycotting the bus line, but it never developed. The Women's Political Council already had a network of volunteers in place and had preprinted flyers; they needed only a time and place for a meeting.

About six o'clock that evening, Parks was arrested and sent to jail. She was later released on a one-hundred-dollar bond, and her trial was scheduled for December 5. Parks agreed to allow her case to become the focus for a struggle against the system of segregation. On December 2, the Women's Political Council distributed more than 52,000 flyers throughout Montgomery calling for a one-day bus boycott on the day of Parks's trial. There was a mass meeting of more than 7,000 blacks at the Holt Street Baptist Church. The black community formed the Montgomery Improvement Association and elected Martin Luther King, Jr., president. The success of the bus boycott on December 5 led to its continuation. In the second month it was almost one hundred percent effective, involving 30,000 black riders. When Parks was tried, she was found guilty and fined ten dollars plus court costs of four dollars. She refused to pay and appealed the case to the Montgomery Circuit Court.

Following her release from jail, Parks went back to work but later lost her job, as did her husband. At home, the couple had to deal with

Parks •

triggers

Montgomery

bus boycott

407 •

threatening telephone calls. Rosa Parks devoted her time to arranging rides in support of the boycott. Blacks were harassed and intimidated by the authorities in Montgomery, and there was an attempt to break up their carpools. Parks served for a time on the board of directors of the Montgomery Improvement Association, and often was invited elsewhere to speak about the boycott.

On February 1, 1956, in an attempt to have the Alabama segregation laws declared unconstitutional, the Montgomery Improvement Association filed a suit in the United States District Court in the names of four women and on behalf of all who had suffered indignities on the buses. On June 2 the lower court declared segregated seating on the buses unconstitutional. The Supreme Court upheld the lower court order that Montgomery buses must be integrated, and on December 20, 1956, the order was served on Montgomery officials. After 381 days of boycotting, resulting in extreme financial loss to the bus company, segregation and other discriminatory practices were outlawed on the city buses. Parks's refusal to give up her seat on a bus was the beginning of the civil rights movement of the 1950s and 1960s. Her action marked the beginning of a time of struggle by black Americans and their supporters as they sought to become an integral part of America.

With the notoriety surrounding her name, Parks was unable to find employment in Montgomery. Her husband became ill and could not work, so Parks, her husband, and mother moved to Detroit in 1957 to join Parks's brother. Since Raymond did not have a Michigan barber's license, he worked in a training school for barbers. In 1958 Parks accepted a position at Hampton Institute in Virginia for one year, after which she returned to Detroit and worked as a seamstress. She continued her efforts to improve life for the black community, working with the Southern Christian Leadership Conference in Detroit. In 1965 Parks became a staff assistant in the Detroit office of United States Representative John Conyers; she retired in 1988.

Rosa Parks has been called "the first lady of civil rights" and "the mother of the freedom movement." The *New York Times* reported that Coretta Scott King and former diplomat Andrew Young assured Parks that "she had a permanent place in history." With the publication in 1992 of *Rosa Parks: My Story*, an autobiography written with Jim Haskins, children and readers of all ages can read Parks's firsthand account of her early life and contribution to the civil rights movement.

Parks is the recipient of many awards, including the NAACP's Spingarn Medal, bestowed in 1979. In 1980 Parks was the ninth person, and the first woman, to receive the Martin Luther King, Jr., Nonviolent Peace Prize, accepting it from Coretta Scott King, Martin Luther King's widow. She holds ten honorary degrees, including one from Shaw College in Detroit. The citation for an honorary degree from Mount Holyoke College in 1981 read in part, "When you led, you had no way of knowing if anyone would follow." In 1984 Parks was the recipient of a special award, the Eleanor Roosevelt Women of Courage Award, from the Wonder Woman Foundation. In 1986 as part of the celebration for the Statue of Liberty's one-hundredth birthday, Parks was one of eighty people to receive a medal of honor for their contributions to American ethnic diversity.

Parks continues to make speeches across the country to raise money for the NAACP, and she speaks to young people about the civil rights movement. She is still active in the Southern Christian Leadership Conference, which since 1963 has sponsored the annual Rosa Parks Freedom Award. Her many honors in Detroit have included the naming of Rosa Parks Boulevard, which runs through the black community, and the Rosa Parks Art Center. In 1987 she established the Rosa and Raymond Parks Institute for Self-Development, incorporated as a nonprofit organization in Detroit, to work with young people between the ages of eleven and fifteen. In January 1988 the Museum of African-American History in Detroit unveiled a portrait of Parks on her seventy-fifth birthday. On June 30, 1989, the twenty-fifth anniversary of the Civil Rights Act, she attended ceremonies at the White House. The National Committee for the Rosa Parks Shrine is soliciting money for a home on Rosa Parks Boulevard for Parks after her retirement. It will also serve as a library for her personal papers. And in 1990, Parks's seventy-seventh birthday was celebrated in Washington, D.C., by three thousand black leaders, government dignitaries, entertainers, and social leaders. Rosa Parks took the occasion to speak again on behalf of freedom and equality, saying, "Pray and work for the freedom of Nelson Mandela and all of our sisters and brothers in South Africa."

**Profile by
Ruth Edmonds Hill**

CARRIE SAXON PERRY

W omen in general—and in Hartford, Connecticut, in particu-

lar—congratulated a history-maker when Carrie Saxon Perry became

the first black woman mayor of the city. Explaining her desire to use the

political process to combat racism, sexism, and other forms of oppres-

sion, Perry says, "The idea of community embraces a diversity of

individuals, groups, experiences, interests and viewpoints. Believing

that diversity strengthens the community I strongly support efforts to

make the political process more representative and responsive to all

constituencies of the community."

1931- •

politician, •

social

worker

Perry was born on August 10, 1931, in Hartford, Connecticut, the only child of Mabel Lee Saxon. The mother and daughter found themselves in a circle of poverty, as did many black families during the depression of the thirties. Perry considers her mother her greatest asset throughout her life. To provide comfort, warmth, and protection, her mother used ingenuity and hard work. In spite of the poverty around them, they found beauty in their family relationships. Perry says that her grandmother and aunt served as role models and gave her continuous encouragement in her life's goals. Perry graduated from the Hartford public schools and attended Howard University in Washington, D.C., as an undergraduate political science major in 1949. She also studied two years at Howard's School of Law, and then returned to Hartford. She married James Perry, Sr., and they had one son, James Perry, Jr. They later divorced.

After her return to Hartford, Perry became a social worker for the state of Connecticut, an administrator for the Community Renewal Team of Greater Hartford, and executive director of Amistad House. Through this work, she became more conscious of the conditions that have an impact on lower economic families and their rearing of children. She found that poverty affects the attitudes, self-esteem, values, code of conduct, job training opportunities, and family activities of poor people. Perry feels that black families should develop a sense of pride and confidence, perpetuate memories of black leaders and heroes, and disseminate information on black history to their children.

In 1976 Perry decided to run for the General Assembly of the Connecticut State Legislature. With the help of her son, she jumped in the race and did quite well, although she was not endorsed by anyone. In 1980, however, Perry ran successfully. She was reelected state representative to the Connecticut State Legislature three times.

Ernest N. Abate, speaker of the House, appointed Perry assistant majority leader of the House in her freshman year. A member of the Education Committee and the Finance, Revenue, and Bonding Committee throughout her tenure at the capitol, Perry also chaired the House Subcommittee on Bonding. In this position, she used her persuasive powers to obtain funds for the Riverfront Recapture, the Artists' Collective, and the Old State House Restoration. Furthermore, she was able to assist in the allocation of funds for minority contractors in the state. Concerned with human rights in the United States as well as abroad, she convinced the state legislature to divest state funds linked to the apartheid-supporting government of South Africa. Continuing her sensitivity for the disadvantaged in the community, Perry supported programs and legislation for quality education for Hartford's schools, job training programs to reduce high school dropout rates, and programs to prevent teenage pregnancies and the high rate of infant mortality. She also fought for the homeless to have the right to vote.

A member of the Democratic party, Perry served as alternate delegate from Connecticut to the Democratic National Convention in San Francisco in 1984, while in 1988 she served as state vice-chair for the Connecticut delegation at the Democratic National Convention in Atlanta, Georgia. In Atlanta she spoke in the nationally televised platform debate on funding for social programs and limited funding for the military.

Perry was elected the sixtieth mayor of Hartford on November 3, 1987, and inaugurated on December 1 of that year. Her election followed that of Thurman Milner, who was New England's first black mayor. Becoming the first black female mayor of a northeastern city, she defeated her white male Republican opponent by a vote of 10,304 to 7,613. Responding to the question of why she ran for mayor, Perry said: "I thought about it. And the fact that Mount Everest is there, why not climb it? It was a challenge, an opportunity."

Hartford, the capitol of Connecticut and the insurance capitol of the world, housed a population of 136,000 in 1990. More than a third of the citizens were black, while twenty-two percent were Hispanic. Both groups have worked diligently to achieve political power. In 1990 the city council included three black and two Hispanic members out of nine. In 1989 the public schools of Hartford were approximately ninety percent black and Puerto Rican, while outside the city limits the schools were decidedly white.

In Hartford, urban poverty is contrasted with New England affluence. According to the 1980 census, Perry is mayor of the nation's fourth-poorest city among those with populations of more than 100,000. Conscious of poverty, racism, and sexism, Perry is aware that changes must take place in society in order for a birth of new ideas and directions to take place. She proclaimed in *I Dream a World:*

Perry attacks •

city's problems

as mayor

> I believe that you have to force change. It doesn't always have to be by violence. You rebel, you organize, you force issues, you threaten the status quo, you show numbers, you promise upheaval: there are numbers of things you have to do. You have to be committed to long distance and accept the fact that it doesn't happen overnight, and that you're doing it probably for another generation.

Perry has demonstrated as much interest in the cultural and business life of Hartford as in its social problems. At a conference on American Cities in Crisis held at Bryn Mawr College in Pennsylvania in

1989, Perry called the state of our cities "more of a threat to our national security than the Warsaw Pact." Because of her concern, she has allocated funds for after-school and weekend recreation programs to provide wholesome outlets for underprivileged youth. Disturbed by the value system that she had seen developing among some inner-city school children, she felt the need to form Operation Bridge, which targets potential dropouts and those with negative behavior patterns.

Sensitive to the plight of the deprived, Perry constantly uses innovative programs to uplift these persons to a level where they can compete with the middle class in Hartford. Since her election as mayor, she walks into community meetings unannounced and listens to her constituents. She attended a community meeting in Clay Hall, a North End neighborhood known for its drug dealers and drug addicts, to let the people know that she cares and is on their side. She made no speeches nor promises.

• *Perry*

advocates

women as

political

leaders

According to Perry, women have established themselves in greater numbers in the American political scene, but a very few have made it to the upper levels. Female politicians encounter what has been called the "glass ceiling" syndrome. They were free to lick stamps and stuff envelopes but were seldom elected to the senior positions in the political arena. At a conference on "Gender, Authority and Leadership" held at Smith College, Perry urged women to become aware of the change for women in politics:

> It is very lonely being a woman in politics. We have to become much more comfortable with these positions. Women, African-American women in particular, have to consider public office as a position that is most honorable.

To succeed as political leaders, Perry feels that women have to change their attitudes toward men, power, and politics. She is concerned that women frequently fail to assert themselves in politics for fear of appearing aggressive. When men and women work together in decision making, the women may become reticent.

Although she is proud of her visibility around Hartford, Perry feels that she could do more if the city charter were revised so the office of the mayor had more power. As it is written now, the mayor's office represents influence rather than power. If reelected, she has vowed to push to have a vote on the council, add another member to maintain an uneven number of council votes, lengthen the mayor's term to four years, and stagger four-year terms for council members.

Perry's colleagues and constituents find her friendly and congenial. They exhort her to be outspoken and forceful since their city is in decline and needs strong leadership. At this point she has not faced any issues with the council that have caused confrontations. Instead of fighting the city council, Perry works harmoniously with them to a degree that has not been seen in recent years.

Perry is also known for the hats she wears, though she claims that she is not trying to make a fashion statement. She simply has such a busy schedule that she "does not have time to comb her hair," according to *Ebony*. Nevertheless, her hats have become her trademark, and her office includes an antique brass hat rack for her broad-brimmed trademarks.

As a social worker, member of the House of Representatives for the State of Connecticut, and mayor of Hartford, Perry has risen to the challenge with vision and intelligence. In these positions she has had the chance to interact with the poor and disadvantaged, the middle class, and prominent, political, educational, civic and business leaders of the state. She has shared her thoughts and opinions and discussed answers to today's tough problems. Perry hopes to bring together a diversity of people, programs, and resources in order to improve the lives of her community.

**Profile by
Joan Curl Elliott**

LEONTYNE PRICE

1927- •

opera singer •

Mary Violet Leontyne Price, the first black lyric soprano to achieve international diva status in our time, emerged as a major artist in the 1950s. She was recognized as an extraordinary talent from her student performances at Juilliard School of Music. When Frederick Cohen, director of Juilliard's opera department, first heard her sing, he proclaimed hers "the voice of the century." Internationally acclaimed by music critics and fans, Price has been crowned "A Prima Donna Assoluta" of the international world of music, "the Stradivarius of singers," and "the prototypical . . . black singer, to whose pinnacle all who have followed aspire." Her preeminent career opened the international operatic stages to younger black singers.

Price—whose name was originally spelled *Leontine*—was born in Laurel, Mississippi, on February 10, 1927. Her brother George was born two years later. They grew up during the depression and were reared by hardworking, proud, self-reliant, and deeply religious parents—James Anthony and Katherine (Kate) Baker Price.

A stimulus for Price's ambitions occurred at the age of nine when she accompanied her mother to hear Marian Anderson at a concert in Jackson, Mississippi: "It accomplished exactly what she wanted it to accomplish," Price recalled in *Ebony*. "I woke up! I was excited! I was thrilled with this woman's manner, her carriage, her pride, her voice." As Price listened to Anderson, her ambition became focused: "When I first heard Marian Anderson, it was a vision of elegance and nobility. . . . I can't tell you how inspired I was to do something even similar to what she was doing. That was what you might call the original kick-off," she is quoted in *Current Biography*.

This strong guidance in Price's early life paid off, for at the age of eleven she was an accomplished pianist, playing for the Sunday school, church services, and at community affairs. Price entered the sixth grade at Oak Park Vocational High School in the fall of 1937, firmly committed to a career in music. She sang first soprano with the prestigious Oak Park Choral Group and was selected to play for all school concerts. On December 17, 1943, she presented her first recital.

After graduating cum laude from Oak Park Vocational High School, Price was awarded a full four-year scholarship at Wilberforce College in Ohio. Initially she sang alto, unaware of the full potential of her vocal range. As Price's visibility increased, her professors realized that there was something special about her abilities and advised her to change her major to voice and to seek expert voice training. When a visiting pianist encouraged Price to sing a song written for a lyric rather than mezzo soprano, she realized for the first time that she had a vocal instrument for a professional career.

Enrolling at Juilliard in the fall of 1948, Price's classmates included an impressive group of promising talent: Andrew Frierson, Martha Flowers, Billie Lynn Daniels, Gloria Davy, and Mary Robbs, many of whom remained Price's lifelong friends. Even more important to Price was the opportunity to study vocal technique with Florence Page Kimball, a former concert singer, who was her teacher for four years and her lifetime adviser, coach, and friend. Initially, Kimball was not impressed by Price's voice but was encouraged by her seriousness, determination, and charm. After the first year, Kimball's confidence in the young soprano was manifest in inviting noted film composer Max

• Marian

Anderson

influences

Price

Steiner to hear a concert. His recognition of Price's superb vocal power was immediate. Steiner, looking for someone to cast as Bess in his revival of Gershwin's *Porgy and Bess*, promptly invited Price to star in the role.

While a student at Juilliard, the excitement that Price experienced when she attended her first operatic performances—Puccini's *Turandot* at the City Center in New York City and Strauss's *Salome* at the Metropolitan—thoroughly convinced her to become an opera singer, in spite of the limited roles for blacks in the standard repertoire. At Juilliard's Opera Workshop, Frederick Cohen immediately recognized Price's extraordinary, powerful talent. Price's first role, that of Aunt Nella in Puccini's *Gianni Schicchi,* was followed by an appearance as Mistress Ford in Verdi's *Falstaff.* After hearing her, composer and critic Virgil Thompson cast her as Saint Cecilia in a revival of his *Four Saints in Three Acts*, a production that ran in New York and Paris in the spring of 1952. That same year she made her triumphant international debut as Bess in Gershwin's *Porgy and Bess.*

Price makes •

operatic debut

Between 1952 and 1954, Price and baritone William Warfield (then her husband) made international headlines. John Rosenfield of the *Saturday Review* declared: "The voice, a bright and focused soprano, has great impact, but even this is only half of it. She brought a lively theatrical imagination to the role . . . and . . . such vivid detail that the first night audience lost its composure when she took her final curtain call." David Hume of the *Washington Post* observed: "Leontyne Price sings the most exciting and thrilling Bess we have heard. . . . But when she is available for other music, she will have a dramatic career. And her acting is as fiery as her singing."

In 1955, Price's appearance in the role of Flora Tosca on a nationally televised production by NBC-TV Opera Workshop was historic—she was the first black to appear in opera on television—and won for her a succession of leading roles in subsequent NBC productions, such as Mozart's *The Magic Flute* in 1956 and *Don Giovanni* in 1960. Price made her American operatic debut on September 20, 1957, with the San Francisco Opera, as Madame Liodine in *Dialogues of the Carmelites.* In subsequent seasons she starred in such diverse operas as Verdi's *Aida* and *Il Trovatore*, Orff's *The Wise Maiden*, Mozart's *Don Giovanni*, and Massenet's *Thaïs*, performing in major opera houses throughout the United States. Her European reputation was established when conductor Herbert von Karajan cast her as Aida with the Vienna State Opera in 1958, after which Price appeared in a succession of roles at the Vienna Arena, the Salzburg Festival, and London's Covent Garden. When she sang *Aida* at La Scala in 1960, Price emerged as *the* Verdi soprano. One

Italian critic exclaimed in *Time:* "our great Verdi would have found her the ideal Aida."

• *Price debuts*

at the Met

Price was well prepared when she made her historic debut as Leonora in Verdi's *Il Trovatore* at New York's Metropolitan Opera on January 27, 1961. As the fifth black artist to sing a major role at the Met since Marian Anderson made the breakthrough in 1955, Price was triumphant. A review in the *New Yorker* stated: "Her interpretation was virtually without flaws." At the conclusion of the performance, Price received "an unprecedented forty-two minute ovation," according to *Ebony.* In this extraordinary season she had five starring roles.

Price's grace and regal appearance also gained her considerable attention. "Her best features are her almost translucent brown skin, high cheekbones and expressive eyes set in charcoal shadows," Hugh Lee Lyon declared in his book *Leontyne Price: Highlights of a Prima Donna.* Critics acclaimed her as a statuesque Aida, the most impressive they had seen in years. According to Ross Parmenter of the *New York Times,* "She was Aida of such physical attractiveness that, for once, it was thoroughly understandable that Radames should prefer her to the highborn princess."

Although a veteran of 118 Metropolitan performances between 1961 and 1969, Price reduced her appearances at the Met considerably during the 1970s. She explained in *Divas:*

> I feel that you rest the voice and avoid pressure for considerable periods. You have to reflect too. . . . I think a career, if it is good, should be handled like something really beautiful. . . . I'm beginning to forget what I started out with—the completely natural joy of singing. It's almost coming back, and I'm trying not to lose it.

• *Price returns*

to recitals

From the late 1970s until her retirement in 1985, Price concentrated on her "first love," recitals, which allowed her to "indulge a long standing predilection both for spirituals and for songs by such contemporary composers as Samuel Barber, John LaMontaine, Ned Rorem, Margaret Bonds, and Dominick Argento," according to *Time.*

Price bade farewell to the opera stage on January 3, 1985, singing *Aida* to a tumultuous ovation. Robert Jacobson sums up her distinguished reign in *Opera News:* "Perhaps *the* opera event of 1985 was the stage farewell of Leontyne Price who bid adieu with *Aida* . . . on the stage of the Metropolitan Opera—a fitting platform for the Mississippi born soprano, who over the decades had become *the* American prima donna personified. . . ."

Among Price's many awards are the Presidential Medal of Freedom and an American Academy of Arts and Sciences' Fellow. She was awarded honorary doctorates from Dartmouth College, Howard University, Fordham University, Central State University, and Rust College. Besides being a trustee and member of the Board of Directors of International House and a member of the Advisory Board of the National Cultural Center, Washington, D.C., Price also has served as honorary vice-chairperson of the U.S. National Committee of UNESCO. She received the Spirit of Achievement Award from Albert Einstein College of Medicine and the NAACP's Spingarn Medal, as well as the Order of Merit from the Republic of Italy. During her career she was presented twenty Grammy awards from the National Academy of Recording Arts and Sciences.

Since 1958, Price has recorded almost exclusively for RCA Victor. Her records include Negro spirituals, pop tunes, Christmas carols, hymns, American, French, and German art songs, and complete operas.

Price lives in a spacious federal-era townhouse in New York's Greenwich Village. Relishing her privacy, she enjoys working with her neighborhood block association and gardening. Price continues, however, to accept new challenges; in addition to her recitals, she is working on her autobiography and is actively involved with civic organizations. Of interest to both young readers and adults is the 1990 book *Aida*, told by Price and illustrated by Leo and Diane Dillon, which captures the thrill of the opera as told by a diva.

Price is especially proud of the part she has played in opening the world's stages to younger black singers. She insists in *Opera News:* "to the end of time . . . I will be the vehicle for major exposure for young black artists—sopranos, baritones, the whole thing."

**Profile by
Jacquelyn Jackson**

ERNESTA G. PROCOPE

*E*rnesta Gertrude Foster Bowman Procope is the founder and presi-

insurance •

dent of the nation's largest black-owned insurance brokerage agency,

brokerage

E. G. Bowman Company, with an estimated thirty million dollars in

executive

annual premium sales and a client list that includes more than fifty

Fortune 500 corporations. She is married to John Procope, publisher

and editor of the Amsterdam News, *the nation's largest weekly newspa-*

per for blacks, who also serves as chief executive officer of E. G. Bowman

Company.

Procope was born in Brooklyn, New York, the only daughter among the four children born to West Indian immigrants Clarence and Elvira Lord Foster, who entered the Bedford-Stuyvesant section of Brooklyn in the 1910s. She studied music at an early age, performing in concert with eight other students at Carnegie Hall. She graduated from the New York High School of Music and Art, attended Brooklyn College for a short time, and then entered Pohs Institute of Insurance and Real Estate. In 1950 she gained her real estate license.

Procope began her career in insurance as a result of the encouragement she received from her first husband, Albin Bowman, a real estate developer whom she married in the late 1940s. Many neighborhoods in which he owned property, including his own office building in the Bedford-Stuyvesant neighborhood, were poor. Because insurance for these buildings was difficult to obtain, he decided to insure them himself. Bowman encouraged his wife to enter the Pohs Institute in 1950, and at the time of Bowman's death in 1952 Procope was handling all their insurance needs. She formed the E. G. Bowman Company in 1953. At the time, hers was one of only a handful of companies providing insurance to black families for new and existing homes.

During the late 1960s, most of Procope's business centered around Bedford-Stuyvesant. Insurance companies, fearful of the urban rioting going on elsewhere and threatening in that area, canceled some 80 percent of her clients' insurance. She then became actively involved in the Bedford-Stuyvesant Restoration Corporation, a community-based economic development program founded in 1967 to stem the rapid deterioration of the area. By 1968 Procope was handling all the property-casualty insurance of the program. She kept her office in this section of Brooklyn until 1979.

In 1970, Procope began courting the commercial insurance market accounts, expanding her client list to include corporate enterprises. She also successfully bid for the entire employee benefits package of the Community Development Agency (CDA), an umbrella organization for the city's antipoverty agencies. She established a subdivision, Bowman-Procope Associates, to oversee those benefit programs, which now cover seventeen thousand employees.

Procope began innovative programs including a data-processing system to solve the problems of reporting and documentation at the CDA, employee education programs about health and safety, and an approach to corporate accounts that included a scripted cassette called "We Can't Let George Do It Anymore," pointing out the need for managers to be more cautious and responsible for safety and programming. "These demonstrated not only her commitment to providing clients with adequate insurance coverage, but her concern with keeping costs within the client cost at a minimum by preventing loss," according to *Nation's Business*. Applying affirmative-action program techniques and innovative employment policies to the acquisition of corporate accounts resulted in a client list that now includes such giants as Control Data, Pepsi-Co, IBM, General Motors, and Gulf Oil.

During the early 1970s, Procope was instrumental in the passage of the New York State Fair Plan, which guaranteed homeowner's insurance in poor neighborhoods. Keeping her ties to the old Bedford-Stuyvesant neighborhood, Procope continues to insure churches, organizations, and schools such as Howard University, although these clients and personal-property and casualty insurance make up only five percent of her current business. In 1972 she was named "Woman of the Year" by the black newspaper supplement *Tuesday at Home.* By 1973, Avon Products had become a client, and in 1974 she joined its board of directors. Procope was honored to serve as the United States representative to Gambia's tenth anniversary celebration in 1975. In 1979, she moved her company to new offices at 97 Wall Street, a move she felt would bring her company into the mainstream of commercial insurance brokerage. Her continuing aim is to stress cost reduction, emphasize risk analysis, and encourage clients to improve on-the-job-safety techniques. She is also on the board of directors of many other corporations and organizations, including the Salvation Army, Chubb Corporation, and the Urban National Corporation, which invests in minority businesses nationwide.

From the very start of her career, Procope's business philosophy has reflected her concern for the need to provide insurance to all client companies, regardless of size. Although she founded her company primarily to handle the needs of her first husband's investment properties, she soon branched out into the areas of homeowner's and business insurance sales as word of her abilities spread.

Insurance •

company

reflects

business

philosophy

From the beginning, Procope's primary business goal has been to build a professional insurance company that would be accepted and respected by the mainstream American business establishment. This goal, she knew, was a lofty one for a small, black-owned agency operating in a ghetto and run by a woman, but Procope persevered, never forgetting the commitment she made in the early years to serve the needs of her traditional clients. Even with that commitment, she knew the firm would have to grow and expand if it was going to be financially successful.

Developing the necessary skills to make her company a success, Procope says, was a combination of her formal education at the Pohs Institute and what she refers to in *Working Woman* as on-the-job-training:

> In order to develop an insurance-brokerage agency, the skill one must have is the ability to sell. When I first became interested in insurance, I didn't really equate it with sales—that came later. But, if you have a product to offer, you have to sell it.

Continuing skills development remains Procope's major concern, both for herself and her staff, who regularly attend seminars and keep abreast of changes in the industry by reading periodicals and professional journals. "It's a dynamic field—it changes almost daily," Procope continued. The challenge of staying ahead of these changes and incorporating new ideas into the company's way of doing business has helped to create a firm to be reckoned with. She attributes her success to a willingness to work hard and show tenacity in the face of seemingly insurmountable odds, she told *Working Woman:*

> I don't think the fact that I'm a woman has hindered me, but I do believe that being black has been somewhat of a deterrent in moving ahead. To build the company, I needed to get large commercial accounts. I could get in the door because I'm black and a woman and they were curious to see what I'm all about. That doesn't necessarily mean I would be able to sell the account. I think it was harder to sell commercial accounts because my company was small and black-owned rather than because of the fact that it was owned by a woman.

Procope believes in building a strong organization in support of existing management, a cue she took from large corporations, and in encouraging other women to enter the insurance field. Regular employee seminars and a predominantly female staff are the legacy of these efforts. "I think it's important to create a dialogue among employees—it makes them feel involved with the company," Procope continued. "It's constructive communication: we get their input about how they feel about the company and where they want to go within it, and they keep up-to-date on what the company is doing."

Procope believes her exposure to the inner workings of large corporations has provided her an opportunity to benefit from their success, particularly in the area of structural organization. This exposure, she added in *Working Woman,* "has been a great experience for me—just in that area if nothing else. I believe in perpetuity. I want to build an organization that is not here just while I'm here. That is why I've always attempted to build people behind me. I want this organization to prosper, and I want it to become a meaningful entity in this country."

While she is modest about her own accomplishments and the role she has played in the phenomenal growth of her company, Procope is vocal about her pride in serving on the boards of directors of numerous organizations and corporations, especially the Urban National Corporation. "Being on boards of directors is a very important role," Procope explained in *Sepia*. "The board oversees what management does, setting up committees such as compensation, which examines salaries, pension plans and benefits. It's very much how the government works." She feels uniquely qualified to advise other board members about possible improvements and innovations in insurance needs because she understands what both the insurance carriers and the employees require concerning coverage. It is this balanced perspective and her goal to provide consistent improvement that have enabled Procope to gain a voice in the process of creating quality insurance coverage, as well as gain the respect and admiration of her peers and business associates.

Ambitious, energetic, and unwilling to settle for the success her firm has earned to date, Procope keeps a firm hand on the present and an ever-watchful eye on the future. Having made great strides in developing a solid customer base nationwide, she says the next step is to expand the company beyond the boundaries of the fifty states, particularly to Puerto Rico and Canada. She admits her goals may seem lofty, but told *Sepia* she feels they are attainable:

> It falls to us to convince major corporations that we can handle their needs—effectively and competently . . . the key word is exposure. We know our own capabilities and when to stop. All we ask is an opportunity, because one day we might be in a position to be worldwide ourselves.

**Profile by
Thura R. Mack**

BARBARA GARDNER PROCTOR

Barbara Gardner Proctor's career as an advertising entrepreneur is

marked by her courage to maintain high standards, her unwavering

belief in her own abilities and talents, and her willingness to assume

risks. Through determination, she has been able to overcome discrimi-

natory barriers, becoming a highly respected business leader whose

resilience, forthrightness, individualism, and style have become her

trademarks in the advertising business.

1933- •

advertising •

executive

Proctor was born November 30, 1933, in Black Mountain, North Carolina, the only child of a single mother. She was raised by her grandmother and an uncle. Proctor's early academic achievements led to a scholarship at Talladega College in Alabama, which she attended in the 1950s, earning a bachelor's degree in English education and another in psychology and social science. There she was a recipient of the Armstrong Creative Writing Award in 1954.

Proctor's transition from college to the multimillion-dollar career she is presently involved in was a gradual one. She has worked as jazz music critic and contributing editor of *Downbeat* magazine and international director of Vee-Jay Records, as well as holding positions at various advertising agencies in Chicago. Proctor has a strong belief in the need for quality and equality in advertising. Armed with her degrees, her professional experience, and the will to succeed, she formed her own firm in 1971. Now chief executive officer, founder-president, and creative director of Proctor & Gardner Advertising, Proctor has demonstrated successful performances with impressive blue-chip clients, boards of directors, and varied industries.

Proctor's credibility, vivacious personality, and leadership skills put her in constant demand in the business arena; a demand evidenced by her service on the boards of directors of Illinois Bell Telephone Company, Northwestern Hospital, the 1988 Illinois Olympic Committee, the council of the Chicago Better Business Bureau, the *Louisville Courier-Journal*, the Girl Scouts of Chicago, and the Economic Club. In 1983 and 1984, Proctor served, by special appointment from the governor of Illinois, as co-chairperson of the Gannon-Proctor Commission; she is also a governing council member of the Illinois State Bar Association's Institute for Public Affairs. Her contributions to the American marketplace and to her community have earned numerous awards, citations, and honors. She is also a recipient of more than twenty advertising industry awards for excellence, including Clio Awards from the American Television Commercial Festival.

• **Advertising**

firm developed

early

Proctor's willingness to take on tough challenges has allowed her to realize her dream: a timely entrance into the entrepreneurial sphere of the 1970s made for a dynamic beginning for her advertising firm. According to *Contemporary Newsmakers:*

> The climate was right for a minority agency; commercial awareness of the black consumer marker was gradually mounting. Thus, Proctor & Gardner was able to tap into a virtually untouched market, totaling millions of dollars annually, and at the same time had the opportunity to improve the public's perception of blacks by creatively casting them in a positive and constructive manner.

Proctor's career has been marked by clear direction, while her refusal to play it safe is an example of her leadership ability, her intense desire to succeed, and her willingness to reach beyond barriers. At her agency, Proctor has been successful in creating a relaxed atmosphere for staff and clients. She thrives on countering problems through timely innovations and strategic planning. A prime example of her clever planning is her choice of a name for the firm, Proctor & Gardner. "I found the advertising world wasn't ready for a female" in charge of the firm, she explains in the *New Orleans Times-Picayune,* "so I called my agency Proctor and Gardner. I'm both of them, but men assumed there was a Mr. Gardner back running the company."

Undaunted by early setbacks, Proctor obtained her first account after being in business for six months. Having created her agency through the assistance of a loan from the Small Business Administration and finding herself in need of additional working capital at the end of four years, Proctor again approached the SBA. Following her request, she says, "They sent an accountant to review my books, and he said I'd be out of business in three years. I didn't know it. I just kept going to work."

"In advertising, the only thing worse than being a woman was being an old woman," Proctor continued. "I was over 30, female, and black. I had so many things wrong with me that it would have taken all day to figure out which one to blame for my rejections. So I decided not to spend any time worrying about it."

True to her belief in the power of positive thinking, Proctor falls back on earlier successes as her ace in the hole for handling setbacks and conflicts. "In every case where something would have been an obstacle, I've found a way to turn it to an advantage," she notes. "I cannot buy the concept that anyone outside is responsible."

Rather than being a hindrance to her success, Proctor believes being black and female helped her to get that first SBA loan. "I think blacks have a different acceptance of reality than white people," she told *Working Woman.* "We're more realistic. There is less fear. Being poor was good for me. Once you've been poor and black and you survive, there's nothing left to be afraid of. Most people are afraid of taking risks."

As a business leader, Proctor encourages women to seek viable opportunities and make good use of them. "Risk is one trademark in business," she pointed out in *Working Woman,* adding that women have often been afraid to fail and are too quick to blame others for their own lack of success in the business world:

> One of the things women fear is risk. They don't want to risk anything; they want guarantees. If you are able to risk, able to lose, then you will gain. When women get to the point where they take the risk, fail and try again, without any loss of self-esteem, they will be free.

Women urged •

to enter

business world

431 •

In the *New Orleans Times-Picayune,* Proctor holds that women have assets, talents, and skills they often overlook or do not emphasize:

> I think women are more multi-talented and have less self-esteem (than men), so they don't worry about being above doing things that need to be done. I brought my baby with me everywhere. I did my work in bed. I did what I had to do. I think women have this sort of flexibility.

Exercising this flexibility and learning to use teamwork, which she says is often not a part of women's early training, can lead to dynamic performance. "Women learn very early to count on individual effort, but we continue to draw on our differences from other women rather than on our similarities with other executives," Proctor continued. Once women have overcome barriers in their own thinking, she believes, no door will be closed to them and there is no limit to the amount of success women can achieve.

Proctor points out that while women have made significant gains in the workplace over the past twenty years, many have not reached the pinnacle of success because they have been taught that power is unfeminine. She urges women to abandon the attitudes of self-effacement and self-sacrifice that have sabotaged them. In part, this effort requires inspiring others to succeed, just as she was inspired through the early influence of the grandmother who raised her. She recalled in *Working Woman:*

> My grandmother always thought I would do something. She taught me what is important isn't on the outside, but inside. She said it was important to put something inside you, some courage, knowledge, and a skill, things that no one can take from you.

With these thoughts to sustain and bolster her confidence from an early age, Proctor has yet to find a door she cannot open and has maintained a sense of pride.

But one use to which she will not lend her talents is what she refers to as "ethically dubious advertising pitches" aimed at women and minorities. She is unrepentant in her criticism of advertising by drug, tobacco, and alcohol companies that target women and minorities, believing these companies have been responsible for the increased use of psychoactive drugs, sleep-inducing medications, and tobacco among the target groups. Her firm refuses liquor and cigarette accounts, choosing to handle accounts that reflect family values and lend themselves to quality promotional ideas. This policy cost Proctor her first job in the advertising business in 1970. According to Proctor, the agency came up with the concept of a television commercial that parodied the civil rights marches and sit-ins, "a mass demonstration of housewives running down the street waving a can demanding that their hairdressers foam their hair," as she described it in *Forbes*. She found the commercial's concept tasteless and offensive, particularly to blacks, and was fired for her refusal to work on the project. Again, timing was an important force behind the success of her agency: the 1970s reflected an increasing awareness of the black consumer market.

Proctor continues to maintain accounts that reflect her own high standards. "Advertising is the single most important way of reaching everyone in America, and I feel a deep sense of responsibility for my work," she told *Working Woman*. She has no fear of turning away business that she believes provides reinforcement of negative stereotypes of women and blacks.

**Profile by
Thura R. Mack**

BERNICE J. REAGON

*I*nspired by the civil rights movement of the 1960s, Bernice Johnson

Reagon has woven her skills as a singer, writer, and historian into a life's

work to make the field of black studies credible. From a modern

perspective, the struggles of black pioneers may be taken for granted. Yet

in fighting for a bus to take children to school or in risking their lives to

cast a ballot, heroic black Americans have fought for and defended the

individual rights Americans cherish. Children like Reagon looked on,

grew up, and continued the struggle.

1942- •

musician, •

writer,

historian

Reagon was born on October 4, 1942, to the Reverend Jessie Johnson and Beatrice (Wise) Johnson, the third of their eight children. In the little cluster of homes near Albany, Georgia, where they lived, the Johnson family were black pioneers. Reagon began to distinguish herself as a singer at age five in her father's church and credits him, a singer also, for her style. But for her, the church meant more than singing. Her heart heard the collective voice of people united in struggle.

Entering Albany State College, Georgia, in 1959 as a music major, she studied German leider and Italian arias. But soon the rising voices of the civil rights struggle caught her attention. Her political activities led her to hold the office of secretary of the local NAACP Youth Chapter. Later, when the Student Nonviolent Coordinating Committee moved into Albany to help organize the community, Reagon found she preferred their confrontational style to the legal battle that the NAACP waged. In December 1961, during her junior year, she participated in a SNCC-coordinated march protesting the arrest of two fellow students. Commenting on the protest in *Essence,* Reagon said:

> The SNCC workers told us we were not supposed to hit back if we were hit. It didn't make sense to me. I had nothing in my brain to absorb the word nonviolence. But the SNCC people gave a long speech on marching with dignity and there was a discussion among them as to whether we would sing. It was decided we would be quiet, marching in pairs around the city jail. I was not moved by nonviolence as a way of life. What I was moved by was the hundreds and thousands of people in the streets. I was moved by hearing songs, and after hearing them all my life, for the first time, I understood what they meant. They were saying what I was feeling. Somehow, it felt like all those words that Black people had been praying and saying was a language for us, a language we could not understand unless we were involved in practical, everyday struggle. I remember feeling incomplete and humble, yet really powerful. It was the most powerful thing that happened to me.

For her part in these activities, Reagon was suspended from school, and on the third day of the Albany march she was arrested. What held her together in jail, she says, was music—unaccompanied vocal music sung by the forty to fifty incarcerated women. Before leaving Albany State College, where she was the school's highest-ranking student, she had changed her major. When she resumed her studies at Spelman College in Atlanta in 1962, she returned to her music, though majoring in nonwestern history.

That same year, Reagon left school to join the Freedom Singers of SNCC. This group of young people sang at mass meetings and in jails, traveled around the country raising money for the movement, and often drew attention to voter registration drives. In 1963 she sang with a group during the March on Washington and later directed the Harambee Singers. Reagon joined the Harambee Singers at a time when she felt herself growing away from the integrationist posture of the civil rights movement and into a separatist posture. She looks back on this as a time when she wrote her most militant songs.

During this period she married Cordell Reagon, an SNCC field worker and Freedom Singer from Nashville, Tennessee, whom she met at Albany State. Before their painful separation, they had a daughter, Toshi, who is now a singer also, and a son, Kwan, who graduated from the Baltimore International Culinary College. Bernice and Cordell Reagon were divorced in 1967.

Folkway Records released Reagon's first solo album of traditional songs, *Songs of the South,* in 1966, and Kintel Records her second, *Sound of Thunder,* in 1967. Following these successes, Reagon began to integrate her music and education. She completed her degree at Spelman in 1970, then moved to Washington, D.C. As vocal director at the District of Columbia Black Repertory Theater, she organized the folk-music group Sweet Honey in the Rock and began her career with the Smithsonian Institution with the program in Black American Culture. By 1975 she had earned a Ph.D. from Howard University with a dissertation about songs of the civil rights movement.

Despite their name, which comes from a gospel song, Sweet Honey in the Rock's message is more often political than religious. "I think everything is political," Reagon stated in *People.* "We are about being accountable." In a review published on October 11, 1978, the *Washington Post* stated:

> This rare composite of a cappella virtuosos, directed by American music historian Bernice Reagon, has just released an important new album of original songs entitled "Believe I'll Run On, See What the End's Gonna Be." In this new album as well as on their earlier disc, the vitality of these ladies' natural singing voices squarely competes with more popularized and exploited music forms.

High Fidelity magazine described the group's singular and uncommercial sound as "breathtaking excursions into harmony singing" while *Downbeat* magazine called it "neck-hair raising." The group has turned down offers from many record labels who wanted to commercialize Sweet Honey's sound.

With eight albums to their credit, Sweet Honey opened to a sold-out performance at Carnegie Hall in May of 1989. The group is presently composed of Reagon, Ysaye Maria Barnwell, Carol Lynn Maillard,

Nitanju Bolade-Casel, Aisha Kahlil, and Shirley Childress Johnson, who signs the group's songs for the hearing impaired. (Since 1979 the group has made sign-language interpretation for the deaf an integral part of their concern.) Over the years, others have joined and left the group for various reasons. One former member, Evelyn Harris, penned several of their songs, though Reagon, too, is a songwriter. Many of her songs are showcased on *Believe I'll Run On, See What the End's Gonna Be*.

Sweet Honey has performed at churches, concerts, and festivals in Washington, D.C., New York City, and Ann Arbor, Michigan. By their fifth anniversary, Sweet Honey's fans filled Washington's All Souls Church. A performance at "Sisterfire" in Washington in 1987, a multicultural outdoor women's arts festival, drew a large following, as did New York's Caribbean Cultural Center's "Tribute to Women of Color." Reagon's humorous storytelling on stage is a part of Sweet Honey's attraction. The group also contributed to an album produced to benefit the environmental and peace movements.

On the international scene, they performed at the New Song Festivals in Ecuador and Mexico; toured Germany, Japan, England, Canada, Australia, and the Caribbean; and served as coordinators of the closing cultural festivities at the United Nations Decade for Women Conference in Nairobi, Kenya, in 1985. In 1990 Sweet Honey in the Rock toured Africa, performing in Uganda, Zimbabwe, Mozambique, Swaziland, and Namibia. They also performed in several events in the United States celebrating the release of Nelson Mandela, South African freedom fighter. "Sweet Honey's song stylizing is to black music what Alex Haley's *Roots* was to black written history. They both offer a much needed legacy of black culture," lauded *Mind Is*.

Even as the fame of Sweet Honey grew, Reagon continued to establish her role as a solo artist on such albums as *Joan Little* and *Give Your Hands to the Struggle*. Her recordings of "We Are Climbing Jacob's Ladder" and "Dixie" are featured in the original soundtrack of the PBS documentary series "The Civil War."

Reagon's career as a scholar has kept pace with her musical career. The *Washington Post* reported, "The Smithsonian Institution has recently come out with a three-record collection called 'Voices of the Civil Rights Movement: Black American Freedom Songs 1960-66.' One of those voices is both on the record and behind it: Dr. Bernice Reagon." The illustrated booklet in the Smithsonian Collection that accompanies the record collection is itself a music history journal.

In a 1978 *Essence* interview, Reagon asserted, "I'm a performer, teacher, researcher and historian with a strong social, political, and economic consciousness." While working as cultural historian for the Smithsonian Institution's Division of Performing Arts/African Diaspora Project, she did extensive research on the black American artistic expression and its relationship to similar Caribbean and African experiences. The result was her article "African Diaspora Women: The Making of Cultural Workers." Here she traces the cultural growth of black women from West Africa, Brazil, and America. As a result of the African diaspora, she says:

> There is the struggle to contend with a new space where . . . people and children are defined in new ways. . . . [The Diaspora] disrupted and threw in severe trauma cultural practices that had been nursed in African societies. Mothering therefore required a kind of nurturing that would both provide food and stamina for survival within a cruel slave society and the passing on of nurturing that would allow for the development of a community that was not of but beyond the slave society. . . . Nurturing was not only reconciling what was passed to them with the day-to-day reality, but also sifting and transforming this experience to feed this child, unborn, this new Black community, in preparation for what it would face.

A future book is planned on Ruby Doris Robinson, a strong supporter of civil rights workers in Mississippi during the movement. Not surprisingly, when filmmakers decided to explore life-changing experiences of people caught up in social change, they called on Reagon to narrate her experiences during the civil rights movement in Albany, Georgia. Reviewers described her presentation as forceful, yet unpretentious. Further showing the range of respect for her talent, Reagon was asked to write the program notes for "A Program of Spirituals," given by Kathleen Battle and Jessye Norman at Carnegie Hall in March 1990. Produced in 1991, the documentary video "The Songs Are Free with Bill Moyers" records Reagon's singing interwoven with a thought-provoking interview.

Until her recent promotion to curator of the National Museum of American History, Reagon served as director of the Smithsonian's program in black American culture. She is credited with bringing black studies into the mainstream. "Her work is of such high scholastic quality that the legitimacy of the field has come to be unquestioned," stated the *Evening Sun*. Speaking of the folks like those she grew up with in the backwoods of Georgia, Reagon said: "If these people have a sense that the National Museum of American History knows they exist, then I know I'm doing my job."

Reagon •

appointed

curator of

National

Museum

**Profile by
Margaret D. Pagan**

439 •

ESLANDA GOODE ROBESON

*A*lthough biographical and critical material abounds on the career **1896-1965** •

of Paul Robeson, a full-length biography of his wife, Eslanda Goode

Robeson, who is astonishing in her own right, has not yet been attempt- **chemist,** •

ed. In addition to her role as Robeson's loving partner and a tireless **anthropologist**

promoter of his career, she distinguished herself equally through her

own endeavors in anthropology and political activism.

Eslanda Cardoza Goode Robeson was born into the black middle-class community of Washington, D.C. Her father, John Goode, had risen above his slave origins and held a position as a clerk in the War Department. Her mother, Eslanda (Cardoza) Goode, was a product of South Carolina's free black community and was descended from the union of Isaac Nuñez Cardozo, a Spanish Jew of considerable wealth, and an octoroon slave woman. His son, Essie Robeson's grandfather, Francis Louis Cardozo, was referred to by Henry Ward Beecher as "the most highly educated Negro in America."

When Robeson, or Essie, as she was known to all her intimates, was six, her father died from the effects of alcoholism and her mother took her and her two brothers to live in New York City, where they would not have to attend segregated schools. Robeson arrived in Harlem at a propitious time, and she was fortunate to see and experience the glorious beginnings of the Harlem Renaissance. She first attended the State University of Illinois but went on to complete her education at Teachers College of Columbia University. She also completed one year at Columbia University Medical School.

Historian Barbara Ransby says that it was during these years that Robeson first became politically active. The Bolshevik Revolution stimulated radical thinking among young intellectuals in New York, and Robeson's natural interest in racial equality propelled her into this realm. She became close friends with John Reed and other activists and developed both left-wing political views and a deepened commitment to social change.

Essie Robeson graduated from Columbia with a bachelor of science degree in chemistry. She immediately made history by becoming the first black person to obtain employment as an analytical chemist and technician in the surgery and pathology department at Columbia Presbyterian Medical Center, where she was in charge of the laboratory.

- ***Paul Robeson***

changes career

Paul and Essie Robeson became friends with some of the show people who were putting on the many musical extravaganzas that were so much a part of the Harlem scene in the 1920s, and Paul once accompanied some of them in some impromptu songs at a party. Essie saw what an impression Paul's powerful baritone voice made on the audience, and she got the idea of channeling her husband into show business. She convinced him to take the lead in a YMCA production of *Simon the Cyrenian,* one of *Three Plays for a Negro Theatre* written by Ridgely Torrence, a white lyric poet. Later, this play would be considered a turning point in the depiction of blacks in American theater, because it was the first time that they were depicted as real people of human depth rather than as comical stereotypes.

Robeson made an impact in this role, and in 1922 he was offered the lead in Mary Hoyt Wyborg's play *Taboo,* produced in London. Success there was followed by another offer in the fall of 1923 to play the leads in Eugene O'Neill's *All God's Chillun Got Wings* and a revival of *The Emperor Jones.* Eslanda Robeson resigned her position at Columbia Presbyterian Medical Center in fall 1925 and accompanied her husband to London. Soon Robeson was the toast of two continents and was regularly performing in both the United States and Europe. By 1926 they were making a European concert tour and Essie had left her career as a chemist to become Paul's full-time manager, booking him into concerts, shows, and motion picture roles.

The adulation Paul Robeson received from white intellectuals, however, did nothing to counteract the effects of daily prejudice, such as being refused service in restaurants. Hamilton notes that "no single situation of their daily lives served to radicalize Paul and Essie more than these endless, petty incidents of racial discrimination and prejudice." Essie Robeson began staying home more, partly in order to avoid these humiliations, but also because they were expecting a child. In 1927 their son, Paul, afterwards known as Pauli, was born.

In April 1928 the pair went to London, where Paul Robeson was starring in *Show Boat,* and decided to settle in London in 1928. In the years that followed, Paul Robeson starred in *Othello,* a role he could never have played in the United States even though the character is black. Essie Robeson also began to come into her own, writing a compelling and at times revealing biography about Paul that came out in 1930. The biography was considered somewhat shocking because she discussed the possibility of Paul's infidelities with other women and lampooned whites who came to tour Harlem. Although the *New Republic* condemned the book, it was nonetheless tremendously successful and made for her a reputation as a writer.

By the mid-thirties, Eslanda Robeson had undertaken a new direction in her life—a growing interest in Africa and the study of anthropology. During her studies at London University and the London School of Economics she began to understand that racism was being fostered by the "interpretation" of the Negro mind and character by white students and teachers. She later derided this thinking in her book *African Journey:*

> After more than a year of very wide reading and intensive study I began to get my intellectual feet wet. I am afraid that I began to be obstreperous. I soon became fed up with white students and teachers "interpreting" the Negro mind and character to me. Especially when I felt, as I did very often, that their interpretation was wrong.

This kind of condescension to Robeson was like adding a spark to fuel. In 1936 she decided to go to Africa to do the field work for her degree. Disturbed that her eight-year-old son, Pauli, had known only a white world, she brought him along to "see a black world, . . . see a black continent."

This trip proved to be a revelation to Robeson as she explored the political, economic, and social realities of this black world. She quickly found that the suffering of the peasant population of this huge continent touched her more deeply than anything else she saw. Ransby tells us that she became a Pan-Africanist in the sense that she recognized the importance of racial pride and unity for the defeat of racism as an ideology. She also saw the need for African people to overcome tribalism and other divisions in order to combat successfully colonialism and imperialism. At the same time, Ransby asserts, she was not a black separatist and never hesitated to link the cause of African peoples with the cause of oppressed minorities the world over.

The Robesons returned to America in September 1939 and, after living on Edgecombe Avenue in Harlem for a couple of years, purchased a rural retreat in Enfield, Connecticut, which they named "The Beeches." Essie Robeson enrolled at Hartford Seminary to begin work on a Ph.D. in anthropology.

- *Pan-Africanist*

condemns

Western

imperialism

Robeson was not content merely to engage in academic life during this period. In 1941 she joined with her husband and other influential black people to found the Council on African Affairs. Eslanda Robeson became one of the most outspoken and articulate members of this organization and was often blunt in her criticism of western colonial powers, which subjugated Africans and other non-white peoples for political and economic reasons. In 1944 she wrote:

> Until this war, the only people who were even vaguely aware of Africans as human beings were missionaries. Tourists, businessmen, government officials, and politicians—with few exceptions—considered the Africans (if they considered them at all) as savages, labor fodder, and pawns.

> This war has changed all that. The people of the world, in fighting for their own freedom, have come at long last to sense that no man can be free until all men are free. . . . I believe there will never be peace in the world until people achieve what they fought and died for.

> *Africans are people.*

The middle forties were to bring more accolades and fame to both of the Robesons and, with the end of World War II, hope for the future. In 1945 Eslanda Robeson's book *African Journey* was published and Paul Robeson was awarded the Spingarn Medal. Paul Robeson was off again to Europe to entertain victorious Allied troops, and Essie Robeson was sent by the Council on African Affairs as a delegate to the San Francisco Conference, which would create the United Nations. In 1946

Essie Robeson returned to Africa and traveled on foot, on horseback, and by car, airplane, and boat throughout the Congo, Ruanda-Urundi, and French Equatorial Africa. She later used the knowledge she gained on this trip to argue and discuss the problems of the region before the United Nations Trusteeship Council. Rayford Logan has mentioned that the support of the Soviet Union to these emerging self-governing and independent nations reinforced Essie Robeson's already strong sympathies for the Soviet Union.

Paul Robeson invited great criticism when he spoke out against racism and pointed to the apparent success of the Soviet Union in producing a system rooted in equality of all peoples. Remarks he made at the Paris World Congress of Partisans of Peace in April 1949 were distorted in the American press, and he was made to seem a subversive voice favoring communism. Robeson was called before the House Un-American Activities Committee, where he was questioned by hostile congressmen about his political sympathies and possible membership in the Communist Party of the United States. Armed only with the force of his personality and intellect and a controlled anger, Robeson fought the committee to a standstill. It was forced to dismiss him without having proven anything against him.

Later Essie Robeson was called before the committee. When questioned regarding her political activities, she, in turn, questioned members of the committee on the lack of civil rights for blacks in the United States. Finally, Senator Joseph McCarthy dismissed her from the stand, saying that only her sex had prevented her from being held in contempt. She got in the last lick, however, writing in *Freedomways* that "before any committee starts yelling for first class loyalty and cooperation from me, they'd better get busy and put me and my Negro people in the first class department by making US first class citizens."

Unable to prove anything against the Robesons, the State Department nonetheless revoked their passports, effectively destroying any opportunity for Paul Robeson to continue his career as a concert singer. Almost overnight their income dropped from more than one hundred thousand dollars a year to about two thousand. They were forced to sell The Beeches in order to live.

Even this did not stop them from speaking out against injustice to others. Not satisfied simply to criticize wrongdoing at home, Eslanda Robeson again took up her pen to criticize American foreign policy in an open letter to President Dwight D. Eisenhower in the March 19, 1953, issue of the *Daily Worker*. Here she attacked the foreign policy that urged friendship with former enemies (Germany and Japan), yet openly supported opposition to Russia and China.

By the end of the fifties, things finally began to turn around. In 1958 Paul Robeson was invited to give his first concert in nearly ten years at Carnegie Hall. That same year the Robesons also finally got back their passports, leaving them free to go first to Great Britain and then to the Soviet Union, where they temporarily settled among people for whom they felt a great gratitude and kinship.

The years and their troubles had taken their toll on both Robesons, however, and in 1959 they were hospitalized for fatigue and other complaints. Still tired and ill, they returned to the United States in 1963, after stopping in East Germany, where Essie Robeson spoke to a crowd of more than twenty thousand and was awarded both the Peace Medal and the Clara Zetkin Medal, an award made by the East German government to women who have been distinguished by their fight for world peace.

Back in the United States, Essie Robeson's health continued to decline, although she remained outspoken in her criticism of both imperialist and colonialist foreign policy and inequality at home and abroad. She died of cancer on December 13, 1965, at Beth Israel Hospital in New York City. Paul Robeson died in 1976.

Eslanda Robeson's career was nothing less than astounding. Although she didn't mind being identified as the wife of Paul Robeson, she was not swallowed up by this role. Her pride of self and of race enabled her to go places and do things from which others would shrink. At the same time, her relationship to Robeson was a deep and close one. Robeson, for all his greatness, was subject to the same frailties as a lesser man, something that placed a strain on, yet did not destroy, their marriage. Her support of his career and of him as her husband was unfaltering in spite of the stresses that inevitably come with a relationship with a man of such towering ego.

R. L. Prattis has noted of Eslanda Goode Robeson that "although a talented woman in her own right, she forgot self in love of her husband. . . . If Paul is great, so was Essie for indeed they were one and the same person."

- *Robeson*

receives

peace medals

**Profile by
Robert E. Skinner**

WILMA RUDOLPH

ilma Goldean Rudolph, one of the world's most noted track stars, was born June 23, 1940, the fifth of eight children born to Ed and Blanche Rudolph in Bethlehem, Tennessee. Given the achievements that she was to make later in life, the physical problems that surrounded her from birth until she was eight years old give cause to wonder how she survived and excelled. Rudolph, who was born with polio, weighed only four-and-a-half pounds at birth. She suffered from double pneumonia twice and scarlet fever by the time she was four years old, and was left with the use of only her right leg from the crippling effect of polio.

1940-

Olympic

gold

medalist

When doctors at Meharry Medical College in Nashville advised the Rudolphs that Wilma might regain the use of her leg through daily therapeutic massages, for two years the mother and daughter made weekly visits to Meharry for heat and water therapy treatment. On all

other days the mother, with the assistance of three of her older children (there were nineteen in all), massaged Rudolph's crippled leg at least four times each day. The hospital and home treatment was to prove immensely beneficial to Rudolph. It was her many rides from Clarksville to Nashville's Meharry Medical College for therapy that left on Rudolph the deepest, most enduring impressions of the place of her race in southern society. The trip was always taken on the segregated Greyhound bus; the route was always the same, and blacks were the ones who sat in the back. The bus station had a separate ticket window, waiting area, and toilet for blacks. Blacks were expected to give up their seats, even those in the back of the bus, and stand in the aisle if the front of the bus became overcrowded with whites. The bus driver enforced the seating arrangement.

At age five, Rudolph was fitted for a steel brace to correct her polio condition, and for the next six years she wore that brace from the time she rose in the morning until she went to bed at night. Psychologically the brace was devastating, since it served as a constant reminder that "something was wrong" with her. She also endured other illnesses and surgeries for the first decade of her life. At age nine, she took off her brace after forcing herself to walk normally by "faking a no-limp walk." Losing her brace liberated Rudolph, as she wrote in her autobiography, *Wilma:*

> From that day on, people were going to start separating me from that brace, start thinking about me differently, start saying that Wilma is a healthy kid, just like the rest of them.

Rudolph entered Cobb Elementary School in Clarksville in 1947 at the age of seven, and although she had missed kindergarten and the first grade because of her physical problems, she was allowed to enter the second grade. Rudolph's first year of school changed her life. "I went from being a sickly kid the other kids teased to a normal person accepted by my peer group, and that was the most important thing that could have happened to me at that point in my life, she wrote later. "I needed to belong, and I finally did."

The seventh grade proved to be the pivotal year of Rudolph's life, for then she was introduced to organized sports, specifically basketball. When she was in the eighth grade, Rudolph's seventh-grade basketball coach, Clinton Gray, decided to resurrect the track team that had been started the previous year, and he invited girls on the school's basketball team to join the track program. Rudolph signed up, although she still preferred basketball and continued to play well into the ninth grade. Rudolph ran in five different events in high school—the fifty meter, seventy-five meter, one-hundred meter, two-hundred meter, and the relay. She was thirteen years old and ran twenty different races that season, winning every one.

In her sophomore year she scored 803 points to set a new record for high school girls' basketball. Her team won the Middle East Tennessee Conference title, which earned them a spot on the Tennessee High School Girls' Championship, played at Pearl High School in Nashville. They lost the second game were eliminated from the tournament. It was at this tournament that Rudolph remembered one of the referees who worked many of the girls' basketball games. He was a track coach at Tennessee State University, Edward Temple. Temple took an interest in Rudolph because he saw her as a good prospect for his women's track team at Tennessee State University.

In her sophomore year at Clarksville's Burt High School Rudolph entered her first serious track meet, held at Tuskegee Institute in Alabama. The meet attracted girls from all over the South, and Rudolph lost every race. This was the first time she had suffered defeat in track; it had a devastating effect on her morale. But this was a sobering experience that made her realize that she could not "always win on natural ability alone, and that there was more to track than just running fast," she recalled. The Tuskegee meet also had a tremendous psychological impact upon her. If it shattered her confidence momentarily, it soon made her determined "to go back the following year and wipe them out."

The May following the Tuskegee meet, Coach Temple came from Nashville to see if Rudolph's parents would allow her to spend the summer at Tennessee State University. He wanted to teach her the techniques of running. At this summer camp, Coach Temple ran his girls "about twenty miles a day, five days a week, cross country to build up endurance." At the end of the summer Temple took his team to the National Amateur Athletic Union (AAU) contest in Philadelphia. Rudolph won all nine races that she entered, and the women from Tennessee State swept the whole junior division of the National AAU. She also demonstrated her potential for the 1956 Olympic Games in Melbourne, Australia.

Rudolph attended the Olympic trials in Seattle as a high school junior and qualified for the United States Olympic Team. As the youngest member of the Olympic Team, she took her first trip to Los Angeles and her first airplane flight in 1956. At the trials, she was looked after by Bill Russell, captain of the United States men's basketball team. In Melbourne, Rudolph was eliminated from the two-hundred meter, but she ran the third leg of the relay, and the team placed third for a United States bronze medal.

The team scored three outstanding firsts in the history of Olympic competition: It was the first time any school or club had six members qualify for Olympic competition in any sport; it was the first time all four members of the women's relay team came from the same team; and it was the first time that three teams broke the world's record in the same event.

In September 1958, Rudolph entered Tennessee State University as a freshman majoring in elementary education and psychology. Although an athlete and soon to become a member of the track team, she did not attend college on an athletic scholarship. Rudolph and other members of the famed "Tigerbelles" helped support their education through a work assistance program. Each athlete worked two hours a day, five days a week, at various jobs all over the campus to stay in school.

In Rudolph's sophomore year, the first stop on the way to the 1960 Olympics was Corpus Christi, Texas, where the National AAU meet was held. The best women athletes were invited to the Olympic trials two weeks later at Texas Christian University. Rudolph set a world record in the two-hundred meter that was to stand for eight years, and she qualified for the Olympic team in three events—the one-hundred meter, two-hundred meter, and relay. In Rome she became the first American woman to win three gold medals. Afterward, she and the whole American team were invited to the Vatican to meet Pope John XXIII.

"Tigerbelle" •

seizes three

gold medals

From Rome, Coach Temple took his winning team to the British Empire Games in London. Rudolph won all of the events she entered. From London the team went to Stuttgart, West Germany, and on to Holland and throughout Europe. Wherever Rudolph went, crowds of admirers came to see her. Journalists in Europe admired her running technique and scissoring stride, and noted: "The French called her 'La Gazelle,' 'La Chattanooga Choo Choo,' and 'La Perle Noire'; to the Italians she became known as 'La Gazzélla Nera'." Rudolph duplicated her previous successes in all of these meets. When she returned to the United States, she and her teammates were honored with a parade in her hometown, Clarksville. More than forty thousand people attended the parade. The event had a social significance beyond the celebration of Rudolph's achievements—it was the first integrated event in Clarksville's segregated history.

From Clarksville Rudolph went to Chicago, where she received the key to the city from Mayor Richard Daley, then on to Detroit, Atlanta,

Philadelphia, and Washington, D.C., where she met Vice President Lyndon B. Johnson and President John F. Kennedy. She was called on to attend numerous banquets, give television appearances, sign autographs, and make countless speeches. Always poised, she met the challenges well.

In 1961, after returning from Rome, Rudolph received the Sullivan Award—given to the top amateur athlete in the United States—and the Female Athlete of the Year Award. She was the first woman to be invited to run in such meets as the New York Athletic Club Meet, the Melrose Games, the Los Angeles Times Games, the Penn Relays, and the Drake Relays. She later ran track against the Russians and made two goodwill trips—one to French West Africa and another with the evangelist Billy Graham and the Baptist Christian Athletes, who went to Japan.

Next to coaches Ed Temple and Clinton Gray, May Faggs was an important influence on Rudolph's athletic career. Faggs held several records in United States Women's Track, and she won medals in the Olympic competitions before Rudolph completed high school. She encouraged Rudolph to "perform as an individual" and not to be concerned with the loss of the friendship of her teammates if she should defeat them.

After graduating from Tennessee State University on May 27, 1963, Rudolph was offered the job as girls' track coach and teacher of the second grade at the elementary school she attended as a child. She married her high school sweetheart, Robert Eldridge, and later moved to Evansville, Indiana, where she became the director of a community center. From Evansville she moved to Boston, where she became involved in the Job Corps program in Poland Springs, Maine.

In 1967 Vice President Hubert Humphrey invited her to work with him in Operation Champion, a program to bring star athletes into sixteen of the largest ghettoes of the United States to give young people training in sports. Ralph Boston, another Tennessee State track star and a graduate of the school, and Rudolph were the track specialists. After this project ended, the Job Corps transferred Rudolph to St. Louis, which allowed her to be closer to her home state. From St. Louis she went to Detroit and took a teaching position at Palham Junior High School. Later, at the advice of Bill Russell, she went to California, where she worked with the Watts Community Action Committee. She returned to Clarksville, Tennessee, in 1977 before her final return to Detroit, where she and her family reside today.

Rudolph is president of the Indianapolis-based Wilma Rudolph Foundation. She and her husband, Robert Eldridge, have two daughters—Yolanda and Djuana—and two sons—Robert, Jr., and Xurry. Rudolph is active in her community as a member of Delta Sigma Theta Sorority, which she joined as a sophomore in college.

A major autobiographical work, *Wilma: The Story of Wilma Rudolph*, published in 1977 and produced as an NBC television movie starring Cicely Tyson, told Wilma Rudolph's story to the world. The book and movie also provided encouragement to handicapped youth to achieve the goals they set for themselves. In 1991, puzzled and angered over the fact that there was no mention of Rudolph in the World Book Encyclopedia, the fourth-grade class of Jessup Elementary School in Jessup, Maryland, wrote to the publisher to urge inclusion. World Book obliged, and its 1991 edition features an entry.

**Profile by
James E. Haney**

GLORIA SCOTT

Gloria Dean Randle Scott, distinguished leader in higher education

1938- •

and an advocate of women's issues, is the second woman chief adminis-

trator of Bennett College, Greensboro, North Carolina. A zoologist by

college •

training, she rose rapidly in academia to hold professorial administra-

president

tive posts outside the field of science. She is known also for her leadership

in Girls Scouts, USA, for which she served as national president.

Born April 14, 1938, in Houston, Texas, Scott is the middle of five children born to Freeman Randle, a Houston cook, and Juanita (Bell) Randle, a domestic and part-time nurse. Gloria's first-grade teacher was a strong influence in her life, reported Kent Demaret in *People.* "She made learning interesting and let us know that, because we were black, we had to be doubly achievement oriented," said Scott. "She had no children of her own, but she would have us to her house, tell us how to study, take us on outings. As a result, I found learning a challenge." Scott graduated from Jack Yates High School in Houston in 1955, where she was salutatorian. She received three degrees from Indiana University: a B.A. in zoology with minors in botany and French, 1959; M.A. in zoology with a minor in botany, in 1960; and a Ph.D. with a major in higher education and minors in zoology and botany, in 1965.

Scott taught at Marian College, Indianapolis, Indiana, from 1961 to 1965 and moved to Knoxville College, Knoxville, Tennessee, in 1965, where she joined the teaching faculty and was also dean of students and deputy director of the Upward Bound program. From 1967 to 1972 Scott was at North Carolina Agricultural and Technical State University, Greensboro, where, in addition to teaching, she developed a ten-year institutional plan for the university and served as director of institutional research.

Moving to Houston, Scott was professor of higher education and assistant to the president for educational planning and evaluation at Texas Southern University. She then spent nine years at Clark College in Atlanta as vice-president. From 1978 to 1987 she taught at several colleges—Clark, Bryn Mawr, Atlanta University, and Grambling State University. In 1987 Scott was elected president of Bennett College, Greensboro, North Carolina, becoming the second woman president in the school's history.

• Black women's

college has a

mission

Scott refers to herself as a "race woman." "Giving something back, influencing what happens to Black people has always been important. . . . I suppose I'm one of the vestiges of what you call 'race women'—people who really believe in African Americans," Joye Mercer quoted her. Scott sees the black college as an institution with a mission to provide an education "that allows economic, social and intellectual mobility," but it is also potentially "a corporate citizen," particularly since black high schools have closed and the community must look elsewhere for advocates for black students. A black woman's college goes a step beyond the coeducational institution. Scott told Mercer: "If you attend a woman's college, you have the opportunity to be everything. . . . You don't have to deal with the competitive personal development issue of whether you challenge the males, or if you're a good student, the question of whether you tailor that so you won't appear to be too smart."

Scott is as much concerned with the black community and black students in the schools as she is with Bennett College and higher education. She is troubled over a national problem that seems to defy resolution—the countless numbers of black students who need good higher education but are unable to get it. "Black students need to see some validation about what they can do." Black teachers also make a tremendous impact on white youth, "who need to know that blacks are leaders too," she said.

In the area of governance, Scott's experiences have come from her academic background as well as from affiliations with other institutions and agencies. She was a founding member and secretary of Persons

Responsive to Educational Problems from 1966 to 1982. Since then she has served as board member for the Southern Education Foundation, 1967-1977; and vice-chair of the National Advisory Committee on Black Higher Education and Black Colleges and Universities (to the United States Department of Education and the office of Health, Education, and Welfare), 1976-1983.

In 1975 she was on the Education Commissions of States Task Force on Equal Education Opportunity for Women. President Gerald Ford and later President Jimmy Carter appointed Scott to the National Commission on International Women's Year, from 1976 to 1978, and for the next two years Carter appointed her to serve the National Commission on International Year of the Child. For nearly a decade she was chairperson of the education committee and member of the board of directors of the National Urban League. Professional organizations and regional agencies have benefited extensively from Scott's leadership ability. She has been active in extensive program development for the Southern Regional Education Board, the Council on Social Work Education, professional regional accreditation agencies, and miscellaneous education-related groups. Currently she serves on the external review board for Stanford University's Minority Participation and Presence.

Scott is well known for her work with the Girl Scouts, USA. Her interest in scouting was nurtured while she was growing up in Houston, and she saw it as both an opportunity for personal development and a means of enhancing the lives of poor and minority children. Her nature trips, which she took during her early teens as a Girl Scout, created an abiding interest in the outdoors. She has been a member of the board of directors of the Girl Scouts since 1969. From 1969 to 1972 she served as chair of the Program Committee and member of the Minority Task Force. From 1972 to 1975 she was first vice-president, and from 1975 to 1978 she was national president—the first black in the organization's history of more than sixty-five years.

Scott rises to •

helm of

Girl Scouts

Scott directed an unprecedented array of innovations early in her term as Girl Scout president. In Florida a statewide scout conference explored women's issues, land use, and justice for juveniles. Scouts in North Dakota who were interested in law, politics, and public administration became state legislative interns. Baltimore scouts organized a coalition to increase the participation of black youth and adults in the movement. Leadership training for black and Puerto Rican teenagers was held in Hartford, Connecticut; therapeutic programs for mentally handicapped girls as well as those with psychiatric problems were held in Nashville, Tennessee; and scouts in Maine attended classes on venereal disease.

Volunteer and other civic activities have come to Scott's attention, and she has devoted tireless service to these groups. Of special interest for Scott are women's issues. She participated in the Women in Passage Conference in 1975 sponsored by *Good Housekeeping,* and Phase II: Women in Passage—The Male Point of View in May 1977. In November of that year she was the official presiding chair for the opening of the National Women's Conference held in Houston, Texas, and she was national cochairperson of the 1981 Black Women's Summit in Washington, D.C., in July 1981. When Clark College held its Conference on American Black Women titled "Have We Come a Long Way, Baby? A Report on the Status of America's First Female Work Force" in 1985, she was conference convener and led a delegation to the International Women's Decade meeting in Nairobi, Kenya. Honors and awards for Scott, including several "woman of the year" citations, have been numerous.

Scott is "an activist president" who manages by visiting other offices on campus for conferences. "In moving back and forth, I see things on campus, and get a better sense of what's going on," she explained to M. Colleen Jones. She is a carefully spoken, dynamic leader with will and determination, quiet reserve, and a wry sense of humor. Rarely is she without pencil and notepad to record conversations and meeting highlights; she uses the information for planning, action, and evaluation. An early riser, she walks three miles around the campus each day as much for exercise as to examine the campus and its condition. In 1959 Scott married Will Braxton Scott, currently a professor of sociology and social work at Bennett College. While they have no children, they have been surrogate parents to more than three million Girl Scouts and hundreds of former students.

**Profile by
Jessie Carney Smith**

NTOZAKE SHANGE

*I*n the early 1970s, Ntozake Shange, a brilliant poet, playwright,

1948- •

performer, and novelist, changed her name to one that in Zulu means

"She who comes with her own things/ she who walks with lions." It was

poet, •

for colored girls who have considered suicide / when the rainbow is

playwright,

enuf, *Shange's prize-winning, controversial choreopoem, that cata-*

performer

pulted her to fame. Nominated for Tony, Emmy, and Grammy Awards

in 1977, for colored girls *won the Outer Circle Critics Award and three*

Obie awards. A feminist statement on behalf of black women, the

Broadway production was a combination of music, dance, and poetry

in the form of soliloquies, dialogue, stories, and chants performed by an

ensemble of seven black actresses.

Ntozake Shange was born October 18, 1948, in Trenton, New Jersey. The daughter of Paul T. Williams, an air force surgeon, and Eloise Owens Williams, a psychiatric social worker and educator, Shange was originally named Paulette Williams, after her father. The eldest of four children, she spent her childhood with her family in upstate New York and in Saint Louis, Missouri.

By all accounts—including her own in the autobiographical *Betsey Brown: A Novel*—Shange had an interesting, even extraordinary, childhood. Paul and Eloise Williams were able to provide for their children upper-middle-class comfort and social standing and access to their American and African-American cultural heritage. Their foreign travel to such destinations as Cuba, Haiti, Mexico, and Europe; Eloise Williams's wide reading, which encompassed the major works of the African-American canon and which she shared with her children; and Paul Williams's love of the rich and varied musical expression of Africa all contributed to an intellectually and aurally stimulating childhood. There was "always different music in our house all the time," noted Shange in an interview with Stella Dong. The Williams children came into frequent contact with numerous visiting musicians, writers, and thinkers, a reflection of their parents' interests. Dizzy Gillespie, Chuck Berry, Miles Davis, and Chico Hamilton were among the well-known musical guests at the Williams's home. One evening, according to family lore, only the renowned scholar W. E. B. DuBois could coax the reluctant young Shange into going to bed.

The day-by-day presence of musical expression, the constant reading and declamation of black poetry and prose, the family's attendance at concerts, dance performances, and the ballet, the impact of foreign travel, and the intellectual vibrancy of the Williams's household all had an early and profound effect on Shange's development as a writer. "I live in language / sound falls round me like rain on other folks," she wrote in *Nappy Edges*. The anger that infuses Shange's poems, novels, and plays stems in part from her awakening as a child to the racial cruelty that she unavoidably witnessed and endured at the newly integrated school she attended in St. Louis, Missouri, following the 1954 Supreme Court desegregation decision. And the fierce and protective love for young black American girls that also pervades her work can be explained by her other painful awakening to the concomitant oppression of women.

A writer all of her life, even as a child, Shange has most recently published *The Love Space Demands (a continuing saga)*, a collection of poems set in the city where women struggle to survive and find love in a loveless, dangerous world. *Ridin' the Moon in Texas* is a collection of

461 •

poetry and prose inspired by the creations of fourteen visual artists. Shange's full-length books of poetry include *Nappy Edges*, *A Daughter's Geography* and *From Okra to Greens*. Her novels to date are *Sassafrass, Cypress & Indigo* and *Betsey Brown*. Shange has written and directed many theater pieces, including the poem-play *A Photograph: A Study in Cruelty, Boogie Woogie Landscapes*, and *Spell #7: A Geechee Quick Magic Trance Manual*. In addition to directing and sometimes performing in her own theater pieces, Shange has directed those of others, among them Richard Wesley's *The Mighty Gents* in 1979 at the New York Shakespeare Festival and *Tribute to Sojourner Truth*, a work coauthored by poet June Jordan and scholar/performer Bernice Reagon.

• *Choreopoem*

combines

artistic forms

Shange achieved fame in the late 1970s with her acclaimed choreographed poem *for colored girls,* which ran for two years on Broadway and traveled to major cities throughout the United States as well as abroad. *for colored girls* was first published as a book of twenty poems in 1975 and was adapted for an "American Playhouse" public television series in 1982.

In the foreword to the 1976 edition of *for colored girls,* Shange explains the genesis of the play. While living and working in northern California in the early 1970s, she began writing a series of poems about the reality of the lives of seven different kinds of women. The poems were first presented at Bacchanal, a women's bar near Berkeley and one of a number of bars and clubs in the area where poetry, dance, and music were being experimentally combined to form a dynamic women's theater. In fact, the vitality of the emergent women's movement during this period was a significant factor in helping to define Shange's feminist point of view. She writes in the foreword that her three-year association with the women's studies program at Sonoma State College was "inextricably bound" to the development of her sense of the world, herself, and women's language. Shange also credits as influential the poetry readings then being staged by small women's presses such as Shameless Hussy Press, The Oakland Women's Press, and Third World Communications. She had much in common with other women writers whose energies were being directed "toward clarifying our lives—& the lives of our mothers, daughters, & grandmothers—as women."

Shange was involved at the same time in the theory and practice of African-American dance as student, teacher, and performer, another aspect of her California residence that contributed to her development as a performance artist and writer. She danced in Halifu Osumure's all-female dance troupe and taught theater and dance in San Francisco and Berkeley public schools. "Just as women's studies had rooted me to an articulated female heritage & imperative," she wrote in *for colored girls,* "so dance as explicated by Raymond Sawyer & Ed Mock insisted that everything African, everything halfway colloquial, a grimace, a strut, an arched back over a yawn, waz mine." Similar to the Afrocentric dance she learned, performed, and taught, Shange's own writing is infused with and ordered by African-American cultural elements—literary, musical, and folk.

The mother of a daughter, Shange writes also out of a trenchant sense of obligation to young African-American women for whom she hopes to provide "information I did not have." Passionately, she proclaims: "When I die, I will not be guilty of having left a generation of girls behind thinking that anyone can tend to their emotional health other than themselves." She says in the dedication to her novella *Sassafras* that she wrote the story "to make her daughter's dreams as real as her menses." Still, in spite of her special concern for black women, Shange's work displays great empathy for other categories of the oppressed. Her extensive travel and sympathy with peoples of Latin America and the Caribbean are readily apparent in her poems.

The polemical force and impact of her creative efforts notwithstanding, Shange's purpose and achievement is that of the true artist. At a national Afro-American writers conference held in 1977 at Howard University, she insisted:

> When I take my voice into a poem or a story / i am trying desperately to give you that. i am not trying to give you a history of my family / the struggle of black people all over the world or the fight goin on upstairs tween Susie and Matt. i am giving you a moment / like an alto solo in december in nashville in 1937. as we demand to be heard / we want you to hear us. we come to you the way leroi jenkins comes or cecil taylor / or b. b. king. we come to you alone / in the theatre / in the story / & the poem. like with billie holiday or betty carter / we shd give you a moment that cannot be recreated / a specificity that cannot be confused. our language shd let you know who's talkin, what we're talking abt & how we cant stop saying this to you. some urgency accompanies the text. something important is going on. we are speaking. reaching for yr person / we cannot hold it / we dont wanna sell it / we give you ourselves / if you listen.

Shange attended Barnard College in New York and graduated with honors in 1970; she received an M.A. in American Studies in 1973 from the University of Southern California, Los Angeles, and has pursued other graduate study at the University of Southern California.

Throughout her career as a writer, performer, and director, Shange has taught courses in women's studies, creative writing, drama, and related subjects at colleges and universities across the United States. In 1981 she received a Guggenheim Fellowship for writing and the Medal of Excellence from Columbia University. Among other awards, she has received the Pushcart Prize, the *Los Angeles Times* Book Prize for Poetry for *Three Pieces*, and an Obie for *Mother Courage and Her Children*, her adaptation of Bertolt Brecht's play.

**Profile by
Carole
McAlpine Watson**

Shange currently lives in Philadelphia, works as a performance artist and is artist-in-residence at Villanova University. She is writing a novel and adapting Harriet Beecher Stowe's *Uncle Tom's Cabin* for performance by the San Francisco Mime Troupes.

ALTHEA T. L. SIMMONS

*A*lthea T. L. Simmons demonstrated a fierce and uncompromising **1924-1990** •

desire to remove apartheid-like conditions wherever they existed. From

her experiences as fieldworker for the NAACP, she rose in the ranks of the **lawyer,** •

organization to head its Washington Bureau and became its chief **organization**

lobbyist. She fought relentlessly for legislation to support civil rights. Her **official**

faithfulness to the cause also led to voting rights extensions, a strengthened

Fair Housing Law, and a bill to establish the Martin Luther King Holiday,

later made into law. A fierce fighter, uncompromising expert on

civil rights issues, and faithful servant of the NAACP, Simmons wrestled

with the organization's problems efficiently and effectively for more

than twenty-eight years. Above all, she spent a lifetime fighting racism.

Simmons was born in Shreveport, Louisiana, on April 17, 1924, the daughter of M. M. Simmons, a high school principal, and Lillian (Littleton) Simmons, a high school teacher. Since kindergarten days she has used the initials "T. L." When asked to define the initials, she responded, "That's one secret I will keep." She grew up in a family of an older brother and a younger sister. She received her bachelor of science degree with honors from the black, state-supported institution Southern University in New Orleans, Louisiana, 1945; a master's degree in marketing from the University of Illinois, Urbana, 1951; and a law degree from Howard University, Washington, D.C., 1956. She pursued further study in contract compliance at the University of California, Los Angeles, and took additional work at the American Society for Training Development, the American Management Association, the New School for Social Work in New York City, and the National Training Laboratory. This training was necessary for Simmons, who after graduation from law school, immediately set her sights on climbing unclimbable mountains and achieving the seemingly unachievable, with a particular interest in eliminating the color, gender, and economic barriers to racial unity.

Simmons was associated with the W. J. Durham law office from 1956 to 1961. A former college teacher and journalist, in 1961 Simmons began twenty-eight years of service to the NAACP. Before that she had been an NAACP volunteer as executive secretary of the Texas State Conference of NAACP branches and chairperson of the executive committee of the Dallas branch. From 1961 to 1964 she was field secretary and worked out of the NAACP subregional office in Los Angeles. When Medgar Evers was assassinated on June 11, 1963, the NAACP sent her to work with Evers's wife, Myrlie, and the Evers family and to relocate them to California. "Her quiet courage and demeanor was a source of strength to Myrlie and the children," said Benjamin L. Hooks.

In 1964 a management consultant firm submitted a reorganization plan to the NAACP Board of Directors calling for an office of secretary for training. Roy L. Wilkins, then executive director, appointed Simmons to the newly created position of secretary for training, a position that she held until 1974.

In 1964 Simmons was also director of the NAACP's National Voter Registration Drive. Later, as NAACP national education director, 1974-1977, she developed handbooks, pamphlets, programs, and other instructional materials designed to uplift black youth. As associate director of branch and field services, 1977-1979, she supervised the NAACP's nationwide network of branches, field staff, and the membership and youth and college division.

- *Chief NAACP*

lobbyist named

In 1979 Simmons was appointed director of the Washington Bureau and chief lobbyist for the NAACP. She had already excelled in her various assignments with the organization and she said that her years of field service within the NAACP "taught her the value of grassroots mobilization." It was in Washington that Simmons's work finally gained her the national respect and recognition that she had earned considerably earlier. But the shadow of her predecessor, legendary Clarence Mitchell, remained, and her stewardship was often compared to his. There were those who disregarded her as a worthy successor to Mitchell and who opposed her on the basis of her gender, "convinced that being black and female would be a double liability in a predominantly white male world," wrote Lena Williams.

None of this would deter Simmons, for she had a mission and her own agenda, and she knew that the larger problem dealt with the organization's civil rights agenda. Immediately she began her usual pattern of working tirelessly and incessantly, late in the evenings and on weekends, to get the job done. She never viewed her role as one of self-glorification. She was an expert on civil rights and had a comprehensive understanding of the civil rights agenda. Thus, the fierce, determined, and uncompromising Simmons buttonholed congressmen and senators and "cajoled them . . . into supporting Civil Rights legislation," according to *Crisis*. Her forceful determination also helped to bring about extensions of voting rights, passage of the Fair Housing Act, and a bill to establish a Martin Luther King, Jr., national holiday. Simmons played a pivotal role in causing Congress to deny Robert Bork's appointment to the United States Supreme Court. She was "one of the most effective, intelligent lobbyists on the Hill," said Senator Orrin G. Hatch, Republican of Utah. She facilitated the work of the Resolutions Committee at the NAACP conventions in planning summits, conferences, marches, and various protests and demonstrations.

Simmons's commitment to social action was manifest in other positions that she held outside of the NAACP. She was a member of the National Manpower Advisory Committee for United States Department of Labor, vice-president of the American Society for Training and Development, and vice-president of NOW's Legal Defense and Education Fund, among many other positions. Also during her distinguished career, Simmons received a number of awards and recognitions professionally and in community service, including the 1988 Leadership Award from the National Association for Equal Opportunity in Education.

Tall and stately, Simmons had the bearing of an African queen with the forcefulness and resolve that made her an awesome opponent and a fearless leader. She was straightforward and to the point in her transactions. She had a brisk walk, always appearing to be in a hurry. Though ill for a number of months, Simmons set up office in her Howard University Hospital room to continue her work rather than take leave. "The job must go on. There is little time for rest," she said. After a long illness, she died in her hospital room on September 13, 1990. She left a legacy in the civil rights struggle that may never be equalled.

**Profile by
Jessie Carney Smith**

CAROLE SIMPSON

*C*arole Simpson has made outstanding contributions to the field of

journalism and, through her work, to society at large. Though not

allowing herself to be pigeonholed as a reporter only of "black" news—

indeed, since 1988 she has been anchor of ABC's "World News Satur-

day"—she has brought sensitivity and perspective to her coverage of

news and features concerning black America.

1940- •

broadcast •

journalist

Carole Simpson Marshall was born on December 7, 1940, in Chicago, Illinois. Simpson graduated from the University of Michigan in 1962 with a bachelor of arts degree in journalism and did graduate study in journalism at the University of Iowa. Simpson is married to James Marshall and has two children, a daughter named Mallika and a son named Adam.

Simpson is a well-respected journalist and news anchor with more than twenty years of experience covering a wide array of topics, including Capitol Hill, health care, housing, education, the environment, and the release of Nelson Mandela. Early in her career, Simpson worked as a stringer correspondent for Voice of America. She then spent two years as a journalism instructor and director of the Information Bureau at Tuskegee Institute in Alabama.

From 1965 to 1968 she worked as a news reporter and anchor as well as a movie and book reviewer for WCFL Radio in Chicago. From 1968 to 1970, Simpson served as a special correspondent and weekend anchor at WBBM Radio in Chicago. While serving in that capacity, Simpson also performed as a commentator on "Our People," a minority affairs program on WTTW-TV, a public television station in Chicago. From there, Simpson became Chicago's first black woman television reporter.

Simpson continued to make strides in her career. She became a television news correspondent for WMAQ-TV and worked at that station from 1970 to 1974. At the same time, she worked as a journalism instructor for Northwestern University's Medill School of Journalism from 1971 to 1974. While working at WMAQ-TV, Simpson had her priorities concerning the types of stories she covered. Although she enjoyed covering hard news stories, she preferred feature stories "that allow more creativity," she told *Ebony*. She also stated at that time the following regarding the coverage of black stories:

> I want to cover black stories because I feel I bring them
> sensitivity and a perspective that white reporters don't
> have. I wouldn't want to cover just black news though,
> because you often lose your credibility that way.

Simpson continued to rise in the area of television news and earned her credibility through excellence in her work.

• *Simpson*

receives

presidential

assignment

Moving on to Washington, D.C., Simpson worked as a host of a women's public affairs program called "Her-Rah," which aired on WRC-TV, an NBC Washington affiliate television station. She then became a substitute anchor for "NBC Nightly News" and also anchored NBC's "Newsbreak" on the weekends. Simpson's news delivery style, camera presence, and finesse on the air evolved, and she was selected to cover Capitol Hill as a news correspondent; she performed in that position from 1978 to 1981. Simpson was then chosen to serve as a perimeter reporter during the Republican and Democratic conventions in 1980. The visibility she received on Capitol Hill as well as her coverage during the conventions earned Simpson respect and a national reputation. In 1982, Simpson joined ABC in Washington as a general assignment correspondent.

Simpson has been covering George Bush since 1980. She has accompanied him on domestic and foreign trips since his vice-presidency. In 1984 Simpson covered his vice-presidential reelection campaign and in 1988 his bid for the presidency. She also served as a perimeter reporter during the 1988 Republican Convention in New Orleans.

Simpson is articulate and has a rhythmic flow in her news delivery in addition to a manner that exhibits confidence. Her excellent skills, combined with her many years of experience in the news business, are apparent in her role as anchor of ABC's "World News Saturday." Simpson was named anchor in June, 1988. In addition to her performance as news anchor, she contributed to reports concerning family issues for the "American Agenda" segment on "World News Tonight" with Peter Jennings. Some of her "American Agenda" segments include stories on children under stress, battered women, teen pregnancy, and a 1988 report on children with AIDS that earned her an Emmy nomination. Simpson can also be seen on "Nightline" and "20/20."

Simpson is a versatile journalist. Besides anchoring half-hour news shows and doing news segments, Simpson has also anchored three hour-long ABC news specials: "The Changing American Family," "Public Schools in Conflict," and "Sex and Violence in the Media." Simpson reported the release of Nelson Mandela, who had been imprisoned in South Africa for twenty-seven years. While covering Mandela, Simpson also did a special report on South African women. However, Simpson was assaulted by a South African police officer during a disturbance in Johannesburg while she was covering a church service the day before the African National Congress leader was released. According to *Jet,* Simpson says she "will not return to the country until its apartheid policy ends."

Simpson served as president of the Radio and Television Correspondents Association from 1982 to 1983, and in 1986 she was elected chairperson of the ABC News Women's Advisory Board. In 1988 she was the recipient of the Milestone Award in Broadcast Journalism from the National Commission on Working Women and received the Silver Bell Award from the Ad Council in 1989.

**Profile by
Dhyana Ziegler**

NAOMI SIMS

aomi Sims's haute couture modeling career, which included the

1948- •

first prominent fashion magazine covers featuring a black model,

changed the fashion industry and the national perception of beauty.

model, •

Never before had a woman of such deep, rich color been used to

entrepreneur

exemplify beauty. Upon leaving modeling, Sims rose to become one of

the nation's premier black woman entrepreneurs and the author of

several books.

Sims was born March 30, 1948, in Oxford, Mississippi. The product of a broken home, Sims had only faint memories of her father, who divorced her mother when Sims was a baby. Her mother suffered a nervous breakdown when Sims was only eight. The subsequent separation from her mother and her other sisters, Betty and Doris, and shifts from one home to another, created a lonely childhood for young Naomi Sims. She therefore spent many nights longing for her natural mother and the security of the fairy tale that could always be found in the elementary readers. She was never returned to her natural mother; instead, she was placed with loving foster parents who raised her.

Young Sims continued to battle the usual adolescent insecurities that were magnified by a height that would one day propel her to the pinnacle of a modeling career. The insecurity remained for years, but her sense of self-reliance assisted her in transforming the gangling adolescent into a striking teenager. "At 13, Naomi Sims was already 5 feet 10 inches in height. She felt tall, dark, and different," reported Barbara Summers in *Essence*. At fourteen, Sims's proclivity for modeling and fashion was recognized by friends who suggested modeling as a career. It was a natural suggestion; by Sims's admission, she had "always been a clotheshorse," wrote Diane Lurie. After graduating from Westinghouse High School in Pittsburgh, Sims enrolled in New York's Fashion Institute of Technology. A shortage of money precipitated Sims's foray into modeling. She began posing for a fashion illustrator at $6 an hour. To further increase her earnings, Sims had to take drastic measures. At this time she did the unheard-of, and it ended up launching her modeling career. Without benefit of an agent or an introduction, she boldly telephoned prominent fashion photographer Gosta Peterson. Her purpose was served and the association led to a marked increase in her earnings. She went from six to sixty dollars an hour. Sims found the juggling of a growing modeling career and the study demands of school too taxing; consequently, she left school.

- ***Model breaks***

down social

barriers

Notwithstanding the tenfold increase in her modeling fees, the road to success was still to be an uphill struggle. Sims went through weeks of unemployment, living on borrowed money from the modeling agency that was then representing her. Not surprisingly, Sims eagerly accepted the *New York Times* assignment that placed her on the cover of its *Fashion of the Times* supplement—the first for a black model. Fashion designer Halston understood the significance of the exposure of Sims. He surmised that "she was the great ambassador for all black people. . . . She broke down all the social barriers," noted Barbara Keveles in *People*. While it was an optimistic overstatement to say that she broke down "all" of the social barriers, many did fall as she appeared in the AT&T commercial and became the first black model published on the covers and pages of such Anglo-American bastions of fashion as *Vogue, Ladies Home Journal, Life,* and *Cosmopolitan*.

Despite her success in her chosen career, Sims found the fashion world superficial, boring, and unnatural. In a 1968 interview for *Ladies Home Journal,* Sims said:

> I can't see myself modeling at 30—it's too competitive and often shallow. When you're young its great because you can make fantastic money. I like money. . . . But I think I can be happy just making enough to buy

what I want. Once you've got success, it's empty. The
fun is in reaching for it.

At the age of twenty-four, Sims had experienced tremendous
success in modeling and gave it up to reach for success in her own
business. Her goal in her private enterprise was to manufacture quality
wigs that were complimentary to women of color. Utilizing a synthetic
fiber she invented and patented, Kanekalon Presselle, she attempted to
place her wigs on the market. Many businesses were reluctant to carry
her line. In her typical take-charge stance, Sims explained to Summers
the procedure for opening the market: "I took a slide show to those in
the industry who resisted and gave them an education. I told them if they
would just leave me and Black women alone, it would be fine." In spite
of the obvious risks in any new business, the Naomi Sims Collection was
more than just "fine"; it was a financial success that assured Sims' status
as an accomplished businesswoman. Naomi Sims Beauty Products was
incorporated in 1985 with Sims serving as founder and chairperson of
the board. The company expanded to include a complete line of beauty
products for women of color that could be found in department and
specialty stores in the United States and the Bahamas.

The company business was just one aspect of Sims's busy life. As
wife to art dealer Michael Findlay and mother to their son, John Phillip,
Sims felt that nurturing the family was important, and she sought to keep
her private life sheltered. However, that did not hinder her public and
civic participation as she attempted to give back to her community and
her people. She used her fashion and beauty expertise to write several
books. Her first, *All about Health and Beauty for the Black Woman*,
published in 1975 by Doubleday, became the health and beauty reference book for black women. After multiple printings, Sims published a
revised edition in 1986. She also wrote *How to Be a Top Model* (1979), *All
about Hair Care for the Black Woman* (1982), and *All about Success for
the Black Woman* (1983), all published by Doubleday. She contributed
regularly to *Right On!*, a magazine with a nationwide black teenage
audience. Her insightfulness and ability to speak cast her as lecturer and
participant in numerous seminars, panel discussions, and gatherings on
topics as diverse as drug abuse, sickle-cell anemia, and education, as
well as health and beauty.

Sims has been a member of the board of directors of the Northside
Center Child Development in Harlem, and a participant in the Sickle-
Cell Anemia Drive and the New York State Drug Habilitation Program.
In 1980 she was invited to be executive-in-residence for the School of
Business Administration of Georgetown University in Washington, D.C.
Her business acumen was recognized again in 1984 when she was

Sims opens •

manufacturing

business

selected as a participant in the President's Panel at the Twelfth Annual Career/Alumni Conference of the Harvard Business School.

Long absent from the modeling world, Sims has continued to be a model for humanity—a complementary ensemble of social conscience, community involvement, religious faith, and family love.

**Profile by
Bonnie Shipp**

BESSIE SMITH

*T*hey called her the *"Empress of the Blues."* Born into poverty April

15, 1894, in Chattanooga, Tennessee, to William and Laura Smith,

Bessie Smith began singing for coins on street corners and rose to

was her vocal style in person, reinforced as it was by her under-

when she appeared. Those outside the theaters clamored to get in; those

inside refused to leave without hearing more. At two critical points, she

cy. While at her peak, in 1925, Smith bought a custom-designed

railroad car for herself and her troupe on which they could travel and

1894-

blues singer

live. This luxury allowed her to circumvent some of the dispiriting effects of the racism found in both Northern and Southern states as she traveled with her own tent show or with the Theater Owners' Booking Association shows throughout much of the country, commanding a weekly salary that peaked at $2,000.

One of the many myths about Smith is that she was tutored (some versions claim kidnapped) by Ma Rainey, the prototype blues singer, and forced to tour with Rainey's show. In fact, Rainey didn't have her own show until after 1916, long after Smith had achieved independent success through her apprenticeships in a variety of minstrel and tent shows. Rainey and Smith worked together and established a friendship as early as 1912, and no doubt Smith absorbed vocal ideas during her early association with the "Mother of the Blues." Originally hired as a dancer, Smith rapidly polished her skills as a singer and often combined the two, weaving in a natural flair for comedy. From the beginning, communication with her audience was a hallmark of the young singer. Her voice was remarkable. Able to fill the largest hall without amplification, it reached out to each listener with its earthiness and beauty. In *Jazz People,* Dan Morgenstern quotes guitarist Danny Barker: "Bessie Smith was a fabulous deal to watch. She was a large, pretty woman and she dominated the stage. You didn't turn your head when she went on. You just watched Bessie. If you had any church background like people who came from the South as I did, you would recognize a similarity between what she was doing and what those preachers and evangelists from there did, and how they moved people. She could bring about mass hypnotism."

When Mamie Smith (no relation) recorded the first vocal blues in 1920 and sold 100,000 copies in the first month, record executives discovered a new market and the "race record" was born. Shipped only to the South and selected areas of the North where blacks congregated, these recordings of black performers found an eager audience, a surprising segment of which was made up of white Southerners to whose ears sounds of the blues were quite natural. Smith's first effective recording date, February 16, 1923, produced "Down-Hearted Blues" and "Gulf Coast Blues," with no accompaniment by Clarence Williams. The public bought an astounding 780,000 copies within six months. Smith's contract paid her $125 per usable recording, with no provision for royalties. Frank Walker, who supervised all of Smith's recordings with Columbia through 1931, quickly negotiated new contracts calling first for twelve new recordings at $150 each, then twelve more at $200— and Smith's fabulous recording career of 160 titles was successfully launched. On the brink of receivership in 1923, Columbia recovered

Birth of the •

"race record"

481 •

largely through the sale of recordings by Eddie Cantor, Ted Lewis, Bert Williams, and its hottest-selling artist, Bessie Smith.

During her ten-year recording career, the first six of which produced most of her output, Smith recorded with a variety of accompanists, including some of the most famous names in jazz and some of the most obscure. Among the elite were pianists Fred Longshaw, Porter Grainger, and Fletcher Henderson; saxophonists Coleman Hawkins and Sidney Bechet; trombonist Charlie Green; clarinetists Buster Bailey and Don Redman; and cornetist Joe Smith. Perhaps her most empathetic backing came from Green and Smith, as well as from Louis Armstrong and piano giant James P. Johnson. Examples of the support given her by Green and Smith may be found on such songs as "The Yellow Blues," "Empty Bed Blues," "Trombone Cholly," "Lost Your Head Blues," and "Young Woman's Blues." When Smith and Louis Armstrong first teamed up for 1925's brilliant "St. Louis Blues" and "Cold in Hand Blues," it marked the end of the acoustic recording era, with Smith's first electrically recorded sides coming on May 6, 1925. Other standouts with Armstrong include "Careless Love Blues," "Nashville Woman's Blues," and "I Ain't Gonna Play No Second Fiddle." Johnson's accompaniment sparkles on 1927's "Preachin' the Blues" and "Back Water Blues," as well as a number of 1929 efforts, "He's Got Me Goin'," "Worn Out Papa Blues," and "You Don't Understand."

Feeding on the popularity of her records, Smith's personal-appearance schedule escalated. As she moved from her home base of Philadelphia to Detroit, Chicago, Washington, Atlanta, and New York, adoring crowds greeted her at each stop. Extra police details to control the enthusiasm became the norm. What was the attraction? Critic and promoter John Hammond wrote in 1937: "Bessie Smith was the greatest artist American jazz ever produced; in fact, I'm not sure that her art did not reach beyond the limits of the term 'jazz.' She was one of those rare beings, a completely integrated artist capable of projecting her whole personality into music. She was blessed not only with great emotion but with a tremendous voice that could penetrate the inner recesses of the listener."

In *Early Jazz*, Gunther Schuller listed the components of Smith's vocal style: "a remarkable ear for and control of intonation, in all its subtlest functions; a perfectly centered, naturally produced voice (in her prime); an extreme sensitivity to word meaning and the sensory, almost physical, feeling of a word; and, related to this, superb diction and what singers call projection. She was certainly the first singer on jazz records to value diction, not for itself, but as a vehicle for conveying emotional states. . . . Perhaps even more remarkable was her pitch control. She handled this with such ease and naturalness that one is apt to take it for granted. Smith's fine microtonal shadings . . . are all part of a personal, masterful technique of great subtlety, despite the frequently boisterous mood or language." Further, Schuller heralds Smith as "the first complete jazz singer," whose influence on Billie Holiday and a whole generation of jazz singers cannot be overestimated.

In spite of her commercial success, Smith's personal life never strayed far from the blues theme. Her marriage to Jack Gee was stormy, punctuated by frequent fights and breakups, and, despite the 1926 adoption of Jack Gee, Jr., it ended in a bitter separation in 1929, after which Gee contrived to keep the boy from Smith for years by moving him from one boarding home to another. Another battle Smith waged was with the liquor bottle. Though able to abstain from drinking for considerable periods, Smith often indulged in binges that were infamous among her troupe and family. Equally well known to her intimates was Smith's bisexual promiscuity.

Smith rode the crest of recording popularity until about 1929, when the three-pronged fork of radio, talking pictures, and the Great Depression pitched the entire recording industry onto the critical list. Though her personal-appearance schedule continued at a brisk pace, the prices she could demand dipped, she was forced to sell her beloved railroad car, and the smaller towns she played housed theaters whose general quality and facilities were a burden. Even so, she starred in a 1929 two-reel film, "St. Louis Blues," a near-autobiographical effort that received some exposure until 1932.

Smith's lean years were coming to an end in the summer of 1937. The recording industry's revival soared on the craziness of the early Swing Era, spearheaded by the success of the Benny Goodman band. Smith had proved adaptable in her repertoire and could certainly swing with the best of them; even better, blues singing was experiencing a revival in popular taste. Smith's only appearance on New York's famed Fifty-second Street came on a cold February Sunday afternoon in 1936 at the Famous Door, when she was backed by Bunny Berigan, Joe Bushkin, and other regulars of the "Door" band. The impact of her singing that day has remained with those present for more than half a century. Much was made of the fact that Mildred Bailey wisely refused to follow Smith's performance. Further, that one afternoon's singing gave rise to other possible Smith appearances with popular swing performers: John Hammond claimed that a 1937 record date teaming Smith and members of the Basie band was in the works; Lionel Hampton recalled Goodman's eagerness to record with Smith. Another film was planned.

Even Smith's personal life was on the upswing in 1937 with the steady and loving influence of companion Richard Morgan.

Early in the morning of September 26, 1937, Smith and Morgan were driving from a Memphis performance to Darling, Mississippi, for the next day's show. Near Clarksdale, Mississippi, their car was involved in an accident that was fatal to Bessie. One of the persistent myths about Smith is that she bled to death because a white hospital refused to admit her. This story was given impetus by the unfortunate 1937 *downbeat* story by John Hammond, and was perpetuated by Edward Albee's 1960 play, *The Death of Bessie Smith*. Author Chris Albertson puts this myth firmly to rest. Albertson won a Grammy award for his booklet that accompanied the 1970 Columbia reissue of Smith's complete works (their second major reissue project). He was spurred to deeper investigation, resulting in his acclaimed 1972 biography, *Bessie*.

Albertson describes Smith's funeral: "On Monday, October 4, 1937, Philadelphia witnessed one of the most spectacular funerals in its history. Bessie Smith, a black super-star of the previous decade—a 'has been,' fatally injured on a dark Mississippi road eight days earlier—was given a send-off befitting the star she had never really ceased to be. . . . When word of her death reached the black community, the body had to be moved [to another location] which more readily accommodated the estimated ten thousand admirers who filed past her bier on Sunday, October 3. . . . The crowd outside was now seven thousand strong, and policemen were having a hard time holding it back. To those who had known Bessie in her better days, the sight was familiar."

**Profile by
Robert Dupuis**

JUANITA KIDD STOUT

*J*uanita Kidd Stout, retired Justice of the Supreme Court of Pennsyl-

1919- •

vania, is the first black woman to serve on the highest appellate court of

any state. Upon her election in 1959 to the Municipal—the name was

judge •

later changed to County—Court of Philadelphia, she became the first

black woman to be elected to a court of record in the United States. She

later served on the Court of Common Pleas, the court of general trial

jurisdiction, and the Supreme Court of Pennsylvania. Upon reaching

the mandatory retirement age of seventy, Stout retired from the Supreme

Court and returned to the Court of Common Pleas as a senior judge in

the homicide division.

Stout was born on March 7, 1919, in Wewoka, Oklahoma, the only
child of Henry M. and Mary Chandler Kidd. From her parents, who were

schoolteachers, she learned to be obedient, studious and, above all, "useful," her mother's favorite word. Her parents taught her to read by the time she was three and, when she was six, she started school in the third grade. She graduated at the head of her class in grade school and high school but had to leave Oklahoma at age sixteen to attend an accredited college. For two years, beginning in 1935, she studied at Lincoln University in Jefferson City, Missouri, then transferred to the University of Iowa in Iowa City to study music. Stout had studied piano diligently since she was five and she received a bachelor of arts degree in music in 1939. For two summers she did graduate study in piano at the University of Colorado in Boulder, Colorado, and at the University of Minnesota in Minneapolis.

At the age of twenty, Stout began her career as a teacher in Seminole, Oklahoma, where she taught grade school and high school music for two years at the Booker T. Washington High School. She also taught one year at Sand Springs, near Tulsa, Oklahoma. It was there she met her future husband, Charles Otis Stout, who taught history and Spanish and also assisted as boys' counselor. Although a few of Stout's students were older than she, and most of them were larger—she weighed only eighty-eight pounds—she believed that the first prerequisite for learning was order in the classroom and "order I was determined to have." Discipline, however, was the one shortcoming of her principal, "a wonderful, kindly man," who had built an excellent school with an enthusiastic faculty. Because of her future husband's commanding physical presence, she formed the habit of sending "the large boys who were troublesome" to him, and her discipline problems "began to fade away."

The relationship between the two teachers grew closer than either realized at that time. They spent much of their spare time together playing the piano and singing and playing bridge. After a year of teaching together, World War II broke out and they went their separate ways: he to the army and she to Washington, D.C., with another teacher from Sand Springs, Eula Mae Smith, and found employment as a secretary.

The two young ladies, in their early twenties, found Washington more exciting then Sand Springs, and decided to remain there. For a very brief period, Stout took a job with the National Housing Authority. After passing the examination for a job as junior professional assistant, which was the only qualification for the job, Stout observed that others were being given these jobs while she was not. After a heated and futile discussion with the personnel manager, Stout decided to quit rather than to stay in a job paying only eighteen hundred dollars a year. Good fortune, however, awaited her. That evening Smith told her that she had learned that the prominent law firm of Houston, Houston, and Hastie was seeking an additional secretary. Because Stout was excellent in typing and shorthand and also because she loved the law, she was hired. She worked directly with Charles Hamilton Houston, who inspired her and whom she still describes as "the best lawyer I have ever met."

When Stout left Sand Springs there were no plans for marriage. Before his first leave, however, her future husband located her through their former school principal. On his first leave, he went to Washington to renew his relationship with her. She says, "He never asked me to marry him. He just walked in and said 'We're getting married.' He never gave me a chance to say 'No'." On June 23, 1942, they were married.

• *Aspirations to*

law began early

Stout knew she wanted to be a lawyer from the time she was three years old. She had "never even seen a woman lawyer, never mind a black woman lawyer," she says. "I can't explain it even today. It was my dream."

Stout's legal training began at Howard University, but she transferred to Indiana University in Bloomington, Indiana, where her husband was completing his doctoral studies. This arrangement proved to be her golden opportunity to accomplish her dream of becoming a lawyer. She earned two law degrees: a doctor of jurisprudence in 1948 and a master of law, specializing in legislation, in 1954.

Stout passed the grueling Pennsylvania Bar examination in 1954 and went into private practice with Mabel G. Turner, who later became assistant U.S. attorney. In April 1956 Stout joined the Philadelphia district attorney's office. Three-and-one-half years later she was promoted to chief of the Appeals, Pardons, and Parole Division. During her tenure in this office she still maintained a private practice, limited to civil cases. Stout became the first black woman to sit on the bench in Philadelphia. Her appointment as judge of the municipal court was made by Governor David L. Lawrence in September 1959. In November of that year she ran in a citywide election and won a ten-year term—beating her opponent by a two-to-one margin—and thus became the nation's first elected black woman judge.

During the mid-1960s, while serving a brief period in the juvenile division of the court, Stout attracted national attention because of her handling of youth gang problems, which turned some neighborhoods into battlegrounds. *Life* magazine featured her in an article titled "Her Honor Bops the Hoodlums," which paid a special tribute to Philadelphia for having a "tough" but fair judge on the bench. However, she was criticized by the American Civil Liberties Union, which felt she paid insufficient attention to the "constitutional niceties" in meting out her "swift justice," according to *Time* magazine. Despite this criticism, which Stout says she doesn't understand, she has earned a reputation for her intellectual prowess. Many of her colleagues, *Ebony* reports, say that her special talent "is that she knows when to take the long-term view."

Stout is known among her peers for the clarity of her legal writing and opinions. She has published several articles, and she has been active in many professional and civic organizations. These include the American Judicature Society, American Bar Association, National Association of Women Lawyers, and the American Judges Association. She has held board memberships with Rockford College, Saint Augustine's College, the National Conference of Christians and Jews, and the Women's Medical College of Pennsylvania.

Stout's unique ability has been recognized by eleven universities that have awarded her honorary degrees, and she has received more than two hundred awards from professional and civic organizations. Recently, she was named the justice of the year by the National Association of Women Judges in 1988, and in 1989 she was awarded the Gimbel Award for Humanitarian Services by the Medical College of Pennsylvania and was named a distinguished daughter of Pennsylvania by Governor Robert P. Casey. Presidents John F. Kennedy and Lyndon B. Johnson each named her to missions to Africa. And on November 16, 1981, a very special event occurred: Her home state of Oklahoma—which had not admitted her to any of its accredited colleges or to its law school—inducted her into its Hall of Fame. She was inducted into the Oklahoma Women's Hall of Fame on November 18, 1983.

Stout is cognizant that her accomplishments are unprecedented but attributes them to the many people who have helped her along the way, especially her parents, who taught her the value of education and moral living, and to the unswerving support of her husband, Charles Otis Stout, who died August 15, 1988. Stout continues to find pleasure in forming new legal theories and in applying the law in a manner "that will serve people, make for the overall good, and be useful to American society."

**Profile by
Emery Wimbish, Jr.**

NIARA SUDARKASA

*O*n September 29, 1986, the Board of Trustees at Lincoln University

announced that from a field of 103 candidates, Niara Sudarkasa had

been unanimously chosen as president of that historic black academic

institution. Lincoln, founded in 1854, is the oldest of America's black

colleges established and maintained on the original site to develop into a

baccalaureate degree-granting institution. In the history of this famed

institution, Sudarkasa is the first woman to be appointed president. Her

inauguration was held on October 1, 1987. At the ceremony one of the

committee members said, "When we looked around to find the best man

we could for this position, we discovered that he was a woman."

Sudarkasa's devotion to higher education for people of African
descent is only one of her many qualifications; she is a guiding light for

1938- •

university •

president,

anthropologist

black scholars whose future has been jeopardized by political decisions and racism. She values higher learning but places the importance of peace above that of education: "As concerned as we are about education, our paramount concern is for peace."

On August 14, 1938, in Fort Lauderdale, Florida, Gloria Albertha Marshall was born to George and Rowena Marshall. She has three brothers. Her mother was a silkfinisher and presser in New York City, and her father was in the United States Army. They later separated and then divorced. Her stepfather, Alex Charlton, owned a cocktail lounge in Fort Lauderdale. Growing up in Florida, Sudarkasa was often called a "Nassau" because her grandparents were from the Bahamas.

While living in Florida, Sudarkasa attended Dillard High School from 1948 to 1952, where she was an honor student. At age fourteen she won a Ford Foundation Early Entrant Scholarship to Fisk University in Nashville, Tennessee. In her junior year at Fisk she went to Oberlin College as a semester exchange student, where she subsequently decided to apply for admission to the college of arts and science, and Oberlin accepted her as a transfer student. She became active with WOBC (Oberlin's radio station), the Interracial Committee, and the Young Democrats.

At the age of eighteen in 1957, Sudarkasa graduated from Oberlin College with a bachelor of arts degree in sociology, ranking in the top ten percent of her class. She went to Columbia University in New York, where she earned a master's degree in anthropology in 1959, after which she was awarded the John Hay Whitney Opportunity Fellowship to pursue a Ph.D. In 1960-63 she received a Ford Foundation Foreign Area Training Fellowship to study the Yoruba language and the role of Yoruba women in the markets, first at the University of London School of Oriental and African Studies, then in Nigeria. In 1963-64 she became a fellow with the Carnegie Foundation Study of New Nations at the University of Chicago, where she served on the Committee for the Comparative Study of New Nations. Sudarkasa received her Ph.D. in anthropology from Columbia University in 1964.

Sudarkasa taught at Columbia University as a visiting faculty member and then at New York University in 1964. In 1967 she moved to the University of Michigan in Ann Arbor, where she served for twenty years and became the first black woman to be promoted to full professor in the division of arts and sciences.

Sudarkasa's academic activities at the University of Michigan were matched by her political activism. Describing her role in *I Dream a World,* she stated:

- *Sudarkasa*

promoted in

academia

I was a vocal spokesperson for all the things that the students were advocating in those days, the early seventies: black studies, more black and minority students in the university. At Michigan I became the activist I had not been in the sixties, and most people knew me there as an activist-scholar.

Sudarkasa's academic research has made her an internationally acclaimed anthropologist. She has more than thirty scholarly publications to her credit. Further, she has conducted research in Nigeria, Ghana, and the Republic of Benin. She is a recognized authority in the fields of African women, especially Yoruba women traders, West African migration, and the African-American and African family. Sudarkasa has applied her study of West African culture to that of the African-American family structure, with emphasis on the role of black women within the family and society. She has also studied higher education policies for black Americans and other minorities, and she is an advocate for minority access to education at the university level.

Anthropologist •

studies Yoruba

women

Like the black family, black women have been severely criticized and blamed because of their roles in the family and society. Sudarkasa's research shows that African-American women's active participation has roots in pre-colonial Africa. Unlike their European counterparts, African women traditionally have been more active in economic and social activities outside the home, and they participate equally in family responsibilities.

Sudarkasa notes also that the sexism that is prevalent in Africa today is a result of Western disruption of traditional economic systems. Introduction of Western technology eliminated many traditional jobs; thus, women have been denied access to the necessary education to qualify for the new types of employment. With distribution of jobs on the basis of sex, those jobs that women dominate are classified as low status and are poorly financed. Sudarkasa stresses that Africa cannot expect to advance if the importance of women's contribution is denied and women are deprived of their rights in the social and economic sphere.

Sudarkasa also stresses that in order for black Americans to achieve in the United States, black students must have access to quality higher education. She has devoted her life to ensuring that educational opportunities are available to blacks and other minority students. She strongly believes in the necessity of black institutions of higher learning because they are unique in their ability to teach students of African descent to survive in a racist society.

493 •

Since 1977 Sudarkasa has shared her life with her husband, John L. Clark, an inventor, sculptor, and contractor, and their son, Michael, born on August 5, 1964. Of her husband, she said to Elsie B. Washington: "Everybody has told me that he is the anchor I needed." Sudarkasa and Clark are both willing to compromise for the other when necessary. Before Sudarkasa was asked to accept the presidency at Lincoln, John Clark wanted to relocate to the Republic of Benin to start a construction company and to work on his inventions. They agreed that whoever got the opportunity first would accept it and the other would follow. Her offer from Lincoln came first, so they moved to Lincoln University, Pennsylvania.

• *Sudarkasa*

assumes

university

presidency

As president of Lincoln University, Sudarkasa intends to carry its long tradition of educational excellence into the twenty-first century. She promotes the university's strong science reputation and its international studies program. She makes herself accessible to the students, who fondly refer to her as Madame President.

Sudarkasa's mission is to prepare Lincoln graduates to walk in the shoes of alumni like Thurgood Marshall and Nnamdi Azikiwe: "These men graduated with a sense of mission. . . . They wanted to make a contribution to African people—to better our condition." She would like to convey this same sense of urgency to today's students. Sudarkasa also plans to preserve the institution's ties to the African continent.

The cultural ties with Africa that she discovered at Oberlin College led Sudarkasa to affirm her association with the African continent. Brian Lanker records her feeling that the continent is the home she does not have in America: "I felt that [America] was my country but not my land. But when I went to West Africa, I had the deep sense not only of belonging, but of possession. This was ours! The whole continent was ours!" She adopted an African name, in addition to Gloria Marshall Clark, to symbolize her ties to the continent. "The word 'nia' in Swahili means purpose. So Niara was an adaptation and the name was given to me to mean a woman of high purpose." The name "Sudarkasa" came by marriage.

President Sudarkasa's inaugural gown also symbolized her ties to Africa. It is royal-blue appliqued and trimmed with blue and gold kente, with matching cap. The kente cloth was given to her mother, who is now deceased, when she visited Ghana in 1968. Sudarkasa used some of that kente cloth for her inaugural robe in 1987, as she told Washington:

> Something told me to use the kente in the robe. I saw it
> as a way of having my mother always with me. I also
> reflected on the connections of the kente with Ghana

and Kwame Nkrumah, that country's first president and one of Lincoln's greatest sons. Having the kente on my robe was a magnificent coming together of many things.

Sudarkasa has received numerous awards, fellowships, and grants, and she has long been active in a number of organizations, including the American Anthropological Association, the Association of Black Anthropologists, the American Ethnological Society, and the African Studies Association.

**Profile by
D. Stewart and
A. L. Jones**

SUSAN L. TAYLOR

Something so delicious is happening in Black America. We're only

120 years up from slavery. We are doing incredibly well if we look at the

fact that the people we're comparing ourselves with have been in this [rat]

race for 400 years with all of the assets, all of the support. We've been

running that same race with shackles on our ankles trying to hold us

back."

1946- •

editor, •

television

host

Few American women of any race have the style and finesse of Susan L. Taylor, who wrote the above passage in 1986. As editor-in-chief of *Essence* magazine, she exudes a glowing personal energy that enhances her strikingly beautiful appearance. This magnetism, coupled with old-fashioned intelligence and foresight, has gotten Taylor where she is today. Along with editing *Essence,* she is also vice president of Essence Communications and past host and producer of the Essence television show. The magazine has a readership of fifty thousand, with revenues of more than twenty million. The television show was the first nationally syndicated black-oriented magazine show and ran for four seasons in more than sixty countries.

This is a far cry from Taylor's early days. Born on January 23, 1946, in Harlem, the daughter of a shopkeeper and a homemaker, she became a licensed cosmetologist and dabbled in acting with the Negro Ensemble Company before joining *Essence* as a free-lance beauty writer in 1970. A year later she was named the magazine's beauty editor, and the following year her position was expanded to include both fashion and beauty.

Much of Taylor's life exemplifies the kinds of triumphant struggles *Essence* readers know intimately. The determination to advance personally and professionally and the desire to promote positive images and take pride in one's accomplishments are values Taylor shares with her readers. These are reflected in her editorial column "In the Spirit" and in the kinds of topics regularly covered by *Essence*. Taylor notes that the magazine was among the first to deal editorially with incest, cocaine, heroin, and rape. Recent issues have run the gamut from an interview with Winnie Mandela to romantic meals for two, male/female relationships, hair styling tips, spa and European vacations, and facial bleaching.

She sees the two Essences—magazine and television show—as having two different missions, as she told the *Detroit News:* "The magazine is a hands-on, how-to vehicle for helping black women move their lives forward," she said, while "the television show [was] aimed at everyone to project a positive image of black Americans. People tend to have negative views of what black people are all about."

Taylor, who has been a strong source of inspiration at many college seminars, shares her secret of inner strength in *Excel:*

> My day starts with quiet time about 6 a.m. I meditate. It's not any formal kind of meditation. It's just getting centered. I try to tap into that spiritual side of me. Cause when I go out without that intact, I get crazy, befuddled, and depressed. I read some psalms or the Lord's Prayer just to affirm some things for myself; that I am gonna move through this day from the highest perspective—that I'm going to be a problem solver and not fall victim to the things I see. That's what I have to tell myself.

● *Lifestyle*

magazine for

black women

When asked what *Essence* means to her personally, she has often pointed to society's negligence: "Imagine yourself as a white woman, wanting to buy a magazine and seeing black faces on every cover," she once told the *Detroit News*. "Wouldn't you feel isolated and ignored?" Evoking this uncomfortable picture clearly tells all of Taylor's frustration before spring 1970, when *Essence* became the first lifestyle magazine devoted to black women. The *Los Angeles Times* quoted her:

I was so happy I didn't know whether to read it or hug it. Let's be real. We live in a racist society, and that makes it difficult to keep our faith high. . . . There is little to remind us daily of how powerful and capable we are, so we must do that for ourselves and for each other. . . . We can make a difference in our lives and in the world. We black folks have to believe this is true. It's time to dream big dreams and make them real.

Taylor likes to talk with people about taking charge of their lives and moving forward so that they can begin to believe they can excel. Explaining in the *Los Angeles Times* what life was like when she became a single mother, she said:

I've come from a place where I didn't believe in myself. I had no money, no man, my car was broken. I was making $500 a month working at *Essence* and paying $368 a month for rent. I could not see tomorrow.

What turned it around for her, she said, was a conversation with a minister who implored her to believe in herself. "Nobody had ever said that to me," she said.

Taylor personifies the *Essence* woman in much the same way Helen Gurley Brown personifies *Cosmopolitan*. But she still remains close to home in her heart. "There's still that little girl in me that jumped double-dutch on 116th Street. I want to keep her alive."

Taylor is a member of the National Association of Black Journalists, the Society of Professional Journalists, the American Society of Magazine Editors, the Alliance Directors Resource Council for the National Women's Economic Alliance Foundation, and Women in Communications. She is a board member of the Edwin Gould Services for Children, an adoption and foster-care agency. She has received the Women in Communications Matrix Award and an honorary Doctorate of Humane Letters from Lincoln University in 1988, among many other awards.

Her personal commitment is to empower the poor, to work with women in prison, and to work with teenage mothers to help them realize their strengths and take charge of their lives. She earned a bachelor's degree in social science and economics from Fordham University in 1990 in New York City. Recently married to Kephera Burns, she has one daughter, Shana, age twenty-one.

**Profile by
Dianne Marshall**

SUSIE BAKER KING TAYLOR

*A*mong the legacies of the nineteenth century, the names of only a

few women of color are found in American history books. Harriet

Tubman, the fugitive slave, Underground Railroad conductor, Civil

War spy and nurse, and women's activist, is usually considered to be the

most prominent woman of her era. Other worthy black women frequent-

ly listed include Mary McLeod Bethune and Sojourner Truth. Susie

Baker King Taylor, however, is rarely mentioned, although her writings

alone warrant attention. This former slave, Civil War nurse, teacher,

and author is one of the many unsung heroes of the late nineteenth

century.

1848-1912 •

nurse, •

activist,

author

    Like many of her counterparts, Taylor was born a slave and died a
free woman. Unlike most of her contemporaries, she was raised in an

intact household that was able to maintain the family structure. She knew her family as well as its history, which extended back to a great-great-grandmother. This young woman grew up a member of a proud family, and she displayed abilities normally denied to the slave community. Taylor was able to leave the plantation to visit and eventually live with her grandmother, and she could read, write, and sew before she was nine.

In 1820 Taylor's maternal grandmother, Dolly, was born. She married Fortune Lambert Reed some thirteen years later and gave birth to two children: James, who died when he was twelve, and Hagar Ann, Taylor's mother. Born in 1834, Hagar Ann married Raymond Baker in 1847. They had nine children; six survived. While it is not clear whether Raymond Baker was a slave, his wife and children were held in bondage. Susie, born on August 5, 1848, was their first child. Apparently she lived with her mother on the Grest farm on the Isle of Wight in Liberty County, Georgia, some thirty-five miles from the city of Savannah. Both Dolly Reed and Hagar Baker developed important relationships with their masters that were crucial to Taylor's development. Dolly Reed was hired out and allowed to live in Savannah under the supervision of a guardian. Similarly, Hagar Ann Baker was a well-liked house servant and privy to special considerations.

- *Young slave*

taught to read

and write

When Taylor was seven, Mr. Grest allowed Dolly Reed to take her and a younger sister and brother to raise in Savannah. Although it was against the law, their grandmother sent Taylor and her brother to a free woman's home to learn to read and write. In 1860 Taylor began her informal education, sometimes turning to neighboring white children. The first of these illegal tutors was Katie O'Connor, who volunteered to teach Taylor if she promised not to tell her father; the two young women met every evening over a four-month period until O'Connor entered a convent. James Blouis, the son of Dolly Reed's landlord, served as the second tutor until he was sent to the battlefront in the middle of 1861.

From the onset of the Civil War, Dolly Reed went to meetings and discussed current events with other knowledgeable citizens. On several occasions, Taylor accompanied her grandmother and developed her own opinions. Almost immediately, Taylor was pressed into action and used her skills by writing passes for slaves and free blacks alike. Unfortunately, such contributions came to an abrupt end following a police raid on a suburban church meeting, where Dolly Reed was arrested and handed over to her guardian. On April 1, 1862, Taylor was sent back to her mother on the Grest farm.

As the war raged around Savannah and several area forts, the fear of the Yankees increased. When Fort Pulaski fell to the Union troops,

Taylor, an uncle, and several members of his family escaped to St. Catherine Island. They were placed under the protection of the Union fleet and remained on the island for roughly two weeks. With thirty other African-Americans, Taylor and her family were then transported to St. Simon's Island.

During the voyage to St. Simon's Island, Taylor had her first conversation with a Yankee, Captain Whitmore, the commander of the boat. He asked the fourteen-year-old Taylor where she was from and if she could read or write or sew. When convinced of her abilities, the captain replied, "You seem to be so different from the other colored people who came from the same place you did." Taylor responded, "No! The only difference is, they were reared in the country and I in the city."

Just three days after her arrival on St. Simon's Island, a Commodore Goldsborough approached Taylor about operating a small school on the island. Upon receiving the necessary supplies, she started a school at Gaston Bluff. Her earliest groups consisted of two sessions. She taught forty children during the day and a handful of eager adults at night; the school operated for most of 1862.

Unknown to Taylor and the other African-American refugees on the Sea Islands, they were part of an experiment in freedom. While President Lincoln maintained a strict policy of retaining slavery to preserve the Union, the Union officers clearly disregarded the orders. With the assistance of northern missionaries, the soldiers distributed some of the confiscated lands and convinced blacks to resume cotton production. In her role as a teacher, Taylor made an important contribution by preparing members of her race for their eventual emancipation.

Slaves •

prepared for

emancipation

As the war waged on along the Georgia coast, it became obvious to the Union officers that the outpost on St. Simon's Island was not secure. In the late fall of 1862, a decision was made to evacuate the black residents, and Taylor was relocated to Camp Saxton in Beauford, South Carolina. The school came to an end, and Taylor was recruited to serve as a laundress. She was assigned to Company E, the First South Carolina Volunteers, an all-black unit led by white officers and the first black regiment formed in the South, an outgrowth of the experiments waged by Lincoln's pro-abolition generals. Supported by General David Hunter, General Rufus Saxton formed the regiment from free blacks and fugitive slaves who wanted to fight for the freedom of their race. Captain, later Colonel, C. T. Trowbridge was responsible for the enlistment of many of the recruits, and in 1863, Harvard-educated Thomas Wentworth Higginson took command of the regiment.

Following the response to the reading of the Emancipation Proclamation in 1863, President Lincoln agreed to the involvement of blacks in the conflict and authorized the formation of the United States Colored Troops. The USCT became the all-black regiments under the control of the Union army. They would be led by northern white officers, including colonels Robert Gould Shaw and Thomas Wentworth Higginson, Bostonians of great social prominence. Company E became the Thirty-third Regiment of the USCT. While morale in these regiments was extremely high, conditions were poor. Taylor reported that despite the support of their commanding officers, the black troops were ill-clad, were not paid for eighteen months, and then were given a lower salary than were white troops. She proudly related that although General Saxton provided services to some of the needier soldiers from his own funds, the men refused their wages until they received equal compensation.

Taylor remained with the regiment throughout the course of the war and dedicated all her time and energies to those who fought for freedom. Members of her family, including several uncles and cousins, joined the regiment. However, in her eyes, the most important member of the regiment was Sergeant Edward King. Also from Georgia, Edward King had lived in the city. After escaping from his master, he joined the First South Carolina Volunteers. Although Taylor had known Sergeant King before arriving in Beaufort, the two became very close during the war, and they eventually married.

• *King becomes*

camp nurse

Taylor, now fifteen, was gaining responsibilities beyond her original charge. She was taught how to use and care for a rifle, and during her spare time she cooked meals for the wounded and taught eager soldiers how to read and write. As the war pressed on, these duties multiplied. Due to an increasing number of casualties, Taylor began a new occupation as a camp nurse, an indirect result of her participation as a laundress. While caring for the uniforms, bandages, and other supplies, she began to assist the military surgeons. Her voluntary duties included the soothing of the sick and other tasks assigned by the doctors. Later, when the need for competent persons increased, she donated the majority of her time to this task. She proved to be an excellent practitioner, and the soldiers were constantly thanking her for her care. Regardless of their company, she treated all of the men the same. When her kindness was noted, Taylor replied, "You are all doing the same duty, and I will do just the same for you."

Perhaps one of her greatest memories of the war was meeting Clara Barton, the founder of the American Red Cross. The two met during Barton's stay at the hospital in Beaufort in the summer of 1863. In the course of Taylor's hospital visits, the two women conversed. Taylor enjoyed these encounters and wrote: "Miss Barton was always very cordial toward me, and I honored her for her devotion and care of those men."

Despite her efforts during the war, Taylor received no pay or certificate of service, and since she was not officially credited as a Union nurse, she was also denied a post-war pension. Following the Union victory, however, the Kings started their life together. They returned to Savannah, where Taylor settled in as a housewife, and—due to racial prejudice—Edward took a job as a longshoreman although he was a boss carpenter by trade. Taylor's inactivity was short-lived, however. Since there was no school for black Americans within the community, she established one in her home, with twenty day pupils and several night students, each of whom she charged a dollar per month.

On September 16, 1866, Taylor's world was shattered. Edward King was killed in an accident unloading vessels at the pier. Not yet twenty, Taylor was a widow and an expectant mother. In December her condition and the arrival of the Beach Institute, a free school, forced her to stop teaching. Shortly after the birth of her son, she resumed her work, briefly operating a country school in Liberty County. Within a year, however, she relinquished control of the school to a Susie Carter.

Once back in Savannah, her enthusiasm returned. With the assistance of her brother-in-law, Taylor ran a night school for adults, but the following year this school was also forced to close when the Beach Institute started another free evening program. Facing mounting financial difficulties, Taylor sought assistance. She placed her son with her mother and applied for Edward King's army pension of one hundred dollars. Upon receiving the money, she placed some of it in the Freedmen's Bank, only to lose her savings when the bank collapsed.

While waiting for her claim, she worked as a laundress for Mrs. Charles Green. In 1873 the Greens relocated to Rye Beach for the summer and took Taylor as their cook. It was her first time in the North, a place she had only heard about from the white officers. To Taylor, Boston was a magical city, and she was captivated by its charm and relative lack of prejudice. This first exposure to northern living left a lasting impression. In 1874 she returned to Boston, this time in the employ of the James Barnards. Although she would make several trips back to the South, Boston became her home. In 1879 she met and married Russell L. Taylor.

As late as 1886, Susie Taylor was still influenced by the Civil War. In that year her undying patriotic fever led to the organization of Corps Sixty-seven, Women's Relief Corps, auxiliary to the Grand Army of the

Republic. Taylor was loyal to the organization she helped to found, serving as a guard, secretary, treasurer, and in 1893 as president. In 1896 she was involved in another war-related venture: she compiled a list of war veterans living in Massachusetts, locating both black and white soldiers who had been forgotten by their peers. Her work was respected and within the veteran's association she was highly admired.

Tragedy struck again in 1898. Taylor lost her father in 1867, her grandmother in 1889, and she learned that her son was seriously ill in Louisiana. He was an actor traveling with Nickens and Company and had been performing in *The Lion's Bride* when he was taken ill in January and became bedridden in Shreveport. As he could not travel to Boston, Taylor went south to take care of him. A great hatred of southern culture stirred within Taylor upon encountering racist behavior during her rail trip to Shreveport, and after the lynching she witnessed on her return home after her son's death.

- ***Autobiography***

relates racial

progress

In 1901 Taylor finished a manuscript about her life. The book, *Reminiscences of My Life in Camp*, was more than an autobiography; it was a personal account of the struggles and achievements of Americans, particularly black Americans, from the Civil War to the turn of the century. Although she highlighted some of the accomplishments of blacks since the war, the legacy of racism and discrimination was a theme in the second half of the work. Many of her comments were influenced by her travels, especially the trip to Shreveport. Taylor believed that racism was a national problem but felt it was much more pronounced in the South. On the subject of racism and progress she wrote:

> I wonder if our white fellow men realize the true sense or meaning of brotherhood? For two hundred years we had toiled for them; the war of 1861 came and was ended, and we thought our race was forever free from bondage, and that the two races could live in unity with each other, but when we read almost every day of what is done to my race by some whites in the South, I sometimes ask, "Was the war in vain? Has it brought freedom, in the full sense of the word, or has it not made our condition more hopeless?"

> In this "land of the free" we are burned, tortured, and denied a fair trial, murdered for any imaginary wrong conceived in the brain of the negro-hating white man. There is no redress for us from a government which promised to protect all under its flag. . . . No, we

cannot sing, "My country 'tis of thee, Sweet land of Liberty!" It is hollow mockery.

Taylor published the manuscript in 1902. Although there were no reviewers of the work or records of its sales, presumably distribution was limited. Most of the purchases were probably made by fellow clubwomen and their families.

Following the publication of *Reminiscences,* there is virtually nothing known about the activities of Taylor. In all probability, she continued to work as a domestic and spent her free time involved with war organizations. Before the publication of the book, Russell Taylor died, and it is apparent that Taylor remained alone. On the morning of October 6, 1912, the landlady making her rounds at the rooming house where Taylor lived found her body slumped near her bed. Taylor was buried in Boston's Mount Hope Cemetery with an unmarked headstone. The local papers did not carry an obituary or a funeral notice for this teacher, nurse, author, and organizer.

**Profile by
Leslie Wilson**

MARY CHURCH TERRELL

*D*uring Mary Church Terrell's long and notable life, it seemed that

1863-1954 •

there was very little she didn't attempt in order to improve the social,

economic, and political conditions of black Americans. Her excellent

writer, •

education and her travels abroad helped equip her for a career that

lecturer,

began with teaching and continued with leadership positions in the

educator

Colored Women's League and later the National Association of Colored

Women. Terrell worked vigorously for women's suffrage and women's

rights, particularly black women's rights.

She was an internationally known speaker and lecturer, a widely published writer, a member of numerous boards and associations, a founding member of a church in Washington, D.C., an active member of the Republican party, and a charter member of the NAACP. Terrell led and won the fight to desegregate Washington, D.C., a struggle that was finally resolved in 1953, just a year before her death.

Mary Eliza Church Terrell, born in Memphis, Tennessee, on September 23, 1863, was the eldest child of Louisa (Ayers) Church and Robert Reed Church, both former slaves. Terrell's early schooling was in Memphis, but schools for black children there were so inadequate that her parents decided to send her to the Antioch College Model School in Yellow Springs, Ohio, when she was about six years old, where she was often the only black child among her classmates. She boarded with a kind black family, the Hunsters, and when she was older, divided her summers between her parents' homes. After two years at the Model School, Mary attended public school in Yellow Springs, then began eighth grade at the public high school in Oberlin, Ohio, graduating in 1879.

At Oberlin College, Terrell was one of several black students. One of the few integrated institutions of higher learning in the United States, it had first opened its doors to blacks in 1835. Most women at Oberlin chose the two-year ladies' curriculum, but Terrell decided to pursue the "gentleman's course"—four years of classical studies. She performed well in classes and was active in many campus activities, including bible studies, the church choir, literary societies, and various recreational activities such as dancing. She graduated in 1884, and in 1929 she was named among the one hundred most successful students to graduate from Oberlin.

• Teaching

career

launched

When she accepted a job in Ohio at Wilberforce College in 1885, her father was livid and refused to speak to her for almost a year—he had strictly forbidden her to pursue a career. Although pained by the estrangement, Terrell nevertheless pursued her goal, teaching five different courses and acting as the college secretary. They did eventually reconcile, however, and he later relinquished all efforts to keep her from a professional career.

Following Wilberforce, Terrell accepted a position in the Latin department of the Colored High School in Washington, D.C. There she worked under the direction of Robert Heberton Terrell, who had graduated with honors from Harvard College in 1884. While she was working in the District of Columbia she completed the requirements for a master of arts degree from Oberlin, which she received in 1888. She spent two years—from 1888 to 1890—traveling and studying in France, Germany, Switzerland, Italy, and England, relishing the cultural opportunities that were open to her in Europe because of the freedom from racial tensions.

After she returned to the United States, she was soon convinced that she should marry Terrell, who had finished his law degree at Howard University while she was gone. She was momentarily tempted to postpone the planning for the wedding because she received an offer to work as the registrar at Oberlin College, a position of responsibility that she believed no other black person had ever held at any predominantly white institution of higher education. However, she decided to marry Terrell as scheduled in October 1891. Her father gave her an elaborate ceremony in Memphis that received favorable coverage in both white- and black-owned newspapers.

Robert Terrell taught at M Street High School in Washington, D.C., from 1884 to 1889 and served as principal of the school ten years later from 1899 to 1901. He was admitted to the bar in 1883 and opened a law firm with John Roy Lynch, a black man who had served in the United States House of Representatives during the Reconstruction period. In 1889 he was appointed chief of division, Office of the Fourth Auditor of the Treasury Department. From 1911 until 1925, Terrell was an instructor in law at Howard University, but his most outstanding accomplishment was his appointment in 1902 as judge of the District of Columbia Municipal Court (called Justice of the Peace Courts until 1901), a position to which he was appointed consecutively by four presidents—Democrat and Republican—until his death in 1925.

Because married women were legally barred from working as teachers, Terrell dedicated herself to managing her household. During the early years of her marriage, she was depressed by three miscarriages that she attributed to poor medical facilities for blacks and finally traveled to New York to be with her mother when she gave birth to a healthy baby girl, Phyllis (named after Phillis Wheatley, the black poet), in 1898. Later, in 1905, the Terrells adopted her brother Thomas's daughter, who had been named after her aunt, Terrell Church.

The primary event that drove Terrell back into the political and professional arena was the 1892 lynching of her lifelong friend from Memphis, Tom Moss, who was murdered by whites jealous of the success of his grocery store. Never had such blatant injustice struck Terrell so personally. She and Frederick Douglass were able to make an appointment with President Benjamin Harrison to urge him to speak out forcibly about such racial violence. Although the president gave them a sympathetic hearing, he made no public statement.

In the same year, 1892, Terrell assumed the leadership of a new group formed in the District of Columbia, the Colored Women's League. Three years later black women in Boston under the leadership of Josephine St. Pierre Ruffin formed the Federation of Afro-American Women. Margaret Murray Washington, the wife of Booker T. Washington, was elected president of the Boston organization. In 1896 the two groups, along with other black women's organizations, merged to become the National Association of Colored Women and elected Terrell as the first president. Thus began one of the endeavors for which Terrell would become most well-known—the fight for equal rights for women in general and black women in particular. She was later elected to a second and a third term and then named honorary president for life. One of the women's early endeavors was to establish kindergartens and day nurseries for black working mothers—an effort that continues to this day. They also were concerned with equal rights for blacks, work opportunities for black women, female suffrage, and the criminal justice system. During her many years of work with the association, Terrell came into contact with most of the black women leaders, such as Mary McLeod Bethune and Nannie Helen Burroughs.

In 1898 she delivered a speech before the National American Women's Suffrage Association entitled "The Progress of Colored Women" and in 1900 gave a thirty-minute presentation before the same group entitled "Justice of Women Suffrage." In 1904 she spoke at the Berlin International Congress of Women, at which she was the only representative of the darker races of the world; she impressed audiences with her ability to speak French and German. In 1919 she addressed the delegates of the International League for Peace and Freedom, meeting in Zurich, and in 1937 she represented black American women at the World Fellowship of Faiths held in London. Meeting with women's groups both at home and abroad, Terrell had the opportunity to become acquainted with many of the leaders of suffrage organizations, including Susan B. Anthony, Alice Paul, Carrie Chapman Catt, and Jane Addams. In the years leading up to the passage of the Nineteenth Amendment, Terrell and her daughter marched with suffrage groups, picketed in front of the White House, and pointed out to some of their white counterparts the inconsistency of their lukewarm stance about suffrage for black women.

In addition to Terrell's ongoing work with both black and white women's organizations, she was recruited in the 1890s by the Slayton Lyceum Bureau (also called the Eastern Lyceum) to be a professional lecturer. She composed a number of speeches on subjects such as black women's progress since Emancipation, racial injustice, lynching, female suffrage, economics, crime, and various aspects of black history and culture. While preparing and practicing her addresses Terrell became interested in publishing articles on a wide variety of social issues. Early in her career she wrote under the pen name Euphemia Kirk, but soon abandoned it and used her own name. Copies of many of her publications are among the Mary Church Terrell papers in the Manuscript Division of the Library of Congress.

In 1895 Terrell was appointed to the District of Columbia School Board, served until 1901, was reappointed in 1906 and served five more years until 1911. One of the first black women in the country to serve in such a capacity, she was worked for equal treatment of black students and faculty members in Washington's segregated school system. She was also the first black woman to be elected to the presidency of the Bethel Literary and Historical Association in Washington, D.C., serving the 1892-93 term, and was one of the early members of the Association for the Study of Negro (later Afro-American) Life and History, which was organized in 1915.

Terrell vacillated in her feelings toward the Booker T. Washington philosophy of accommodation and industrial education, but after visiting Tuskegee Institute she decided that Washington was doing great work; thereafter she generally supported his strategies and programs. However, several years later, in 1901, when the NAACP was organized, Terrell became a charter member of that organization at the invitation of W. E. B. DuBois, Washington's intellectual rival, and cooperated with DuBois's more militant political tactics.

In 1911 Terrell helped organize a birthday centenary celebration in memory of abolitionist Harriet Beecher Stowe, author of *Uncle Tom's Cabin*. A few years later, after the United States entered World War I, Terrell worked at the War Risk Insurance Bureau, where she soon became involved in a protest about the treatment of black women. Soon after the armistice, Terrell worked for a short time with the War Camp Community Service as the director of work among black women and girls. In 1920 she was asked by the Republican National Committee to be the supervisor of the work among black women in the east. Terrell continued to work with the Republican party, campaigning in 1929 for Ruth Hannah McCormick, who ran unsuccessfully for United States senator from Illinois. In 1932 Terrell served as an advisor to the Republican National Committee during the Hoover campaign. She remained a Republican until 1952, when she decided to vote for Democratic presidential candidate Adlai Stevenson.

In 1940, the culmination of Terrell's writing career involved the publication of her autobiography, *A Colored Woman in a White World*, with a preface by H. G. Wells. In this work she traced her life from early childhood days, emphasizing her experiences growing up and living in white-dominated America. In 1949, Terrell was elected chair of the Coordinating Committee for the Enforcement of District of Columbia Anti-Discrimination Laws. These laws, forbidding discrimination in the district's public accommodations, had been passed in 1872 and 1873 and never repealed. Segregated public facilities had become the norm in the

Famous •

book

published

nation's capital, and blacks who attempted to integrate were fined or jailed. The coordinating committee, under Terrell's direction, decided to test the laws both in practice and in court. Terrell joined a small demonstration in the city targeting Thompson's Restaurant, which refused to serve the group. The group sued, and the case went all the way to the Supreme Court, where Terrell had the opportunity to testify in behalf of the cause of equal accommodations. The committee won the case in 1953, and the desegregation of the capital was set in motion.

One of Terrell's last major crusades was in behalf of Rosa Ingram, a black sharecropper from Georgia, who was sentenced to death along with her two sons for killing a white man who had assaulted them. Terrell agreed to head the National Committee to Free the Ingram Family. She led a delegation to the United Nations where she spoke in the Ingram's behalf and then traveled to Georgia in an unsuccessful attempt to win a pardon from the state governor. After a decade-long campaign, the Ingrams were finally freed in 1959, five years after Terrell's death.

Terrell died on July 24, 1954, a scant two months after the Supreme Court's *Brown* v. *Board of Education* decision sounded the death knell of segregation in the United States. Her funeral was held on Thursday, July 29, at one o'clock in the afternoon at the Lincoln Temple Congregational Church, where she had been a member for many years. She was buried in Lincoln Memorial Cemetery.

Terrell had been honored many times during her long life for her accomplishments and had received honorary doctorates from Howard University, Wilberforce and Oberlin colleges, and numerous citations and plaques from the organizations she had worked with or supported. A Washington, D.C., school was named in her honor, and many black women's clubs are named in her memory.

**Profile by
Debra
Newman Ham**

JACKIE TORRENCE

ackie Torrence has been on the road as a teller of tales for the past

seventeen years. She has been described as "a new breed of storyteller—

the professional—who chooses to make a living travelling throughout

the nation spinning tales to all who will listen." What prompted her to

use her creative talents as an outstanding exponent of the oral tradition

is a story containing within itself some of the essential ingredients

inherent in a folktale.

1944- •

"The Story Lady" •

Born February 12, 1944, in Chicago, Illinois, Torrence spent much of her early childhood on Second Creek near Salisbury, North Carolina. Living in this farming settlement with her grandparents, she experienced both happiness and sadness. Through a warm family relationship with her older kin, she remembered being "surrounded by a family who told lovely old stories," she recounted in *Homespun.* With fondness she recalled her grandfather, Jim Carson, son of a slave. Known affectionately as "Mister Jim," he spun innumerable tales to her as they spent hours together. While her grandmother baked bread in an old wood cookstove, she responded with more tales to her ever-curious, questioning grand-

515 •

daughter. From such a legacy Torrence can rightfully claim, "I know stories Uncle Remus never heard of."

Her departure from Second Creek occurred when she was ready to enter school in Salisbury. Living with her Aunt Mildred, who had never married, she was a lonely girl who was limited in opportunities to make friends. In school she endured the taunts and ridicule of her classmates because of a speech impediment. Fortunately for Torrence, she found an outlet from these traumatic experiences through the sensitive intervention of two dedicated teachers. In a poignant reflective note, she recalls in *Homespun* these bittersweet days:

> You see, I was a fat child, had no daddy, and felt unattractive. . . . In the fifth grade, I realized I didn't talk like everyone else. I had a speech impediment [and] . . . whenever I began to talk, it sounded as though I had rocks in my mouth, and the other kids laughed at me. I was shattered.

Helping her to overcome this obstacle and to regain a sense of self-worth, her teacher, Pauline Pharr, encouraged her to write stories that she would read to the class as a substitute for Torrence. Together, these two shared her creative efforts with the other children, and, for once, Torrence became a figure in her own right.

Through an accident when she was struck in her mouth with a thrown bottle, it was discovered that Torrence had a dental abnormality. She had impacted teeth—an unusual occurrence of a complete set of extra teeth in her mouth that prevented her from speaking clearly. When this defect was corrected, her ability to express herself improved over the next four years in high school. This progress occurred during and after school hours with the careful guidance and selfless support of her English teacher, Abna Aggrey Lancaster. In a personal tribute to this extraordinary individual, Torrence called her "one of the most incredible people I have ever met." In Brian Lanker's *I Dream a World,* Torrence explained: "She will tell you that she never taught school, she taught students. . . . Mrs. Lancaster gave me the courage to stand in front of an audience and to say what I wanted to say and do what I wanted to do."

The ability to perform before an audience was nurtured during her high school years when she read the Scriptures in the school assembly programs. Completing her secondary education, Torrence matriculated at Livingstone College. Finding sororities too expensive, she became a member of the Drama Club, where she starred in Lorraine Hansberry's play *A Raisin in the Sun.* Encouraged by her success in this venture, she cherished the afterglow of this event; however, her college days ended before she graduated. Marrying a ministerial student, Torrence was confronted with the rigors of a difficult existence as she and her husband went from one southern community to another, from one impoverished church to another.

For a period of eight years their church-related odyssey compelled them to travel throughout Georgia, Mississippi, Arkansas, Oklahoma, and Texas. It was in Little Rock, Arkansas, that Torrence assumed a new role during the absence of her husband. She fulfilled the pastoral duties, reading the Scriptures, praying, and usually relating a religious story. She recalled in *Homespun:*

> When I told the congregation a Bible story, I thought I was teaching. I didn't know—didn't have no idea under the sun—that I was *storytelling.*

Realizing with regret that her marriage was unsuccessful, Torrence returned to North Carolina, where she had left her daughter, Lori, in the care of her mother in Granite Quarry. Seeking employment in High Point, North Carolina, she became an uncertified reference librarian in the public library until a chance event helped to chart for her a new and exciting future.

• **Storytelling**

On a snowy day in 1972 the children's librarian was ill, and the library director approached her. The scenario remains vivid in her memory, recorded in *Homespun:*

career evolves

> He said, "The storyteller's not here. There's nobody to tell and the children are yellin' and screamin'. Will you tell 'em a story?"

> I was a reference librarian. I had never told a story at the library before. "No, I have a stack of questions to answer and telephone calls to make."

> But he begged me. Then he bribed me, "I'll give you an extra hour off, any time you choose, if you'll just do it for me!" So, reluctantly, I went into the children's department. . . . I was terrified.

What followed next had far-reaching repercussions for Torrence. The youngsters' reception of her stories from Richard Chase's *The Grandfather Tales* was overwhelming. From this well-received storytime with three- and four-year-old children, a new career eventually evolved. In subsequent weeks Torrence charmed countless audiences in the library as she became the full-time storyteller, known affectionately as "The Story Lady." With a fast-growing reputation and repertoire of stories, Torrence lured large crowds into the library, eager to fall under the spell of her telling. Within a short time her skills as a raconteur brought her numerous requests to present programs in neighboring communities. Now she was faced with a dilemma. She had a choice of relinquishing her free-lance engagements and confining her storytelling activities to the library or of resigning. Faced with this decision and experiencing some trepidation, Torrence severed her relationship with the library.

In succeeding years Torrence has excelled as a storyteller, giving unstintingly of herself and adding luster to the revival of the old art of storytelling. Traveling throughout the United States, Canada, Hawaii, England, and Mexico, she has revealed hitherto unexplored worlds of wonder to eager listeners in storytelling festivals, at schools, colleges and universities, and through radio, television, and recordings. In an April 1980 article from the *Wall Street Journal* titled "Br'er Possum, Meet Br'er Snake, but You Better Be Careful," Torrence remarked:

> many people think storytelling and storytellers are weird. Somehow they think it's not a legitimate thing to do. It's like being a shepherd. What do you say to a shepherd? "Where's your flock?"

On the stage she notes: "I can't wait to tell the stories." When the performance ends, she says, "I feel like I'm waking up from a very beautiful night's sleep."

What does a storyteller of Torrence's stature relate? Her selections are broad and come from varied sources; however, she is well-known for her retelling of tall tales, ghost stories, African-American tales, and Appalachian lore. Recognizing the reluctance of many tellers to use the Uncle Remus stories as recorded in heavy dialect by Joel Chandler Harris, she feels that these tales are an indigenous part of American lore and the legacy of the African-American:

> As a teaching tool, the tales implied great morals when they told of the sly ways the slaves had outsmarted the master; they were warning devices and were used as signals to those who were hiding—needing information about people who could and would help.
>
> Why do we resent them now? The fact that the tales came from the evil days of slavery could be a major reason. We also seem to be uncomfortable with the imagery in the stories, and we seem to be uncomfort-

able with the dialect and with their overall ideals. Whatever the reason, we are making a grave mistake. These stories are important to the black as well as to the white heritage of America.

A distinguished raconteur, Torrence has insights on the merits and value of perpetuating the art of storytelling. Considering the use of language as a vehicle to transport listeners into distant times and places, she realizes that understanding will come when the heart is touched. In tribute to her heritage, she acknowledges in *I Dream a World*:

> I am proud to know that my ancestry was from Africa. I'm proud that my great-grandparents were slaves and they made it through. They must have been strong, because I'm here. . . . If it had not been for storytelling, the black family would not have survived. . . . I wish you could see all my uncles and aunts when we get together and the stories come out. They are storytellers on a higher level than I will ever be.

Profile by Spencer G. Shaw

An audience waits, their eyes focused upon Torrence, who sits comfortably; then, in a quiet moment, all are mesmerized as they hear her say, "Once upon a time. . . ."

SOJOURNER TRUTH

S ojourner Truth, one of the most famous nineteenth-century black

American women, was an uneducated former slave known for active

opposition to slavery. A tall, raw-boned woman, Truth was admired for

her ability to voice fearlessly and pungently the necessary truths that her

fellow, self-censoring abolitionists and feminists probably dared not

conceive and certainly could not utter. Over the years she has stood for

the nexus connecting race and sex in liberal reform.

1797-1883 •

abolitionist, •

feminist,

religious leader

As a symbol of the unintimidated, articulate black woman, Truth both reminds black Americans that black women have gender- as well as race-based interests and refuses to let white feminists forget that black women *are* women. Even though she never learned to read or write and could not generate the books, letters, or other historical documents that usually guarantee historical longevity, her reputation has endured for more than a century after her death.

Having begun to gain recognition as a gifted preacher around New York City in the 1830s, Isabella Van Wagenen, or Sojourner Truth, is

remembered today as a prophetic presence on the antislavery and women's rights lecture circuit in the 1840s and 1850s. Truth symbolized enslaved black women in predominantly white reform movements that portrayed "the slave" as male and "woman" as middle- or upper-class and white.

Truth was born a slave to James and Elizabeth (Mau-Mau Bett) Baumfree in 1797 in Ulster County, New York, the second youngest of ten or twelve children. As a child, Truth belonged to several owners before being sold in 1810 to her longtime master, John Dumont of New Paltz. At an unknown date, Truth married an older slave named Thomas, who also belonged to Dumont, with whom she had five children. Shortly after her emancipation by New York State law in 1827, Truth left her children with her husband on Dumont's place. Several years later Thomas died in a workhouse.

Truth had three pivotal experiences in 1826 and 1827. Her youngest child, Peter, was sold and transported illegally to Alabama. She secured the assistance of Ulster County Quakers, who helped her successfully bring suit to secure his return. In 1826 she also seized her own freedom by leaving John Dumont and spending a year in the employ of Maria and Isaac Van Wagenen. During this same period she underwent a conversion experience, in which she recognized Jesus as her "intercessor" to the more remote figure of God. Following this, Truth joined a Methodist church in Kingston where she made the acquaintance of a Miss Grear, who took her to New York City in about 1828.

In New York, Truth attended the predominantly white John Street Methodist Church and the black African Methodist Episcopal Zion Church. She also began to forge a reputation as a gifted Methodist preacher and visionary at the camp meetings that were frequently held around New York City during the Second Great Awakening.

Truth remained in New York, taking in washing and doing housework. By 1843, however, she was disgruntled with urban life, particularly with the money-grubbing that accompanied the depression following the panic of 1837. As the depression deepened, she was appalled by her own lack of charity toward the poor. Then, she said, God spoke to her, commanding her to leave the city and take a new name, Sojourner. She herself took the last name Truth. On June 1, 1843, she left New York and set out, as God instructed her, toward the East. She spoke at camp meetings on Long Island, then crossed over into Connecticut.

During the year 1843, Millerism—a mass movement in the Northeast that expected the second advent to occur between 1843 and 1844—was at its height. William Miller was a farmer from Vermont and northern

New York who had begun in about 1831 to preach the approaching end of the world. Thanks to the support of a gifted abolitionist organizer from Boston, Miller's message reached hundreds of thousands from Maine to Michigan via a series of widely distributed periodicals and the words of scores of itinerant preachers who held forth at frequent and massive camp meetings.

Hence, when she took the name Sojourner Truth, she did so at a moment when hundreds of Northerners heard God command them to go out and preach their message to others and when large numbers were particularly receptive toward wandering, unlettered, itinerant preachers of many sorts and both sexes. Truth was joining an established tradition of Quaker and Methodist itinerant women preachers, some of whom, like Zilpha Elaw and Jarena Lee, were black.

Once she took to the road, Truth was immediately able to reach large, ready-made audiences at Millerite camp meetings at which she was welcome to preach. Truth was not a Millerite, and in Connecticut she denounced second adventism as totally wrongheaded. Despite the tongue-lashing, Millerites thought her a gifted, inspired preacher and singer. Through invitations that she received at second advent meetings at which she preached, Truth followed a Millerite network up the Connecticut River valley into western Massachusetts.

Millerites steered Truth to the utopian Northampton Association, which seems odd, for second adventists, expecting the world to end momentarily, were not motivated to improve it. But many of them had been active in moral reform, such as antislavery, and the connection between Millerite millennialism and utopianism was also close. When the world failed to end by 1844, disappointed second adventists flocked to utopian communities. In the Northampton Association, Sojourner Truth lived with well-off, well-educated people whose main concerns were political. Although she later became disillusioned with this version of communal life, at Northampton she encountered Garrisonian abolitionism for the first time, and abolitionists and supporters of women's rights like Garrison and Frederick Douglass were frequent visitors. Truth embraced abolitionism and women's rights and, when she was ready to leave the commune, she found a new means of subsistence in reform-minded audiences. In the late 1840s, she joined the antislavery lecture circuit, speaking and selling personal mementos.

Truth fed and clothed herself and paid off the mortgage on her house in Massachusetts through the sale of *The Narrative of Sojourner Truth*, which an abolitionist, Olive Gilbert, had taken down and which Truth published herself in 1850. A friend in Battle Creek, Michigan, Frances Titus, added new material and published a second edition of the

Narrative around 1875. For the rest of Truth's life, she supported herself through sales and charitable contributions, which she solicited through antislavery newspapers and collected from the reform-minded audiences who were her market. After she moved to Battle Creek, Michigan, in 1856, she was able to repay mortgages on two buildings through money earned from the Freedmen's Bureau and contributions.

Truth started out on the abolitionist circuit in the late 1840s, initially in company with the British antislavery member of Parliament, George Thompson. In 1850 she attended her first women's rights convention in Worcester, Massachusetts, where she and another former slave soon to gain great prominence, Frederick Douglass, were listed as representatives of the "enslaved African race."

Truth joins the • abolitionist circuit

In 1851 Truth spoke her first (and now most famous) lines at a women's rights conference in Akron, Ohio, which she had attended primarily to sell copies of her *Narrative.* The standard account of Truth's appearance in Akron (rendered in dialect) is by Frances Dana Gage, who chaired the meeting, and is reprinted in the second edition of Truth's *Narrative* and in the first volume of *History of Woman Suffrage.*

Gage says that Truth sat on the steps of the pulpit—the rest of the audience was in the pews—and said nothing the first day. Several ministers in the audience had denied women's claim to equal rights on account of women's lack of intelligence, the fact that Jesus Christ was a man, not a woman, and the sex of Eve, who had tempted man into original sin. None of the white women in the convention was brave enough to respond to these charges publicly. On the second day, Sojourner Truth stood up and spoke. Her words are well-known, but what is not usually appreciated is the contrast between her self-confidence and the timidity of the white women who had organized the meeting. Whereas Gage herself was apprehensive about chairing a meeting for the first time, Truth had boldly taken a seat at the front of the room. The white women had failed to answer the ministers who trounced women's rights, but Truth, an uninvited speaker, defended all women in phrases that silenced the male opposition. She said:

> Dat man over dar say dat womin needs to be helped into carriages, and lifted over ditches, and to hab de best place everywhar. Nobody eber helps me into carriages, or ober mud-puddles, or gibs me any best place! And a'n't I a woman? Look at me! Look at my arm! (and she bared her right arm to the shoulder, showing her tremendous muscular power). I have ploughed, and planted, and gathered into barns, and no man could head me! And a'n't I a woman? I could

work as much and eat as much as a man—when I could get it—and bear de lash as well! And a'n't I a woman? I have borne thirteen chilern, and seen 'em mos' all sold off to slavery, and when I cried out with my mother's grief, none but Jesus heard me! And a'n't I a woman?

Before her 1851 audience, Truth asserted her identity as a woman, even though she was working-class and black. She demanded the broadening of the category of "woman" to include not only those who were treated as ladies but those who, enslaved, could not protect their children. Interestingly enough, in this speech Truth appropriated her mother's tragic experience: Mau-Mau Bett had lost ten or twelve children who were sold away from her. But none of Truth's five children had been sold away from her permanently. This was not to be the only time that Truth heightened the drama of her life as a slave for rhetorical power. In the 1870s she routinely claimed that she had been a slave for forty years—instead of thirty—and that she had suckled white infants, which was more common practice on southern plantations than in Ulster County, New York. As early as 1851, Truth was making herself into the emblematic slave woman.

In Indiana in the fall of 1858 Truth made another memorable gesture before an audience of both sexes, again related to gender. According to a report published in the abolitionist newspaper, the *Boston Liberator*, and republished in the second edition of Truth's *Narrative*, after a hostile minister claimed she was a man:

> Sojourner told them that her breasts had suckled many a white babe, to the exclusion of her own offspring; that some of those white babies had grown to man's estate; that, although they had sucked her colored breasts, they were, in her estimation, far more manly than they (her persecutors) appeared to be; and she quietly asked them, as she disrobed her bosom, if they, too, wished to suck! In vindication of her truthfulness, she told them that she would show her breast to the whole congregation; that it was not to her shame that she uncovered her breast before them, but to their shame.

Again, the demand was to be seen as a woman, despite her strength.

In the late twentieth century, Truth's remarks and gestures regarding gender, race, and class are her signature. But during the nineteenth century her most famous remark was religious. Today the rhetorical question through which she would not let Frederick Douglass forget God's ultimate goodness is no longer so well-appreciated. It appears in an essay that made Truth widely known in her own lifetime, Harriet Beecher Stowe's "The Libyan Sibyl," which was published in the April 1863 issue of the *Atlantic Monthly*.

According to Stowe's report and Douglass's remembrances in his *Life and Times of Frederick Douglass*, Douglass was a speaker at a meeting in Boston. Following the passage of the Fugitive Slave Act of 1850, Douglass had been influenced by the reasoning of his friend, John Brown, who subsequently attempted to instigate a slave revolt in Virginia in 1859. Douglass began to exhort southern slaves to seize their own freedom by force of arms. His advocacy of violent action and his despair shocked Truth, whose faith in God's power was boundless. From the front row of the audience, she asked a rhetorical question that carried all over Faneuil Hall: "Frederick, is God dead?"

During the debates over black and women's suffrage that surrounded the drafting and ratification of the Fourteenth Amendment to the United States Constitution, Truth was one of a minority of black American abolitionists who favored the inclusion of women in the provisions for widened citizenship. While most male and black abolitionists agreed with Frederick Douglass that Reconstruction was the "Negro's hour" and that women should not imperil black suffrage by insisting on women's suffrage immediately, Truth sided with white feminists who advocated the deletion of the word "male" from the Fourteenth Amendment. At an 1867 equal rights convention she noted that in debates over enfranchising black men, no one had thought about black women. Truth held that if black men but not women were enfranchised, "colored men will be masters over the women, and it will be just as bad as it was before."

Truth lived many more years and was active in public life as an advocate of the cause of ex-slave refugees, but this part of her history has not entered the realm of black American or feminist history. In 1864 she recovered from a bout of ill health and went to Washington, D.C., where she met President Abraham Lincoln. Truth remained in the Washington area for several years, working alongside former abolitionist colleagues like Josephine Griffing. Ministering to the needs of the freed refugees in the District, Truth worked with the Freedmen's Bureau of the federal government and the private, New York-based National Freedmen's Relief Association in the Freedmen's Village at Arlington Heights, Virginia, and at Freedmen's Hospital.

By the late 1860s she became discouraged about the future of unemployed and impoverished freedpeople in the District of Columbia.

Together with friends and colleagues in Battle Creek, Michigan (such as Quaker Henry Willis), and Rochester, New York (such as Isaac and Amy Post), Truth helped several freedpeople relocate and find employment. Distressed that this piecemeal approach could never solve the overwhelming social and economic problems of the black poor in the Washington area, Truth conceived of a plan by which freedpeople would be allocated government lands in the West. She had a petition drafted to submit to Congress and solicited signatures, beginning in Providence, Rhode Island, in 1870. In the following year she accepted an invitation from a supportive Kansan and visited the state that eight years later would become the goal of migrants from the deep South fearing reenslavement after the end of Reconstruction. She was never able to persuade Congress to take action on her petition.

By the time of the exodus to Kansas in 1879, however, Truth's health had deteriorated badly. Her grandson, Sammy Banks, who had accompanied her over the years and written her letters, had died in Battle Creek in 1875. After several years' painful suffering, Truth died in Battle Creek in 1883 of ulcerated sores on her legs, perhaps from diabetes or gangrene. She is buried in Battle Creek, Michigan.

Profile by
Nell Irvin Painter

HARRIET TUBMAN

I *had crossed the line of which I had so long been dreaming. I was*

c. 1820-1913 •

free; but there was no one to welcome me to the land of freedom," Harriet

Tubman spoke of her accomplishment and the intense loneliness that

Underground •

led to her resolve to free her family and other slaves. Although she

Railroad

escaped from slavery, her heart was "down in the old cabin quarters,

conductor

with the old folks and my brothers and sisters." With this resolve she

began her work as a conductor on the Underground Railroad, a venture

that lasted ten years and earned for her the title "Moses"—emancipator

of slaves. Tubman made at least fifteen trips from the North into

southern slave states, leading over two hundred slaves into free northern

states. On her first trip into slave territory, she led her sister, Mary Ann

529 •

Bowley, and two children to freedom in the North, eventually freeing all her brothers and sisters as well as her parents. Although Tubman achieved historical importance primarily in this role, she was also a spy, nurse, feminist, and social reformer—if indeed these terms can adequately describe her various activities during a period of profound racial, social, and economic upheaval in the United States in the nineteenth century.

The term conductor was, of course, a euphemism for guide or leader, as the Underground Railroad was for the illegal transportation of escaped slaves. These terms have a romantic ring today, but Tubman's work was far from romantic; it was extremely dangerous and demanded great strength and endurance, both physically and mentally. Tubman's physical appearance was decidedly unimposing, unlike that of Sojourner Truth, a slave who became a famous orator and feminist. Tubman was of slight build and only five feet tall. Even more curious for a person whose leadership depended upon physical action, Tubman suffered from seizures of sudden and deep sleep because of a head injury received as a young girl. Nevertheless, she possessed leadership qualities that were quickly recognized by the slaves she led to freedom and the abolitionists with whom she worked. Thomas Wentworth Higginson, the author and reformer, called her "the greatest heroine of the age," in an 1859 letter to his mother, quoted by biographer Carl Conrad. "Her tales of adventure are beyond anything in fiction and her ingenuity and generalship are extraordinary. I have known her for some time—the slaves call her Moses."

Tubman made up for her small size through the expedient of carrying a long rifle—a weapon she used to encourage any slaves who became fainthearted during their journey north as well as to discourage pro-slavers—and with her innate leadership abilities. She was not taught to read or write but relied upon her memory, knowledge of nature, and natural shrewdness. When some whites expressed unusual curiosity while observing Tubman and some slaves in a small southern town, she bought railway tickets for a train going south. What slave attempting to escape from a southern state would travel south? The ploy was one of many Tubman used to elude authorities. She was well versed in the Bible, music, and folklore of her time and place in the South, and her repertoire of biblical verse and song was important in communicating. Tubman used her strong singing voice to announce her presence to slaves in the South and to communicate danger or safety to hidden slaves while she scouted their surroundings.

Of her childhood, Tubman said, "I grew up like a neglected weed— ignorant of liberty, having no experience of it," when she was interviewed by Benjamin Drew, an educator and part-time journalist, in St. Catherines, Ontario, in the summer of 1855. Although as a slave Tubman lacked liberty, she was nurtured and cared for in a large family. Born in 1820 in Dorchester County near Cambridge, Maryland, one of eleven children of Benjamin and Harriet (Green) Ross, Tubman was called Araminta as a child but later adopted the name of her mother. Tubman experienced relative stability while growing up, unlike some slaves who were sold to landowners in the deep South, although that stability was constantly under threat. Tubman was hired out for housework for families living near her owner at various times as a young child but was always returned to her family between jobs. While she and her family were subject to the orders of their owner and hired out to neighboring farmers, they were a family unit in which care and support were given and in which religion and folklore were shared.

Tubman was returned to the care of her family after the severe head injury which caused her recurring seizures. When she was about thirteen years of age and working in the field one autumn, one of her fellow slaves left his field work early and went to the general store. The overseer caught up with the man in the store and attempted to bind him for a whipping. As the slave ran out the door, Tubman attempted to shield the man and was knocked unconscious by a two-pound weight the angry overseer had thrown at the running slave. She recovered from the blow, but the injury to her head was serious, and her convalescence was slow. While her body was healing, Tubman, raised in a deeply religious family, began praying. While seeking a solution to her condition as a slave, she began to examine the institution of slavery from a philosophical and practical perspective.

Speaking of this recovery period in her youth to her friend and biographer, Sarah Elizabeth Bradford, Tubman said: "And so, as I lay so sick on my bed, from Christmas till March, I was always praying for poor old master. Oh, dear Lord, change that man's heart, and make him a Christian." Tubman's prayers changed when she heard that she and her brothers were to be sent to a chain gang in the deep South. She prayed, "Lord, if you ain't never going to change that man's heart, kill him, Lord, and take him out of the way, so he won't do no more mischief." When her owner died shortly afterwards, Tubman again changed her prayers. She began praying in different ways and at different times for the Lord to "cleanse her heart of sin," beginning the process of taking control, as much as she could, of her life rather than passively accepting things as they were.

During this period of illness and prayer, Tubman began to formulate a personal philosophy that transcended the laws of men. She trusted herself, God, and Divine Providence, in that order. Although she did not formulate this philosophy in a stroke of flashing illumination, it is probable that Tubman's character and intelligence, combined with the experience of her illness, prayer, and changing circumstances, produced an individual who, through both desire and necessity, developed self-reliance, courage, and strength of purpose.

Tubman had a calm respite after she slowly healed from her injury. It was during this period that two significant events took place: she married a free black man, and she discovered that her mother legally should have been freed years earlier upon the death of her former owner. Shortly after her recovery, her father became a valuable laborer for a neighboring timber operator, and Tubman began working for the man, slowly regaining her strength. In 1844, she married John Tubman, a free black in the Cambridge area. Little is known about Tubman's relationship with her husband, but there are reports that he was not an ambitious man and that he thought his wife worried too much about her condition as a slave. About a year after marrying, while she was still a slave, Tubman's curiosity about legal matters affecting the status of blacks led her to hire a lawyer to trace her mother's history in slavery. She discovered that her mother should have been legally free at one time because of the untimely death of one of her owners, a young woman named Mary Patterson who died young and unmarried, leaving no provisions for Harriet Green Ross. It was the lawyer's opinion that Tubman's mother was emancipated at that time. No one informed Harriet Ross of her rights, and she remained a slave. Although Tubman realized that literacy had been denied her, she began to understand the social order that enslaved her.

In 1849 Tubman escaped to freedom in Pennsylvania alone and unaided. She began supporting herself economically, and within a year of her escape, she began the task of freeing her relatives. Tubman's first stop was Baltimore, Maryland, for her sister and two children. Tubman embarked on her career as an Underground Railroad conductor simply by working as a cook and domestic in Philadelphia until she had saved enough money to meet her needs. She provided for herself in between her trips to the South before the Civil War and also between her political interventions after the war.

By 1857 she had freed her entire family, including her aging parents. John Bell Robinson, a pro-slavery advocate, criticized Tubman's work in his book *Pictures of Slavery and Freedom*, stating, "The most noted point in this act of horror was the bringing away from ease and comfortable homes two old slaves over seventy years of age." Pro-slavery writing criticizing Tubman was not only indicative of the economic damage she was responsible for in the South but also intended to correct the increasing agitation in the North to abolish slavery. While Tubman began the work of leading her family and others from slavery to freedom in the North single-handedly after her own escape, she soon worked in concert with other abolitionists in the North, both black and white.

Tubman's primary goal was to work for the freedom of slaves, and her career led her to associate with people who shared her goal regardless of the boundaries of gender, color, and socioeconomic status. She became closely associated with John Brown before his raid on the federal arsenal at Harper's Ferry and admired him enormously all of her life. Other white leaders she personally knew were Thomas Garrett and William H. Seward, as well as Susan B. Anthony, Ralph Waldo Emerson, and the Alcotts. The settlement and growth of the western states led to increased agitation over the institution of slavery, and white progressive leaders supported Tubman's work financially and welcomed her into their homes when she needed shelter. As the controversy over slavery intensified, Tubman became an effective and acknowledged leader in the abolitionist movement, which had a strong and effective organization in Philadelphia.

- *Tubman and*

William Still

join forces

As Boston was the center of progressive thought in New England, so Philadelphia was the center of progressive social thought and action further south on the Atlantic seaboard. It was in Philadelphia that Tubman became acquainted with William Still and other well-known and well-organized abolitionists. The first organized society against slavery was established in Philadelphia in 1775, the Pennsylvania Society for Promoting the Abolition of Slavery, the Relief of Free Negroes Unlawfully Held in Bondage, and for Improving the Condition of the African Race. Tubman became closely associated with Still, the energetic and active executive director of the General Vigilance Committee. The Underground Railroad was effectively organized into networks for the safe transport of slaves, and communication between leaders and workers in the system was necessary for safety and efficiency. On the other hand, written records were dangerous to keep, as abolitionists learned when John Brown's papers were seized after the Harper's Ferry raid. Although many written records and letters were destroyed, Still kept a chronicle that has survived. Of Tubman he later wrote, "She was a woman of no pretensions; indeed, a more ordinary specimen of humanity could hardly be found among the most unfortunate-looking farm hands of the South. Yet in point of courage, shrewdness, and disinterested exertions to rescue her fellow-man, she was without equal."

William Still and the other members of the General Vigilance Committee worked closely with Tubman, and through their organization she met Thomas Garrett, a prominent white Quaker abolitionist in Wilmington, Delaware. Garrett thought highly of Tubman and her work and provided her with shelter, money, and whatever else she needed for her trips on the Underground Railroad, especially when she was leading groups of slaves into Canada. He corresponded with friends united in the abolitionist movement as far away as Scotland, describing the activities of antislavers in the United States, as well as Tubman's activities, and raising money for her needs. His help was especially important as she freed members of her family from Delaware and began taking slaves to St. Catherines in western Canada for complete safety "under the lion's paw" of England. Passage of the Fugitive Slave Law in 1850 made freedom precarious for blacks in the North.

After living intermittently in St. Catherines, Ontario, from 1851 until 1857, Tubman moved to Auburn, New York, eventually settling there with her parents after the Civil War. Auburn was the center of progressive thought in New York, and abolition and women's suffrage thrived there. In addition, it was the home of one of Tubman's strongest supporters, William H. Seward, governor of New York, and a publishing center for abolitionist literature. Seward sold Tubman a home in Auburn on generous terms, for which she paid through unsolicited donations from supporters. At the annual meeting of the Massachusetts Anti-Slavery Society in 1859, the president, Thomas Wentworth Higginson, asked for a collection to assist her in buying the house so "her father and mother could support themselves, and enable her to resume the practice of her profession!" There was much "laughter and applause" after Higginson's announcement, reports Conrad.

Tubman's profession changed little during the Civil War. She was sent to Beaufort after the fall of Port Royal, South Carolina, in 1862 for Reconstruction work by Governor Andrew of Massachusetts. Tubman nursed the sick and wounded soldiers and taught newly-freed blacks strategies for self-sufficiency. She was sent to Florida for a time to nurse soldiers who were ill with fever. After her return to South Carolina, she resumed her nursing duties there. When the young schoolteacher, Charlotte L. Forten, visited Beaufort, she enthusiastically wrote the following entry in her diary on 31 January 1863: "We spent all our time at Harriet Tubman's. She is a wonderful woman—a real heroine." Tubman also organized a group of eight black men to scout the inland waterway area of South Carolina for Union raids under the direction of Colonel James Montgomery. She personally assisted Colonel Montgomery when he led a raid in the Combahee area, coming under fire herself from Confederate troops in the battle.

Returning to Auburn after the Civil War, Tubman devoted herself to caring for her parents, raising funds for schools for former slaves, collecting clothes for destitute children, and helping the poor and disabled. She worked closely with black churches that had provided overnight shelter for runaway slaves on the Underground Railroad and raised money for Tubman's work as a conductor. Always concerned with the most vulnerable—children and the elderly—Tubman was the agent of her church in collecting clothes for destitute children and was concerned with homes for the elderly. With her characteristic penchant for action, Tubman purchased twenty-five acres of land adjoining her house in 1896. The Harriet Tubman Home for Aged and Indigent Colored People was built there in 1903, with the assistance of the AME Zion church, and formally opened in 1908.

- **Racial and**

women's

liberation

linked

Tubman resumed her affiliation with women's groups, because she viewed racial liberation and women's liberation as being closely linked. Tubman had a long-lasting and cordial relationship with suffragist pioneer and leader Susan B. Anthony, both being active in the New England Anti-Slavery Society. Tubman strongly believed that the greatest strides toward equality could be achieved when blacks and whites worked together. She was a delegate to the first annual convention of the National Federation of Afro-American Women in 1896, and when she was asked to give a talk at this first meeting, her theme was "More Homes for Our Aged." Victoria Earle Matthews, chairperson of the evening session, introduced Mother Harriet, as she was called, and commented on the great services that she had rendered to the causes of freedom and equality. Tubman's initial appearance before the delegates as speaker was a momentous occasion, as the convention records attest:

> Mrs. Tubman stood alone on the front of the rostrum; the audience, which not only filled every seat, but also much of the standing room in the aisles, rose as one person and greeted her with the waving of handkerchiefs and clapping of hands. This was kept up for at least one minute, and Mrs. Tubman was much affected by the hearty reception given her.

While Tubman was active in Reconstruction work, women's rights organizations, and in caring for her parents in her home, she also remarried. Her first husband, John Tubman, did not join her after her dash for freedom, and he died in 1867. In 1869 Tubman married a Union soldier, Nelson Davis, a black man twenty-two years younger than she. Little is known of Davis except that he was a former slave who served in the Union Army. The facts that have survived him are a result of his war service record, documentation that enabled Tubman to draw a pension after his death as the widow of a Civil War veteran.

Tubman died of pneumonia on March 10, 1913, after a two-year residence in the Harriet Tubman Home for Aged and Indigent Colored People. A memorial service was held a year later by the citizens of Auburn, at which time a tablet erected in her honor was unveiled. Booker T. Washington was the featured speaker at the evening service. Although biographies of Tubman contain elements of myth as well as fact, her fame has endured, most recently because of new interest in the role of women in history and in literature. A liberty ship was christened the *Harriet Tubman* during World War II, and in 1978 the United States Postal Service issued a Harriet Tubman commemorative stamp, the first in a Black Heritage USA series. Poets, artists, and musicians have written, portrayed, and sung their admiration of this nineteenth-century hero. Harriet Tubman personified strength and the quest for freedom, and her fame is enduring.

**Profile by
Nancy A. Davidson**

SARAH VAUGHAN

*R*eviewers called Sarah Vaughan "The Divine." Some of her friends

called her by the nickname "Sassy." The former name was first used by

Dave Garroway, the latter by accompanist John Malachi. She was well

known as a "musician's singer," both because of her vocal precision

and because it was rare that a performance did not meet with praise.

1924-1990 •

jazz singer •

Vaughan was born on March 27, 1924, in Newark, New Jersey, to Ada and Asbury Vaughan. She went to Arts High School and sang at Mount Zion Baptist Church in Newark. Appropriately, a student from Arts High School, Kwan Nelson, sang "Precious Lord" at her funeral, held on April 9, 1990, at Mount Zion Church, where more than a thousand people came to pay their respects.

Vaughan was married four times: to George Treadwell in 1956, George Atkins in 1959, Marshall Fisher in 1971, and Waymon Reed in 1978. The first three marriages ended in divorce. George Treadwell, a trumpeter and subsequently her manager, had a strong effect on her early career development, as did trumpeter and manager Waymon Reed in her later career. She had an adopted daughter, Deborah, and she lived with her mother and husband on the Vaughan estate in Hidden Hills, California, until her death in April 1990.

Vaughan's musical training began early. Her father was an amateur guitarist and pianist, and her mother sang in the choir at Mount Zion. She joined her mother in the choir and began piano and organ lessons at the age of eight. She was an organist at Mount Zion at the age of twelve. Her interest in music theory began from her days playing piano in the band at Arts High School, teaching herself to analyze the music and discovering new and different ways to sing melodies.

It was during her school days that Vaughan's interest in jazz performance began. She reported later that she learned from other musicians, particularly horn players. She used to sneak into a bar in her neighborhood and listen to trumpet player Jabbo Smith. Charlie Parker and Dizzy Gillespie were other early mentors. She met them in 1943, during her first year in show business.

Vaughan's career started fortuitously in 1942. On a friend's dare, she entered a jazz contest at Harlem's Apollo Theatre and won first prize with her performance of "Body and Soul": ten dollars and a week's engagement at the Apollo. Billy Eckstein, the great vocalist, heard her there and recommended her to his bandleader, Earl "Fatha" Hines. She was hired as vocalist and pianist, playing with him at the Apollo and traveling with the band for a year. Eckstein then formed his own bop-oriented big band and hired her as vocalist. Subsequent engagements followed with John Kirby and the J. C. Heard sextet.

Early champions of Vaughan's career included critic and pianist Leonard Feather, who arranged her first solo recording session with Continental Records. Dave Garroway heard her and featured her on radio and television shows. Successful appearances and recordings followed that led to her winning *Downbeat* magazine's best female singer award in 1947 through 1952 and similar awards from *Metronome* magazine in 1948 through 1953.

Concerning her typical tour experiences, Vaughan's accompanist at that time, John Malachi, is quoted in *Current Biography:*

> You'd play a few key cities—New York, Washington, Philadelphia, Pittsburgh, Chicago—and then you'd go on tour and play tobacco warehouses and barns all through the South. We'd be on the road for three to eight months of the year. I can remember the times when Sarah was cussin' every minute. She had this beautiful voice and they weren't paying her any attention. They wanted to hear Billy Eckstein. Billy had the hit records as far as the black circuit was concerned.

Being a black girl, you know, had definite limitations in
those days.

Initially Vaughan was often viewed as a vocalist accompanied by a
stage band or studio orchestra. She was usually featured in soulful
ballads in which her sultry voice with its beautiful nuances of vibrato
could be heard and enjoyed. Her range, precision, and musical ability
were important trademarks, along with personalized interpretations.
She also appeared with small ensembles and jazz groups, tending to
favor this setting more in later years. As a jazz singer, her reputation was
first solidified with her recording of "Lover Man" in 1945 with Charlie
Parker and Dizzy Gillespie, followed by "Body and Soul" in 1946.

Various attempts have been made to classify her art. Vaughan was
above all else a jazz singer in the deepest meaning of the term. The
dimensions of jazz were always broad enough to allow her to find the
expressive quality she sought for a particular song, and the pages of
countless reviews are full of exclamations of praise for the particular
insights and nuances she brought to her music. What does one expect of
a jazz singer? Improvisation? Interpretation? Vocal technique used for
expressive purposes? Word-painting? A studied grasp of the art of
variation? She had these, and more.

Perhaps versatility, beyond the hackneyed present-day use of the
word "crossover," might be a point of departure to use in drawing a
musical sketch of Vaughan's art form. She could take a pop song like "I
Left My Heart in San Francisco" and paint it a new and different hue. Her
1950s "Mean to Me" shows her early skill in improvising a new second
melody to fit the prescribed changes. Can "Tenderly" be colored blue?
Listen to hers. Her "Misty" and "Foggy Day" touch your skin with the
impressionistic texture she conveys in them. Her "April in Paris" is a jazz
tour de force. Do you want up-tempo? Try her "Sweet Georgia Brown."
Slow? Try one of her mournful blues renditions. Bossa? Try her "If You
Went Away."

For Vaughan, boundaries seemingly didn't exist for jazz. She wasn't
"crossing" to reach for the audience; they came to her. Of her rendition
of the Broadway show tune "Dancing in the Dark," critic Martin Williams
commented that it was "a gloriously dramatic version, in which every
note seems to be bursting out of the confines of that song."

Vaughan's career may be seen as moving along several tracks with
some shifts and turns in the process. She performed in virtually all
available settings, from solo appearances to small combos to concerts
accompanied by a full symphony orchestra. She performed in small
clubs, theaters, concert halls, and large stadiums; at jazz festivals, for

presidents, and on college campuses; from New York's Cafe Society Downtown to Copenhagen's Tivoli Gardens to the Hollywood Bowl to New York's Avery Fisher Hall to the Copacabana to Mister Kelly's in Chicago.

Her accompanying groups have ranged from combos featuring jazz artists the caliber of Ray Brown, Oscar Peterson, Joe Pass, and Louis Bellson, to orchestras including the Los Angeles Philharmonic, National Symphony Orchestra, and Duke Ellington's Orchestra. Her first European tour was in 1953, and subsequent European and international tours included an extensive tour in the 1960s with the Count Basie Orchestra, and tours to South America, Japan, Africa, Australia, and England. As a result, her acclaim extended widely abroad and won her the Downbeat International Jazz Critics award for world's best female singer during the years 1973 and 1975 to 1979, and she headed the 1990 list of inductees into the Jazz Hall of Fame.

In describing Vaughan's vocal abilities, one should begin with Ella Fitzgerald's affirmative statement: "The greatest singing talent in the world today is Sarah Vaughan." Gifted with a wide-ranging voice centered primarily in the contralto register, Vaughan made excellent use of all of her vocal strengths. Her control was strong throughout her range. There was a sultry, soulful nature to the lower voice, great strength in the mid-range, and a more pointed, clear, and bell-like quality to the upper register.

- *Improvisation*

called

Vaughan's

greatest gift

An early discovery of the potentials of vibrato led to her use of this technique to color her lower range with dark, whispery caresses, or bright dynamic colorations in her higher ranges, and to use these nuances for a beautifully embroidered painting of notes, ideas, and moods. Precise musicianship enabled her to complete slides and embellishments with pinpoint accuracy. The art of improvisation was one of her greatest gifts. Perhaps Martin Williams best summarizes her technical prowess:

> Her voice has range, body, volume. More important, her control of her voice is phenomenal. Her pitch is just about impeccable, and she can jump the most difficult intervals and land true. No other singer has such an effortless command of dynamics. I know of no one who can move from a whisper to full volume in the course of a few notes and make the move sound less affected than Sarah Vaughan.

Bill Cosby recounts a humorous event, recorded in *Jazziz,* that shows another, lighter dimension of this versatile personality. At a performance on Vaughan's birthday, she apparently had celebrated a bit too much, but nevertheless went ahead with a high-speed virtuoso rendition of "Sweet Georgia Brown." She forgot the words, but improvised all kinds of impossible words and sounds to fit the notes, always homing in on "Sweet Georgia Brown," to the point where Camille Cosby fell on the floor, overcome with laughter. Cosby comments that, "My wife, though she's married to a comedian, never laughed so hard in all her life."

Another revealing Cosby anecdote is this bit of gallows humor: Vaughan's husband, Wayman Reed, was talking to Cosby on the night Vaughn died and said, "No, you have to listen to me. I have your singing album." Cosby said, "What?" He said, "Yeah, I have your singing album." Cosby said, "Oh, man. Well, don't play it." He said, "No man, I won't play it because you can't sing worth a beep-t-beep, you know." Cosby replied, "Yeah, but after Sarah dies you can play it again, because there'll be nothing to measure great singing with."

**Profile by
Darius L. Thieme**

Mother CHARLESZETTA WADDLES

n Detroit, a city plagued with problems of severe magnitude, the

Reverend Mother Charleszetta Waddles has devoted her life to uplifting

the human spirit and bettering the human condition in a ministry to

others that has earned her the name "Mother" Waddles. An ordained

Pentecostal minister and a visionary, Mother Waddles believes that God

reveals His grace through the good works of people: "It's not me that's

doing the good, it's God."

1912- ●

religious leader ●

She has guided the Mother Waddles's Perpetual Help Mission for more than three decades. The mission has grown from a collection point for food for the hungry located in the basement of Waddle's home to ten urban missions, including two in Africa. They answer the needs of more than one hundred thousand people a year, providing assistance ranging from job training and placement to health care and counseling to providing food, utility payments, or other solutions to emergency situations. Her nonprofit mission has its headquarters at 12479 Grand River on Detroit's commercial west side, and Mother Waddles is on call around the clock, regularly putting in twelve-hour days for the needy.

She befriends people submerged in poverty and personal tragedy, but it is not just her love she gives away; she teaches people to hope. She believes that all unresolved human conflicts and problems result from myopia—incorrect vision or thinking. Her optimistic attitude, faith, and vision keep her from being overwhelmed by the privations of the many hungry and needy people who come to her for help.

Charleszetta Lena Campbell was born on October 7, 1912, in Saint Louis, Missouri. She was the oldest of Henry Campbell and Ella (Brown) Campbell's seven children, only three of whom survived to adulthood. Her parents' third child lives in California; her youngest sister, born three months after her father's death, and Mother Waddles both reside in Detroit. Of her philanthropic calling, Waddles says:

> I remember when I was eleven or twelve years old, my mother used to say, "I wish I had a heart like you." I guess up until the time I did get the calling, all through my younger years and the times I married and remarried, and went through the changes that young people go through, I considered myself freehearted. Then I found out that there's no such animal. There are no freehearted persons, that all good is God, whether you recognize it or not. God was working through me; I just didn't understand it.

Although her father's death forced her to leave school at twelve, Mother Waddles has become self-educated through her wide-ranging and productive experience and diligent Bible study. Even though life seemed to have dealt her a heavy blow at an early age, Charleszetta Waddles says that having to leave school to go to work to help support her family because of her mother's heart condition was no burden: "It just didn't bother me. I had started doing little chores in the neighborhood and washing windows for people when I was nine years old and I would take food to the fair."

Mother Waddles believes that the death of a loved one is not the worst experience that can happen to someone. Her father's rejection by church members after his earnings declined and his resultant feelings of dejection had a greater impact on her than his death and helped prepare her for her life's work:

> I had the experience of watching my dad go from affluence to dejection. He had a person who came in [to the barber shop] and he had impetigo. My dad was not a learned barber. He did not go to school to learn

about impetigo, so he lost his trade, by not being aware. I saw him go from that business to working in a black shop where there was no money to be made. And I watched the people in our church, go from saying "Come here, darling," to "Not now, I'm in a hurry." And, boy, I felt that. I saw my dad go stand on corners, for hours at a time. And, so many, many times, I saw my mother cry. When my father died, there weren't hardly any of those people from the church at his funeral. . . . I think that was the foundation for what I am today.

Her faith has seen her through what others might believe to be impossible odds. Married and a mother by the age of fourteen, she was treated as a "little toy" by her first husband, Clifford Walker, who was nineteen at that time—a man whom she says loved her, but who was a man of the streets and was "not what he said he was." Mother Waddles faced the harsh reality of widowhood at the age of nineteen. By the time she was twenty-one, she was married again, this time to a man twice her age. Like her father, this husband experienced financial setbacks. Expecting to get a good job, he decided to leave Saint Louis, with twenty-four-year-old Charleszetta and her child, for Detroit, where he landed a job in a restaurant making eleven dollars a week. Believing her second husband to be unchallenged and uninspired to strive for a better life, Mother Waddles left with her seven children and returned to Saint Louis to help care for her ailing mother. After ending that marriage, she had a short common-law relationship, with which alcohol interfered.

After the death of her mother, she returned to Detroit. Eventually, Mother Waddles found satisfaction in a marriage to Payton Waddles, whom she believes God sent to her and her nine children at a time when they were living on welfare and having trouble making ends meet. By the time she was seventy-nine, she was the mother of ten children, grandmother of thirty-seven, and great-grandmother of twenty-three.

From her early years, Waddles took risks to help those in need. This behavior came to be her way of life. Years later, despite her limited resources as a mother alone with nine children after several bad experiences with marriage and living on Aid to Dependent Children, Charleszetta Waddles once again stepped forward to answer a need. One of her friends, the mother of two children, was about to lose her home, so Waddles gave up her own house, moved in to her friend's unfinished basement, and helped her keep the home. It was in the basement of this house that Mother Waddles, at the age of thirty-six, had her first vision directing her to "create a church that had a social conscience, that would feed the hungry, clothe the naked, and take folks in from outdoors."

A woman with drive, creativity, and spirit, Mother Waddles undertook to raise money for a church function. She was selling barbecue at the church when a man on his way to gamble stopped to buy something to eat. Mother Waddles recalls, "I'd never seen that man before in my life. But, I married that man. He not only got the barbecue, he got me and my nine children . . . and today, I draw his social security; he passed away in 1980. I've never been back on welfare, and I'm still living off the love that he gave me."

Mother Waddles believes that God made it possible for her to submit to His will. He had sent her a man to help her carry out the work. She began to have prayer meetings at her house. She would tell the small group of ladies gathered that they were never too poor to give to the less fortunate, that they could take a can of food from the shelf and give it to someone in need. She says, "You can create a thing, and it can be a step. I wanted a black, religious, charitable church . . . one that tended to the earthly things as well as the heavenly things."

- **Church and**

charitable

mission opened

In 1950 Mother Waddles opened a "thirty-five-cent restaurant," where all meals cost just thirty-five cents. Mother Waddles did the cooking, the laundry, and almost everything that had to be done for the restaurant. A few years later, while reading the newspaper, Mother Waddles found an advertisement that read "Store for Rent, two months rent free." In responding, however, she learned that the occupant would have to pay two months rent up front before receiving the two months free. Mother Waddles told the owner, "I have nothing but an idea, and I just happened to see the two months free rent." Impressed by her determination, the owner let her have the space. And thus began her black religious charitable church, the Perpetual Help Mission.

Mother Waddles is a living testament to her conviction about the importance of love and service to others. Many people have assisted her in carrying out her mission: "That's how I keep my business going. Some give food, some give clothes, some give shoes." Being creative and resourceful, Mother Waddles has also written a philosophy book, a book on self-awareness and self-esteem, and two cookbooks. She has sold more than 85,000 copies of the latter over the past thirty years; the proceeds go to help continue her work.

Mother Waddles seeks to bring hope to desperate, destitute, and dispossessed persons caught in the web of poverty and deprivation, the thousands of men, women, and youths who find themselves entrapped in the vicious whirlwind of drugs and associated crimes. She insists that many of life's tragedies could be circumvented if people would develop positive attitudes towards living and learn to help themselves. About many situations, she says, "We've got to help them to help themselves." Mother Waddles also knows the value of education and strongly encourages young people to stay in school to acquire the skills they will need to realize their potential. She hopes to join a speaking circuit to talk to young people about the importance of family, relationships, and marriage.

She is also concerned about the obstacles many men face in this society, especially those who live in large urban areas experiencing economic woes, such as Detroit. With threats to the automobile industry all around, she has opened a school to retrain people who have lost their jobs through plant closings and permanent layoffs. She is keenly aware of the technological advances made in this society and the shift to industrial production with highly technical skill requirements. While she is taking steps to move the mission into the future, she has not abandoned her founding purpose. The school will offer classes in adult basic education, as well.

Mother Waddles was the featured subject of a 1989 PBS documentary on her endless devotion to the needy. The thirty-minute *Ya Done Good,* described her endeavors and commitment to those who need help and to those who have "fallen through the cracks" of other social service systems. The program's producer and director, Daphne Boyd Kilgore, said in an article in the *Detroit Free Press* that "there's strong interest in Hollywood for a miniseries docudrama."

Mother Waddles has accomplished much in the eight decades since her mission began. Municipalities and civic, service, and social organizations have recognized her leadership and contributions, presenting her with more than three hundred awards, plaques, and honoraria. Many of her weekly sermons have been published and are available to the public, as are her cookbooks and book of philosophy. She uses the proceeds from her writings to continue the work of her mission.

Mother Waddles says she is a simple person, doing the Lord's work because it is her calling to serve the needs of others. She says, "I think that's why He picked me. Because I was simple. I didn't have all that technical knowledge, and He didn't let me get it. I had to get down to the nitty-gritty. . . . So, I've kept my feet on the ground and stayed with the people. I'm the one God gave [the calling] to. If I don't keep doing it until the day I die, then I have lived beneath my privilege." Asked what she would be if she were not a missionary, she replied, "I'd be a revolutionary."

**Profile by
Helen C. Cooks**

ALICE WALKER

A *prolific writer of poetry and fiction, Alice Malsenior Walker has*

1944- •

captured the essence of African-American life for more than twenty-five

years in her work. A number of her novels, short stories, and poems

writer, poet •

reflect the struggles of African-American women as they search for

happiness and justice in an oppressive society. She won the Pulitzer

Prize for Fiction in 1983 but generally refuses many academic awards

and honorary degrees, valuing instead the satisfaction she derives from

writing about African-American experiences. By writing, Walker

explains, "I'm really paying homage to the people I love, the people who

are thought to be dumb and backward but who taught me to see

beauty."

Walker was born on February 8, 1944, in Eatonton, Georgia. Her parents, Willie Lee and Minnie Tallulah (Grant) Walker, were sharecroppers and dairy farmers who supported their eight children—of whom Alice was the youngest—on limited resources. In 1952 Alice Walker suffered temporary disfigurement and permanent blindness in her right eye when one of her brothers shot her with a B.B. gun. Although the injury caused her to become shy and introspective, it nevertheless marked the emergence of the creative spirit lying dormant in the young girl. Walker later stated the salutary effects of the accident:

> I believe, though, that it was from this period—from my solitary, lonely position of an outcast—that I began really to see people and things, really to notice relationships and to learn to be patient enough to care about how they turned out. I no longer felt like the little girl I was. I felt old, and because I felt I was unpleasant to look at, filled with shame. I retreated into solitude, and read stories, and began to write poems.

Much of Walker's literary talent is devoted to expressing this "inner" vision. In her works, especially in her poetry, Walker illustrates her sensitivity to, and insistence upon, the worth of the individual and of human relationships. Since her teenage years, Walker has read widely in the literature of many cultures; however, she prefers to focus on presenting and interpreting the tradition of African Americans, especially African-American women. According to *American Women Writers,* which quotes Walker, "To her, to lose those traditions is not only to lose 'our literary and cultural heritage, but, more insidiously, to lose ourselves'."

Walker did not share a close relationship with her father but did establish a strong bond with her mother, who quietly encouraged her to pursue a literary career. Although her mother was earning less than twenty dollars a week, she bought Alice several gifts, including a typewriter, which symbolized to Walker her mother's message—"Go write your ass off." Greatly affected by her mother, Walker regarded her as a forerunner to the women's movement, according to *Current Biography:*

> I grew up believing that there was nothing, literally nothing, my mother couldn't do once she set her mind to it . . . so in a way when . . . the women's movement happened, I was really delighted because I felt they were trying to go where my mother was and where I always assumed I would go.

After graduating from high school as valedictorian and senior class queen, Alice Walker enrolled at Spelman College but did not feel comfortable at the elite black women's college because of its "puritanical atmosphere." Leaving Spelman after completing her sophomore year, she enrolled in the more liberal Sarah Lawrence College in Bronxville, New York.

After completing her junior year at Sarah Lawrence, Walker spent the summer in Africa, an experience that provided her with some of the material for her first collection of poetry, *Once.* Written when Walker, having returned from Africa, was pregnant and contemplating suicide, the volume contains poetry about influential experiences surrounding a critical moment when she decided to have an abortion. Specifically, the poems touch upon subjects such as love, suicide, Africa, and the civil rights movement. With the help of her teacher, she had the volume published in 1968.

Walker's poems show influences of Zen epigrams and Japanese haiku—"simple brief and mysterious poems about love, pain, struggle, and the joy of being alive and whole," according to *American Women Writers.* This collection of poems has a special significance for Walker herself, who explained the genesis of the poems in an interview:

> I have gone into this memory because I think it might
> be important for other women to share. I don't enjoy
> contemplating it; I wish it had never happened. But if it
> had not, I firmly believe I would never have survived to
> be a writer. I know I would not have survived at all.

Walker received her bachelor's degree from Sarah Lawrence College in 1965. Later, while involved in the civil rights movement in Mississippi, she met Melvyn Rosenman Leventhal, a Jewish attorney, whom she married on March 17, 1967. They lived in Mississippi for seven years as the first legally married interracial couple in the state and raised their daughter, who was born in 1969. In 1984 Walker told *People Weekly* that her interracial marriage had a negative effect on her career: "My own work was often dismissed by black reviewers because of my lifestyle: a euphemism for my interracial marriage." She and her husband were divorced amicably in 1977.

During the next few years, Walker established herself on the literary scene with several important works. In 1967 Walker wrote her first novel, *The Third Life of Grange Copeland,* while on a fellowship at the MacDowell Colony in New Hampshire. According to Walker, *The Third Life of Grange Copeland* is "a grave book in which the characters see the world as almost entirely menacing," wrote one reviewer. The novel received mixed reviews with some critics feeling that the characters lack the depth of analysis seen in Walker's later works.

In the early 1970s Walker moved to Massachusetts, while her husband remained in Mississippi. In 1973 she released a collection of short stories titled *In Love and Trouble,* According to critic Lillie P. Howard, the stories in the volume deal with "the oppressions, the insanities, the loyalties, and the triumphs of black women," the only people she respects "collectively and with no reservations." In 1974, *In Love and Trouble* won the American Academy and Institute of Arts and Letters Rosenthal Award.

In the same year she released *Revolutionary Petunias and Other Poems,* written "in honor of incorrect people like Sammy Lou, the heroine of the title poem who struggled against oppression and won," according to *American Women Writers.* The autobiographical work, which contains poems about revolution and love, was nominated for the National Book Award and won the Lillian Smith Award of the Southern Regional Council in 1974.

After having two biographies published in the mid-1970s, Walker released her second novel, *Meridian,* which has been praised "as one of the finest novels to come out of the civil-rights movement." Abandoning the realism seen in *The Third Life,* Walker attempted a more evocative rendering of the life of a civil rights worker named Meridian. In an interview with Claudia Tate, Walker explained the reason for the nonlinear structure of her second novel:

> All I was thinking of when I wrote *Meridian,* in terms of structure, was that I wanted one that would continue to be interesting to me. The chronological sequence in *The Third Life of Grange Copeland* was interesting as a one-time shot, since I had never before written a novel. So when I wrote *Meridian,* I realized that the chronological sequence is not one that permits me the kind of freedom I need in order to create.

Between 1979 and 1982, Walker put out several more works, including *Good Night, Willie Lee, I'll See You in the Morning,* a poetry volume whose title work was inspired by her mother's last words to Alice's father.

Released in 1982, Walker's third novel, *The Color Purple,* established her as a major American writer. It remained on *The New York Times* best-seller list for twenty-five weeks and claimed the American Book Award as well as the Pulitzer Prize for Fiction in 1983. An epistolary novel, it recounts the life of Celie, a young, sexually abused black woman living in the rural South. *The Color Purple* opens with her plaintive expostulation: "Dear God, I am fourteen years old. I have always been a good girl. Maybe you can give me a sign letting me know what is happening to me." The novel includes Celie's letters to God, her later letters to her sister, Nettie, and Nettie's letters to Celie. In an essay included in *Black Women Writers,* Walker recounts the initial difficulty that she had in writing *The Color Purple.* Although Walker conceived of the novel while living in New York, she states that her characters weren't comfortable among the tall buildings of the city: "'What is this tall shit, anyway?' they would say." Listening to her characters, Walker moved to California in 1978, where she could write about them more easily.

Walker told *People Weekly* that Celie is the voice of her step-grandmother, Rachel: "I tried very hard to record her voice for America because America doesn't really hear Rachel's voice." *The Color Purple* illustrates the writer's feminist allegiance as well as the black woman's tenuous place in American society. Celie's emergence as a strong woman, despite her early incestuous rape and marriage of convenience to an abusive man, gives testimony to the tenacity of black women in a male-dominated society. The critical acclaim of *The Color Purple* prompted Walker to remark, "I think to many people I could not be a name brand until I was certified by the Pulitzer people. I understand it and I'm not angry at all." Warner Brothers later paid Walker $350,000 for movie rights to *The Color Purple.*

Since the publication of *The Color Purple,* Walker has written several works, including two volumes of poetry and nonfiction works such as *In Search of Our Mother's Gardens*, a collection of essays, articles, reviews, and statements written between 1966 and 1982. The subtitle of the second collection, "Womanist Prose," defines Walker's work as a "black feminist." Walker prefers the term "womanist" to "feminist," explaining to David Bradley her use of the designation:

> I just like to have words that describe things *correctly*. Now, to me, "black feminist" does not do that. I need a word that is organic, that really comes out of the culture, that really expresses the spirit that we see in black women. And it's just that . . . *womanist.*

Walker calls

herself

"womanist"

In the late 1980s and early 1990s, Walker released two more novels. After the publication of *The Temple of My Familiar* in 1989, she wrote *Possessing the Secret of Joy,* which focuses on a young woman who must undergo circumcision as part of an African tribal ritual that claimed the life of her sister many years before. In an interview published in *USA Today,* Walker argued for the dignified treatment of women in contem-

**Profile by
Grace E. Collins**

porary society, stating that "the unsanitary ritual" described in the novel, which is still a custom in many African countries, "is part of the global problem of men trying to control women's sexuality, mobility, and selfhood."

MADAME C. J. WALKER

Among the early entrepreneurs of the twentieth century, no one is

1867-1919 •

more intriguing than the black beauty-culture genius Madame C. J.

Walker—not only because of her development of the "hot" comb but

entrepreneur, •

because of her remarkable business acumen. A black woman with one

philanthropist

dollar and fifty cents in her pocket in 1904, Walker was the first woman

in the United States to become a millionaire through her own efforts.

Walker burst on the scene in 1904 and changed the way business people

marketed their products. She also revolutionized the methods for treat-

ing black hair.

Sarah Breedlove McWilliams Walker, later known as Madame C. J. Walker, was born in 1867 in Louisiana and died on May 12, 1919, in New York. Born to Owen and Minerva Breedlove, indigent former slaves, Walker lived in a dilapidated shack with her parents on the

Burney family plantation in Delta, Louisiana, on the Mississippi River. Her parents worked as sharecroppers on the plantation until their deaths. As a child and an adult, Walker toiled in the cotton fields with other black laborers.

During the Reconstruction era, 1865-1898, Walker could not have lived in a more hostile environment. Although blacks had moved from being slaves to being sharecroppers, nothing on the plantation had changed. Walker experienced extreme poverty in all aspects of her daily life. The windowless shack in which she lived had one door, no water, no toilet, and a dirt floor. She and other family members slept on the ground. As a child, she received the coarse materials for one dress a year that was handed out by the plantation owner and suffered the humiliations and indignities common to blacks at that time.

After her parents died in her childhood, Walker moved to Mississippi with her married sister Louvenia and Louvenia's husband, at which time she experienced domestic violence and abuse. Insensitive and tyrannical, the brother-in-law showered only cruelty on seven-year-old Sarah. She eventually moved away and married Moses McWilliams at the age of fourteen. In 1885, she had a daughter, Lelia. Two years later when Sarah McWilliams was twenty years old, it is said that her husband was killed by a lynch mob.

Her difficulties continued to mount as she became a single parent with a two-year-old child to rear. Vicksburg, Mississippi, was not an ideal place for blacks. Since they had the best chance for employment and education in urban areas, Walker moved to Saint Louis, Missouri, where she had relatives, found work as a cook and a laundress, and supported her daughter with her meager earnings. Although she was unable to read and write at the time, she sent her daughter, Lelia Walker, not only to school but to Knoxville College, a private black college located in Knoxville, Tennessee. As an uneducated black, Walker was proud of this accomplishment.

Poverty continued to haunt Walker. At the same time she began to experience baldness due to the stressful wrap and twist method then used to straighten the hair of blacks. This method caused only pain. With intimate knowledge of hair loss, agony, and the inconvenience of black hair care, Walker set out to address the problems black women faced with their hair. Using patent medicines of the day and her own secret ingredients (supposedly sulfur), she stopped her own hair loss. She was amazed how quickly her hair grew back. Her friends, using the products, were intrigued by her efforts and became enthusiastic customers. According to A'Lelia Bundles in *Ms.* magazine, Walker said her formula came to her in a dream after she had prayed to God to save her hair:

Walker •

finds her

system

He answered my prayer, for one night I had a dream, and in that dream a big black man appeared to me and told me what to mix up for my hair. Some of the remedy was grown in Africa, but I sent for it, mixed it, put it on my scalp, and in a few weeks my hair was coming in faster than it had ever fallen out. I tried it on my friends; it helped them. I made up my mind to begin to sell it.

Black people needed methods for handling hair since no running water, supplies, and equipment existed for them. Bringing water from outdoors and placing the body in awkward positions to shampoo the hair, Walker and other black women found taking care of their hair was one more arduous task to deal with. Walker went on to develop the hot comb and her Wonderful Hair Grower. Faced with the prospect of domestic and laundry work for life, she took her chance with destiny and became a successful businesswoman.

- *Walker*

establishes a

hair

preparations

company

After the death of her brother, Walker moved to Denver, Colorado, to live with her sister-in-law and her four nieces. With one dollar and fifty cents, she began a hair preparations company. She gradually moved away from working as a domestic to manufacturing hair products. Encouraged by the success of her formula on the hair of other black women, she, her daughter, her sister-in-law, and her nieces began to fill jars with the hair preparations in the attic of their home. Six months after her arrival in Denver, she married C. J. Walker, a newspaper man with knowledge of advertising and mail order procedures, which she used successfully.

Although the business gradually became successful, she experienced incompatible differences with her husband, who failed to share the dream for the company she envisioned. Following the dissolution of her marriage, she continued to use the initials of his name. At the time whites called all black women by their first names no matter who they were, so black women frequently kept their first names a secret, if possible. Hence, she is referred to as Madame C. J. Walker rather than Sarah Breedlove Walker.

Like most inventors, no one is totally original, for the inventor responds to a situation, improves upon it, and draws from the environment around him or her. Walker was not the first to organize a hair preparations company, since Annie N. Turnbo Malone with her Poro Company and "Wonderful Hair Grower" preceded her in 1900. Some sources suggest that Walker was first an agent for Malone and later her rival in the beauty empire business. Walker was also not the first to heat a comb to straighten hair, since the French Jews pressed hair in the early eighteenth century. Nor was she the first to send products through the mail, for many white companies had used this strategy with much success. However, she was the first woman to organize supplies for black hair preparations, develop a steel comb with teeth spaced to comb the strands of blacks, place the comb on a hot stove, send the products through the mail, organize door-to-door agents, and develop her own beauty school. From a combination of these ideas she nursed her company and it grew.

In spite of her early struggles as a single parent, her daughter, Lelia Walker, became her chief asset in the business. Working side by side with her mother, she assisted in the product manufacturing, helped with business decisions, trained the students in the Walker method, and traveled around the country to sell the products. In 1906, Walker placed her daughter in charge of the mail-order operation while she continued to introduce the products in different parts of the South and East. By 1908 mother and daughter moved to Pittsburgh, Pennsylvania, and set up a beauty school, Lelia College, to train cosmetologists in the Walker method. Lelia Walker handled the manufacture of the hair products as well as the beauty school, while Madame Walker continued to sell the products personally to black women around the country. Through her personal endeavors and travels she contacted thousands of women who became Walker agents. During one of her stops in 1910 she decided that Indianapolis, centrally located in mid-America, would be an ideal location for the company's headquarters; Lelia Walker moved part of the business operations to New York in 1913 and set up another Lelia College.

Although she began her company with door-to-door selling techniques, Walker eventually sold on a national level. She established a chain of beauty parlors throughout the United States, the Caribbean, and South America, and she built her own factories and laboratories. By 1910 Walker had five thousand black agents selling her products on a commission basis. These agents averaged over one thousand dollars a day, seven days a week. In addition, they removed themselves from the tyranny of domestic work.

Walker's career as an entrepreneur continued as an odyssey of personal discovery. She continued to expand her distribution by recruiting and retaining her sales force of black women, who used, demonstrated, and sold the products. Her agents taught other women to set up beauty shops in their homes and to learn techniques of bookkeeping. By 1919, 25,000 women called themselves Walker agents.

Many in the black community denounced Walker for trying to make black women resemble white women. The conservatives spoke against

Walker

becomes a

millionaire

this artificially straightened hair, accusing her of trying to remake black women into an imitation of white Europeans. Even the church became an opposing force. Walker believed that she could make contact with large groups of black women if she approached churches. The churches, in many instances, rejected her. Black clergymen claimed that if God meant for blacks to have straight hair, he would have endowed them with it. Notwithstanding, black women turned to these products in an effort to eliminate the stigma assigned to the hair of the lower socioeconomic caste.

Illiteracy was another negative force which Walker overcame; unable to read and write, she surrounded herself with educators and lawyers to assist in her business transactions. Indeed, for a while she wrote her name in an illegible script on checks and bank documents. As she gradually became financially able, she employed tutors to teach her to read and write.

After she became wealthy, Walker built a palatial mansion on the Hudson River in Irvington, New York. She named the mansion Villa Lewaro, after her daughter Lelia Walker Robinson, now married, using the first syllables from the first, middle, and last names. Madame Walker and A'Lelia Walker Robinson (Lelia added an *A'* to her name) invited leaders of the black community to socials, soirées, and dinners at the mansion. She bequeathed the mansion to her daughter, A'Lelia, at her death, with the idea that the NAACP would inherit it from A'Lelia. Due to the depression the NAACP could not support the mansion, which it sold for the proceeds.

• Walker

becomes

benefactor

Even at the height of her success, Walker was unable to forget the black experience that had produced her. She contributed to philanthropic causes and black educational institutions. She donated five thousand dollars to Mary McLeod Bethune's school in Florida, Daytona Normal and Industrial Institute for Negro Girls; she left five thousand dollars to Lucy Laney's Haines Institute in Augusta, Georgia; she sponsored a teacher at Charlotte Hawkins Brown's Palmer Memorial Institute, a black preparatory school in Sedalia, North Carolina; and she gave five hundred dollars to redeem and restore Frederick Douglass's home, Cedar Hill, in southeastern Washington, D.C.—a project sponsored by the National Association of Colored Women's Clubs.

Although Walker placed emphasis on education, she also promoted the idea of black economic self-help, recounted Bundles. If women could develop a business, Walker reasoned, they could manage their lives:

The girls and women of our race must not be afraid to take hold of business endeavors. I started in business eight years ago with one dollar and fifty cents. [Now I am] giving employment to more than a thousand women. . . . I have made it possible for many colored women to abandon the washtub for a more pleasant and profitable occupation.

Walker, faced with prejudice throughout her life, remembered her roots, became a social activist, and supported causes which fought racism. She provided funds for Monroe Trotter's National Equal Rights League and supported to the NAACP's anti-lynching drive. In 1917 she accompanied other black leaders from Harlem to the White House to attempt to confront President Woodrow Wilson concerning federal anti-lynching legislation. Wilson pretended he was too busy to see the black coalition, but at the Walker agents' convention in 1917, the women sent a telegram encouraging President Wilson to give support to the federal anti-lynching legislation. These women also voiced their concern over the killing of black people in a riot in East St. Louis, Illinois.

Gender bias in the workplace was a force Walker experienced all of her life. Limited to working as a laundress and maid, she dared to take a chance and developed her company. Even after she became a success she still faced the male chauvinism of black men. At the National Negro Business League in 1912, Booker T. Washington and other men at the convention did not intend to let her speak. As Washington praised a black male banker for his bank's operations, Walker proceeded to the podium and stated emphatically:

I am a woman who came from the cotton fields of the South. I was promoted from there to the washtub. Then I was promoted to the cook kitchen, and from there I PROMOTED MYSELF into the business of manufacturing hair goods and preparations. . . . I have built my own factory on my own ground.

At the 1913 convention Walker was a presenter on the program.

Walker had a decided influence on people—an effect that made many people feel that their lives had been changed, deepened, and enriched. A letter from a Walker agent stated:

You have opened up a trade for hundreds of colored women to make an honest and profitable living where they make as much in one week as a month's salary would bring from any other position that a colored woman can secure.

Her company was not just her expression of her own possibilities, but became an ethnic statement giving credence to the ingenuity of black people. Walker proved to the world that a black could overcome lack of white business support and lack of capital with a creative idea. Her dramatic commercial success was intriguing to her people. News articles invariably stressed her wealth and material acquisitions, as they have always done when discussing a folk-derived entrepreneur who has made it big. Admittedly, Walker's earnings and investments were enough to attract anyone's notice. By 1914 her gross from company earnings were over a million dollars.

Walker died on May 25, 1919. Funeral services were conducted in the Villa Lewaro by the pastor of her church, the Mother Zion African Methodist Episcopal Zion Church of New York, and she was buried in Woodlawn Cemetery in the Bronx.

**Profile by
Joan Curl Elliott**

MAGGIE L. WALKER

*M*aggie Lena Walker was born black in a society governed by

1867-1934 •

prejudice, female in a society dominated by male achievement, and

poor in a nation of comparative wealth, yet she became the country's   **bank president** •

first woman bank president and used her economic and social position

to fight for greater educational opportunities, for black pride, and for

women's rights.

On December 18, 1934, the *Richmond News Leader* ran a lengthy obituary for Maggie Lena Walker. Its praise was noteworthy: "Maggie Walker was the greatest of all Negro leaders of Richmond. She probably was the most distinguished Negress ever born in Richmond and, in solid achievement, one of three or four ablest women her race ever produced in America."

Elizabeth Draper Mitchell, an ex-slave, was a cook's helper in the Van Lew mansion on Church Hill in Richmond, Virginia. Her mistress was both an eccentric spinster and an ardent abolitionist. Maggie Walker was born to Elizabeth on July 15, 1867, and spent her early years at the elegant home in free-spirited happiness. "The household afforded its servants not only an exceptionally good education, but unusual

encouragements to enterprise as well," wrote Caroline Bird in *Enterprising Women*. William Mitchell, Elizabeth's husband, who was a butler in the mansion, decided that opportunities were greater in downtown Richmond, so the family moved to a small clapboard house there.

Maggie learned well her mother's lessons of industry and became an extremely conscientious child. Her sense of responsibility was tested in the first of her life's several tragedies. William Mitchell, who worked as a head waiter at the Saint Charles Hotel, mysteriously disappeared. Five days later, he was found floating in the James River, apparently the victim of robbery and murder. As support for her family, Elizabeth Mitchell increased her laundry business; to her young daughter fell the responsibility of caring for a rambunctious younger brother and of carrying laundry back and forth to her mother's white clients.

Walker's adolescence was filled with school, work, church, and her involvement with the Order of Saint Luke. Educated in the segregated Richmond public school system, Walker led her class at Armstrong Normal and High School. Her senior class protest was a foreshadowing of the aggressive stand for racial equality that she would later espouse. The 1883 black graduating class objected strongly to receiving diplomas in a church and wanted to join their white counterparts who would march in a theater. Told by their principal that they could do so only if separate seating were accorded white and black audience members, the students decided to graduate from their school auditorium. Wendell Dabney, who also participated in this protest, claims that "this event stands recorded as the first school strike of Negroes in America."

Walker never left school during her childhood, but she did devote much time and energy to helping her mother support her family. She shopped, carried baskets of laundry, did washing and ironing. Side by side with her beloved mother, she learned the rewards of drive and endeavor. She grew up as one of two women who supported a family, and all her life she realized the virtues of her black sisters. In 1909 she spoke of this appreciation:

> And the great all absorbing interest, this thing which has driven sleep from my eyes and fatigue from my body, is the love I bear women, our Negro women, hemmed, circumscribed with every imaginable obstacle in our way, blocked and held down by the fears and prejudices of the whites, ridiculed and sneered at by the intelligent blacks.

Walker's passionate plea to young women was that they work diligently and find in themselves the source of female power she so admired: "I wish to God that I could imbue you with the spirit of push and energy that would awaken your dormant powers." For Walker, the industry of women was mandatory if racial progress was to be made. Perhaps it was the absence of William Mitchell during her formative years; perhaps it was the carefree indolence of her brother; perhaps it was the frustration and pain she saw in the community's menfolk who were so severely beaten by the racist system—whatever the factors, Walker repeatedly urged women to better themselves educationally and economically. She saw this industry as necessary not only for personal improvement but also for racial progress:

> The timidity and retiring disposition of women unfit them for the strife, competition and worry of business life. But, we must do something. We are up and doing, working and suffering because our needs and necessities and our ambitions force us to enter the world and contend for a living. . . .

> If our men are so slothful and indifferent as to sleep upon their opportunities, I am here to-day to ask the women of North Carolina to awake, gird their armor and go to work for race uplift and betterment.

Walker was an ardent feminist but she was careful to explain that she was not "an advocate for what is called 'New Woman and the Bachelor Girl'." She enjoyed men and loved her family dearly. What she called for was the fulfillment of women as individuals in a time when they were often merely appendages of their husbands.

As a child Walker joined the Old First Baptist Church and became very active in the Thursday night Sunday school meetings. It was at one of these meetings that she met a young contractor, Armstead Walker, who would become her husband. She was active in the church and soon took charge of a Sunday school class. For Walker, belief in God was not posture and was not superficial; she held a deep abiding faith that carried her through many difficulties. Walker spoke often at churches, and she remained a forceful presence in the religious community of Jackson Ward.

At fourteen, Walker joined the Independent Order of Saint Luke (IOSL). In 1886, when she and Armstead Walker were married, she stopped teaching to devote herself to her new family. An ever-active woman, she filled the void of not teaching by increasing her activities in the order. Basically an insurance company started by Mary Prout in 1867 in Baltimore, the IOSL was created for blacks to help the sick and bury the dead during the post-Civil War period. It also encouraged self-help and racial solidarity—two goals that appealed to Walker. The order proved a natural outlet for her unbridled energy; she moved through the ranks from secretary of a Good Idea Council to appointment as delegate to the annual convention in Petersburg, and finally to Grand Sentinel. In 1890 the Magdelena Council, Number 125, was named in her honor. Eventually, she became Right Worthy Grand Secretary, succeeding William T. Forrester in 1899. When she accepted the post at a reduced salary of eight dollars per month, the treasury contained $31.61 against a stack of unpaid bills, and there were only 1,080 members. Through increased memberships, through the formation of a department store and a bank, and through the charismatic competency of its secretary treasurer, the order expanded tremendously. A *Richmond Times Dispatch* news article of August 23, 1924, reports that "the $31 that was placed in her hands has grown until the order has collected $3,480,540.19." But the black beneficent society was more than just economic; according to Elsa Barkley Brown, "the Order demonstrated a special commitment to expanding the economic opportunities within the community in the face of racism and sexism." The organization also operated in a religious spirit. The Independent Order of Saint Luke, then, proved an ideal organization in which Walker could channel her energies; it bought her beliefs about education, religion, race, and sexism under the umbrella of economic enterprise.

The young woman who emerged at the turn of the century was a confident, articulate champion of her strong beliefs who became a visible force in the community. Through the Order of Saint Luke, she established *The St. Luke Herald* on March 29, 1902, to provide increased communication between the community and the order and to illuminate black concerns. "The first issue espoused lofty ideals and came out foresquare against injustice, mob law, Jim Crow laws, the curtailment of public school privileges and the enactment and enforcement of laws that constricted the roles of blacks in Virginia politics," explained Daniel Jordan in *Commonwealth*. As a forum for community and national issues, the paper squarely faced controversy. A reader would expect no less; for three decades, Walker served as editor of the weekly journal.

In 1903 Walker determined the order needed a bank. In its Historical Overview, the currently named Consolidated Bank and Trust Company—built diagonally across the street from the original Saint Luke's Penny Thrift Savings Bank—relates Walker's purpose in founding the institution: she "persuaded the Richmond-based organization (I.O.S.L.) to establish a bank to monitor and house funds accruing from its expanding operations in states along the Atlantic seaboard." She also sought a bank to help black people turn pennies and nickels into dollars and to finance black home ownership. Walker was proud of this

Walker founds •

savings bank

mortgaging success and observed that by 1920, 645 black homes were paid for because of help from the bank. This enterprise had a marked effect on the quality of black life in Richmond. Walker served as president of the bank until poor health dictated her retirement in 1932, at which time she became chairman of the board. She had seen the bank through a name change to the Saint Luke Bank and Trust Company after the Virginia Banking Division forced the separation of secret orders and their banks, and through a second name change after two mergers. When she died, she left an institution strong enough to weather the Great Depression and exist today. For Walker, this bank—black-owned and run—was another way to help her race. The bank's slogan reflects this intention of keeping black people's money in black people's pockets: "Bring It All Back Home."

Children always held a special place in Walker's heart, and she used the bank and the IOSL to help them. She encouraged a sense of thrift in the children of Jackson Ward by providing small cardboard boxes in which they were encouraged to save pennies; when the pennies had reached a dollar, the children were praised for opening bank accounts. Walker proudly reported their progress, quoted by Sadie Iola Daniel: "Numbers of children have bank accounts from one hundred to four hundred dollars. They sell papers, cut grass, do chores, run errands, and work in stores on Saturdays." Walker also used the juvenile division of the order to instill values of industry, thrift, and generosity.

Walker's vast community contributions extended far beyond the confines of the Saint Luke order. Her many varied activities and honors reflected the concerns she held closest: racial improvement and educa-tion. She was instrumental in establishing and maintaining a Community House in Richmond, in securing and keeping a visiting nurse for blacks, and in supporting and advising the Piedmont Tuberculosis Sanitorium for Negroes in Burkeville. She was active in many organizations to promote black interests, serving as founder and president of the Council of Colored Women, cofounder of the Richmond branch of the NAACP, vice-president of the Negro Organization Society of Virginia, and board member of several organizations, including the national NAACP, Col-ored Women's Clubs, National Urban League, and the Virginia Interra-cial Committee. She served in various groups, including the State Federation of Colored Women, the International Council of Women of the Darker Races, and the National Association of Wage Earners.

Walked joined other women in the community in the battle for women's suffrage, in voter registration campaigns after the passage of the Nineteenth Amendment, and in the formation of the Virginia Lily-Black Republican Party. The Lily-Blacks were a splinter faction of the

Virginia Republican party. They not only created their own platform but also nominated their own candidates. Walker ran unsuccessfully for state superintendent of public instruction. She also was active in the National League of Republican Colored Women and handled that organization's funds.

Domestically, Walker's life was both rich and tragic. While she married on September 14, 1886, her views on marriage were rather advanced for the turn of the century:

> And since marriage is an equal partnership, I believe that the woman and the man are equal in power and should by consultation and agreement, mutually decide as to the conduct of the home and the government of the children.

Three sons were born to Walker: Russell Ecles Talmage, one who died in infancy, and Melvin DeWitt. Walker enjoyed being surrounded by her extended family, but tragedies did mar her happiness. In 1915 her husband died in an accident when Russell mistook his father for a prowler on the porch and shot him. During his ensuing trials, his mother remained a steadfast support. Russell was acquitted of the murder charge but never quite recovered from the ordeal. He died in 1923, leaving his wife and child to live with Maggie. Her beloved mother, Elizabeth, also passed away. In 1907 Walker fell on the front steps of her home and injured her knees, damaging several nerves and tendons. She subsequently suffered severe pain and, during her last ten years, spent much time in an upstairs suite and on a window-enclosed porch from which she would greet neighbors. In 1928 she was confined to a wheelchair and made two major accommodations to the inconvenience: a hand-operated elevator at the back of her home and a 1929 eight-passenger Packard modified to accept her chair.

Walker was hostess to many important people. She loved to entertain, choosing personally her china and menus, and famous visitors graced her home, including W. E. B. Du Bois, Langston Hughes, and Mary McLeod Bethune.

Walker's brilliance shone in so many lives that awards in later life were profuse. Among them were a 1924 "testimonial of life" celebration for her at City Auditorium given by the people of Richmond and the IOSL, an honorary master of science degree from Virginia Union, and, posthumously, a high school bearing her name. An October 4, 1934, *Richmond News Leader* article discusses the creation of "Maggie Walker Month" (October) by black organizations across the country "in recognition of her outstanding achievements as Christian mother, fraternalist, banker, philanthropist, and minister of inter-racial good will."

Two months later, Walker died, her death certificate citing "diabetes gangrene" as the cause of death. The service at First American Baptist Church was one of the largest in Richmond history. She was buried on Wednesday, December 19, in the family section of Evergreen cemetery.

**Profile by
Margaret
Duckworth**

FAYE WATTLETON

*F*aye Wattleton has been one of the most influential black American

women in the area of reproductive rights. As president of the Planned

Parenthood Federation of America from 1978 to 1992, she transformed

a declining service-oriented organization into a high-profile, aggres-

sive proponent of women's right to reproductive choice. As one admirer

remarked, "Her political savvy and her remarkable ability to communi-

cate difficult issues have made her a giant in the ongoing battle to

preserve American's fundamental liberties."

1943- •

reproductive •

rights

activist

The only child of George Edward and Ozie (Garrett) Wattleton, Alyce Faye Wattleton was born on July 8, 1943, in St. Louis, Missouri. George Wattleton, who died in 1970, was a factory worker. Ozie Wattleton—one of Faye Wattleton's role models, along with Martin Luther King, Jr., and John F. Kennedy—was a seamstress and minister of the Church of God. Living one's politics was important in the

Wattleton family. Her father, for example, refused to buy gas from a service station that failed to provide bathroom facilities for blacks.

Faye Wattleton's family was poor but stressed the importance of helping those who were even less fortunate. She "was expected to become a missionary helping 'the poor and maimed' of Africa," according to Helen Epstein. At the age of sixteen she entered Ohio State University Nursing School, and in 1964 she became the first person in her family to receive a college degree. Her first postgraduate job was as a maternity nursing instructor for the Miami Valley Hospital School of Nursing in Dayton, Ohio. It was during her two years there that she was first exposed "to the medical and emotional complications of women who had life-threatening illegal abortions," wrote Constance M. Green in *Black Enterprise*. In 1966 Wattleton moved to New York to study at Columbia University on a government stipend; a year later she received an M.S. in maternal and infant health care, with certification as a nurse-midwife. While a student at Columbia, she was an intern at Harlem Hospital, where the importance of access to safe abortion became clear to her. As she recalled to Epstein: "One of the cases I remember in Harlem was a really beautiful 17-year-old girl. She and her mother had decided to induce an abortion by inserting a Lysol douche into her uterus. It killed her."

In 1967 Wattleton moved to Dayton, Ohio, to work as consultant and assistant director of Public Health Nursing Services in the City of Dayton Public Health Department. She was asked to join the local Planned Parenthood board and a year and a half later, at the age of twenty-seven, was asked to serve as its executive director. Under her leadership, the number of clients tripled, and the budget increased from less than four hundred thousand dollars to almost one million dollars.

In 1973 Wattleton married Franklin Gordon, a social worker raised in Roxbury, Massachusetts. Two years later she not only gave birth to her daughter, Felicia, but also became chairwoman of the national executive director's Council of Planned Parenthood Federation of America (PPFA). In fact, Wattleton was in labor when she won the election to the position. Three years later, in 1978, she was appointed president of PPFA.

As the first black person, first woman, and youngest individual to head the organization, Wattleton shocked many people with her appointment. According to one local director, "Nobody believed our board would settle on 'a little nurse from Dayton' with no national experience for the highest-paid job [seventy thousand dollars a year] in the largest voluntary health agency in the country." How, then, did the board decide to appoint a woman, particularly a black woman, as president? In Wattleton's opinion, there were at least three factors

Wattleton heads •

Planned

Parenthood

involved: her demonstrated compassion for human suffering, the organization's realization that its primary reason for existence was women's issues, and her competence.

Even Wattleton, however, could not have imagined just how tough her job would be. The Hyde Amendment, passed in 1977 and "aimed to prohibit the use of any federal funding for abortion, unless the life of the mother was endangered," was one of the early indicators that anti-abortion or Right to Life groups were having a significant influence on the political process. During that same year, Planned Parenthood of Miami Valley came under attack from a local Baptist group and Right to Life chapter and also was subjected to a federal inquiry into its use of government financing. In addition, Planned Parenthood clinics in Minnesota, Virginia, Nebraska, Vermont, and Ohio were burned or bombed. Thus the anti-choice stage had been set. One of the ongoing efforts of the Reagan administration was an attempt to repeal the United States family planning program, Title I of the Public Health Service Act. As family planning services and their funding were being threatened, Wattleton worked to bring PPFA into public view. She appeared on radio and television talk shows, including "Donahue," to rally support around her cause. In fact, Phil Donahue called Wattleton "a talk show host's dream guest" because she got to the point and was always well-informed.

President Reagan attempted to enact a "squeal rule," which would have required federally funded clinics to receive parental consent before distributing diaphragms, intra-uterine devices, or birth control pills to minors. Wattleton, however, argued that the mandatory notification of parents would merely lead to an increase in teen pregnancies. A "gag rule," which would have prevented abortion counseling by federally funded family-planning agencies, was also proposed and vigorously fought by Wattleton.

Because PPFA served men and women in the developing countries of Africa, Asia, and Latin America, the Reagan administration's "Mexico City" policy particularly disturbed Wattleton. In essence, the policy was an attempt to restrict United States family-planning aid to foreign organizations that referred, performed, or advocated abortion. However, according to Wattleton and the majority of Americans who participated in the 1988 Harris poll, the United States should provide family-planning funds to developing nations—even those nations where abortion was a legal option.

"By engaging in political activism, Ms. Wattleton has brought Planned Parenthood full circle," observed Nancy Rubin in *Savvy Woman*. When Margaret Sanger, also a public health nurse, opened the nation's first birth control clinic in 1916, she was jailed, and contraceptives were confiscated. The early 1900s were a time when "contraceptives were classified as 'obscene materials'; when Kotex was not yet on the market and when most women were 'prisoners of their own fecundity'," wrote Epstein. Because of early efforts, such as those of Sanger and her associates, the distribution of information about birth control became widely accepted by the medical establishment.

Almost seventy years later, Wattleton had to struggle to keep family planning on the national agenda. By this time, Planned Parenthood had lost much of its attraction among middle- and upper-class women. Most of the organization's clients were poor or of the working class and thus were particularly vulnerable to reductions in federal funding, such as Medicaid. The Hyde Amendment, for example, cut off Medicaid abortion funding, which meant that hundreds of thousands of poor women could no longer have their abortions paid for by Medicaid. As Epstein notes, Wattleton argued that poor people, like the rich, should have access to the full range of health care services:

> The women who came to my hospitals under less than dignified circumstances were not affluent. That girl in Harlem who died was not affluent. . . . *That's* when I became aware of the political significance of these people. If they really cared about equity and fairness in life they would say that as long as abortion is legal in this country, poor people should have the same access as the rich.

Equal access was not the only issue raised concerning reproductive choice and freedom. Wattleton attempted to locate the reproductive issue in a wider context of federal neglect. In her view, the Reagan-Bush administration tried to dismantle programs designed to confront not only the issue of inadequate health care but also homelessness and poor education. Thus, one had to look at the circumstances under which so many women chose to end their pregnancies—many of which were unintended.

One of the major setbacks for PPFA as well as other advocates of reproductive choice was the Supreme Court's ruling in the *Webster v. Reproductive Health Services*. The case challenged certain aspects of *Roe v. Wade*, the 1973 Supreme Court decision that legalized abortion. On July 3, 1989, the Supreme Court gave states the right to limit access to abortion. Although this event may have signaled defeat to even the most resolute leader, noted Marianne Szegedy-Maszak, Wattleton confidently asserted after hearing the decision, "my commitment and my determination is in no way diminished. I am furious as can be."

Planned Parenthood is dedicated to working for a society where unintended pregnancies would be reduced, and sex education and information about contraceptives are very important elements of this commitment. Under Wattleton's leadership the agency "expanded its public advocacy drive through newspaper and television advertisements geared toward educating teens, parents, and public officials on the financial and human costs of runaway teen pregnancy," Green reported. Wattleton also co-authored a book entitled *How to Talk to Your Child about Sex*, which sold more than thirty thousand copies. It angered her, however, that by 1989 "no major network [would] accept contraceptive advertising [and] only 17 states and the District of Columbia require[d] sex education in their school systems," wrote Marcia Ann Gillespie in *Ms.* In Wattleton's view, children needed to be taught about sexuality before they became adolescents. Wattleton attributes the increase of teen pregnancies to children's contradictory exposure to sex: children are bombarded with sexual messages and exploitation by a society that is, for the most part, sexually illiterate.

Wattleton's demanding role as president of PPFA unfortunately took its toll on her personal life. Although she commuted from New York to Dayton on weekends to be with her husband and daughter, her marriage to Franklin Gordon crumbled in 1981. In retrospect, Wattleton said that her demanding schedule "probably accelerated" the demise of an already shaky marriage. In spite of her personal problems, however, her calm and rational outward demeanor were not shaken. In fact, cool composure and articulation have become her trademarks, and these qualities have allowed her to disarm enemies and inspire supporters.

In January 1992, Wattleton announced her resignation as president of PPFA, saying that she would begin hosting a Chicago talk show dealing with a variety of women's issues. Of her resignation, Planned Parenthood board chairman Kenneth Edelin said, "There was a gasp all the way from Texas." And Arthur J. Kropp, president of People for the American way, remarked: "Faye Wattleton's departure is a significant loss to the choice community. Her political savvy and her remarkable ability to communicate difficult issues have made her a giant in the ongoing battle to preserve American's fundamental liberties."

Wattleton's awards and accomplishments are impressive, coming from such organizations as the World Institute of Black Communication, the American Nursing Association, the Better World Society, and the American Public Health Association.

**Profile by
C. Cunningham and
A. L. Jones**

IDA B. WELLS BARNETT

C haracterized by the print media as courageous, determined,

forceful, fearless, fiery, and militant, Ida Bell Wells Barnett came of age

during the post-Reconstruction period and spent her adult life fighting

to redress the inequities brought about by Jim Crow. She was born a slave

on July 16, 1862, in Holly Springs, Mississippi, to James Wells and

Elizabeth (Bell) Wells. Her mother was the child of a slave mother and

an Indian father. The oldest in a family of four boys and four girls, Ida

Wells Barnett attended Rust College, a freedmen's high school and

industrial school formerly called Shaw University.

1862-1931 •

"Crusader •

for

Justice"

The yellow fever epidemic of 1878, which ravaged Memphis, Tennessee, and northern Mississippi, claimed the lives of Ida Wells Barnett's parents and that of her youngest brother. At the age of sixteen she assumed responsibility for her siblings and taught for a short time in the

rural district of Holly Springs. In the 1880s, Wells Barnett engaged her brothers and sisters in apprenticeships and with her two younger sisters moved to Memphis to be close to her father's sister and to obtain a better-paying teaching position.

A train ride from Memphis to Woodstock was the beginning of Wells Barnett's lifelong public campaign against the inequities and injustices faced by blacks throughout the South. In May 1884 she purchased a first-class ticket on a local Memphis-to-Woodstock line operated by the Chesapeake, Ohio, and Southwestern Railroad Company. Taking a seat in the ladies' coach, she was asked by the conductor to move to the forward car, a smoker. Wells Barnett refused, got off the train, returned to Memphis, and subsequently filed suit against the railroad company for refusing to provide her the first-class accommodations for which she had paid.

Legal suit •

filed against

railroad

In December 1884 the Memphis circuit court ruled in favor of Wells Barnett, levied the maximum fine of three hundred dollars against the railroad company, and awarded her personal damages of five hundred dollars. Headlines in the Christmas edition of the Memphis *Daily Appeal* read, "A Darky Damsel Obtains a Verdict for Damages Against the Chesapeake and Ohio Railroad—What It Cost to Put a Colored Teacher in a Smoking Car—Verdict for $500." Wells Barnett's success against the railroad company was short-lived. The railroad appealed the case to the Tennessee Supreme Court, which on April 5, 1887, reversed the lower court's decision on the grounds that the railroad had satisfied the statutory requirements to provide "like accommodations." Six days after the court's decision, Wells Barnett noted in *Crusader for Justice:*

> I felt so disappointed because I had hoped [for] such great things from my suit for my people generally. I [had] firmly believed all along that the law was on our side and would, when we appealed to it, give us justice. I feel shorn of that belief and utterly discouraged, and just now, if it were possible, I would gather my race in my arms and fly away with them.

Wells Barnett taught in the Memphis city schools from 1884 to 1891, attending summer sessions at Fisk University in Nashville to sharpen her skills. She met weekly with other teachers at the Memphis Vance Street Christian Church to play music, give recitals, read essays, and engage in debates. These literary meetings closed with the reading of the *Evening Star*, an internal journal of current events that Wells Barnett went on to edit. While serving in this capacity, she became known throughout the community and in 1887 wrote for the *Living Way*, a religious weekly. She also began writing regularly for the black press throughout the country. At the 1889 meeting of the Colored Press Association, later called the Afro-American Press Association, she was elected secretary. During this same year, the "Princess of the Press," was invited to become editor of and partner in the *Free Speech and Headlight,* a militant journal owned by the Reverend Taylor Nightingale, pastor of the Beale Street Baptist Church, and J. L. Fleming.

● *Wells Barnett*

called a

fearless

journalist

Wells Barnett gained a reputation for fearlessness because of the scathing and militant opinions she openly expressed in print. In 1891 Wells Barnett openly sanctioned retaliatory violence by blacks in George-town, Kentucky, who avenged the lynching of a black man by setting fire to the town. Because Wells Barnett wrote an editorial critical of the Memphis Board of Education and its unequal distribution of resources allocated to the segregated black schools, the board dismissed her from its employment in 1891. Disheartened but not discouraged, Wells Barnett devoted all her energy to the paper, shortening its name to the *Free Speech* and working diligently to expand its circulation, which she increased by 38 percent.

In 1892 events in Memphis changed the course of Wells Barnett's life. Thomas Moss, Calvin McDowell, and William Stewart, all friends of hers, opened the People's Grocery Store in a black section of Memphis. The black entrepreneurs successfully competed with white merchant W. H. Barrett, who operated a grocery store across the street. Barrett retaliated against the new competition with violence, and after several episodes, the Shelby County grand jury indicted the owners of People's for maintaining a nuisance. On Saturday, March 5, after dark, when nine deputy sheriffs dressed in civilian attire converged upon the grocery store owners, the deputies were taken for a mob and fired upon by a group of blacks determined to protect the owners. Three deputies were wounded; McDowell, Stewart, Moss, and scores of other accused rioters were arrested.

Judge Dubose of the Shelby County criminal court illegally dis-armed the Tennessee Rifles, a black state militia company that guarded the jail for three nights in an attempt to protect the prisoners. On Wednesday, March 9, 1892, nine white men abducted Moss, McDowell, and Stewart from the jail, carried them one mile north, and barbarously shot them to death. *Crusader for Justice* contains Wells Barnett's reaction:

> The city of Memphis had demonstrated that neither character nor standing avails the Negro if he dares to protect himself against the white man or become his rival. There is nothing we can do now about the lynching, as we are out-numbered and without arms.

The white mob could help itself to ammunition without pay, but the order was rigidly enforced against the selling of guns to Negroes. There is therefore only one thing left that we can do; save our money and leave a town which will neither protect our lives and property, nor give us a fair trial in the courts, but take us out and murder us in cold blood when accused by a white person.

The black community encouraged all who could to leave the Bluff City, and those who stayed to refrain from patronizing the City Railroad Company. Prodded by angry editorials in the *Free Speech* and calls of "On to Oklahoma," two thousand blacks left Memphis and put the streetcar company in dire financial straits. Throughout the following weeks and into the spring, Wells Barnett's editorials "demanded that the murders of Moss, McDowell, and Stewart be brought to justice."

In May 1892, Wells Barnett wrote an editorial in the *Free Speech* provoked by the lynching of eight more blacks. Her fiery pen punctured the ego of white men of the South, calling into question the hackneyed excuses used by whites for executing blacks without due process of the law by inferring that white women of the South were sexually attracted to black men. In response, terroristic statements poured forth from the local papers, the *Free Speech* presses and offices were destroyed on May 27, 1892, and Wells Barnett was warned not to return to Memphis.

Exiled from the South, Wells Barnett persevered in her struggle against racial injustice and the lynching of blacks as a columnist for the *New York Age*, a paper owned and edited by T. Thomas Fortune and Jerome B. Patterson. On June 7, 1892, the *New York Age* published a detailed analysis of lynching, refuting the myth that the white men in Memphis intended to shield white women against rape and providing a history of black and other lynchings since 1863.

Fiery journalist •

exiled from

the South

Discontented with narrating the story in the black press, Wells Barnett began lecturing throughout the Northeast. This lecture circuit brought her international attention, and in 1893 Catherine Impey, the British editor of the *Anti-Caste*, invited her to speak in England. Wells Barnett left the United States on April 5, 1893, and lectured throughout England, Scotland, and Wales, with the tour ending in May 1893.

While abroad, Wells Barnett learned of the enterprising endeavors of the women of England through their civic groups. Upon her return home she strongly advised her sisters to become more involved in the matters of their communities, cities, and the nation through organized civic groups. According to Gerder Lerner, on the eve of Wells Barnett's departure for England she spoke at a fund-raising rally a group of prominent New York women organized in her support. This meeting had a profound effect on the black women's club movement:

> This 1892 meeting, which brought together Mrs. Josephine St. Pierre Ruffin of Boston, Victoria Earle Matthews of New York and Dr. Susan McKinney of Brooklyn, inspired the formation of the first two black women's clubs. The New York and Brooklyn women formed the Women's Loyal Union and somewhat later, Mrs. St. Pierre Ruffin organized the Woman's Era Club of Boston.

Josephine Pierre Ruffin in 1895 had actively promoted a national organization, the First National Conference of Colored Women. In that same year, the National Federation of Afro-American Women was founded with Mary Margaret Washington as president.

Wells Barnett moved to Chicago in 1893 and began working for the *Chicago Conservator*, the first black American paper in the city, founded by Ferdinand L. Barnett. She continued her interest in women's clubs and organized Chicago's first civic club for black women, which was later named in her honor. In February 1894 she returned to England. During her six-month stay, a Chicago daily paper, the *Inter-Ocean*, edited by William Penn Nixon, published her articles in a column entitled "Ida B. Wells Abroad." While there, she spoke widely on the increasing occurrences and savageness of lynchings in the South and of the negligence of regional authorities. Wells Barnett was the impetus behind the Britons' formation of an anti-lynching committee for the purpose of investigating and publicizing the persecution of blacks in America's South.

On June 27, 1895, Wells Barnett married Ferdinand L. Barnett, a black attorney and editor and founder of the *Chicago Conservator*. Barnett shared his wife's interests, and together they championed the black cause for equal rights. They had four children: Charles Aked, Herman Kohlsaat, Ida B. Wells, and Alfreda.

Domesticity did not detract Ida Wells Barnett from her crusade, however. She continued to write articles and took an interest in local and national affairs. In 1909 Wells Barnett was one of two black women— Mary Church Terrell was the other—who signed the "Call" for a conference on the Negro, which came in response to three days of racial violence in Springfield, Illinois, in August 1908. On May 31, 1909, the conference convened in New York City and led to the formation of the National Association for the Advancement of Colored People (NAACP).

At the close of the conference, Wells Barnett was placed on the NAACP's executive committee and was a strong advocate of the NAACP's having its own publication to express the views of the organization. Thus, *Crisis* was founded in 1910.

Wells Barnett continued to fight injustice and discrimination in Chicago and throughout the United States. The Springfield riots had motivated her, with students in her Sunday School class at Grace Presbyterian Church, to establish an organization called the Negro Fellowship League. Just before the NAACP was chartered in May 1910, the Negro Fellowship League established a settlement house in Chicago. In 1913 Judge Harry Olson of the municipal court appointed Wells Barnett adult probation officer, a job she held until 1916. She worked out of the Fellowship League's social center and contributed her monthly salary of $150 to the center's budget.

Wells Barnett believed in the power of the ballot box and encouraged black men to register and exercise their right to vote. She worked in the women's suffrage movement and on January 30, 1913, founded the Alpha Suffrage Club of Chicago, the first black suffrage organization. Wells Barnett marched in suffrage parades and led her club members in the parade of June 16, when suffragists marched to the Republican National Convention and demanded a plank to give women the right to vote.

In December 1920 Wells Barnett was hospitalized and underwent surgery. After her recovery a year later she again became active in the civic and political affairs of Chicago and was one of the founders of the Cook County League of Women's Clubs. When the National Association of Colored Women met in Chicago in 1924, Wells Barnett ran for president of the organization but was defeated by Mary McLeod Bethune. Six years later, in 1930, Wells Barnett entered Chicago's political arena as an independent candidate for state senator. Running against Warren B. Douglas and Adelbert H. Roberts, she was defeated handily.

On March 21, 1931, she became ill and was rushed to Daily Hospital on Monday, March 23, suffering from uremic poisoning. Two days later, at the age of sixty-nine, the ever-vocal "crusader for justice" died. She was buried in Chicago's Oakwood Cemetery. In 1941 the Chicago Housing Authority opened the Ida B. Wells Housing Project, and in 1950 the City of Chicago named her one of twenty-five outstanding women in the city's history. On July 16, 1987, the 125th anniversary year of her birth and ninety-five years since she had been forced from the "Bluff City," the Memphis Community Relations Commission, through the Tennessee Historical Commission, dedicated a historical marker at the former site of the *Free Speech* newspaper offices.

"Crusader for Justice" continues the struggle

For the 1990 Black History Month observance, the United States Postal Service issued a stamp honoring this civil rights activist. Also, in 1990, the first full-length biography of Wells Barnett, *Ida B. Wells Barnett*, by Mildred Thompson, was published in the sixteen-volume series entitled *Black Women in the United States History: From Colonial Times to the Present.*

**Profile by
Linda T. Wynn**

PHILLIS WHEATLEY

*P*hillis Wheatley, who after her marriage usually signed her name

c. 1753-1784 •

Phillis Peters, was the first black person in America to publish a book

and, after Anne Bradstreet, the second woman to publish poetry. The

poet •

commentary that surrounds Wheatley's life and work describes two

Wheatleys: a pseudo-Wheatley, a person "petted" as a slave (according

to Wheatley, an impossible condition for any human being) while as an

artist called an imitator of Alexander Pope; and a real Wheatley, who

consciously engaged in an unflagging struggle for freedom and who

constructed a poetry that is creative and original. For the past two

hundred years, the pseudo-Wheatley has dominated biographical

critical commentary.

Evidence indicates Pope was only one of many poets Wheatley read, among them the American poets Mather Byles and Samuel Cooper. The recent recovery of her letters and poems reveals Wheatley's unmistakable concern for the problem of slavery, and her poems and her 1773 volume amply reveal that she not only accepted her African origins, but she was proud of them. Interpretation of her published work establishes that the central concern of her writing was the quest for freedom.

Because in "Phillis's Reply" Wheatley identifies Gambia as the land of her birth and because her slender facial features (long forehead, thin lips, well-defined cheekbones, and small nose) resemble those of the present-day Fulani, a people who occupied the region of the Gambia River during the eighteenth century, it is plausible that Wheatley was born of the Gambian Fulani. Since at the time of her purchase in Boston, on or about July 11, 1761, she was losing her front baby teeth, it is suggested that the year of her birth was 1753. The ship that transported her from Africa was the *Phillis*, a name that may have been foisted upon her.

The only memory of her mother Wheatley recalled to her white captors was that of her mother pouring "out water before the sun at his rising," recounted Margarita Matilda Oddell in her 1984 *Memoir*. The life-giving sun subsequently became the central image of her poetry. Wheatley's blend of solar imagery, Judaeo-Christian thought and figures, and images from ancient classicism reveal complex multicultural origins, not the least of which derives from her African heritage.

Another manifestation of Wheatley's African heritage is her practice of the funeral elegy. Among the Akan peoples, a group neighboring the Fula, for example, tradition dictated that all girls sang and composed funeral elegies for the deceased. Wheatley's memories of her African days very likely included performances of dirges sung by young women. As practiced in Africa, however, the oral elegy bears other parallels to Wheatley's. For example, in Africa the singer of the dirge is expected in her performance to point out numerous examples of the departed's wisdom; such references are typically drawn by young women lamenting that they have lost a wise counselor. In her elegies on Joseph Sewall and Samuel Cooper, Wheatley carries out these specifications. Of Joseph Sewall, for example, who was for fifty-six years pastor of the famous Old South Church of Boston and whose services the poet attended until his death in 1769, Wheatley wrote: "I, too have cause this mighty loss to mourn, / For he my monitor will not return."

Wheatley's principal biographer, Margaretta Matilda Oddell, has recorded that Wheatley "was frequently seen" very shortly after her purchase by John and Susanna Wheatley, "endeavoring to make letters

African •

heritage

reflected in

elegies

upon the wall with a piece of chalk or charcoal." Mary Wheatley, one of the Wheatley twins (Nathaniel was the other), instructed Phillis in reading the English Bible. Her master John wrote in a letter dated November 14, 1772, which comprises a portion of the prefatory material of Phillis Wheatley's 1773 *Poems on Various Subjects Religious and Moral*, that "by only what she was taught in the Family, she, in sixteen Months Time from her Arrival, attained the English Language." He also noted that "She has a great Inclination to learn the Latin Tongue, and has made some Progress in it." Wheatley had, by the publication of her 1773 *Poems*, mastered Latin so well that she rendered into heroic couplets the Niobe episode from Ovid's *Metamorphoses* with such dexterity that she created one of the best English translations of this episode.

Wheatley's first noted composition was a letter to Samson Occom, the Mohegan Indian minister, possibly composed in 1765. Her first published poem was printed on December 21, 1767, in the *Newport Mercury*, a colonial newspaper of Newport, Rhode Island, where her black friend Obour Tanner resided. Some have speculated that Wheatley and Tanner came over together on the *Phillis*. In any event, Wheatley corresponded with Tanner with great tenacity. Recent evidence has suggested that these two visited with some frequency as well, with Wheatley traveling from Boston to Newport.

• *Wheatley's*

linguistic talent

recognized

Wheatley's linguistic talent soon brought her to "the attention of the literati of the day," so Oddell observes, "many of whom furnished her with books." Oddell further notes that Wheatley was to be "frequently visited by clergymen, and other individuals of high standing in society." One of those individuals was probably Mather Byles, sometime-poet who became first Congregational minister of the Hollis Street Church. It has been argued that Wheatley designed her 1773 *Poems* after Byles's 1744 *Poems on Several Occasions*.

As a young man Byles carried on an active correspondence with Alexander Pope, who sent Byles copies of his famous translations of the *Iliad* and *Odyssey*. It may be through these that Wheatley was introduced to Pope's couplets. Byles, a Harvard graduate and no stranger to Latin, may have served Wheatley as occasional tutor in the ancient language. His inheritance of the library of his uncle, Cotton Mather—one of the most extensive libraries in the colonies—would have equipped Byles to teach his enthusiastic student.

With the colonies' best libraries and minds available to Wheatley, this developing poet was enabled to pursue her scholarly interests. She probably participated, as well, in the singing schools, thereby meeting the young women whose families later became the subjects of her elegies. But Wheatley was not merely a student-scholar and social participant; she was also a politically active, as her many poems about political events attest. One possible motivation for her political position may well have been her close association with Old South Church. The church was the site of the town meeting held after the Boston Massacre, a meeting that resulted in the expulsion of the royal governor. Wheatley's non-extant poem "On the Affray in King-Street, on the Evening of the 5th of March," was most likely about the Boston Massacre and the martyrdom of Crispus Attucks, the black man who organized the "affray."

The fact that Wheatley was a communicant of the largely-patriot Old South Church, while John and Susanna Wheatley attended the more loyalist New South Church has gone relatively unnoticed. For example, as recently as 1982 J. Saunders Redding published a sketch of Wheatley in which he claimed she was, along with the entire Wheatley family, a faithful British loyalist. However, Wheatley wrote no poetry on behalf of the Tories' predicament. It is true that John and Susanna Wheatley were loyalists, and it is also very likely that their son Nathaniel, who remained in England, was a staunch loyalist. Yet Wheatley did maintain a patriotic stance throughout her career, writing poems dedicated to George Washington, General David Wooster, and the declaration of peace in the 1783 Treaty of Paris.

Such a political position, doubtless known by the citizens of Boston, may have contributed to Wheatley's failure to publish a volume of her poems in Boston in 1772. But whether or not the poet's politics played a role, racism certainly did. As William H. Robinson has demonstrated, the Boston public would not support "anything of the kind" to be printed. Wheatley, however, found a more sympathetic backer in England. Largely because of Wheatley's publication in 1770 of her most famous elegy, "On The Death of the Mr. George Whitefield," a poem widely printed in broadside on both sides of the Atlantic, the poet came to the attention of Selina Hastings, Countess of Huntingdon, a wealthy philanthropist whose personal chaplain Whitefield had been. When the Countess heard that Boston subscribers would not endorse Wheatley's volume, she agreed to finance it in London.

Almost a year and a half passed before the volume went to press. During that interval much of the content was radically altered, so that a 1772 version would have taken on a character different from the later 1773 *Poems*. While the earlier volume would have had much more appeal to an audience of American patriots, the 1773 *Poems* had more of an aesthetic appeal to an audience that would have found pro-American poems inflammatory. The 1772 volume's subject was patriot American politics; if published, Wheatley could arguably have been the author of the first book of Revolutionary War poems, challenging Philip Freneau's claim to this distinction.

● *Poet matures*

as artist

The year and a half between March 1772 and July 1773 was an unusually productive one that saw Wheatley's maturation as a poet. Not yet finding her freedom in the material world, Wheatley turned inward to construct a poetics of liberation. In her poem, "On Imagination," she can, as poet with absolute power over the words of her poems, "with new worlds amaze th'unbounded soul." In the very next line of this piece, she begins immediately to construct a new world not bound by winter's iron bands but one populated by fragrant flowers and forests heavy with verdant leaves. This world into which she escapes is more redolent of her African Gambia than of a Christian paradise. She reluctantly leaves "the pleasing views" and returns to a winter whose most stark reality is the condition of slavery.

After the appearance of Wheatley's *Poems on Various Subjects, Religious and Moral*, however, she was not to endure slavery much longer. When *Poems* appeared in London in early September, the volume was reviewed at least nine times in British newspapers, many reviews expressing indignation for the fact that Wheatley, obviously an extremely talented artist, remained a slave. These notices crossed the Atlantic along with the first copies of Wheatley's *Poems*. It is probable that these notices, which praised the poet but attacked her masters, played a role in bringing about Phillis Wheatley's manumission. Another fact that may have contributed to the poet's release from slavery was the famous Somerset judgment of 1772, which was widely interpreted to mean that any slave who set foot on the English shore was thereafter considered free. Thus, technically Wheatley received manumission when she arrived in London on June 17, 1773.

By the time the poet penned a letter in October 1773 to David Wooster enumerating her activities in London during the past summer, she also announced: "Since my return to America my Master, has at the desire of my friends in England given me my freedom." It is important to note that Wheatley does not say John Wheatley freed her out of his own generosity but at the behest "of my friends in England." This same letter reveals that Wheatley made good use of her limited time in London where she met such dignitaries as Thomas Gibbons, Granville Sharp, Brook Watson, and the Earl of Dartmouth.

Wheatley returned to Boston on July 26, 1773, to be at the side of her mistress, whose health was in a state of rapid decline. While taking care of her, Wheatley carried on active correspondence, writing to such figures as the Countess of Huntingdon; David Wooster, who later became a general in the American revolutionary forces; John Thornton,

British philanthropist and friend of the Countess; Samson Occom, the Mohegan Indian minister and graduate of what later became Dartmouth College; the Reverend Samuel Hopkins; and Obour Tanner. In these letters, Wheatley seized every opportunity to promote her *Poems*. In her epistle to Occom, Wheatley presents her most eloquent and emphatic condemnation of slavery when she declares: "In every human Breast, God has implanted a Principle, which we call Love of Freedom; it is impatient of Oppression, and pants for Deliverance." The letter had more than a dozen reprintings in New England newspapers before 1780.

Despite solicitous care, Susanna Wheatley died on March 3, 1774, at the age of sixty-five. It was about this time that Wheatley began to see John Peters, a free black whom she married on April 1, 1778. Most sources give little time and no kindness to the figure of John Peters. Sidney Kaplan, however, paints a favorable portrait describing Peters as a multi-talented, enterprising man whose vocations included grocer and advocate on behalf of blacks before Massachusetts tribunals. Kaplan said Peters seemed "to have been a black man of dignity, who valued himself, did not kowtow to patronizing whites, struggled to climb the educational and economic ladder and failed." It is largely because of Peter's failure that Wheatley's own fortunes began to deteriorate. Another factor which undeniably contributed to the decline of the Peters family was the American Revolutionary War.

In October of 1775, Wheatley wrote a poem in honor of George Washington, which she mailed to the commander-in-chief of the Continental Army, receiving an enthusiastic reply and an invitation to visit him at his headquarters. Washington passed on Wheatley's tribute to a friend; subsequently the poem was printed several times as an instrument for the patriot cause. Wheatley did visit Washington at his Cambridge headquarters, and some surmise that she told him that Jefferson was grossly unjust in his assertion that blacks had intelligence and aesthetic capacities inferior to those of whites.

Wheatley's final years were marred by multiple disappointments. In 1778, the year of her marriage to Peters, John Wheatley died, leaving her with greatly limited resources. The very next year, one senses a desperation behind her decision to publish a set of proposals for a new volume of poems. Surely this attempt failed not because of racist reasons alone, but largely because a country in revolution has little time or money for poetry. Even so, this volume projects some three hundred pages of poetry, only a small portion of which has been reclaimed. Until that manuscript is recovered (many think John Peters took the manuscript south to Philadelphia after his wife's death), poems by Wheatley will probably continue to surface. During the last year of her life, she published what is perhaps her most moving funeral elegy, this one on the death of her mentor, Samuel Cooper, a poem celebrating the victory and peace of the American Revolution, and another elegy.

While neither of these poems suggests a weakening of Wheatley's poetic ability, "An Elegy on Leaving —————" does imply that the poet's career may indeed be coming to an end, for she bids farewell to "friendly bow'rs" and streams, protesting that she leaves "with sorrow each sequester'd seat." On December 5, 1784, Phillis Wheatley Peters died in Boston, unattended, of complications arising from the birth of her third child, who died with her.

**Profile by
John C. Shields**

OPRAH WINFREY

Nearly everyone knows Oprah Winfrey from a television talk show

1954- •

that draws seventeen thousand viewers each weekday, from her films, or

more recently from her passionate testimony before Congress on the

talk show •

subject of child abuse. Winfrey's swift rise to stardom is an extraordi-

host,

nary story of personal achievement, and she is among the best-known

actress

women now performing on national television.

Oprah Gail Winfrey was born on January 29, 1954, in Kosciusko, Mississippi, a small town seventy miles north of Jackson. Her parents, Vernita Lee and Vernon Winfrey, never married. Vernon Winfrey was twenty years old and in the service when his daughter was born. He had been on furlough from Fort Rucker in Alabama in 1953 and had returned to his military duties when his leave ended. He had no knowledge of his fatherhood until Vernita Lee mailed a card to him announcing the baby's arrival and scrawled across it a request for clothing for the infant. Lee had intended to name her daughter "Orpah" after the Biblical woman in the Book of Ruth, but someone, perhaps the midwife who attended the delivery, the clerk at the courthouse, or even Vernita Lee herself, misspelled the name by transposing the *p* and the *r*.

There was little work for a young black woman in Kosciusko who had no specific skills and no advanced training in any area of employment. Lee had heard that jobs were more plentiful in Milwaukee and better paid. Shortly after Oprah's birth, she moved to Milwaukee, Wisconsin, leaving the baby in the care of Vernon Winfrey's mother. She hoped to find a job as a domestic worker at wages of fifty dollars a week.

Grandmother Winfrey was a woman of strong, disciplined character, closely attached to her church. Much of Oprah Winfrey's early life was spent at church, which furnished her with her first opportunities to display her talents. She made her first speaking appearance in an Easter program. Later, at Christmas, she was on the program again. She was three years old. At home, however, the vocal Oprah Winfrey was made to understand that she was not to be heard so readily. She spent a great deal of time with adults and was to be quiet when in their presence. This kind of restraint was very difficult and discomfiting to an articulate child who longed for the company and attention of the people around her.

When she recalls her childhood, Winfrey indicates that she began to wish she were white when she was about six years old. She relates that she slept with a clothespin on her nose and prayed for corkscrew curls. Though she viewed her life as unsatisfactory, her spirit was not broken. She would not be subdued, and her grandmother would not compromise.

Eventually, Winfrey joined her mother in Milwaukee and found the life there decidedly different from the semi-rural life she had known in Mississippi. Her mother had only a room in another woman's house and had to work so hard that she had little time or energy to devote to the care of her child. The combination of welfare money and her wages as a maid was still insufficient to afford her and her daughter even the minimal comforts of a home. As she became more and more aware of city life, Winfrey became increasingly rebellious and resentful of the lack of material comforts and simple diversions that marked her life with her mother. As she had proven to be too much for her grandmother to control, so too was she more than her mother could handle.

It was Vernon Winfrey's turn now. Perhaps the influence of a father might be brought to bear upon this difficult child with greater success than either grandmother or mother had been able to realize. He had moved to Nashville, Tennessee, upon completing his military commitment, married, and established a home with his wife. The couple welcomed Oprah Winfrey during the summer of 1962, just after she had finished first grade. They were pleased to have Vernon Winfrey's daughter with them, but Winfrey was soon to find that she could not wear them down as she had her mother and grandmother. The little girl's stepmother quickly discovered that in spite of her skills in reading, speaking, and writing, Winfrey lacked mastery of basic arithmetic, so she was firmly set to work at strengthening her performance in computation. The ensuing school year went well.

The church was still a major influence in her life. Vernon Winfrey was active in his church, Progressive Baptist, and brought his daughter with him for Sunday church services, youth activities, holiday programs, and church-sponsored community activities. Oprah Winfrey was a dependable performer in religious pageants, choral presentations, and the activities of the various organizations within the church. Finally it was summer again, and Vernita Lee wanted to see her daughter. Despite misgivings, Vernon Winfrey and his wife agreed. Months later, their fears of a summertime visit proved well-founded: when summer ended and Vernon went to retrieve his daughter, he found both her and her mother reluctant to resume the arrangement of the previous year.

Vernita Lee had persuaded Oprah Winfrey that life "at home" could now be much more pleasant than it had been earlier. She was soon to marry a Milwaukee man with whom she had maintained a relationship for several years. The new family would include the man's two children, a son and a daughter. It was for the Winfreys quite a blow to return Oprah Winfrey to an environment they knew did not offer the support and discipline she needed and deserved, but they felt a certain respect for Lee's wishes. The return to Milwaukee represented a downturn in Oprah Winfrey's fortunes, and the negative aspects of her life became more intolerable to her as she grew older.

- **Winfrey suffers**

in silence

Again Winfrey developed a painful concern relating to skin color and standards of physical attractiveness. She became convinced that she was neglected in favor of her lighter-skinned stepsister. She felt cast off, and her pain was all the more intense because it seemed to her that her mother was as guilty of her mistreatment as anyone else.

It was also during this period, beginning as early as her ninth year, that Winfrey alleges she was subjected to frequent sexual abuse, initially by a cousin, then by a family friend, and finally by a favorite uncle. She found the attacks confusing and frightening but suffered them in silence because she did not know what else to do and because she thought she was somehow to blame. Today she realizes that children are never to blame for such treatment at the hands of adults, and her early experiences have led her to step forward as a dedicated spokesperson on the subject of child abuse.

In spite of her miserable home life, Winfrey remained a good student. Gene Abrams, one of her teachers at the inner-city Lincoln

Middle School, recognized her exceptional abilities and took an active interest in her. He helped her get a scholarship to a prestigious suburban school in the affluent Fox Point area. Winfrey encountered few scholastic difficulties there, but her emotional problems were proliferating and her behavior was reflecting the chaos she was experiencing. Out of her fertile mind, Winfrey was hatching and staging one preposterous scheme after another. On several occasions she destroyed family belongings and pretended that their apartment had been burglarized in order to get herself a more fashionable pair of glasses. Twice she ran away from home. Winfrey's mother was constantly bewildered by her increasingly frequent escapades and again had to acknowledge her inability to deal with her rebellious daughter. During the summer of 1968 Oprah Winfrey, now fourteen, returned to her father and his wife in Nashville.

It was a vastly different Oprah Winfrey who returned to Nashville after five years in Milwaukee. Early adolescence is a period of rapid growth and change for any individual, but the circumstances under which Winfrey had lived had brought great negative influences into her life, which forced her to grow up exceptionally quickly. Adjustment between father and daughter was not easy, but Vernon Winfrey prevailed. He set high standards of conduct and achievement for his daughter and saw that she met them. She enrolled in Nashville's East High School and was soon involved in numerous school activities, especially those having to do with public speaking and dramatics.

Life takes a •

new course

By the time Winfrey entered her senior year of 1970-1971, she knew that her future lay in the performing arts. She was chosen to attend the 1970 White House Conference on Youth in Washington. She went to Los Angeles to speak at a church and toured Hollywood while she was there. A local radio station, WVOL, managed and operated by blacks, hired Winfrey to read the news. She was soon ready to enter college and hoped to attend an institution far removed from Nashville, perhaps in New England. Once again, Vernon Winfrey made a decision that countered his daughter's preferences, and she attended Tennessee State University in Nashville.

Winfrey continued her work as a news announcer at WVOL and was soon hired away by WLAC, a major radio station. It was not long before she moved to WLAC-TV (later WTVF) as a reporter-anchor. Although she was earning a five-figure salary while she was in college, her father had not softened his strict requirements of her in terms of conduct or scholarship, and with each succeeding year she was finding his restraints on her social life harder and harder to accept. She began to look beyond Nashville and found a new position at WJZ-TV in Baltimore, Maryland, in 1976. She was only a few months short of her college graduation when she left Nashville and Tennessee State University without having received her bachelor's degree.

Winfrey's tenure in Baltimore began less auspiciously than she would have liked. She became the object of an intensive makeover effort on the part of her station management, which sought to develop an entirely new persona. The attempt was not completely successful. She had little formal training in journalism or mass communication, and her reporting often failed to achieve the desired degree of objectivity. Indeed, she resisted the necessity to be objective, preferring to approach a story from the inside and react to it in a subjective manner. She had never before accustomed herself to a self-disciplined point of view and seemed unable or unwilling to do so now.

- ***Winfrey finds***

  her niche

Winfrey was well-protected by the contract she had with the station, and management was forced to find a better use of her talents. She was assigned to cohost a local morning show called "People Are Talking." Neither she nor her employers recognized the fact immediately, but Winfrey had found her niche. Her engaging personality and her amazing ability to communicate with a diverse audience were indisputable assets in her new assignment. Sherry Burns, who was producer of the show, said of her, "Oprah is a wonderful, wonderful person. Who she is on-camera is exactly what she is off-camera. . . . She's a totally approachable, real, warm person." The very traits of emotionalism and subjectivity that had hampered her efforts as a reporter helped make her an effective and stimulating interviewer.

As the popularity of her show began to grow, as well as her satisfaction with and enjoyment of the program, Oprah Winfrey began sending tapes of her broadcasts to other markets around the country. She sensed that she was ready for big-time broadcasting. The woman who had been coproducer of "People Are Talking" left Baltimore in 1984 for a new position on "A.M. Chicago," a morning talk show broadcast by the ABC-TV Chicago affiliate, WLS-TV. The station manager had observed Winfrey on some of the tapes his new producer had screened for him and quickly decided to hire her for "A.M. Chicago," which would compete with the "Phil Donahue Show," the well-established favorite in the local and national market. With Winfrey's coming, "A.M. Chicago" took off and quickly outdistanced Donahue in the ratings. In early 1985 Phil Donahue moved his show to New York and left Chicago to Winfrey.

In high school and college Winfrey had pursued an interest in dramatics and had attracted favorable attention as an actress, so she found the idea of portraying Sofia in the 1985 Quincy Jones/Steven Spielberg film production of Alice Walker's novel *The Color Purple* appealing. She took leave from her show and went south to create her role. The film opened to mixed reviews and much controversial discussion, but most professional critics praised Winfrey's performance, and it earned her an Academy Award nomination. Close on the heels of *The Color Purple*, she appeared in 1986 in a motion picture based on Richard Wright's novel *Native Son*. Hers was not a major role, and the film, which was neither a critical success nor a popular one, was not widely distributed.

Winfrey's "A.M. Chicago" having become such a sensation, WLS-TV decided to allot it a full hour instead of its former thirty minutes and changed its title to "The Oprah Winfrey Show." By late 1986 the show was in syndication. It was reported that the deal grossed $125,000,000 and that its star would receive more than $30,000,000 in 1987-1988 and become the highest-paid performer in show business. A five-year contract secured her position as a television host through the 1990-1991 season.

Winfrey had become one of the best-known figures of the 1980s. She could finally devote much of her prodigious energy to the pursuit of the numerous dreams she had cherished throughout the years of her swift professional ascent. Since the achievement of her full-blown success, Winfrey has formed her own company, Harpo (Oprah spelled backwards) Productions and purchased a gigantic studio to house its operations. Harpo, Inc., has taken over the ownership and production of "The Oprah Winfrey Show," over which she maintains full control and responsibility. The company plans to bring to the screen productions that convey important social and spiritual messages that might not be deemed commercially promising by others, and has already brought television audiences a movie version of Gloria Naylor's *The Women of Brewster Place*. Plans call for productions of Toni Morrison's Pulitzer Prize-winning novel *Beloved*, Mark Mathabane's autobiographical *Kaffir Boy*, and Zora Neale Hurston's much-admired *Their Eyes Were Watching God*.

Winfrey forms •

Harpo, Inc.

In 1988 Winfrey was invited to deliver the main address at commencement exercises at Tennessee State University. At that ceremony the university awarded her a diploma in recognition of her accomplishments, although she left the institution without having completed degree requirements. For her part, Winfrey established a scholarship fund at her alma mater that will furnish payment of expenses for ten students enrolled in the university each year. Characteristically, she reserves the right to choose the students who receive these annual awards, then maintains a personal relationship with each recipient and requires that each student maintain a "B" average.

Winfrey speaks to numerous youth groups and urges her audiences on to higher achievement, pressing them to strive for higher standards. She seeks to raise the level of confidence and self-esteem of her female listeners of all ages and speaks of helping women to win self-empowerment. She serves as a mentor to girls from a Chicago housing project and also as an advocate for children, appearing before Congress in 1991 to urge passage of proposed protective legislation—the National Child Protection Act—which would create a national registry of convicted child-abusers. The registry would allow day-care center staff to conduct background checks on potential employees—no idle need, since in the six states which already use such registers, 6,200 convicted criminals were discovered seeking work in child-care in a given year. Winfrey also hopes that legislators eventually will put into place nationwide mandatory sentencing for child abusers, with no plea bargaining nor parole permitted.

She also anticipates establishing a center that would offer counseling and support to women who need assistance. Says Winfrey, "I want to be able to spread the message that you are responsible for your life and to set up a format to teach people how to do that." It is difficult to envision a more able teacher of that lesson than Oprah Winfrey.

**Profile by
Lois L. Dunn**

A CLOSER LOOK

● *MARIAN ANDERSON*

Abdul, Raoul. *Blacks in Classical Music: A Personal History*. Dodd, Mead, 1977.

————. "Marian Anderson: Symbolic Challenge of Culture in America." *New York Amsterdam News*, 6 February 1982.

"The Age of the Black Diva." *Ebony*, August 1991: 74, 76.

Allen, Cleveland G. "Marian Anderson Given Tremendous Ovation." *Pittsburgh Courier*, 5 September 1925.

Anderson, Marian. *My Lord, What a Morning: An Autobiography*. Viking Press, 1956.

————. "Hall Johnson, 1888-1970." *The New York Times*, 24 May 1970.

"At Home with Marian Anderson." *Ebony* 9 (February 1954): 52-59.

Bogle, Donald. *Brown Sugar: Eighty Years of America's Black Female Superstars*. Harmony Books, 1980.

Collins, Leslie M. *A Song, A Dance, and A Play: An Interpretative Study of Three American Artists*. Ph.D. Dissertation. Case Western Reserve University, 1945.

Current Biography Yearbook. H. W. Wilson, *1940*: 17-19, *1950*: 8-10.

De Coverley, Roy. "Marian Anderson in Denmark: An Appreciation." *Opportunity* 12 (September 1934): 270-271.

De Schauenesee, Max. "Marian Anderson." *The New Grove Dictionary of Music and Musicians*. Vol. 1. Edited by Stanley Sadie. Grove's Dictionaries of Music, 1981.

Embree, Edwin R. *13 Against the Odds*. Viking Press, 1944.

Ewen, David. "Marian Anderson." *The Negro in Music and Art*. Edited by Lindsay Patterson. Publishers Company, 1967.

————. *Musicians Since 1900: Performers in Concert and Opera*. H. W . Wilson, 1978.

"An 80th Birthday Tribute to Marian Anderson." *Ebony* 37 (May 1982): 48-50.

Fisher, Isaac. "Marian Anderson: Ambassador of Beauty from Her Race." *Southern Workman* 65 (March 1936): 72-80.

Fogel, Henry. Review of "The Art of Marian Anderson." *Fanfare* 10 (September/October 1986): 276-277.

Fraser, C. Gerald. "Marian Anderson: A National Treasure is Saluted at 75." *The New York Times*, 25 February 1977.

Gibbs, Margaret. *The DAR*. Holt, Rinehart & Winston, 1969.

Hare, Maud Cuney. *Negro Musicians and Their Music*. Associated Publishers, 1936.

Heylbut, Rose. "Some Reflections on Singing." *Etude* 57 (October 1939): 631-632.

Hughes, Langston. *Black Magic: A Pictorial History of the Negro in American Entertainment*. Englewood Cliffs, N.J.: Prentice-Hall, 1967.

————. *Famous Negro Music Makers*. Dodd, Mead, 1955.

Hurok, Sol. *Impresario, a Memoir*. Random House, 1946.

Klaw, Barbara. "'A Voice One Hears Once in a Hundred Years': An Interview with Marian Anderson." *American Heritage* 28 (February 1977): 50-57.

Kuyper, George. "Marian Anderson." *Southern Workman* 61 (March 1932): 125-27.

"Lady from Philadelphia: Marian Anderson's Far East Trip is Television's Finest Hour." *Ebony* 13 (March 1958): 31-32.

Lebow, Bernard, and Stephen Fassett, eds. *The American Record Index*. Elaine Music Shop, 1950.

Lovinggood, Penman. *Famous Modern Negro Musicians*. Press Forum Co., 1921.

"Marian Anderson, American Product." *The Bulletin* (1 April 1929): 1.

Moe, Michael. "12 Years After: Marian Anderson Comes Back Home—A Laundress' Daughter Whose Voice Thrilled All Europe." *Philadelphia Record*, 8 May 1937.

"NAACP Salutes a Living Legend." *Crisis* 89 (April 1982): 25.

Neal, Steve. "Marian Anderson Cherishes Her Privacy." *Philadelphia Inquirer*, 23 February 1975.

Noble, Jeanne L. *Beautiful, Also, Are the Souls of My Black Sisters: A History of the Black Woman in America*. Prentice-Hall, 1982.

Novak, Benjamin J. "Opening Doors in Music." *Negro History Bulletin* 34 (January 1971): 1-14.

"'Of Men and Music': Story of Marian Anderson is Told in Series of Music Films." *Ebony* 6 (May 1951): 49-50.

Reif, Rita. "Marian Anderson at 70: 'We Never Felt Poor.'" *New York Times*, 28 February 1972.

Robinson, Wilhelmena S. *Historical Negro Biographies*. 2d ed., rev. Publishers Co., 1969.

Rogers, Joel Augustus. *World's Great Men of Color*. Edited by John Henrik Clarke. Vol. 2. Macmillan, 1972.

Sims, Janet L. *Marian Anderson: An Annotated Bibliography and Discography*. Greenwood Press, 1981.

Steane, John B. *The Grand Tradition: Seventy Years of Singing on Record*. Scribner, 1974.

Stecklow, Steve. "Marian Anderson Returns with Memories, Thanks." Philadelphia *Evening Bulletin*, 13 May 1977.

"Story of Marian Anderson." *Literary Digest* 123 (May 22, 1937): 30.

Story, Rosalyn M. *And So I Sing: African-American Divas of Opera and Concert*. Warner Books, 1990.

Sweeley, Michael. "The First Lady." *National Review* 41 (September 29, 1989): 65-66.

Thompson, Bill. "To Penn, Fondly, from Marian Anderson." *Philadelphia Inquirer*, 14 April 1977.

"A Tribute to Marian Anderson." *Ebony* 45 (November 1989): 182.

"Triumphs in Berlin." *Norfolk Journal and Guide*, 8 November 1930.

Turner, Patricia. *Afro-American Singers: An Index and Preliminary Discography of Long-Playing Recordings of Opera, Choral Music and Song*. Challenge Productions, 1977.

———. *Dictionary of Afro-American Performers, 78 RPM and Cylinder Recordings @1900 to 1949*. Garland, 1990. 3-25.

Vehanen, Kosti. *Marian Anderson: A Portrait*. Whittlesey House, 1941.

Westlake, Neda M., and Otto E. Albrecht. *Marian Anderson: A Catalog of the Collection at the University of Pennsylvania Library*. University of Pennsylvania Press, 1981.

White, Al. "Triumph of Marian Anderson." *Our World* 10 (April 1955): 60-67.

White, Lucien H. Review of New York concert. *New York Age*, 7 August 1920.

Williams, Juan. Review. *Variety*, May 13, 1991.

● *MAYA ANGELOU*

Angelou, Maya. *The Heart of a Woman*. Bantam Books, 1982.

———. *I Know Why the Caged Bird Sings*. Bantam Books, 1970.

Bloom, Lynn Z. "Maya Angelou." *Afro-American Writers after 1955: Dramatists and Prose Writers*. Edited by Thadious M. Davis and Trudier Harris. Gale Research, 1985.

Collier, Eugenia. "Maya Angelou: From *Caged Bird* to *All God's Childen*." *New Directions* 13 (October 1986): 22-27.

Cudjoe, Selwyn R. "Maya Angelou and the Autobiographical Statement." In *Black Women Writers (1950-1980): A Critical Evaluation*. Edited by Mari Evans. Doubleday, 1984. 6-24.

Current Biography. H. W. Wilson, 1974. 12-15.

Grossman, Mary Ann. "Maya Angelou's Life Is a Touch of Elegance." *St. Paul Pioneer Press Dispatch* 18 June 1989.

"Maya Angelou." *Tampa Tribune* 17 March 1989.

McPherson, Dolly A. "Order Out of Chaos: The Autobiographical Works of Maya Angelou." *Studies in African and African American Culture.* Vol. 1. Edited by James L. Hill. Peter Lang, 1990.

• *JOSEPHINE BAKER*

Ehrlich, Karla (producer). *Chasing a Rainbow: The Life of Josephine Baker* (video). Csaky Production, 1986.

Haney, Lynn. *Naked at the Feast.* Dodd, Mead, 1981.

Papich, Steven. *Remembering Josephine.* Bobbs-Merrill, 1976.

Rose, Phyllis. "Exactly What Is It about Josephine Baker?" *New York Times* 10 March, 1991.

————. *Jazz Cleopatra: Josephine Baker in Her Time.* Doubleday, 1989.

Spradling, Mary Mace. *In Black and White.* 3rd ed. Vol. 1. Gale Research, 1980. Supplement, 1985.

• *MARGUERITE ROSS BARNETT*

Chronicle of Higher Education 37 (6 March 1991): A-3.

New York Times (27 February 1992): A-17.

• *DAISY BATES*

Bates, Daisy. *The Long Shadow of Little Rock.* McKay, 1962.

Blossom, Virgil T. *It Has Happened Here.* Harper, 1959.

Freyer, Tony. *The Little Rock Crisis: A Constitutional Interpretation.* Greenwood Press, 1984.

Huckaby, Elizabeth. *Crisis at Central High School: Little Rock, 1957-1958.* Louisiana State University Press, 1980.

Jacoway, Elizabeth. "Taken By Surprise: Little Rock Business Leaders and Desegregation." In *Southern Businessmen and Desegregation.* Edited by Elizabeth Jacoway and David Colburn. Louisiana State University Press, 1982.

New York Times, 23-30 September 1957.

Record, Wilson and Jane C. Record, eds. *Little Rock, U.S.A.: Material for Analysis.* Chandler Pub. Co., 1960.

Williams, C. Fred., et al. *A Documentary History of Arkansas.* University of Arkansas Press, 1984.

Williams, Juan. *Eyes on the Prize: America's Civil Rights Years, 1954-1965.* Penguin Books, 1987.

• *MARY FRANCES BERRY*

Berry, Mary Frances. *Black Resistance/White Law.* Prentice-Hall, 1971.

————. "A Love-Hate Relationship with the National Archives." In *Afro-American History: Sources for Research.* Edited by Robert Clarke, Howard University, 1981.

————. *Stability, Security, and Continuity.* Greenwood Press, 1978.

————. *Why ERA Failed.* Indiana University Press, 1986.

Carroll, Susan J. Review Essay. *American Political Science Review* 81 (December 1987): 1339-41.

Choice 19 (June 1982): 1477.

Guidepost, 22 December 1977.

Harris, Ron. "The Turning Point, That Changed Their Lives." *Ebony* 34 (January 1979): 80, 82.

Lanker, Brian. *I Dream a World.* Stewart, Tabori and Chang, 1989.

Library Journal 106 (December 1981): 2390.

Pinderhughes, Dianne M. "Black Women and National Educational Policy." *Journal of Negro Education* 51 (Summer 1982): 301-307.

Poinsette, Alex. "Colorado University's Chancellor." *Ebony* 30 (January 1977): 58-60, 65-66.

Quarles, Benjamin. Review of *Military Necessity and Civil Rights Policy. Journal of American History* 45 (September 1978): 478.

Reynolds, Barbara. "The Woman the President Couldn't Fire." *Essence* 15 (October 1984): 12, 158.

"Rights Panel Backs Reagan in Opposing Quota." *Washington Post,* 18 January 1984.

Smith, Carol Hobson. "Black Female Achievers in Academe." *Journal of Negro History* 51 (Summer 1982): 323-27.

Wattenberg, Ben. Editorial. *Washington Post,* 16 September 1983.

Williams, Richard. Review of *Stability, Security, and Continuity. Journal of American Studies* 14 (April 1980): 167.

MARY McLEOD BETHUNE

Daniel, Sadie Iola. *Women Builders*. Associated Publishers, 1931.

Germani, Clara. "Bronze Tribute to a Black Leader Balances Lincoln Park Monument." *The Christian Science Monitor*, 18 January, 1991.

Holt, Rackham. *Mary McLeod Bethune: A Biography*. Doubleday, 1964.

Leffall, Dolores C., and Janet L. Sims. "Mary McLeod Bethune—The Educator." *Journal of Negro Education* 45 (Summer 1976): 342-59.

Ludlow, Helen W. "The Bethune School." *Southern Workman* 41 (March 1912): 144-54.

Peare, Owen. *Mary McLeod Bethune*. Vanguard Press, 1951.

Ross, B. Joyce. "Mary McLeod Bethune and the National Youth Administration: A Case Study of Power Relationships in the Black Cabinet of Franklin D. Roosevelt." *Journal of Negro History* 60 (January 1975): 1-28.

Smith, Elaine M. "Mary McLeod Bethune and the National Youth Administration." In Mabel E. Deutrich and Virginia C. Purdy, eds. *Clio Was a Woman: Studies in the History of American Women*. Howard University Press, 1980.

————. "Mary McLeod Bethune." *Notable American Women: The Modern Period*. Vol. I. Harvard University Press, 1980.

GWENDOLYN BROOKS

Baker, Houston A., Jr. "The Achievement of Gwendolyn Brooks." *CLA Journal* (September 1972): 23-31.

Brooks, Gwendolyn. *Report from Part One*. Broadside Press, 1972.

————. *The World of Gwendolyn Brooks*. Harper & Row, 1971.

Kent, George E. *A Life of Gwendolyn Brooks*. University Press of Kentucky, 1989.

Madhubuti, Haki, ed. *Say That the River Turns: The Impact of Gwendolyn Brooks*. Third World Press, 1987.

Melhem, D. H. *Gwendolyn Brooks: Poetry and the Heroic Voice*. University Press of Kentucky, 1987.

Mphahlele, Ezekiel. *Voices in the Whirlwind, and Other Essays*. Hill and Wang, 1972.

New Yorker 21 (22 September 1945): 88.

Tate, Claudia, ed. *Black Women Writers at Work*. Continuum, 1983.

Washington, Mary Helen. "Taming All That Anger Down: Rage and Silence in Gwendolyn Brooks's *Maud Martha*." *Black Literature and Literary Theory*. Edited by Henry Louis Gates, Jr. Methuen, 1984.

Wilder, Amos N. "Sketches from Life." *Poetry* 67 (December 1945): 164-66.

MARGARET TAYLOR BURROUGHS

Atkinson, Edward J. *Black Dimensions in Contemporary Art*. New American Library, 1979.

Barbour, Floyd, ed. *The Black Seventies*. Sargent, 1970.

Bontemps, Jacqueline Fonvielle. *Forever Free: Art by African American Women, 1862-1980*. Stephenson, 1980.

Burroughs, Margaret T. *What Shall I Tell My Children Who Are Black?* MAAH Press, 1968. 29.

Celebrating Negro History and Brotherhood: A Folio of Prints by Chicago Artists. Seven Arts Workshop, 1956.

Contemporary Authors. Gale, 1977.

Dickerson, Mary Jane. "Margaret T. G. Burroughs." In *Dictionary of Literary Biography*. Vol. 41: *Afro-American Poets Since 1985*. Eds. Trudier Harris and Thadious M. Davis. Gale, 1985.

Dover, Cedric. *American Negro Art*. New York Graphic Society, 1969.

Ebony Success Library. Vol. 1. *1,000 Successful Blacks*. Johnson Pub. Co., 1973.

Edwards, Audrey. "They Made It Happen." *Black Enterprise* (May 1980): 33-40.

Lewis, Samella S., and Ruth G. Waddy. *Black Artists on Art*. Vol. 2. Contemporary Crafts, 1971.

"Prints by Margaret G. Burroughs." *Freedomways* 1 (Spring 1961): 107-109.

Rush, Theresa Gonnels, Carol Fairbanks Myers, and Esther Spring Arata. *Black American Writers Past and Present*. Scarecrow Press, 1975.

Stoelting, Winifred. *Hale Woodruff: 50 Years of His Art*. Studio Museum of Harlem, April 29-June 24, 1979.

Tibbs, Thurlow E., Jr. *Margaret Burroughs/Marion Perkins: A Retrospective*. Evans-Tibbs Collection, 1980s.

• MARY ELIZABETH CARNEGIE

Carnegie, M. E. *Contemporary Minority Leaders in Nursing*. American Nurses' Association, 1983.

———. *Making Choices; Taking Chances*. Edited by T. Schorr and A. Zimmerman. C. V. Mosby, 1988.

———. *The Path We Tread: Blacks in Nursing, 1854-1984*. Lippincott, 1986.

———. "The Path We Tread." *International Nursing Review* 9 (October 1962).

Dannett, Sylvia G. L. *Profiles of Negro Womanhood*. Vol. 2. Educational Heritage, 1966.

Staupers, Mabel K. *No Time for Prejudices*. Macmillan, 1961.

• ELIZABETH CATLETT

Bontemps, Jacqueline Fonville. *Forever Free: Art by African-American Women 1862-1980*. Stephenson, 1980. 68-69, 174-76.

Brown, B. A. "Expressing Social Concerns." *Artweek* 17 (March 1986): 5.

Cotter, Holland. "Black Artists: Three Shows." *Art in America* (March 1990): 165-71, 217.

de la Cuesta, M. Durand. "Elizabeth Catlett, Outstanding Sculptor of Our Epoch." *Nosotros* (Mexico) (July 1962).

Dover, Cedric. *American Negro Art*. New York Graphic Society, 1960.

Driskell, David C., and Fred F. Bond. *An Exhibition of Sculptures and Prints by Elizabeth Catlett*. The Carl Van Vechten Gallery of Fine Arts, Fisk University, 1973.

Fax, Elton Clay. *Seventeen Black Artists*. Dodd, Mead, 1971.

Gedeon, Lucinda. *Sculpture, Elizabeth Catlett / Francisco Mora, Watercolors*. Tempe, Ariz.: University Art Museum, January 11-February 15, 1987.

Goldman, Shifra M. "Six Women Artists of Mexico." *Women's Art Journal* 3 (Fall-Winter 1982-1983): 1-9.

Gouma-Peterson, Thalia. "Elizabeth Catlett: 'The Power of Human Feeling and of Art.'" *Woman's Art Journal* 4 (Spring/Summer 1983): 48-56. Also in *Arts Quarterly* 5 (October-December 1983): 26-31.

Hewitt, Mary Jane. "Elizabeth Catlett." *The International Review of African-American Art* 7 (1987).

Lewis, Samella. *Art: African-American*. Harcourt Brace Jovanovich, 1978.

———. *The Art of Elizabeth Catlett*. Hancraft Studios, 1984.

"My Art Speaks for Both My Peoples." *Ebony* 54 (February 1970): 94-96.

Oliver, Stephanie Stokes. "Elizabeth Catlett: Portrait of a Master Sculptor." *Essence* 16 (June 1985): 85-88.

Paintings, Sculpture, and Prints of the Negro Woman by Elizabeth Catlett. Introduction by Gwendolyn Bennett. Washington, D.C.: Barnett Aden Gallery, December 1947-January 1948.

Rodilles, Ignacio Marques. "Betty Catlett: Artists de un Mondo Anhelante." *El Sol de Mexico* (Sunday supplement) 9 March 1975.

Rubenstein, Charlotte Streifer. *American Women Artists*. G. K. Hall, 1982.

• BARBARA CHASE-RIBOUD

Barbara Chase-Riboud. Bertha Schaefer Gallery, February 1970.

Bontemps, Arna Alexander, and Jacqueline Fonveille-Bontemps. *Forever Free: Art by African-American Women 1882-1980*. Stephenson, 1980.

Chase-Riboud, Barbara. *Echo of Lions*. William Morrow, 1989.

———. *From Memphis to Peking*. Random House, 1974.

———. "The Life and Death of Josephine Baker." *Essence* 6 (February 1976): 36-37.

———. *Sally Hemings, a Novel*. Viking, 1979.

———. *Portrait of a Nude Woman as Cleopatra, a Meloloque*. William Morrow, 1988.

———. *Echo of Lions*. William Morrow, 1989.

———. "Le Plaisir d'Etre Étrangère." *Le Monde* (23 January 1983).

———. *Valide: A Novel of the Harem*. William Morrow, 1986.

———. "Why Paris?" *Essence* 18 (October 1987): 65-66.

Contemporary Artists. St. James Press, 1975.

Dover, Cedric. *American Negro Art*. New York Graphic Society, 1960.

Fine, Elsa Honig. "Mainstream, Blackstream and the Black Art Movement." *Art Journal* (Spring 1971).

Heller, Nancy G. *Women Artists: An Illustrated History*. Abbeville Press, 1987.

Igoe, Lynn M. *Two-Hundred Fifty Years of Afro-American Art: An Annotated Bibliography*. Bowker, 1961.

Kisselgoff, A. "Watching China from the Inside." *New York Times* (4 April 1967).

Lewis, I. "People: Barbara Chase-Riboud." *Essence* 1 (June 1970): 62, 71.

Lewis, Samella. *Art: African American*. Harcourt Brace Jovanovich, 1978.

Munro, Eleanor. *Originals: American Women Artists*. Simon and Schuster, 1979.

Naylor, Colin, and Genesis P-Orridge, eds. *Contemporary Artists*. St. Martin's Press, 1977.

Newton, Edmund. "Now Showing: The Artist at Work." *Los Angeles Times* (3 May 1990).

Nora, Françoise. "From Another Country." *Art News* 71 (March 1972): 60-64.

Nora-Cachin, Françoise, Pol Bury, and Barbara Chase-Riboud. *Barbara Chase-Riboud*. Paris: Musée d'art moderne de la ville Paris, 25 avril-2 juin, 1974.

Palmer, A. "Jewelry Mirrors Her Sculpture." *New York Times* (29 April 1972).

Richardson, Marilyn. "Barbara Chase-Riboud." In Thadious M. Davis and Trudier Harris, eds. *Dictionary of Literary Biography*, Vol. 33: *Afro-American Fiction Writers After 1955*. Gale Research, 1984.

Rubenstein, Charlotte Streifer. *American Women Artists: From Early Indian Times to the Present*. Avon, 1982.

————. *Barbara Chase-Riboud* (exhibition catalogue). Pasadena City College, April 1-28, 1990.

University Art Museum, Berkeley. *Chase-Riboud*. January 17-February 25, 1973.

Wilson, Judith. "Barbara Chase-Riboud: Sculpting Our History." *Essence* (December 1979): 12-13.

• *SHIRLEY CHISHOLM*

Brownmiller, Susan. *Shirley Chisholm: A Biography*. Doubleday, 1970.

Chisholm, Shirley. *The Good Fight*. Harper and Row, 1973.

————. *Unbought and Unbossed*. Houghton Mifflin, 1970.

Christopher, Maurine. *America's Black Congressmen*. Crowell, 1971.

Ehrenhalt, Alan, ed. *Politics in America: Members of Congress in Washington and At Home*. Congressional Quarterly, 1981.

Flynn, James J. *Negroes of Achievement in Modern America*. Dodd, Mead, 1970.

Scheader, Catherine. *Shirley Chisholm: Teacher and Congresswoman*. Enslow Publishers, 1990.

• *JEWEL PLUMMER COBB*

Cobb, Jewel Plummer. "Filters for Women in Science." *Annals of the New York Academy of Sciences*. Vol. 323, 1979.

• *JOHNNETTA BETSCH COLE*

Bateson, Catherine. *Composing a Life*, The Atlanta Monthly Press, 1989.

Bernstein, Alison. "Johnnetta Cole: Serving By Example." *Change Magazine* 19 (September/ October 1987): 45-55.

Edwards, Audrey. "The Inspiring Leader of Scholars and Dollars." *Working Woman* 14 (June 1989): 68-74.

Giddings, Paula. "A Conversation with Johnnetta Betsch Cole." *SAGE: A Scholarly Journal on Black Women* 5 (Fall 1988): 56-59.

————. "Johnnetta B. Cole, 'Sister President.'" *Essence* 18 (November 1987): 35.

McHenry, Susan. "Sister President." *Ms.* 16 (October 1987): 58-61.

McKinney, Rhoda E. "'Sister' Presidents." *Ebony* 43 (February 1988): 82-88.

• *BESSIE COLEMAN*

"First Monument Recognizing Black Aviators Is Unveiled." *Jet* 78 (3 September 1990): 34.

Goodrich, James. "Salute to Bessie Coleman." *Negro Digest* 8 (May 1950): 82-83.

Holden, Henry M. "Brave Bessie, the Barnstormer." *Sisters* 2 (Spring 1989): 6-8.

King, Anita. "Brave Bessie; First Black Pilot." *Essence* 7 (May 1976): 36; 7 (June 1976): 48.

Patterson, Elois. *Memoirs of the Late Bessie Coleman, Aviatrix*. Privately published, 1969.

Powell, William J. *Black Wings*. Los Angeles: Ivan Deach, Jr., 1934.

Robinson, Nancy. "Black Wings Made to Fly." *Sepia* 30 (June 1981): 56-57.

St. Laurent, Philip. "Bessie Coleman, Aviator." *Tuesday* (9 January 1973): 10, 12.

"They Take to the Sky." *Ebony* 32 (May 1977): 88-90.

• *CARDISS COLLINS*

Barone, Michael and Grant Ujifusa. *The Almanac of American Politics, 1990.* Washington, D.C.: National Journal, 1989.

Biographical Directory of the United States Congress, 1774-1989. Bicentennial ed. Washington: Government Printing Office, 1989.

"Black Caucus Examines U.S. Relations with Caribbean." *Jet* 59 (25 December 1980): 38.

"A Black Woman's Place Is in the House ... of Representatives." *Ebony* 46 (January 1991): 104-105, 108, 110.

Booker, Simeon. "Washington Notebook." *Ebony* 34 (April 1979): 30.

"Cardiss Collins Named to Powerful House Panel." *Jet* 67 (14 January 1985): 4.

Christopher, Maurine. *Black Americans in Congress.* Rev. ed. New York: Crowell, 1976.

Collins, Cardiss. "A Plea for Respect." *Ebony* 36 (July 1981): 78.

———. "U.S. Support for Israel." *Encore* 4 (August 1975): 52.

"Collins: United Airlines Must Hire More Blacks." *Jet* 71 (23 March 1987): 8.

Congressional Directory, 1989-90. 101st Congress. Washington, D.C.: Government Printing Office, 1989.

Congressional Quarterly's Guide to Congress. 3rd ed. Washington, D.C.: Congressional Quarterly Service, 1982.

Cummings, Bernice and Victoria Schuck. *Women Organizing: An Anthology.* Metuchen, N.J.: Scarecrow Press, 1979.

Duncan, Phil, ed. *Congressional Quarterly's Politics in America, 1990.* 101st Congress. Washington, D.C.: Congressional Quarterly Service, 1989.

Edwards, Audrey. "Cardiss Collins: Do Your Votes Count?" *Essence Magazine* 11 (November 1980): 84-85, 102, 105, 107.

Fleming, Robert. "Congressional Black Caucus: Cardiss Collins Promises More Clout." *Encore* 8 (April 1979): 20-21.

"45 Years from Today: What's Ahead for Blacks and Whites." *Ebony* 46 (November 1990): 54-77.

Glaser, Vera and Laura Elliott. "Woman Power." *Washingtonian* 18 (May 1983): 156-164.

Harris, Jessica B. "More Political Victories for Black Women." *Encore* 2 (August 1973): 20.

Kurtz, Howard. "Hill Hearing on Amtrak Is Cancelled." *Washington Post,* 8 March 1985. A-5.

Malone, Julia. "Folks Back Home Speak Their Piece to Representatives." *Christian Science Monitor,* 8 September 1983. 1, 12.

"Our New Men in the House: Congressional Black Caucus Picks Up Four New Members, Loses One in General Election." *Ebony* 36 (January 1981): 40-42.

Parker, Laura. "Hijack Alert Issued Before Lockerbie." *Washington Post* 20 March 1989.

Poinsett, Alex. "The New Cardiss Collins." *Ebony* 35 (December 1979): 63-68.

Ragsdale, Bruce A. and Joel D. Treese. *Black Americans in Congress, 1870-1989.* Washington, D.C.: Government Printing Office, 1990.

"Rep. Collins Delivers Ultimatum to Carter: Change Jobs Policies." *Jet* 58 (26 June 1980): 6.

"Rep. Collins Urges More Access for Blacks in Media." *Jet* 60 (19 March 1981): 29.

Reynolds, Barbara. "Cardiss Collins Chairperson." *Black Collegian* 9 (May-June 1979): 36-37.

"Seven Caucus Members are Perfect to Women's League." *Jet* 60 (2 April 1981): 6.

Stineman, Esther. *American Political Women: Contemporary and Historical Profiles.* Littleton, Colo.: Libraries Unlimited, 1980.

"Three U.S. Agencies Facing Action Over Hiring Goals." *New York Times,* 22 August 1984.

Tolchin, Martin. "Congressional Blacks Vow to Stir Campaign Against Budget Cuts." *New York Times,* 1 March 1979.

Trescott, Jacqueline. "Another Widow in the House: Mrs. George Collins Takes Over Husband's Seat in Congress." *Sunday Star and Daily News,* 1 July 1973.

———. "The Coming Out of Cardiss Collins." *Washington Post,* 21 September 1979.

"Two House Members Call for Outside Inquiry on F.A.A. Doctor." *New York Times,* 21 December 1986.

"U.S. Rep. Collins' Mother Dies After Brief Illness." *Jet* 75 (12 December 1988): 12.

"Women in Government." *Ebony* 32 (August 1977): 91.

Wynter, Leon E. "Can Colgate Ward Off a Threatened Boycott?" *Wall Street Journal*, 29 March 1990.

"Young Saves Face for Carter at China Dinner." *Jet* 55 (15 February 1979): 5.

• *JANET COLLINS*

The Concise Oxford Dictionary of Ballet. 2nd ed. London: Oxford University Press, 1982.

Clancy, Joseph P. "The Dancer." *Commonweal* 75 (February 1962): 516.

The Dance Encyclopedia. New York: Simon and Schuster, 1967.

"Dunham Dance Graduates." *Ebony* 78 (June 1953): 48-53.

Gilbert, Morris. "Up and Coming." *New York Times Magazine* 1 February 1953.

"Janet Collins." *Ebony* 4 (September 1949): 43-54.

"Janet Collins' Dance School." *Ebony* 11 (January 1956): 28-30.

Milton, Nerissa. "The Young People's Corner." *Negro History Bulletin* 18 (December 1954): 68-69.

Stahl, Norma. "The First Lady of the Metropolitan Opera Ballet." *Dance Magazine* 28 (February 1954): 27-29.

"U.S. Progress Inspires Gains Abroad." *Ebony* 11 (November 1955): 138.

"Women in Arts." *Ebony* 21 (August 1966): 93-95.

• *MARVA COLLINS*

Adler, Jerry, and Donna Foote. "The Marva Collins Story." *Newsweek* (8 March 1982): 64-65.

Collins, Marva, and Civia Tamarkin. *Marva Collins' Way.* J. P. Tarcher, 1982.

Current Biography Yearbook. H. W. Wilson, 1987. 95.

Keerdoja, Eileen, and others. "Report Card on Marva Collins." *Newsweek* (27 June 1983): 13.

Lanker, Brian. *I Dream a World.* Stewart, Tabori and Chang, 1989. 74-75.

Marshall, Marilyn. "Marva Collins: Weathering the Story." *Ebony* 40 (February 1985): 77-78, 82.

Reynolds, Barbara A. "Something Good Is Happening Here." *Essence* 12 (October 1981): 106-108, 162, 167.

Smikle, Ken. "Trashing Marva Collins." *Black Enterprise* 12 (June 1982): 46.

• *ANNIE J. COOPER*

Bogin, Ruth, and Bert Loewenberg, eds. *Black Women in Nineteenth-Century American Life: Their Words, Their Thoughts, Their Feelings.* University Park: Pennsylvania State University Press, 1985.

Cooper, Anna Julia. *L'Attitude de la France à l'égard de l'esclavage pendant la Révolution.* Paris: Imprimerie de la Cour d'Appel, 1925. Translated by Frances Richardson Keller as *Slavery and the French Revolutionists (1788-1805).* Lewiston, N.Y.: Edwin Mellen Press, 1988.

———. *Life and Writings of the Grimké Family.* 1951.

———. *Le Pèlerinage de Charlemagne.* Paris: A. Lahure, Imprimeur-Editeur, 1925.

———. *The Third Step.* c. 1950.

———. *A Voice from the South: By a Black Woman from the South.* New York: Oxford University Press, 1988.

Gabel, Leona Christine. *From Slavery to the Sorbonne and Beyond: The Life and Writings of Anna J. Cooper.* Introduction by Sidney Kaplan. Northampton, Mass.: Department of History of Smith College, 1982.

Giddings, Paula. *When and Where I Enter.* New York: Morrow, 1984.

Harley, Sharon. "Anna J. Cooper: A Voice for Black Women." In *The Afro-American Woman: Struggles and Images.* Eds. Sharon Harley and Rosalyn Terborg-Penn. Port Washington, N.Y.: Kennikat Press, 1978.

Hooks, Bell. *Ain't I a Woman?: Black Women and Feminism.* Boston: South End Press, 1981.

Hutchinson, Louise Daniel. *Anna J. Cooper: A Voice from the South.* Washington, D.C.: Smithsonian Press, 1981.

Klein, Félix (Abbé). *Au pays de "La Vie intense."* Paris: Plon, Nourrit et Cie., 1907.

Sewall, May Wright. *World's Congress of Representative Women.* Chicago, 1893.

Shockley, Ann Allen. *Afro-American Women Writers, 1746-1933*. Boston: G. K. Hall, 1988.

• *ELIZABETH "LIBBA" COTTEN*

Baggelaar, Kristin, and Donald Milton. *Folk Music: More Than a Song*. Crowell, 1976.

Bastin, Bruce. *Red River Blues: The Blues Tradition in the Southeast*. University of Illinois Press, 1986.

Chalmers, Wilma Grand. *$2 at the Door: Folk, Ethnic and Bluegrass Music in the Northwest*. Broadsheet Publications, 1981.

Cotten, Elizabeth. *Elizabeth Cotten Live!* Arhoolie. 1983.

"For These 'Youngsters' Life Begins at 80." *Ebony* 36 (February 1981): 60.

Funaro, Arti, and Artie Tatum. *Chicago Blues Guitar*. Oak, 1983.

Gerrard, Alice. "Libba Cotten." *Frets* 2 (January 1980): 26-29.

Groom, Bob. *The Blues Revival*. Studio Vista Limited, 1971.

Harris, Sheldon. *Blues Who's Who:* Da Capo Press, 1979.

Lanker, Brian. *I Dream a World*. Stewart, Tabori and Chang, 1989. 156-57

Michelson, Stephen. Liner notes to *Music from the Hills of Caldwell County*. Physical. Silver Spring, Md.

The New Grove Dictionary of American Music. Edited by H. Wiley Hitchcock and Stanley Sudie. Macmillan, 1986.

"Ordinary Women of Grace: Subjects of the I Dream a World Photography Exhibit." *U.S. News and World Report* 106 (13 February 1989).

Seeger, Pete. *The Incompleat Folksinger*. Simon and Schuster, 1972.

Smith, Janet. "The Music of Libba Cotten." *Frets* 2 (January 1980): 30-31.

Southern, Eileen. *Biographical Dictionary of Afro-American and African Musicians*. Greenwood Press, 1982.

• *ELLEN CRAFT*

Blassingame, John, ed. *Slave Testimony: Two Centuries of Letters, Speeches, Interviews, and Autobiographies*. Louisiana State University Press, 1977.

Craft, William, and Ellen Craft. *Running a Thousand Miles for Freedom*. London: Tweedie, 1860. Reprinted. *Great Slave Narratives*. Ed. Arna Bontemps. Beacon Press, 1969.

Dannett, Sylvia G. L. *Profiles of Negro Womanhood, 1916-1900*. Vol. 1. Educational Heritage, 1964.

Gara, Larry. "Ellen Craft." *Notable American Women*. Vol. 1. Harvard University Press, 1971.

Nichols, Charles H. *Many Thousand Gone: The Ex-Slaves' Account of Their Bondage and Freedom*. Indiana University Press, 1963.

Quarles, Benjamin. *Black Abolitionists*. Oxford University Press, 1969. 62-63, 134, 137, 150, 202-204.

Starling, Marion Wilson. *The Slave Narrative: Its Place in American History*. 2nd ed. Howard University Press, 1988.

Sterling, Dorothy, ed. *We Are Your Sisters: Black Women in the Nineteenth Century*. Norton, 1984. 62-64.

Still, William. *Underground Railroad Records*. Rev. ed. William Still, 1886.

Woodson, Carter G., ed. *The Mind of the Negro as Reflected in Letters Written During the Crisis, 1800-1860*. Washington, D.C.: Association for the Study of Negro Life and History, 1926.

• *ANGELA DAVIS*

Abbott, D. "Revolution by Other Means." Interview with Angela Davis. *New Statesman* 114 (14 August 1987): 16-17.

Davis, Angela. *Angela Davis: An Autobiography*. Random House, 1974.

———. *If They Come in the Morning: Voices of Resistance*. Third Press, 1971.

———. "Lifting As We Climb: Radical Perspectives on the Empowerment of Afro-American Women." *Harvard Educational Review* (Summer 1988).

———. *Women, Culture and Politics*. Random House, 1988.

———. *Women, Race and Class*. Random House, 1982.

Giddings, Paula. *When and Where I Enter: The Impact of Black Women on Race and Sex in America*. William Morrow, 1984.

"Making of a Revolutionary." *Sepia* 19 (December 1970): 9-11.

• JULIETTE DERRICOTTE

Cuthbert, Marion V. *Juliette Derricotte.* Woman's Press, 1933.

Derricotte, Juliette. "The Student Conference at Mysore, India." *Crisis* 36 (August, 1929): 267, 280-83.

Du Bois, W. E. B., "Dalton, Georgia." *Crisis* (March 1932): 85-87.

Jeanness, Mary. *Twelve Negro Americans.* Friendship Press, 1925.

Leffall, Dolores. "Juliette [Aline] Derricotte." *Dictionary of American Negro Biography.* Edited by Rayford Logan and Michael Winston. Norton, 1982.

Richardson, Joe M. *A History of Fisk University, 1865-1946.* University of Alabama Press, 1980.

White, Walter. *New York Herald Tribune,* 31 December 1931.

Wygal, Winifred. "Juliette Derricotte, Her Character and Martyrdom: An Interpretation." *Crisis* 39 (March, 1932): 84-85.

• KATHERINE DUNHAM

Dannett, Sylvia G. L. *Profiles of Negro Womanhood.* Vol. 2. Yonkers, N.Y.: Educational Heritage, 1966.

Harnan, Terry. *African Rhythm-American Dance.* Knopf, 1974.

Mangione, Jerre. *The Dream and the Deal: The Federal Writers' Project, 1935-1943.* Little, Brown, 1972.

Rush, Theressa Gunnels, Carol Fairbanks, and Esther Spring Arata. *Black American Writers, Past and Present.* Vol. 1. Scarecrow Press, 1975.

• RAMONA HOAGE EDELIN

Campbell, Gail A. "Targeting Urban Ills: The First Woman Chief of the National Urban Coalition." *Washington Times,* 13 July 1988.

Du Bois, W. E. B. *The Souls of Black Folk.* Fisk University Diamond Jubilee Edition. Nashville: Fisk University Press, 1979.

Edelin, Ramona. "African America in the Year 2000." *The World & I* (January 1990): 558-69.

———. "Toward an African-American Agenda: An Inward Look." In *The State of Black America 1990.* New York: National Urban League, 1990.

• MARIAN WRIGHT EDELMAN

"By Marian Wright." *Spelman Messenger* 76 (May 1960): 5-6.

"Letters from Two Merrill Scholars." *Spelman Messenger* 75 (November 1958): 18-19.

Tomkins, Calvin. "Profiles: A Sense of Urgency." *New Yorker* (March 1989): 48-74.

Traver, N. "They Cannot Fend for Themselves." *Time* 129 (23 March 1987): 27.

Washington-Blair, Angela. Review of *The Measure of Our Success: A Letter to My Children and Yours* by Marian Wright Edelman. *Library Journal* (1 May 1992).

• EFFIE O'NEAL ELLIS

Baltimore *Evening Bulletin,* 12 February 1952.

• ELLA FITZGERALD

Bogle, Donald. *Brown Sugar: Eighty Years of America's Black Female Superstars.* Harmony Books, 1980.

Colin, Sid. *Ella: The Life and Times of Ella Fitzgerald.* Elm Tree Brooks, 1986.

The Continuum Dictionary of Women's Biography. Ed. Jennifer S. Uglow. Continuum, 1989.

"Ella Fitzgerald Saluted at New York City Gala." *Jet,* 7 (March 5, 1990): 56-67.

McHenry, Robert, ed. *Famous American Women.* Dover, 1980. 133.

Nolden, R. *Ella Fitzgerald: ihre Leben, ihre Musik, ihre Schallplatten.* Gauting, Germany: 1986.

Pleasants, Henry. *The Great American Popular Singers.* Simon & Schuster, 1974.

• ARETHA FRANKLIN

"Aretha Gives Christmas Benefit Show for Needy." *Jet* 77 (26 December 1989): 26.

Bego, Mark. *Aretha Franklin.* St. Martin's Press, 1989.

Current Biography Yearbook. H. W. Wilson, 1968. 132-34.

Feather, Leonard. *The Encyclopedia of Jazz in the Sixties.* Bonanza Books, 1966. 119.

Feather, Leonard and Ira Gitler. *The Encyclopedia of Jazz in the Seventies*. Horizon, 1976. 138.

Garland, Phyl. *The Sound of Soul*. Regnery, 1969. 24, 128-29, 191-203.

"Lady Soul: Singing It Like It Is." *Time* 91 (21 June 1968): 62-66.

Low, W. Augustus, and Virgil A. Clift. *Encyclopedia of Black America*. McGraw-Hill, 1981. 393.

Miller, Jim. "Cruising the Freeway of Love." *Newsweek* (26 August 1985): 69.

Miller, Jim. "Aretha Franklin." *New Grove Dictionary of American Music*. Edited by H. Wiley Hitchcock and Stanley Sadie. Macmillan, 1986. 163-64.

"More Respect." *Jet* 79 (7 January 1991): 10.

Moses, Mark. *New Yorker* 63 (1 February 1988): 84-87.

"A Native of Detroit." *Jet* 76 (7 August 1989): 59.

"Queen of Soul's Brother Rev. Cecil Franklin Dies of Heart Attack in Detroit." *Jet* 77 (15 January 1990): 14.

Southern, Eileen. *Biographical Dictionary of Afro-American and African Musicians*. Greenwood Press, 1982. 137.

• *MARY HATWOOD FUTRELL*

Bender, Steve. "They Teach Our Children Well." *Southern Living* 25 (June 1990): 85-90.

Blount, Carolyne S. "Initiating Qualitative Educational Issues." *About Time* 17 (November 1989): 13-16.

Futrell, Mary Hatwood. "President's Viewpoint." *NEA Today* 7 (February, March, April, May 1989): 2. 7 (March, April, May, September, November, December 1988): 2. 6 (March, April, May 1988): 2. 6 (March, April 1988): 2. 5 (March, June, November 1987): 2.

————. "Mama and Miss Jordan." *Reader's Digest* 135 (July 1989): 75-80.

Howard, Michael E. "A Conversation with Mary Hatwood Futrell." *Black Enterprise* 20 (October 1989): 30.

• *ZELMA WATSON GEORGE*

Abdul, Raoul. *Blacks in Classical Music*. New York: Dodd, Mead, 1977.

"Battissi Names Three to Help Monitors." *Cleveland Plain Dealer*, 2 June 1985.

Bean, Don. "A Minority Report by Zelma George." *Cleveland Plain Dealer*, 25 May 1985.

Current Biography. New York: H. W. Wilson, 1961. 171-73.

Davis, Marianne W., ed. *Contributions of Black Women to America*. Vol. 1. Columbia, S.C.: Kenday Press, 1982. 88.

Eyman, Scott. "The Life and Times of the Determined and Gifted—and Indomitable—Zelma George." *Cleveland Magazine* (1 March 1983): 68.

"Five Black Women Discuss Achievements." *Cleveland Plain Dealer*, 15 April 1986.

Gard, Connie Schultz. "It's a Wonderful Life." *Plain Dealer Magazine* (22 July 1990).

Garland, Phyl. "The Miracle on Ansel Road." *Ebony* 7 (May 1968): 90-100.

Jelliffe, Rowena Woodham, and others. *Here's Zelma*. Cleveland: Job Corps Center Committee, 10 September 1971.

Keegan, Frank L. *Blacktown U.S.A.* "Two Black Women and a Newspaperman: Zelma George." Boston: Little, Brown, 1971.

Peery, Richard. "A Life's Work Honored." *Cleveland Plain Dealer*, 22 November 1985.

Ploski, Harry A. and James Williams, ed. *The Negro Almanac:* 4th ed. New York: Wiley 1983.

Robinson, Tracey L. "Zelma George: The Power of One." *Cleveland Plain Dealer*, 13 June 1985.

"Scholarship Named for Civic Leader Dr. Zelma George." *Cleveland Plain Dealer*, 28 February 1987.

"Two to be Honored During Women's Week." *Cleveland Plain Dealer*, 3 March 1985.

"Women of Courage." *Ebony* 16 (April 1961): 70-77.

• *ALTHEA GIBSON*

Ashe, Arthur R., Jr. *A Hard Road to Glory: A History of the African-American Athlete Since 1946*. Vol. 3. Warner Books, 1988.

"Althea Gibson Shares Her Knowledge with Collegians." *Jet* 58 (1980).

Casabona, Helen, and Alice Dawson. "Winners Circle: Outstanding Women Athletes of the Past 65 Years." *Women Sports and Fitness* 6 (1984): 5.

Dannett, Sylvia G. L. *Profiles of Negro Womanhood*. Vol. 2. Educational Heritage, 1966.

Davis, Marianna W., ed. *Contributions of Black Women to America*. Vol. 1. Kenday Press, 1982. 503-509; 573, 575.

Dawson, Alice. "Matches to Remember: Women of the U.S. Open." *Women's Sports and Fitness* 7 (August 1985): 22-23, 45.

"First Black Wimbledon Champ, Althea Gibson, Recognized in England." *Jet* 66 (23 July 1984): 46-48.

"Former Wimbledon Tennis Champion Althea Gibson Interviewed." *San Francisco Chronicle*, 15 November 1984.

Forsee, Aylesa. *Women Who Reach for Tomorrow*. Macrae Smith Company, 1960.

Gibson, Althea. *I Always Wanted to Be Somebody*. Harper, 1958.

———. *So Much to Live For*. Putnam, 1968.

Grimsley, Will. *Tennis: Its History, People and Events*. Prentice-Hall, 1971.

Henderson, Edwin B., and others. *The Black Athlete: Emergence and Arrival*. Publishers Agency, 1976.

Lumpkin, Angela. *A Guide to the Literature of Tennis*. Greenwood Press, 1985.

1,000 Successful Blacks. Vol. 1, *Ebony Success Library*. Johnson Pub. Co., 1973. 123.

Pizer, Vernon. *Glorious Triumphs: Athletes Who Conquered Adversity*. Dodd, Mead, 1968.

Reasons, George. *They Had a Dream*. Los Angeles Times Syndicate, 1970.

• *NIKKI GIOVANNI*

Bailey, Peter. "Nikki Giovanni: 'I Am Black, Female, Polite....'" *Ebony* 27 (February 1972): 48-56.

Black Writers. Gale Research, 1989.

Collins, L. M. *Images of the Afro-American Woman: A Bibliographic Profile*. Introduction by Nikki Giovanni. Fisk University Press, 1980.

Evans, Mari, ed. *Black Women Writers (1950-1980)*. Doubleday, 1984.

Giovanni, Nikki. "Campus Racism 101." *Essence*, August 1991: 71-72.

Mitchell, Mozella G. "Nikki Giovanni." *Dictionary of Literary Biography*. Vol. 41. *Afro-*

American Poets Since 1955. Edited by Trudier Harris and Thadious M. Davis. Gale Research, 1985.

Rush, Theresa Gunnels, Carol Fairbanks Myers, and Esther Spring Arata. *Black American Writers Past and Present*. Vol. 1. Scarecrow Press, 1975.

Shockley, Ann Allen, and Sue P. Chandler. *Living Black American Authors*. Bowker, 1973.

Stetson, Erlene. *Black Sister: Poetry by Black American Women, 1746-1980*. Indiana University Press, 1981.

Tate, Claudia, ed. *Black Women Writers at Work*. Continuum, 1984.

• *WHOOPI GOLDBERG*

Current Biography. New York: Wilson, 1985.

Dworkin, Susan, "Whoopi Goldberg—in Performance." *Ms.* 12 (May 1984): 20.

Gill, Brendan. "The Theater." *New Yorker* 60 (5 November 1984): 155.

McGuigan, Cathleen. "Whoopee for Whoopi." *Newsweek* 106 (30 December 1985): 60.

Noel, Pamela. "Who Is Whoopi Goldberg and What Is She Doing on Broadway?" *Ebony* 40 (March 1985): 27-28, 30, 34.

Randolph, Laura B. "The Whoopi Goldberg Nobody Knows." *Ebony* 46 (March 1991): 110-12, 114-16.

"23rd NAACP Awards Presented." *Tennessean*, 3 December 1990.

Unterbrink, Mary. *Funny Women: American Comediennes, 1860-1985*. New York: McFarland, 1987.

"Whoopi and Jean Rap." *McCalls* (November 1990): 110-114.

"Whoopi Goldberg and Jean Stapleton: Actresses Star in TV's New Bagdad Cafe." *Jet* 78 (23 April 1990): 58-60.

"Whoopi Goldberg Makes Her Funniest Film in 'Burglar.'" *Jet* 72 (20 April 1987): 56-57.

"Whoopi Wins Excellence Award." *Tennessean*, 28 October 1990.

• *ANGELINA WELD GRIMKÉ*

Adolf, Arnold, ed. *Poetry of Black America: Anthology of the Twentieth Century*. Harper, 1973.

Bond, Frederick. *The Negro and the Drama*. Associated Publishers, 1940.

Eliot, T. S.. *Four Quartets, III, The Complete Poems and Plays, 1909-1950*. Harcourt, 1962.

Greene, Michael. "Angelina Weld Grimké." *Dictionary of Literary Biography*. Vol. 50: Afro-American Writers Before the Harlem Renaissance. Ed. Trudier Harris. Gale Research, 1986.

Grimké, Angelina Weld. Poems anthologized in *Caroling Dusk*. Edited by Countee Cullen. Harper, 1927.

————. "A Biographical Sketch of Archibald H. Grimké." *Opportunity* 3 (February 1925): 44-47.

————. "The Closing Door." *Birth Control Review* 3 (September 1919): 10-14.

————. "To Keep the Memory of Charlotte Forten Grimké." *Crisis* 3 (January 1915): 134.

Hatch, James V. *Black Theatre, U.S.A.: Forty-Five Plays by Black Americans, 1847-1874*. Free Press, 1974.

Hull, Gloria. *Color, Sex, and Poetry*. Indiana University Press, 1987.

Kerlin, Robert T., ed. *Negro Poets and Their Poems*. Associated, 1935.

Locke, Alain, and Gregory Montgomery. *Plays of Negro Life: 1886-1954*. 1927. Reprinted. Negro Universities Press, 1970.

New York Times, 11 June 1958.

Stetson, Erlene, ed. *Black Sister: Poetry by Black American Women*. Indiana University Press, 1981.

• CLARA HALE

"Chronicle-Clara Hale." *New York Times*, 5 December 1990.

Current Biography Yearbook. H. W. Wilson, 1985.

Johnson, Herschel. "Clara (Mother) Hale: Healing Baby 'Junkies' with Love." *Ebony* 41 (May 1986): 84.

Kastor, Elizabeth. "The Hour of the Heroes." *Washington Post*, 8 February 1985.

Lanker, Brian. *I Dream a World*. Stewart, Tabori and Chang, 1989.

Stanley, Alessandra. "Hale House Fights City Hall for Babies' Fate." *New York Times*, 23 September 1990.

• FANNIE LOU HAMER

"Black Voices of the South." *Ebony* 26 (August 1971): 51.

Collum, Danny. "The Life of Fannie Lou Hamer." *Sojourners*, 2 December 1982.

Crawford, Vicki L., Jacqueline Anne Rouse, and Barbara Woods. *Women in the Civil Rights Movement*. Brooklyn: Carlson Publishing, 1990.

DeMuth, Jerry. "'Tired of Being Sick and Tired.'" *Nation* 198 (1 June 1964): 548-551.

Dorsey, L. C. "An Action Memorial." Mississippi Council of Human Relations *Newsletter*, March 1977.

————. "Fannie Lou Hamer." *Jackson Advocate*, 31 August 1978: 8.

Hamer, Fannie Lou. Black Oral History Interview. Fisk University Library, Fisk University, 6 October 1962.

————. "It's in Your Hands." Selection from "The Special Plight and the Role of Black Woman." Speech given at the NAACP Legal Defense Fund Institute, New York City, May 7, 1971. In *Black Women in White America*." Edited by Gerda Lerner. Pantheon Books, 1972.

O'Dell, J. H. "Life in Mississippi: An Interview with Fannie Lou Hamer." *Freedomways* 5 (Second Quarter, 1965): 231-42.

Sewell, George. "Fannie Lou Hamer." *The Black Collegian*, May-June 1978: 20.

————. "Fannie Lou Hamer's Light Still Shines." *Encore American and Worldwide News* 18 (July 1977): 3.

Wright, Robert. "Interview with Fannie Lou Hamer," 9 August 1968. Civil Rights Documentation Project, Moorland-Spingarn Research Center, Howard University.

• VIRGINIA HAMILTON

Hamilton, Virginia. "The Mind of a Novel: The Heart of the Book." *Children's Literature Quarterly* 8 (Winter 1983): 10-13.

————. "Newbery Award Acceptance." *Horn Book* 51 (August 1975): 337-343.

————. "On Being a Black Writer in America." *The Lion and the Unicorn* 10 (1986): 15-17.

————. *Paul Robeson: The Life and Times of a Free Black Man*. Harper, 1975.

———. "The Known, the Remembered, and the Imagined: Celebrating Afro-American Folk Tales." *Children's Literature in Education* 18 (Summer): 67-75.

Something about the Author. Vol. 56. Gale Research, 1989.

• *LORRAINE HANSBERRY*

Abramson, Doris E. *Negro Playwrights in the American Theatre: 1925-1959*. Columbia University Press, 1969.

Baldwin, James. "Lorraine Hansberry at the Summit." *Freedomways* 19 (1979): 269-72.

Baraka, Imamu Amiri. "Raisin in the Sun's Enduring Passion." *Washington Post*, 16 November 1986.

Bigsby, C. W. E. *Confrontation and Commitment: A Study of Contemporary American Drama, 1959-1966*. MacGibbon & Kee, 1967.

Brown, Lloyd W. "Lorraine Hansberry as Ironist." *Journal of Black Studies* 4 (March 1974): 237-247.

Carter, Steven R. "Commitment Amid Complexity: Lorraine Hansberry's Life-in-Action." MELUS 7 (Fall 1980): 39-53.

Cruse, Harold. *The Crisis of the Negro Intellectual*. William Morrow, 1967.

Haisteon, Loyle. "Lorraine Hansberry: Portrait of an Angry Young Writer." *Crisis* 86 (April 1979): 123-124, 126, 128.

Lorraine Hansberry Speaks Out: Art and the Black Revolution. Caedmon Records, 1972.

Marre, Diana. *Traditions and Departures: Lorraine Hansberry and Black Americans in Theatre*. Ph.D. dissertation. The University of California, Berkeley, 1987.

Ness, David E. "The Sign in Sidney Brustein's Window: A Black Playwright Looks at White America." *Freedomways* 11 (Fourth Quarter 1971): 359-366.

New York Times, March 1959.

Terkel, Studs. "An Interview with Lorraine Hansberry." WFMT Chicago Five Arts Guide, 10 (April 1961): 8-14.

Wilkerson, Margaret B., ed. *Nine Plays by Black Women*. New American Library, 1986.

• *BARBARA HARRIS*

Boston Globe, 12 February 1989.

Charlotte Observer, 26 September 1988.

Cincinnati Enquirer, 12 February 1989; 13 February 1989.

CLASS, May 1989.

Esquire, August 1989.

Interchange, Diocese of Southern Ohio, October 1988, March 1989.

Jet, 13 February 1989; 29 February 1989.

Journal-News (Philadelphia), 12 February 1989.

Lexington Herald Leader, 12 February 1989.

Linkage, December 1985/January 1986.

Newsweek, 13 February 1989.

Tennessean, 25 September 1988; 26 September 1988; 5 February 1989; 13 February 1989; 17 February 1989; 25 February 1989.

Time, 26 December 1968.

U.S. News & World Report, 19 June 1989.

USA Today, 26 September 1988; 30 September 1988.

Witness, September 1984, June 1985, April 1989.

• *MARCELITE J. HARRIS*

"Dunn-Landry Papers." *Amistad* 2 (August 1984): 1, 3.

"Harris First Black Female General in U.S. Air Force." *Jet* 79 (12 November 1990): 7.

• *PATRICIA HARRIS*

Ambassador for Progress: Black Americans in Government. Buckingham Learning Corp., 1969.

"Ambassador Harris Cites Needs for Racial Progress in Marketing 99th Anniversary of [Howard] University." *Howard University Magazine* (4 April 1966): 8.

"Black Woman Joins Three Boards." *Business Week* (29 May 1971): 22.

Greenfield, Meg. "The Brief Saga of Dean Harris." *Washington Post*, 23 March 1969.

Harris, Patricia Roberts. "Building Stronger Urban Economics." Speech Before Editors of Trade Union Publications, 4 May 1978.

———. "Exporting American Ideals." Speech Before the Conference Board, New York, 18 May 1978.

————. Speech Before the National Women's Political Caucus Convention, Cincinnati, Ohio, 14 June 1979.

————. Speech Before the National Committee Against Discrimination in Housing), Washington, D.C., 17 April 1978.

————. Testimonial Speech for Honorable Henry S. Reuss, Milwaukee, Wisconsin, 13 October 1977.

"Honorable Patricia Roberts Harris." *Vogue* (May 1966): 202-203.

"Howard Says Farewell to Patricia Roberts Harris." *Capstone* 6 (April 1985): 1.

"Ladies Home Journal Woman of the Year 1974." *Ladies Home Journal* (April 1974): 83.

Murray, Pauli. *Song in a Weary Throat.* New York: Harper, 1987.

Principle Officers of Department of State and United States Chiefs of Mission. U.S. Department of State, 1988.

"A $200 Billion Budget." *Dawn Magazine* (March 1980): 4.

• DOROTHY HEIGHT

"American Airlines Advertisement." *Ebony* 19 (November 1963): 118.

Booker, Simeon. "Washington Notebook." *Ebony* 33 (May 1978): 29.

Contributions of Black Women to America. Vol. 2. Ed. Marianna W. Davis. Kenday Press, 1982.

Current Biography Yearbook. H. W. Wilson, 1972.

Encyclopedia of Black America. Edited by W. Augustus Low and Virgil A. Clift. McGraw-Hill, 1981.

"Family Affair." *Wall Street Journal* 20 September 1988.

Giddings, Paula. *In Search of Sisterhood.* William Morris, 1988.

Manning, Beverly. *We Shall Be Heard.* Scarecrow Press, 1988.

Noble, Jeanne. *Beautiful, Also, Are the Souls of My Black Sisters.* Prentice-Hall, 1978.

Rowan, Carl T. "Crusade of Hope." *Washington Post* (1 September 1987): A-23.

"Senate Panel Probes Plight of Black Males in America." *Jet* 8 April 1991.

• AILEEN HERNANDEZ

Christmas, Walter. *Negroes in Public Affairs and Government.* Vol. 1. Yonkers, N.Y.: Educational Heritage Year, 1966.

"Conversation: Ida Lewis and Aileen Hernandez." *Essence* (February 1971): 20-25, 74-75.

Current Biography. New York: H. W. Wilson Co., 1971.

Dreyfurs, Joel. "Civil Rights and the Women's Movement." *Black Enterprise* 8 (September 1977): 36-37, 45.

King, Helen. "The Black Woman and Women's Lib." *Ebony* (March 1971): 68-70, 75-76.

• CLEMENTINE HUNTER

Bailey, Mildred H. *"Clementine Hunter." Four Women of Cane River—Their Contributions to the Cultural Life of the Area.* Natchitoches Parish Library, 1980.

Black Women Oral History Project Interview with Clementine Hunter. Schlesinger Library, Radcliffe College, 1979.

"Cane River Memo." *Natchitoches Times,* 20 February 1968.

Dowdy, Verdis. "Louisiana's Primitive Artist Is Like a Black Grandma Moses." (New Orleans) *Clarion Herald,* 14 August 1969.

Knight, Margaret R. "On a Sunday Morning at Clementine Hunter's." (New Orleans) *Times Picayune Dixie-Roto* Magazine, 17 October 1976.

Lamothe, Eva. "A Visit with Clementine Hunter: Painter of Visions and Dreams." New Orleans *Arts Quarterly* 7 April/May/June 1985): 32-34.

Miller, Herschel. "Clementine Hunter—American Primitive." *New Orleans Magazine* (December 1968): 6-11.

New Orleans Times-Picayune, 3 April 1974.

Plantation Menu: Plantation Life in Louisiana, 1950-70, and Other Matters. Edited by Oral Garland Williams. Baton Rouge, 1972.

Rankin, Allen. "The Hidden Genius of Melrose Plantation." *Reader's Digest* 107 (December 1975): 118-22.

Visit to Melrose Plantation with François Mignon. Louisiana Heritage Association, Alexandria, Louisiana. LP record No. S737, 1967.

Willard, Charlotte. "Innocence Regained." *Look* 17 (16 June 1953): 102-105.

Wilson, James L. *Clementine Hunter: American Folk Artist.* Pelican Pub. Co., 1988.

• *ZORA NEALE HURSTON*

Boas, Franz. Preface. *Mules and Men.* Indiana University Press, 1978.

Bontemps, Arna. "From Eatonville, Florida, to Harlem." *New York Herald Tribune* (22 November 1942).

Brown, Sterling. Review of *Mules and Men.* Unidentified clipping, James Weldon Johnson Collection, Yale University. Cited in Robert Hemenway. *Zora Neale Hurston: A Literary Biography.* University of Illinois Press, 1977.

Hemenway, Robert. *Zora Neale Hurston: A Literary Biography.* University of Illinois Press, 1977.

Howard, Lillie P. *Zora Neale Hurston.* Twayne Publishers, 1980.

Hurston, Zora Neale. "Crazy for This Democracy." *Negro Digest* 4 (December 1942): 45-48.

———. "How It Feels to Be Colored Me." *World Tomorrow* 11 (May 1928): 215-16.

Levine, Lawrence. *Black Culture, Black Consciousness.* Oxford University Press, 1977.

Walker, Alice, ed. *I Love Myself When I Am Laughing...: A Zora Neale Hurston Reader.* The Feminist Press, 1979.

• *MAE C. JEMISON*

Johnson, Maria C. "Upward with Worldly Lessons." *Greensboro News and Record*, 28 January 1991.

Marshall, Marilyn. "Child of the '60s Set to Become First Black Woman in Space." *Ebony* 44 (August 1989): 50, 52, 54-55.

The Missing Piece 3 (Summer/Fall 1990): 1.

"Monument Recognizing Black Aviators Is Unveiled." *Jet* 78 (September 1990): 34.

"1988 Essence Awards." *Essence* 19 (October 1988): 59-60.

"Space Is Her Destination." *Ebony* 42 (October 1987): 93-98.

• *BARBARA JORDAN*

Angelo, Bonnie. "An Ethical Guru Monitors Morality." *Time* 137 (3 June 1991): 9-10.

Brown, Ray B., ed. *Contemporary Heroes and Heroines.* Gale Research, 1990. 225-29.

Contemporary Authors. Vol. 113. Gale Research, 1985. Vol. 123, 1988.

Current Biography. H. W. Wilson, 1974. 189-92.

Ebony Success Library. Vol. 2, *Famous Blacks Give Secrets of Success.* Johnson Pub. Co., 1973. 146-49.

Jordan, Barbara and Shelby Hearn. *Barbara Jordan: A Self Portrait.* Doubleday, 1979.

Sanders, Charles L. "Barbara Jordan: Texan Is a New Power on Capitol Hill." *Ebony* 30 (February 1975): 136-42.

United States House of Representatives. Commission on the Bicentenary. *Women in Congress.* United States Government Printing Office, 1991. 117-18.

• *The JOYNERS*

Axthelm, Pete. "A Star Blazes in the Fast Lane." *Newsweek,* September 19, 1988: 55-57.

Brennan, Christine. "Drug Claims Denied by Griffith Joyner." *Washington Post,* September 22, 1989: sec D, 1, 9.

Browne, Ray B., ed. *Contemporary Heroes and Heroines.* Gale Research, 1990: 185-89, 230-33.

Cart, Julie. "Asthma Is Joyner-Kersee's Toughest Foe." *Los Angeles Times,* June 6, 1991: sec C, 10.

Connors, Martin, Diane L. Dupuis, and Brad Morgan. *The Olympics Factbook.* Visible Ink Press, 1992: 505-06.

Ebony, April 1989: 96, 98, 100.

Gabriel, Alice. "Bound for Glory." *Rolling Stone,* September 22, 1988: 93.

Griggs, Lee, Kumiko Makihara, and Ellie McGrath. "Final Frames of the Games." *Time,* October 10, 1988: 78-79.

Hersh, Phil. "FloJo Sobs, but Track Is Hurting." *Chicago Tribune,* February 27, 1989: sec C, 12.

Jordan, Pat. "Wonder Woman: No Man Is a Better Bet than Jackie Joyner-Kersee." *Life,* October 1988: 89-95.

Mansfield, Stephanie. "Go with the Flo." *Vogue,* April 1989: 402-05, 454.

Masback, Craig A. "Siren of Speed." *Ms.,* October 1988: 34-35.

• ELIZABETH KECKLEY

"A Black Woman's View of Mary Todd Lincoln." *Ebony* 25 (March 1970): 98-100.

Black Women in Nineteenth Century American Life. Bert James Loewenberg and Ruth Bogin, eds. Pennsylvania State University Press, 1976. 70-77.

Brown, Hallie W. *Homespun Heroines and Other Women of Distinction.* Aldine Pub. Co., 1926. Reprinted: Oxford University Press, 1974. 174-77.

Dannett, Sylvia G. L. *Profiles of Negro Womanhood.* Vol. 1. Educational Heritage, 1974. 174-77.

Davis, Arthur P. and J. Saunders Redding, eds. *Calvacade: Negro American Writing from 1760 to the Present.* Houghton Mifflin, 1971. 132.

Fry, Smith D, "Lincoln Liked Her." *Minneapolis Register* 6 July 1901.

Grimké, Francis J. *The Works of Frances J. Grimké.* Ed. Carter G. Woodson. Associated Publishers, 1942. 544-49.

Keckley, Elizabeth. *Behind the Scenes: Thirty Years a Slave and Four Years in the White House.* G. W. Carleton, 1868. Reprinted: Arno Press and the *New York Times,* 1968.

Kickley, Betsey, pseud. *Behind the Seams.* National News, 1868.

Logan, Rayford W. "Elizabeth Keckley." *Dictionary of American Negro Biography.* Edited by Rayford W. Logan and Michael R. Winston. Norton, 1982. 375-76.

Loggins, Vernon. *The Negro Author: His Development in American to 1900.* Kennikat Press, 1964. 258-61.

Miers, Earl S. *Lincoln Day by Day: A Chronology, 1809-1865.* Vol. 3. Lincoln Sesquicentennial Commission, 1960. 148, 326-27.

Millstein, Beth and Jeanne Bodin. *We, The American Women: A Documentary History.* Science Research Associates, 1977. 136-37.

Noble, Jeanne. *Beautiful, Also, Are the Souls of My Black Sisters: A History of the Black Women in America.* Prentice-Hall, 1978. 50-54.

Quarles, Benjamin. "Elizabeth Keckley." *Notable American Women, 1607-1950: A Biographical Dictionary.* Vol. 2. Harvard University Press, 1971. 310-11.

Randall, Ruth Painter. *Mary Lincoln: Biography of a Marriage.* Little, Brown, 1953.

Sandburg, Carl. *Abraham Lincoln: The War Years.* Scribner, 1939: Vol. 1, 457-58, 547-48; Vol. 2, 212, 259-60; Vol. 3, 345-46; Vol. 4, 120-21.

Sims, Naomi. "A Gift Truly Liberating." *Encore* 4 (June 23/July 4, 1975): 56-58.

Washington, John E. *They Knew Lincoln.* Dutton, 1942. 53-55, 85, 205-41.

Washington Star, 11 November 1935; 15 November 1935.

Wefer, Marion. "Another Assassination, Another Widow, Another Embattled Book." *American Heritage* 18 (August 1967): 79-88.

Woodson, Carter G. "Communications." *Journal of Negro History* 21 (January 1936); 56-57.

• LEONTINE KELLY

"Bishop Kelly to Head New National Network on AIDS." *Holston United Methodist Church Reporter* (19 August 1988).

Cincinnati's Black Peoples: A Chronology and Bibliography, 1787-1982. University of Cincinnati, June 1986.

"Ex-Cincinnatian Becomes First Black Female Bishop." *Cincinnati Enquirer,* 8 August 1984.

Tutu, Desmond M. B. "God's Kingdom of Righteousness." *Proceedings of the Fifteenth World Conference.* Nairobi, Kenya, July 23-29, 1986. Published by the World Methodist Council, 1987. 160-69.

"Leontine Kelly to be First Woman to Preach on National Radio Pulpit." *Afro-American* (National Edition) (10 March 1984): 11.

Jet 75 (16 January 1989): 40.

Lincoln, C. Eric, and Lawrence H. Mamiya. *The Black Church in the African-American Experience.* Duke University Press, 1990.

"L. Kelly and Woodie White Become United Methodist Bishops." *Michigan Chronicle,* 11 August 1984. B-6.

Macklin, Beth. "Colorful Bishops." Tulsa *World* (5 August 1984).

"Methodist Bishop, Leontine Kelly, Records Album of Stories." *Los Angeles Sentinel,* 23 August 1984. C-9.

"Methodist Bishop Records 'New Testament Stories' Album." *Afro-American,* 18 August 1984. 12.

"Methodists Elect First Black Woman." *Los Angeles Sentinel Times,* 2 August 1984. C-10.

"Methodists Elect 19 to Leadership." *New York Times,* 29 July 1984. 19.

"Methodists Vote for Bishops." *Washington Post,* 20 July 1984. B-3.

Reed. W. A. "Methodist Women Pastors Receive Promise of Equality." *Tennessean,* 25 July 1984.

Richardson, Harry V. *Dark Salvation: The Story of Methodism as It Developed among Blacks in America.* Doubleday, 1976.

"United Methodist Church Names Bishops." *Afro-American,* 28 July 1984. 15.

Weston, Rubin F. *Blacks in Ohio History.* Ohio Historical Society, 1976.

• SHARON PRATT KELLY

"Election Results: Blacks Make New Gains Across U.S." *Jet* 79 (26 November 1990): 12-15.

"Sharon Pratt-Dixon: Fresh Alternative." *Georgetowner* 35 (29 June-12 July, 1990): 1, 8, 17.

Washington Times, 17 April 1990.

"Why Not a Ms. Mayor?" *Washington Post* 10 July 1990.

• FLO KENNEDY

"Activist, Attorney Flo Kennedy Roasted on 70th Birthday." *Jet* 70 (31 March 1986): 6.

Acton, Jay, Alan LeMond and Parker Hodges. *MUG Shots: Who's Who in the New Earth.* World Pub. Co., 1972.

Burstein, Patricia. "Lawyer Flo Kennedy Enjoys Her Reputation as Radicalism's Rudest Mouth." *People Weekly* 3 (14 April 1974): 54.

"Flo Speaks Out." *The Megaphone.* Southwestern University, 9 October 1975.

Kennedy, Flo. *Color Me Flo: My Hard Life and Good Times.* Prentice-Hall, 1976.

King, Helen H. "The Black Woman and Women's Lib." *Ebony* (March 1971): 68-70, 75-76.

• CORETTA SCOTT KING

Assensoh, A. B. *Rev. Dr. Martin Luther King, Jr., and America's Quest for Racial Integration.* Arthur H. Stockwell, 1987.

Caldwell, Earl. "50,000 March in Capital to Support Demand by Poor for Sharing of Affluence." *New York Times,* 20 June 1968.

"Dr. King is Honored." *New York Times,* 12 July 1977.

"Dr. King's Widow in London." *New York Times,* 17 March 1969.

Garrow, David J. *Bearing the Cross: Martin Luther King, Jr., and the Southern Christian Leadership Conference.* Morrow, 1986.

King, Coretta Scott. *My Life with Martin Luther King, Jr.* Holt, 1969.

Lanker, Brian. *I Dream a World.* Stewart, Tabori and Chang, 1989. 80-81.

Lewis, David Levering. *King: A Critical Biography.* Praeger, 1970.

Lukas, J. Anthony. "Mrs. King Asks Peaceful Society." *New York Times,* 9 April 1968.

Norment, Lynn. "The King Family." *Ebony,* (January 1987): 25-26.

• KING and SHABAZZ

Bailey, A. Peter. "The Ties That Bind." *Essence,* January 1982: 78, 102, 107-08.

Christon, Lawrence. "Going Her Way." *Los Angeles Times,* March 1, 1992: sec CAL, 5, 84.

Clayton, Dawn. "The Daughters of Malcolm X and Martin Luther King Team Up to Bring a Play of Hope to Kids." *People,* September 5, 1983: 99-101.

Ebony, May 1979: 166-68.

Hopkins, Ellen. "Their Fathers' Daughters." *Rolling Stone,* November 30, 1989: 76-84, 120, 123-24.

Johnson, Robert E. "World-Respected Leader Was Just 'Daddy' to His Four Youngsters." *Ebony,* April 1972: 74-82.

Norment, Lynn. "The King Family: Keepers of the Dream." *Ebony,* January 1987: 25-28, 30, 32, 34.

Pool, Bob. "Daughters of King, Malcolm X Also Have a Message." *Los Angeles Times,* April 9, 1988: sec II, 3-4.

• JEWEL STRADFORD LAFONTANT

"Attorney Jewel Lafontant Joins 114 Lawyer Firm." *Jet* (3 October 1983): 33.

Contributions of Black Women to America. Volume 1. Ed. Marianna W. Davis. Kenday Press, 1982.

Ebony Success Library. Volume 1. *1,000 Successful Blacks.* Johnson Pub. Co. 1973.

Encyclopedia of Black America. Eds. W. Augustus Low and Virgil A. Clift. McGraw Hill, 1981.

"Executive Changes." *New York Times*, 16 March 1972.

"Former Business and Professional Honoree to Chair Salute to Women." *Dollars and Sense* 14 (April/May 1988): 9.

Hine, Darlene Clark and Patrick Kay Bidelman. *Black Women in the Middle West Project: A Comprehensive Resource Guide*. Indiana Historical Society and Purdue University, 1986.

"An Interview with Jewel S. Lafontant." *Dollars and Sense* 8 (December 1982/January 1983): 18-22.

"Jewel Lafontant Named to High Post by Nixon." *Jet* 43 (4 January 1973): 10.

"Jewel Lafontant to Chair Salute to 100 Women." *Dollars and Sense* 14 (February/March 1988): 9.

"Lafontant Oversees Refugee Affairs in New State Post." *Jet* 76 (7 August 1989): 9.

"The Lawyer Is Truly a Lady: J. Lafontant, U. S. Deputy Solicitor General." *Ebony* 28 (April 1973): 146-152.

"Nixon Plan for Black Woman for Appeals Court Set Back." *Washington Post* 2 February 1974.

"Praising a Woman Lawyer." *Washington Post*, 18 April 1973.

Washington Star News, 4 April 1974.

● *ELMA LEWIS*

Bailey, Peter. "Black Art's Amazing Fund-Raiser." *Ebony* 25 (June 1970): 70-78.

Bailey, Susan. "The Undeferred Dream of Elma Lewis." *Essence* 4 (July 1973): 40-41.

Boston Globe, 30 January, 22 September 1971; 26 February, 21 June 1974; 1 January, 31 January, 3 February, 1975.

Boston Herald Traveler, 27 April 12 June, 8 November 1971.

Editors of Ebony. *Ebony Success Library*. Vol. 1. *1,000 Successful Blacks*. Johnson Pub. Co., 1973.

Garfinkel, Perry. "Big Boom in Black Arts and Culture." *Sepia* 25 (September 1976): 66-72.

Guralnick, Estelle Bond. "The Private Elma Lewis. *Boston Sunday Globe,* 23 January 1977.

Korzenik, Diana. "A Blend of Marcus Garvey and the 92nd Street Y: An Interview with Elma Lewis." *Art Education* 35 (March 1982): 24-26.

Lewis, Elma. "Celebrating Little People." *Boston Review of the Arts* 2 (September 1972): 89-92.

Merchant, Zarine. "Elma Lewis School of Fine Arts: The Fountainhead of Black Culture in Boston Started as a School and Is Now a Mini-Empire." *Black Enterprise* 6 (August 1975): 29-31.

New York Times, 17 November 1968; 19 April 1968; 19 November 1968; 16 December 1969; 20 September 1970; 24 June 1974; 19 May, 25 May 1981; 10 July 1986.

Quinn, Susan. "Elma Lewis: Keeping African Culture Alive in Boston." *Ms.* 5 (May 1977): 14-15.

Record American (Boston) 25 May 1971.

Southern, Eileen. *Biographical Dictionary of Afro-American and African Musicians*. Greenwood Press, 1982.

Spradling, Mary Mace. *In Black and White*. 3rd ed. Vol. 1. Gale Research, 1980. Supplement, 1985.

Vogue 153 (May 1969): 173.

Washington Post, 10 September 1975.

● *AUDRE LORDE*

Black Writers. Gale Research, 1989.

Evans, Mari. *Black Women Writers: A Critical Evaluation*. Doubleday, 1984.

Lorde, Audre. *The Black Unicorn*. Norton, 1978.

————. *Burst of Light*. Firebrand Books, 1988.

————. *Sister Outsider*. Crossing Press, 1984.

————. *Zami: A New Spelling of My Name*. Crossing Press, 1982.

● *ANNIE TURNBO MALONE*

Bowles, Eva. "Opportunities for the Educated Colored Woman." *Opportunity* 1 (March 1923).

Embree, Edwin R. *Brown Americans: The Story of a Tenth of the Nation*. Viking, 1946. 161, 163.

Frazier, E. Franklin. *The Negro in the United States*. Macmillan, 1968.

"Missouri Women in History: Annie Turnbo Malone." *Missouri Historical Review* (July 1973).

Mongold, Jeanne Conway. "Annie Minerva Turnbo-Malone." *Notable American Women: The Modern Period.* Harvard University Press, 1980. 700-702.

Kleitzing, Henry F., and William Crogman. *Progress of a Race.* J. L. Nichols, 1898.

Porter, Gladys L. *Three Negro Pioneers in Beauty Culture.* Vantage Press, 1966.

Woodson, Carter G. *The Negro in Our History.* 4th ed. Associated Publishers, 1927. 461.

• *BIDDY MASON*

Beasley, Delilah L. *The Negro Trailblazers in California.* Times Mirror Printing and Binding House, 1919.

Bunch, Lonnie G. *Black Angelenos: The Afro-American in Los Angeles, 1850-1950.* Exhibit catalog. California Afro-American Museum, 1988.

Crouch, Gregory. "Early Black Heroine of L.A. Finally Receives Her Due." *Los Angeles Times,* 28 March 1988.

Hayden, Dolores. "Biddy Mason's Los Angeles, 1856-1891." *California History,* 68 (Fall 1989): 86-99.

Oliver, Myrna. "A Lot of History." *Los Angeles Times,* 17 November 1989.

• *Queen Mother AUDLEY MOORE*

Black Scholar (March-April 1973): 47-55.

Gilkes, Cheryl Townsend. "Interview with Queen Mother Audley Moore." *Black Women Oral History Collection.* Schlesinger Library, Radcliffe College, 1980.

Lanker, Brian. *I Dream a World: Portraits of Black Women Who Changed America.* Stewart, Tabori and Chang, 1989. 102-103.

Women of Courage: An Exhibition of Photographs by Judith Sedwick. Schlesinger Library, Radcliffe College, 1984. 59.

• *TONI MORRISON*

Dictionary of Literary Biography. Vol. 33. *Afro-American Fiction Writers After 1955.* Ed. Thadious M. Davis. Gale Research, 1984. 194.

McKay, Nellie. "An Interview with Toni Morrison." *Contemporary Literature* 24 (Winter 1983): 413-39.

Morrison, Toni. "Rootedness: The Ancestor as Foundation." *Black Women Writers.* Ed. Mari Evans. Anchor Books, 1983. 339-45.

Stepto, Robert B. "'Intimate Things in Place': A Conversation with Toni Morrison." *Chant of Saints.* Eds. Michael S. Harper and Robert B. Stepto. University of Illinois Press, 1979. 213-29.

Ruas, Charles. "Toni Morrison." *Conversations with American Writers.* Knopf, 1985. 215-43.

Strouse, Jean. "Toni Morrison's Black Magic." *Newsweek* 97 (30 March 1981): 52-57.

• *CONSTANCE BAKER MOTLEY*

Berry, Bill. "Husbands of Well Known Women." *Ebony* 33 (April 1987): 154, 156-58.

Dannett, Sylvia G. *Profiles of Negro Womanhood.* Vol. 2. Educational Heritage, 1964. 320-27.

Duckett, Alfred A. *Changing of the Guard: The New Breed of Black Politicians.* Coward McCann and Geoghegan, 1972. 108-12.

Lamson, Peggy. *Few Are Chosen; American Women in Political Life.* Houghton Mifflin, 1968. 127-61.

Lerner, Gerda. Ed. *Black Women in White America: A Documentary History.* Vintage Books, 1973. 323.

Low, Augustus W. *Encyclopedia of Black Americans.* McGraw-Hill, 1981. 582.

"Mme. Borough President: Constance Baker Motley." *Crisis* 72 (April 1965): 224-25.

Motley, Constance Baker. "James Meredith in Perspective." *Crisis* 70 (January 1963): 5-11.

Ploski, Harry A., and James Williams, comps. and eds. *The Negro Almanac: A Reference Work on the African American.* Gale Research, 1989. 38, 345-46.

Reasons, George and Sam Patrick. *They Had a Dream.* New American Library, 1971. 42.

Robinson, Wilhelmena S. *Historical Afro-American Biographies.* Publishers Agency, 1978. 230-31.

Spiegler, Charles, Ed. *They Were First.* C. E. Merrill, 1968. 85-89.

Smythe, Mable M., Ed. *The Black American Reference Book.* Prentice-Hall, 1976. 95-121.

• *PAULI MURRAY*

Contemporary Authors. Gale Research, 1989. 352-354.

Diamonstein, Barbaralee. *Open Secrets: Ninety-four Women in Touch With Our Time.* Viking, 1972. 289-294.

Leland, Elizabeth. "Pauli Murray Returns to Fulfill A Prophesy." *The Chapel Hill Newspaper,* 14 February 1977.

McKay, Nellie. "Pauli Murray." *Dictionary of Literary Biography.* Vol. 41, *Afro-American Poets Since 1955.* Gale Research, 1985. 248-251.

McNeil, Genna Rae. "Interview with Pauli Murray, February 12, 1976, Alexandria, Virginia." Southern Historical Collection and Manuscripts, Wilson Library, University of North Carolina, Chapel Hill.

Murray, Pauli. *Proud Shoes: The Story of an American Family.* Harper and Row, 1956.

————. *Song in a Weary Throat: An American Pilgrimage.* Harper, 1987.

Thomas, Gwendolyn. "Pauli Murray." *American Women Writers.* Vol. 125. Frederick Ungar, 1981. 241-243.

• *ELEANOR HOLMES NORTON*

Afro-American Encyclopedia. Vol. 3. Educational Book Publishers, 1974.

Ayres, Drummond B. "Women Nominated for Capital Mayor." *New York Times* 12 September 1990.

"Candidate Owing Back Taxes Won't Quit Race." *New York Times* 10 September 1990.

Current Biography. H. W. Wilson, 1976.

Dionne, E. J. "Two Party Insiders to Lead Jackson's Convention Drive." *New York Times* 14 May 1988.

Dreifus, Claudia. "'I Hope I'm Not a Token.'" *McCall's* 99 (October 1971): 51.

"Gaining Ground." *New Republic* 200 (5 June 1989): 10, 11.

Haywood, Richetta. "Eleanor Holmes Norton Takes D.C. Seat." *Ebony* 46 (January 1991): 105-106.

Jenkins, Kent, Jr. "First Year Brings Norton A Reversal of Fortune." *Washington Post* 12 January 1992.

Norton, Eleanor Holmes. "... And the Language Is Race." *Ms.* 4 (January-February 1992): 43-45.

Ploski, Harry. *The Negro Almanac.* Bellwether Pub. Co., 1976.

Pyatt, Richard I. "Eleanor Holmes Norton: From Human Rights to Equal Opportunity." *Encore* 6 (20 June 1977): 47, 48.

Villarosa, Linda. "What Have They Done For Us Lately." *Essence* 21 (May 1990): 66-68.

Walker, Greta. "Eleanor Holmes Norton." *Women Today* (1975): 29.

Watts, Daud. "The American Dilemma Has Not Been Solved." *Black Enterprise* 19 (October 1989): 26. Includes photograph.

• *ROSA PARKS*

Bennett, Lerone, Jr. *Wade in the Water.* Johnson Publishing Co., 1979.

"Interview with Rosa Parks." *Black Women Oral History Project.* Schlesinger Library, Radcliffe College, 1984.

Boston Globe, 25 May 1981.

Current Biography Yearbook. H. W. Wilson, 1989.

Giddings, Paula. *When and Where I Enter.* Morrow, 1984.

Hymowitz, Carol and Michaele Weissman. *A History of Women in America.* Bantam Books, 1978.

Metcalf, George R. *Black Profiles.* McGraw-Hill, 1988.

Miller, Judi. *Women Who Changed America.* Manor Books, 1976.

New York Times, 15 January 1980.

New York Times Book Review, 2 February 1992.

People's Almanac 2. Morrow, 1978.

Raines, Howell. *My Soul Is Rested.* Penguin Books, 1983.

Robinson, Jo Ann. *The Montgomery Bus Boycott and the Women Who Started It.* University of Tennessee Press, 1987.

Sunday News Magazine, New York, 24 May 1981.

USA Today, 1 February 1988.

Washington Post, 6 February 1990.

• *CARRIE SAXON PERRY*

Condon, Tom. "Mayor Merits a Little Heart in Hartford." *Hartford Courant,* 8 February 1990.

Fahy, Anne. "Mayor Urges Rescue Efforts for Cities." *Philadelphia Inquirer* 3 December 1989.

Graham, George. "Hartford Mayor Foresees Opportunities for Women." *Union News,* 21 February 1990.

Johnson, Kirk. "In Hartford, Drug Violence May Draw Region's Concern." *New York Times*, 11 November 1989.

Keveney, Bill and Mary Pazniokas. "Mellow Style Suits Perry." *Hartford Courant*, 31 May 1988.

Lanker, Brian. *I Dream a World.* New York: Stewart, Tabori, and Chang, 1989.

Marshall, Marilyn. "Carrie Saxon Perry: More Than a Pretty Hat." *Ebony* 43 (April 1988): 60.

Moser, Matthew. "Inmates Cheer Hartford Mayor." *Hartford Courant*, 15 February 1990.

Perry, Carrie Saxon."Gender, Authority and Leadership: Perspectives from the Political World." Speech delivered at Smith College, 20 February 1990.

————. Inaugural Address: Hartford, Connecticut, 5 December 1989.

Richardson, Lisa. "Choice for Mayor of Hartford." Editorial. *Hartford Courant*, 29 October 1987.

"Speaking Out: What Must be Done. (Four Black Leaders' Opinions on Government's Anti-drug Efforts) (War! The Drug Crisis: Programs and Solutions.)" *Ebony* 44 (August 1989): 156.

"What Did Rainbow Tuesday Mean? (Race as a Factor in American Politics)." *Ebony* 45 (February 1990): 32.

● *LEONTYNE PRICE*

Bloomfield, Arthur. *San Francisco Examiner*, 20 October 1977.

Current Biography. H. W. Wilson Co., 1978.

Eaton, Quaintance. *The Miracle of the Met.* Meredith Press, 1968.

Frankenstein, Alfred. *San Francisco Chronicle.* Quoted in Hugh Lee Lyon. *Leontyne Price: Highlights of a Prima Donna.* Vantage Press, 1973.

Garland, Phyl. "Leontyne Price: Getting Out At the Top." *Ebony* (June 1985): 31-36.

Harrison, Jay. *New York Herald Tribune*, 18 November 1954. Quoted in *Current Biography*, 1978. 330.

Hume, David. *Washington Post* August 1952. Quoted in Lyon, 66.

"I'm Just a Girl from Laurel Mississippi." *Ebony* 30 (February 1975): 40-41.

Jacobson, Robert. "Collard Greens and Caviar." *Opera News* 50 (July 1985): 18-23.

Lanker, Brian. *I Dream a World.* Stewart, Tabori and Chang, 1989.

Lyon, Hugh Lee. *Leontyne Price: Highlights of a Prima Donna.* Vantage Press, 1973.

Parmenter, Ross. *New York Times.* Quoted in Lyons, 101.

Rosenfield, John. "A New Porgy in Dallas." *Saturday Review*, 28 June 1952: 44.

Sargeant, Winthrop. *Divas.* Coward, McCann & Geoghean, 1973.

————. "Musical Events. A Great Night." The *New Yorker* 4 February 1961: 102.

Schonberg, Harold. "A New and Handsome Aida Opens at Met." *New York Times*, 4 February, 1961.

Story, Rosalyn M. *And So I Sing: Afro-American Divas of Opera and Concert.* Warner Books, 1990.

Walsh, Maurice. "What Price Glory, Leontyne!" *Time* 14 January 1985.

● *ERNESTA G. PROCOPE*

"A View From the Top." *Black Enterprise* 5 (June 1975): 79.

Gayle, Rosalie. "Procope: Premium Power Broker." *Working Woman* 4 (December 1978): 21, 22.

Iverem, Esther. "Wall Street Success Story: How One Woman Guided Her Insurance Company to the Top." *Essence* 19 (October 1988): 130.

McLeod, Douglas. "Small Fish Swims in Exclusive Pond of Corporate Clients." *Crains New York Business*, 25 July 1988.

Mourges-Rudolph, Denise. "Ernesta Procope: No. 1 in Insurance." *Sepia* 27 (May 1978): 27, 31.

Prufer, Diana. "A Premium Life: Ernesta Procope Battled Scandal and Racism to Build a Twenty-five Million Dollar Insurance Brokerage." *Savvy* 9 (October 1988): 40.

Schwab, Priscilla. "A Little Tokenism Can Help." *Nation's Business* 67 (December 1979): 121.

Wansley, Joy. "Opening Doors, Especially on Wall Street, is no Easy Task, but Ernesta Procope Managed It." *People Weekly* (December 1978): 203.

• BARBARA GARDNER PROCTOR

"Advertising Exec. Barbara Proctor Discusses Her Career." *New Orleans Times-Picayune*, 30 April 1984.

Ball, Millie. "Ad Whiz Was on Her Way with Her First SBA Loan." *New Orleans Times-Picayune*, 30 April 1984.

Bergen, Michele. "They Are Owners, Bosses, Workers." *Ebony* 32 (August 1977): 122.

Brown, Michelle. "Barbara Gardner Proctor." *Contemporary Newsmakers*. Gale Research, 1986.

Dudley, Percy. "Entrepreneur Urges Women to Take Control of Their Lives." *Atlanta Constitution*, 24 September 1987.

Francke, Richie L. "Proctor Takes a Gamble and Hits the Jackpot." *Working Woman* 4 (August 1979): 19.

Gottschalk, Earl C., Jr. "More Women Start Up Their Own Business with Major Successes." *Wall Street Journal*, 17 May 1983.

Klose, Kevin. "In the Spirit of Enterprise: Barbara Proctor and Her Presidential Mention." *Washington Post*, 27 January 1984.

McFadden, Robert D. "President's 5 Heroes for the 80's Seek to Share Their Spotlight." *New York Times*, 27 January 1984.

Morton, Carol A. "Black Women in Corporate America." *Ebony* 32 (November 1975): 107.

"Profile of Chicagoan Barbara Proctor." *Chicago Tribune*, 26 January 1984.

Runde, Robert. "The Ad Agency Chief." *Money* 10 (September 1981): 50.

Stravro, Barry. "The Best Collateral (Barbara Gardner Proctor)." *Forbes* 132 (21 November 1983): 124.

Winako, Bess. "Success Wasn't So Elusive for These Black Women." *Chicago Tribune*, 5 September 1971.

• BERNICE J. REAGON

Camacho, Mildred. "The Other Side." *High Fidelity* (April 1986): 82.

"Coda." *Ms.* 13 (May 1985): 53.

DeVeaux, Alexis. "Bernice Reagon." *Essence* 11 (June 1980: 92-93, 142, 145, 148, 150.

Dratch-Kovler, Carol. "Video Reviews." *Library Journal* 15 February 1992.

Dretzka, Gary. "'The Civil War' Original Soundtrack." *Chicago Tribune* 21 February 1991.

"Inspired by Gospel and African Rhythms, Sweet Honey in the Rock Delivers Political Punch A Capella." *People* 33 (28 May 1990): 108.

"Limelight." *Washington Post* 16 November 1980. M-3.

McHenry, Susan. "Stepping across the Line: Voter Registration Then and Now." *Ms.* 13 (November 1984): 86.

Morris, Rachel. "Essence Women." *Essence* 8 (February 1978): 40.

Palmer, Don. "Sweet Honey in the Rock: Live at Carnegie Hall." *Downbeat* (May 1989): 74.

"Performer, Researcher, Curator: Her Life Is a Commitment to African-American Culture." Baltimore *Evening Sun* (30 July 1989). G-1.

Reagon, Bernice J. "African Diaspora Women: The Making of Cultural Workers." *Black Women's History*. Vol. 2. Edited by Darlene Clark-Hine. Carlson Pub. Co.

"Reagon Makes Sweet Music." *A Mind Is a Terrible Thing to Waste* 1 (Winter 1991): 24-25, 40.

"Sweet Honey Runs on with a Strong New Album." *Washington Post*, 11 October 1978.

Wood, Peter H. "You Got to Move." Movie review. *Journal of American History* 74 (December 1987): 1117.

Young, Ivy. "Sweet Honey in the Rock." *Essence* 18 (May 1987): 92.

• ESLANDA GOODE ROBESON

Duberman, Martin Bauml. *Paul Robeson: A Biography*. Knopf, 1988.

Golden, Lillie. "Remembrances of Eslanda." *Freedomways* Fourth Quarter 1966): 330-32.

Graham, Shirley. *Paul Robeson: Citizen of the World*. Messner, 1946.

Hamilton, Virginia. *Paul Robeson: The Life and Times of a Free Black Man*. Harper, 1974.

Logan, Rayford W. "Eslanda Cardoza Goode Robeson." *Dictionary of American Negro Biography*. Eds. Rayford W. Logan and Michael R. Winston. Norton, 1982. 527-28.

Prattis, R. L. "Remembrances of Eslanda." *Freedomways* Fourth Quarter 1966): 337-38.

Ransby, Barbara. "Eslanda Goode Robeson, Pan-Africanist." *Sage* 3 Fall 1986): 22-26.

Robeson, Eslanda Goode. "African Journey." *Freedomways* Fourth Quarter 1966): 346-47.

———. "African Journey" [condensation]. *Negro Digest* 3 October 1945): 86-93.

———. *Paul Robeson, Negro.* Harper and Brothers, 1930.

———. "Re the Assassination of Harry T. Moore and His Wife at Mims, Florida, Christmas, 1951." *Freedomways* Fourth Quarter 1966): 350-53.

———. "What Do the People of Africa Want?" Quoted in Barbara Ransby, "Eslanda Goode Robeson, Pan-Africanist." *Sage* 3 Fall 1986): 22.

Sullivan, Patricia. "Eslanda Cardoza Goode Robeson." *Notable Black American Women: The Modern Period.* Harvard University Press, 1980. 583-84.

• WILMA RUDOLPH

Biracree, Tom. *Wilma Rudolph.* Chelsea House, 1988.

Current Biography. H. W. Wilson, 1961. 399-401.

Jacobs, Linda. *Wilma Rudolph: Run for Glory.* Eric Corp., 1975.

Lanker, Brian. *I Dream a World.* Stewart, Tabori and Chang, 1989. 140-41.

Lewis, Dwight, and Susan Thomas. *A Will to Win.* Cumberland Press, 1983.

Rudolph, Wilma. *Wilma: The Story of Wilma Rudolph.* New American Library, 1977.

Time 19 September 1960.

"Track Star Wilma Rudolph Will Be in World Book Thanks to Jessup Students." *Jet,* 1 July 1991.

• GLORIA SCOTT

"Bush's Black College Board Lauds Call for Review of Minority Scholarship Plan." *Jet* 79 (21 January 1991): 33.

Contributions of Black Women to America. Vol. II. Ed. Marianna W. Davis. Kenday Press, 1982.

Demaret, Kent. "The Old Girl Scout Cookie Crumbling?." *People* (25 July 1977): 38-39.

"Essence Women." *Essence* 8 (January 1978): 6.

Jones, M. Colleen. "An Interview with Gloria Scott." Special Issue: "Black Women in Higher Education." *Journal of the National Association of Women Deans, Administrators, and Counselors* 53 (Spring 1999): 29-32.

Ladies' Home Journal (June 1977): 75-76.

Lanker, Brian. *I Dream a World.* Stewart, Tabori and Chang, 1989. 118-19.

Mercer, Joye. "Difficult Winds Ahead: Five Women Chart the Course for HBCUs in the 1990s." *Black Issues in Higher Education* 7 (27 September 1990): 10-15.

People (3 October 1977): 69.

"Speaking of People." *Ebony* 32 (August 1977): 3.

• NTOZAKE SHANGE

Betsko, Kathleen, and Rachel Koenig, eds. *Interviews with Contemporary Women Playwrights.* Beech Tree Books, 1987.

Chambers, Gordon. "Book Mark." *Essence* (August, 1991).

Christ, Carol P. *Diving Deep and Surfacing: Women Writers on Spiritual Quest.* Beacon Press, 1980.

Contemporary Authors: New Revision Series. Vol. 27. Gale Research, 1989.

Contemporary Literary Criticism. Vol. 8. 1978; Vol. 25, 1983; Vol. 38, 1986. Gale Research.

Dictionary of Literary Biography. Vol. 38, Afro-American Writers after 1955: Dramatists and Prose Writers. Gale Research, 1985.

Dong, Stella. "Ntozake Shange." *Publishers Weekly* (5 May 1985): 74-75.

Shange, Ntozake. *See No Evil: Prefaces, Essays and Accounts, 1976-1983.* Momo's Press, 1984.

———. *A Daughter's Geography.* St. Martin's Press, 1983.

———. *for colored girls who have considered suicide/ when the rainbow is enuf.* St. Martin's Press, 1976.

———. *From Okra to Greens.* Coffee House Press, 1972.

———. *Nappy Edges.* St. Martin's Press, 1972.

———. *Ridin' the Moon in Texas.* St. Martin's Press, 1987.

———. *Sassafras.* Shameless Hussy Press, 1976.

———. *Sassafrass, Cypress & Indigo.* St. Martin's Press, 1982.

Squier, Susan Merrill, ed. *Women Writers and the City: Essays in Feminist Literary Criticism.* University of Tennessee Press, 1984.

Tate, Claudia, ed. *Black Women Writers at Work.* Continuum Publishing Company, 1983.

• *ALTHEA T. L. SIMMONS*

"Althea Simmons Runs Civil Rights Drive from Hospital." *Jet* 78 (16 April 1990): 7.

Booker, Simeon. "Ticker Tape U.S.A." *Jet* 78 (10 April 1990): 10.

Guess, Jerry M. "Reflections on a Life." *Crisis* 97 (October 1990): 37-40, 51.

Lanker, Brian. *I Dream a World.* Stewart, Tabori and Chang, 1989.

"Miss Simmons in New Post." *Crisis* 72 (March 1965): 166-67.

"Statement of Benjamin L. Hooks on the Death of Althea T. L. Simmons." *Crisis* 97 (October 1990): 41, 51-52.

Williams, Lena. "Black and Female, and Now Deemed Effective." *New York Times*, 30 June 1987.

• *CAROLE SIMPSON*

"ABC News' Carole Simpson Won't Return to South Africa." *Jet* 768 (30 April 1990): 12.

"Upsurge in TV News." *Ebony* 26 (June 1971) 168, 170.

"Tops in TV Newscasters." *Ebony* 34 (January 1979): 111.

• *NAOMI SIMS*

Kevels, Barbara. "From Cover Girl to Cover Up: Naomi Sims Turns Wigs into Millions." *People* (22 August 1977): 14-19.

Lurie, Diane. "Naomi." *Ladies Home Journal* (November 1968): 114.

Summers, Barbara. "Naomi Sims." *Essence* 16 (January 1986): 41.

• *BESSIE SMITH*

Albertson, Chris, *Bessie,* Stein and Day, 1972.

Donaldson, Norman, and Betty Donaldson, *How Did They Die?* St. Martin's Press, 1980.

Esquire, June 1969.

High Fidelity Magazine, October 1970; May 1975.

Kinkle, Roger D., *The Complete Encyclopedia of Popular Music and Jazz 1900-1950,* Volume 3, Arlington House, 1974

Morgenstern, Dan, *Jazz People,* Harry N. Abrams, 1976.

National Review, July 1, 1961.

Newsweek, February 1, 1971; January 22,1973.

Rust, Brian, *Jazz Records 1897-1942,* 5th Revised and Enlarged Edition, Volume 2, Storyville Publications, 1982.

Saturday Review, December 29, 1951; February 26, 1972.

Schuller, Gunther, *Early Jazz,* Oxford University Press, 1968.

Schuller, Gunther, *The Swing Era,* Oxford University Press, 1989.

Shapiro, Nat, and Nat Hentoff, Editors, *The Jazz Makers* (Bessie Smith chapter by George Hoefer), Rinehart & Co.,1957.

Terkel, Studs, and Millie Hawk Daniel, *Giants of Jazz,* revised edition. Thomas Y. Crowell Company, 1975.

• *JUANITA KIDD STOUT*

"A Career of Firsts." *Ebony* 44 (February 1989): 76, 78, 80.

Dannett, Sylvia G. L. *Profiles of Negro Womanhood.* Vol. 2. Educational Heritage, 1966.

"Her Honor Bops the Hoodlums." *Life* 59 (9 July, 1965): 74.

Philadelphia Inquirer (7 March 1988) F-1; (30 October 1989) F-6.

"Unfrightened Crusader." *Time* 85 (16 April 1965): 47.

• *NIARA SUDARKASA*

Lanker, Brian. *I Dream a World.* Stewart, Tabori and Chang, 1989.

McKinney, Rhoda E. "'Sister' Presidents." *Ebony* 43 (February 1988): 82-88.

Reynolds, Rhoda E. "Inquiry: Black Colleges." *USA Today* 12 October 1987.

Sudarkasa, Niara. "An Exposition on the Value Premises Underlying Black Family Studies." *Journal of the National Medical Association* 67 (May 1975).

————. "Female Employment and Family Organization in West Africa." In *The Black*

Woman Cross-Culturally. Edited by Filomina Steady. Schenkman Publishing, 1981.

————. "Sex Roles, Education and Development in Africa." *Anthropology and Education Quarterly* 13 (Fall 1982): 278-88.

Washington, Elsie B. "Niara Sudarkasa: Educator for the 1990's." *Essence* 20 (May 1989): 106-108.

• *SUSAN L. TAYLOR*

Detroit News, 30 October 1986.

Excel 2 (Fall 1986): 13-15.

Los Angeles Times, 13 April 1986.

• *SUSIE BAKER KING TAYLOR*

Black Women in Nineteenth-Century American Life: Their Words, Their Thoughts, Their Feelings. Eds. Bert James Loewenberg and Ruth Bogin. Pennsylvania State University Press, 1976. 898-894.

Booker, Simeon. *Susie King Taylor: Civil War Nurse*. McGraw-Hill, 1969.

Burchard, Peter. *One Gallant Rush: Robert Gould Shaw and His Brave Black Regiment*. St. Martin's Press, 1965.

Carnegie, Mary Elizabeth. *The Path We Tread: Blacks in Nursing 1854-1984*. Lippincott, 1986.

Dannett, Sylvia G. L. *Profiles of Negro Womanhood*. Vol. 1. Educational Heritage, 1964.

Driver, Paul J. *Black Giants in Science*. Vantage Press, 1978.

Gaines, Edith M. *Terrible Tuesday*. New Day Press, 1972.

Higginson, Thomas Wentworth. *Army Life in a Black Regiment*. Reprinted. Norton, 1984.

Lerner, Gerda, ed. *Black Women in White America*. Pantheon Books, 1972.

Merriam, Eve. *Growing Up Female in America: Ten Lives*. Doubleday, 1917.

Risjord, Normal K. *America: A History of the United States*. Prentice-Hall, 1985.

Taylor, Susie King. *Reminiscences of My Life in Camp*. Boston: privately printed, 1902. Reprinted: Arno Press, 1968.

"Teen-age Civil War Nurse: Susie King Taylor." *Ebony* 24 (February 1970): 96-102.

• *MARY CHURCH TERRELL*

Current Biography H. W. Wilson, 1942, 1954.

The Delta 10 (January 1941): 4.

Giddings, Paula. *When and Where I Enter; The Impact of Black Women on Race and Sex in America*. Morrow, 1984.

Jones, Beverly Washington. *Quest for Equality: The Life and Writings of Mary Church Terrell*. Carlson Publishers, 1990.

New York Times, 29 July 1954.

Shepperd, Gladys B. *Mary Church Terrell—Respectable Person*. Human Relations Press, 1959.

Sterling, Dorothy. *Black Foremothers*. Feminist Press, 1979. Revised 1988. A children's book.

————. "Mary Church Terrell." *Notable American Women: The Modern Period*. Vol. 4. Harvard University Press, 1980.

Terrell, Mary Church. *A Colored Woman in a White World*. Ransdell, 1940. Reprinted. Arno Press, 1980.

Washington Post, 25 July 1954.

Washington Star, 25 July 1954.

Wesley, Charles H. *History of the National Association of Colored Women's Clubs, Inc., A Legacy of Service*. National Association of Colored Women's Clubs, 1984.

• *JACKIE TORRENCE*

"Br'er Possum, Meet Br'er Snake, but You Better Be Careful." *Wall Street Journal*, 4 April 1980.

Lanker, Brian. *I Dream a World*. Stewart, Tabori and Chang, 1989.

National Directory of Storytelling, 1990. National Association for the Preservation and Perpetuation of Storytelling, 1990.

Smith, Jimmy Neil, ed. *Homespun: Tales from America's Favorite Storytellers*. Crown, 1988.

Storytelling, 1990, Catalog of Storytelling Resources. National Association for the Preservation and Perpetuation on Storytelling, 1990.

Torrence, Jackie. "Storytelling." *Horn Book* 69 (February 1983): 280-283.

Wellner, Cathy. "Paying Your Dues: An Interview with Jackie Torrence." *National Storytelling Journal* 2 (Summer 1985): 12-13.

• SOJOURNER TRUTH

Douglass, Frederick. *Life and Times of Frederick Douglass.* 1892. Reprinted. Bonanza Books, 1962.

Stanton, Elizabeth Cady, et al., eds. *History of Woman Suffrage.* 2 vols. Fowler and Wells, 1881-82.

Stowe, Harriet Beecher. "The Libyan Sibyl." *Atlantic Monthly* 11 (April 1863): 473-81.

Truth, Sojourner, and Olive Gilbert. *The Narrative of Sojourner Truth.* By Olive Gilbert. Privately printed, 1850. Privately printed (edited by Frances Titus). 1875/78.

• HARRIET TUBMAN

Bradford, Sarah. *Harriet Tubman: The Moses of Her People.* 1886. Reprinted: Corinth, 1961.

Conrad, Carl. *Harriet Tubman.* Erickson, 1943.

Contributions of Black Women to America. Vol. 2. Edited by Marianna W. Davis. Kenday Press.

A History of the Club Movement among the Colored Women of the United States of America. Washington, 1902.

McPherson, James M., et. al. *Blacks in America: Bibliographic Essays.* Doubleday, 1971.

Quarles, Benjamin. "Harriet Tubman's Unlikely Leadership." *Black Leaders of the Nineteenth Century.* Edited by Leon Litwack and August Meier. University of Illinois Press, 1988.

Williams, Lorraine A. "Harriet Tubman." *Dictionary of American Negro Biography.* Edited by Rayford W. Logan and Michael R. Winston. Norton, 1982.

• SARAH VAUGHAN

Aldred, Michael, "The Divine Sarah Vaughan—The Columbia Years, 1949-1955." *Audio* 73 (October 1989): 172.

Balliett, Whitney. "Jazz Giants." *The New Yorker* 66 (October 1990): 89-90.

Cosby, Bill, "Sarah Vaughan." *Jazziz* 7 (June/July 1990): 67-68.

Current Biography. H. W. Wilson, 1980.

Driggs, Frank. "Everything I Have Is Yours—The MGM Years." *Audio* 71 (October 1987): 41.

Feather, Leonard. *Pleasures of Jazz.* Horizon, 1976.

Gelly, Dave. *The Giants of Jazz.* Schirmer, 1986.

Jones, Max. *Talking Jazz.* Norton, 1988.

Kernfeld, Barry. "Sarah Vaughan." *The New Grove Dictionary of American Music.* Macmillan, 1986.

————. "Sarah Vaughan." *The New Grove Dictionary of Jazz.* Macmillan, 1988.

Leydi, Roberto. *Sarah Vaughan.* G. Ricordi, 1961.

Liska, James. "Sarah Vaughan: I'm Not a Jazz Singer." *Down Beat* 49 (May 1982): 19-21.

Lyons, Leonard, and Don Perlo. *Jazz Portraits.* Morrow, 1989.

McDonough, J. "50th Annual Down Beat Readers Poll." *Down Beat* 52 (December 1985): 22-24.

Morgenstern, Dan. *Jazz People.* Prentice-Hall, 1976.

Morrison, Allan. "Sarah Vaughan Adopts a Baby." *Ebony* 16 (September 1961): 88-94.

Quinn, B. "Sassy '67." *Down Beat* 34 (1967): 20.

Reisner, Robert. *Jazz Titans.* DaCapo Press, 1977.

Robinson, Louie. "The Divine Sarah." *Ebony* 30 (April 1975): 94-102.

"Sarah Vaughan." *Variety* 330 (20 April 1988): 140. (Concert review, Sydney, Australia, Opera House).

"Sarah Vaughan Inducted Into Jazz Hall of Fame." *Jet* 78 (8 October 1990): 56.

Shaw, Arnold. *Black Popular Music in America.* Schirmer, 1986.

Simon, George T. *Best of the Music Makers.* Doubleday, 1979.

"Singer Sarah Vaughan Dies." *The Tennessean,* 5 April 1990.

Southern, Eileen, ed. *Biographical Dictionary of African and Afro-American Musicians.* Greenwood Press, 1982.

Watrous, Peter. "Sarah Vaughan Is Eulogized in Church Where She Sang as a Child." *New York Times,* 10 April 1990.

Williams, Martin. "Words for Sarah Vaughan." *Saturday Review* 50 (26 August 1967): 81.

Williams, Martin, ed. *Smithsonian Collection of Classic Jazz*. Washington, D.C.: Smithsonian Institution and Norton, 1973.

Woodward, Richard B. "The Jazz Singer." *Connoisseur* 219 (March 1989): 146-49.

• *Mother CHARLESZETTA WADDLES*

Briscoe, Stephen. "Mother Waddles: City's Poor 'Worse than Ever.'" *Michigan Chronicle* 3-9 October 1990.

Chargot, Patricia. "Mother Waddles, City's Helper of Poor, Stars in Documentary." *Detroit Free Press* 16 February 1990.

"Mother Waddles: One Woman's War on Poverty." *Essence* 21 (October 1990): 48.

Nagy, Mike. "Mother Waddles Speaks at the University of Detroit about Charity and Self-Esteem." University of Detroit *Student Illustrated* 10 February 1988.

• *ALICE WALKER*

Bradley, David. "Telling the Black Woman's Story." *New York Times*, 8 January 1984. 24-37.

Christian, Barbara. "Alice Walker: The Black Woman Artist as Wayward." In *Black Women Writers (1950-1980): A Critical Evaluation*. Ed. Mari Evans. Anchor, 1984. 457-77.

Current Biography. H. W. Wilson, 1984.

Donahue, Diedre. "Walker's Disturbing Secret." *USA Today* (18 June, 1992): D1.

Mainiero, Linda, ed. *American Women Writers*. Vol. 4. Vois, N.Y.: Frederick Ungar, 1982.

O'Connor, William Van. *The Tangled Fire of William Faulkner*. University of Minnesota Press, 1954.

Tate, Claudia, ed. *Black Women Writers at Work: Conversations*. Continuum, 1983. 175-87.

Walker, Alice. *The Color Purple*. Washington Square Press, 1982.

———. *Good Night, Willie Lee, I'll See You in the Morning*. Harcourt, 1979.

———. *In Search of Our Mothers' Gardens: Womanist Prose*. Harvest, 1983.

———. "Letters to God are Postmarked with a Pulitzer." *People Weekly* 20 (2 January 1984): 85-86.

———. *Living by the Word*. Harcourt, 1988.

———. "Writing the Color Purple." *Black Women Writers (1950-1980): A Critical Evaluation*. Ed. Mari Evans. Anchor, 1984.

Washington, Mary Helen. "Her Mother's Gifts." *Ms.* 10 (June 1982): 38.

Wolcott, James. "Party of Animals." *New Republic* 200 (29 May 1989): 28-30.

• *MADAME C. J. WALKER*

Bundles, A'Lelia. "America's First Self-Made Woman Millionaire." *Radcliffe Quarterly* (December 1987): 11-12.

———. "Black Foremothers: Our Trail Blazers." *Spelman Messenger*. 18-19.

———. "Madame C. J. Walker—Cosmetics Tycoon." *Ms.* July 1983: 91-94.

———. "Madame C. J. Walker to Her Daughter A'Lelia Walker—The Last Letter." *Sage* 1 (Fall 1984): 34-35.

Doyle, Kathleen. "Madame C. J. Walker: First Black Woman Millionaire." *Illustrated* March 1989: 24-26.

Fisher, Walter. "Sarah Breedlove Walker." *Notable American Women*. Vol. 3. Harvard University Press, 1971.

"Henry Bundles and the Madame C. J. Walker Co." *Shoptalk* Spring Journal, 1989: 108.

Higgins, Will. "On the Verge of Big Growth? 76-year-old Madame Walker Firm Considers Leaving Indianapolis." *Indianapolis Business Journal* 29 June 1987: 9-11.

Hughes, Langston. *The Big Sea: An Autobiography*. Thunder's Mouth Press, 1940.

Lewis, David Levering. *When Harlem Was in Vogue*. Knopf, 1981.

Logan, Rayford W. "Madame C. J. Walker [Sarah Breedlove]." *Dictionary of American Negro Biography*." Eds. Rayford W. Logan and Michael R. Winston. Norton, 1982.

Lyons, Douglas C. "History Children: Descendants of Legendary Figures Continue The Tradition." *Ebony* (February 1988): 33-37.

The Madame C. J. Walker Beauty Manual. Mme. C. J. Walker Manufacturing Co. 1925.

"Mme. C. J. Walker Honored: The Rebirth of the Walker Theatre." *Jet* (October 1988): 54.

Nelson, Jill. "The Fortune That Madame Built." *Essence* (June 1983): (June 1983): 84-89.

The Story of a Remarkable Woman. Mme. C. J. Walker Manufacturing Co., 1970.

Trescott, Jacqueline. "The Hair Way to Success: The Business Dynasty of Madame Walker." *Washington Post* 25 May 1973.

Wells, Ida B. *Crusade for Justice*. University of Chicago Press, 1970.

• MAGGIE L. WALKER

Bird, Caroline. "The Innovators: Maggie Walker, Kate Gleason." *Enterprising Women*. Norton, 1976.

"A Brief History of Consolidated Bank and Trust Company in Richmond, Virginia." Historical Overview.

Brown, Elsa Barkley. "Maggie Lena Walker." *Encyclopedia of Southern Culture*. Edited by Charles Wilson and William Ferris. University of North Carolina Press, 1989.

Chandler, Sally. *Maggie Walker: An Abstract of Her Life and Activities*. Bound Study. 28 April 1975.

Dabney, Wendell. *Maggie L. Walker and the I.O. of St. Luke*. Dabney, 1927.

Daniel, Sadie Iola. *Women Builders*. The Associated Publishers, 1931.

Field, Sue and Stephanie Halloran. "Maggie Walker—Lifting as We Climb." Richmond, Virginia, January 1976. Maggie Walker Papers, Maggie Walker National Historic Site.

Jordan, Daniel. "Indomitable Maggie Walker." *Commonwealth* 48 (March 1981): 32-4.

"'Maggie Walker Month Set Apart." *Richmond News Leader*, 4 October 1934.

"Negro Leader's Rites Arranged." *Richmond News Leader*, 17 December 1934.

Pettiger, Betty. "Maggie Walker House: Park Service to Rescue." *Richmond Times Dispatch*, 28 July 1981.

Richmond News Leader, 18 December 1934. Obituary.

Richmond Times Dispatch, 23 August 1924.

Walker, Maggie. *Addresses—Maggie Walker*. 1909, 1921, 1931. Maggie Walker National Historic Site, Richmond, Va.

————. *Diaries of Maggie Walker*. 1921, 1931. Maggie Walker National Historic Site, Richmond, Va.

White, Pam. "Famous Grandma Walker was 'Full of Fun.'" *Richmond News Leader*, 16 July 1979.

• FAYE WATTLETON

Dionne, E. J., Jr. "On Both Sides, Advocates Predict a 50-State Battle." *New York Times*, 4 July 1989.

Epstein, Helen. "Abortion: An Issue That Won't Go Away." *New York Times Magazine*, 20 March 1980.

Gillespie, Marcia Ann. "Repro Woman." *Ms.* 18 (October 1989): 50-53.

Green, Constance M. "A View from the Top." *Black Enterprise* 17 (April 1987): 40-48.

Greenhouse, Linda. "Change in Course." *New York Times*, 4 July 1989.

Lanker, Brian. *I Dream a World*. Stewart, Tabori and Chang, 1989.

Leavitt, Judith A. *American Women Managers and Administrators*. Greenwood Press, 1985.

Lewin, Tamar. "Planned Parenthood Chief Resigns to Be a TV Host." *New York Times*, 9 January 1992.

Lewis, Shawn D. "Family Planning's Top Advocate." *Ebony* 33 (September 1978): 85-86.

"Planned Parenthood Federation." *Wall Street Journal*, 9 January 1992.

Reynolds, Barbara. *And Still We Rise: Interviews with 50 Black Role Models*. USA Today Books, Gannett Co., 1988.

Rubin, Nancy. "The Politics of Parenthood." *Savvy Woman* (April 1989): 81-83.

Szegedy-Maszak, Marianne. "Calm, Cool and Beleaguered." *New York Times Magazine*, 6 August 1989. 16-19.

• IDA B. WELLS BARNETT

Cartwright, Joseph H. *The Triumph of Jim Crow: Tennessee Race Relations in the 1880s*. University of Tennessee Press, 1976.

Church, Annette E., and Roberta Church. *The Robert R. Churches of Memphis*. Edwards Brothers, 1974.

Church, Roberta, and Ronald Walter. *Nineteenth Century Memphis Families of Color, 1850-1900*. Murdock Printing Co., 1987.

Duster, Alfreda M., ed. *Crusader for Justice, the Autobiography of Ida B. Wells*. University of Chicago Press, 1970.

Flexner, Eleanor. "Ida B. Wells-Barnett." *Notable American Women 1607-1950*. Vol. 3. Harvard University Press, 1971.

Free Speech, 21 May 1892.

Holt, Thomas C. "The Lonely Warrior: Ida B. Wells Barnett and the Struggle for Black Leadership." *Black Leaders of the Twentieth Century.* Edited by John Hope Franklin and August Meier. University of Illinois Press, 1982.

Lerner, Gerda. "Early Community Work of Black Club Women." *Journal of Negro History* 59 (April 1954): 158-167.

Manchester Guardian, 8 May 1893.

Memphis Commercial, 25 May 1892.

Memphis Daily Appeal, 25 December 1884.

Memphis Scimitar, 25 May 1892.

Nashville American, 26 May 1892.

Neverdon-Morton, Cynthia. *Afro-American Women of the South and the Advancement of Race, 1895-1925.* University of Tennessee Press, 1989.

Pacyga, Dominic A., and Ellen Skerrett. *Chicago: City of Neighborhood Histories & Tours.* Loyola University Press, 1986.

Sterling, Dorothy. *Black Foremothers: Three Lives.* Old Feminist Press, 1979.

Thompson, Mildred. *Ida B. Wells-Barnett: An Exploratory Story of an American Black Woman, 1893-1930.* Vol.16 *Black Women in United States History.* Edited by Darlene Clark-Hine. Carlson Publishing Co., 1990.

Tucker, David M. *Black Pastors and Leaders: The Memphis Clergy 1819-1972.* Memphis State University, 1975.

———. "Miss Ida B. Wells and Memphis Lynching." *Phylon* 32 (Summer 1971):

Wilson, Charles R., and William Ferris. *Encyclopedia of Southern Culture.* University of North Carolina Press, 1989.

• PHILLIS WHEATLEY

Franklin, Benjamin. *The Papers of Benjamin Franklin.* Edited by William B. Willcox. Yale University Press, 1976.

Kaplan, Sidney, and Emma Nogrady Kaplan. *The Black Presence in the Era of the American Revolution.* Rev. ed. University of Massachusetts Press, 1989.

McKay, David P., and Richard Crawford. *William Billings of Boston: Eighteenth-Century Composer.* Princeton University Press, 1975.

Oddell, Margarita Matilda. *Memoir.* Boston, 1834.

Redding, J. Saunders. "Phillis Wheatley." *Dictionary of American Negro Biography.* Edited by Rayford W. Logan and Michael R. Winston. Norton, 1982.

Robinson, William H. *Black New England Letters.* Boston Public Library, 1977.

———. *Phillis Wheatley and Her Writings.* Garland Publishing, 1984.

Shields, John C. "Phillis Wheatley and Mather Byles: A Study in Literary Relationship." *College Language Association Journal* 23 (June 1980): 377-390.

Wheatley, Phillis. *The Collected Works of Phillis Wheatley.* Ed. John C. Shields. Oxford University Press, 1988.

• OPRAH WINFREY

Anderson, Chris,"Meet Oprah Winfrey." *Good Housekeeping*, August 1986.

Angelou, Maya. "Oprah Winfrey (Woman of the Year)." *Ms.* 17 (January/February 1989): 88.

Chapelle, Tony. "The Reigning Queen of TV Talk: Oprah!" *Black Collegian*, 21 (November-December 1990): 136

Edwards, Audrey. "Stealing the Show," *Essence* (October 1986): 50-52, 123.

Gillespie, Marcia Ann. "Winfrey Wakes All." *Ms.* 17 (November 1988): 50.

Gross, Linden. "Oprah Winfrey: Wonder Woman." *Ladies Home Journal* 105 (December 1988): 40.

Harrison, Barbara. "The Importance of Being Oprah." *The New York Times Magazine* 138 (June 11, 1989): 28.

King, Norman. *Everybody Loves Oprah!* Morrow, 1987.

Mills, David. "Oprah, Children's Crusader." *The Washington Post*, 13 November 1991.

Sanders, Charles L. "At Home with Oprah Winfrey." *Ebony* 43 (October 1988).

● *Making a*

difference

Making a ●

difference

Making a

difference

Making a ●

difference

bout the Author

"As a librarian, you save every sliver of information you can find

• *Jessie*   *on a subject that fascinates you, because you never know when that*

Carney   *information will come in handy."*

Smith

Noted author and scholar Jessie Carney Smith has been university librarian and professor at Fisk University in Nashville, Tennessee, for the past 25 years. Recognized for her outstanding educational and community achievements, as well as her numerous published works on black American life and culture, Dr. Smith is the recipient of 1992's Women's National Book Association Award, the Candace Award for excellence in education, and *SAGE* magazine's Anna J. Cooper Award for her monumental work, *Notable Black American Women*.